The Writings of the New Testament

The Writings of the New Testament

An Interpretation

Revised Edition

Luke Timothy Johnson

with the assistance of Todd C. Penner

SCM Press

Cover art: "Saint Mark Writing the Gospel" from the Pierpont Morgan Library/Art Resource, N.Y. Greek manuscript, Constantinople, 2nd half 11th century. M.639, F.218. The Pierpont Morgan Library, New York, N.Y., U.S.A.

Material from Religious Studies R220: The Christian Church in New Testament Times is reprinted courtesy of Indiana University, School of Continuing Studies.

0 334 02787 X

First published 1999
by SCM Press
9-17 St Albans Place, London N1 0NX

SCM Press is a division of SCM-Canterbury Press Ltd

Printed in the United States of America

To Joy

Contents

Preface to Revised Edition

THE FIRST EDITION of *The Writings of the New Testament: An Interpretation* appeared in 1986. The manuscript for that edition was completed in 1984. The bibliographies were fairly up-to-date but included only a few items from 1984. The contents of the book are therefore almost fifteen years old. Despite the usefulness of the first edition—it went through 13 printings—it is clearly time for a new edition.

I have not changed the basic philosophy or design of the book. I have simply tried to update and improve it. The updating takes two basic forms. The first is the completely revised bibliographies. Some older items are eliminated, many more recent items are included. I have continued to use only English-language references for the reasons stated in the first edition. The second updating is found in two appendices. One deals with newer methods that have developed over the past fifteen years; it is only a sketch but it shows the general lines of development and its bibliography provides some starting points for reading. The other appendix deals with the question of the Historical Jesus. I explain why I continue to omit this topic from the body of the book, and try to indicate some of the critical questions and sources to consult.

The improvement of the book is found in the line-by-line editing. Every sentence has been assessed for accuracy and clarity. Many passages have been rewritten, some have been omitted, some added. The argument of each chapter remains the same, though I hope it is clearer and more accessible. All of the references have been checked and corrected. I have also added study questions at the end of each chapter to make the book an even better teaching tool.

I could not have completed this arduous work without the help of two associates in particular. Todd Penner is given credit on the title page. His assistance has involved all of the improvements. He has read every word and made suggestions that I followed or rejected. I stand behind every change made, but the credit for many of them goes to Todd. He is even more responsible for the enlarged bibliographies. I am grateful for his talented and cheerful collaboration. My thanks also to David Charnon, who undertook the arduous work of checking all internal references and making corrections when necessary. It was Ann Schechter who first alerted me to the number of these that were in error in the first edition (blessings on readers who actually follow out cross-references!); it was David who carried out the brutal task. I am grateful.

In addition to the thanks expressed in the preface to the first edition, I want to add a heartfelt word of appreciation to the many readers, both teachers and students, who have used this book, especially those who reported to me things that worked and things that did not. Special thanks as well to Marshall Johnson of Fortress Press, who authorized this new edition; Michael West, who has overseen its production; and K. C. Hanson, who edited it.

Luke Timothy Johnson
Atlanta, Georgia
January 26, 1998

Preface to First Edition

I HAVE WRITTEN this book for those who want to understand the origin and shape of the New Testament writings but are unable to find a comprehensive introduction that is neither repellingly technical nor appallingly trivial. I have called it an interpretation rather than an introduction for the simple reason that most volumes going by the name of introduction are either handbooks devoted to the communication of information concerning a narrow range of scholarly issues or popularized versions of conventional scholarly wisdom for college students. In contrast to both, I have tried to provide a genuine interpretation of Christianity's earliest writings. By so doing I draw the reader into the most important critical questions concerning their understanding. In this sense, every interpretation is also an introduction. By no means is every introduction an interpretation.

The organization of this book, its argument, and the choice of topics have all been dictated by the desire to make these writings intelligible and alive for the contemporary reader who wants to meet and understand them more than scholarly discussions of them. I have considered all the critical issues pertinent to the understanding of the writings, but I have gone beyond presenting a consensus of scholarly opinion. The reader will find in these pages a single "reading" of the evidence from beginning to end—my own. My approach to the writings and the critical issues is independent. It is not, I think, idiosyncratic. I have learned more than I can ever credit to my teachers and to the reading of other scholars. But in this book I advance my own understanding of the New Testament in its origin, in each of its parts, and as a collection. Sometimes I agree with the majority of scholars; sometimes I disagree. I have tried to indicate the reasons for both. As in every attempt to deal with the whole of a subject within a reasonable space, much has been eliminated or abbreviated. More advanced readers should recognize in my sometimes elliptical remarks a thoughtful response to critical scholarship.

In order to keep my argument and presentation clean I have not used footnotes, nor do I refer to other scholars by name in the text. The reader will, I hope, forgive the inevitable air of omniscience that results. It seemed better to restrict references to primary sources, above all to the texts of the New Testament itself. Occasionally even these are so numerous as to make the detection of decent prose a problem. At the end of each chapter I have provided an annotated bibliography. Some entries support my presentation, others provide alternative points of view, still others give the reader additional resources for study. With very few exceptions I have included only literature in

English, since the notes are meant to be an aid to the reader rather than a demonstration of learning. Given the rate of translation, not that much of great value is missing. I have also tried to refer to literature that is reasonably available. Translations of primary sources are acknowledged at the head of each bibliographical section.

In everything I write, I discover again and in an ever more humbling degree how much I owe to my teachers. The bibliographical entries do not reveal how much I have taken from Nils Dahl, Wayne Meeks, Abraham Malherbe, as well as Rowan Greer, Brevard Childs, Judah Goldin, Henry Fischel, and Frederick Wisse. For the constant encouragement to stay immersed in the text, my contemporaries William Kurz, Dennis Hamm, Halvor Moxnes, and Jerome Neyrey are owed particular thanks. This book began as lectures at Yale Divinity School. The first stages were worked out together with my good friend and colleague Carl R. Holladay. Our endless debates and our shared passion for the chase mean more to me than I can adequately state. Carl deserves credit for much that might be good in this book. Among my teaching assistants at Yale who went on to become excellent scholars and who offered me much criticism of this point or another are Jouette Bassler, John Fitzgerald, Michael White, David Worley, Tim Polk, Jacqueline Williams, Alan Mitchell, Stan Stowers, Ann McGuire, Tony Lewis, and David Rensberger. Of my students at Yale whose responses to my ideas made a real difference, I must single out Kenneth Frazier, Sam Candler, Mark Burton-Schantz, Jan Fuller, Bill Shepherd, Julie Galambush, and most of all, Nancy Heslin.

My colleagues in the Department of Religious Studies at Indiana University have been outstandingly supportive of this project. To them I owe additional time for writing, as well as support for an Indiana University Summer Faculty Fellowship, which enabled me to complete the first draft of the manuscript. I must thank in particular Sam Preus, David Smith, and Jim Ackerman.

Norman A. Hjelm of Fortress Press was willing to take a chance on supporting this project when it was just a sheaf of lecture outlines. Since then my editor, John A. Hollar, has provided me and the manuscript with unfailingly kind and critical attention. Dr. Barry Blose at Fortress Press gave careful attention to the entire manuscript and greatly improved its prose. My wife, Joy, and my daughter, Tiffany, make all things possible and almost everything a pleasure.

Luke Timothy Johnson
Bloomington, Indiana
June 26, 1985

Abbreviations

AB	Anchor Bible
ABD	*Anchor Bible Dictionary*, 6 vols., ed. D. N. Freedman
AGJU	Arbeiten zur Geschichte des antiken Judentums und des Urchristentums
AnB	Analecta Biblica
ANRW	*Aufstieg und Niedergang der Romischen Welt*, ed. J. Temporini and W. Haase
ATR	*Anglican Theological Review*
BETL	Bibliotheca ephemeridum theologicarum lovaniensium
Bib	*Biblica*
BJRL	*Bulletin of the John Rylands University Library of Manchester*
BJS	Brown Judaic Studies
BO	Biblica et Orientalia
BS	The Biblical Seminar
BTB	*Biblical Theology Bulletin*
BZNW	Beihefte zur *ZNW*
CBQ	*Catholic Biblical Quarterly*
CBQMS	Catholic Biblical Quarterly-Monograph Series
CGTC	Cambridge Greek Testament Commentaries
ConBNT	Coniectanea biblica, New Testament
CR:BS	*Currents in Research: Biblical Studies*
CRINT	Compendia rerum iudaicarum ad novum testamentum
ETL	*Ephemerides theologicae lovanienses*
ExpTim	*Expository Times*
GBS	Guides to Biblical Scholarship
HDR	Harvard Dissertations in Religion
HNTC	Harper's NT Commentaries
HSM	Harvard Semitic Monographs
HTR	*Harvard Theological Review*
HTS	Harvard Theological Studies
IBS	*Irish Biblical Studies*
ICC	International Critical Commentary
IDBSup	*Interpreter's Dictionary of the Bible Supplementary Volume*, ed. K. Crim
Int	*Interpretation*

IRT	Issues in Religion and Theology
JAAR	*Journal of the American Academy of Religion*
JBL	*Journal of Biblical Literature*
JCS-D	*Jewish and Christian Self-Definition*, eds. E. P. Sanders, A. I. Baumgarten, A. Mendelson, and B. F. Meyer, 3 vols. (Philadelphia: Fortress Press)
JJS	*Journal of Jewish Studies*
JR	*Journal of Religion*
JRH	*Journal of Religious History*
JRS	*Journal of Roman Studies*
JSJ	*Journal for the Study of Judaism in the Persian, Hellenistic, and Roman Period*
JSNT	*Journal for the Study of the New Testament*
JSNTSup	Journal for the Study of the New Testament Supplement Series
JSOTS	Journal for the Study of the Old Testament, Supplement Series
JSPSS	Journal for the Study of the Pseudepigrapha, Supplement Series
JSS	*Journal of Semitic Studies*
JTC	Journal for Theology and the Church
JTS	*Journal of Theological Studies*
NCB	New Century Bible
Neot	*Neotestamentica*
NICNT	New International Commentary on the New Testament
NIGTC	New International Greek Testament Commentary
NovT	*Novum Testamentum*
NovTSup	Novum Testamentum Supplements
NTS	*New Testament Studies*
NTTS	New Testament Tools and Studies
RB	*Revue biblique*
RQ	*Restoration Quarterly*
SBL	Society of Biblical Literature
SBLDS	Society of Biblical Literature Dissertation Series
SBLMS	Society of Biblical Literature Monograph Series
SBLSBS	Society of Biblical Literature: Sources for Biblical Study
SBLSP	*Society of Biblical Literature Seminar Papers*
SBLSS	Society of Biblical Literature Symposium Series
SBS	Stuttgarter Bibelstudien
SC	*Second Century*
SE	*Studia Evangelica*
SFSHJ	South Florida Studies in the History of Judaism
SJLA	Studies in Judaism in Late Antiquity
SJT	*Scottish Journal of Theology*

SNTSMS	Society for New Testament Studies M
SP	Sacra Pagina
SPB	Studia postbiblica
SR	*Studies in Religion/Sciences religieuses*
TDNT	*Theological Dictionary of the New Testamen*
	and G. Friedrich
TS	*Theological Studies*
TU	Texte und Untersuchungen
USFSHJ	University of South Florida Studies in the History
VC	*Vigiliae christianae*
WBC	Word Biblical Commentary
WUNT	Wissenschaftliche Untersuchungen zum Neuen Testan
ZNW	*Zeitschrift für die neutestamentliche Wissenschaft*

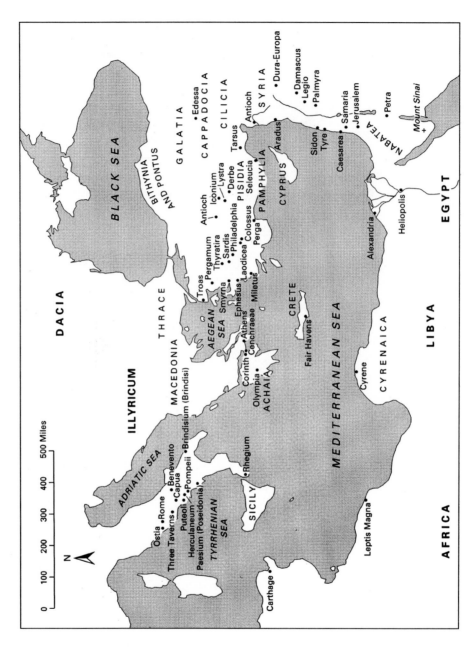

Central and eastern Roman Empire during the first century

Introduction

THIS BOOK SERVES as an introduction to the writings of the New Testament (NT). Its subject is a set of writings ordinarily found with another collection in the large anthology called the Bible. These writings came to birth in a specific time and place and were generated by specific causes. It may seem odd to think of the "birth" of literature, but the word is a reminder that what the reader now meets as an ancient text began as a living expression of living experience, and entered the world with a still visible parentage.

The twenty-seven compositions in the NT are not, at first sight, terribly impressive. There are four narratives about Jesus called "Gospels," and one about his followers entitled "The Acts of the Apostles," some occasional correspondence by one apostle (Paul), a handful of letters by other more or less anonymous leaders, and a strange apocalyptic vision. They claim no great literary merit. None directly claims inspiration for itself. But their impact has been disproportionate to their size or claims. For two thousand years they have been regarded by much of the western world as inspired by God, part of a revelation that was recognized as the definitive norm by which life's meaning is to be measured. Such disparity between cause and effect justifies the study of these specific writings and demands that fundamental questions be put to them. It is surprising that such questions are so seldom explicitly asked.

The first question is why these writings should exist at all. The question of sheer existence is one natural to poets and philosophers, who first allow themselves to be stunned by the realization that there are such things as trees and flowers before they try to describe and explain them. The existential question pertains to the NT in a fairly obvious way. It is not at all necessary that religious movements produce writings, still less that they in a short period of time certify those writings as sacred texts. Not every failed messianic figure generates a literature that insists he is still alive, and apparently makes this absurd claim plausible to others. Not all communities expecting the imminent end of the world produce documents remarkably unconcerned with timetables for demolition and more concerned with interpreting the past than predicting the future. The production of these writings should be a shock. The poet or philosopher would conclude from such an effect a commensurate cause, whether natural or magical. Something happened that gave birth to these writings.

A second question concerns the type of writings we find in the collection. Why four Gospels? They have unceasingly raised problems because of their odd combination of

1

agreement and dissonance, because of their refusal to be either simply biographies or simply legends, because of their uncanny verisimilitude and realism, even when their hero is doing patently impossible things. And why these particular letters? Romans, we might understand, and even the Corinthian correspondence. But why three pastoral letters, so alike yet so subtly different from each other, so Pauline yet seemingly so unlike Paul? Why both 2 Peter and Jude? Why, above all, Philemon? When we look closely at the writings, we are impressed most of all by their variety in outlook, form, and symbol. We sense the diversity of the movement that gave them birth, and wonder at the perceived coherence among them that made the community choose these writings as normative and not others.

Why do these writings look the way they do? This question is really two, each requiring equal stress. The first part asks: Why does the NT look so much like the Old Testament (OT)? Of all the obvious and important observations that are seldom expressed, this is the most significant: without any explanation or theoretical justification, these writings continue with the same characters and symbols as the Hebrew Scriptures (OT). The NT writings must be seen as Hellenistic literature, it is true. But their immediate parentage is unmistakable. Little in these documents would be intelligible if not read against the backdrop of the Jewish Scripture: Torah, Prophets, and Writings. It was neither accident nor violence that made the NT part of the Bible. The second part of the question, though, is equally important: Why does the NT look so different from the Old? The differences are not minor. Taking the NT seriously demands understanding the OT in an entirely different way. The symbols are the same, yet are radically reworked. The combination of continuity and contrast is expressed in the Pauline phrase "Grace to you and peace from God our Father and the Lord Jesus Christ." An adequate analysis of that phrase would lead to the enigmatic heart of the NT. By taking seriously the dialectic of similarity and difference between the NT and OT, we gain our surest entry into the distinctive character of these writings. But further distinctions must first be made.

Ways Not Taken

The basic questions concerning the origin and appearance of the NT writings have been answered previously in ways that, in their inadequacy, help sharpen the focus of this book.

Some have answered the questions by appealing to direct divine inspiration. According to them, the NT looks like the OT because it has the same author, God. The human writers were passive recipients of the divine impulse, secretaries taking down dictation. God simply shifted from Hebrew to Greek. In this explanation, human causality is eliminated. There is, therefore, nothing to explain, for there is no problem. But this position, while attempting to take seriously the religious conviction that these writings are authoritative, distorts the equally important Christian conviction that God works through human freedom, not through its suppression. One can, moreover, assert that these writings are authoritative, or even inspired, without using such a crude model of inspiration.

At the other extreme are conspiracy theories for the origin of Christianity and therefore of the NT. According to these theories, the writings serve to cover up what really happened. There are, naturally, several versions of what really happened. Some theories suggest that Jesus did not die on the cross but survived to continue teaching; others, that he died but that his disciples stole his body to give the impression that he had been raised. A further refinement (a more plausible one) has it that Jesus was in fact a revolutionary but that the Gospels portray him, for politically expedient reasons, as a religious teacher.

The conspiracy theories agree that the disciples manipulated the events of Jesus' life and death, as well as the messianic prophecies from the OT, in order to convince others that he was the expected messiah. Like all conspiracy theories, these tend to attribute at once too much and too little cleverness to the conspirators. Lucian of Samosata's parody, *Alexander the False Prophet*, shows us how a really successful religious scam could be pulled off in that time. It is unlikely that the disciples would have invented a messiah who fulfilled the prophecies so inadequately: Jesus did not match most of the important texts traditionally thought to refer to the messiah, nor was it suggested he did. It is hard to conceive that the disciples would have conjured up traditions that treated them as harshly as they are treated in the Gospels. And it goes beyond comprehension why they would have invented a movement that offered them nothing but the same fate as their master's, rejection and death.

Still, conspiracy theories all have germs of truth that give them plausibility. It *is* difficult to discern the "real" Jesus beneath the layers of interpretation in the Gospels. And there was a human process involved in the rereading of OT prophecies and the applying of them to Jesus. Indeed, this process is one of the keys to understanding the character of the writings. The process, however, had nothing to do with fraud or deception. It arose from the human impulse to interpret transforming experiences in the light of available symbols.

Other explanations are less radical than the supernaturalistic or paranoid options, but share the tendency to reduce Christianity to some cause other than religious. One explanation makes Christianity begin in the hallucinations of the disciples. This credits the disciples with sincerity but not with rationality. The writings of the NT are thereby seen as rather elaborate rationalizations of delusion. A classic expression of this view says that Jesus did not rise on Easter, faith did. There is, of course, a sense in which this can be asserted. I concentrate in this book on the pivotal importance of Easter faith as the catalyst *both* of the movement *and* of its interpretation. Psychological reduction, however, fails to deal with genuine religious experience and tends to read the texts themselves rather casually.

Another sort of explanation regards Christianity as the distillate of first-century political, social, and economic forces. According to this explanation, the NT writings are the propaganda and ideology of a proletarian movement that, because of its success, had to reinvent itself not as the critic but as the support of society. Or the explanation holds that the Christian movement succeeded because it matched the social needs of the age better than its rivals, such as Judaism and Mithraism. There is, again, some truth here: the social world of early Christianity is undoubtedly of great importance, especially for the explanation of its growth and eventual dominance. The attempt to locate the *cause* of the movement in specific economic or social factors, however, is less successful.

In each of these approaches the attempt to explain results in the loss of richness and complexity. When the religious element of the writings is asserted, the social dimension is lost; when the psychological dimension is emphasized, the religious disappears. Each explanation has merit, but each is too partial to allow for an adequate grasp of the writings. The narrowness of each approach reduces and distorts the writings themselves.

In this introduction, I offer another sort of explanation, namely that the writings of the NT emerged from powerful religious experiences that demanded the reinterpretation of a symbolic world. To grasp that sort of explanation, the reader must shift from a search for a single and simple explanation to a more complex understanding. Rather than a simple explanation, I offer here a model of interpretation.

The Search for an Interpretive Model

If the writings of the NT are to be grasped adequately, they must be approached as much as possible on their own terms. Readers must take seriously the writings' self-presentation and adjust their questions to them, rather than force the writings to the readers' preconceptions. What is needed above all is an adequate *model* for understanding the texts; one flexible enough to respect the variety of the individual writings, yet sufficiently definite to deal with them as parts of a coherent whole.

What do I mean by a model? A model is a paradigm within which the data appropriate to a discipline make sense. The adequacy of the paradigm can be measured both by the way it covers the data and by the way it enables further investigation. A model in this sense differs from a method insofar as it represents a sort of imaginative construal of the materials being studied, a structured picture of both process and product, within which the parts are seen not only to fit but also to function. A model can employ a variety of methods. But methods can themselves easily become unwitting models if we employ our methods without critical self-awareness. That is, a particular way of questioning data can unintentionally become an implicit but comprehensive understanding of what the material is about. When this happens, both data and method can become distorted.

Models and methods can be variously appropriate to the tasks they are asked to perform. A given subject can be made to fit several different models, but this is not to say that every model is equally adaptable. Likewise, a subject can be questioned using the tools of different methods, but not every method is appropriate to every purpose. Moreover, a specific model may be asked to do what it cannot, or a particular method of studying texts may fail to raise or respond to the questions deemed significant. When this happens, it is possible that a shift in models or methods is required.

An adequate model for the NT considered as canon would provide an explanatory framework for the birth and development of the writings in the first place (Why do they exist?) and for their specific shape (Why do they look the way they do?). It would enable us to deal with the documents as writings (that is, as literary productions) and not simply as sources of information. It would account for the process of their development as well as their final literary shape. The model would allow for the anthropological, historical, literary, and religious dimensions of the texts to be maintained in their integrity and to survive analysis.

Anthropological

By "anthropological," I mean at the simplest level that the writings must be taken seriously as fully *human* productions. Divine inspiration is not excluded, but inspiration is not a fact available for study. Second, the term "anthropological" asserts that these are *fully* human writings, and that intrinsic to being human are religious experiences and ideas. Indeed, much of what anthropologists have traditionally studied has involved the way religions structure the lives of people. Third, the term has a more specific application: in the production of these writings, we find operative the universal dynamics of the human search for meaning. In particular, we find in them the interplay of myth and experience in the shaping of symbolic worlds (see pp. 10–16).

Historical

For the moment, I merely note that the NT writings must be read within their first-century Mediterranean setting, and in particular within the matrix of first-century Judaism. The NT came to birth among social structures and symbols different from our own. The writings are conditioned linguistically by that historical setting. Their linguistic code is not only alien but also only partially available to us. Precisely the "things that go without saying" are not accessible. Every responsible reading therefore demands historical adjustment. The writings are very much conditioned both by the times and places of their origin and by the settings and intentions of their authors. The more we can reconstruct those settings and intentions, the better readers we are. If the anthropological pattern of myth and experience provides the broad framework for the model I am proposing, then the specific application of it is found within the historical setting of first-century Judaism.

Literary

An adequate model for the interpretation of the NT must deal with the documents as compositions. This means first that however important the prehistory of texts may be, however helpful the distinctions between tradition and redaction, the complete and finished literary form of the writing is what demands interpretation within the canon. Second, attention must be given to the literary conventions of the age of composition. The reader must take into account the implications of genre and the uses of rhetoric. Third, the writings must be read in terms of their self-presentation rather than reduced to the status of sources for another body of information. Finally, the model must seek for a fit between the form of a writing and its function, between literary structure and substance. What the term "literary" does not mean is a concern only for aesthetic techniques.

Religious

The writings of the NT are first and foremost religious writings. They were generated by a specifically religious movement, and were written by and for adherents of that movement. These assertions should not meet dispute, but some further distinctions are important.

I do not mean to equate "religious" with "theological." There is theology in the NT, but it is not of a scholastic or self-conscious sort. There were philosophers and theologians in that age doing what we do not find being done in the NT: writing systematic treatises on virtues, for example, and composing extended commentaries on authoritative texts. The theology found in the NT is closer to what we would call *practical* theology. It works out the implications of religious experience and conviction for life in the community and world. It does not resemble what we call systematic theology, which correlates the propositions of belief with more comprehensive philosophical worldviews. The History of Religions School (*Die Religions-geschichtliche Schule*), which flourished in the early years of this century, rightly protested against the tendency to regard the writings of the NT as theological treatises and asserted that they more strongly resembled the writings of popular religion in Hellenistic culture.

The program and promise of the History of Religions School has never been fulfilled. This is partly because scholarship was diverted by the renewal of theology and the resurgence of literary-critical analysis in each postwar period. It may also be partly due to the problems of the program itself. Its understanding of religion tended to be somewhat narrow, at times almost seeming to equate religion with cult. Consequently, more of the NT was explained in terms of cultic activity than is justified. There was also a tendency to *separate* "religion" from theology, ethics, and conscious literary expression—a separation that increasingly appears to be artificial. Finally, the approach tended to be over-rationalistic in its understanding of religious phenomena such as myth and ritual, while showing a reluctance to deal with the actual religious claims of the texts.

I use the term "religious" here to refer to experiences, convictions, and interpretations having to do with what is perceived as ultimate reality. The term points to a way of being human, a way both individual and social that asserts by word and deed that human existence is bound by, and defined in reference to, realities transcending every-day categories. To call these writings religious, therefore, does not prejudge their social setting, literary form, or intellectual sobriety. But it does recognize that they claim to be speaking about life as related to God. Their subject matter concerns what it means to be human in the light of faith, specifically in light of the experience of the Holy that the first Christians claimed to have had in Jesus.

The NT writings approach us as witnesses to and interpretations of specifically religious claims having to do with the experience of God as mediated through Jesus. They never claim, we notice, to mediate that experience themselves. They only witness and interpret. It should go without saying, therefore, that the contemporary reader cannot reach that experience by using the tools of anthropology, history, and literary criticism. But the contemporary reader can claim to come in contact with the witness and interpretation.

Historical Method but Not Historical Model

At this point, a delicate distinction must be drawn. I have already asserted the importance of recognizing the historical dimension of the NT texts. Because of the linguistic conditioning of these writings, because of the peculiar claims of the creed with its specifically historical elements, and because of the nature of the Christian community that claims continuity with a people of the past, such historical appreciation will continue to be desirable, necessary, and inevitable. The use of historical-critical methods therefore is entirely appropriate. Among the tasks necessary to the study of the NT are the attempts to hear the text in its first voice, to distinguish between levels of tradition, to evaluate sources, to determine the time, provenance, and authorship of the writings, and to describe their social settings. On the other hand, these tasks can be carried out within the framework of different models. I am suggesting here that it is not history as method that requires qualification, but history as the overarching model for understanding the NT.

Despite many minor disaffections, the historical model remains dominant in NT scholarship. The historical model provides a distinctive imaginative construal of the writings and the task of studying them. First, the task: in answer to the question,

"What are these writings about?" this model responds, "They are about the history of the primitive Christian movement." The goal set by this model is the description, or possibly even the reconstruction, of that historical development. At least ideally this goal is detachable from the writings themselves. If we could ever achieve a definitive picture of that development, the writings could be consigned to the archives and we could move to the next historical period.

The writings themselves play a secondary role: they are nothing more or less than sources for the reconstruction. The historian evaluates the writings as historical sources (Are they first- or second-hand, authentic or inauthentic?), and asks of them questions that yield specifically historical information. Indeed, this model can use only this type of information. Whether the topic is ideas, rituals, literature, or institutions, the end result is the same: a picture of historical development. This model is neither unsophisticated nor without virtue.

Even taken on its own terms, however, the historical model has a difficult time with the texts of the NT. The problems stem from the paucity of genuine historical data in the writings, and the artificiality of the canonical frame for the historical enterprise. The two problems influence each other. The historical model has traditionally worked within the canon. It was obvious, of course, that as historical sources, the canonical writings were greatly deficient: they were fragmentary and biased. But the need to do history, with the stakes being regarded as theologically significant, led generations of investigators to proceed as though these pieces of the puzzle were the only ones. They were like people hunched over a hundred-piece jigsaw puzzle with only twenty-seven pieces in hand, and constrained to fit the pieces into some pattern of dependence and development. Not surprisingly, the resulting pictures were sometimes grotesque.

The interplay between dating and development was especially problematic. History lives off chronology but is never content with chronology. It seeks causality, which is to say, development. The historical model is not satisfied with a rich but disjointed collection of vignettes of the NT period. It reaches insatiably for sequence, for the possibility of a narrative. In fact, however, the NT canon offers, and will always offer, only scattered vignettes of the earliest Christian period. Worse, Christianity was at first so unnoticed by outsiders that there is little external framework for dating the writings so that they could securely be used as sources for a developmental picture.

Faced with the irreducible deficiency of their sources and the goal of doing history, investigators did the best they could. But the lack of data and controls led them inevitably to a focus on data that were assumed to be traceable, namely ideas. Even this, however, was made possible only by the employment of developmental models that helped fill in the gaps between documents. The process was circular, of course. The circularity was only occasionally broken by scholars who time and again allowed the stubbornly fragmentary data to upset the symmetry of developmental schemes.

These observations on the historical model are not novel. It has been more vigorously and acutely criticized by its practitioners than by its detractors. The critics have

First of all, my symbolic world not only helps me interpret my experience after the fact; it actually gives me the capacity to perceive (i.e., to have my experience in the first place). Symbols shape my experience. Because of my symbolic world I perceive the rotation of the earth on its axis in relation to the sun as the sun rising. I do not perceive the same phenomenon as a god rising from the death of night, although someone in another symbolic world might well perceive it that way. The same point can be illustrated by an indefinite series of examples. I extend my hand to greet a stranger, and smile. The stranger approaches me the same way. Because of our shared symbolic world, we both perceive the interchange as friendly. In the ordinary course of things, it is—and the experience confirms the perception. When it does, the symbolic world is strengthened, and the symbolic structure that legitimates handshakes is renewed.

But the process can go the other way. What if the stranger should grasp my hand violently and slap me in handcuffs? What if he seizes my hand and cuts it off at the wrist? Then my experience radically disconfirms my symbolic world, which says that handshakes are signs of friendship. This experience shakes my view of the world, and the symbolic structure is threatened. In light of this experience, I must now struggle to find meaning where it appears to be absent. The quest for meaning is relentless; life cannot continue without it. We try first to stretch our symbols to cover the experience. Perhaps the stranger was an enemy in disguise, and his handshake was a camouflage. That makes his act of violence anomalous, the exception that proves the rule. Thus our myth is saved, our world secure.

Myths stretch to cover experience, and sometimes stretch exceedingly far. For example, remote islanders, with only a simple set of stories to norm their woodland existence, were visited by anthropologists who descended in helicopters, waving candy bars and cameras. Then the anthropologists departed, and the islanders stretched their simple stories to include such a totally other experience: they now had sky visitors and gift bearers in their symbolic world.

The elastic capacity of myths and symbols is, however, finite. Some experiences are so powerful and radical that they threaten to collapse the very structure of the world, the very structure of meaning. In our time, there is no better example of this than the Holocaust. The systematic murder of six million people guilty only of being Jewish tore to shreds the symbolic world of Judaism as it existed before that event. This social experience created a massive displacement in a symbolic structure two thousand years and more in the making. It did this so decisively that the basic symbols of Torah and messiah became, in a decade, empty of their previous content for millions of people. We can go further and state without paradox that the Holocaust was a religious experience in the proper sense of that word. Evil, too, is a religious category. And this was an experience of the "otherness" of evil so powerful that it shattered the capacity to explain or even intelligently to perceive it.

Yet, the search for meaning continues. Even in the face of apparently limitless and meaningless evil, there is the human struggle to understand. But what can be used once the myths have been destroyed? Some have responded to the Holocaust with silence, insisting that any words will distort the event by diminishing it. Others have begun to interpret the experience of the Holocaust with words, using the bits and pieces of the myths that now lie scattered about. Torah will eventually encompass even the Holocaust. The myth, of course, will no longer look the same as it did before. The old symbols will be there, but they will be read in an entirely new way because of the event that forced the process of reinterpretation in the first place. And it will take time for the new interpretation itself to acquire the force of myth, that is, have the power to shape new experiences in a way that seems natural and even inevitable. Already some Jewish scholars have pointed to the birth of the State of Israel as a "resurrection of the just" following upon the death of the people at Auschwitz.

This dialectic of experience and interpretation is the basic model I am proposing for the understanding of the writings of the NT. It allows us to answer the fundamental questions of origin and shape: why the documents were written and why they look the way they do. It places the birth of the NT within the symbolic world of first-century Judaism. It allows us to ask about the experience that generated, indeed necessitated, the process of interpretation. And it enables us to read each of the writings of the NT as specific *modes* of interpretation: the reshaping of the symbols of Judaism in light of the experience of a crucified and raised Messiah.

The model also gives us the framework for our investigation. We need to ask first about the shape of the symbolic world of first-century Judaism within Hellenistic culture. Then, we need to look at the experience of the first Christians that forced the reshaping of that symbolic world. Next, we need to look in detail at each of the writings as specific ways of interpreting those new religious convictions and experiences. Finally, we need to explore the implications of the fact that those writings were gathered into a normative canon.

Study Questions

1. Why is each dimension of the New Testament (anthropological, historical, literary, religious) critical to its interpretation?

2. What is meant by the distinction between historical methods in the reading of the New Testament and a "historical model"?

3. How is an understanding of the social construction of reality—the making of symbolic worlds—helpful for reading religious literature?

4. What are basic features of the "experience interpretation" model used in this book?

Bibliographical Note

Among standard scholarly introductions to the NT, that of T. Zahn, *Introduction to the New Testament*, 3 vols. (New York: Charles Scribner's Sons, 1909 [1905]) is still unmatched for the depth and vigor of its textual analysis. The most useful one-volume compendium is W. G. Kümmel, *Introduction to the New Testament*, trans. H. C. Kee (Nashville: Abingdon Press, 1975). Although uneven in quality, H. Koester's *Introduction to the New Testament*, 2 vols. (Philadelphia: Fortress Press, 1982), contains much useful information, particularly in its first volume, *History, Culture, and Religion of the Hellenistic Age* (2nd ed., 1995). Also quite helpful is the survey of modern NT research in E. J. Epp and G. W. MacRae (eds.), *The New Testament and Its Modern Interpreters* (Philadelphia: Fortress Press, 1989). Among textbook introductions, R. E. Brown, *An Introduction to the New Testament* (New York: Doubleday, 1997), and B. D. Ehrman, *The New Testament: A Historical Introduction to the Early Christian Writings* (New York: Oxford Univ. Press, 1996), are worth consulting. For treatments of the development of the NT, see Hans von Campenhausen, *The Formation of the Christian Bible*, trans. J. A. Baker (Philadelphia: Fortress Press, 1972); A. von Harnack, *The Origin of the New Testament*, trans. J. R. Wilkinson (New York: Macmillan Co., 1925); and C. F. D. Moule, *The Birth of the New Testament*, 3rd ed. (San Francisco: Harper & Row, 1982).

The basic pattern of conspiracy explanations of early Christianity has remained rather constant. One can compare H. S. Reimarus, *The Goal of Jesus and His Disciples*, trans. G. W. Buchanan (Leiden: E. J. Brill, 1970 [written before 1768]) and H. Schonfield, *The Passover Plot* (New York: Bantam Books, 1966). The options are laid out with customary verve by D. Strauss, *The Life of Jesus Critically Examined*, ed. R. Hodgson (Philadelphia: Fortress Press, 1973 [1835]), 735–44. Strauss himself developed a mythological approach to the NT that is very close to the one I use, but with significant differences. Strauss was hampered by rigid presuppositions and relatively undeveloped critical tools, but his insight was nevertheless acute.

For examples of psychological reductionism, see E. Fromm, *The Dogma of Christ* (New York: Holt, Rinehart & Winston, 1955), and R. L. Rubenstein, *Paul My Brother* (New York: Harper & Row, 1972). For a reading of earliest Christian history from the perspective of a Marxist reduction, see K. Kautsky, *Foundations of Christianity*, trans. H. F. Mins (New York: S. A. Russell, 1953).

On the development and history of the historical-critical model, see W. Baird, *History of New Testament Research; Volume 1: From Deism to Tübingen* (Minneapolis: Fortress Press, 1992); R. A. Harrisville and W. Sundberg, *The Bible in Modern Culture: Theology and Historical-Critical Method from Spinoza to Käsemann* (Grand Rapids: Wm. B. Eerdmans, 1995); W. G. Kümmel, *The New Testament: The History of the Investigation of Its Problems*, trans. S. MacL. Gilmour and H. C. Kee (Nashville: Abingdon Press, 1972); S. Neill and N. T Wright, *The Interpretation of the New Testament*

1861–1986 (New York: Oxford Univ. Press, 1988); and J. K. Riches, *A Century of New Testament Study* (Valley Forge, Pa.: Trinity Press Int'l, 1993). Criticism of the method by scholars taking it very seriously is exemplified by J. A. T. Robinson, *Redating the New Testament* (Philadelphia: Westminster Press, 1976), and N. T. Wright, *The New Testament and the People of God* (Minneapolis: Fortress Press, 1992), 3–120.

The classic expressions of the History of Religions School approach to the NT are W. Bousset, *Kyrios Christos: A History of the Belief in Christ from the Beginnings of Christianity to Irenaeus,* trans. J. Steely (Nashville: Abingdon Press, 1970), and R. Bultmann, *Theology of the New Testament,* 2 vols., trans. K. Grobel (New York: Charles Scribner's Sons, 1951–55). On this approach, see L. W. Hurtado, "New Testament Christology: A Critique of Bousset's Influence," *TS* 40 (1979): 306–17.

The movement to treat the history of earliest Christianity without regard to considerations of canon was given great impetus by W. Bauer's *Orthodoxy and Heresy in Earliest Christianity,* ed. R. A. Kraft and G. Krodel, trans. P. J. Achtemeier et al. (Philadelphia: Fortress Press, 1971), and given programmatic expression by J. M. Robinson and H. Koester in *Trajectories Through Early Christianity* (Philadelphia: Fortress Press, 1971). See also B. L. Mack, *Who Wrote the New Testament?: The Making of the Christian Myth* (San Francisco: HarperCollins, 1995). For a challenge to this view, see H. J. Hultgren, *The Rise of Normative Christianity* (Minneapolis: Fortress Press, 1994).

The so-called sociological approach to early Christianity is not entirely novel (cf. S. J. Case, *The Social Origins of Christianity* [Chicago: Univ. of Chicago Press, 1923]), but it has come into its own. For a popular treatment, see H. C. Kee, *Christian Origins in Sociological Perspective* (Philadelphia: Westminster Press, 1980), and for a review of the options, H. E. Remus, "Sociology of Knowledge and the Study of Early Christianity," *SR* 11 (1982): 45–56. To date, the theoretically oriented approaches of J. G. Gager, *Kingdom and Community: The Social World of Early Christianity* (Englewood Cliffs, N.J.: Prentice-Hall, 1975); R. A. Horsley, *Sociology and the Jesus Movement,* 2nd ed. (New York: Continuum, 1994); and G. Theissen, *Sociology of Early Palestinian Christianity,* trans. J. Bowden (Philadelphia: Fortress Press, 1977) have received more attention than the carefully crafted studies of E. A. Judge, *The Social Pattern of Christian Groups in the First Century* (London: Tyndale Press, 1960); A. J. Malherbe, *Social Aspects of Early Christianity,* 2nd ed. (Philadelphia: Fortress Press, 1983); W. A. Meeks, *The First Urban Christians: The Social World of the Apostle Paul* (New Haven: Yale Univ. Press, 1982); and G. Theissen, *The Social Setting of Pauline Christianity: Essays on Corinth,* trans. and ed. J. Schütz (Philadelphia: Fortress Press, 1981). For a summary of the issues involved, see B. Holmberg, *Sociology and the New Testament: An Appraisal* (Minneapolis: Fortress Press, 1990).

As for the now burgeoning literary approach to the NT, see appendix 1 for further bibliography.

For examples of Jewish response to the Holocaust and reinterpretation of the traditional Jewish symbols, see the very different approaches by R. L. Rubenstein, *After Auschwitz: Radical Theology and Contemporary Judaism* (Indianapolis: Bobbs-Merrill Co., 1966), and E. L. Fackenheim, *The Jewish Bible after the Holocaust: A Re-reading* (Bloomington: Indiana Univ. Press, 1990).

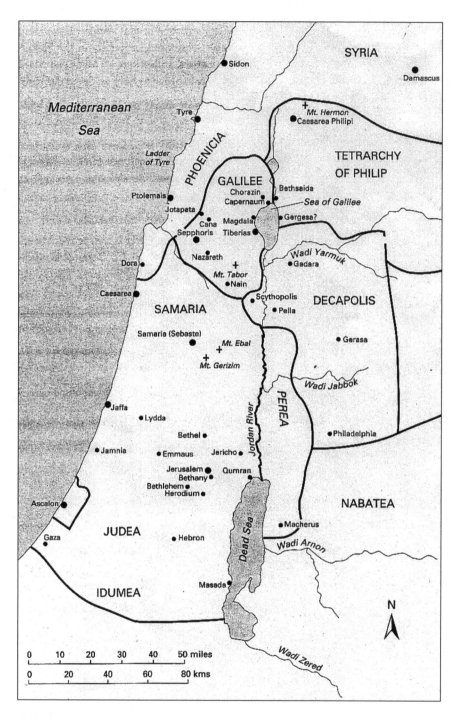

Palestine in the Roman era

PART ONE

The Symbolic World of the New Testament

A SYMBOLIC WORLD is made up of the social structures in which people live, and the symbols attached to and supporting those structures. In the case of the NT, it might be better to speak of the symbolic *worlds*, so complex and pluralistic was its setting. The pluralism was constituted by the diverse combinations of four elements: Mediterranean culture, Roman rule, Hellenistic civilization, and the religious symbols of Judaism. A carefully calibrated description of each is beyond the scope of this, or any single, book. There is scarcely an observation on this world that cannot be countered by another bit of evidence. Beneath the welter of specific phenomena, however, some recognizable patterns can be discerned.

The reader will do well to recognize the selectivity of the present description and investigate further the matters touched on. The better one's grasp of this symbolic world, the more intelligent will be one's reading of the NT. My focus here is on those aspects of the symbolic world that illustrate the dynamics of experience and interpretation I described in the Introduction. The writers of the NT were doing exactly what others were doing in that first-century world: seeking to interpret their religious experience with the available symbols.

Further cautionary remarks are appropriate. The symbolic world of the NT is more than a background, as though the influence went only in one direction, or stopped once Christianity began. Judaism and Hellenism continued to exist after the writing of the NT. Judaism, of course, looked different at least in part because of its negative response to the messianic claims of the Christians. And Hellenism received back its symbols reshaped, so that in the course of centuries Hellenism itself became a

Christian culture. The interactions between the symbols of Hellenism, Judaism, and Christianity were complex and ongoing.

Despite a wealth of information available to us about this world, we should not overestimate our ability to understand it. Our sources are fragmentary; we do not have everything that was written. The sources, furthermore, are sometimes difficult to date, as are the traditions they contain. We do better, therefore, at impressionistic, composite sketches than at precise delineations. Our sources are partial in another sense: they represent the perspectives of the more literate and therefore more sophisticated adherents of religious or philosophical movements and, since they were moved to write, also the more wholeheartedly committed to their ideals. Our notions of that symbolic world are inevitably affected by the accidents of historical preservation. We do not always know what ordinary people were doing, but we might suspect they did not always meet the idealized pictures given to us by our sources.

For that matter, it is good to remember that the construction of symbolic worlds—especially of religious symbols—did not occupy all or even the best efforts of those committed to the task. Their symbolic world involved politics, economics, and warfare as much as magic and mystery cults. However much religious symbols legitimated and expressed those other activities, it was probably true then, as now, that greater effort went into making a living than into the interpretation of living. The rabbis complain of the difficulties of manual labor and the troubles caused by gossiping wives. Paul's letters suggest he spent more time journeying and at his workbench than in evangelization. And people of that age continued for the most part to have the good sense to mate and procreate, so that energy given to symbolic structuring had to be taken from those more engrossing occupations.

1. The Greco-Roman World

WE CAN BEGIN to describe the world of the NT by indicating some of its limits. Geographically, it was the world of the Mediterranean, those territories embracing the inland sea that for the ancients made up the known and civilized world, the *oikoumenē*. What lay outside this world was both fascinating and frightening, and all the more for being so little known. Those responsible for the security of the *oikoumenē* worried about the threat of invasion from the Parthians to the east and various tribes to the north, but the NT reveals nothing of such awareness or concern. Temporally, this world began with the conquests of Alexander the Great (356–323 B.C.E.) and continued at least until the mid-second century of the Common Era. Although Hellenism is given a new frame by the Roman Empire, beginning with the accession of Augustus in 31 B.C.E., Hellenistic civilization continues well through the time of the early empire, so that we can accurately designate the most encompassing symbolic world of the NT as Greco-Roman culture.

Politically, it was a world shaped by empire. By his conquests, Alexander had created an empire but died before it could be stabilized. His successors fought for control of the pieces, and for two hundred years Antigonids (rulers of Achaia and Macedonia), Seleucids (masters of Asia and Syria), and Ptolemies (rulers of Egypt) battled for supremacy. The critical land bridge formed by Palestine made it, as always, a prime battleground. These internecine battles reflected disagreement not over the virtues of Hellenism or empire, but over who should rule the *oikoumenē*.

During these conflicts, another power slowly but steadily came to dominate the Mediterranean. Rome had begun its territorial conquests during the time of the late republic and accelerated them by the competition between Caesar and Pompey. From the middle of the second century B.C.E., Rome commanded the *oikoumenē*, and the explicit assumption of imperial prerogatives by Augustus only ratified that fact. Rome gave political stability to the ideals of Hellenization that had already been diffused by the conquests of Alexander.

Yet Greece and Rome built on a foundation that preceded and survived them both. The distinctive cultural patterns of the Mediterranean were not eliminated by these empires, only modulated. Among the features of this world we can include an economy based primarily in agriculture and villages, a taste for trade and for warfare, a delight in display and a love for language, a desire for honor and a fear of shame. It was a world of large households run by patriarchs, a world of slaves and owners. It was a world whose severe disparities in status were negotiated by a subtle system of patronage shown by benefactors and of honor paid in return by those so assisted; a world in which the demands of *quid pro quo* were mollified by ideals of friendship and harmony. All these social realities were reflected in the pantheon, in the unruly households of the gods and in the intrigues and fratricidal jealousies that so often broke out among these deities. Their power was pervasive, but was distributed among a band of personalities as vivid and varied as those of the humans with whom they so frequently commingled.

Hellenistic Ideals and Realities

When the twenty-two-year-old Alexander crossed the Dardanelles to conquer the Persian East in 334 B.C.E., he intended more than military conquest; he was beginning a mission of cultural hegemony. To that end, he brought with him poets, philosophers, and historians. He had been a student of Aristotle and, considering the Greek way best for all, desired to create one Panhellenic world. He encouraged his soldiers to intermarry with native women to create one race, and set a good example by his marriage to the Indian princess Roxanne. He turned conquered cities into Greek city-states, and in strategic locations he established new cities. He made Greek the universal language and actively encouraged a religious syncretism whereby local deities might be identified, then merged with the gods of the Greek pantheon. His successors, and particularly the Seleucids, continued to cultivate his dream of a Hellenized world.

The city-state, the *polis*, was itself the first tool of Hellenization. It was the symbol of Greek culture and its best expression: a place where citizens could meet, market, debate, and vote. The city was the center for culture (*paideia*), and played an integral role in the communication of that culture through education. The *gymnasion* offered an opportunity for the learning of both physical and intellectual virtue. Training in rhetoric was the staple of education; both letters and morals were learned through the imitation of textual and living exemplars. Such training imbued the young with common cultural values—for example, how friendship demanded the sharing of all things—even as it showed them how to manipulate those values in a life of public discourse and disputation. For young men destined for military careers, there was the *ephēbeion*.

In classical Greece, the *polis* was the center around which religious activity was organized. The rituals and liturgies of the city gave to its citizens a sense of personal and communal identity. One was not Greek so much as one was Athenian or Spartan.

Alexander used the *polis* as a means for disseminating Greek culture. Old cities, such as Jerusalem under the Seleucid Antiochus IV, were made Hellenistic by a change of constitution. New cities, such as Alexandria in Egypt which was founded by Alexander himself, were Hellenistic from the start. The Hellenistic world, then, was conceived of as an *urban* world. Civilization and the city were conterminous.

Such was the ideal. The reality was somewhat harsher. In the first century, the major cities were not small; Rome had a million in population, Alexandria probably half that many. They were so big that the ideal of citizen participation was impossible to achieve. Worse, the cities were not really independent. They existed within an empire of complex bureaucracies, military installations, and sometimes oppressive taxation. The sense of local identity provided by the ancient *polis* declined, together with the protection offered by local deities and the responsibility demanded of citizens.

For some, the fact of a worldwide empire created the possibility of a new and more cosmopolitan identity. Now one could be a citizen of the world. For others, the picture was bleaker; the loss of local roots meant alienation and despair. If one is equally at home everywhere, does one really have a home anywhere? Both reactions colored the religious symbols of the age.

A second tool of Hellenization was language. This was the most powerful tool, for a language bears with it all the symbols of a culture. Greek became the common language (*koinē*) of the *oikoumenē* and remained so even under Rome, with Latin only much later becoming the official imperial language. Greek was the language of trade and government, of philosophy and religion. Even the Hebrew Scriptures were translated into Greek by the mid-second century B.C.E. in Alexandria. This translation, the Septuagint (LXX), became, quite literally, Scripture—for Hellenistic Jews, and later also for the first Christians. The LXX, indeed, formed the basis for an entire corpus of Jewish literature, illustrating the pervasive influence of Greek language and rhetoric.

The use of a single language was of obvious importance for communication; it enabled the rapid diffusion of new ideas and old. In such transmission, symbols both gained and lost resonances through their being clothed in Greek. Still, from the time of Alexander, even the refutation of Greek ways usually demanded the use of the Greek tongue. Not always, however, and not by everyone. Local languages such as Aramaic and Coptic continued to be spoken. The preservation of sacred writings in these tongues enabled local identities to continue and sometimes to become the focal point for resistance to the empire.

The third tool of Hellenization was religious syncretism. Local gods, such as Baal ha Shemaim, the high god of ancient Canaanite mythology, were systematically identified with their Greek counterparts, such as Zeus Olympus. The idea was to reduce local allegiances in favor of more universal ones. Here we recognize a classic case of using religion as a societal glue. The results were various and multiple. The old Greek pantheon was not strengthened by being stretched so violently, and the Greek myths seemed to lose rather than gain credibility by being universalized. On the one hand, syncretism may have hastened a movement toward monotheism—it is not a big step from equating divine powers to deciding there is one divine power diversely manifested. So philosophers could use the language of polytheism, but also speak of a single divine providence.

Less happily, the loss of prestige suffered by the traditional gods together with the alienation fostered by the empire helped create a perception of the world as governed alternatively by fickle chance (*tychē*) or inexorable fate (*heimarmenē*). Such perception gave impetus to the search for religious experiences more profound and personal than were available in the official cults. It is important, however, not to exaggerate this emerging religious spirit.

The impact of empire was felt less dramatically by people at either extreme of the social scale. Those at the upper end were buffered from dramatic change by wealth and power; those at the lower end were equally insulated by poverty and ignorance. Typically, those whose fortunes were most precarious and unpredictable—the traders and scholars, the merchants and travelers, who moved in and out of the empire's great cities—were the ones who most felt the effects of displacement and the threat of cruel fortune.

The goal of Hellenization was somewhat self-contradictory from the outset. The genius of classical Greece lay in the vibrancy of its local traditions. Trying to universalize that genius meant inevitably to distort it. The results of Hellenization were therefore mixed and ambiguous. Certainly, something new came into being. Whether the East had been made Greek, or whether Greece had been orientalized, Hellenistic culture was very different from that of classical Greece. The ideals may have been the same, but they were diffused and subtly altered by the new realities of life. Chief among these realities was the fact of empire. It changed everything. Above all, empire established a world in which the individual person had little direct control over his or her life. In response, both religion and philosophy in the Hellenistic period gave increased attention to the individual.

Roman Rule

Rome was preoccupied with power and used it with unprecedented efficiency. The Roman version of empire provided both security and the framework of legal legitimization for the force it required. Emperors after Augustus may have been bizarre in their behavior and increasingly desirous of accolades due the divine, but they maintained a remarkably long-lasting peace through a complex system of governance. The empire ruled the relatively safe areas, like Africa and Asia, as senatorial provinces—run, at least ostensibly, by the senate through its governors. Territories like Palestine that were refractory or threatened with invasion, however, were under the explicitly military governance of prefects or procurators. There were, in fact, military colonies and installations throughout the empire, and their troops were used to quell local disturbances. But Rome did not rely entirely on violence to enhance its power. It extended the right of citizenship ever more widely, so that by the middle of the first century members of military colonies, former soldiers, even local personages like the Jews of some provincial cities, could enjoy citizenship.

The empire grew by conquest, however, and two significant aspects of life within it were shaped by that fact. First, an already stratified society had its lower levels swelled by large numbers of slaves and other persons displaced by wars. They congregated in the cities and dangerously distended their populations. Such uprooted peoples were often ready for rebellion or religion or both, and tested the toleration of the empire for deviance. They also placed extreme pressure on the empire's ability to feed them. The public dole was a fact of life. Rome was fed at the expense of the provinces, especially of Egypt, the breadbasket of the empire. Rome experienced periodic crises caused by the delay of shipments or the failure of crops.

The second aspect was the constant pressure of taxation on the provinces. Taxes levied on subject peoples were especially severe. In Galilee under Julius Caesar, as much as a quarter of a year's harvest could go as taxes to Rome. Add to that the amount skimmed by local chieftains like Herod and the agents hired to do the collecting—the publicans—and the amount gouged from local populations was even greater. Small wonder the agents of Rome were hated.

Governance and trade required efficient transportation and communication. The Roman roads were extensive—about fifty thousand miles paved by the year 100 c.e.— and well maintained. Between May and October (after which weather made passage perilous) the Mediterranean could quickly and easily be crossed. The travels of Paul and his companions show that frequent and relatively safe travel was common, though still arduous and very expensive. Hostels were often also brothels, so a mobile and separatist group such as the first Christians needed to make hospitality a prime virtue. The availability and security of travel also encouraged communication. An efficient postal system made letter writing commonplace for commerce, friendship, and literary exercise, as we can see in the correspondence of Cicero, Seneca, and Pliny the Younger. Letters were also written for mutual encouragement and support between philosophical communities.

Everyday life in the empire could be harsh. Away from the wide public spaces—and for those not enjoying aristocratic privileges—life even in the capital was difficult (see Juvenal *Satires* III.190–320). Streets were narrow, crowded, and dirty; food was simple when not scarce, with meat considered a luxury item. The security offered by the totalitarian state, moreover, exacted a price in freedom.

But on balance, the Roman Empire was a significant and positive force in the spread of the Christian movement. One universally used language enabled the preaching and acceptance of the message. Great urban centers, filled with mobile and often disaffected populations, encouraged the rapid diffusion of new cults and teachings. Rapid, safe, and frequent travel and letter writing were available. All of these were enabled by the freedom from war and internal danger that marked the *Pax Romana*.

The Pagan World

The NT cannot be trusted to provide a fair and accurate picture either of Jews or of pagans. It was written by converts seeking to demonstrate the superiority of their new life by contrast to both groups. The NT is preoccupied with community concerns and addresses the outside world only insofar as it has impact on the movement. We find in it, for example, no interest in the threat of Parthian invasion that so affected Roman policy in Palestine, demanding the settlement of disturbance at any cost. We discover no sensitivity to the threat the movement itself posed to a hierarchical and patriarchal society through its offer of communal egalitarianism to slaves and women.

The NT treatment of pagan society is overwhelmingly negative, here showing its roots in Judaism. The gentile world is considered morally degenerate and spiritually benighted. The Gospels (see Matt. 6:7, 32; 15:26) and the letters (see Rom. 1:18-32; 1 Pet. 1:14-18) agree that pagan life was "lived in the passions of our flesh," a matter of "following the desires of body and mind" and being "by nature children of wrath" (Eph. 2:3). Pagan satirists and moralists are even more condemning in their descriptions of the general moral decay of their day.

The reality was probably not so dismal. A. D. Nock notes

> It is . . . a grave error to think of the ordinary man in the Roman empire as a depraved and cruel fiend, dividing his hours between the brothel and intoxication, torturing a slave from time to time when he felt bored, and indifferent to the suffering and poverty of others.

The picture of total depravity, after all, comes to us not only from Christians interested in distancing themselves from their former life but from moralists who themselves embodied the highest standards within "pagan" society. Like all moralists, they delighted in exaggerating vices in order to make their appeal to virtue more dramatic, and they found their most vivid examples in those classes of society that could afford the more colorful sins. In fact, Roman law imposed a rather somber standard of morality, at least in public, and Hellenistic culture in general was profoundly, albeit unevenly, religious in its outlook.

Of course, not every religious expression was of the highest order. Rootlessness and resentment, the loss of a personal sense of worth, the lack of community, the sense of passivity before overarching and impersonal forces—these arouse powerful and often primitive religious responses. Magic and astrology were enormously popular even among the educated; they offered direct control, or at least foreknowledge, of the future. Wearing protective amulets was common, as was the casting of curses.

Credulity and superstition could be found among both the simple and the sophisticated (see Lucian of Samosata *The Lover of Lies*). Such religiosity was easily exploited by spiritual frauds and flimflammers. The Hellenistic world was well acquainted with the charlatan (*goēs*), who might appear in the guise of a sophist, rhetorician, philosopher, thaumaturge, or priest—but in every costume was the first-century equivalent of the snake-oil salesman, seducing the fearful crowd for personal profit and prestige. The satirist Lucian of Samosata gives us two sharply drawn portraits of such charlatans and the way they fed on the crowd's credulity (see *Alexander the False Prophet* and *The Passing of Peregrinus*). On the other hand, Philostratus' completely admiring account of another wandering preacher, Apollonius of Tyana, indicates that a fine line separated the fake from the sincere in the realm of popular religion and philosophy.

All was not superstition and magic, however. The development of moral and religious sensitivity in religion and philosophy prepared a soil in which the seed of the Christian message could grow.

Helenistic Religion

Little attention will be given here to traditional Greek or Roman religion, either in the official forms of public liturgies and the taking of auspices in temples or in domestic manifestations such as the burning of incense before household gods and the decorating of country shrines. Neither does the imperial cult require much consideration. Although the NT may contain some implicit polemic against it, as when the title "Lord of lords" is used with reference to Jesus, it remained a minor irritant during the period when the NT was being written. From the first genuflection before Alexander the Great to the deification of Claudius, the imperial cult was for the most part a political form of religious manipulation, never pretending to express the longing of human hearts. Particularly in Asia Minor, however, local enthusiasm for the imperial cult shows that it was by no means entirely a manifestation of Roman megalomania, but functioned positively as a social adhesive. It first became important to Christianity as the test case for the choice between monotheism and idolatry.

Of far greater importance for the NT are the popular developments within Hellenistic religion that responded to the grimmer religious mood created by empire, a mood in which the classical sense of order, which saw the world as cosmos, turned chaotic. Sometimes by renewing older elements of the tradition and sometimes by fusing them with other traditions, these developments shared an emphasis on personal religious experience and the esoteric rather than exoteric. The religious spirit of Hellenism in the early Roman Empire was one hungry for revelation, for transformation, and for a personal allegiance that would give a sense of identity in an alienating world.

Prophecy was held in high honor; not only the official variety, which involved the discernment of entrails, but especially the mantic type. It could be found at ancient oracle sites such as Delphi and Dodonna, and among the priests of foreign mystery cults. It was characterized by ecstasy and speaking in tongues. Frequently it was accompanied by physical rapture and even self-mutilation. Mantic prophecy was held in reverence from ancient times since it was regarded as a literal possession of the human psyche by the divine spirit (*pneuma*), an indwelling of the god (*enthusiasmos*; see Plato *Phaedrus* 244A). The revelations uttered may have been difficult to interpret but they were received as divine oracles (Plutarch *The E at Delphi* 387B).

Transcendent power (*dynamis*) was also manifested in miracles such as healings and exorcisms. Wandering charismatics like Apollonius of Tyana performed wonders and were sometimes regarded as divine men (*theioi andres*; see, e.g., Philostratus *Life of Apollonius of Tyana* IV.45). Healings were regularly accomplished by the savior gods Serapis and Asklepios. At the shrine of Asklepios, sick petitioners received the visitation of the god in their sleep and were healed. Like a first-century Lourdes, the walls of the shrine were adorned with the relics of the limbs and organs that had been restored, as well as plaques attesting the powers (*aretai*) of the god. Devotion to Asklepios could be both deep and personal, and the ritual meals held at the shrines of gods like Serapis offered a sense of community to their devotees.

Mystery cults were a feature of Greek religion for centuries, but their appeal had remained limited to a particular locality or clientele. In the early Roman Empire, the mystery cults gained a far wider appeal. This was partly due to the influx of new deities from the East such as Isis and her consort Osiris from Egypt, and the mother goddess Cybele from Phrygia in Asia Minor, who offered the double attraction of being both exotic and ancient. The wider appeal of the mysteries may have owed as much, though, to the needs of the age, for these cults offered divine revelation, transformation, and a sense of community. We know little about the actual rituals involved, but we do know that the initiates saw themselves as being saved from the inimical powers at work in the structures of the world, and dedicated to the god or goddess who had accomplished their transformation (Plutarch *Isis and Osiris* 382 E).

A similar attraction was at work in that pervasive but indefinable religious response called gnosis. We find elements of this response in the hermetic literature of paganism, the Merkabah mysticism of Judaism, and the gnostic writings of Christianity. At the birth of the NT, gnosis lacked a fully structured form and appears to have become a fully identifiable phenomenon only as the Christian heresy called Gnosticism. In the NT period, though, it was definitely present as a mood and as a variety of inchoate responses to a particular perception of the world.

Beneath all its variations, some elements of gnosis are consistent: a profoundly pessimistic worldview; human life seen as alienated from its true source and imprisoned in materiality; worldly existence seen as captive to cosmic forces inimical to God and to humans (see *Poimandres* 15). The religious response is to seek, through esoteric knowledge and ritual, escape from the power of materiality and the forces of fate at work in the social and political structures of the world. Such an escape cannot be complete until death, when the soul can shed its garments of flesh in its ascent to a heavenly, spiritual home (see *Poimandres* 22–25). But even in life, ecstatic visions can send the soul on a heavenly journey to discover the mysteries of transcendence.

A sense of both the lowest and the highest in Hellenistic religious responses can be found in the *Golden Ass* by Apuleius. On the surface, this is a dazzling romance, filled with fantastic and sometimes bawdy tales. At a deeper level, it is a story of a spiritual journey from alienation to restoration. The protagonist, Lucius, is a curious and cunning young man, fascinated by the possibility of using magic to control Chance (*fortuna*). He drinks a magical potion, thinking thereby to trick Chance, but of course finds himself tricked by her: he drinks the wrong potion and turns into an ass.

As an animal, in a condition symbolizing his spiritual alienation, Lucius is harried by Chance from one stage of degradation to another. At one point, he is sold as a pack animal to an old eunuch priest, "one of the scum that turns the Great Goddess of Syria into a beggar woman, hawking her along the road from town to town to the accompaniment of cymbals and castanets" (*Golden Ass* VIII.24). These priests include a form of mantic prophecy in their show (VIII.27):

> They would throw their heads forward so that their long hair fell down over their faces, then rotate them so rapidly that it wheeled about in a circle . . . they would bite themselves savagely, and as a climax cut their arms with the sharp knives they carried. One of them let himself go more ecstatically than the rest. Heaving deep sighs . . . as if filled with the spirit of the goddess, he pretended to go stark mad.

Chance seems bent on keeping Lucius imprisoned as an animal. His lowest point is reached when he becomes a performer in a sexual sideshow. Then, while at the port of Cenchrae (near Corinth), he has a sudden vision of the goddess Isis: ". . . fortune seemed at last to have made up her mind that I had suffered enough and to be offering me a hope of release."

Lucius prays to the goddess, and she responds with a long recitation of her names and attributes. We see in this scene how syncretism could move toward monotheism and how a mystery could demand an exclusive allegiance. Isis tells him (XI.5):

> You see me here, Lucius, in answer to your prayer. I am nature, the universal mother, mistress of all the elements . . . though I am worshipped in many aspects, known by countless names, and propitiated with all manner of different rites, yet the whole world venerates me. The primeval Phrygians call me the Goddess of Pessinus . . . the Athenians call me . . . the Minerva of Cecrops' citadel . . . and the Egyptians, who excel in ancient learning . . . call me by my true name, namely Queen Isis. I have come in pity of your plight, I have come to favor and aid you. Weep no more, lament no longer; the hour of deliverance, shone over by my watchful light, is at hand. Listen attentively to my orders . . .

She demands from Lucius faith and complete devotion (XI.6):

> . . . from now on until the very last day of your life, you are dedicated to my service. It is only right that you should devote your whole life to the goddess who made you a man again . . . I alone have the power to prolong your life beyond the limits appointed by destiny.

Isis saves him from captivity to Chance, and even from inexorable Fate. She restores him to full humanity, promising him immortality. Being transformed back into his human form, Lucius is initiated into her mystery and that of her consort Osiris. He enjoys the company of fellow initiates. He proudly wears the distinctive garb and hairdress of the initiate as he pursues his now worthwhile life as a lawyer and priest of Osiris (XI.20–30). In short, he has found new life.

The *Golden Ass* reveals the craving of ordinary people for some power over their life and some sense of identity in an alienating world. Those desires could be met only imperfectly by magic and astrology. The mysteries offered much more. The case of Lucius indicates that we can add conversion to the list of Hellenistic religious experiences. The commitment of Lucius to Isis did not preclude his honoring other gods, but it did reverse the direction of his life in a fundamental way, and in return for his lifelong commitment to her he could expect to receive eternal life.

Hellenistic Philosophy

Philosophy had changed since the days of Plato and Aristotle. The philosophical schools continued to compete for adherents and attacked each other polemically. But the "love of wisdom" (*philosophia*) was now equated less with metaphysics and politics and more with the art of living; there was a definite shift from theory to therapy. Philosophy was a way of life. For some, it was a religious calling.

Among the great schools, Stoicism had the most obvious influence. This was surely due in part to the way its concentration on the virtues and duties of the individual fit the societal situation. If Fate, Chance, and the power of the state are beyond our control, then what can we do? We can focus on things in our control: our mind, our desires. Stoicism had an officially positive view of reality: the universe was rational, and divine providence (*pronoia*) governed events (see Epictetus *Discourses* I.6). The person who sought to live according to nature, that is, reasonably, would be virtuous and therefore happy. One could be at home anywhere; the ideal was to be a citizen of the world. Nothing could prevent a person from being a fully realized human being— reasonable, self-controlled, and content—not even slavery or exile. Even death was not to be feared, for it too was natural (Epictetus *Discourses* III.5.8–11). Stoics like Musonius Rufus and Epictetus taught a severe form of virtue, with an extraordinarily strict sexual code and inner-directed morality. The tightness of the Stoic focus, however, was itself an indication that much of life could not be controlled. And the ethics of self-control was a desperate accommodation to a world in which the structures of state and family were often not according to reason.

Philosophy was also syncretistic in the Hellenistic period. All philosophers agreed that theoretical differences were less significant than practical results. And no tradition was more practical and nontheoretical than Cynicism, which especially affected Stoicism during the early empire. Cynicism represented a wholly individualistic approach. It eschewed doctrine in favor of freedom and free speech. Freedom meant living just as one pleased, even when—as was often the case—this meant contravening society's standards. Free speech meant the willingness to revile those who conformed to those same standards. The Cynic responded to an alienating social structure by celebrating an untrammeled individualism. The Cynic hero was Diogenes, and many were the stories that told of his snubs of the great and that demonstrated the excellence of "the free, the open-air, life" (see Lucian *Dialogues of the Dead* and Dio Chrysostom *Oration* 6). The Stoicism of Epictetus was particularly influenced by this Cynic tendency, so much so that his description of the ideal philosopher is really one of the ideal Cynic: Diogenes is for him as important a model as Socrates (Epictetus *Discourses* III.22). Although Stoicism domesticated Cynicism, there remained tensions between the traditions. For the Stoics, perfection was difficult if not impossible to attain; for the Cynics, it was simply defined and easily accomplished: freedom and free speech summed it up.

Small wonder, then, that the Cynics, in particular, attracted people who wanted to be called philosophers but did not want to work at it. Satirists have left us wonderful portraits of these would-be philosophers who had all the right equipment (rough cloak, bag, staff, long hair, and beard) and right speech (reviling the hypocrisy of others) but all the while sought to fulfill their own appetites, thus enjoying the reputation for virtue without paying its price (Lucian *Timon* 54). Many times these charlatans hit the road; from town to town they would go, reviling passersby at street corners and preaching in the marketplace. Apollonius of Tyana was one such wandering wise man (see Philostratus *Life of Apollonius* IV.2). Even more impressive was Dio of Prusa, called Chrysostom, who began as a traveling rhetorician but after a conversion experience (Dio *Oration* 13) became a philosopher. Though he continued to travel and speak, now it was "to aid everyone" (Dio *Oration* 77/78).

Not all philosophers were so mobile. Some, like Seneca, were court counselors. Others, like Musonius and Epictetus, were schoolteachers whose "diatribes" were lively pedagogical exercises. Whatever their social setting, philosophers agreed that the good life was the virtuous life. Much of their energy went into the description and dissection of vice and virtue. Sometimes this was by way of acute psychological analysis: a saying attributed to Socrates ran, "Envy is the ulcer of the soul" (Stobaeus, *Greek Anthology* III.38.48). Sometimes social obligations were systematically displayed, as in the tables of household ethics (see Plutarch *Advice to Bride and Groom* 142E). And at other times the sheer cataloguing of vices made the point that all vice is illness and all virtue is health. Few vice lists were as extravagant as that of Philo Judaeus, who declared that the pleasure lover would also be "unscrupulous, impudent, cross-tempered, unsociable, intractable, lawless, troublesome, passionate, headstrong, coarse, impatient of rebuke, reckless, evil planning," and, some 130 vices later, "a scoffer, a glutton, a simpleton, a mass of misery and misfortune without relief" (Philo *Sacrifice of Cain and Abel* 32).

Vice as illness, virtue as health: medicine was one of the governing metaphors for philosophy in this age. The philosopher was a physician, able to diagnose spiritual illness and prescribe the appropriate remedy (Dio *Oration* 32.14–30). The philosophical school, in turn, was a hospital, and the first step toward getting better was recognizing that one was sick: "The lecture room of the philosopher is a hospital; you ought not to walk out of it in pleasure but in pain" (Epictetus *Discourses* III.23.30).

From healing to salvation is not a large leap, and some philosophers had a deeply religious perception of their calling. Epictetus is the most obvious example—though not the only one (see also Dio *Oration* 32.12). He frequently quotes the *Hymn of Cleanthes*, "Lead me thou on, O Zeus and Destiny" (*Discourses* II.23.42), sees his own life as one of service to God (I.16.21), and uses explicitly religious terminology in his description of the ideal Cynic: he is called by God and "has been sent by Zeus to men, partly as a messenger . . . partly as a scout" (III.22.2, and 23).

Not all philosophers were as pious as Epictetus, but all conceived of philosophy as more than a course of study; it was a way of life. Philosophers dressed and acted differently from most people. Becoming a philosopher meant turning from one way of life to another; the term "conversion" is an appropriate one. Even the satirist Lucian was aware of this convention. At the end of the *Wisdom of Nigrinus*, a description of one of the few philosophers he admired, Lucian portrays a young man, transformed by Nigrinus' words, relating them to a friend. Both conclude that they should return to join the one who had first wounded them so that they might also be healed by him (*Nigrinus* 38).

The religious dimensions of philosophy are even more evident in those schools that brought their students into a full community life, like the Pythagoreans and Epicureans. Both based their communal life on the ideal of spiritual friendship. The Pythagoreans made literal application of the ancient proverb "friends hold all things in common" and pooled their material goods (Iamblichus *Life of Pythagoras* 18). The Epicureans had no organized sharing of possessions but were generous in their expressions of friendship (Epicurus *Fragments* 23, 34, 39, 42). Both schools regarded their founders as virtually divine. Some even paid homage to Epicurus during his lifetime (Plutarch *Against Colotes* 1117 A–D). Both groups saw doctrine as a means of ensuring the soul's bliss and emphasized tradition: the maxims of Pythagoras and Epicurus were memorized by members of the school (Diogenes Laertius *Life of Epicurus* X.12).

The Epicureans also used letter writing as a means of maintaining support among their communities.

It is evident that these philosophical schools offered a sense of identity and a real experience of community that was deeper than any offered by the clubs and associations so common in the Roman Empire. The Epicureans, in fact, concentrated so exclusively on the inner life of the group, advocating the quiet life removed from political activity, that they were sometimes attacked for being misanthropic (Plutarch *Against Colotes* 1125 C–F).

Misunderstanding was not the worst thing philosophers had to suffer. Though often admired by the common people, they were held in suspicion by authorities (Dio Cassius *Roman History* 52.36.4) and exile was a common fate (Philostratus *Life of Apollonius* IV.35). Rome had a complex attitude toward voluntary groups. It was surprisingly tolerant of cults and allowed many other forms of association, from funerary societies to trade guilds. But it was deeply suspicious of any gathering that from Rome's point of view might foment rebellion. Since philosophers were notorious for challenging the social order, they were possible sources of subversion. Hence, they were more generally suspected and more harshly treated than other groups.

The Reinterpretation of Symbols

The Hellenistic period was one of ferment in both religion and philosophy. Religion took many forms, and philosophy was as variegated as its adherents. The causes of change were multiple as well. But if one cause were to be isolated as most pivotal, it would unquestionably be the fact of empire, which fundamentally altered traditional Greek values by changing the social context for their expression. The manifold developments in religion and philosophy were responses to the collapse of traditional norms and symbols caused by an alienating societal structure.

It is important to recognize, however, that these developments did not lead to the invention of new symbols. Rather, they reflect the use and reinterpretation of the traditional symbols that were still available. This new use of the traditional past is most pertinent to our investigation. The religious leaders and philosophers of first-century Hellenism did not conceive of themselves as creating new and better ways. To the contrary, they never questioned the notion held by all that antiquity was far superior to novelty. Their task, therefore, was to establish and demonstrate continuity with the traditions of the past as new challenges were met. Religious leaders, practicing rituals as ancient as their people, would accept gods from abroad when these gods were perceived to be even more ancient than their own, and consequently all the more powerful and worthy of veneration. In fact, openness to barbarian wisdom during this time was rationalized as receptivity to a knowledge older than that available to the Greeks. Philosophers, in turn, saw their own concentration on virtue and self-control as continuing what Socrates had done long ago. This search for ancient precedent and the reinterpretation of symbols can be demonstrated by two features of Hellenistic philosophy: the employment and rereading of authoritative texts, and the use of models from the past.

The Hellenistic world had its sacred texts. Greek culture, in fact, was shaped throughout its long history by the constant reading and rereading of texts from its remote past. It found the ideal of culture (*paideia*) as the noble expression of virtue (*arētē*) first and best expressed in the heroic poems of Homer. In the *Iliad* and *Odyssey*, and to some extent also in Hesiod and the classical dramatists, the Greeks found tales of great deeds and, as well, the involvement of gods in human affairs. The reading and appropriate use of these texts were basic to the education of rhetors and philosophers alike. The texts carried with them self-evident and weighty authority.

Since the writing of the Homeric poems, however, much had changed in society and in the understanding of nobility. No longer was virtue the rustic sort that is valued by warriors. The myths of the gods found in Homer and Hesiod were regarded as offensive in light of greater moral sensitivity and scientific knowledge. Tales that spoke of gods lusting after each other, mating with humans, and engaging in feuds were scandalous. They attributed to gods qualities unacceptable even in humans (see Josephus *Against Apion* II.34.242–49). In other words, the classical texts that had provided Hellenism with its fundamental symbolic framework were at risk of becoming dysfunctional because of new experiences.

The reaction of some was to abandon the texts altogether. Plato admired the poetry of Homer but mistrusted the tales (*Republic* 378 B–E, 595 B–C) and finally denied poetry a place in his ideal state (*Republic* 398A). The Epicureans, who denied the existence of gods anyway, saw all myths as blinding people to a scientific view of the world (Philodemus *On Piety* 18). But those more committed to the ethical and religious values implicit in possessing such normative texts—their antiquity, their divine inspiration—found it important to reclaim the texts by reinterpreting them. How? Precisely in the light of the new scientific and ethical developments that had caused them to be questioned in the first place.

Antisthenes may have been the first to claim that Homer said "some things in accord with fancy and some in accord with reality" (Dio *Oration* 53.5), but it is with the Stoics that we find systematic use of allegory as a way of reclaiming sacred texts. Simply stated, allegorical interpretation claims that the surface (literal) meaning of the text is only a cipher pointing to another meaning. The text says one thing but means another, and the "real" truth can be reached by knowing the system of meaning (scientific or ethical) that will unlock the text. One such system was etymology; Plutarch passes on a common way of using it: "Cronos is but a figurative name for Chronos (time), Hera for air, and . . . the birth of Hephaestus symbolizes the change of air into fire" (*Isis and Osiris* 363D).

In allegorical interpretation, gods were not really fornicating or fighting; rather, the myths were expressing cosmological, psychological, or ethical truths. Thus, in the *Odyssey*, we read of "the loves of Ares and Aphrodite and how they first began their affair in the house of Hephaestus" (VIII.266–366). It is manifestly a tale of adultery. But in the *Homeric Questions* of Heraclitus (no. 69), we see that the union of Ares and Aphrodite is really the combination of strife and love in harmony. The explanation of Cornutus is very similar (*Compendium of Greek Theology* 19). The texts, in short, are still "true" and still authoritative, but only if understood in the proper way.

Allegorical interpretation was not practiced by all who cited these texts, but the principles involved won wide approval. We even see other myths interpreted allegorically, as when Plutarch says of the Egyptian myths (*Isis and Osiris* 355 B–D), "You must not think that any of these tales happened in the manner in which they are related," and goes on to advise:

> if, then, you listen to the stories about the gods in this way, accepting them from those who interpret the story reverently and philosophically [*hosiōs kai philosophikōs*], and if you always perform and observe the established rites of worship . . . you may avoid superstition which is no less an evil than atheism.

This way of rereading sacred texts provided a precedent that was eagerly followed by Hellenistic Jews. They also had ancient, venerable, and sometimes troublesome Scriptures, which were in need of reverent and philosophical interpretation. Allegory came into its own in the scriptural exegesis of Hellenistic Judaism.

One reason classical texts needed to be maintained was that they provided models for life. To an extent that we can scarcely appreciate, Greek culture was built on the imitation of models from the past. The arts of writing and speaking were based on explicit imitation of examples (*paradeigmata*) found in classical sources. The style of the present copied, so far as possible, that of the past. Novelty was not a value.

Imitating models was essential to the learning of virtue as well. The Greeks were convinced that virtue could not be taught by command, but had to be learned from observation of its living expression in parent or teacher. The teacher was to be a living textbook of the virtuous life. That is why charlatans who professed virtue but did not live it were so dangerous: they presented false examples to others.

The classical texts needed to be reinterpreted so that the models might continue to function positively. The ideals of virtue were no longer those of the archaic nobles who fought for honor. Allegory helped the Hellenistic reader discover contemporary virtues beneath those simpler, ruder ones. And in moral discourse, figures from the myths, like Odysseus, took on new dimensions in line with contemporary perceptions. The figure of Heracles, in particular, was developed in a manner that the simple recitals in Hesiod's *Theogony* (450–470) would not lead one to suspect. His labors now were seen as acts of great virtue, and Heracles was the model of the philosopher.

The myth had it that Heracles abandoned his children. Epictetus, however, makes this act of neglect a positive virtue. It showed how Heracles saw Zeus as the father of all and how the philosopher could be happy in any place, even apart from his children (Epictetus *Discourses* III.24.13–17). As the philosopher was a physician and king, so Heracles (III.26.32; see also Dio *Oration* 1.84)

> was ruler and leader of all the land and sea, purging them of injustice and law-lessness, and introducing justice and righteousness, and all this naked and by himself.

Heracles became a "son of God" (II.16.44) and the model of those who achieved immortality and divine status by their virtue. One who imitated Heracles could hope for the same divine elevation (Pseudo-Heraclitus *Epistle* 4).

Not only mythical figures but also philosophers from the past functioned as models. Socrates and Diogenes were the preeminent examples of the philosophic life. For Epictetus, Socrates was a citizen of the world and kin to the gods (I.9.22); he was free in every respect (I.12.23) and the example that others imitated (I.19.6); he held rank next to Heracles (II.18.22). As for Diogenes, Epictetus measured a potential Cynic this way: "Is he a man worthy to carry the staff of Diogenes?" (III.22.57; cf. Dio *Oration* 4.12–39). Even contemporary philosophers could be models for their students (Lucian *Demonax* and *Nigrinus*). The writing of biographies of philosophical founders—by Diogenes Laertius, for example—enabled students to learn their doctrines and imitate their virtues. The ultimate relationship in which the imitation of a model was demonstrated, of course, was that between father and son (Pseudo-Isocrates *To Demonicus* 9).

These developments were complex and often colored by religious perceptions. The lines between hero, demigod, immortal, prophet, sage, and divine man were often obscure. The ambiguity and obscurity indicate that both philosophy and religion were, in that day, open to the transcendent and eager for the experience of transformation.

Study Questions

1. What were the main tools of Hellenization used by Alexander and his successors?

2. What impact did empire have on Greek culture?

3. What is meant by the statement that Hellenistic philosophy turned "from theory to therapy"?

4. What were the importance and roles of prophecy and healing in Hellenistic religion?

5. What was the significance of the "network of communication" (roads and letter-writing) in the Roman empire for the earliest churches?

Bibliographical Note

Unless otherwise noted, all translations from Greek and Latin authors are found in the Loeb Classical Library (Cambridge: Harvard Univ. Press; London: William Heinemann). The sections of Apuleius in this chapter come from *The Golden Ass*, trans. R. Graves (New York: Farrar, Strauss & Giroux, 1951), 187, 190, 262, 264–66. The quotation of A. D. Nock is from *Conversion* (London: Oxford Univ. Press, 1933), 218.

For introductory surveys of the symbolic world of the NT, see R. Bultmann, *Primitive Christianity in Its Contemporary Setting*, trans. R. Fuller (Philadelphia: Fortress Press, 1956); E. Ferguson, *Backgrounds of Early Christianity*, 2nd ed. (Grand Rapids: Eerdmans, 1993); H. Koester, *History, Culture, and Religion of the Hellenistic Age*, 2nd ed. (New York: Walter de Gruyter, 1995); B. Reicke, *The New Testament Era*, trans. D. Green (Philadelphia: Fortress Press, 1980 [1956]); U. Schelle, *The History and Theology of New Testament Writings*, trans. M. E. Boring (Minneapolis: Fortress Press, 1998); and N. T. Wright, *The New Testament and the People of God* (Minneapolis: Fortress Press, 1992). One should also consult the invaluable eight volume series edited by W. A Meeks, *Library of Early Christianity* (Philadelphia: Westminster Press, 1986–87), which explores the Greco-Roman and Jewish backgrounds of the NT. Engaging introductions to the symbols of the NT world are provided by B. J. Malina, *The New Testament World: Insights from Cultural Anthropology*, rev. ed. (Atlanta: John Knox Press, 1993); and R. Rohrbaugh (ed.), *The Social Sciences and New Testament Interpretation* (Peabody, Mass.: Hendrickson Pubs., 1996). Selections of primary texts pertinent to the NT can be found in C. K. Barrett, *The New Testament Background: Writings from Ancient Greece and the Roman Empire That Illuminate Christian Origins*, rev. ed. (New York: Harper & Row, 1987), and E. M. Boring et al. (eds.), *Hellenistic Commentary to the New Testament* (Nashville: Abingdon Press, 1995). Standard treatments of Hellenistic history and culture include M. Hadas, *Hellenistic Culture* (New York: W. W. Norton & Co., 1959); W. W. Tarn, *Hellenistic Civilization*, 3rd rev. ed., with G. T. Griffith (New York: World Pub. Co., 1952); and P. Green, *Alexander to Actium: The Historical Evolution of the Hellenistic Age* (Berkeley: Univ. of California Press, 1990). For the Roman period more specifically, see P. Petit, *Pax Romana*, trans. J. Willis (Berkeley: Univ. of California Press, 1976); and K. Galinsky, *Augustan Culture: An Interpretive Introduction* (Princeton: Princeton Univ. Press, 1996). An indispensable reference work for the history and culture of the ancient world is S. Hornblower and A. Spawforth (eds.), *The Oxford Classical Dictionary*, 3rd ed. (New York: Oxford Univ. Press, 1996).

Classic studies of the Roman context are J. Carcopino, *Daily Life in Ancient Rome*, ed. H. T. Rowell, trans. E. O. Lorimer (New York: Penguin Books, 1985 [1940]), and S. Dill,

Roman Society from Nero to Marcus Aurelius (New York: World Pub. Co., 1956 (1904]). For more recent treatments, see M. Goodman (with J. Sherwood), *The Roman World: 44 BC–AD 180* (New York: Routledge, 1997); P. Garnsey and R. Saller, *The Roman Empire: Economy, Society and Culture* (Berkeley: Univ. of California Press, 1987); R. MacMullen, *Roman Social Relations: 50 B.C. to A.D. 284* (New Haven: Yale Univ. Press, 1974); and P. Veyne (ed.), *A History of Private Life; Volume 1: From Pagan Rome to Byzantium*, trans. A. Goldhammer (Cambridge: Harvard Univ. Press, 1987). A good sense of the imperial atmosphere is given by R. Macmullen, *Enemies of the Roman Order: Treason, Unrest, and Alienation in the Empire* (New York: Routledge, 1992 [1966]). Connections to Christianity are drawn in S. Benko and J. J. O'Rourke (eds.), *The Catacombs and the Coliseum: The Roman Empire as the Setting of Primitive Christianity* (Valley Forge, Pa.: Judson Press, 1971). A selection of primary texts is found in N. Lewis and M. Reinhold, *Roman Civilization: Selected Readings*, 2 vols., 3rd ed. (New York: Columbia Univ. Press, 1990).

Aspects of Hellenistic and Roman religion are considered by G. Anderson, *Sage, Saint and Sophist: Holy Men and Their Associates in the Early Roman Empire* (New York: Routledge, 1994); W. Burkert, *Greek Religion*, trans. J. Raffan (Cambridge: Harvard Univ. Press, 1985); D. Feeney, *Literature and Religion at Rome: Cultures, Contexts, and Beliefs* (Cambridge: Cambridge Univ. Press, 1998)—by far the best book ever done on Roman religion; R. MacMullen, *Paganism in the Roman Empire* (New Haven: Yale Univ. Press, 1981); L. H. Martin, *Hellenistic Religions: An Introduction* (New York: Oxford Univ. Press, 1987); A. D. Nock, *Essays on Religion in the Ancient World*, 2 vols., ed. Z. Stewart (New York: Oxford Univ. Press, 1972); R. M. Ogilvie, *The Romans and Their Gods in the Age of Augustus* (New York: W. W. Norton & Co., 1969); R. Turcan, *The Cults of the Roman Empire*, trans. A. Nevill (Cambridge, Mass.: Blackwell, 1996); and A. Wardman, *Religion and Statecraft Among the Romans* (London: Granada, 1982). Pertinent primary texts are selected in F. C. Grant's two collections: *Ancient Roman Religion* (Indianapolis: Bobbs-Merrill, 1957) and *Hellenistic Religion: The Age of Syncretism* (Indianapolis: Bobbs-Merrill, 1953). Also see M. Beard, et al., *Religions of Rome*, 2 vols. (Cambridge: Cambridge Univ. Press, 1998).

On specific facets of ancient religion, see the following: for the mysteries, W. Burkert, *Ancient Mystery Cults* (Cambridge: Harvard Univ. Press, 1987), the source collection by M. W. Meyer (ed.), *The Ancient Mysteries: A Sourcebook* (San Francisco: Harper & Row, 1987), the classic by R. Reitzenstein, *Hellenistic Mystery Religions: Their Basic Ideas and Significance*, trans. J. E. Steely (Pittsburgh: Pickwick Press, 1978), and D. Ulansey, *The Origins of the Mithraic Mysteries: Cosmology & Salvation in the Ancient World* (New York: Oxford Univ. Press, 1989); for magic, the collection of texts and introductions by G. Luck, *Arcana Mundi: Magic and the Occult in the Greek and Roman Worlds* (Baltimore: Johns Hopkins Univ. Press, 1985), and C. A. Faraone and D. Obbink (eds.), *Magika Hiera: Ancient Christian Magic & Religion* (New York: Oxford Univ. Press, 1991); for the pervasive traditions concerning miracles, W. Cotter, *Miracles in Greco-Roman Antiquity* (New York: Routledge, 1998), H. C. Kee, *Miracle in the Early Christian World: A Study in Sociohistorical Method* (New Haven: Yale Univ. Press, 1983), and H. E. Remus, "Miracle (NT)," *ABD* 4: 859–69; for conversion, A. D. Nock, *Conversion: The Old and New in Religion from Alexander the Great to Augustine of Hippo* (Baltimore: Johns Hopkins Univ. Press, 1998 [1933]), N. Shumate, *Crisis and Conversion in Apuleius' Metamorphoses* (Ann Arbor: Univ. of Michigan Press, 1996), and T. M. Finn, *From Death to Rebirth: Ritual and Conversion in Antiquity* (New York: Paulist Press, 1997); for prayer, M. Kiley et al. (eds.), *Prayer from Alexander to Constantine* (New York: Routledge, 1997), and S. Pulleyn, *Prayer in Greek Religion* (New York: Oxford Univ. Press, 1997); for prophecy, D. E. Aune, *Prophecy in Early Christianity and the Mediterranean World* (Grand Rapids: Eerdmans, 1983), and H. W. Parke, *Sibyls and Sibylline Prophecy in Classical Antiquity*, ed. B. C. McGing (New York: Routledge, 1988); for the imperial cult, S. R. F. Price, *Rituals and Power: The Roman Imperial Cult in Asia Minor* (Cambridge: Cambridge Univ. Press, 1984); for the darker side of Hellenistic religiosity, E. R. Dodds, *The Greeks and the Irrational* (Berkeley: Univ. of California Press, 1966 [1951]), and H. Jonas, *The Gnostic Religion: The Message of the Alien God and the Beginnings of Christianity*, 2nd ed. (Boston: Beacon Press, 1963); and for the often neglected facet of women's religious experience, the source collection by S. Kraemer, *Maenads, Martyrs, Matrons, Monastics: A Sourcebook on Women's Religions in the Greco-Roman World* (Philadelphia: Fortress Press, 1988), and her important synthesis of the material, *Her Share of the Blessings: Women's Religions Among Pagans, Jews, and Christians in the Greco-Roman World* (New York: Oxford Univ. Press, 1992).

For a comprehensive survey of ancient philosophy see G. Reale, *A History of Ancient Philosophy*, 4 vols., trans. J. R. Catan (Albany: State Univ. of New York Press, 1985–90). The emphases of philosophy in the Hellenistic period are treated in J. Annas, *The Morality of Happiness* (New York: Oxford Univ. Press, 1993); P. Bilde et al. (eds.), *Conventional Values of the Hellenistic Greeks* (Stockholm: Almqvist & Wiksell, 1997); R. B. Branham and M. O. Goulet-Cazé (eds.), *The Cynics: The Cynic Movement in Antiquity and Its Legacy* (Berkeley: Univ. of California Press, 1996); A. A. Long, *Hellenistic Philosophy: Stoics, Epicureans, Skeptics*, 2nd ed. (Berkeley: Univ. of California Press, 1986); the source collection, translation, and commentary of A. A. Long and D. N. Sedley (eds.), *The Hellenistic Philosophers*, 2 vols. (Cambridge: Cambridge Univ. Press, 1987); the source collection by A. J. Malherbe, *Moral Exhortation, A Greco-Roman Sourcebook* (Philadelphia: Westminster Press, 1986); M. C. Nussbaum, *The Therapy of Desire: Theory and Practice in Hellenistic Ethics* (Princeton: Princeton Univ. Press, 1994); and R. W. Sharples, *Stoics, Epicureans and Skeptics: An Introduction to Hellenistic Philosophy* (New York: Routledge, 1996). On the importance of imitating models in Hellenistic culture, see W. Jaeger, *Paideia: The Ideals of Greek Culture*, 3 vols., trans. G. Highet (New York: Oxford Univ. Press, 1939–45); H. I. Marrou, *The History of Education in Antiquity*, trans. G. Lamb (New York: Sheed & Ward, 1956); and G. Kennedy, *The Art of Persuasion in Greece* (Princeton: Princeton Univ. Press, 1963).

2. Judaism in Palestine

THE SYMBOLS OF the NT are fundamentally those of Judaism, to the extent that the first Christian writings can fairly be considered part of first-century Jewish literature. As the literature of a separatist Jewish group, however, the NT's use of these symbols is complex: it appropriates the riches of Judaism wholesale, but in its need to demonstrate its exclusive claim to these symbols, it shows hostility to those Jews who remain unenthusiastic about the sect. So intricate is the process of identification and separation that a knowledge of first-century Judaism is a precondition for the intelligent reading of the NT.

In contrast to the remarkably uniform impression made by the talmudic tradition that dominated Judaism for nearly two millennia, the Judaism of the first century was anything but uniform. The strain that represented Judaism's future and that after the destruction of the temple in 70 C.E. became normative, namely, the Pharisaic movement, was in NT days only one variety of Judaism among others. Distinctions within Judaism were partially due to geographical and linguistic factors (see chap. 3, on the forms of Judaism in the Diaspora). In Palestine, however, ideological differences were even more significant in shaping multiform and competing versions of Judaism.

The diversity of first-century Judaism was contained, however, within a consistent framework of self-definition. Pagans could recognize even the most thoroughly Hellenized Jews as members of a "second race." The framework, or symbolic world, shared by all Jews was that found in Torah. In the NT, *torah* is usually translated as "Law," but it is a word infinitely complex in its associations. It refers first to the Sacred Writings of Israel. The first denotation of *Torah* is the five books of Moses (the Law/Pentateuch). *Torah* is also used to designate the other portions of Scripture: the Prophets (*neviim*) and the Writings (*kethuvim*). These were the most ancient Scriptures extant; they expressed God's own word, and in them could be found all needful knowledge and wisdom. Everywhere, Jews based their lives on these texts.

Within Torah as text, Jews in every nation and every generation discovered their identity as a people, a sense given to those who share a common story. When they listened to these narratives, they could consider themselves a people in direct continuity with those called by the Lord from Egypt, redeemed from slavery, gifted by covenant in the wilderness, and more: a people awaiting the complete fulfillment of the promise made at the dawn of history to the patriarch Abraham, that in them, all the nations of the earth would be blessed (Gen. 12:3).

43

Torah also means "commandment," *mitzvah*. When the Lord chose this people out of all the earth, he showed himself as a God of faithfulness and loving kindness (Exod. 34:6). The covenant he made with Israel demanded the same qualities of them. They were to be faithful to the Lord and not turn away to other gods; they were also to show covenantal love to one another (Lev. 19:18). The "love with all their heart" they had toward God (Deut. 6:4-5) was manifested in their attitudes and actions toward other humans. The commandments spelled out those responses, articulating the demands of covenantal fidelity and love (Deut. 6:1-3). And by observing them, Israel was to show all peoples that God is holy, that is, utterly different from any imaginable powers on earth. Israel was to be a "holy nation" (Exod. 19:6), different from other peoples on the earth: "I am the Lord who brought you up out of the land of Egypt, to be your God; you shall therefore be holy, for I am holy" (Lev. 11:45). This aspect of the commandments, however, became increasingly problematic: what did being holy demand?

Whatever their differences, then, all Jews affirmed the symbols provided by Torah. They therefore shared a sense of election as God's special people, and a sense of responsibility for manifesting that election by being a people among whom God's rule (God's kingdom) was effective. Precisely because the symbols of Torah and people were so central and interdependent, they became the focus of unity and diversity among Jews in the NT period.

As we begin to look at the variety of Judaism in Palestine, where both political and religious experiences profoundly altered the shape of these symbols of Torah and people, some caution is required. For the sake of analysis, we will describe traditions and concepts as though they were separate entities. But to speak of apocalyptic thought or rabbinic theology or even Hellenistic Judaism is to name elements that existed not in isolation but in complex combinations. Because there were ideologically divided groups in first-century Palestine, it is extremely tempting to distribute ideas and sects in perfect alignment. However attractive, the impulse should be resisted, for experience teaches us that a single mind is capable of holding in fragile balance many and logically conflicting ideas. Even more so are communities able to calmly and unself-consciously juggle ideologically self-contradictory notions. In the Qumran community, for instance, we see a group equally devoted to law, apocalyptic, wisdom, mysticism, messianism, zealotry, and liturgy. And, in the great Rabbi Akiba, we see a patron saint of the legal tradition who was also an adept of mysticism and who proclaimed Bar Kochba (a second-century c.e. revolutionary) the awaited messiah. Our aim here, then, is to describe some distinguishable features, without pretending that these are all that need to be considered or that they ever existed apart from the living expressions of individuals and communities.

The Political Context

Three factors in particular accounted for the diversity in first-century Palestinian Judaism. First was the pervasive presence and force of Hellenistic culture. Second was the reality of Greek, then Roman, political hegemony. Third was a traditional inter-connection drawn between religious and sociopolitical realities: both ideology and practice had for a long time identified the fulfillment of the promise to Abraham with the people's secure possession of the land (Gen. 50:24; Exod. 3:16-17; Josh. 1:2-4), had coalesced God's rule with the Davidic dynasty (2 Sam. 7:11-16), and had sometimes equated the temple with the presence of God in the land (1 Kings 8:22-53).

Palestine was so strategically located that empire builders needed to secure it if they wished to rule the East. But because it was inhabited by a people with such a pecu-liar sense of itself—"You shall be my own possession among all peoples; for all the earth is mine, and you shall be to me a kingdom of priests and a holy nation" (Exod. 19:6)—Palestine was never a secure imperial possession. From the period of the Mac-cabean revolt (167 B.C.E.) to the collapse of all messianic hope in the Bar Kochba rebellion (135 C.E.), Palestine was violently torn apart by political strife. So tense were the years of Jesus' ministry that his proclamation "the Kingdom of God is at hand" (Mark 1:15) could not help being both inflammatory and deeply ambiguous.

The story can be read as one of a brave and united people fighting off foreign culture and despotic rule. That is part of the story, and it is highlighted in the Jewish propaganda of the period. But that is too simple a reading. The story is also one of a people divided over the issues of Hellenism and empire. The struggle for Jewish iden-tity in Palestine involved opposition to forces hostile to the people of God from with-out, and disagreements over the meaning of being the people of God from within.

The stages of the story are well known and can be quickly noted. Although during the Babylonian exile (586 B.C.E.) an identity was forged that depended exclusively on Torah (Ezra 7:10; Neh. 8:1-8), the return from exile in 538 B.C.E. provided an oppor-tunity to restore the temple (Ezra 3:10-13) and the hope of kingship (Zech. 9:9) to the purified people who had returned to the land (Neh. 13:30). The years after the restora-tion are largely silent, broken only by a few sources that indicate that the problems of pluralism continued (Ezra 10:9-44). Those who fought for the rule of Torah in the land did so with increasing rigidity (Mal. 2:10-16). When the sources speak again, we find the land caught in a struggle between Seleucids and Ptolemies, and the priesthood bought and sold by corrupt Hellenizers (2 Macc. 4:7-16). But when Antiochus IV Epiphanes tried to impose syncretistic worship by placing the statue of Zeus Olympus in the temple and forbidding observance of Torah (1 Macc. 1:41-57; 2 Macc. 6:1-6), the spark of rebellion was struck by Mattathias and those "zealous for the law" (1 Macc. 2:27).

Surprisingly, the revolt succeeded, aided by Rome's timely but fateful support (1 Macc. 8). Quite unexpectedly, then, both kingdom and priesthood were restored in the Hasmonean dynasty (143–37 B.C.E.; see 1 Macc. 13:41). But it was a kingdom dependent on Roman approval and a priesthood increasingly in the hands of venal men, so the dream of a restored inheritance, kingship, priesthood, and consecration as "He promised through the law" (2 Macc. 2:17-18) was diluted by a harsher reality. Years of squabbling over the priesthood brought at long last the decisive Roman intervention by Pompey in his conquest of Judea (63 B.C.E.). This was followed by steadily increasing subjugation, first under the looser control of local chieftains, then (in 6 C.E.) under the sterner hand of provincial procurators. Continued resistance to Roman rule led to the Jewish War of 66–70 C.E., which ended in the ruthless siege of Jerusalem and the destruction of the temple in 70, a date of pivotal importance for the continuing and separate development of Judaism and Christianity. Then, more desperately, sporadic revolts led to the Bar Kochba rebellion, which, once crushed (135 C.E.), ended all hope of identifying the promise to Abraham with the temporal rule of Palestine under a Davidic king guided by Torah.

Throughout this period, Palestinian Jewish ambivalence toward Hellenism was widespread. Hellenism had made significant inroads well before the time of Antiochus IV: some sixteen cities had been Hellenized, and the first steps toward making Jerusalem a *polis* with a gymnasium were taken, not by the Seleucids (as one might expect) but by the leading families of Jerusalem. Many Jews were eager to learn these new and attractive ways: "Let us go and make a covenant with the Gentiles round about us, for since we separated from them many evils have come upon us" (1 Macc. 1:11). The use of Greek was pervasive, especially in Galilee. Aristotle is said to have met a Jew from Coele-Syria who "not only spoke Greek, but had the soul of a Greek" (Josephus *Against Apion* I.179–181). Indeed, Zeno, the founder of Stoicism, was born in Palestine.

Even at the heart of Pharisaic tradition, Greek culture left its mark. It is said, for instance, that Rabbi Gamaliel the Patriarch (early 2nd cent. C.E.) had one thousand students, five hundred of whom studied Torah, and five hundred of whom studied Greek wisdom. The seven rules of midrash introduced into the rabbinic tradition by Hillel are borrowed from Greek logic and there are many Greek loanwords in the midrashic writings. Even the inscription concerning the building of a synagogue by Theodotus, found in the precincts of the Jerusalem temple itself, was written in Greek. As a final irony, it is worth noting that the writings that tell of the heroic resistance against Hellenism by the Maccabees were either composed in Greek or quickly translated into Greek.

By no means, then, was Greek culture entirely rejected. But even those who welcomed Greek ways sometimes balked at the implications. The dividing line for all was syncretism. To be Jewish meant to worship one God alone, a deity who admitted no fellows. When it came to the choice between *paideia* and Torah, the Jew was called to choose Torah. But some did not, while others thought the choice could be avoided. Some even regarded syncretism as compatible with claiming Jewish identity. These responses caused many "loyal" Jews to recoil, hardening them in their conviction that adherence to Torah demanded resistance to Greek culture in all its forms.

Different responses to Roman rule proved even more divisive. The taste of independence under the Hasmoneans caused many to hope for complete restoration of the Davidic line by an anointed ruler (messiah) who would liberate the land from foreign oppression. But not all Jews were convinced that political rule and the kingdom of God should be so closely identified or that Roman administration of the land was necessarily worse than that of the corrupt Hasmoneans or that promised by the zealots: ". . . it seemed a much lighter thing to be ruined by the Romans than by themselves" (Josephus *The Jewish War* [*JW*] IV.3.2). They could argue from Torah that kingship had from the beginning been suspect on religious grounds (1 Sam. 8:4-22; Ezek. 34:1-24). They refused to attach Jewish identity and the hope of restoration under God to a political program.

The first major consequence of the Palestinian political context, then, was the division of Jews into mutually antagonistic parties. The well-known "sects" of first-century Judaism were politically as well as theologically opposed. At the extremes were the people of action. On the far right were those who could be called agents of Roman oppression, the tax collectors; themselves Jewish, they preyed on the people for Rome. On the far left were a variety of nationalistic rebels who have popularly been designated as Zealots. Their messianism was concrete and political (Josephus *Antiquities of the Jews* [*Ant*] XVIII.1.1). They worked actively to overthrow Roman rule by military means, aided by their terrorist wing, the *sicarii*, who carried out assassinations of prominent officials (*JW* II.18; IV.3).

As for those more properly termed sects, the Sadducees—who represented the wealthier and more aristocratic elements including the high priestly families—tended to be cooperative with Rome and positive toward Hellenism. The Pharisees were largely Judean, urban, and middle-class; they began with definite and active political affiliations (see *Ant* XIII.10.5–6; XVII.2.4), but became increasingly apolitical, neither cooperating with Rome (*JW* I.5.2), nor actively opposing it. The Essenes were thoroughly separatist in ideology and rejected all things foreign; those in the community at Qumran (by the Dead Sea) translated this rejection into an active military resistance to Rome at the end of the sect's life. These sects, however, made up only a fraction of the Palestinian population. The rest of the Jews, the people of the land (*am-ha-aretz*), have left us no record of their convictions. Of their political and religious proclivities we learn only what is treated by others.

Divisions were rampant among these groups. The Pharisees, for example, despised the *am-ha-aretz* as sinners for their failure to observe tithes and purity regulations. For that matter, the Essenes could have regarded the Pharisees the same way; it was not enough to purify the body after possible contact with the heathen, it was necessary to withdraw from every possibility of such contact. These divisions were more than disputations over theological niceties. They amounted to opposing claims concerning the nature of God's people.

The second major consequence of the Palestinian political context was the specific transformation of traditional religious symbols. The one most obviously pertinent to the NT is messianism. In this period the hope for an anointed deliverer of the people was neither universal in its appeal nor uniform in its configuration. Moreover, the contrast between an earthly, "Davidic" messiah who would lead a political revolution (the desire of the zealots) and a heavenly "Son of man" who would initiate the reign of God on earth (as suggested by Dan. 7:13-14) is too simplistic, and inadequately supported by the sources. Such emphases were undoubtedly present (see e.g., *Psalms of Solomon* 17 and *1 Enoch* 37–71), but were mixed with other elements. At Qumran, for example, there is clearly the expectation of a priestly messiah (see the Qumran *Rule of the Congregation*, 1Q28a.2), a hope also reflected in other writings (see *Testament of Levi* 8). And at least some versions of messianism appear to have been communal rather than individual in nature (i.e., the messiah corporately represented the people; Dan. 7 may be so interpreted). Precisely the variety of expectations and configurations illustrates that messianism was "in the air" during the first century c.e. in an unprecedented and pervasive way.

Messianism, however, was only one symbol enlivened by this political context. The fact of religious persecution, first unleashed by Antiochus IV, stimulated the development of other convictions that previously had been, at best, only latent in the tradition: martyrdom, resurrection, and individual judgment. In persecution, people were faced with the choice between the dictates of Torah and of the king (2 Macc. 6:18-30). The consequence of obeying Torah was death. Those who chose to be executed rather than abandon Torah wrote their witness in blood, and became the prototypes of those later to be called martyrs (2 Macc. 6:31). They could do this, however, only because of the conviction that such a sacrifice would be repaid by resurrection. God would give back life to those who die for his Word (2 Macc. 7:9):

> You dismiss us from this present life, but the king of the universe will raise us up to an everlasting renewal of life, because we have died for his laws.

Resurrection and martyrdom are correlative, and are connected in turn to an increased emphasis on individual judgment (see Ezek. 18:1-32); the people do not rise and fall together, but as they have kept Torah so will they be judged by God (2 Macc. 7:23):

> The creator of the world . . . will in his mercy give life and breath back to you again, since you now forget yourselves for the sake of his laws.

These developments indicate as well that the symbols of people and Torah were also in the process of transformation. For many Jews of the period, not all who were born

Jewish were really Jews. The people of God was considered to be smaller than the historical Israel. Belonging to God's people was a matter of choice, and it hinged on one's allegiance to Torah. But precisely here was the debate: how was Torah to be understood, and how strictly was it to be observed? These questions led to ever more severe forms of separatism and exclusivity. The logic ran thus: those who kept Torah most rigidly represented the people of God most perfectly.

Finally, we can see how the symbol of the temple was revalued. In the popular mind, the sanctuary and the land were often closely linked (see, e.g., 1 Macc. 3:43, 59). Some calling themselves Jews could apparently live with a statue of Zeus in the temple, but others could not (1 Macc. 1:57). For such as these, the purification and rededication of the temple was crucial (1 Macc. 4:36-59). But when the priesthood again became Hellenized, separatists rejected the temple of Jerusalem completely; it was no longer "holy" (cf. the Qumran texts CD 4, 6; 1QpHab 12). This did not mean that the symbol of the temple was rejected; for many it was impossible to think of a people without a sanctuary. Some longed for a restored, messianic temple (*Jub.* 1.23-29); others dreamed of heavenly temples that were prototypes for an eschatological sanctuary (*2 Bar.* 4:2-7; *1 Enoch* 90.28-29). Still others applied the symbol directly to the purified people itself: the holy remnant was a sanctuary, a temple of God in the land (*Rule of the Community*, 1QS 7.4–10).

Literature in Palestine

We find the transformation of symbols reflected in the various kinds of literature written in Palestine after the Maccabean period. We will look briefly at representative apocalyptic writings, as well as some literature from the emerging rabbinic tradition, liturgical materials from Jewish worship, and some texts from Qumran. In each case we seek to discover how various writers had their understanding of traditional symbols, found originally in Torah, reshaped by distinctive experiences and convictions.

Apocalyptic Literature

Apocalyptic literature is the matrix for many of these symbolic transformations. It is an overstatement to call all the NT apocalyptic, but it is accurate to state that much of it is unintelligible apart from apocalyptic categories. The term "apocalyptic" means "revelational." It refers to a distinctive *outlook* found in many forms of literature, and to a particular type of *writing* produced both by Jews and Jewish Christians. Some of the writings, like the classics Daniel and the NT Book of Revelation, are included in the canon; others, like *1 Enoch* and 4 Ezra, are not and hence are called apocryphal (hidden, noncanonical).

Anticipations of an apocalyptic perspective occur in some of the later Hebrew prophets, such as Zechariah, but the outlook's first full literary expression came in the Book of Daniel (ca. 165 B.C.E.), written in response to the religious persecution under Antiochus IV Epiphanes. Here we already find major conventions of the literature. Daniel is the hero of the book, a young Jew living in Babylonian, then Persian, exile. He has visions that astonishingly predict the events of the Maccabean period. The book is pseudonymous and is written at the same time as the events it purports to predict. The conventions indicate the nature of the writing. It is written in an esoteric code because it is an underground literature aimed at comforting those undergoing persecution, exhorting them to fidelity. Attribution to a prophet of the past was probably a transparent fiction for the readers and served to connect this exhortation to the long-established prophetic tradition.

The first six chapters of Daniel also have a definite connection to the wisdom tradition. They contain folkloric tales of a pious Jewish youth confounding the sages of a foreign culture. The application to contemporary Hellenism was not difficult to make. The moral of each story is much the same: the true Jew does not commit idolatry even when under threat of death (Dan. 3:18; 6:5) but remains faithful to Torah (1:8; 3:18; 6:15). The wisdom found in Torah is superior to gentile wisdom (2:27-28; 4:7-8; 5:13-17), and shows that God is master of history (2:37, 44; 4:25; 5:18-23). The same points are made in Daniel 7–12, but less dramatically. Now, not folk tales but strange nocturnal dreams of the young man carry the message (7:1-4). Here we find the basic literary device of apocalyptic: the vision of things future and things heavenly.

As Daniel interprets the visions, we discover that each one tells basically the same story: the history of the recent past and the emergence of the threatening present. Both the visions and their interpretations tell the reader in a coded way that, despite all evidence to the contrary, God is in control of history. God has, in fact, a divine plan for history: it will seem to go from bad to worse only so that God can intervene to reverse its course, stop the reign of evil, and establish his kingdom among the saints. By what agent will God accomplish this? The visions remain tantalizingly vague. A mysterious figure called Son of man comes on the clouds to receive eternal dominion from the "Ancient of Days" (7:13-14). Who is he? Is he the archangel Michael (12:1-4)? Does the Son of man stand for the people themselves (7:18, 22, 27)? While obviously an impressive symbol, the Son of man remains sufficiently obscure to allow further reinterpretation in light of subsequent experiences and convictions regarding God's intervention to establish a kingdom (cf. 4 Ezra 13; *1 Enoch* 45-53; Mark 13:24-27).

The Book of Daniel inaugurated a long tradition of apocalyptic literature. Although the literature's mood was esoteric and mystical, its production owed little to ecstasy. The visionary apparatus is a literary technique, and the complex symbolism of the writing suggests a self-conscious literary endeavor. It is essentially a written rather than oral literature: the opening, closing, and sealing of heavenly books play a prominent role. The symbolism requires a shared code between writers and readers for the message to be understood. Although they quickly become standardized in the categories of fabulous beasts, significant numbers, and cosmic catastrophes, the code beneath these symbols is that given by Torah itself. Apocalyptic from the first is anthological; it not only claims antiquity, it makes use of earlier written tradition to solidify its claims (e.g., see how Zech. 1:18-20 is utilized in Dan. 7:19-22). It is impossible to allocate the production of this literature to any one sect of first-century Judaism, since the literature enjoyed a wide appeal.

Apocalyptic involves more than a distinctive style. It is a specifically religious response to the experience of persecution from without and erosion from within. In literary terms, apocalyptic answers the question posed by the choice between king and Torah. To those suffering for allegiance to Torah, it says, "be comforted"; to those tempted to apostatize, it declares, "hold fast." But if the message is so simple, why does it require such an elaborate setting? Because fidelity demands a reason, and comfort requires support. The peculiar apocalyptic interpretation of history undergirds the religious message.

The apocalyptic view of history is shaped by the tension between conviction and experience. This may require some explanation. We must remember that, despite Job and Qoheleth, the dominant teaching of Torah on human history said that the Lord was not only master of it generally, but in a specific and highly individualized way. The Deuteronomistic principle was plain: if you keep Torah, you will be blessed with long life, prosperity, and possession of the land; if you abandon Torah, you will lose possessions and children, and die (Deut. 30:1-20). Before there was religious persecution, however, this conviction could be maintained even when experience disconfirmed it. The reason: no experience was so visible and massive enough to dislodge the conviction. It could be assumed that people who appeared to be good yet suffered must really have been secret sinners or suffering for their parents' sins.

But persecution is another sort of experience. People are put to death precisely because they observe Torah. Their children and possessions are ripped away not because of any impiety, but precisely because they are pious. God does not appear to be in charge at all. The forces of evil seem to control history. Those who have abandoned Torah prosper, those who worship idols put the saints to death. The crisis of theodicy created by this conflict between experience (suffering for Torah) and conviction (Torah brings blessings) was real (4 Ezra 6:55-59):

> All this I have spoken before thee, O Lord, because thou hast said that for our sakes thou hast created this world. But as for the other nations, which are descended from Adam, thou hast said that they are nothing, and that they are like unto spittle; and thou hast likened the abundance of them to a drop in a bucket. And now, O Lord, behold these nations which are reputed as nothing, lord it over us and crush us. But we, thy people, whom thou hast called thy first-born, thy only begotten, thy beloved, are given up into their hands. If the

world has indeed been created for our sakes, why do we not enter into possession of our world? How long shall this endure?

How then can the meaning of Torah, and its claim that God controls history, be saved? Only by reinterpreting history itself, and in the process, reinterpreting the symbols of Torah. Though their present experience would argue otherwise, history is meaningful; it moves through successive periods to a divinely appointed goal. The nature of that goal and the precise time of its accomplishment are God's own secret, but they are certain to be realized. It would be a mistake to compress such a wildly diverse literature into a single mold, but a classic scenario, with many permutations, runs something like this: history consists of two great ages. This present age (*ha olam ha zeh*) is dominated by the wicked. Their machinations against the saints are sponsored by cosmic powers inimical to God's reign, frequently represented by the fallen angels (see Gen. 6:1-4). The path of history is like an inverted ellipse; as the power of evil grows more evident, history moves downward toward a situation of absolute evil. But precisely when the nadir of the ellipse is reached, when evil is so overwhelming that there is no human hope, God intervenes and begins the age to come (*ha olam ha ba*). At this time God's rule is definitively established, the wicked crushed, and the saints rewarded. Apocalyptic is preoccupied with periodization (Dan. 9:2, 24-27; 12:5-13, *Jub.* 1.29), because only if history is seen as fulfilling distinct stages can God's control of it be asserted. And only because the end vindicates God's mastery is monotheism saved from the dualistic implications of cosmic conflict between good and evil carried out on apparently equal terms.

Even as it reshaped Torah, apocalyptic perpetuated its symbolic world. It explicitly asserted the centrality of the law and the importance of one's obedience to it for being counted among the elect. It identified Torah as the highest wisdom, based not in human understanding but in divine revelation. In the midst of persecution and apostasy, it spoke a word of prophecy to the people. The visionary apparatus gave even further impetus to the development of other esoteric movements such as Gnosticism, and resembled the expressions of mysticism found among the masters of the Merkabah (speculation and prayer centered on the throne chariot [*Merkabah*] of Ezekiel). It also provided a coherent symbolic framework for those who claimed to have experienced the radical intervention of God in world history, as was the claim of those who first confessed Jesus to be "the Son of man."

Rabbinic Tradition

Apocalyptic is plainly shaped by the very historical events it seeks to interpret. The rabbinic tradition, in contrast, rejects analysis of history altogether and is correspondingly hard to locate historically. Three specific reasons make the description of this movement in NT times difficult. First, the Pharisaic movement survived the catastrophe of the Jewish War (66–70 c.e.) and became the dominant form of Judaism for the next two millennia; understandably, it tends to overemphasize its role in the earlier period. Nevertheless, the Gospels confirm that the Pharisees and scribes were indeed important before 70 c.e., and we find them at the center of disputes with Jesus over Torah (see, e.g., Mark 7:1-13). Second, the whole nature of the movement *was* tradition. Its interest was not in constructing new teaching but in passing on ancient instruction. The oral interpretation of Torah that characterizes the movement was regarded as being as old as the written Torah (*Pirke Aboth* 1):

> Moses received Torah from Sinai and delivered it to Joshua, and Joshua to the elders, and the elders to the prophets, and the prophets delivered it to the men of the great synagogue. These said three things: be deliberate in judging, and raise up many disciples, and make a hedge for the Torah.

The third reason is the nature of the sources. The rabbinic movement began with a focus on oral tradition, and the great compilations of its lore are all considerably later than the NT. Judah the Prince codified the Mishnah in 200 c.e., and this provided the basis for further interpretations, which were crystallized in the two versions of the Talmud, the Palestinian (ca. 350 c.e.) and the more authoritative Babylonian (ca. 450 c.e.). Despite their late date of compilation, the collections do contain much older material.

The process of defining the rabbinic movement is made particularly difficult, moreover, by the timeless atmosphere of the material, which makes it seem as though all the world were a classroom. This is not accidental; the basic social setting for the development of this tradition was the school, with a teacher (rabbi) instructing students in Torah and its interpretation. The Talmud and other rabbinic materials resemble the shorthand notes of a seminar. Topics are picked up and dropped. Ancient opinions are found next to the most recent. The point, it quickly becomes clear, is not systematic thought but the process of discussion itself. This is a tradition based on the study and the living of Torah. The Talmud shows us the insatiable, quirky, profound, and sometimes silly questions and answers of learned men over the connections between Torah and life, in a lively and sometimes unruly centuries-long conversation.

The tradition was based on the religious convictions of the Pharisees concerning Torah and was shaped by the interpretive skills of the scribes (*sopherim* = men of the book), who appeared already in the time of the restoration as interpreters of Torah (Neh. 8:4-8). We have seen that the Pharisees tried to be apolitical. How then did they understand the symbols of Torah and the people? Their specific approach can best be grasped by way of contrast to other groups in the first century.

As noted earlier, little can be said about the vast majority of Jews, the *am-ha-aretz*, for they left behind no records of their convictions. Undoubtedly many of them were pious and devoted to Torah and the cult. So far as the Pharisees were concerned, however, they were ignorant, untrustworthy, and not fully part of the people (cf. *Mishnah Demai* 2.3; *Gittin* 5.9; *Pirke Aboth* 2.6; 5.10). The Samaritans, on the other hand, were a significant part of the Palestinian mix, although their precise importance is harder to weigh. They were of mixed race and custom (*Tractate Kutim* 1.2):

> The usages of the Samaritans are at times like those of the heathens, at times like those of the Israelites, but most of the time like the Israelites.

They were separated from all Jews by their insistence on the priority of Shechem over Jerusalem (see John 4:20), and from the Pharisees in particular by their attitude toward Torah, which was profoundly conservative. The Pharisees' stance toward them is suggested by *Tractate Kutim* 1.2: "This is the principle: [the Samaritans] are not to be trusted in any matter in which they are open to suspicion." On the other hand, the Samaritans' own self-designation as "the protectors/keepers" (*ha Shomrim*) implies that groups like the Pharisees were, in their eyes, all too progressive. A further distinguishing characteristic was their insistence that only the five books of Moses (Genesis through Deuteronomy) were to be considered Scripture. On that basis, however, they developed a lively messianic expectation of their own. It centered on a figure like Moses, for Deut. 18:15-18 had promised that God would "raise up a prophet like you from among your brethren" (e.g., see *Memar Marqah* IV.3).

The Jewish historian Josephus describes the Sadducees, Essenes, and Pharisees as philosophical schools (*JW* II.8.2), and given the degree of Hellenization in Palestine, he may not have been far off. He tells us little about the Sadducees, except that they were vaguely Epicurean in their philosophy (*JW* II.8.14; *Ant* XVIII.1.4) and were conservative in their attitude toward Torah. They "say we are to esteem those observances to be obligatory which are in the written word, but are not to observe what are derived from the tradition of our forefathers" (*Ant* XIII.10.6). This worked well for them, for having a close association with priesthood and temple, they could fulfill the purity laws without special applications. A conservative view of Torah led to the rejection of developments arising in oral tradition, such as belief in resurrection and angels.

The Essenes are greatly admired by Josephus. He describes in considerable detail their community of possessions (*JW* II.8.2–4) and their separatist tendencies based in the desire for purity (8.5–9). It is not surprising that he sees them as Pythagoreans. He also notes that they are concerned for the prophetic aspects of Torah (8.12)—we will see more of this when we look at the Qumran branch of the Essene movement.

The Pharisees look like Stoics in Josephus' treatment, with a belief in providence and free will (*JW* II.8.14). But he emphasizes above all that they were "skillful in the exact application of the laws" (*JW* II.8.14; *Life* 191) and that they sponsored oral tradition (*Ant* XIII.10.6). These characteristics, however, do not explain the survival and eventual dominance of the Pharisaic tradition. Partly, of course, attrition played a role: the Sadducees disappeared with the temple; the Essenes and the zealots were wiped out by war with Rome; the Samaritans remained a quaint relic. But the Pharisees also had the capacity to adjust to new circumstances. They were not tied to any particular location, social institution, or political program. As urban and middle-class people, they were mobile and adaptable. Above all, their perception of the people and Torah was flexible and progressive, and this was what enabled them to represent the future of Judaism.

On the one hand, their view of Torah was strict and demanding. To be part of the people, to take upon oneself the yoke of the kingdom, was to take on the yoke of Torah in all its parts. These laws, particularly those relating to purity and tithing, applied not only to the priests of the temple but to every Jew, for the Jews were a "nation of priests." The Pharisees identified people and Torah, and for this reason above all they were able to survive the loss of priesthood, temple, king, and land.

The genius of the Pharisaic tradition is found in its ability to interpret and apply Torah for all Jews. The matrix of Pharisaic interpretation is once more a conflict between conviction and experience. The conviction is that Torah is God's word and therefore eternal, unchanging, and normative for life. Torah's commandments (*mitzvoth*) make specific demands on every Jew. But tension is created by the fact that life is *not* changeless; it changes continually. The *mitzvoth* for tithes and purity were addressed to a people living an agricultural existence. Torah demands sharing possessions but spells this out in terms of vines, fields, and harvests. Jews who live in cities have very different circumstances: they must buy food from strangers and engage in trade in order to live. How can they now observe the tithes and keep ritually pure? The options are limited. They could simply abandon Torah or regard it as less than an absolute norm, but that would be to degrade God's word. They could change Torah, but again that would amount to treating it as a human word. They could keep Torah by removing themselves from others and trying to reestablish an agricultural society that they can control. Or they could continue to live in the present world but seek to discover in Torah itself the principles that would allow them to maintain its integrity as an absolute norm, yet relate it to the real circumstances of their lives. The Pharisees did not, like the Essenes, leave society for Torah. They stayed in the city and invented midrash.

Midrash (from the verb *darash*, "to search") is a method of contemporizing sacred texts. It is based on the conviction that Torah itself provides the basis for new understanding and contemporary application. Every word and letter of Torah bears the possibility of new meaning; where application is not clear, one searches the text for ways of resolving the difficulty. Without midrash, the text remains dead; with it, the text is enlivened and speaks to the present with new authority. From the time of Hillel (1st cent. B.C.E.) the Pharisees took over rules from Greek logic for adjudicating textual problems. With an exact and comprehensive knowledge of the details of Torah, they used these rules to sort out conflicts and establish priorities among, and find appropriate applications of, the *mitzvoth*.

So central to the tradition was this rereading of the text that the synagogue was also called the house of study (*beth ha midrash*). Study, observance, and worship—all articulated Torah in life. It was Torah that gave meaning to life and enabled it to be, in every act, obedience to God's will. Midrash was applied to the strictly legal material of Torah in order to yield a rule of action called *halakah* (from the verb "to walk," therefore, "way of acting"). When midrash was applied to other texts, it was called *haggadah* (from the verb "to relate," thus, loosely, narratives). Haggadic midrash tended to be freer and more spontaneous, and in it we find much of the spiritual and ethical idealism of Pharisaism. While halachic midrash concerned itself with establishing the precise grounds of righteousness before God, haggadic midrash created the ethos that brought the formal instruction to life.

Halachic midrash was clearly central to the rabbinic tradition, and its earnest religious spirit should not be slighted. A short example of halachic midrash illustrates its true nature. One of the *mitzvoth* in Torah was that farmers should not glean all of the wheat in a field but should leave a "corner" (*peah*) for the poor (Lev. 19:9; 23:22). The intent was to "do justice" by helping the poverty-stricken among the people. But the problems of applying the commandment are immediately evident. Who should qualify as poor? What constitutes a "corner"? How big must it be? And how can this principle be translated to other circumstances? These are not trivial questions. Both the needs of the poor and the legitimate needs of the farmer require consideration; the farmer, already heavily taxed, might not be able to feed his family if the corner takes too much of his small field. In the early midrashic tractate *Sifra*, we find the problem dealt with extensively, and the halachic discussion is carried over to the Mishnah, in the tractate *Peah*. Page after page is given to legal discussion; every detail is considered. Is it all senseless? Not at all, once the premises of the tradition are granted. And at the very head of the tractate (*Mishnah Peah* 1.1) we find this fine expression of those premises:

> These are things whose fruits a man enjoys in this world while the capital is laid up for him in the world to come: honouring father and mother, deeds of loving kindness, making peace between a man and his fellow; and the study of the Law is equal to them all.

Every legal decision can proliferate regulations that appear pointless to outsiders. This is the charge that Jesus brings against the Pharisees in the Gospels, especially concerning Sabbath regulations (see Mark 2:23—3:7). The issue of Sabbath law provides a good foil for this discussion, for it was around the Sabbath that the most extensive body of rules grew. This growth was due in part to the nature of positive commands: it is much harder to set the limits to commands like "keep holy" than it is to commands like "don't kill." The growth was also due to the fact that the Sabbath was so central to the identity of the people. Already in Torah, it is attached to the practice of God himself (Exod. 20:8-11). It was to be a sign of difference, marking the place of holiness in the world. And the Sabbath was a unique institution in the ancient world. By it even pagans recognized the distinctiveness of the Jews and their God, a deity who demanded that one day a week be set aside and consecrated as holy.

But determining the dimensions of the holy is not so simple. This day is to be "different" from the others that are given over to "work"—that is clear enough and is in Torah itself. But what is the meaning of "work"? Midrash located every mention of the term "work" in Torah and came up with a comprehensive list of thirty-nine activities that were designated work-related and thus to be avoided (*Mishnah Shabbat* 7.2). To the outsider, refusal to light a fire or to tear a thread might seem trivial. But such lists "put a hedge around the Torah" in order to ensure that the central commandment itself ("keep the Sabbath holy") would not be broken. The method and its results are open to debate, but the strong religious motivation is not.

The religious impulse of the Pharisaic tradition is also found in some of its theological emphases. God was indeed transcendent, "the Holy One," but his presence was made available to humans. A symbol for this was the Divine Presence (*Shekinah*, from *shakan*, "to dwell"), which was with the people in the desert and Solomon's temple, and was now present in synagogues when Torah was read. Indeed, the study of Torah placed one in this "shadow of God's presence" (*Pirke Aboth* 3.2):

> If two sit together and words of Torah are between them, the Shekinah rests between them . . . and even if one sits and occupies himself with Torah, the Holy One, blessed be He, fixes for him a reward.

Torah, in fact, is God's eternal blueprint for creation and for righteous human behavior. In its study humans find joy, freedom, and wisdom. Yet the emphasis on study does not lead to a neglect of good deeds (*Pirke Aboth* 3.10; cf. *Aboth de Rabbi Nathan* 24):

> Everyone whose deeds are more than his wisdom, his wisdom endures; and everyone whose wisdom is more than his deeds, his wisdom does not endure.

Among these good deeds were the fulfillment of Sabbath and purity regulations, but above all, "deeds of charity," actions by which the covenantal obligations of fidelity and love were expressed toward others, particularly in the help given to the poor and dispossessed (see Babylonian Talmud, *Berakoth* 8a; *Shabbat* 156b).

Torah was a measure that was never perfectly met. Humans were free but subject to drives and impulses that sometimes prevented them from observing Torah in greater as well as smaller ways. The remedy for this was not despair but repentance. A saying attributed to Rabbi Eliezer went "Repent one day before your death . . . let him repent today lest he die on the morrow; let him repent on the morrow lest he die the day after; and thus all his days will be spent in repentance" (*Aboth de Rabbi Nathan* 15).

A passage from the Babylonian Talmud, *Makkoth* 24a, illustrates the spirit of the rabbinic tradition both in its apparent pointlessness and in its deeper seriousness. The passage begins with the statement "Therefore gave he them Torah and many commandments . . ." The discussion begins, naturally, with the question, "How many commandments?":

> R. Simlai, when preaching, said, "Six hundred and thirteen precepts were communicated to Moses, three hundred and sixty-five negative precepts, corresponding to the number of solar days, and two hundred and forty-eight positive commands, corresponding to the number of the members of a man's body . . ."

This may sound a bit frivolous, especially when it is then supported by texts of Torah. But then other traditions are cited, which systematically reduce and compress the commandments into ever tighter and more religiously focused texts. When Isaiah, Micah, and Amos are quoted, the intent of Torah is narrowed down even further, leading us to this conclusion (Babylonian Talmud, *Makkoth* 24a):

> Again came Isaiah and reduced them to two principles, as it is said, "Thus saith the Lord, Keep ye justice and do righteousness. . . ." Amos came and reduced them to one principle, as it is said, "For thus saith the Lord unto the house of Israel, seek ye me and live." To this, R. Nachman b. Isaac demurred, saying, "Might it not be taken as 'seek me by observing the whole Torah and live'?" But it is Habbakuk who came and based them all on one principle, as it is said, "but the righteous shall live by his faith."

The only stronger expression of this sentiment is found in Paul, himself a Pharisee.

Jewish Worship

One of the most important contexts for the development of Jewish symbols was worship. In worship, after all, the convictions of religion come alive and a community expresses its identity in myth and cult. In the NT period, Jewish worship was performed in the temple, synagogue, and home.

The temple continued to be considered one of the architectural marvels of the world and a center for pilgrimages three times a year, at the feasts of Passover, Booths, and Pentecost, when Jews from all over the world would converge on Jerusalem (see Acts 2:5-11). Sacrifices and prayers continued to be offered in its courts, and both Jesus and the first disciples taught in its precincts (Luke 19:47; Acts 3:11—4:2). By the first century, however, the temple was not the center of piety in the way that synagogue and home were.

The origins of the synagogue are obscure. It may have begun in the gatherings of the people to hear Torah while in exile, or it may have started as the local parallel to worship in the temple, with the times of its three daily prayers corresponding to the temple's hours of sacrifice (see *Mishnah Taanith* 4.2-4). By the NT period, the synagogue was an institution found in most villages (see Luke 4:15-17), both in Palestine and in the Diaspora (Acts 13:14-15). According to tradition, Jerusalem was filled with synagogues—there was even one in the precincts of the temple (Babylonian Talmud, *Sukka* 53a).

The synagogue was unique as a place of worship in the ancient world. It offered no animal sacrifices, and ritual actions generally were held to a minimum. Its worship centered wholly on Torah. In NT times, the synagogue and house of study (*beth ha midrash*) (see Sirach 51:23) seem to have been the same, and its space allowed for a casual but regular rhythm of prayer and learning.

Our written sources for the synagogue liturgy are so late (the *Seder Rav Amran Gaon* dates from the 9th cent. c.e.) that we can reconstruct the prayer service only with great caution. Still, the NT writings and the fragmentary discussions of worship in the Mishnah allow us to make some statements (cf. *Mishnah Yoma* 7. 1; *Berakoth* 1–2; *Megillah* 4). The entire service was centered on Torah: the hearing of God's word in the Scripture readings; the proclamation of it in the midrashic homily; and the prayers and petitions that used the very words of Torah.

The classic form of Jewish prayer is the blessing (*breach*). It is the antecedent of prayer forms in the NT and early Christian liturgy (see Eph. 1:3-14; 1 Pet. 1:3-6). Its form is simple though capable of indefinite expansion. It opens with a statement of praise, follows with the reasons for praise, then concludes with renewed praise. The basic form is found already in Psalm 117:

> *Praise the Lord all nations!*
> *Extol him all peoples!*
> *For great is his steadfast love for us*
> *and the faithfulness of the Lord endures forever.*
> *Praise the Lord!*

The morning synagogue service had three lengthy blessings (*berakoth*) which enclosed the central confession of faith, the *Shema*: "Hear O Israel, the Lord your God is One . . ." One of these is the *Berakah Ahabah*:

With abounding love hast thou loved us Lord our God, with great and exceeding pity hast thou pitied us, our Father, our King, for the sake of our fathers who trusted in thee, and whom thou didst teach the statutes of life, be gracious also unto us . . . put it into our hearts to hear, to learn, and to do, all the words of instruction in thy Torah in love . . . and let not thy mercy abandon us forever and ever. Let peace come over us from the four corners of the earth . . . for thou hast chosen us from all peoples and tongues and hast brought us near unto thy great name in love. Blessed be thou Lord, who hast chosen thy people Israel in love.

The *berakah*, we see, is fundamentally an act of remembrance. God is to be praised for the way he has worked in the past. By remembering his deeds, we are moved again to praise him. Remembrance of this sort acts like myth: it makes the past active in the present. Besides uniting past and present, the *berakah* form of prayer also united public worship and private piety. The pious Pharisee would recite up to one hundred smaller *berakoth* privately every day in order to "sanctify time." The sacred space of communal worship was thus also expressed in ordinary life.

Another form of synagogue prayer is the *tefillah*. On normal days there were eighteen of these, from which they received the name "the eighteen benedictions" (*shemone esre*). They were also called the *amidah* because they were recited "standing" (*amad* = to stand). The most characteristic of them is the "Blessing of the Name" (*Qedushat ha shem*):

> From generation to generation give homage to God, for He alone is high and holy, and thy praise, our God, shall not depart from our mouth forever, for a holy and great king thou art. Blessed be thou, O Lord, thou Holy God.

Synagogue worship included the reading of Torah and a sermon. The readings were from the Law and Prophets, and followed a regular sequence (*Mishnah Megilla* 4.1-10). The most important reading was from the Law, which was read in the original Hebrew. Because the majority of Jews no longer understood Hebrew, however, it was necessary to translate the sacred text into Aramaic. As the text was read, a translator would freely render the text for the people in a paraphrastic fashion, clarifying obscurities and pointing out contemporary relevance. Not a little haggadic midrash found its way into such translations, which, when later written down, were called Targums. They provide one more instance in which a text from the past was made relevant for newer contexts. The Hebrew text of Gen. 49:1, for example, reads:

> Then Jacob called his sons and said, "Gather yourselves together that I may tell you what will befall you in days to come.

The Aramaic Targum *Pseudo-Jonathan* rendered Gen. 49:1 thus:

> And Jacob called his sons and said to them: "Purify yourself from uncleanness, and I will show you the mysteries which are hidden, the appointed times

which are concealed, what the recompense of reward for the just, the retribution in store for the wicked, and the joys of Eden are." The twelve tribes gathered together around the bed of gold on which he lay. And after the shekinah of the Lord was revealed, the determined time in which the King Messiah is to come was hidden from him.

This is an extraordinary passage; more than an expanded translation, it is a virtual compendium of symbols, both apocalyptic (hidden secrets, messiah, individual judgment) and rabbinic (*Shekinah*, purification). The truly remarkable part is that pious Jews in the synagogue heard this as the words of Torah itself, made contemporary with the hearers' ways of thinking, believing, and acting. Precisely such reworkings of the text would have been heard by Jesus and his disciples in the synagogues of Galilee.

After the reading from Law and Prophets, a homily followed in which the speaker would midrashically work out the text and its implications. The earliest description of a synagogue service is found in the Gospel of Luke (4:16-30). Coming to his home synagogue in Nazareth, Jesus was asked to read from the prophet Isaiah (61:1-2) and then to preach. He read the words "The spirit of the Lord is upon me because he has anointed me to proclaim good news to the poor. . . ." When he sat down to preach, however, instead of giving a midrashic exposition, he simply said, "Today this scripture has been fulfilled in your hearing" (Luke 4:21).

The third place of Jewish worship in the first century was the domestic liturgy of the meal, such as that celebrated on the Sabbath and at important feasts such as Passover. All meals had a certain sacred character and were accompanied by blessings (*Mishnah Berakoth* 7–8). Meals, furthermore, symbolized fellowship; to eat together signified spiritual unity. The charge against Jesus that he ate with sinners amounted to a charge that he also was a sinner (Luke 7:34; 15:2). It is likely that the Pharisaic fellowships (*haburoth*) celebrated at least festival meals together.

The most significant sacred meal in Judaism was the Passover supper. Though lambs were still slaughtered ritually in the temple, those who came to Jerusalem for this greatest pilgrimage feast ate the lamb together with family and friends in lodgings scattered throughout the city. The last supper of Jesus and his followers was probably such a meal (Mark 14:12, contra John 19:31). Passover celebrated the exodus experience, when the Lord had taken Israel out of the bondage of Egypt, led them through the desert, and brought them to the promised land. This was the paradigmatic experience of redemption, and Passover was a feast of Jewish freedom. The words and rituals of the meal show us texts from the past being reinterpreted. The classic myth and ritual of first-century Judaism is found in the *Passover Haggadah*: "Let each one regard himself as having come out of Egypt." The words recited over the bread at once interpret, and are interpreted by, Torah:

This matzah which we eat, what is the reason for it? Because the dough of our fathers had not yet been leavened when the king over all kings, the Holy One, blessed be He, revealed himself to them and redeemed them. As it is said, "And they baked unleavened cakes of the dough which they brought forth out of Egypt" (Ex. 12:39).

Likewise with the words said over the cups of wine:

Therefore we are bound to thank, praise, laud and glorify . . . him who performed all these miracles for our fathers and for us. He has brought us forth from slavery to freedom, from sorrow to joy, from mourning to holiday, from darkness to great light, and from bondage to redemption. Let us then recite before him a new song, Hallelujah.

In the Passover ritual, the myth of the community is renewed and the symbols of Torah once more establish Jewish identity as a people chosen and saved by God.

Qumran

Despite the warning with which this chapter opened, there still may be the temptation to isolate "apocalyptic," "rabbinic," and "liturgical" aspects of first-century Judaism into airtight compartments. For that reason, one of the greatest contributions made by the Dead Sea Scrolls to the study of Judaism and early Christianity has been to illustrate how these various expressions could be united in the experience of a single concrete community: the congregation of Khirbet Qumran.

We will not recount the history of this fascinating and bizarre group of sectarians, doubtless an extreme form of the Essene movement, who took the logic of separatism so seriously that they retreated to the desert "to prepare a way for the Lord." They accomplished this by wholly devoting themselves to the observance of Torah (1QS 8.13–16) and by completely removing the impure from their midst—not only the heathen but all those Jews who remained in contact with the heathen (1QS 5.1–3; 7.24–25; 8.22–24). We know that they gave special allegiance to a Teacher of Righteousness (CD 20.1; 1QpHab 9.9–10) whom they credited with unique insight into the meaning of Torah (1QpHab 2.2) and its application to their community. We know too that they had a particular hostility for the "wicked priests" in Jerusalem whom they regarded as having profaned the temple and polluted the land (1QpHab 8.9; 9.9). We know, finally, that they saw themselves as the replacement for the priesthood and temple. The community was a "house of holiness" for the Lord, which offered spiritual sacrifices of praise and study (4QFlor 1.6; 1QS 8.6–8; 9.3–11) guided by a leadership of priests and Levites of the order of Zadok (1QS 2.19–20; 5.1–3).

Their application of purity regulations was systematic. Because they could not mingle goods with the impure (1QS 1.11–12; 6.17–22), they had a total community of possessions. This emphasis on purity demanded an elaborate system of punishments (1QS 6.24—7.27) and the extreme penalty of excommunication when one seriously threatened the community's boundaries (1QS 5.14–16; 8.22–26). The community was there in the desert as a purified remnant of the people, a realization of what God wanted Israel to be. All other rival claims to membership in the people were false; only they truly were the people of God. And so they drew to themselves all the symbols of land, Torah, people, and temple. Moreover, they were the anticipation of God's eschatological rule, living proleptically the life of God's future kingdom. Their community organization would be replicated in the time of the messiah (1QSa 1.19–26), and their sacred meals were a foretaste of those to be shared with the one to come (1QSa 2.16). And all of this was legitimated by a rigid and comprehensive mythology that based their separation in a cosmic dualism, a battle between the children of light, whose origin was God, and the children of darkness, whose origin was the prince of darkness (1QS 3.13—4.26).

Immediately after the discovery of these scrolls, elaborate theories abounded as to the dependence of Christianity on the Qumran community. Most of these theories have fallen by the way. There remains reason to think, however, that John the Baptist had some contact with the sect and that certain ideas and practices influenced the earliest Palestinian Christian communities. Hard and direct links, however, have not been established. Qumran is most important not for what it tells us about first-century Christianity but for what it tells us about first-century Palestinian Judaism.

First, in Qumran's library we discover from the reading material that many tendencies we had formerly thought incompatible or even opposed could comfortably find a home here in one tightly knit group. In addition to the texts of Torah, which the group diligently studied, there are remains of many apocalyptic works, some of which were known before the discovery and obviously widely circulated in this period (*Jubilees, 1 Enoch*), as well as others produced by the community itself (such as the *War Scroll,* 1QM). These texts we might have expected. But there are also a number of other texts: scriptural commentaries done in halachic, haggadic, and targumic styles (as in the *Genesis Apocryphon*); liturgical documents (the hymns and the prayers of blessing); treatises on community rules (the *Rule of the Community*); apocryphal additions to Torah, as well as other extra-biblical texts; wisdom poems; treasure maps (the *Copper Scroll*); fragments of astronomical and astrological manuscripts; remains of magical spells; even remnants suggesting the practice of Merkabah mysticism. The Qumran library makes clear to us what we should already have suspected: there is not a one-to-one alignment of texts and communities. Given a coherent ideology of its own, a particular group can read and assimilate, in accordance with its normative ideology, a variety of apparently divergent traditions.

Second, the Qumran writings have had an impact on scholarly presuppositions concerning cultural influence and doctrinal development in both Judaism and Christianity. One of the primary areas of impact was in the reevaluation of the nature of

Hellenism in Palestine. Perhaps Josephus was not far wrong when he depicted the Essenes as Jewish Pythagoreans. Certainly their practice of a total "community of goods" for the sake of purity bears far more resemblance to the practice of Greek philosophy than to anything in Torah. If this is so, then these ways were not foreign to Palestine—indicating the high degree of Hellenistic influence in this region.

Likewise with some of the Qumran symbols: formerly the dualistic language of John's Gospel (truth/falsehood; light/darkness) was thought to be indebted to Hellenism, which meant a setting outside Palestine, which, in turn, implied a late dating of the document. Since Qumran, such reasoning does not hold. Hellenistic influence may have been available to the writer of the Fourth Gospel, as it was to Qumran, within Palestine during the first century.

Another area of impact is the matter of community structure. Developmental theories of early Christianity were fond of attributing any organization or authority, especially if it was rationalized and self-conscious, to the passage of time and the waning of eschatological fervor and charismatic leadership. Qumran shows us a first-century Jewish community that, while it maintained an elaborate and highly rationalized organization and authority structure, together with a strict legalism and a penal code, also had an acute eschatological tension far more explicit and time-conscious than anything found in the NT. It should no longer be possible to suggest seriously that order and charism are incompatible, or that legalism and eschatology cannot coexist.

Third, and perhaps most significant, Qumran provides an early and striking analogy to the early Christian community. We find in the writings of the group an example of the same sort of dialectic between experience and interpretation that we find in the NT. Two aspects of this similarity are especially significant: (1) the community's consciousness of being opposed to mainstream Judaism, together with the conviction that it alone represents the authentic and eschatological Israel; (2) its attempt to establish the basis of that consciousness in an idiosyncratic interpretation of Torah.

The community is intensely conscious that it has separated itself from the rest of Judaism. It alone is holy precisely because it has separated itself from the "sons of the pit" (CD 6.14—7.6) to form the remnant that God will save (CD 4.19–23). The community's ideology, in turn, appears to be rooted in formative experiences. This is of great importance. We find suggestions that in the past a concrete conflict with the "wicked priest" in Jerusalem led to the despoiling of the property of the community members (1QpHab 8.8–12; 11.1–6; 12.9–12). There are only hints, but it seems that the historical experience was, in time, elaborated into a comprehensive and cosmic myth of the war between the children of light and the children of darkness.

More fascinating still is the fact that this experience provides the basis for the community's reading of Torah. We find it especially in the distinctive haggadic midrash called *pesher* ("interpretation"). Torah is interpreted as applying directly and explicitly to the existence and calling of this group; it is what Torah is all about! Prophecy-fulfillment is applied not to Israel as a whole but to this small group that sees itself as the authentic and true Israel. A good example is the *pesher* on Hab. 2:17. The passage from the prophet reads:

> For the violence done to Lebanon shall overwhelm you and the destruction of beasts shall terrify you because of the blood of men and the violence done to the land, the city, and all its inhabitants.

And here is the interpretation (1QpHab 12.2-9):

> This saying concerns the wicked priest inasmuch as he shall be paid for the reward which he himself tendered to the poor. For *Lebanon* is the council of the community; and the *beasts* are the simple of Judah who keep the law. . . . [I]nterpreted, the *city* is Jerusalem where the wicked priests committed abominable deeds and defiled the temple of God.

Like allegorical interpretation, *pesher* supplies a new code for the reading of the passage. But it is not one derived from ethics or cosmology. It comes from the *experience* of the group itself. Another example is the interpretation of a passage that will be important for Paul (Rom. 1:17), namely Hab. 2:4b: "The righteous will live by his faith." How does Qumran understand this text? According to 1QpHab 8.1-3,

> this concerns all those who observe the Torah in the house of Judah, whom God will deliver from the house of judgment because of their suffering and because of their faith in the Teacher of Righteousness.

The sectarians read their own history in the texts of Torah, employing a method of exegesis that makes the *meaning* of the prophecies to be their fulfillment in present events. The analogy to the practice of the first Christians is both unmistakable and instructive.

In the writings of Qumran, then, as well as in apocalyptic literature, Rabbinic midrash, and the prayers of Jewish worship, we see how particular experiences and convictions lead to specific interpretations of the symbolic world contained in Torah. The symbolic world of Torah is shared by all; the process of Torah interpretation is everywhere. Therefore, the cause for diversity must be sought in the generative and formative nature of the experiences and convictions themselves.

Study Questions

1. What did all Jews have in common during the Hellenistic period?

2. What were the political and religious convictions of the Pharisees?

3. What functions did the synagogue serve? What was the importance of the synagogue for Judaism and the earliest churches?

4. What are the characteristics of "apocalyptic" literature, and how does it defend God's control of history?

5. What was the importance of meals in ancient Judaism?

Bibliographical Note

In this chapter, I have written out the titles of Jewish primary sources whenever possible. For the Qumran writings this is too complex, so I have used the abbreviations found in the Society of Biblical Literature's Member's Handbook, 1994.

The translation of 4 Ezra is by G. H. Box in *Apocrypha and Pseudepigrapha of the Old Testament*, vol. 2, ed. R. H. Charles (Oxford: At the Clarendon Press, 1913), 579; that of the Mishnah is from *The Mishnah*, trans. H. Danby (London: Oxford Univ. Press, 1933), 10–11, except for Pirke Aboth, which comes from R. Travers Herford, *The Ethics of the Talmud: Sayings of the Fathers* (New York: Schocken Books, 1962), 19, 66, 77. The Rabbi Eliezer citation comes from *The Fathers According to Rabbi Nathan*, trans. J. Goldin (New Haven: Yale Univ. Press, 1955), 82. *Tractate Kutim* is translated by Michael Higger, as found in S. W. Baron and J. L. Blau (eds.), *Judaism: Postbiblical and Talmudic Period* (Indianapolis: Bobbs-Merrill, 1954), 68–69. The translation of Babylonian Talmud, *Makkoth*, is by H. M. Lazarus in I. Epstein (ed.), *The Babylonian Talmud* (London: Soncino Press, 1935), 30:169–73. The blessings are translated by D. Hedegard, *Seder Rav Amran Gaon*, pt. 1 (Lund: C. W. K. Gleerup, 1951). The selections from the *Passover Haggadah* are translated by J. Sloan, *The Passover Haggadah*, rev. ed. (New York: Schocken Books, 1953), 49, 51. The selection from Targum *Pseudo-Jonathan* is translated by M. McNamara in *Targum and Testament* (Grand Rapids: Wm. B. Eerdmans, 1972), 140. The Habakkuk Pesher from Qumran is translated by G. Vermes in *The Dead Sea Scrolls in English*, 2nd ed. (New York: Penguin Books, 1975), 242, 239.

Standard historical surveys of Judaism in Palestine are available in W. D. Davies and L. Finkelstein (eds.), *Cambridge History of Judaism* (Cambridge: Cambridge Univ. Press), Vol. 1: *Introduction: The Persian Period* (1984) and Vol. 2, W. D. Davies (ed.), *The Hellenistic Age* (1989); as well as in L. L. Grabbe, *Judaism from Cyrus to Hadrian*, 2 vols. (Minneapolis: Fortress Press, 1992). Of particular value is E. M. Smallwood, *The Jews Under Roman Rule from Pompey to Diocletian* (Leiden: E. J. Brill, 1976). For a general survey of the region, see F. Miller, *The Roman Near East: 31 BC—AD 337* (Cambridge: Harvard Univ. Press, 1993); J. H. Hayes & S. R. Mandell, *The Jewish People in Classical Antiquity: From Alexander to Bar Kochba* (Louisville: Westminster John Knox

Press, 1998). A condensed survey of the historical period is found in E. Bickerman, *From Ezra to the Last of the Maccabees* (New York: Schocken Books, 1949). For a thorough treatment of the history and the literature of the period, see E. Schürer, *A History of the Jewish People in the Time of Jesus*, 4 vols., rev. ed., ed. G. Vermes et al. (Edinburgh: T. & T. Clark, 1973–87), and the series CRINT (Assen: Van Gorcum; Philadelphia/Minneapolis: Fortress Press): Sect. 1: S. Safrai and M. Stern (eds.), *The Jewish People in the First Century*, 2 vols. (1974–76); Sect. 2.1: M. J. Mulder (ed.), *Mikra: Text, Translation, Reading and Interpretation of the Hebrew Bible in Ancient Judaism and Early Christianity* (1988); Sect. 2.2: M. E. Stone (ed.), *Jewish Writings of the Second Temple Period* (1984); and Sect. 3.1: S. Safrai (ed.), *Literature of the Sages* (1987). Also noteworthy is the survey of modern scholarship in R. A. Kraft and G. W. E. Nickelsburg (eds.), *Early Judaism and Its Modern Interpreters* (Atlanta: Scholars Press, 1986). For a more general treatment of the literature of the period, see G. W. E. Nickelsburg, *Jewish Literature Between the Bible and the Mishnah* (Philadelphia: Fortress Press, 1981). An important handbook on the relationship of thisliterature to the NT is C. A. Evans, *Noncanonical Writings and New Testament Interpretation* (Peabody, Mass.: Hendrickson Pubs., 1992).

Several specific studies on Palestine are worth noting: D. Mendels, *The Rise and Fall of Jewish Nationalism: Jewish and Christian Ethnicity in Ancient Palestine* (New York: Doubleday, 1992); D. M. Rhoads, *Israel in Revolution 6–74 C.E.* (Philadelphia: Fortress Press, 1976); Z. Safrai, *The Economy of Roman Palestine* (New York: Routledge, 1994); S. Freyne, *Galilee; from Alexander the Great to Hadrian 323 B.C.E. to 135 C.E.: A Study of Second Temple Judaism* (Wilmington, Del.: Michael Glazier; Notre Dame: Univ. of Notre Dame Press, 1980); R. A. Horsley, *Archaeology, History, and Society in Galilee: The Social Context of Jesus and the Rabbis* (Valley Forge, Pa.: Trinity Press Int'l, 1996); L. I. Levine (ed.), *The Galilee in Late Antiquity* (New York: Jewish Theological Seminary of America, 1992); P. Richardson and S. Westerholm (eds.), *Law in Religious Communities in the Roman Period* (Waterloo, Ont.: Wilfrid Laurier Univ. Press, 1991); and T. Ilan, *Jewish Women in Greco-Roman Palestine* (Peabody, Mass.: Hendrickson Pubs., 1996 [1995]). For general cultural information, see J. J. Rousseau and R. Arav, *Jesus and His World: An Archaeological and Cultural Dictionary* (Minneapolis: Fortress Press, 1995). Also, see Appendix 1 for a bibliography on culture in the time of Jesus. On general aspects of Judaism of the period, see S. J. D. Cohen, *From the Maccabees to the Mishnah* (Philadelphia: Westminster Press, 1987).

Special attention is given to the relation of Judaism to Hellenism in M. Hengel, *Judaism and Hellenism*, 2 vols., trans. J. Bowden (Philadelphia: Fortress Press, 1974); J. Goldstein, "Jewish Acceptance and Rejection of Hellenism," in *JCS-D*, 2:64–87; and H. Fischel (ed.), *Essays in Greco-Roman and Related Talmudic Literature* (New York: Ktav Pub. House, 1977). On the sects, see G. Stemberger, *Jewish Contemporaries of Jesus: Pharisees, Sadducees, Essenes*, trans. A. W. Mahnke (Minneapolis: Fortress Press, 1995); L. Finkelstein, *The Pharisees: The Sociological Background of Their Faith*, 2 vols., 3rd ed.

(Philadelphia: Jewish Publication Soc. of Am., 1966); J. Neusner, *From Politics to Piety: The Emergence of Pharisaic Judaism* (Englewood Cliffs, N.J.: Prentice-Hall, 1973); A. J. Saldarini, *Pharisees, Scribes and Sadducees in Palestinian Society: A Sociological Approach* (Wilmington, Del.: Michael Glazier, 1988); R. J. Coggins, *Samaritans and Jews: The Origins of Samaritanism Reconsidered* (Atlanta: John Knox Press, 1975); R. A. Horsley (with J. S. Hanson), *Bandits, Prophets, and Messiahs: Popular Religious Movements at the Time of Jesus* (San Francisco: Harper & Row, 1985); and M. Hengel, *The Zealots*, trans. D. Smith (Edinburgh: T. & T. Clark, 1989). An important work which surveys the practice and beliefs of all the sects, including the *am-ha-aretz*, is E. P. Sanders, *Judaism: Practice & Belief 63 BCE–66 CE* (London: SCM; Philadelphia: Trinity Press Int'l, 1992).

On apocalyptic, see J. J. Collins, *The Apocalyptic Imagination: An Introduction to the Jewish Matrix of Christianity* (New York: Crossroad, 1984; 2d ed. [Grand Rapids: Eerdmans, 1998]); A. Yarbro Collins (ed.), *Early Christian Apocalypticism: Genre and Social Setting; Semeia* 36 (1986); B. McGinn, et al., *Encyclopedia of Apocalyticism;* vol. 1: *The Origins of Apocalypticism in Judaism and Christianity* (New York: Continuum, 1998); C. Rowland, *The Open Heaven: A Study of Apocalyptic in Judaism and Early Christianity* (London: SPCK Press, 1982); D. S. Russell, *The Method and Message of Jewish Apocalyptic* (Philadelphia: Westminster Press, 1964); and P. Sacchi, *Jewish Apocalyptic and Its History*, trans. W. J. Short (JSPSS, 20; Sheffield: Sheffield Academic Press, 1996 [1990]). See also the detailed studies in D. Hellholm (ed.), *Apocalypticism in the Mediterranean World and the Near East* (Tübingen: J. C. B. Mohr [Paul Siebeck], 1983). On resurrection, see G. W. E. Nickelsburg, *Resurrection, Immortality, and Eternal Life in Intertestamental Judaism* (HTS, 26; Cambridge, Mass.: Harvard Univ. Press, 1972). For messianism, see J. H. Charlesworth (ed.), *The Messiah: Developments in Earliest Judaism and Christianity* (Minneapolis: Fortress Press, 1992); J. J. Collins, *The Scepter and the Star: The Messiahs of the Dead Sea Scrolls and Other Ancient Literature* (New York: Doubleday, 1995); and G. S. Oegema, *The Anointed and His People: Messianic Expectations from the Maccabees to Bar Kochba* (JSPSS, 27; Sheffield: Sheffield Academic Press, 1998). On the Book of Daniel, see J. J. Collins, *The Apocalyptic Vision of the Book of Daniel* (HSM, 16; Missoula, Mont.: Scholars Press, 1977). On the Jewish wisdom tradition in both Palestine and the Diaspora (next chapter), see J. J. Collins, *Jewish Wisdom in the Hellenistic Age* (Louisville: Westminster John Knox Press, 1997).

On aspects of Jewish worship, see B. M. Bosker, *The Origins of the Seder: The Passover Rite and Early Rabbinic Judaism* (Berkeley: Univ. of California Press, 1984), and L. A. Hoffman, *The Canonization of the Synagogue Service* (Notre Dame: Univ. of Notre Dame Press, 1979). On the temple, see C. T. R. Hayward, *The Jewish Temple: A Non-Biblical Sourcebook* (New York: Routledge, 1996). On the synagogue, see S. Fine (ed.), *Sacred Realm: The Emergence of the Synagogue in the Ancient World* (Oxford: Oxford Univ. Press, 1996); and idem, *This Holy Place: On the Sanctity of the Synagogue during the Greco–Roman Period* (Notre Dame, Ind.: Univ. of Notre Dame

Press, 1998); J. Gutmann (ed.), *The Synagogue: Studies in Origins, Archeology, and Architecture* (New York: Ktav Pub. House, 1975); and L. I. Levine (ed.), *The Synagogue in Late Antiquity* (Philadelphia: The American Schools of Oriental Research, 1987). On the Targums, see D. R. G. Beattie and M. J. McNamara (eds.), *The Aramaic Bible: Targums in their Historical Context* (JSOTS, 166: Sheffield: Sheffield Academic Press, 1994); E. G. Clarke, "The Bible and Translation: The Targums," in B. H. McLean (ed.), *Origins and Method: Towards a New Understanding of Judaism and Christianity* (JSNTSup, 86; Sheffield: Sheffield Academic Press, 1993), 380–93; and A. D. York, "The Targum in the Synagogue and in the School," *JSJ* 10 (1979): 74–86.

For an introduction to the rabbinic tradition, see G. F. Moore, *Judaism in the First Centuries of the Christian Era*, 2 vols. (New York: Schocken Books, 1927); S. Schechter, *Aspects of Rabbinic Theology* (New York: Schocken Books, 1961); H. L. Strack and G. Stemberger, *Introduction to the Talmud and Midrash*, 2nd rev. ed., trans. M. Bockmuehl (Edinburgh: T & T Clark, 1991); and E. E. Urbach, *The Sages: Their Concepts and Beliefs*, 2 vols., trans. I. Abrahams (Jerusalem: Magnes Press, 1975). For more recent scholarship, see J. Neusner, "The Formation of Rabbinic Judaism: Yavneh (Jamnia) from A.D. 70 to 100," *ANRW* II.19.2 (1979): 3–42. On the development of midrash, see G. Vermes, *Scripture and Tradition in Judaism*, 2nd rev. ed. (Leiden: E. J. Brill, 1973); G. Porten, "Midrash: Palestinian Jews and the Hebrew Bible in the Greco-Roman Period," *ANRW* II.19.2 (1979): 103–38; and A. G. Wright, *The Literary Genre Midrash* (New York: Alba House, 1967). On the literature, see J. Neusner, *Introduction to Rabbinic Literature* (New York: Doubleday, 1994). For the history, see G. Alon, *The Jews in Their Land in the Talmudic Age 70–640 C.E.*, trans. G. Levi (Cambridge, Mass.: Harvard Univ. Press, 1989). On the role of women, see P. J. Haas (ed.), *Recovering the Role of Women: Power and Authority in Rabbinic Jewish Society* (Atlanta: Scholars Press, 1992), and J. R. Wegner, *Chattel or Person? The Status of Women in the Mishnah* (New York: Oxford Univ. Press, 1988).

On the Dead Sea Scrolls and the community at Qumran, see G. Boccaccini, *Beyond the Essene Hypothesis* (Grand Rapids: Eerdmans, 1998); G. J. Brooke, *The Bible and Its Interpretation* (London: Routledge, 1998); J. J. Collins, *Apocalypticism in the Dead Sea Scrolls* (New York: Routledge, 1997); F. M. Cross, *The Ancient Library at Qumran and Modern Biblical Studies*, 3rd ed. (Minneapolis: Fortress Press, 1995); P. W. Flint and J. C. Vanderkam (eds.), *The Dead Sea Scrolls after Fifty Years*, 2 vols. (Leiden: Brill, 1998); F. García Martínez and J. Trebolle Barrera, *The People of the Dead Sea Scrolls: Their Writings, Beliefs, and Practices*, trans. W. G. E. Watson (Leiden: E. J. Brill, 1995); D. Harrington, *Wisdom Texts from Qumran* (New York: Routledge, 1996); S. E. Porter and C. A. Evans (eds.), *The Scrolls and the Scriptures: Qumran Fifty Years After* (JSPSS, 26; Sheffield: Sheffield Academic Press, 1997); L. H. Schiffman, *Reclaiming the Dead Sea Scrolls* (Philadelphia: Jewish Publication Society, 1994); E. Ulrich and J. Vanderkam (eds.), *The Community of the Renewed Covenant* (Notre Dame: Univ. of Notre Dame Press, 1994); and J. C. Vanderkam, *The Dead Sea Scrolls Today* (Grand Rapids:

Eerdmans, 1994). On women, see E. M. Schuller, "Women in the Dead Sea Scrolls," in M. O. Wise et al. (eds.), *Methods of Investigation of the Dead Sea Scrolls and the Khirbet Qumran Site* (New York: The New York Academy of Sciences, 1994), 115–31.

For a selection of primary texts, see C. Montefiore and H. Loewe, *A Rabbinic Anthology* (New York: Schocken Books, 1974), and G. W. E. Nickelsburg and M. E. Stone, *Faith and Piety in Early Judaism: Texts and Documents* (Philadelphia: Fortress Press, 1983). For full editions of primary texts, see the following: for the Jewish pseudepigraphic writings, J. H. Charlesworth (ed.), *The Old Testament Pseudepigrapha*, 2 vols. (New York: Doubleday, 1983, 1985); for the targums, the series *The Aramaic Bible* (Collegeville, Minn.: Liturgical Press, 1987–); for the mishnah, J. Neusner, *The Mishnah: A New Translation* (New Haven: Yale Univ. Press, 1988); for the Babylonian Talmud, both I. Epstein (ed.), *The Babylonian Talmud* (London: Soncino Press, 1935–52), and A. Steinsaltz (ed.), *Talmud: The Steinsaltz Edition* (New York: Random House, 1989–); for the Palestinian Talmud, *Talmud of the Land of Israel: A Preliminary Translation and Explanation*, ed. J. Neusner (Chicago: Univ. of Chicago Press); and for the Qumran texts, both F. García Martínez, *The Dead Sea Scrolls Translated: The Qumran Texts in English*, 2nd ed., trans. W. G. E. Watson (Leiden: E. J. Brill; Grand Rapids: Eerdmans, 1996), and M. Wise et al., *The Dead Sea Scrolls: A New Translation* (San Francisco: HarperCollins, 1996).

3. Diaspora Judaism

IN THE FIRST CENTURY, far more Jews lived outside Palestine than within, and the forms of Judaism prevalent in the Diaspora are of great importance for the understanding of the NT. The term "Diaspora Judaism," however, is not equivalent to "Hellenistic Judaism." In the first place, Hellenization was a significant part of Judaism in Palestine. There were various expressions of Judaism in the Diaspora, and not all were necessarily Hellenistic. The tendency to identify Diaspora and Hellenistic derives from the state of our sources. Most of the information about first-century Diaspora Judaism comes from Alexandria, and it was indeed Hellenistic, not only because it was written in Greek but even more because it appropriated Greek culture in distinctive ways. Not even this Hellenistic Judaism, however, is completely uniform; in addition to Philo, it produced the *Sibylline Oracles*, with their messianic and apocalyptic overtones.

If Hellenistic and Diaspora are not interchangeable, what value is there in distinguishing between Palestinian and Diaspora Judaism? The distinction recognizes that the development of Jewish life and symbols was directly influenced by social and political contexts. Diaspora Judaism was not continually forced to equate religious and political symbols. The perennial problem facing all Jews, the tension between assimilation and separation, was worked out in a setting less colored by religious persecution and political oppression. Although no less intense in their devotion to the homeland, those living outside Palestine could deal with pluralism in a way unavailable to those for whom territory and religion were unavoidably interconnected.

This sketch of some aspects of Diaspora Judaism, therefore, is deliberately selective. It leaves aside the East, for which we have only later sources, in favor of the West, for which we have extensive contemporary records. The primary reason for this is that Christianity developed westward, encountering first the Greek forms of Diaspora Judaism, and being most deeply and permanently marked by them.

Extent and Importance of Diaspora Judaism

The Diaspora situation was not a recent development for Jews of the NT period. Already in the days of David and Solomon, Jews went abroad to serve in military garrisons (2 Sam. 8:6) or for purposes of trade (1 Kings 5:14; 9:26-28; 10:15, 22). The exiles of 722 and 586 B.C.E., of course, involved the deportation of many Jews to Assyria and Babylon and also caused some to migrate to Egypt (Jer. 43:6-7). The majority of those who went into exile did not return to the land. As a consequence, by the first century the Diaspora was the natural, accepted, and centuries-old context for the transmission of Jewish identity for the majority of Jews in the world.

In Mesopotamia, the Jewish population was so large and well organized that it became the new center for Jewish scholarship and remained so into the medieval period. Syria had large numbers of Jews, especially in the cities of Damascus and Antioch (*JW* VII.3.3; cf. also Acts 9:2, 19-20). Cyrene in North Africa had been settled with Jews during the time of Ptolemy I (*Ant* XIV.7.2). Its thriving Jewish culture is shown by the production of the multi-volume history of the Maccabees by Jason (2 Macc. 2:23), and the strength of its Jewish populace is evidenced by the people's temporary success in the revolt of 115–17 C.E. Two thousand Jewish families were transported from Babylon to Asia Minor at the end of the third century B.C.E., forming the basis for an extensive Jewish life there (*Ant* XII.3.4; Acts 13:14; 14:1, 6, 24-25; 16:1). Achaia and Macedonia had synagogues in most important urban centers by the first century (see Philo *Embassy to Gaius* 281–82; Acts 16:13; 17:1, 10, 17; 18:4), and there was a large Jewish community at Rome (Acts 28:17-24).

The Jewish population in Egypt goes back to the sixth century B.C.E., and was repeatedly enriched by emigration from Palestine. Philo says that there were a million Jews in Egypt (*Against Flaccus* 43). During the Maccabean period, opponents of the Jerusalem priests erected a rival temple at Hierapolis (*Ant* XIII.3.1–3), and even earlier, there was an Aramaic-speaking military colony of Jews at Elephantine. Most Egyptian Jews lived in Alexandria, from which comes our richest literary evidence. Since Alexandria was the intellectual capital of the Hellenistic world, with its great library and museum, it is not surprising that these writings reveal a lively and positive engagement with Hellenistic thought. In Alexandria, above all, we find distinctively Greek culture entering into creative dialogue with Jewish thought and practice.

Demographic figures for the ancient world are difficult to establish, but by some estimates there were seven million Jews in the first century; of these, two million were in Palestine and five million in the Diaspora. More significant than the specific number is the proportion. The Jews were a visible presence in the Diaspora. In the eastern empire, they may have constituted as much as fifteen percent of the population, and no doubt their visibility would have been heightened by their close community life. This perception of Jewish prominence is clear when Josephus quotes the late first century B.C.E. Greek historian Strabo (*Ant* XIV.7.2; cf. Philo *Embassy* 281–82):

> The Jewish people had already come into every city, and one cannot readily find any place in the world which has not received this tribe and been taken possession of by it.

This great flow of Jewish people into the wider world was not regarded by the Jews as a great tragedy or a circumstance that prevented their singing a song to the Lord in a foreign land (Ps. 137:4). At least since the second century B.C.E., Palestine was overcrowded (Philo *Flaccus* 45–46), and most Jews were content to be where they were. They filled a variety of social roles. Some were mercenary soldiers (as those at the Elephantine colony), others farmers, still others were craftsmen and traders, ranging from simple peddlers to entrepreneurs. Some Jews enjoyed both wealth and civic importance. Such was the case with the family of Philo. His younger brother Alexander was an Alabarch (*Ant* XVIII.8.1), and Philo himself led a delegation that was received by the emperor Caligula. Jews in the Diaspora were found at every level of society.

The direct and considerable importance of Diaspora Judaism to Christianity can be summed up in one word: synagogue. In Acts 15:21, James says,

> For from early generations Moses has had in every city those who preach him,
> for he is read every sabbath in the synagogues.

Synagogues were established wherever Jews migrated. In the first century, a vast and intricate network of synagogues (often called "houses of prayer" in the Diaspora) covered the Mediterranean world. The synagogues were the center for the maintenance of Jewish identity (*Flaccus* 48), providing the context for the problems and possibilities facing a minority group that sought to maintain its singularity in a highly pluralistic environment.

It was this network of common Jewish centers that became the stepping stone from which Christianity moved into the gentile world. From the synagogue Christianity inherited a well-established tradition of preaching, teaching, and worship, carried out in the midst of Greek culture (*Embassy* 312). It was from the synagogue as well that the early Christians received the Greek Bible (Septuagint), which was read and studied in the synagogues week by week (Josephus *Against Apion* II.175). It was this Greek version of Torah that provided the primary symbolic framework for the development of a specifically Christian self-understanding. The synagogue also aided later Christian evangelization by spreading, throughout the gentile world, an awareness of the peculiar and exclusive nature of Jewish monotheism, of the high moral code of Torah, and of the attractive claim of being a people called by God. It was among those Gentiles first attracted to the synagogue (*Apion* II.282–86) that Christian preachers found their initial missionary successes in the Diaspora (Acts 13:42-44, 48, 14:1; 17:4).

No less than the Jews in Palestine, those in the Diaspora looked to the texts of Torah for the symbolic expression of their identity. Their understanding of the symbols, however, was shaped by their experience of reading them within a very different sort of world. Jews of the Diaspora were immeasurably freer with regard to Hellenistic culture. They were not so frequently required to choose between God and king. In the first century, there were sporadic and sometimes violently repressive measures taken against the Jews by emperors or local rulers (*Flaccus* 58–95; *JW* VII.3.2–4), but these seem to have been the exception and a rather recent innovation. Before and during the first century c.e., Jews of the Diaspora were given the right to autonomy within the city-state (*polis*) of their residence, and to live according to their ancestral customs (a point noted in Claudius' famous letter to the Alexandrians in 41 c.e. [P. Lond. 1912]).

The exact legal status of Jews in the empire is difficult to determine. Many individual Jews enjoyed full citizenship (*Flaccus* 53; *Embassy* 349), and Jews as a group seemed to fall into the category of a *politeuma*, that is, a group of aliens of the same ethnic origin who were allowed to follow their own customs and worship their own gods (see *Apion* II.35–47). In Alexandria, Jews were apparently governed by a body of elders (*gerousia*), which functioned as a court for settling disputes (*Ant* XIV.7.2). Since physical proximity made the observance of Torah easier, Jews tended to live close together (*Flaccus* 55), though this was not required.

Not only did Jews enjoy freedom, they also were significantly privileged. It appears, for example, that Jews were exempt from the obligation to observe syncretistic worship such as would be required of other members of the polis. There is no firm documentary evidence for this, but the outrage expressed when the exemption was in danger of being suspended suggests that it was a privilege of some consistency and antiquity (*Flaccus* 47; *Embassy* 117, 134; *Apion* II.71–72). The Jews were allowed to meet regularly in their synagogues (*Embassy* 312) and they could take a day off work for Sabbath observance (*Embassy* 156). Jews were exempt from military duty (since it inevitably involved marching under the images of gods), although many of them served voluntarily (*Apion* I.200–204). Most remarkably, the empire recognized the yearly temple tax paid by Jews from around the world to Jerusalem as a sacred fund and protected its transportation to Jerusalem (*Embassy* 216, 313). In short, Diaspora Jews had remarkable freedom to follow Torah and shape their identity by its symbols. The preservation of that identity was complicated, however, by the fact of their being a minority in a pluralistic culture.

The Religious and Cultural Tensions of Diaspora Life

Like all intentional communities, first-century Judaism in the Diaspora was pulled between opposing attractions. On one side was the powerful appeal of the dominant culture, which invited assimilation. On the other side was the call of the ancestral ways, which demanded that the Jews remain a separate people. Every community and every individual resolved the tension differently. Each resolution inevitably involved some conflict.

Assimilation into the dominant cultural context is a natural and understandable need. Societies demand a high price from those who would be deviant, either as individuals or groups. It is extraordinarily difficult to appear to be, and indeed to be, different. Assimilation to Greek culture began with the use of a Greek name. Sometimes this was simply a Greek "public" form of a Hebrew name, such as Paul for Saul (Acts 13:9). Other times, full Greek names were adopted, as we see with Jason in 2 Macc. 4:7, and with Stephen, Philip, and the other "Hellenists" in Acts 6:5.

Changing names represented a level of acceptance of the dominant language of the culture. By the first century, most Jews in the Diaspora did not know Hebrew, having spoken nothing but Greek for generations. For them, Greek was not a foreign tongue, it was their native language. So ancient was this situation that the Septuagint translation (LXX) of Torah was already some two hundred years old by the time of Philo (see *Life of Moses* II.25–40).

Translation of Torah into Greek was a massive, and at the same time subtle, transformation of symbols. Every translation is an interpretation. Even when the LXX sought to be scrupulously literal in its rendering, something was both lost and gained in the transition from Hebrew forms to Greek ones. The syntax of the two languages is sufficiently different to give a distinctive structuring even to narratives. Even at the level of individual words, the process of losing some resonances and gaining others is clear. For instance, the word "glory" lost some of the nuance of "weight" and "presence" that was rooted in the Hebrew, but gained some further sense of "appearance" and "radiance" from other Greek usages. The Greek word for "law" (*nomos*) had a different set of associations and implications than did the Hebrew word *torah*, resulting in subtle shifts in meaning when the former was used to translate the latter. Losses and gains alike would be imperceptible to Greek-speaking Jews, for they lacked any standard of comparison. Thus, despite the ambiguity in the Hebrew text of Isa. 7:14 (*almah* can mean either "young woman" or "virgin"), the Diaspora Jew, reading in the Septuagint translation that a *parthenos* would bear a son, had no doubt that the individual in question was a virgin. In places, moreover, where the LXX itself was much freer in translation, it became something of a Greek Targum, but one unperceived as such by those who heard it in the synagogue. The text of the Septuagint was Scripture for Jews in the Diaspora, and so the meaning and reading of the "original" Hebrew was not a concern.

Another social structure that worked on behalf of assimilation was education. A Jew like Philo, growing up in Alexandria, would have regarded a fully Greek education as completely normal and certainly not contrary to Torah. In fact, Torah itself expressed Greek wisdom (*sophia*), especially in writings like the Wisdom of Solomon. Study or exercise in the gymnasium did not represent a break with ancestral ways as it did in Palestine (cf. 2 Macc. 4:10-17). The study of Greek poetry and philosophy was not incompatible with the study of Torah, and in Torah itself was found sufficient corrective to the negative side of Greek literature, namely, its associations with idolatry.

In such a context, the synthesis of Jewish and Greek symbols was inevitable, unconscious, and natural. It would have been impossible for Philo, growing up where and when he did (Alexandria, ca. 20 B.C.E. to 50 C.E.), to look at the heroes of faith in Torah and *not* see them as models of the philosophical life. It was impossible for him, when confronted with the difficulties presented by the literal meaning of Torah, *not* to use the allegorical method he had learned in his reading of the Homeric poems and in the commentaries on them.

The opposite pole of attraction was separation. However Hellenized Jews became, they remained a distinct and identifiable presence among the pagans. To a remarkable degree, they maintained active contacts with Palestine. They paid the yearly temple tax and went up to Jerusalem whenever possible for the pilgrimage feasts, swelling the city with their presence (Acts 2:5-11). They followed the political fortunes of the homeland with lively interest (*Embassy* 188–89), and were an eager market for Jewish propaganda like the histories of Jason and Josephus.

Their allegiance to Torah as the ultimate norm for their lives was what truly separated them from their pagan neighbors, for that allegiance implied certain convictions and demanded particular responses that were alien to Hellenistic culture as a whole. Diaspora Jews might find beauty in Homer, but true wisdom could be found only in Moses; they could read about utopia in Plato but could find the frame for a priestly people only in Torah. Torah they heard read in the synagogue, and Torah provided the words for their prayers. Because of Torah, they kept the Sabbath day holy and observed the other feasts (*Flaccus* 116) even when societal pressure made it difficult. Because of Torah, they observed special dietary practices and practiced circumcision (*Embassy* 361) even when such practices were regarded as barbarous by their neighbors. Because they shared the same symbolic world of Torah, Diaspora Jews maintained close ties with Palestinian Jews, even sending announcements of marriages to the temple archives (*Apion* I.32–36), although such connections might make them suspect at home. Perhaps even more emphatically than Jews in Palestine, those in the Diaspora remained a part of the people because of their intense and exclusive allegiance to Torah (*Apion* II.232–35).

No other cult was so exclusive in its claims; no school of philosophy was so inclusive in its demands. The distinctiveness of Diaspora Jews generated among their gentile neighbors a mixed response. One side of the response was positive, especially among rulers and the better-educated. Sophisticated Greeks were fascinated by "barbarians" generally, and the Chaldeans ranked with the Egyptians as main objects of interest. Philosophers saw Judaism as an ancient and praiseworthy form of wisdom. And the strong community ties of the Jews undoubtedly attracted many proselytes and God-fearers from among the pagans (*Apion* II.179–96). Judaism in the first century was an aggressive and growing phenomenon.

Among those threatened by Jewish claims, such as the priests of other cults, and among those less sophisticated in their tastes, the Jews were a constant irritant because of their difference. Popular resentment could easily turn to hostile action (*Embassy* 120–26; *Apion* II.32). The official privileges enjoyed by the Jews seemed to have been particularly offensive to some. They saw that the Jews took from the *polis* but did not give to it. They were exempt from worshiping the civic gods on whose protection the safety of the city depended (*Apion* II.65). Indeed, the monies that should have been given in support of the public service (*leiturgeia*) of the city were sent to a foreign temple. The Jews had all the privileges of Hellenistic culture but not the responsibilities. Even the regular Sabbath observance could prove disruptive for the economy in a world that did not have weekends. The mix of imperial privilege and local resentment was a volatile one, and Jews could be charged with the refusal to mingle with others (*amixia*) and hatred of humankind (*misanthropia*) by those who viewed their separateness as a scandal.

Anti-Semitism as an explicit and articulate response to Judaism seems to have originated in Alexandria in the time of Ptolemy II. An Egyptian priest named Manetho wrote a history of Egypt in which the Jews played an ignoble role (*Apion* I.227–50): the account was filled with scurrilous suggestions concerning both Moses and the Jews (I.249) that were already familiar by the first century. For instance, it was said that Jews were really atheists, for they did not worship the gods, and their own deity was invisible. Other rumor-like charges abounded: they really worshiped an ass's head (II.80); or Gentiles were captured by Jews to be killed and eaten (II.92–96). All the customs of the Jews were fair game for mockery and innuendo (II.137–42). The most persistent charge, however, reveals the genuine source of irritation: misanthropy (II.121–24, 291). In a pluralistic world, a group that kept to itself and claimed exclusive possession of the truth was bound to be resented by many. Similar charges of misanthropy and failure to mix were made, in fact, against the other two groups who most combined dogmatic claims and strong community ties: the Epicureans and the Christians.

The Response of Jewish Apologetic

A minority group under attack for its distinctiveness can react in three ways. It can intensify the efforts to assimilate and become indistinguishable from its critics; it can intensify its separatist qualities and cultivate an insider-against-outsider mentality; or it can seek to defend and explain its way of life to others. This last is the way of *apologetic*. In broadest terms, nearly all the flood of writing from Alexandrian Judaism can be called apologetic, in the sense that it attempted to demonstrate the beauty of the distinctive way of Torah to those who shared the same language but worshiped different gods.

Jewish apologetic literature helps us understand early Christian writings by its choice of topics and marshaling of arguments, but most of all by the very nature of the enterprise. Apologetic makes a statement about the group's view of outsiders; it presumes a world of good will and openness to rational argument. The writing of apologetic may have been the greatest oblique compliment paid by Jews and Christians to that corrupt pagan world. Something is also said about insiders: they are people open to the wider world, eager to bridge the misunderstandings separating them from others and confident that their shared culture will enable such bridge-building.

Ostensibly addressed to outsiders for purposes of persuasion, apologetic is in reality aimed equally at insiders. The attempt to make ourselves intelligible to others helps make us intelligible to ourselves. Apologetic strengthens community identity even as it seeks to communicate it. In the process, however, the community's symbols themselves become transformed. To make our position clear to outsiders, we must use language and symbols familiar to them since our aim is to garner greater understanding and tolerance. Inevitably, we color our self-portrait in shades familiar and acceptable. Continuity and commonality are stressed more than dissension and distinction.

To a large extent, then, the categories of the discussion are provided by the outsiders. For Alexandrian Jews, that meant the categories of Greek wisdom. In apologetic literature, therefore, Judaism appears as another, though infinitely superior, form of Greek philosophy. The most obvious example is the description of Palestinian Jewish sects by Josephus (*JW* II.8.2). He refers to them as schools of philosophy and aligns their teachings with those of the Stoics, Epicureans, and Pythagoreans. By so doing, he not only makes them intelligible to Greek readers, but also reinterprets them for his fellow Jews, causing them to see themselves as philosophers.

In the Wisdom of Solomon (1st cent. B.C.E.), the ancient wisdom tradition of the Jews is recast in a distinctively Hellenistic mold. Not only does language about vice and virtue abound and the concept of immortality assume an important role, but the whole history of Israel from creation to the wilderness (chaps. 10–19) is told as the work of a personified Wisdom (*Sophia*), which, according to 7:25-26, is

> a breath of the power of God, and a pure emanation of the glory of the almighty . . . a reflection of eternal light, a spotless mirror of the working of God and an image of his goodness.

In the middle of the account of the exodus, the author makes an extended attack on idolatry (chaps. 13–16), saying that "all men who were ignorant of God were foolish by nature" (13:1). Such attacks were of course standard fare in the Prophets (cf. Isa. 44:9-20), but in Wisdom, we find a sympathy for the plight of the pagan that the prophets never had (13:5-7):

> . . . for from the greatness and beauty of created things comes a corresponding perception of their creator. Yet perhaps these men are little to be blamed, for perhaps they go astray while seeking God and desiring to find him. For as they live among his works, they keep searching, and they trust in what they see, because the things that are seen are beautiful.

In a wonderfully succinct fashion, those few lines demonstrate just how thoroughly Jewish convictions were wedded to profoundly Hellenistic perceptions.

Certain themes recur frequently in Hellenistic Jewish apologetic literature. In a culture where old was better than new, and East better than West, the antiquity and oriental roots of Judaism were attractive. The purity and beauty of synagogue worship were favorably contrasted to pagan cults. And to counter the charge of misanthropy, the laws of Torah were shown to be philanthropic.

The theme of antiquity could in its crudest form become a kind of cultural competition. The claim that one tradition was older than another, if proved, carried considerable weight (*Apion* I.7–8), especially when combined with the claim that the Greeks also borrowed key beliefs and practices from Israel (II.168). In some texts, it is suggested that Moses was not only older than the Greek gods but was the founder of Greek culture itself. Thus, Josephus claims that Pythagoras learned from Moses (*Apion* I.164–65) and that all the philosophers borrowed from Hebrew wisdom (*Apion* II.281). Nowhere is this claim made in more startling fashion than in fragment 3 by the Alexandrian Jew, Artapanus (mid-2nd cent. B.C.E.):

> Moreover this Moses became the teacher of Orpheus. On reaching manhood, he made many useful contributions to mankind; and in fact he invented ships, machines for laying stones, Egyptian weapons, implements for drawing water, implements for fighting, and the study of Philosophy. He also divided the state into thirty-six Nomes, and assigned which god was to be worshipped in each. He also assigned the sacred books to the priests.

In addition to the antiquity of Moses and his being the source of Greek philosophy (not to mention Egyptian idolatry!), the usefulness and philanthropy of his inventions are stressed. This theme of antiquity is repeatedly stressed by Josephus (his history of the Jews was not accidentally named *Antiquities*). In *Ant* I.16 (proem), he states that Moses, the author of the Pentateuch,

> was born two thousand years ago, to which ancient date the poets never ventured to refer even the birth of their gods, much less the actions or laws of mortals.

Lest we think such cultural competition was found only in the Diaspora, there is this fragment from a mid-second century B.C.E. Palestinian Jew, Eupolemus (frag. 1):

> Moses became the first wise man and was the first to pass along the alphabet to the Jews. And the Phoenicians received it from the Jews, and the Greeks received it from the Phoenicians. And Moses was the first to write laws for the Jews.

As these passages make clear, Moses was a central figure for Jewish apologetic. And in the descriptions of Moses, we find the transformation of the biblical figure into one shaped by Hellenistic perceptions. The same thing that happened to Heracles in Stoic-Cynic philosophy (and in Philo; cf. *Embassy* 81, 90) happened to Moses in Hellenistic Jewish apologetic: the hero of the past is perceived through the symbols of present experience and conviction. Moses comes to resemble the philosopher-king.

Already in Plato's *Republic* (473D, 540D–E), the ideal ruler was seen as both philosopher and king. He could rule wisely because he himself was a wise man (*sophos*), one who personified virtue. The same theme is found in the treatises on kingship in the Hellenistic period (Dio *Oration* 1.34–35; 2.26; 4.78–139). And we find it once again in the Hellenistic Jewish *Letter of Aristeas*. This purports to tell the story of the translation of the Septuagint, but is also a piece of Jewish propaganda. It appropriates the symposium motif from Plato: the king invites the seventy-two Jewish translators to a banquet (181), during which he poses questions to them concerning virtue (187–293). Their answers, predictably, astound the king and demonstrate the superiority of Jewish wisdom: "They were far superior to them [the Greek philosophers] both in conduct and in argument since they always made God their starting point" (235).

Many of the questions posed by the king have to do with the qualities of kingship and good statecraft (211, 222, 265, 271, 279). The scholars respond with typical observations concerning the virtues of an ideal king, with this addition: what characterizes the true *sophos* is the fear of God and the keeping of his commandments. In this writing, there is the use of a thoroughly Hellenistic literary genre and philosophical topic (*topos*) placed in the service of Jewish ethical teaching. It is within this context that the representation of Moses as the perfect philosopher-king begins to make sense, for he surely was a leader of the people (king) and revealed his wisdom in Torah (philosopher). In this argument, Moses was the model of the wise ruler long before Plato expounded it. Thus, when Josephus describes the death of Moses, he does so in these terms (*Ant* IV.8.49):

> He lived in all one hundred and twenty years . . . having surpassed in understanding all men that ever lived and put to noblest use the fruit of his reflections. In speech and in addresses to a crowd he found favor in every way, but chiefly through his thorough command of his passions, which was such that he seemed to have no place for them at all in his soul, and only knew their names through seeing them in others rather than in himself. As a general he had few to equal him, and as prophet none, insomuch that in all his utterances one seemed to hear the speech of God himself.

Except for the mention of Moses as a prophet, Josephus has described the *sophos* skilled in rhetoric; a learned and controlled individual, who is virtuous in legislation and a leader in battle. Such a perception was not unique to Josephus. In his *Life of Moses*, Philo shows the ways Moses perfectly fills the office of lawgiver (II.8–65), high priest (II.66–186), and prophet (II.187–291). While all of these are biblical categories, Philo introduces them through the consideration of Moses as king (*Moses* I.148):

> The appointed leader of all these was Moses, invested with his office and kingship, not like some of those who thrust themselves into positions of power by means of arms and engines of war and strength of infantry, cavalry and navy, but on account of his goodness and his nobility of conduct and the universal benevolence which he never failed to show. Further, his office was bestowed upon him by God, the lover of virtue and nobility, as the reward due to him.

In Philo, not only Moses but all the patriarchs are transformed into *sophoi*, each of whom in his fashion embodies some aspect of virtue and wisdom (cf. *The Testaments of the Twelve Patriarchs*). Moses, however, was the embodiment of all virtue and a model for others to follow, both in his legislation and in his life (*Moses* I.158-59):

> For he was named god and king of the whole nation, and entered, we are told, into the darkness where God was [Ex. 20:21], that is into the unseen, invisible, incorporeal and archetypal essence of existing things. Thus he beheld what is hidden from the sight of mortal nature, and, in himself and his life displayed for all to see, he has set before us, like some well-wrought picture, a piece of work beautiful and god-like, a model for those who are willing to copy it. Happy are they who imprint, or strive to imprint, that image in their souls.

It would be a mistake to think of Josephus, Philo, and the other Hellenistic Jewish writers as engaging in a deliberate distortion of the biblical witness in order to win friends for the Jews. Nowhere is such a motivation suggested. Indeed, Josephus tells us he is the soberest of all historians, neither deleting nor embellishing (*Ant* I.17 [proem]). What then is at work? Simply this: the transformation of the symbols of Torah, accomplished in what was in all likelihood an unconscious and intuitive process of translating Torah into terms the readers—both Gentile and Jewish—best understood. When Josephus and Philo describe the patriarchs as *sophoi*, they are only telling us what they themselves see in the text. Such descriptions, in fact, show just how far into Greek culture these staunch defenders of Judaism were assimilated.

Philo of Alexandria

Philo of Alexandria (d. ca. 50 C.E.) is, next to Paul, the most visible and ambiguous figure in first-century Diaspora Judaism. The difficulty in assessing his importance is connected to the state of our sources. Philo was well loved by the early Christian writers, and they preserved much of his voluminous work. With the possible exception of Josephus, he remains, in our limited sources, the only fully rounded Jewish figure of his time. Consequently, we do not know whether he should be regarded as a unique case or as a representative figure. There is evidence that much of what we find in Philo is paralleled in other places, but he seems to have combined elements in a manner distinctive to himself.

Philo's importance for the understanding of the NT does not lie in the way some of his concepts seem to anticipate those found in the early Christian writings, as striking as those sometimes are: the notion of the *Logos* ("Word") as the intermediary between God and humans, for example (see, e.g., *Who Is the Heir?* 205–6; cf. John 1:1-2; Heb. 1:1-3), and the idea that the demands of Torah can be embodied even by those who have not received the law of Moses (*On Abraham*; cf. Rom. 2:12-16). Nor is his significance to be found in the way ideas similar to his appear to be presupposed by NT arguments, such as in the contrast between the two Adams in 1 Cor. 15:45-50, or the use of etymology in Heb. 7:4-9. As impressive as those connections sometimes are, they remain isolated threads of similarity in greatly dissimilar fabrics.

The greatest significance of Philo for the study of the NT is analogous to the importance of Qumran. Much as the Qumran community showed us how diverse traditions could coexist in a single setting, Philo illustrates how the mind and heart of a single Diaspora Jew could bring together many diverse traditions and viewpoints, molding them into a single coherent vision. Knowing how Philo could be so many things at once helps us understand how another multifaceted Diaspora Jew, Saul of Tarsus, could also contain within himself seemingly contradictory elements. And seeing how the communal heritage and personal experience of Philo could issue in a distinctive reinterpretation of Torah helps us grasp how the author of the Letter to the Hebrews could combine a similar heritage and quite a different religious experience, deriving a hauntingly similar yet clearly divergent reinterpretation of Torah.

Philo was totally at home within Greek culture. He knew little if any Hebrew and read Torah in the Septuagint (LXX) translation. He could quote Plato, Homer, and Euripides as easily as Torah and sometimes cited them side by side (cf. *On Dreams* 139–63). He was also well acquainted with the sort of allegorical interpretations that had been applied to Homer (*Embassy* 93–113; *On the Decalogue* 54). He was not a systematic thinker, though he was conversant with philosophical opinions and used them in a typically eclectic fashion. With the Pythagoreans he shared a fascination with numbers and was always delighted when Torah provided him the opportunity to expound their deeper sense (*Decalogue* 20–31). Platonism had an obvious influence on him. In Genesis (1:26-27; 2:7), for example, when confronted by two accounts of the creation of humans, he suggested that the first creation was of the heavenly prototype and thus androgynous in nature. It was only in the secondary material creation, he argued, that one found division into sexes (see *Allegorical Interpretation* I.31; *Questions on Genesis* I.4). Likewise, the LXX rendering of Exod. 25:40, where God tells Moses to make a tabernacle "according to the image" shown on the mountain, is exploited by Philo in thoroughly Platonic fashion, as it also was by the author of Hebrews (cf. *Questions and Answers on Exodus* 82; *Allegorical Interpretation* III.102; Heb. 8:5).

It is in his interpretation of Torah that Philo's Hellenistic culture is most evident. Just as the Stoics used allegory to deal with the difficulties presented by the Homeric poems, so Philo used allegorical interpretation to underscore and develop the deeper meaning of Torah. The literal meaning of the text remains important to him but sometimes presents insurmountable difficulties: contradictions, impossibilities, even scandals. The true meaning of Torah must be found at the level of the Spirit that guided Moses in the composition of Torah, that is, in a spiritual interpretation. This, for Philo, was an allegorical reading. In *On the Posterity and Exile of Cain* 1–11, Philo starts his comments on Gen. 4:16 ("And Cain went out from the face of God") with these words (1–2, 7):

> Let us here raise the question whether in the books in which Moses acts as God's interpreter we ought to take his statements figuratively, since the impression made by the words in their literal sense is greatly at variance with truth. For if the Existent Being has a face ... what ground have we for rejecting the impious doctrines of Epicurus, or the atheism of the Egyptians or the mythical plots of play and poem of which the world is full? ... [T]he only thing left for us to do is make up our minds that none of the propositions put forward is literally intended and to take the path of figurative interpretation so dear to philosophical souls ...

Philo is perfectly capable of a literal interpretation, and in many of his writings (e.g., in the *Life of Moses*) he carefully expounds the surface narrative. But he is never far from an allegorical interpretation. As with his predecessors in this approach, he made much of etymologies; thus, in *On Joseph* 28 he writes:

> After this literal account of the story, it will be well to explain the underlying meaning, for, broadly speaking, all or most of the law-book is an allegory. The kind of character then here under discussion is called in Hebrew "Joseph," but in our language [Greek] is "*addition of a lord,*" a most significant title well suited to the thing which it indicates, since polity as seen in the various peoples is an *addition* to nature who is invested with a universal *lord*ship.

Philo does not have a consistent framework for his allegorical interpretations, but one aspect of his interpretive task demands attention: its mystical connotations. Philo suggests that he himself was a mystic. When speaking of the creation of humanity, and the way in which the mind is the true image of God, he moves into a near rhapsodic passage, which seems clearly to be autobiographical. In *On the Creation* 71, he says that the mind at times

> is seized by a sober intoxication, like those filled with Corybantic frenzy, and is inspired, possessed with a longing far other than theirs and a nobler desire. Wafted by this to the topnotch ark of the things perceptible to mind, it seems to be on its way to the great King himself; but amid its longing to see him, pure and untempered rays of concentrated light stream forth like a torrent, so that by its gleams the eye of the understanding is dazzled.

There is, furthermore, a connection between his mystical experiences and his reading of Torah. For Philo, it appears that Torah itself contains the possibility of leading the soul into these deeper recesses of the divine reality. He is capable of speaking of it in terms suggestive of a mystery religion, as in *On the Cherubim* 48:

> I myself was initiated under Moses the God-Beloved into his greater mysteries, yet when I saw the prophet Jeremiah and knew him to be not only himself enlightened but a worthy minister of the holy secrets, I was not slow to become his disciple.

It is extraordinarily difficult to evaluate such statements—are they part of an elaborate literary metaphor or do they point to a form of esoteric Jewish mysticism that read the same Torah as the uninitiated, but with different eyes? Certainly, there were mystics in first-century Judaism such as the practitioners of Merkabah mysticism among the Pharisees; and when Philo speaks of being "on the way to the great King himself" he is using language strongly reminiscent of that used of the heavenly throne chariot.

What is clear is that his personal experience did not draw him away from Judaism. He was a leader of the Jewish community in Alexandria, and represented it before the emperor Caligula in a time of crisis (*Embassy* 178–83; cf. Josephus *Ant* XVIII.8.1). When the Alexandrian community was threatened, he responded with the polemical tractate *Against Flaccus*. Moreover, he expended a great deal of energy in his writings interpreting Judaism for the sympathetic outsider, opposing idolatry wherever possible. While some have characterized these writings as taking a liberal attitude toward Jewish belief and practice, it is evident that Philo had no use for those who abandoned the literal observance of Torah, maintaining that literal fulfillment of the commandments was incumbent upon all Jews (*On the Migration of Abraham* 89–93; Embassy 209–12; cf. Josephus *Apion* I.42–43).

As a mystic, however, he could never be satisfied with the surface meaning of the text. For Philo, genuine religion had to do with contemplative experience. He shows great admiration for the Essenes (*Hypothetica* 11.1–18) and, if he had not been needed by the Alexandrian community in an active role, might well have joined the Egyptian counterparts to the Essenes, the Therapeutae (*On the Contemplative Life* 14–18). Instead, he allegorizes the text of Torah so that it reveals, beneath its literal stories, a shimmering world of symbols pointing to mystical realities. Indeed, he may well have regarded his interpretation as a religious service. He says, for instance (*On the Special Laws* III.6):

> Yet it is well for me to give thanks to God even for this, that though submerged I am not sucked down into the depths, but can also open the soul's eyes, which in my despair of comforting hope I thought had now lost their sight, and am irradiated by the light of wisdom, and am not given over to lifelong darkness. So behold me daring, not only to read the sacred messages of Moses, but also in my love of knowledge to peer into each of them and unfold and reveal what is not known to the multitude.

Philo's reading of Torah was shaped by his cultural heritage as a Hellenistic Jew and by his personal experiences as a mystic. In his writings, we find as serious an attention given to the text of Torah as in any Palestinian midrash. His life is as defined by the symbols of Torah as was that of any Pharisee. Yet his understanding of Torah is very different. In Philo we find nothing of apocalyptic, no preoccupation with halachic matters, no expectation of a messiah, and no emphasis on martyrdom. Instead of resurrection, one of the core elements of Palestinian Judaism, one finds immortality of the soul. For Philo, in the end, Jewish righteousness looks very much like Greek virtue. One wonders, in fact, if the Pharisee Hillel and the apologist Philo really would have recognized each other as cultural and religious siblings.

Conclusion

We have seen how normative symbols of the first century were being transformed by the experiences and convictions of those to whom they mattered. We have paid special attention to the ways in which Jews who shared the same texts and symbols in Torah could derive such diverse understandings of them. There was a constant: the same symbolic world and the same process of seeking to understand those texts in terms of specific experiences. Yet in each case the differences were derived from the respective nature of the experiences and convictions. The differing cultural, political, and social contexts gave rise to disparate interpretations and applications of Torah. Now this same symbolic world of Torah was shared by those who wrote the NT. To understand their distinctive reshaping of those symbols, then, it is necessary to learn what we can of their experiences and convictions. In this way we can begin to bridge that gap which lies between the Jewish and Greco-Roman background of the NT and the NT writings themselves.

Study Questions

1. What is the significance of distinguishing between Palestinian Judaism and Diaspora Judaism?

2. How do the dates of Philo of Alexandria comport with the writings of the New Testament? What was his importance as a Diaspora Jewish author?

3. Why did Jews in the Diaspora encounter hostility? What forms did it take?

4. What does it mean to call Hellenistic Jewish literature "apologetic"?

Bibliographical Note

The translations from Greek sources in this chapter are from the Loeb Classical Library, except for the citation from *Aristeas*, by H. T. Andrews, in R. H. Charles (ed.), *Apocrypha and Pseudepigrapha of the Old Testament* (Oxford: Oxford Univ. Press, 1913), 2:115.

For historical surveys of the Diaspora, see J. M. G. Barclay, *Jews in the Mediterranean Diaspora: From Alexander to Trajan (323 BCE–117 CE)* (Edinburgh: T. & T. Clark, 1996); E. J. Bickerman, *The Jews in the Greek Age* (Cambridge, Mass.: Harvard Univ. Press, 1988); E. Schürer, *The History of the Jewish People in the Age of Jesus Christ* III.1, rev. ed., ed. G. Vermes et al. (Edinburgh: T. & T. Clark, 1986), 1–176; E. M. Smallwood, *The Jews Under Roman Rule from Pompey to Diocletian* (Leiden: E. J. Brill, 1976), 121–43, 220–55; and, above all, V. Tcherikover, *Hellenistic Civilization and the Jews*, trans. S. Appelbaum (New York: Antheneum, 1970).

On the variety of literature produced by Jews in the Diaspora, see the survey of modern scholarship in R. A. Kraft and G. W. E. Nickelsburg (eds.), *Early Judaism and Its Modern Interpreters* (Atlanta: Scholars Press, 1986); the relevant studies in M. E. Stone (ed.), *Jewish Writings of the Second Temple Period* (CRINT, 2.2; Philadelphia: Fortress Press; Assen: Van Gorcum, 1984); and sections in Schürer, *The History of the Jewish People*, III.1/III.2 (1986, 1987). For a general treatment of all the literature, see J. J. Collins, *Between Athens and Jerusalem: Jewish Identity in the Hellenistic Diaspora* (New York: Crossroad, 1983).

For discussion of the self-definition of Jews in the Diaspora, see the collection of essays in S. J. D. Cohen and E. S. Frerichs (eds.), *Diasporas in Antiquity* (BJS, 288; Atlanta: Scholars Press, 1993); as well as C. R. Holladay, "Jewish Responses to Hellenistic Culture," in P. Bilde et al. (eds.), *Ethnicity in Hellenistic Egypt* (Aarhus: Aarhus Univ. Press, 1992), 139–63; and J. Z. Smith, "Fences and Neighbors: Some Contours of Early Judaism," reprinted in *Imagining Religion: From Babylon to Jonestown* (Chicago: Univ. of Chicago Press, 1982), 1–18, 135–39.

On various aspects of Jewish life and thought in the Diaspora, see the essays in J. A. Overman and R. S. MacLennan, *Diaspora Jews and Judaism* (SFSHJ, 41; Atlanta: Scholars Press, 1992); as well as C. H. Dodd, *The Bible and the Greeks* (London: Hodder & Stoughton, 1935); J. N. Lightstone, *The Commerce of the Sacred: Mediation of the Divine among Jews in the Greco-Roman Diaspora* (BJS, 59; Chico, Calif.: Scholars Press, 1984); and L. M. White, *Building God's House in the Roman World: Architectural Adaptation among Pagans, Jews, and Christians* (Baltimore: Johns Hopkins Univ. Press, 1990), 60–101, 174–87. Although one should use it with a degree of caution, the magnum opus by E. R. Goodenough, *The Jewish Symbols in the Greco-Roman Period*, 13 vols. (New York: Pantheon Books, 1953–68), should not be neglected (for a general synthesis, see particularly *Vol. 12: Summary and Conclusions*, and the abridged version: E. R. Goodenough, *Jewish Symbols in the Greco-Roman Period*, ed. J. Neusner [Princeton: Princeton Univ. Press, 1988]). On Diaspora religious practice, see L. V. Rutgers, *The Hidden Heritage of Diaspora Judaism: Essays on Jewish Cultural Identity in the Roman World* (Leuven: Peeters, 1998); and E. P. Sanders, "Purity, Food and Offerings in the Greek-Speaking Diaspora," in *Jewish Law from Jesus to the Mishnah: Five Studies* (London: SCM Press; Philadelphia: Trinity Press Int'l, 1990), 255–308, 359–68.

On the Septuagint (LXX), see S. Jellicoe (ed.), *Studies in the Septuagint: Origins, Recensions, and Interpretations; Selected Essays* (New York: Ktav Pub. House, 1974); and M. K. H. Peters, "Septuagint," *ABD* 5: 1093–1104. On the debated issue of Jewish proselytizing of Gentiles, see M. Goodman, *Mission and Conversion: Proselytizing in the Religious History of the Roman Empire* (Oxford: Clarendon Press, 1994); and S. McKnight, *A Light among the Gentiles: Jewish Missionary Activity in the Second Temple Period* (Minneapolis: Fortress Press, 1991). On the general relationships between Jews and Gentiles in antiquity, see L. H. Feldman, *Jew & Gentile in the Ancient World: Attitudes and Interactions from Alexander to Justinian* (Princeton: Princeton Univ. Press, 1993); J. Gager, *The Origins of Anti-Semitism: Attitudes Toward Judaism in Pagan and Christian Antiquity* (New York: Oxford Univ. Press, 1985); P. Schäfer, *Judeophobia: Attitudes Toward the Jews in the Ancient World* (Cambridge, Mass.: Harvard Univ. Press, 1997); and J. N. Sevenster, *The Roots of Pagan Anti-Semitism in the Ancient World* (NovTSup, 41; Leiden: E. J. Brill, 1975).

On Josephus, see P. Bilde, *Flavius Josephus between Jerusalem and Rome: His Life, His Works, and their Importance* (JSPSS, 2; Sheffield: Sheffield Academic Press, 1988); S. Cohen, *Josephus in Galilee and Rome: His Vita and Development as a Historian* (Leiden: E. J. Brill, 1979); L. H. Feldman, "Flavius Josephus Revisited: the Man, His Writings, and His Significance," *ANRW* II.21.2 (1984): 763–862; idem, *Josephus' Interpretation of the Bible* (Berkeley: Univ. of California Press, 1998); S. Mason, ed., *Understanding Josephus* (JSPSS, 32; Sheffield: Sheffield Academic Press, 1998); and T. Rajak, *Josephus: The Historian and Society* (Philadelphia: Fortress Press, 1984). Also useful are the two volumes of essays edited by L. H. Feldman and G. Hata (Detroit: Wayne State Univ. Press): *Josephus, Judaism, and Christianity* (1987) and *Josephus, the*

Bible, and History (1989). Invaluable is the survey of modern scholarship on Josephus by L. H. Feldman, *Josephus and Modern Scholarship (1937–1980)* (New York: Walter de Gruyter, 1984). For Josephus' portrayal of women, see C. A. Brown, *No Longer Be Silent: First Century Portraits of Jewish Women* (Louisville: Westminster/John Knox Press, 1992).

For introductions to Philo, see E. J. Goodenough, *An Introduction to Philo Judaeus*, 2nd rev. ed. (New York: Barnes & Noble, 1963); S. Sandmel, *Philo of Alexandria: An Introduction* (New York: Oxford Univ. Press, 1979); idem, "Philo Judaeus: An Introduction to the Man, his Writings, and his Significance," *ANRW* II.21.1 (1984): 3–46; R. Williamson, *Jews in the Hellenistic World: Philo* (Cambridge: Cambridge Univ. Press, 1989); and H. A. Wolfson, *Philo: Foundations of Religious Philosophy in Judaism, Christianity, and Islam*, 2 vols. (Cambridge, Mass.: Harvard Univ. Press, 1947). Also on Philo, but involving as well an interpretation of much of Hellenistic Jewish literature, see E. J. Goodenough, *By Light, Light: The Mystic Gospel of Hellenistic Judaism* (New Haven: Yale Univ. Press, 1935). On Philo's dual Greek and Jewish identities, see the two books by A. Mendelson: *Secular Education in Philo of Alexandria* (Cincinnati: Hebrew Union College Press, 1982) and *Philo's Jewish Identity* (BJS, 161; Atlanta: Scholars Press, 1988). On Philo's portrayal of women, see J. R. Wegner, "Philo's Portrayal of Women—Hebraic or Hellenic?," in A.-J. Levine (ed.), *"Women Like This": New Perspectives on Jewish Women in the Greco-Roman World* (Atlanta: Scholars Press, 1991), 41–66; and D. Sly, *Philo's Perception of Women* (BJS, 209; Atlanta: Scholars Press, 1990). On the ancient city of Alexandria, an important center of Diaspora Judaism, see C. Haas, *Alexandria in Late Antiquity: Topography and Social Conflict* (Baltimore: Johns Hopkins Univ. Press, 1997), and D. Sly, *Philo's Alexandria* (New York: Routledge, 1996).

On Jewish apologetic literature and figures such as Artapanus and Eupolemus, see B. Bar-Kochva, *Pseudo-Hecataeus "On the Jews": Legitimizing the Jewish Diaspora* (Berkeley: Univ. of California Press, 1996); H. Conzelmann, *Gentiles, Jews, Christians: Polemics and Apologetics in the Greco-Roman Era*, trans. M. E. Boring (Minneapolis: Fortress Press, 1992); R. Doran, "The Jewish Hellenistic Historians Before Josephus," *ANRW* II.20.1 (1987): 246–97; E. S. Gruen, *Heritage and Hellenism: The Reinvention of Jewish Tradition* (Berkeley: Univ. of California Press, 1998); idem, "Fact and Fiction: Jewish Legends in a Hellenistic Context," in P. Cartledge (ed.), *Hellenistic Constructs: Essays in Culture, History, and Historiography* (Berkeley: Univ. of California Press, 1997), 72–88; G. E. Sterling, *Historiography & Self-definition: Josephus, Luke-Acts & Apologetic Historiography* (NovTSup, 64; Leiden: E. J. Brill, 1992); and B. Z. Wacholder, *Eupolemus: A Study of Judaeo-Greek Literature* (Cincinnati: Hebrew Union College Press, 1974). For the way in which the figure of Moses was interpreted in this tradition, see D. Tiede, *The Charismatic Figure as Miracle Worker* (SBLDS, 1; Missoula, Mont.: Scholars Press, 1972); C. R. Holladay, *Theios Anēr in Hellenistic Judaism* (SBLDS, 40; Missoula, Mont.: Scholars Press, 1977); and W. A. Meeks, *The Prophet-King: Moses Tra-*

ditions and the Johannine Christology (NovTSup, 14; Leiden: E. J. Brill, 1967), 100–75. Also see the important collection of essays on Josephus' apologetic work *Against Apion*: L. H. Feldman and J. R. Levison (eds.), *Josephus' Contra Apionem* (AGJU, 34; Leiden: E. J. Brill, 1996).

For a selection of primary sources related to the life and thought of Jews in the Greco-Roman world, see L. H. Feldman and M. Reinhold (eds.), *Jewish Life and Thought among Greeks and Romans* (Minneapolis: Fortress Press, 1996), and M. Williams, *The Jews among the Greeks and Romans: A Diasporan Sourcebook* (Baltimore: Johns Hopkins Univ. Press, 1998). For primary sources, see the following: for most of the Hellenistic Jewish literature, J. H. Charlesworth (ed.), *The Old Testament Pseudepigrapha*, 2 vols. (New York: Doubleday, 1983, 1985); for both Josephus and Philo, the Loeb Classical Library editions; and for Greco-Roman texts on Jews and Judaism, M. Stern (ed. and trans.), *Greek and Latin Authors on Jews and Judaism*, 3 vols. (Jerusalem: The Israel Academy of Sciences and Humanities, 1974–1984). For the diverse witness from Jewish inscriptions and attestation of various Jewish communities and general practice in the Diaspora, see the following: B. J. Brooten, *Women Leaders in the Ancient Synagogue: Inscriptional Evidence and Background Issues* (BJS, 36; Atlanta: Scholars Press, 1982); J. W. van Henten and P. W. van der Horst (eds.), *Studies in Early Jewish Epigraphy* (AGJU, 21; Leiden: E. J. Brill, 1994); P. W. van der Horst, *Ancient Jewish Epitaphs: An Introductory Survey of a Millennium of Jewish Funerary Epigraphy (300 BCE–700 CE)* (Kampen: Kok Pharos Pub. House, 1991); L. Kant, "Jewish Inscriptions in Greek and Latin," *ANRW* II.20.2 (1987): 671–713; H. J. Leon, *The Jews in Ancient Rome*, rev. ed., with C. Osiek (Peabody, Mass.: Hendrickson Pubs., 1995); and P. Trebilco, *Jewish Communities in Asia Minor* (SNTSMS, 69; Cambridge: Cambridge Univ. Press, 1991). For excellent introductions and commentary on the fragmentary Hellenistic Jewish authors and texts, consult the series by C. R. Holladay, *Fragments from Hellenistic Jewish Authors* (Atlanta: Scholars Press): *Vol. I: Historians* (1983); *Vol. II: Poets* (1989); Vol. *III: Aristobulus* (1995); *Vol. IV: Orphica* (1996); and *Vol. V: Pseudo-Greek Poets* (1998).

*Jesus weeping over Jerusalem; miniature evangelistary of Otto III c. 1000
(Munich, SB, Clm 4453, fol 188v)*

PART TWO

The Christian Experience

IN WHAT IS both a critical and a difficult stage of this investigation, we turn now to the character of early Christian experience. We have surveyed some of the symbols Gentiles and Jews used to interpret their lives, and in the process discovered how such symbols both gave shape to, and were shaped by, changing experiences. In light of the previous discussion it is evident that if we are to engage the NT as a fully human document, we cannot move from the symbolic "background" to the Christian writings without giving some consideration to the question most demanding an answer: why were these texts written in the first place? Between the symbolic world of the first century and the symbolic world found in the NT, *something happened*. What was it that created so distinctive a displacement in the symbolic world of the first century? Can we responsibly say anything about the experience or experiences that caused small groups of Jews and Gentiles in the middle of the first century to dramatically reinterpret the symbols of Hellenism and Judaism?

The very term "experience" is not without obscurity. How does one isolate an experience? Science understandably resists such ill-defined and elusive subjects. And if the definition of experience is difficult, describing "religious experience" is worse. Is there such a thing, and how do we know it when we see it? Do religious experiences belong in a separate category, or should they be explained in sociologically or psychologically reductive terms? It is clear that our approach must be cautious and circumspect, for the subject has many ambiguities. How can one speak about experiences that are at best only implicit in the writings themselves? To entertain this subject at all, one must be willing to move behind explicit statements to their tacit presuppositions. The language of the NT represents a secondary reflection on primary experiences that are now inaccessible to us. Yet, these primary experiences have left their trace everywhere throughout the writings of the NT, and we can catch glimpses through an analysis of the basic claims of the first Christians.

93

The reader should therefore stand warned. What follows demands a willingness to imagine what cannot absolutely be demonstrated. While I do not pretend to give an adequate and full account of what these writings claim, I do think that they are claiming what I outline in the following chapters. In writing this section, then, I do not answer all the questions concerning the original and generative Christian experience. But I do suggest that these are the right sort of questions to ask if we are to understand the NT. Moreover, I hold that by uncovering the claims of the first Christians we are best able to recover, in however rudimentary a form, those initial religious impulses that so dramatically and irrevocably caused the reshaping of the symbolic worlds of both Jews and Greeks. In the end, of course, the secondary reflection on the primary experiences has itself been shaped and framed by the symbolic world that was appropriated, and thus we are constantly moving in circular patterns: from experience to interpretation, from interpretation to experience.

4. The Claims of the First Christians

THE QUESTION "What happened?" is forced on us by the realization of how remarkable this phenomenon really was. Christianity began in obscurity. Its putative founder was executed and its first adherents scattered in fear and confusion. Its first missionaries were commoners, whose message appeared as nonsense to the sophisticated. With some exceptions, its chief appeal was to the outcast and marginal elements of society, finding significant numbers of converts among transients, slaves, and women. From the first, it was violently persecuted. Yet, in the course of four centuries, Christianity became the dominant religious force of Hellenistic culture. It swept all before it, becoming the established cult of the empire that had sought to extirpate it, the very form of wisdom for the sages who had reviled it, a movement with such resilient and universal embrace that it gathered all the charms of its cultic and philosophical rivals into a triumphant procession, in the end securing the allegiance of the cultured, the rich, and the powerful.

An explanation for this phenomenon must be sought, for such unlikely success stories are rare in history. Political, social, and economic factors undoubtedly aided the movement's success, but they do not account for everything. Nor can the unparalleled growth of the movement be credited to its being a more profound religion than others, a higher form of ethics, or a unique offer of salvation. Hellenistic moralists taught an ethics just as pure and far more coherent. Judaism was a religion just as profound and far more ancient. The mystery religions offered a revelation just as transcendent and far more esoteric. The key to Christianity's success lay not in its teaching but in its experience of power. What distinguishes the movement is its claim to have actualized the "good news of God" to humans. What accounts for its spread is its ability to make the claim plausible, persuasive, and even present, for others.

The NT provides a window through which we can observe the movement in the period before it achieved political and cultural acceptance, yet at a time when it had already begun to shape its distinctive self-consciousness. We do well, therefore, to locate in these writings the claims being made by the Christians, and contrast them to the perception of the movement by its first outside observers. The disparity is startling. Naturally one expects some divergence, for there is always distance between a group's self-appreciation and its reputation. What insiders see as an army of liberation appears to outsiders as a gang of terrorists; a cult regarded by its adherents as the vanguard of eschatological battle is perceived by outsiders as a band of self-deluded visionaries.

In the case of the NT, however, the disparity is particularly strong. Precisely because of the movement's success and since all contemporary readers are to some extent themselves shaped by a world fundamentally altered by that success, an imaginative leap is required to perceive how surprising and even outrageous the claims of the first Christians were. If it had remained that which at first it appeared destined to be—one more odd cult from the East—then we could see with fresh eyes the bizarre nature of its claims, just as the fragments from Qumran seem all the more singular in their self-aggrandizement since the traces of the community disappeared beneath the sand two thousand years ago. To place the Christian claims in proper perspective, we must begin from the outside and look in.

Christianity from the Outside

The insignificance of the Christian movement in the eyes of the world during the NT period is shown most clearly by its being so systematically ignored by both Jewish and Hellenistic writers. Among Jewish writers, there is next to nothing on early Christians. The historian Josephus thoroughly describes all the Jewish sects in first-century Palestine, but of the Christians he either knew or chose to say very little. He gives favorable notice to John the Baptist and recounts his death under Herod but makes no connection between John and Christianity (*Ant* XVIII.5.2). He briefly mentions Jesus in a passage dealing with the interregnum between the procurators Festus and Albinus. During that time, Josephus says (*Ant* XX.9.1), the high priest Ananus took the occasion to summon the Sanhedrin, the Jewish governing council,

> and brought before them the brother of Jesus who was called Christ, whose name was James, and some others; and when he had formed an accusation against them as breakers of the law, he delivered them to be stoned. . . .

Another passage (*Ant* XVIII.3.3) is so reworked by Christian interpolations that we can say, at most, that Josephus placed Jesus in the period of unrest during the procuratorship of Pontius Pilate, recognized him as a teacher, and knew of a movement that lived on after him.

The Talmud contains only a few obscure references to Jesus and Christians. Later censors may have had a hand in excising other, unflattering notices. In the present Talmudim, some passages appear to mention Jesus directly (e.g., Babylonian Talmud, *Sanhedrin* 43a, b; 103a; 107b), others apparently allude to him (e.g., *Sanhedrin* 106b), but none is indisputably about Jesus. Still other rabbinic materials speak unfavorably about a category of heretics called the *minim*, and we can sometimes correlate those descriptions with what we know about the Christians (e.g., *Koheleth Rabbah* 1.8; Babylonian Talmud, *Sanhedrin* 43a; *Mekilta* par. 66b). So veiled are these references, however, that only because we know of Jesus and the Christians from the NT can we detect them. Even the clearest, moreover, are late, and do not constitute independent contemporary testimony about the movement. However compelling they may be to the Christian reader, they are insignificant compared to the size of the Talmud. In sum, we learn next to nothing about Jesus and the first Christians from those we would expect to be most interested in them.

Greco-Roman sources contain slightly more information. In Suetonius' *Life of Claudius* (early 2nd cent. C.E.), one line appears in a passage describing the emperor Claudius' handling of various foreign peoples (V.25.4):

> Since the Jews constantly made disturbances at the instigation of Chrestus [sic], he expelled them from Rome.

This notice corresponds with Acts 18:2, which tells us that Paul met in Corinth a Jew

> called Aquila whose family came from Pontus. He and his wife Priscilla had recently left Italy because an edict of Claudius had expelled all Jews from Rome.

We know nothing regarding the identity of "Chrestus," and apparently neither did Suetonius. Is this a garbled reminiscence of a commotion caused by preaching about Christ? If so, it was still primarily a Jewish matter to this Roman historian, and Christians were not yet perceived as a separate group (although cf. Suetonius' *Life of Nero*, VI.16.2).

A fuller account is found in Tacitus' *Annals* (early 2nd cent. C.E.). He recounts the great fire in Rome under Nero, and says (XV.44.2–8):

> Nero fastened the guilt and afflicted the most exquisite tortures on a class hated for their abominations, called Christians by the populace. Christus, from whom the name had its origin, suffered the extreme penalty during the reign of Tiberius at the hands of one of our procurators, Pontius Pilate, and a deadly superstition, thus checked for the moment, again broke out, not only in Judaea, the first source of the evil, but also in the city, where all things hideous and shameful from every part of the world meet and become popular.

Tacitus knows of the Christians as an identifiable group, not simply as part of Judaism. They are numerous enough at Rome in the sixties to be noticeable, yet sufficiently a minority to offer no resistance to the violent whim of an emperor. Tacitus provides significant details concerning the execution of Jesus, but for this conservative Roman, the sect is simply a noxious superstition, typical of the bizarre cults that flowed to Rome from the East (cf. Juvenal *Satires* III.62).

The earliest firsthand pagan report about Christians still in our possession was filed by Pliny the Younger, governor of Bithynia (ca. 112 C.E.). Pliny is worried about the great numbers this sect is attracting. He writes to the emperor Trajan for advice. He doesn't know quite how to handle the situation. Should he execute Christians only if they are guilty of other crimes as well, or simply because they bear the name "Christian," or only if they prove to be obstinate when offered the chance to recant? By means of torture, he was able to obtain information, which he passes on to Trajan (*Letter* X.96):

> They maintained, moreover, that the amount of their fault or error had been this, that it was their habit on a fixed day to assemble before daylight and recite by turns a form of words to Christ as to a god; and that they bound themselves with an oath, not for any crime, but not to commit theft or robbery or adultery, not to break their word, and not to deny a deposit when demanded. After this was done, it was their custom to depart, and to meet again to take food, but ordinary and harmless food. . . . I discovered nothing else than a perverse and extravagant superstition.

A final Hellenistic account of the Christian movement before the end of the second century comes from the satirist Lucian of Samosata (120–80). In his *Passing of Peregrinus*, he attacks the charlatan Cynic philosopher Proteus Peregrinus, whom Lucian considers to be striking virtuous poses out of vainglory. Among those duped by Peregrinus was a group of Christians (*Peregrinus* 11–13):

> It was then he learned the wondrous lore of the Christians by associating with their priests and scribes in Palestine. And—how else could it be—in a trice he made them all look like children; for he was prophet, cult leader, head of the synagogue, and everything, all by himself. He interpreted and explained some of their books, and even composed many, and they revered him as a god, made use of him as a lawgiver, and set him down as a protector, next after that other, to be sure, whom they still worship, the man who was crucified in Palestine because he introduced this new cult into the world.
>
> Then at length Proteus was apprehended for this and thrown into prison, which itself gave him no little reputation as an asset in his future career and the charlatanism and notoriety-seeking that he was enamoured of. Well, when he had been imprisoned, the Christians, regarding the incident as a calamity, left nothing undone in the effort to rescue him. Then, as this was impossible, every other form of attention was shown him, not in any casual way, but with assiduity; . . . people even came from the cities of Asia, sent by the Christians

at their common expense, to succor and defend and encourage the hero. They show incredible speed whenever any such public action is undertaken; for in no time at all, they lavish their all. So it was, then, in the case of Peregrinus; much money came to him from them by reason of his imprisonment, and he procured not a little revenue from it. The poor wretches have convinced themselves, first and foremost, that they are going to be immortal and live for all time, in consequence of which they despise death, and even willingly give themselves into custody, most of them. Furthermore their first lawgiver persuaded them that they are all brothers of one another after they transgressed once for all by denying the Greek gods and by worshipping the crucified sophist himself and living under his laws. Therefore they despise all things indiscriminately and consider them common property, receiving such doctrines traditionally and without any definite evidence. So if any charlatan and trickster able to profit by occasions comes among them, he quickly acquires sudden wealth by imposing on simple folk.

Even though Lucian confuses some aspects of Christian teaching and practice, regarding Christians as simple-minded and easily gulled followers of a superstition, he witnesses, however hazily, to certain aspects of Christianity as they are found in the NT: community possessions, sacred books, faith, prophets, belief in life after death. He also has a certain grudging respect for these "simple folk."

Out of all the writings of the first and second century that have come down to us, then, such are the references to Jesus and Christians: a sentence here, a paragraph there. The picture of Christianity is vague and confused. It is connected to Judaism. It has a crucified founder. Its adherents are stubborn, unenlightened, and perverse. All in all, it is a particularly odious form of superstition. The appropriate attitude to be taken toward them is one of contempt. Christianity is regarded as insignificant and powerless, one among many cults with dubious pasts and no futures. The full impact of this casual dismissal comes only when we realize that all these accounts come from a period after the writing of all, or nearly all, the NT texts. The shock is even greater when we turn to the claims being made by those first Christian writers themselves.

Claims of the Christians

The pagan perception of the first Christians was not totally inaccurate. These Christians did sing hymns to Christ as to a god (see Phil. 2:6-11; Col. 1:15-20; Rev. 5:11-16). Some of them, at least, put their possessions into a community of goods (Acts 4:32-36), or generously contributed to the needs of other communities (Acts 11:27-30; Rom. 15:25-29). They did share common meals (Acts 2:42; 1 Cor. 11:18-34). They were stubborn in their convictions, even when persecuted (2 Cor. 11:23-29; 1 Thess. 2:14-3:10; Heb. 10:32-39) and they expected to "live forever" (Rom. 6:23; Gal. 6:8; 1 Tim. 1:16; 1 John 5:11). These characteristics do not, however, by themselves distinguish Christians from other communities in the Hellenistic world. Such activities and attitudes were found among many others.

Had their pagan observers read the Christian writings, however, they would have been astonished at the extraordinary claims the movement made about itself. Far from regarding itself as a benighted group of fanatics doomed to disappear, it staked for itself—apparently from the very first—a claim on the fortunes of the whole world. Its message would extend to the ends of the earth (Acts 1:8) and would make followers from among all nations (Matt. 28:19). It saw itself as enjoying a real ascendancy over the world. Paul tells the Corinthians that (1 Cor. 3:22)

> the world or life or death or the present or the future, all are yours; and you are Christ's; and Christ is God's.

He goes on to write to members of the Corinthian church who were going to court with suits against each other (1 Cor. 6:2-3):

> Do you not know that the saints will judge the world? And if the world is to be judged by you, are you incompetent to try trivial cases? Do you not know that we are to judge angels?

The Christians play a pivotal role in the future of the world. They help reconcile the world to God (Rom. 11:15; 2 Cor. 5:19) and anticipate the whole world's rebirth into freedom (Rom. 8:20-22). The Christian community is the place where God's purpose for the world is revealed (Eph. 3:9-10):

> The plan of the mystery hidden for ages in God who created all things; that through the church the manifold wisdom of God might now be made known to the principalities and powers in the heavenly places.

Indeed, the community participates already in a victory over the world (1 John 5:4-5):

> This is the victory that overcomes the world, our faith. Who is it that overcomes the world but he who believes that Jesus is the Son of God?

This victory will come to complete accomplishment (Rev. 11:15):

> The kingdom of this world has become the kingdom of our Lord and of his Christ, and he shall reign for ever and ever.

The seer John has this vision of the end (Rev. 22:3-5):

> The throne of God and of the lamb shall be in it, and his servants shall worship him; they shall see his face, and his name shall be on their foreheads. And night shall be no more; they need no light of lamp or sun, for the Lord God will be their light, and they shall reign for ever and ever.

What can we make of these claims? Were the first Christians megalomaniacal? All these statements antedate by decades the first casual notice of the group by outsiders. It would be as though the North American colonies in 1690 declared themselves to be a world political power. Faced with the distance between the worldly circumstances of this group and its cosmic claims, it is necessary to look at the basis for these claims. What did Christians offer in support of such statements?

The claims of the first Christians were based *on their experience*. Their claims expressed realities that they said they currently enjoyed. But what was that experience? It is impossible to cut entirely beneath the variety of literary contexts and symbolic expressions in the NT to isolate, in a physical or psychic sense, a core experience. But we can describe some aspects of that experience by observing a number of its effects.

The experience led to a fundamental release from the cosmic forces that, in the perceptions of the age, dominated human existence. Christians were no longer subject to these "powers and principalities" (Rom. 8:38; 1 Cor. 2:6-10; Eph. 2:1-10; Col. 1:13; 1 Pet. 3:22). It meant as well a release from repressive systems of law, which those "elements of the universe" had used to keep humans in bondage (Rom. 6:15-23; 2 Cor. 3:6-18; Gal. 3:23—4:7; Col. 2:8-23). At a more personal level, it involved an escape from the fear of death, which, it was argued, led to the bondage of sin (Rom. 8:14-15; Heb. 2:14-15; 1 John 4:17-21). A central symbol for this experience was, therefore, salvation. When the Christians spoke of salvation, they meant not only something that would happen but something that had in some way already happened to them (Rom. 1:16; 10:10; 1 Cor. 1:18, 21; 15:2; Eph. 2:5-8; Phil. 1:28; Titus 3:5; James 1:21; 1 Pet. 3:21; 2 Pet. 3:15; Jude 3; Rev. 12:10).

Can we get any closer to the nature of this experience? What did salvation mean in terms of concrete human life in this world? We can discern certain qualities ascribed to Christians, which are also found in the writings of Hellenistic philosophy. Thus, the Christians experience freedom (*eleutheria*; see Rom. 6:18-22; 1 Cor. 9:1, 19; 2 Cor. 3:17; Gal. 5:1, 13; James 1:25; 1 Pet. 2:16) and free speech or boldness (*parrēsia*; Acts 2:29; 4:13, 29, 31; 2 Cor. 3:12; Eph. 3:12; 1 Thess. 2:2; Phlm. 8; Heb. 4:16). The ideas of freedom, release, redemption, liberation, and salvation connote a transfer from a negative condition to a positive one, in which they have certain dispositions and capacities: "For freedom Christ has freed you" (Gal. 5:1). Free speech indicates an empowerment, a capacity to confront opposition without fear, to express one's identity in a variety of circumstances with courage and confidence. These are listed in the texts not as ideals for which to strive but as realities: Christians "have" freedom and free speech; they exercise these capacities in their lives.

The Christians also spoke of certain states in which they found themselves. These included peace (Rom. 5:1; 14:17; 1 Cor. 7:15; 2 Cor. 13:11; Eph. 2:17; 4:3; Phil. 4:7; Col. 3:15; James 3:18) and joy (Acts 13:52; Rom. 5:3; Gal. 5:22; Phil. 2:2; 1 Pet. 4:13; 1 John 1:4). Peace is a relationship not only with other humans but also with God—a relationship or state that is not challenged by temporal conflicts. Joy is a state that transcends the conditioned nature of happiness and is found even in the midst of tribulation and suffering (1 Thess. 3:6-9; Heb. 12:1-3; James 1:2; 1 Pet. 4:13). Accompanying these states were certain dispositions, such as faith, hope, and love (1 Cor. 13:13; 1 Thess. 1:2-3; 1 Pet. 1:3-9). These were not abstract terms but living qualities that could be described behaviorally in terms of attitudes and actions. Thus, hope did not grieve at the death of community members (1 Thess. 4:13), faith resisted temptation and persecution (1 Pet. 5:9), and love was not arrogant or rude (1 Cor. 13:5).

If we try to cut deeper beneath the symbolization, we see that the Christian experience had to do with *power*: the Christians said they had been touched by an awesome force that in turn empowered them—a particularly paradoxical claim given their circumstances. The terms for this power are various. It can be called an authority (*exousia*; see John 1:12; 1 Cor. 8:9; 9:4; 2 Cor. 10:8; 13:10; 2 Thess. 3:9), an energy (*energeia*; see 1 Cor. 12:6, 11; Gal. 3:5; 5:6; Eph. 3:20-21; Col. 1:29; 1 Thess. 2:13; Phlm. 6; Heb. 4:12), or a power (*dynamis*; see Rom. 1:16; 15:13, 19; 1 Cor. 1:18; 6:14; 2 Cor. 6:7; 13:4; Gal. 3:5; Eph. 3:20; Col. 1:29; 1 Thess. 1:5; 2 Thess. 1:11; 2 Tim. 1:7; Heb. 2:4; 2 Pet. 1:16). This power manifested itself outwardly in certain "signs and wonders" (Acts 4:30; 5:12; 14:3; Rom. 15:19; 2 Cor. 12:12; Heb. 2:4) such as healings, prophecies, and spiritual utterances, but above all in the proclamation of the "good news" (Rom. 1:16; 1 Cor. 1:18; 2:4; 2 Cor. 4:7; 1 Thess. 1:5; 2 Tim. 1:8; James 1:21). It also manifested itself inwardly by the spiritual transformation of those who received it (Rom. 12:2; 1 Cor. 2:16; 2 Cor. 3:18; Gal. 3:5; Eph. 4:23; Col. 3:10; 1 Pet. 1:22). This power, finally, was not of their own doing, but was transmitted to them from another to whom it properly belonged (Rom. 1:4; 16:25; 1 Cor. 1:24; 5:4; 12:3; 2 Cor. 1:4; 6:7; 12:9; 13:4; Eph. 3:16, 20; Phil. 3:10, 20-21; 2 Tim. 1:7; Heb. 5:7; James 4:12; 1 Pet. 1:5; 2 Pet. 1:16; Jude 24). None of the elements listed here is found in the NT as a goal for which one is to strive; rather, each appears as a dimension of one's present life. The relationships, states, dispositions, and transformations are *experienced*, not just desired. The case is succinctly stated by Paul: "The Kingdom of God does not consist in talk but in power" (1 Cor. 4:20).

Because of this new empowerment, Christians believed they represented something entirely new in the world. They shared in a new covenant with God (1 Cor. 11:25; 2 Cor. 3:7-18; Heb. 9:15) and were given new life (Rom. 6:4; Eph. 4:24). Indeed, they were part of an entirely new creation: "If anyone is in Christ, there is a new creation; the old has passed away, behold, the new has come. All this is from God . . ." (2 Cor. 5:17-18).

And this was the key point: their experience, they said, was not self-generated, but came from God, who always created anew (Rom. 4:17; 1 Cor. 1:28-30; 2 Cor. 4:6). The Christian experience anticipated the completion of God's renewal of the world: "According to his promise we wait for new heavens and a new earth, in which righteousness dwells" (2 Pet. 3:13). Or, as the seer John says, "Then I saw a new heaven and a new earth, for the first heaven and the first earth had vanished, and there was no longer any sea . . . then He who sat upon the throne said, 'Behold, I am making all things new' " (Rev. 21:1, 5). The note of newness is distinctive. The Christians meant by it not mere novelty, but a fundamental transformation. In an atmosphere in which antiquity was so prized, this stress on newness is all the more striking.

The emphasis on experience decisively set the first Christians apart in the world they shared with Greeks and Jews. Greek philosophy offered wisdom, but particularly in Stoicism, it was achieved at great cost of time and effort, and available only to the sophisticated in society. Even the more direct route followed by the Cynics was still regarded by them as being only for the elite. The Christians, in contrast, claimed a superior wisdom that came by way of revelation in the present from God, that was available by gift to all persons, and was not the result of effort or study (see 1 Cor. 1:30; 2:7; Eph. 1:8; 3:10; Col. 1:9; James 3:15-17). The authority of Christian leaders and teachers did not rest, as with the rabbis, on age, education, or the unbroken chain of tradition from the past. Even a Hillel was required, notwithstanding his brilliance, to cite precedents for his opinions. For Christians, however, authority came immediately from God (Rom. 1:1; 1 Cor. 7:40; Gal. 1:1; Eph. 3:3; 1 Tim. 1:18; 1 Pet. 5:1) and the voice of prophecy was alive in the community (1 Cor. 12-14; 1 Thess. 5:20; Rev. 1–3).

The Christian prayers of blessing shared with Judaism did not simply recall God's mercies of the distant past in the hope of their renewal in the future. Christians gave thanks for God's present and continuing work among them, and prayed that what he had begun, he would complete in them (Rom. 1:8-14; 1 Cor. 1:4-9; 2 Cor. 1:3-7; Eph. 1:3-14; Phil. 1:3-11; 1 Thess. 1:3-5; 1 Pet. 1:3-8). Much of the exhortation (*paraenesis*) of the NT, consequently, is based not on norms provided by past precedent, whether written or oral, but on the measure provided by the gift given them in the present: "Become in fact what you already are" (cf. Eph. 4:1—5:20; Phil. 2:1-13; Col. 2:20—3:17; 2 Tim. 1:6-8; Heb. 12:18—13:17; 1 Pet. 1:21—2:3; 1 John 3:16-18).

Like the sectarians of Qumran and other apocalypticists, the Christians looked forward to an eschatological climax to history (1 Cor. 15:20-57; 1 Thess. 4:13—5:3; 2 Thess. 2:8-12; Heb. 9:28; James 5:7-11; 1 Pet. 1:7-9; 2 Pet. 3:10-13; Rev. 21:1—22:5). But unlike them, the Christians saw the beginning of that culmination in their present experience; in addition to a "not yet," there was a definite "already." Indeed, the distinctiveness of the experiential basis for the Christian movement can be traced in the usage of the simple word "now" through the texts of the NT. In the Letter to the Romans, for instance, Paul writes that *now* God's righteousness is being revealed (3:21, 26), *now* they have been made righteous (5:9), *now* they have been reconciled to God

(5:11), *now* they are freed from sin (6:22), *now* they are discharged from the law (7:6), *now* there is no condemnation for God's people (8:1), and *now* the mystery of God is being revealed (16:26). Or, as Paul writes in another place, "Behold, *now* is the acceptable time, behold *now* is the day of salvation" (2 Cor. 6:2; cf. Gal. 4:9; Eph. 2:2; 3:5; Col. 1:22, 26; 2 Tim. 1:10; Heb. 9:26; 1 Pet. 1:12; 2:25; 3:21; 1 John 3:2).

Finally, in contrast to those Jewish sects that bolstered their own claims of being the remnant of God's people by excluding others—whether pagans, apostates from Torah, or associates of either—Christians claimed that their experience of God's favor was available not just to one nation, or to an elite group within it, but to all humans: "All those who call on the name of the Lord shall be saved" (Acts 2:21, 39; Rom. 10:11-13).

It is in the experience of the first believers that the origin of Christianity and of the NT must be sought. *Something happened* in the lives of real women and men; something that caused them to perceive their lives in a new and radically altered fashion, compelling them to interpret the experience by means of available symbols. The NT is incomprehensible if seen as a collection of theological writings in an abstract or theoretical mode. The NT is the furthest thing from such a scholastic enterprise. There is theology to be found in it, to be sure, but it is a theology that consists not in working out corollaries to propositions but in pursuing reflection on a present and continuing experience of the most fundamental sort—religious experience. It was because men and women of the first-century Mediterranean world, both Jews and Greeks, found their lives suddenly and inexplicably transformed by a new and unsuspected power from a new and confusing source that they were forced to reflect on their lives in a new way and infuse the symbols of their world with new content.

If we grant that something happened, however, then we must face the still harder question: What happened? What experience could be profound and powerful enough to generate such bold and prophetic leaders? What power could transform a zealous persecutor into a fervent apostle? What unseen hand shaped, out of the unpromising materials of Galilean *am-ha-aretz* and Corinthian transients, a community that would eventually change the contours of the known world through its proclamation of "good news from God" (1 Thess. 2:2)? We must turn next to that question, knowing full well that it is impossible to answer entirely. Something happened, but what?

Study Questions

1. What do the writings of non-Christians from the first century add to our understanding of the the earliest churches and their practices?

2. What did "salvation" mean specifically for the early followers of Jesus?

3. In what senses did the experiences of the earliest Christians relate to "power"?

4. What did the earliest Christians share in common with other groups in first-century Palestine? How did they differ?

Bibliographical Note

Translations from Latin and Greek authors are from the Loeb Classical Library.

Reviews of the evidence concerning Jesus and Christians from Jewish and pagan sources are found in F. F. Bruce, *Jesus and Christian Origins Outside the New Testament* (Grand Rapids: Eerdmans, 1974); C. A. Evans, "Jesus in Non-Christian Sources," in B. Chilton and C. A. Evans (eds.), *Studying the Historical Jesus: Evaluations of the State of Current Research* (NTTS, 19; Leiden: E. J. Brill, 1994), 443–78; and J. P. Meier, *A Marginal Jew: Rethinking the Historical Jesus* (New York: Doubleday, 1991), 56–111. For Jewish perceptions of Christianity, including discussion of their mutual interaction, see R. T. Herford, *Christianity in Talmud and Midrash* (New York: Ktav Pub. House, 1903); J. Lauterbach, "Jesus in the Talmud," in *Rabbinic Essays* (Cincinnati: Hebrew Union College Press, 1951), 473–570; A. F. Segal, *Two Powers in Heaven: Early Rabbinic Reports about Christianity and Gnosticism* (Leiden: E. J. Brill, 1977); and M. Simon, *Verus Israel: A Study of the Relations between Christians and Jews in the Roman Empire (AD 135–425)*, trans. H. McKeating (New York: Oxford Univ. Press, 1986). For the Roman side, see S. Benko, *Pagan Rome and the Early Christians* (Bloomington: Indiana Univ. Press, 1984); M. Whittaker, *Jews & Christians: Graeco-Roman Views* (Cambridge: Cambridge Univ. Press, 1984); and R. L. Wilken, *The Christians as the Romans Saw Them* (New Haven: Yale Univ. Press, 1984). For shorter treatments, see L. Schiffmann, "At The Crossroads: Tannaitic Perspectives on the Jewish Christian Schism," in *JCS-D* 2:115–56; R. Wilken, "The Christians as the Romans (and Greeks) Saw Them," in *JCS-D* 1:100–125; and H. W. Basser, "Allusions to Christian and Gnostic Practices in the Talmudic Tradition," *JSJ* 12 (1981): 87–105. On the religious claims and experiences reflected in the NT texts, see L. T. Johnson, *Religious Experience: A Missing Dimension of New Testament Studies* (Minneapolis: Fortress Press, 1998).

5. The Resurrection Faith

TURNING TO THE question "What happened?" means facing the most difficult part of this inquiry. It is one thing to collect statements that make it clear that some sort of powerful experience generated the movement. It is quite another to attempt a description of that experience.

Part of the problem is conceptual. Describing the nature of experience becomes more difficult the more exact one tries to be. Experience is always embodied and thus always subjective. When we hear a report of someone's personal experience, we expect both a reference to something outside the subject and an element of interpretation. It is not always possible to distinguish the elements of objectivity and subjectivity in the report itself.

The problems of description and definition are even greater when we deal with religious experience. How is it distinguished from other experiences? Does it have unique components? Can it be reduced to other, nonreligious factors, or is it an irreducible, unique sort of human event?

Religious experiences must be placed in a continuum of all life experience. The religious dimension emerges from, and responds to, other aspects of life. No single kind of event can thus automatically be designated religious. The religious aspect of life is as pervasive as the economic and is equally commingled with psychological, sociological, and cultural realities.

Personal testimony may here count for more than logical analysis, as it does also in the case of the aesthetic. Most of us work with a rough-and-ready sense of the human experience of beauty. We recognize that, when it is real, the response to beauty cannot be collapsed into the appetitive or aggressive drives of the human animal. Yet the more we try to pin down such a response conceptually, the more it recedes. Thus, some experiences cannot be adequately defined, even when we all "have" and "know" them.

Recognizing the inevitably subjective and allusive character of the task, then, we can begin to speak of religious experience, although this is made all the more difficult because of the plethora of experiences sharing similar features. As one examines religious phenomena, it becomes apparent that religious experience can be distorted in many ways, and precisely the variety of things labeled "religious" makes one cautious. Experience should here be taken to exclude that which is purely momentary, sensory, or emotive in nature. Nor does it refer only to so-called "peak experiences." Far from removing a person from "real life," religious experience is about what is perceived to be most real in life. Far from being localized in the emotions, intellect, or will, religious experience involves the whole person—emotions, will, and mind—in a response to what is understood to be most real.

Response is an important element in this definition, for it distinguishes authentic religious experience from projection, fantasy, or autosuggestion. Whereas magic is rooted in the attempt to control one's environment, religious experience is grounded in the subject's reduction to powerlessness by a force outside a person's control. That which is experienced is not a puzzle to be solved but a frightening mystery that escapes human manipulation and refuses to be grasped by human knowledge. It must be added, of course, that realistically much religious practice is indistinguishable from the practice of magic.

Religious experience involves an encounter with the holy, the mystery of the totally other that opens like a chasm before humans in unexpected ways, making impossible the denial of its presence. The human being is inexplicably caught in a tension between attraction and repulsion. The awesome power confronting the person is dangerous yet seductive. It organizes existence around itself, and above all, it demands attention. It carries with itself the weight of an absolutely authoritative presence.

Obviously, this description is culturally conditioned. Not everything called "religious" carries this sense of being a response to something "totally other." In some traditions this sense of otherness and transcendence is much diminished. It is doubtful, however, that it is ever totally absent. In this depiction, I am myself shaped by the symbols I seek to describe and can therefore only affirm that the experiences of Moses before the burning bush (Exod. 3:1-21), Isaiah in the temple (Isa. 6:1-13), and Job before the whirlwind (Job 42:1-6) correspond to something real that reappears in the writings of the NT. In this tradition, the power that intrudes into the realm of the ordinary with threatening force and dangerous charm is always the One Power who, however named, is God—who reduces to insignificance all pretension to glory and reaffirms the creatureliness of humanity.

The human response to such a powerful presence is characterized by intensity and inclusiveness. Although often spectacular and extraordinary, it need not be. A more consistent characteristic is the power's ability to organize life around itself and impress a sense of a "necessity" to act. Genuine religious experience, in other words, is not only felt, it is acted out in a consistent pattern. When I speak about religious experience as being the cause of the Christian movement and therefore of the NT, this is the sort of experience I mean.

But the description is still too idealized. It makes overly consistent a phenomenon often fragmentary and contradictory. It gives the impression that the phenomenon is a matter of pyrotechnics, rather than sometimes the result of a still small voice (cf. 1 Kings 19:1-19), or that it is invariably positive and beneficent rather than sometimes negative and harmful, or that it is exhaustive and once and for all—whereas no human experience has such finality. To understand the religious experience of the NT in particular, further qualifications are necessary.

Religious experiences are conditioned by the subject's degree of awareness, by the situation in which the experience occurs, and by the experience's degree of intensity. It is possible to speak of a community experience, but the character and quality of that experience will be different for each member. The Holocaust provides a helpful analogy. Certainly, all Jews since 1933 have "experienced" the Holocaust. Some "went through it" by being gathered into ghettos, forced to emigrate, dispossessed, killed, or by surviving work and extermination camps. Other Jews went through it differently, by having relatives killed or hearing how they survived, or by receiving education in home, school, or synagogue. Even those who went through it physically and therefore experienced it most intensely had widely different experiences. Some suffered the final indignities in an almost subhuman way. Others maintained their awareness and sensitivity to the very end. For some the intensity of religious faith did not diminish at all, and Hasidic songs were sung by some as they marched to the gas chambers. For others that same march brought only the bitter confirmation that faith was illusory and God was dead.

A similar diversity is found in the religious experiences of the first Christians. Some had experiences that were immediate, profound, and intense, while others had their experience mediated to them by witnesses. Moreover, the NT testifies to the mixed motives, desires, and conflicts, not to mention levels of awareness, that were present in first-generation communities. Not all Christians had religious experiences of the same intensity and authenticity.

Human experiences are also mediated by the available symbols of a person's world. In the very act of perception—in the experience itself—there is already a form of interpretation. There is no naked experience of the holy. The totally other is mediated by that which is not totally other: human symbols. The more powerful the encounter, of course, the more those symbols will stretch and possibly even shatter.

Any attempt to isolate a religious experience in the NT at the purely physical or psychic level, or to find an experience that is not already interpreted, is therefore doomed to fail. Experience needs the clothing of language in order to be reported at all. Whatever the physical or psychic components of the experience of power undergone by the first Christians may be, the power was perceived by them as that of the Holy Spirit.

The NT writings show us a variety of religious experiences, but behind them all is the first and fundamental experience, which found expression in this conviction: Jesus is raised from the dead. This is the one experience without which there would be no Christian movement and therefore nothing to explain or interpret.

The Resurrection Experience

At its core Christianity is not a religion of mystical enlightenment. Jesus is not revered as a sage who reached union with the divine and then showed others the way to that same unity. The generative Christian experience is not understood to be the experiencing of what Jesus himself experienced; that is regarded as unique to Jesus. Christianity, rather, begins with Jesus' followers experiencing Jesus after his death in an entirely new way. Like Judaism, Christianity is a religion of personal encounter with the Other. The primitive Christian experience consisted in encountering the Other in the risen Jesus. *The resurrection faith is the birth of Christianity.*

In the earliest extant Christian writing (ca. 50 C.E.), Paul writes to the young Thessalonian church and reminds its members (1 Thess. 1:9-10) of the terms of their conversion and how they

> turned to God from idols to serve a living and true God, and to wait for his son from heaven, whom he raised from the dead, Jesus, who delivers us from the wrath to come.

Paul goes on to write that this conviction is the basis for their own hope of a future life (1 Thess. 4:14):

> Since we believe that Jesus died and rose again, even so, through Jesus, God will bring with him those who have fallen asleep.

Writing to the Corinthian church some five years later, Paul recalls for them the basic framework of the "good news" (1 Cor. 15:3-8):

> For I delivered to you as of first importance what I also received, that Christ died for our sins in accordance with the scriptures, that he was buried, that he was raised on the third day in accordance with the scriptures, and that he appeared to Cephas, then to the Twelve. Then he appeared to more than five hundred brethren at one time, most of whom are still alive, though some have fallen asleep. Then he appeared to James, then to all the apostles. Last of all, as to one untimely born, he appeared also to me.

This recital bears the marks of a traditional formulation. Paul "received" it himself and "passed it on" to them. Its importance is indicated by his insistence that they are at present being saved by this message and must remain faithful to it (1 Cor. 15:2). The odd phrase "in accordance with the scriptures" will occupy our attention later. For now, we note that Paul is here relating the *experiential base* of the "good news." He has delivered to the Corinthians not only a conviction, "He was raised," but also the report of something experienced by others, "He appeared" (or, "He was seen"). It was something experienced by over five hundred people, some of whom were still alive and able to verify their experience. Nor is this simply an experience Paul heard about from others; he had it himself. Although Paul had not known Jesus when he was alive, he now reports that "he appeared also to me." Here we have a firsthand witness of the resurrection experience.

Paul does not describe his experience in physical or psychological terms, only with religious symbols. He characteristically associates his experience of the risen Lord with his call to be an apostle: "Am I not free? Am I not an apostle? Have I not *seen* the Lord Jesus?" (1 Cor. 9:1). And in a statement defending his call to be an apostle, he says (Gal. 1:11-12, 15-16):

> For I would have you know, brethren, that the gospel which was preached by me is not man's gospel. For I did not receive it from a man, nor was I taught it, but it came through a revelation of Jesus Christ.... But when He who had set me apart before I was born, and had called me through his grace, was pleased to reveal his son to [in] me, in order that I might preach him among the Gentiles, I did not confer with flesh and blood ...

Finally, there is the strange account in 2 Cor. 12:1-5, in which, with language strongly reminiscent of Jewish Merkabah mysticism, Paul speaks of "visions and revelations of the Lord" experienced by a "certain man" fourteen years previous, visions that brought him to the "third heaven" and revealed to him things "that cannot be told." Again, Paul says nothing about the psychic dimensions of the experience, except with the enigmatic line: "whether in the body or out of the body I do not know" (12:3). We cannot say for certain that Paul is referring here to his experience of the risen Jesus, although it is surely possible.

The Acts of the Apostles provides three accounts of Paul's encounter with the risen Jesus, once in direct narrative (9:3-8), and twice as reported by Paul in his defense speeches (22:6-11; 26:12-18). The accounts diverge in some of their details (e.g., in 9:7, his companions hear the voice but see no one; in 22:9, they see the light but hear nothing), but they all agree that it was an encounter with Jesus that resulted in Paul's being sent to proclaim the "good news" to the Gentiles. In this, they also fundamentally agree with Gal. 1:15-16.

Attempts to explain Paul's turnabout from persecutor to missionary on the basis of psychological categories have the charm of familiarity to contemporary readers. It does not seem implausible to us that Paul could have consciously rejected the messianic movement, yet, tortured in his conscience, have been unconsciously drawn to it until at last this internal tension broke him. Then, in a classic reversal of psychological denial, he embraced zealously that which he had fanatically detested. Unfortunately, Paul does not appear to have been a tormented soul. When he talks about his former life, he seems untroubled and even smug (Gal. 1:13-14; Phil. 3:4-6). And while Paul's blindness could be called a hysterical reaction (Acts 9:8-17), such a diagnosis does not significantly clarify the nature of his experience.

Moreover, attention to the psychological dynamics of Paul's experience distracts us from the aspect of the event regarded as most significant by both Paul and the author of Acts: Paul *did not* encounter a Jesus who was still living in an ordinary, human way.

He encountered a *Lord*, that is, a transcendent and commanding presence. This is the most consistent feature of all the resurrection accounts: the commanding and empowering word that comes from the risen one. Jesus' presence, furthermore, was not mediated by some symbol, but by a personal, spiritual encounter. We notice that in Gal. 1:16, Paul says that God was pleased "to reveal his son *to me*," but the Greek phrase can also be rendered "*in me*." Paul's experience was not of an object but of another subject who was exercising personal power over Paul. In the Acts narrative, the voice asks Paul, "Why are you persecuting *me*?" when in fact Paul was persecuting not the human Jesus but the messianic community. But the voice insists, "I am Jesus, whom you are persecuting" (Acts 9:5). Paul experiences Jesus as one who is alive and powerfully present in the messianic community.

Paul reports that his experience of the risen Lord was not unique. Over five hundred people, many of them still alive some twenty years after the event, could say, "I have experienced the risen Jesus; he appeared to me." In the Gospels, we find narratives that recount a handful of these experiences. It should be noted that these narratives are not to be identified with either the number or the nature of the resurrection experiences. They tell us nothing, for example, about an appearance "to more than five hundred brethren at one time" or an appearance "to James." The Gospel narratives are ancient and stem at least in part from eyewitness accounts. But in their present form, they are shaped by the continuing experience of the believing community over a period of some forty years, and in them the resurrection event is given a particular cast in line with the literary and religious purposes of the Gospels. The point here is simple: the Gospel narratives are selective and are shaped to instruct the community; the *claim* to have encountered the risen Lord or to have experienced the power of his presence is not coextensive with these *stories*. While the experience does not derive from these accounts, they seek to express the experience.

The Gospels contain two basic kinds of resurrection narratives. The first is called an empty-tomb account (see Mark 16:1-8; Matt. 28:1-8; Luke 24:1-11; John 20:1-10). The basic form is this: followers of Jesus come to the tomb to anoint him after his death and discover that he is not there; they are told by one or more messengers to deliver to the disciples the news that "He is raised." The empty-tomb stories make several points that can be recognized as responses to charges that the resurrection was a hoax perpetrated by the disciples, a charge made explicit in Matt. 28:11-15 (see 27:62-66). Thus, the stone was too heavy to be rolled away by any human, and the empty tomb is a complete surprise to the visitors. Indeed, when the other disciples are informed of the fact, they are incredulous. These elements, however, do not exhaust the significance of the empty-tomb accounts. The main point is that Jesus is absent from the place of death and that he goes "before them" (see Mark 16:7). Like the tomb itself, these narratives lie open for new encounters with Jesus. He is not where he was buried (his old life is closed), but his new life cannot be defined precisely in time and space (he goes before them). The linens left behind bear mute testimony to one freed from the bonds of death (John 20:6-9).

The second basic type of resurrection narrative is called an appearance account (see Mark 16:9-20; Matt. 28:9-10, 16-20; Luke 24:13-49; John 20:11—21:23). These narratives, too, reveal certain apologetic emphases. Thus, some stress the reality of Jesus' resurrection body in order to make two points: that the one who now lives is to be identified with the one who died (John 20:26-28) and that the experience of his presence is not that of a ghost or a phantom (Luke 24:36-43). Beyond this, however, they also show the sudden, surprising, and unmanipulated nature of these encounters. Jesus intrudes into their midst. They do not make him present. They are frightened when he does appear. Furthermore, he is there not as a shadow of his former self but as a more powerful and commanding presence. These stories are dominated by the words spoken by Jesus. He interprets the Scripture and commands them to proclaim the message to others. In these accounts especially, we can detect the characteristics of religious experience: the sudden intrusion of power, the reaction of fascination and fear, and the sense of being commissioned. The experience of the holy leads to action; the experience of the risen Lord leads to proclamation.

It is useless to tease such narratives into saying something other than what they say. They tell us the tale not of a great psychological struggle that issued in conviction, but of a surprising and totally unexpected encounter that issued in mission. Great insight into the experience of the first believers is not gained from the cynical romanticism of E. Renan, who, trying to account for the resurrection faith, finally pins most of it on Mary Magdalene:

> Let us say, however, that the strong imagination of Mary Magdalene played an important part in this circumstance. Divine power of love! Sacred moments in which the passion of one possessed gave to the world a resuscitated God!

Less facile, though ultimately just as inadequate, is the conclusion of A. Loisy, who said that Jesus did not rise on Easter, but faith did:

> Thus did belief in the resurrection of Jesus come to its birth, and the manner of it may be called spontaneous. The faith of his disciples in his messianic future was too strong to admit of self-contradiction, too strong to give way under the refutation thrown upon it by the ignominy of the cross. Faith raised Jesus into the glory he expected; faith declared him living forever, because faith itself was determined never to die. Quickened by the ordeal, faith produced out of itself visions that brought balm to its anguish and strength to its affirmations. With the fragments of a shattered hope, and building on the death of Jesus, which might have killed their faith outright, the disciples founded the religion of Jesus the Christ. Unconsciously, faith produces for herself all the illusions she needs.

Such explanations place the birth of Christianity in neurosis and illusion. Resurrection is simply the coming to life of a vain hope or an infatuated love. Like conspiracy theories, such explanations appeal to the hermeneutics of suspicion, to the presupposition that religious texts fundamentally function to camouflage other, less noble human appetites. And as with conspiracy theories, there is little in the texts themselves to support such interpretations. We know absolutely nothing of Mary Magdalene's emotional stability, even if she were the only one who had the experience. And the statement that the disciples' faith was too strong to die simply flies in the face of the texts, which agree on little but are unanimous on this: the disciples had little faith in Jesus and abandoned him completely at the end. Furthermore, these explanations show little understanding of the nature of religious experience, and thus miss entirely the import of the texts and the real nature of the Christian confession of the resurrection of Jesus.

The experience of the resurrection is not about vague and vaporous visions. It is not a belief that Jesus was resuscitated and then resumed his former way of living. It does not derive from moments of insight into Jesus' life. The Christian witness of the resurrection does not say that Jesus was spotted in passing by a few people before disappearing. Even the narrative that has Jesus ascending into heaven (Acts 1:9-11) is misread if understood in this way. In Acts, the presence of the resurrected Lord is just as strong after the ascension as before it, indeed stronger; but it is a presence in a new mode.

It is clear, then, that the resurrection experience cannot be confined to the narratives of the Gospels, for the fundamental experience and conviction were available to those who neither saw the tomb nor had a vision of Jesus. The experience of his powerful presence was possible because he was alive and caused it. If we were to compress these observations, we could say that the resurrection experience which gave birth to the Christian movement was the experience of the continuing presence of a personal, transcendent, and transforming power within the community.

This understanding of the resurrection is given expression in the Gospel narratives. In John 20:21-23, the risen Jesus tells the disciples, "As the father has sent me, even so I send you,"

> and when he had said this, he breathed on them and said to them, "Receive the Holy Spirit. If you forgive the sins of any, they are forgiven; if you retain the sins of any, they are retained."

This clearly states that the empowerment of the disciples, which enables them to carry on the mission of Jesus in the world, derives from a Holy Spirit, which comes directly from Jesus himself (see John 14:18-31). The command of the risen Lord in Luke 24:47-49 is similar:

> You are witnesses of these things. And behold, I send the promise of my father upon you; but stay in the city, until you are clothed with power from on high.

Here, the commission to be witnesses finds its empowerment from Jesus.

In Acts 2:1-4, Luke provides a narrative symbolization of this empowerment on the day of Pentecost:

> They were all filled with the Holy Spirit and began to speak in other tongues, as the Spirit gave them utterance.

This is followed by the first proclamation of Jesus as risen Lord in Peter's speech. What requires interpretation by Peter first of all is the ecstatic state of the disciples (Acts 2:12-13). It was their experience of power that demanded explanation. Peter says that this experience is a fulfillment of *prophecy* (Joel 2:28-32; Acts 2:17-21):

> In the last days I will pour out my spirit and they shall prophesy before the day of the Lord comes . . . and whoever calls on the name of the Lord shall be saved.

This text, in turn, is itself interpreted through the recital of the death and resurrection of Jesus (2:22-31). The experience and the conviction are brought together in Acts 2:32-33:

> This *Jesus*, God *raised up*, and of that we are all *witnesses*. Being therefore exalted at the right hand of God, and having received from the father the promise of the *Holy Spirit*, he has poured out *this which you see and hear.*

Beginning with the experience, the interpretation involves the understanding of Torah in the light of the death and resurrection, and returns again to the starting point, the experience of power. *The possession of the Holy Spirit is the experiential correlative to the confession that Jesus is Lord.* Peter concludes (Acts 2:36):

> Let all the house of Israel therefore know assuredly that God has made him both Christ and Lord, this Jesus whom you crucified.

When we turn our attention from the narrative material to statements found in other NT writings, we find these relationships even more clearly delineated. In chapter 4, I showed how the first Christians claimed freedom, boldness, joy, perseverance in suffering, and newness of life. All of these claims, I suggested, were connected to statements about the experience of power. Now we can observe that the source of this power is said to be, with remarkable consistency, the Holy Spirit. Indeed, for all practical purposes, we can say that the symbol of the Holy Spirit in these writings corresponds to the experiential term "power."

According to Acts 2:38 (cf. Matt. 28:19), the Holy Spirit was bestowed upon believers when they entered into the community:

Repent, be baptized, every one of you, in the name of Jesus Christ for the forgiveness of your sins, and you shall receive the gift of the Holy Spirit.

It was the Holy Spirit that worked mighty deeds among believers (Gal. 3:3-5), empowering them to proclaim (Acts 4:8; 1 Thess. 1:5; 2 Tim. 1:6) and indeed to confess their faith in the first place. Paul writes in 1 Cor. 12:3:

No one speaking by the Spirit can say, "Jesus be cursed," and no one can say, "Jesus is Lord," except by the Holy Spirit.

And it was the Holy Spirit that brought about this transformation of their consciousness (1 Cor. 2:12; Titus 3:5).

This Holy Spirit is not an impersonal force; it is the life-giving presence of the risen Lord: "Because you are sons, God has sent the Spirit of his son into our hearts, crying, Abba, Father" (Gal. 4:6). This comes across even more clearly in 2 Cor. 3:17-18:

Now the Lord is the Spirit, and where the Spirit of the Lord is, there is freedom. And we all, with unveiled faces, beholding the glory of the Lord, are being changed into his likeness from one degree of glory into another; for this comes from the Lord, who is the Spirit.

The connection between the Holy Spirit and the presence of Jesus is drawn again by Paul in 1 Cor. 2:12 and 16. He states first the origin of the Spirit, "We have not received the spirit of the world, but the Spirit which is from God," and closes the discussion with the statement, "We have the mind of Christ." In Rom. 8:11 the connection is made explicitly to the resurrection:

If the Spirit of Him who raised Jesus from the dead dwells in you, He who raised Jesus from the dead will give life to your mortal bodies also through his Spirit which dwells in you.

Finally, in the context of an extended discussion of the resurrection (1 Cor. 15:45), Paul makes this summarizing statement:

The first man became a living being; the last Adam became a life-giving spirit.

As these references indicate, the explicit correlation between the resurrection confession ("Jesus is Lord") and the experience of the Holy Spirit is a prominent feature of Paul's theology. But it is not exclusively a Pauline preoccupation (see Heb. 2:4; 4:12; 6:4; James 4:5; 1 Pet. 1:12; 3:18; 4:6; 1 John 3:24; 4:13; 5:8; Jude 19, 20; Rev. 2:7; 4:2; 19:10).

The resurrection faith, then, was not the conviction that Jesus had resumed his life for a time and appeared to some of his followers. It was a conviction, corroborated by the present experience of his power even years after his death, that he was alive in a new and powerful way; that he shared, indeed, God's life. He was Lord, and his lordship was exercised in the world through his life-giving Spirit.

This confession, we should note, was no less scandalous in that world than in ours. It did not take the development of modern physics to make the resurrection a dubious proposition to sophisticated minds. Paul was mocked by some among his Stoic and Epicurean audience when he tried to preach Jesus' resurrection in Athens (Acts 17:32). The death and resurrection of Jesus was as paradoxical then as now, eluding logic and fleeing any response but faith or incredulity.

For the sake of clarity, we can reduce the proposition to its simplest form. First, a man everyone knew was killed is now alive. Second, what happened and is still happening in this singular historical person affects radically and powerfully the existence of every human being, because that man now shares the life of the ultimate, transcendent power of God.

The second part of the proposition was particularly offensive to the Christian messianists' fellow Jews. The shape of their objection helps us see the distinctive nature of the resurrection faith. At least one important sect of first-century Judaism, the Pharisees, believed fervently in the resurrection of the dead (see Acts 23:8). At least as a proposition, the resurrection would not have bothered them. The resurrection they awaited, however, was one destined for the just, and it was to be the eschatological manifestation of God's kingdom. The confession that Jesus was resurrected was impossible for them because, by the norm of Torah, he was not a just man; indeed his death was one that Torah declared cursed by God (Deut. 21:23; cf. Gal. 3:13). Even less could his resurrection be considered the eschatological event, for history manifestly continued on its course. Also implicit in the Christian confession was the claim to represent the authentic Israel on the basis of having received the promise of the Spirit (see Acts 2:33; Gal. 3:14). That was an implication most Jews could not accept. Ultimately, it was not the confession of Jesus as Messiah that divided Christians from other Jews, for it was possible for Jews to make such confessions—as Rabbi Akiba did in the case of Bar Kochba—without apostatizing from Torah. It was the confession of a crucified sinner as resurrected Lord that was divisive. This points us once more to the centrality of this confession for the birth of the Christian movement.

The conviction that Jesus is alive and powerfully active in the believing community is the implicit, and sometimes explicit, presupposition of all the writings of the NT. The Jesus of the Gospels is not simply a past figure who is fondly remembered. He is the living Lord confessed and experienced in the community, whose words now address believers in the present. The Jesus of the NT letters and the Book of Revelation is not a static moral teacher or exemplar, but a living and active presence, shaping the community's identity through his spirit: speaking through the church's prophets, teaching through its teachers, and healing through the hands of the believers.

From the conviction that Jesus is alive and is now the commanding Lord came the motivation to proclaim the "good news," not alone on the basis of past commission but also on the basis of present command (Acts 13:2):

> While they were worshiping the Lord and fasting, the Holy Spirit said, "Set apart for me Barnabas and Paul for the work to which I have called them."

Moreover, it was from the conviction that the risen Lord was present to them through the Spirit of God that the church derived its sense of itself as the authentic Israel upon which had come the spiritual fulfillment of the promises to Abraham (see Acts 2:33, 38-39; Gal. 3:14). Thus the church was the faithful remnant of the people of God (Rom. 9:22-33), the dwelling place of God's Spirit, and therefore the temple of his presence (1 Cor. 3:16-17; Eph. 2:19-22; 1 Pet. 2:4-10).

The conviction that Jesus was alive and active gave rise to the expectation of his return to establish the kingdom among his people. We have already seen the connection Paul drew between the resurrection and Christ's coming (*parousia*) in 1 Thess. 4:14. It is also in connection with the resurrection that he states in 1 Cor. 15:24-28:

> Then comes the end, when he delivers the kingdom to God the father after destroying every rule and every authority and power. For he must reign until he has put all enemies beneath his feet. . . . When all things are subjected to him, then the son himself will also be subjected to him who puts all things under him, that God may be everything to everyone.

The author of Hebrews, for whom the resurrection means precisely that Jesus is alive and making continual intercession for believers, says (9:27-28):
> Just as it is appointed for men to die once and after that comes judgment, so Christ, having been offered once to bear the sins of many, will appear a second time, not to deal with sin, but to save those who are eagerly awaiting him.

It is thus evident that the presence of the resurrected Jesus in the power of the Holy Spirit fundamentally shaped early Christian beliefs and expectations. In the final analysis, then, if we were to ask which came first, the conviction that Jesus was alive or the gift of the Spirit that touched the believers with that life, we would be asking a question impossible to answer. The narratives suggest that the conviction, based on appearances, came first, and the empowerment by the Spirit came after. And this order respects the line of causality: the Spirit is given to humans because Jesus is raised. But which occurred first in the experience of the Christians, we cannot say. From the first, experience and conviction, power and confession, were inextricably mixed, and together they formed the generative experience of Christianity.

The Need for Interpretation

If the resurrection faith gave birth to the Christian movement, it also created the need for interpretation. This is because the resurrection faith is rooted in paradox: a man who died is now alive and the source of power for all humans; a person who died a sinner's death is now the source of the forgiveness of sins for all others. It is a conviction and an experience that creates multiple and vexing problems for human understanding, specifically for those touched by this experience and committed to this conviction. I can here only indicate a few of the questions that had to occur to those who committed themselves to this crucified and raised Messiah.

Was Jesus' death on the cross really the death of a sinner and one cursed by God, as Torah would seem to indicate? If so, how do we reconcile our experience of life through him and our understanding of Torah? Must we choose between the legitimacy of Jesus' messiahship and the ultimacy of Torah? Or if he was not a sinner, then what is sin, and what is the meaning of justice? What was it about the man Jesus that caused God to raise him from the dead and install him as Lord?

If Jesus is Lord as we confess, then what is his relation to the God we call Father? Can there be two powers in heaven? Can God have partners and still be one? And what is Jesus' relation to the world and to this community? Is the presence of his spirit so final and strong that it cannot be broken? If we in this church share the power of his resurrected life through the gift of his spirit, why should we have to die? And, more pertinent, how should we then live? Since he is present to us in power and his kingdom is somehow actual in his dominion as Lord, what more is there to look for?

How can we reconcile the presence of the Holy Spirit among us and the continuing presence of sin as well? If God is victorious over evil in the resurrection of Jesus, why then are we powerless in a hostile world? And if we are the authentic Israel, what does that mean for the historical people of God? If they have rejected Jesus as Messiah, does that mean they are rejected by God? And if so, does that mean God does not keep his promises? And if he has not kept his word to Israel, how can we be sure he will keep his word to us?

It was not enough for the first Christians to experience the transforming transcendent power of the Spirit and proclaim that Jesus was Lord. They also had to interpret their lives in the light of this overwhelming experience. Out of the struggle of the first believers to find meaning in the paradox of the mediation of the holy through the death of a man, there emerged the interpretation of their existence. The symbolic world of Torah, which they shared with their fellow Jews, was the world of symbols toward which they inevitably turned. The paradox of the dead and raised Messiah was the interpretive key for their new reading.

Study Questions

1. Why are people's religious experiences not identical? What factors help us account for the differences?

2. What does it mean to say that the resurrection was "a new way of experiencing Jesus"?

3. What types of narratives about encounters with the resurrected Jesus does the New Testament recount? How are they different?

4. What was distinctive about Paul's experience of the resurrected Jesus? How did it affect Paul?

5. Why was the symbol of the Holy Spirit so central to the early followers of Jesus?

6. In what sense did Jesus' death create a problem for those who confessed him as risen Lord?

Bibliographical Note

The citations on page 113 comes from E. Renan, *The Life of Jesus*, trans. J. H. Holmes (New York: Modern Library, 1927 [1863]), 357, and from A. Loisy, *The Birth of the Christian Religion and the Origins of Christianity*, trans. L. P. Jacks (New York: University Books, 1962 [1933, 1936]), 97–98.

The bald statement that Christianity came to birth with the resurrection experience represents a strong, but also disputed, reading of the evidence, particularly within contemporary scholarship devoted to Christian origins. When I speak of the "birth of Christianity," I do not, of course, suggest that the scattered, fragmentary, and allusive experiences and convictions reported in these pages as yet constituted a uniform and distinctive "religion." But I do claim that what eventually developed into that religion found both its point of origin and its self-definition precisely in these experiences and convictions.

Among some of the older, classic discussions of the resurrection faith, see D. Strauss, *The Life of Jesus Critically Examined*, ed. P. Hodgson (Philadelphia: Fortress Press, 1973 [1835]), 735–44, for a full range of naturalistic explanations. In contrast, F. C. Baur is terse and circumspect in *The Church History of the First Three Centuries*, ed. A. Menzies (London: Williams & Norgate, 1878 [1853]), 1:42: "The view we take of the resurrection is of minor importance for the History." The discussion by J. Weiss in *Earliest Christianity*, ed. E C. Grant (New York: Harper & Row, 1959 [1914]), 1:14–44, is full, critical, but ultimately psychologizing.

At least the older discussions took the issue seriously. Many recent histories of Christianity reduce treatment of the resurrection to a single line or less; see, e.g., W. H. C. Frend, *The Rise of Christianity* (Philadelphia: Fortress Press, 1984), 86; P. Johnson, *A History of Christianity* (New York: Atheneum, 1979), 32; H. Chadwick, *The Early Church* (New York: Penguin Books, 1967); and H. Conzelmann, *History of Primitive Christianity*, trans. J. Steely (Nashville: Abingdon Press, 1973), 38–42. In contrast, see the serious treatment by L. Goppelt, *Apostolic and Post-Apostolic Times*, trans. R. A. Guelich (Grand Rapids: Baker Book House, 1970), 8–24.

Some contemporary historical studies challenge the importance of the resurrection from several directions, all of which share a refusal to take religious experience seriously. The tradition of E. Renan lives on in contemporary explanations of the resurrections as a psychological "event" that takes place in the mind of Peter (at the popular level, see J. Spong, *Resurrection: Myth or Reality?* [San Francisco: HarperCollins, 1994]; and at the scholarly level see both G. Luedemann, *The Resurrection of Jesus: History, Experience, Theology* [Minneapolis: Fortress Press, 1994], and W. Marxsen, *The Resurrection of Jesus of Nazareth*, trans. M. Kohl [Philadelphia: Fortress Press, 1970]). The tradition of Loisy lives on in studies that attribute belief in the resurrection to the resolution of cognitive dissonance. These place the dissonance in a different sequence than I do here. Rather than thinking that the dissonance is caused by the disciples' hopes being shattered by the crucifixion, I locate it in the experience of the resurrection, which shatters their symbolic world. Similar to Loisy are the positions taken by H. Jackson, "The Resurrection Belief of the Earliest Church: A Response to the Failure of Prophecy?" *JR* 55 (1975): 415–25; and U. Wernick, "Frustrated Beliefs and Early Christianity," *Numen* 22 (1975): 96–130.

Pushing the matter even further, the resurrection of Jesus is considered a disease of language according to P. E. Devenish, "The So-Called Resurrection of Jesus and Explicit Christian Faith: Wittgenstein's Philosophy and Marxsen's Exegesis as Linguistic Therapy," *JAAR* 51 (1983): 171–90. In contrast, P. Lapide, *The Resurrection of Jesus: A Jewish Perspective* (Minneapolis: Augsburg, 1983), despite arguing that since the world continued without change Jesus could not be the Messiah, nevertheless affirms the centrality of the resurrection experience for the first Christians.

More recently, some scholars have insisted that diversity in various "Jesus movements" was even more profound than the NT suggests, to the extent that some post-death followers of Jesus knew nothing of the resurrection and based their lives only on his words and deeds (see B. L. Mack, *Who Wrote the New Testament? The Making of the Christian Myth* [San Francisco: HarperCollins, 1995], and J. Z. Smith, *Drudgery Divine: On the Comparison of Early Christianities and the Religions of Late Antiquity* (Chicago: Univ. of Chicago Press, 1990). Such radical disintegration of the Christian movement in its earliest stages simply creates a historical problem of a different order.

On the form and context of the resurrection accounts, see J. E. Alsup, *The Post-Resurrection Appearance Stories of the Gospel Tradition: A History-of-Tradition Analy-*

sis (London: SPCK, 1975), and C. H. Dodd, "The Appearance of the Risen Christ: An Essay in Form-Criticism of the Gospels," in D. Nineham (ed.), *Studies in the Gospels* (Oxford: Basil Blackwell, 1955), 9–35. On issues of redaction by the evangelists, see the conservative but still helpful treatment by G. R. Osborne, *The Resurrection Narratives: A Redactional Study* (Grand Rapids: Baker Book House, 1984). On the NT traditions of the resurrection of Jesus, see H. von Campenhausen, "The Events of Easter and the Empty Tomb," in *Tradition and Life in the Church: Essays and Lectures in Church History*, trans. A. V. Littledale (Philadelphia: Fortress Press, 1968), 42–89; C. F. Evans, *Resurrection and the New Testament* (London: SCM Press, 1970); R. Fuller, *The Formation of the Resurrection Narratives* (Philadelphia: Fortress Press, 1971); P. Perkins, *Resurrection: New Testament Witness and Contemporary Reflection* (New York: Doubleday, 1984); idem, "The Resurrection of Jesus of Nazareth," in B. Chilton and C. A. Evans (eds.), *Studying the Historical Jesus: Evaluations of the State of Current Research* (NTTS, 19; Leiden: E. J. Brill, 1994), 423–42; and U. Wilckens, *Resurrection*, trans. A. M. Stewart (Atlanta: John Knox Press, 1978). A useful review of approaches is found in T. Lorenzen, *Resurrection and Discipleship: Interpretive Models, Biblical Reflections, Theological Consequences* (Maryknoll: Orbis Books, 1995), 1–111.

For background to the remarks made in this chapter on religious experience, see R. Otto, *The Idea of the Holy*, trans. J. W. Harvey (London: Oxford Univ. Press, 1950); W. James, *The Varieties of Religious Experience* (New York: Macmillan Co., 1961 [1902]); J. Wach, *The Comparative Study of Religions*, ed. J. Kitagawa (New York: Columbia Univ. Press, 1958); M. Eliade, *Myth and Reality*, trans. W. Trask (New York: Harper & Row, 1963); G. Van der Leeuw, *Religion in Essence and Manifestation*, 2 vols. (New York: Harper & Row, 1968); G. Marcel, *Mystery of Being: Vol. 1: Reflection and Mystery*, trans. G. S. Fraser (Chicago: Henry Regnery Co., 1969); and idem, *Creative Fidelity*, trans. R. Rosthal (New York: Farrar, Straus & Giroux, 1964).

6. Jesus in the Memory of the Church

THE NATURE OF the Christian experience demanded interpretation as well as proclamation, and this interpretation inevitably centered on the person of Jesus. The reason is simple: the one who appeared to the disciples as the risen Lord was identified with the same Jesus who had died by execution on the cross. The man they had known as one who preached, healed, and suffered, they now knew as the powerful bestower of the Spirit. If the community was to advance its own story, it was necessary first to come to grips with Jesus' story. The identity of the community and the living memory of Jesus were, therefore, inextricably intertwined. It is to the shaping of that memory that our investigation now turns.

Anamnesis

In quite different ways, the letters and Gospels of the NT represent crystallizations of memory, the literary distillation of traditions about Jesus that were transmitted and developed during the years after Jesus' death and resurrection. In the Gospels, the story of Jesus is obviously central and explicit, while the instruction of the church and the interpretation of its story are only implicit. Our present consideration of the memory of Jesus in the early church therefore serves as a natural transition to the reading of those documents. But it should be asserted that the memory of Jesus was no less important for the Book of Revelation and the epistolary writings. Though the instruction of the church and the interpretation of its story are central and explicit in them, the memory of Jesus still plays an integral, albeit implicit, role.

When we speak of the memory of Jesus in the church, we do not mean simply a mechanical recalling of information from the past. We mean, rather, the sort of memory expressed by the Greek term *anamnēsis* (cf. Luke 22:19; 1 Cor. 11:24, 25). It is a recollection of the past that enlivens and empowers the present. Such memory is not restricted to the mental activity of individuals; it is found above all in the ritual and verbal activity of communities. We found that such was the case in the Jewish Passover Haggadah: the recital of the events of the exodus long ago made the power of those events contemporaneous to the present generation ("Let everyone regard themselves as having come out of Egypt"). Anamnesis in earliest Christianity was even more complex, for the one remembered from the past was also being experienced as present here and now. Jesus was not simply called back from the past by mental activity. Thus the present experience of his power threw constant light on the recollection of him from the past.

Memory such as this is intimately bound up with the *identity* of both individuals and communities. An individual's story defines one as a person. The myth of a people defines it as a community. Individual or communal amnesia is a terrifying phenomenon precisely because anamnesis *is* identity. Without a past, we have no present and little hope for a future. The early church's identity was bound up with the memory of Jesus. It sought an understanding of its present in his past, just as it was motivated to search out his past by the experience of his presence.

Personal memory is inevitably *selective*. Not all of the past is remembered, for not all of the past is pertinent to the present. But selectivity is not random; it derives from the continuing experience of those who remember. The present situation stimulates the memory of the past. It was at least partially because the church faced opposition from its fellow Jews that it remembered how Jesus faced such opposition and responded to it. Some things are remembered, of course, simply because they were so important and impressive then, and continue to be important and formative now. It did not take the breaking of bread to make Christians remember what Jesus said and did at his last meal with his disciples, though the breaking of bread was an appropriate occasion for perpetuating that memory.

The memory of the past is also *shaped* by the continuing experience of the community. As new experiences place old ones in different perspective, the human story is constantly revised. As our present situation shapes our past, that which was formerly obscure becomes clear and that which was previously insignificant now looms large. The meaning of a past crisis is affected by our present perception of it as preparatory or analogous to the crisis we are now going through. Our grasp of the present moment enables us to perceive a more intelligible and universal shape in past events.

So also was the memory of Jesus selected and shaped by the continuing experience of Christian communities. The process was made more complex by the distinctive nature of their continuing experience: the one they remembered was present to them now in power. Everything the believers remembered about his past words and deeds was colored by their standing on the other side of the resurrection experience. However faithful they intended to be to the past, their memory could not help being marked by their present perception. The one who spoke then in parables, speaks now through prophets; the one who healed then, now heals through the hands of believers. The interpenetration of past and present experience made the development of Jesus traditions extraordinarily complex.

Nor was the memory of Jesus unaffected by contact with the diverse and changing circumstances of the first Christians. Their need to confront themselves, one another, and their world during a period of turbulent growth and conflict also colored their perceptions of Jesus. A number of these circumstances are located in the social contexts of the early church. What were these social contexts and how could they help select and shape the memory of Jesus?

The Social Contexts of Tradition

The specific social settings of earliest Christianity must themselves be placed within the framework of the missionary expansion over the forty-year period preceding the writing of the first Gospel. The Acts of the Apostles provides the only sustained narrative of the spread of the gospel. Its treatment is selective and affected by its theological purposes, but it provides invaluable information that is corroborated by other NT writings.

In Acts 1:8, Jesus tells the apostles, "You shall receive power when the Holy Spirit comes upon you; and you shall be my witnesses in Jerusalem, and in all Judea and Samaria, and to the end of the earth." Luke uses this prophecy as an organizing principle for his narrative. He shows the "word of God" progressing from its center in Jerusalem (chaps. 1–8) to Judea and Samaria (chaps. 8–10), then to Antioch (chap. 11), and from there, through the missionary work of Paul and his companions (chaps. 13–28), to Rome, the "end of the earth" (28:16). Luke's theological concern accounts for two emphases in this picture: he demonstrates the peaceful continuity of the mission from Jerusalem to the gentile world; and, he shows that the preaching began in synagogues and moved to the Gentiles only after its rejection there (13:46-47; 18:6; 28:25-28).

Acts oversimplifies in many ways. It tells us nothing about missionary activity in some areas of obvious historical interest. Concerning Egyptian or Galilean Christianity, Luke tells us almost nothing (see Acts 9:31); of Syrian Christianity (apart from the brief notes on Damascus and Antioch), very little. As a good Hellenistic author, furthermore, Luke is interested mainly in cities; he never mentions rural evangelization. His irenic purpose leads him to downplay conflict and discord in the earliest communities, even though they can be spotted readily between the lines of his narrative (Acts 6:1-7; 9:26; 11:2; 15:1-21, 39; 21:21). And from Acts 13 onward, his focus is so tightly on Paul that all other developments vanish. The reader discovers that when Paul arrives in Rome as a prisoner, there is already a Christian community there (28:16) even though Luke did not describe the evangelization of the empire's capital city!

Despite its limitations, however, Acts provides an important framework for understanding the spread of Christianity. First, it makes clear that the movement grew by the establishment of churches. Christianity was a movement of social groups. The social setting for tradition is, therefore, intrinsic to the nature of the movement itself. Second, Acts shows how rapidly the message sped across vast geographic areas. Within seven or eight years after the death of Jesus, separate communities existed in

Jerusalem, Judea, Samaria, and Syria. In twenty years there were communities in Cyprus and Asia Minor; after twenty-five years, communities flourished throughout Macedonia, Achaia, and possibly Dalmatia. Thirty years after Jesus was killed, there was a Christian community in Rome. These are conservative estimates, and the time frame could be even shorter.

The rapidity of Christianity's growth had real implications for the memory of Jesus. It meant that his memory had to be transmitted and preserved through new and changing circumstances. An immediate and fundamental transition was from a pre-dominantly rural setting—presupposed by most of Jesus' words—to the urban contexts addressed by Paul and Peter. Some linguistic adjustments were also required. Greek was spoken throughout the empire, and there were Greek-speaking Christians even in the earliest Jerusalem community. But the present Greek form of Jesus' words often suggests the presence of an Aramaic substratum. Insofar as his words required translation, therefore, subtle shadings of meaning would be both gained and lost. The movement's rapid spread into the pluralistic culture of the Diaspora meant as well that the memory of Jesus could be affected by contact with other traditions, such as those of Diaspora Judaism and Hellenistic philosophy and religion.

The point of these observations is simple: the evidence of the NT does *not* suggest that after the resurrection there was a long period of tranquil recollection and interpretation carried out under the tight control of a single stable community that, having forged the memory of Jesus into a coherent and consistent form, transmitted it to other lands, languages, and cultures. The evidence points in the opposite direction: there was no long period of tranquillity. The first community was from the beginning harassed and persecuted. The spread of the movement was carried out by many messengers and required flexible adjustment to new circumstances. In the light of this evidence, what is surprising is not the diversity found in the traditions concerning Jesus but that there is any consistency at all!

Three community contexts were particularly important for both the growth and the stabilization of the Jesus traditions in the early church: preaching, worship, and teaching for the common life. To these we now turn.

Preaching

The historical importance of this context is clear, but the determination of how much Christian preaching found its way into the NT writings or how much it transmitted the memory of Jesus is very difficult. Early Christianity was a missionary movement, and the proclamation (*kēryssein* = to proclaim) or *kerygma* (the content of what is proclaimed) of what God had done in the death and resurrection of Jesus soon brought communities into existence (see Gal. 4:13; Phil. 1:5; Col. 1:3-7; 1 Thess. 1:5; Heb. 2:1-4; James 1:21; 1 Pet. 1:22-25).

Because letters were written to churches already in existence, they presuppose, but do not contain, that earliest proclamation. Even letters like Hebrews and 1 Peter, which may have originated as homilies, move well beyond the first stage of missionary preaching (see Heb. 6:1-3; 1 Pet. 2:2). These sermonic letters do, however, pay relatively explicit attention to the significance of Jesus' earthly life and suffering (see Heb. 5:7-10; 12:1-3; 1 Pet. 2:21-25). Paul also appears to make reference to the narration of Jesus' death in his mention of the initial preaching made to the Galatian churches, "before whose eyes Jesus Christ was publicly displayed as crucified" (Gal. 3:1). Otherwise, we find only fragments of actual preaching (see 1 Cor. 15:1-8; Rom. 10:14-17; Gal. 4:4-7; and 1 Thess. 1:9-10). These texts suggest that preaching was what turned hearers from their former lives to belief and commitment to the God who made Jesus both Christ and Lord (Acts 2:37; 10:44; Gal. 3:2-5; Heb. 6:1; 1 Pet. 1:13-22). It is in this sense that preaching was foundational for early Christianity: faith came through "hearing" (Rom. 10:5-17; Gal. 3:5).

But how important was preaching for the preservation or formation of the memory of Jesus? A decision on this depends to some extent on one's judgment concerning the missionary speeches found in the Acts of the Apostles. Similar speeches are put into the mouth of both Peter (Acts 2:16-36; 3:12-26; 10:34-43) and Paul (Acts 13:16-41; 17:22-31). Paul's sermon to a pagan audience in Athens (17:22-31) is distinctive, but the others are strikingly similar. They maintain with more or less consistency that the age of fulfillment has dawned in Jesus, who, as a descendant of David, carried out a ministry among the people of Israel; that he was crucified and raised by God as the messiah; that the Holy Spirit confirmed God's vindication of Jesus; and that Jesus would return again to judge the world. On the basis of this message, a call is made for repentance. In Peter's speech of Acts 10:34-43, moreover, one can discern an outline resembling the Synoptic account of Jesus' ministry.

The critical question here is the extent to which Acts uses genuinely traditional materials or patterns of preaching. The answer is made more difficult by observing Luke's substantial literary creativity. That both Paul and Peter follow this pattern of preaching would seem to indicate its traditional character. But then we notice that Luke has Peter and Paul work very similar miracles and that, together with all the first leaders of the community, they are described in stereotypical terms for theological purposes of Luke's own. We further observe that Luke, as a Hellenistic historian, uses speeches to interpret and advance his narrative; that he systematically reworks any source he uses; and that he is generally fond of archaizing the language, especially in the sayings material (see the canticles of Luke 1–2). On purely literary grounds, determining what is traditional and what is not becomes nearly impossible.

To challenge the antiquity of the speeches, however, does not deny that their *pattern* may have been traditional. In their focus on the death and resurrection of the Messiah in fulfillment of the Scripture as the basis for repentance, they agree with the summary statements of the kerygma one finds in the NT letters. Further than this one cannot go.

While it is more than likely that some account of Jesus' words and deeds was found even in the initial preaching, it is not possible to specify more closely what sort of materials would have been used, whether they would have been part of a standard repertoire, or what function they might have performed.

A somewhat surer point of contact between the activity of preaching and the memory of Jesus may be found in the apologetic function of preaching. At least some early Christian preaching was done in Jewish synagogues (Acts 13:13-16; 14:1; 17:1-3; 18:4-5; 19:8). At times, it led to disputation with Jews who opposed this proclamation of a crucified messiah. Acts mentions several public controversies between the Christian messianists and their fellow Jews (6:9-10; 9:22, 29; 18:4, 28). In two of them it is explicitly stated that the argument was over the messianic claims of Jesus, involving a disputation over the proper understanding of Torah (Acts 17:1-3; 18:4-5). Early Christian preachers would have been required to respond to objections from other Jews such as we find answered in the Passion narratives of the Gospels: Was Jesus a sinner and a criminal? Did he die as one cursed by God? Was he rightly condemned as a seducer of the people by a legal Jewish court? Was his body stolen from the tomb by his disciples to perpetrate a fraud? If the death and resurrection of the Messiah was the focus of the early kerygma, it would also be the obvious point of attack for those rejecting its message, and therefore the first part of Jesus' story requiring interpretation.

Worship

In worship, the convictions and experiences of religion come alive, and this context was integral for developing the memory of Jesus in the church. The community's ritual and myth centered on what God had done through the death and resurrection of Jesus, so its memory of him played a significant role in its worship.

PLACES OF WORSHIP

The Christian community remembered that Jesus had cleansed the temple as a prophetic act (Mark 11:15-18; pars.) and had taught in its precincts before his death (Mark 11:27; 12:35, 41; pars.). In the narrative about the earliest Jerusalem church, Acts depicts the disciples attending temple services together (2:46; 3:1) and the apostles both preaching and healing in its courts (3:11-12; 5:42). We cannot be sure how long this continued, though it obviously came to an end with the destruction of the temple in 70 c.e. The practice seems to have had little effect on the memory of Jesus or even on the use of temple symbolism, which was employed early on (see 1 Cor. 3:16-17; Eph. 2:19-22; Heb. 10:19-25; 1 Pet. 2:4-8; Rev. 21:22).

Both in Jerusalem and in the Diaspora, Jewish Christians shared in the worship of the synagogue, at least for a time. Acts portrays Christians as preaching Jesus in that context. At least some early messianists remained in the synagogue, since references in the NT indicate that these Christians were expelled from the synagogues by other Jews (Mark 13:9; Matt. 23:34; John 9:22; 12:42; 16:2; Acts 6:11-15; 18:7-17)—a practice that preceded the formal composition of the *birkat ha minim* (the "benedictions against the heretics" formulated sometime after 85 C.E., which finally forced the Christians out altogether). In the NT, "synagogue" is used only once for the Christian worship assembly (James 2:2; although cf. *Proseuchē*, "place of prayer," in Acts 16:13, 16). The usual term is *ekklēsia* (e.g., 1 Cor. 14:23; 1 Thess. 1:1). The main contribution of the synagogue to Christian worship was to supply the forms of prayer and the practice of reading and interpreting Torah.

The dominant place for Christian worship in the NT period was the house (*oikia, oikos*). Even before Pentecost, Acts shows us the Galilean disciples gathering in an "upper room" for prayer (Acts 1:13), and the first believers who attended temple services were also "breaking bread in their houses" (Acts 2:46). People gathered in households to hear preaching and break bread (Acts 10:33; 16:32; 18:7; 20:7-12) and to pray (12:12). Since the basic societal unit in the Roman Empire was the household, it is not by chance that "whole households" converted at once to the Christian faith (Acts 11:14; 16:15, 31; 18:8; John 4:53; 1 Cor. 1:16), with the heads of such households probably providing the place for worship as well as leadership. In the NT, we find repeated mention of "the church" that meets at a certain individual's house (Rom. 16:5; 1 Cor. 16:15, 19; Col. 4:15; Phlm. 2).

The house setting probably had some impact on the self-identification of the community as the "household of God" (Eph. 2:19; 1 Tim. 3:15; 1 Pet. 4:17) and on the use of household ethics for exhortation, such as were employed in Hellenistic moral philosophy (see Col. 3:18-4:6; Eph. 5:21—6:9; Titus 2:1-10; 1 Pet. 2:13-3:7). Moreover, this setting also had an influence on the use of terms like "edification" (*oikodomein*), which was used for the activity of establishing and maintaining community identity (Matt. 16:18; Rom. 14:19; 15:2, 20; 1 Cor. 3:9; 8:1; 10:23; 14:4, 17; 2 Cor. 10:8; 13:10; Eph. 4:16; 1 Thess. 5:11), and "steward,"(*oikonomos*), which was used for the leadership role within the community (1 Cor. 4:1; 9:17; Col. 1:25; Titus 1:7; 1 Pet. 4:10). This context is also reflected in some of Jesus' sayings, where the household, the steward, and the master of the household all figure prominently (Mark 10:29-30; 13:34-35; Matt. 7:24-27; 12:25-29; 13:27, 52; 20:1; Luke 12:39-48; John 8:35; 14:2).

FORMS OF WORSHIP

Cult. Cultic actions are natural occasions for the transmission of communal memory. The two main cultic activities of the early church were baptism and the Lord's Supper. Each attracted to itself a body of tradition. Baptism, of course, was the ritual of initiation into the community (Matt. 28:19; Acts 2:38, 41; 8:12, 36; 9:18; 10:48; 16:15, 33; 1 Cor. 1:15-16) that, over time, replaced the Jewish ritual of circumcision (Col. 2:11-12). Aspects of the ritual action may be reflected in symbols of washing (Acts 22:16; 1 Cor. 6:11; Eph. 5:26; Titus 3:5; Heb. 10:22), light (Eph. 1:18; 5:8-9, 14; 2 Tim. 1:10;

Heb. 6:4; 1 Pet. 2:9), the taking off and putting on of garments (Gal. 3:27; Eph. 4:22-25; Col. 3:8-10; James 1:21; 1 Pet. 2:1), and the unification of opposites (1 Cor. 12:13; Gal. 3:28; Col. 3:11). The symbolism of death and rising appears to be connected to baptism even before Paul (Rom. 6:3-11; Col. 2:12) and is implied by the sayings of Jesus (Mark 10:39) as well as by the accounts of his baptism by John in the Jordan (Mark 1:9; Matt. 3:16; Luke 3:21; John 1:32-33). The Christian experience of baptism also provided a perspective for the reinterpretation of Torah, as in the typological reading of the exodus story in 1 Cor. 10:1-5 and of the Noah story in 1 Pet. 3:20-21.

The second cultic context for the development of the memory of Jesus was the meal. Acts lists "breaking bread in houses" as one of the activities of the first believers (2:42, 46) and describes one occasion of such activity at which time Paul also preached (Acts 20:7, 11; cf. 27:35). This meal was celebrated on the first day of the week (Sunday), which Paul also specifies as a "day of assembly" (1 Cor. 16:2) and the Book of Revelation calls the "Lord's day" (Rev. 1:10). As we have seen, all meals in Judaism had a certain sacred character and were accompanied by blessings. Such was undoubtedly also the case with these special meals, which are called love feasts (*agapai*) in Jude 12 (cf. 2 Pet. 2:13, where there is a pun on this word in the Greek). Some if not all of these meals derived their special character from the remembrance of Jesus' final meal with his disciples. Paul calls such a meal the Lord's Supper (*kyriakon deipnon*; 1 Cor. 11:20), and specifically connects the sharing of bread and wine at it to the actions and words of Jesus the night before his death (1 Cor. 11:23-25):

> I received from the Lord Jesus what I also delivered to you, that the Lord on the night when he was betrayed took bread, and when he had given thanks, he broke it and said, "This is my body . . ."

As the remembrance of the exodus at the Passover meal made that event real for every Jew, so the remembrance of Jesus' words and gestures at his last meal makes effective the presence of the Lord.

Three types of stories about Jesus would naturally attach themselves to this setting of the Lord's Supper. First, Paul's use of this tradition is obviously close to the accounts of the last meal at which time Jesus performed those actions and said those words (Mark 14:22-25; Matt. 26:26-29; Luke 22:19-20). Second, the meal context was also an appropriate setting for the memory of Jesus' miraculous feeding of the multitudes (notice the language of blessing and breaking in these accounts; Mark 6:34-44; 8:1-10; Matt. 14:15-21; 15:32-39; Luke 9:10-17; John 6:1-14, 53-58). Third, the conviction that Jesus was truly present as risen Lord among those who shared these meals (cf. 1 Cor. 11:27-32) made them a fitting setting for the remembrance of the resurrection accounts in which Jesus ate and drank with those to whom he appeared (Luke 24:28-35, 41-43; John 21:9-14; cf. Acts 10:40-41).

Prayer. Communal worship also involved the use of set prayer forms. In these we find the influence of the synagogue liturgy on early Christianity, as well as the decisive impact of the experience of Jesus in the lives of believers. This is seen at once in the blessing formula (*berakah*), which, as we saw, was the standard form of Jewish prayer (cf. Rom 1:25; 9:5; 2 Cor. 1:3-7; Eph. 1:3-14; 1 Pet. 1:3-9). In the NT occurrences, the stereotypical opening of "Blessed be the Lord" is fundamentally modified by the Christian conviction that Jesus is somehow also Lord ("Jesus is Lord"; Rom. 10:9; 1 Cor. 12:3; Phil. 2:11), so that these blessings begin, "Blessed be the God and father of our Lord Jesus Christ." The special filial relationship between Jesus and God is woven into this prayer formula (cf. Rom. 15:6; 1 Cor. 8:6; 2 Cor. 11:31; Col. 1:3; 2 John 3).

A similar blessing formula is found in a prayer of Jesus, wherein he addresses God as Father (Luke 10:21; cf. Matt. 11:25-26):

> I thank [*exhomologoumai*] thee Father, Lord of heaven and earth, that thou hast hidden these things from the wise and understanding and revealed them to babes; yes, Father, for such was thy gracious will.

God is also addressed as Father in the prayer that, according to Luke 11:2-4 and Matt. 6:9-13, Jesus taught to his disciples. The two versions of the prayer are different, and Matthew's seven-sectioned rendering more closely resembles the form of Jewish prayer. On major feasts, the *amidah* (prayers said while standing) consisted of seven rather than eighteen benedictions. The phrases of the Matthean version (esp. the fifth, sixth, and ninth) resemble parts of those benedictions, especially the doxological *kaddish* (sanctification of the name): "Magnified and sanctified be his great name in the world which he created according to his will. May he establish his kingdom during your life." The use of set prayer forms seems to have been a persistent feature of early Christian worship.

The mutual influence of the prayer forms of the early church and the living memory of Jesus can be seen especially in the preservation of three Hebrew and Aramaic expressions in early Christian worship. In 1 Cor. 16:22, writing to a Greek-speaking, largely gentile community, Paul says, "If anyone has no love for the Lord, let him be accursed. Our Lord, come." The phrase "our Lord, come!" (*maranatha)* is in Aramaic. That Paul can employ the Aramaic in this context and presume its intelligibility is fascinating. It indicates first that it was a foreign-language phrase used by the community itself, in all likelihood in its liturgy of the Lord's Supper (cf. 1 Cor. 11:26: ". . . you proclaim the Lord's death until he comes"). Second, it means that Paul, who founded the community, handed on to it a tradition (cf. 1 Cor. 11:23) that had its origin in Aramaic-speaking circles, probably in Palestine. Third, it indicates that Jesus was called Lord (*maran*) in the early Palestinian communities as well as in the Diaspora.

A second Aramaic expression quoted by Paul is "abba," an affectionate term for "father." Paul cites it in Gal. 4:6 (cf. Rom. 8:15):

> Because you are sons, God has sent the spirit of his son into our hearts, cry-
> ing "Abba, Father."

This is probably also a liturgical expression, as indicated by the context in Galatians (see 3:23-29). What is most striking here is not simply that the Spirit enables the cry, or that it is spoken in Aramaic by Greek-speaking Christians, but that the content of the cry, "Abba," is most distinctively associated with Jesus in his earthly life. The most significant occurrence is when Jesus prays to God before his death (Mark 14:36):

> Abba, Father, all things are possible to thee; remove this cup from me. Yet, not
> what I will, but what thou wilt.

The third expression is in Hebrew, and in it the interrelationship of the church's prayer and the memory of Jesus is particularly complicated. It is the simple word "amen." As used in Jewish prayer, it expressed an affirmative response ("so be it" see, e.g., 1 Cor. 14:16) to a statement or wish made by others or to a prayer said by oneself. Typically it came at the end of a statement and in this form is used throughout the epistolary writings of the NT (Rom. 1:25; 11:36; 15:33; 1 Cor. 16:24; Gal. 1:5; Eph. 3:21; Phil. 4:20; 1 Thess. 3:13; 1 Tim. 1:17; Heb. 13:21; 1 Pet. 4:11; 2 Pet. 3:18; Jude 25; Rev. 1:6-7). On the other hand, one of the most distinctive aspects of Jesus' own speech, as reported in all four Gospels, is his use of "amen." Jesus, however, used it to affirm the truth not of another's statement but always of his own, and he never said it at the end of a declaration but always at the beginning: "Amen, I say to you" (see, e.g., Mark 8:12; 11:23; Matt. 5:18; 16:28; Luke 4:24; 21:32; John 1:51; 5:19). In the light of this, one can only wonder at the characterization found in Rev. 3:14. The risen Lord, seen in a vision, employs the phrase "The words of the Amen, the faithful and true witness, the beginning of God's creation." And in 2 Cor. 1:18-20, again with specific reference to Jesus, Paul says,

> As surely as God is faithful, our word to you has not been yes and no. For the
> son of God, Jesus Christ, whom we preached among you, Silvanus and Timo-
> thy and I, was not yes and no; but in him it is always yes. For all the promises
> of God find their yes in him. That is why we utter the Amen through him, to
> the glory of God.

Alongside the prayers, the Christians also sang "hymns" to Christ (see the interest-ing reference to this practice in Pliny the Younger *Letters* 10.96.7). The worship services undoubtedly included the singing of songs, psalms, and hymns (1 Cor. 14:26; Eph. 5:19; Col. 3:16; Rev. 5:9; 14:3; 15:3). Through certain formal features—use of an intro-ductory relative pronoun and rhythmic strophes—it is possible to detect at least frag-ments of such hymns in the NT epistolary literature, where they are used as the basis for exhortation (Phil. 2:6-11; Col. 1:15-20; 1 Tim. 3:16; 1 Pet. 1:22-25; 3:18, 22). Of these, the hymns in 1 Peter and Philippians show the clearest interest in, and resemblance to, the memory of Jesus as described in the Gospels. Several of the hymns in the Book of Revelation (e.g., 4:11; 5:9) are addressed to both God and "the Lamb," and are almost purely songs of praise.

Spiritual Utterances. The pervasiveness and importance of this aspect of early Christian worship are difficult to assess. There is scattered evidence of speaking in tongues and prophecy in several writings (see Mark 16:17; Acts 2:4; 11:27; 21:9-10; Rom. 12:6; 1 Thess. 5:20; 1 Tim. 4:14; Rev. 19:10). We also hear of prophets as persons with gifts sufficiently regular in their manifestation to be recognized together with apostles and teachers (Acts 13:1; 1 Cor. 12:28; Eph. 2:20; Rev. 10:7). We find a detailed account of these activities, however, only in 1 Cor. 12:1-14:40, which is devoted to the problems generated by an unstructured expression of these gifts. We cannot even say whether the manifestation of these gifts took place in conjunction with, or separate from, other forms of worship, such as the Lord's Supper. The distinctive feature of these forms of speech is that they are regarded as directly inspired by the Holy Spirit—in effect, by the Spirit of Jesus (1 Cor. 12:4-11). Speaking in tongues was fundamentally an ecstatic mode of prayer (see 1 Cor. 14:2, 14-16). Prophecy, in contrast, although it was equally inspired (1 Cor. 12:10), had a rational element to it (1 Cor. 14:19) and issued in speech intelligible to others (1 Cor. 14:16). Paul therefore views prophecy as speech that can build up (*oikodomein*) the community in its faith (1 Cor. 14:4-5, 12, 17, 24-25). This much is clear.

More difficult to determine is the content of prophetic "revelations" (1 Cor. 14:26, 30) and the relationship of these sayings to the memory of Jesus. If, on the pattern of oracles in Torah (Isa. 1:10; Jer. 2:2; Amos 7:16), "prophetic words" (2 Pet. 1:19) were introduced as a "word" (2 Thess. 2:2), or the "word of God" (Rev. 1:2, 9; 19:9), or the "word of the Lord" (1 Thess. 4:15), then there could easily develop complex relationships between what came from the Lord as life-giving Spirit now present to the community (see 2 Cor. 3:18) and what came from the Lord by way of the memory of what Jesus said in his earthly ministry (cf. the ambiguity in 1 Cor. 7:10; 11:23; 14:37; 1 Thess. 4:2; 2 Thess. 3:6).

An example of such complexity is the saying that Jesus would return "like a thief." In Rev. 3:3b, we find it as a statement of the risen Lord, delivered through prophecy to the church:

> If you will not awake, I will come like a thief, and you will not know at what hour I will come upon you.

It appears as a classic case of prophetic revelation. Yet, immediately before it, comes "Remember then what you received and heard; keep that and repent" (Rev. 3:3a). Is the prophet repeating an earlier tradition in his own prophetic utterance? If so, what was its source? Next, we find the tradition in a letter by Paul, who tells the Thessalonians (1 Thess. 5:2; cf. 2 Pet. 3:10):

> You yourselves well know that the day of the Lord will come like a thief in the night.

Finally, we find it in the Gospels. In an eschatological discourse of the earthly Jesus (Matt. 24:42-43; Luke 12:39), there is this variation:

> Watch, therefore, for you do not know on what day your Lord is coming. But know this, if the householder had known in what part of the night the thief was coming, he would have watched and not let his house be broken into.

The possible relations between these versions are obviously manifold. The prophetic utterance to the community could have initiated the saying, subsequently becoming part of the memory of Jesus reported in the Gospels. Or the prophetic word could have recalled in the power of the Spirit a word said by Jesus during his ministry, and this prophetic utterance then might have affected the way it was reported in the Gospel narrative. We cannot, it goes without saying, determine the direction of the flow of influence. But we can observe the complexity, learning from it how the memory of Jesus was undoubtedly influenced by what was said by him in the past as teacher and what was perceived to be coming from him in the present as risen Lord. The process is made even more complex when we remember that the memory of Jesus could also have been affected by cultural parallels.

In another example—the expression "the judge is at the door"—the point is made even clearer. In Rev. 3:20, there is a prophetic message of the risen Lord:

> Behold, I *stand at the door* and knock; if anyone hears my voice and opens the door, I will come in to him and eat with him and him with me.

In the Letter of James 5:8-9, we find the same image in an eschatological warning:

> Establish your hearts, for the coming of the Lord is at hand. Do not grumble, brethren, against one another, that you may not be judged. Behold, *the judge is standing at the doors*.

We also find the image in an eschatological saying of Jesus (Matt. 24:33; Mark 13:29):

> So also, when you see these things, you know that he is near, *at the very doors*.

The same image, in sum, occurs in a prophetic utterance of the risen Lord, in a paraenetic letter, and in the Gospels. It is thus evident that an interrelation exists between prophetic utterances in the community and the narrative development of the memory of Jesus in the early church.

Reading and Preaching. Here in all probability is a case of a practice being so well established that we find little specific evidence for it. The church remembered that Jesus had read and preached in the synagogue (Luke 4:16-30; cf. Mark 6:1-6; Matt. 13:53-58; John 6:59), as Paul had also done (Acts 13:13-16). Indeed, Acts includes an episode of Paul preaching to an assembly gathered for the Lord's Supper (20:7-9). Yet we have no specific report of the reading of Torah in the Christian assembly for the earliest period, although Paul tells Timothy to "attend to the reading, prayer, and teaching" in the church at Ephesus in his absence (1 Tim. 4:13). The practice was so much a part of synagogue worship that we can assume its continuance in Christian worship with some confidence, particularly since it continued down into the period for which we have ample documentation (3rd and 4th centuries). Furthermore, the reading of Paul's letters out loud to the gathered assembly (2 Cor. 7:8; Col. 4:16; 1 Thess. 5:27; 2 Thess. 3:14) suggests that a precedent existed for such public reading. The two NT letters that have often been thought to have originated as sermons— 1 Peter and Hebrews—are marked by a very vigorous use of scriptural interpretation, such as would be appropriate for homiletic midrash. It would seem that such a context could account for the creative formation of some Gospel narratives in which Torah has shaped—both explicitly and implicitly—stories about Jesus. Beyond such suggestive remarks, however, one cannot go.

Teaching for the Common Life

The memory of Jesus was also selected and shaped by the experience of churches as they tried to live out the implications of their new identity within the structures of the world. The question of how to live in the light of their transcendent and powerful transformation was real. But equally pressing were the questions posed by their mundane circumstances. The first Christians had to deal with critical and obviously spiritual issues such as the discernment of true prophecy from counterfeit (1 Cor. 14:29; 1 Thess. 5:19-21; 1 John 4:1-3), but they were equally required to answer questions about the manifestations of the Spirit in their life together (Gal. 5:13-26), a life that included the realms of political and social structures, work, leisure, diet, and sexual activity. Did their new experience of God in Jesus have any implications for these aspects of their lives?

The necessity of coming to terms with such areas accounts for the development of teaching (*didaskalia, didachē*) in the early church. Teaching is an activity with many functions and settings, and the traditions that can be associated with it are extensive.

In Acts 19:9-10, Paul is said to have spent two years in Ephesus debating in the lecture hall of Tyrannus. From Paul's writings, it is clear that he saw himself as a teacher to his communities (1 Cor. 4:17; cf. 1 Tim. 2:7; 2 Tim. 1:11). If he followed the practice of some Cynic philosophers, he may even have taught his close followers while practicing his trade as a leather worker (Acts 18:3; 1 Thess. 2:9; 2 Thess. 3:6-12). Paul also taught his communities through trusted delegates whom he sent to remind them of his teachings and instructions (1 Cor. 4:17; Phil. 2:19-24; 1 Tim. 4:11; 2 Tim. 2:2; Titus 2:1). There were local teachers as well in the Pauline and other early Christian churches (Acts 13:1; 1 Cor. 12:28; Rom. 12:7; Gal. 6:6; Eph. 4:11; 1 Thess. 5:12; James 3:1). In 1 Cor. 14:26, "teaching" is placed among charismatic gifts such as tongues and prophecy, although most teaching was probably carried out in a non-ecstatic context.

Some communities may have followed the synagogue practice in which the study of Torah and prayer flowed naturally into each other; thus the synagogue was both a house of study and place of prayer. If Christian teaching took place in this context, we can locate such communal activities as midrash and diatribe, both of which appear in NT writings as the literary residue of an individual author, but also presuppose a prior process that is communal and scholastic in nature.

Such a context allows us to make some sense of the Pauline prohibitions against women speaking in the assembly (1 Cor. 14:34-36; 1 Tim. 2:11-15), even though it is clear that they are already praying and prophesying during worship (1 Cor. 11:5). If we take seriously the mention of teaching (1 Cor. 14:26) and learning (1 Tim. 2:11-12) in these passages, we may find Paul (cf. 1 Cor. 11:2-16) clinging to the cultural perception that moral teaching was a distinctively masculine obligation, specifically associated with the transmission of moral precepts from father to son (see 1 Cor. 4:14-15), whereas motherhood was the culturally appropriate mode for women to exercise influence over children's formation (1 Tim. 2:15). Despite this, it is clear that women were in fact also teaching—otherwise there would be no need for correction—and taking an active part in the Pauline mission (Rom. 16:1, 3, 6, 12).

The ambiguities of life together, combined with the need to clarify the relationship of that life to the gospel, proved to be influential in shaping the memory of Jesus. The questions formed by the church's life stimulated the memory of what Jesus had said and done, and the framing of those questions inevitably had impact on the eventual shape of the memory as it was passed on. At the same time, there was undoubtedly something to remember. The process was not one of untrammeled creative fantasy. The first generation of believers was not so caught up in a charismatic cloud that it could not distinguish between its own handiwork and tradition, or that it thought that such a distinction was unimportant.

The best example is Paul's carefully qualified discussion of virginity and marriage in 1 Cor. 7. In successive sentences, he distinguishes relative degrees of authority for his statements. In 7:8, he says "To the unmarried and widows, *I say* . . ."; but in 7:10, he asserts, "To the married I give charge, *not I but the Lord*, that a wife should not separate from her husband . . ." We see here that Paul distinguishes what he offers on his own authority and what is backed by a command of the Lord. We find, in fact, such an absolute prohibition against divorce enunciated by Jesus in the Gospels (Mark 10:11; cf. Matt. 5:31-32; 19:3-9; Luke 16:18). We do not know, unfortunately, whether Paul had that command by oral tradition from the past or by prophetic announcement in the present—or both. But he makes clear he did not invent the saying. This is made even more obvious when he continues in 7:12, "To the rest I say, *not the Lord . . . ,*" while in 7:25 he writes, "Concerning the unmarried, I have *no command of the Lord,* but I give *my opinion.*"

In response to the questions raised by their worldly circumstances, teachers sought to find precedent for the community's own practices (Why do we act this way?), and guidance for the community's decisions (What should we do in this situation?). They sought to find both in the words and deeds of Jesus. That they did so is the clearest sign of the importance of the memory of Jesus for the identity of the Christian community.

The community could, for example, find precedents for its practice of sending out preachers two by two (Acts 13:2; 15:40; 18:5; 1 Cor. 9:6) and for the shaking the dust off their feet when rejected by their hearers (Acts 13:51) in the practice and commands of Jesus (Mark 6:7-12; Matt. 10:14; Luke 9:5; 10:1, 11). Or, as the preachers exercised gifts of healing within the community (1 Cor. 12:9, 28-30), they could find the pattern of their healing by prayer and their anointing for forgiveness of sins (James 5:14-15) in the healing deeds of Jesus that led to the forgiveness of sins (Mark 2:9-10; pars). When they did not observe the Sabbath the way other Jews did but met together on the resurrection day, they could find precedent for their freedom from the Sabbath law in the deeds and words of Jesus (Mark 2:23-28; pars.; John 5:2-9). Those who chose not to observe days of fasting (Gal. 4:10; Rom. 14:5-6) found an example in the freedom of Jesus from fasting (Mark 2:18-21; pars.). Those who did choose to fast could also find warrant in the words of Jesus (Mark 2:19; Matt. 6:16-18). Those who enjoyed open fellowship with Jew and Gentile alike (Gal. 2:12-13; Acts 11:1-18) found a precedent in the free fellowship Jesus enjoyed with sinners and tax collectors (Mark 2:15-17; pars.). In cases like these, it is impossible for us to determine whether the practice came from the narrative example or whether the narrative example was at least partially shaped by the practice.

Teaching also sought to provide guidance for future practice, since the demands of the gospel were not obvious in every circumstance. Paul was able, we have seen, to apply a saying of the Lord to one aspect of sexual behavior, namely, divorce, and he could call on the whole range of Jewish precedent to exclude obvious sexual immorality (see 1 Cor. 5:1-5; 1 Thess. 4:3-8). But for other aspects of sexual behavior, he could offer only advice. We see a similar situation with regard to work. Should Christians who expect the imminent return of the Lord continue in their worldly occupations, making a living and earning money for their families? The answer was not obvious (1 Cor. 7:29-31). Paul faced a critical instance of the problem in Thessalonica (1 Thess.

4:11; 2 Thess. 3:6-12). Here he reminds the community not only of his own example of working for a living (2 Thess. 3:7-9) but also of his earlier command that all should work (3:10), a directive he refers to as part of the *tradition* they had received from him (3:6). Following upon this, he emphatically repeats the phrase, "in the Lord Jesus Christ" (3:12). Had Paul handed on to them sayings of the Lord regarding work? He was certainly aware of specific commands of Jesus concerning such practical matters as support for the gospel (see 1 Cor. 9:14; 1 Tim. 5:18). And if so, did these commands resemble the sort of sayings we find in Luke 10:7; 12:37-48; and 17:7-10? We cannot be certain, but it is possible.

Another example is provided by the problem of diet in Corinth. Did Christians need to establish alternative sources for their food to ensure its purity, or could they purchase and eat their food anywhere without regard for its possible contact with idols? In Paul's careful discussion of this issue (1 Corinthians 8–10), he does not refer to any decision made by the church as a whole (cf. Acts 15:23-29), nor does he refer to any sayings of Jesus. In some communities, however, a similar problem must have activated the memory of a teaching by Jesus on just this point, for in Jesus' controversy with the Pharisees over purification, the direction of Jesus' teaching is succinctly summarized: "Thus he declared all foods clean" (Mark 7:19).

Still other practical questions required answering. How were Christians to use their material possessions? Were the commandments of Torah binding on them, and if so, how? Their memory of Jesus made it clear that the love of God and neighbor was at the heart of their obligation (Mark 12:28-34; Matt. 22:34-40; Luke 10:25-28; Gal. 5:14; Rom. 13:8-10; James 2:8). But what did that mean in specific cases? Who was the neighbor? These issues are raised in the epistolary literature, and we find teachings on these issues in the sayings and stories of the gospel tradition (see, e.g., Luke 10:25-37; 12:13-34; 16:1-13). The precise connection between the questions and the apparent answers reflected in the narratives about Jesus cannot, however, be firmly established.

Today's critical reader, therefore, faces a very real problem: it is impossible to sort out exactly what came from the earthly Jesus and what originated in the spirit-filled utterances from the "risen Lord." This was not, however, a problem for those who lived by these utterances. For them, the same Holy Spirit at work in the deeds and words of Jesus in the past was at work among them now. Both the present worship of Jesus as Lord and the memory of Jesus as teacher shaped the identity of the church. The selecting and shaping of that memory were regarded not as betrayal or distortion but as a deeper insight and understanding of the past by those who continued to live in the presence of the beloved (see John 2:22; 7:39; 12:16; 20:9-10). The words of Jesus in his last discourse in the Fourth Gospel (John 14:25-26) give accurate expression to the religious understanding that underlies this development of tradition concerning Jesus:

These things I have spoken to you, while I am still with you. But the Counselor, the Holy Spirit, whom the father will send in my name, he will teach you all things, and bring to your remembrance all that I have said to you.

The Forms of Memory: Speech and Writing

Present-day readers of the NT encounter finished literary compositions. Trying to recover the process by which those compositions came into existence involves close analysis as well as a certain amount of guesswork. As the previous sections of this chapter have shown, it is possible to suggest plausible social settings within which the memory of Jesus was shaped and transmitted. More difficult is determining the mix of oral and written elements in the process. Certainly there is strong evidence to suggest that the memory of Jesus was conveyed orally in a variety of settings. But it must be remembered as well that the Christian movement was literary from the start—as evidenced by Paul's letters (our earliest evidence for the existence of Christianity) as well as the letters from other early Christian leaders.

But to what extent were the memories concerning Jesus written down before being included in the compositions we call Gospels? Scholars remain divided on this issue, some emphasizing the oral process, others the written. To some extent, a rigid bifurcation is a distortion, since we know that in both Jewish and Greco-Roman cultures, literary and oral activities often overlapped: Rabbis kept notes on halachic debates that were later codified; rhetoricians wrote out speeches that were later delivered orally; correspondents read aloud the written letters that were initially dictated orally to scribes; and the lectures of philosophers were transcribed. Furthermore, in antiquity all "reading" was a form of oral performance. The distinction between "oral" and "scribal" culture, therefore, should not be made too sharply, and is useful mainly as a reminder that these modes of expression interacted in complex ways.

In the following discussion, we look first at those parts of the memory about Jesus that fit most obviously within the framework of oral tradition, without thereby denying that aspects of writing may have been at work. Then we turn to an examination of that part of the gospel story in which the process of writing, or scribal, activity may most easily be seen, without thereby implying that there was no antecedent oral tradition.

Oral Memory and the Stories About Jesus

The memory of Jesus was affected not only by the social contexts of the early Christian churches, but also by certain persistent habits of human memory, particularly by the way it molds the past into usable pieces for the present. An awareness of these patterns—together with the simple observation that in the various canonical Gospels we find individual short segments of material of striking similarity being used in quite different arrangements—leads us to the recognition that the Gospels are written compositions that employ diverse traditions handed down by both oral and written transmission over a period of some forty years. Oral traditions were passed on, furthermore, not in ordered or sustained narratives, but in short sayings and stories. Their stereotypical patterns result from the process of telling and retelling in community contexts. We turn, then, to some consideration of those sayings and stories in which the memory of Jesus was mediated to the Gospel writers. The process of transmission may be grasped in its essential lines by developing a rather extended analogy, one whose anachronistic character and simplicity will remind us that these observations are not a matter of science but of appreciating the art of storytelling.

We can imagine a family remembering its recently deceased matriarch. The family as a social group engages in this sort of recollection especially at ritual occasions, such as holiday meals and ceremonies of passage like graduations, weddings, and funerals. The occasion, or some part of the ritual, triggers the process of remembrance. Someone will begin, "Remember how Grandma used to say . . . ," and then all join in. The basic form of remembrance is the short tale or anecdote. Even Grandma's wise sayings or memorable mannerisms are related to tales that set up the significant point.

Many of the stories sound alike. The matriarch quite likely repeated herself in word and action in her long life and was observed by different witnesses on various occasions. Her repeated and characteristic behavior in the past, therefore, aids the process of forging her memory into set forms. While the stories are being told, there is also mutual correction taking place. Older members with longer memories correct errors of sequence ("No, she said that *after* Grandpa died") and false attribution ("Grandma didn't say that; Aunt Hilda did"). When eyewitnesses are no longer around, the next generation is dependent on the form and sequence of the stories that the earlier process of criticism left as established. Then an even more formal shape is given to the memories: there is a collection of Our Grandmother stories capable of being told and retold even by generations who never knew her at all except as mediated by these tales.

Closer analysis of the casual family stories shows that they tend to fall into categories. The largest of the categories are those of Things Said and Things Done. Repeated settings and patterns provide the basis for further categories: "Arguing with Grandpa" or "Advice to the Grandchildren" stories. There might even be a loose collection of Grandma's One-Liners, sayings whose occasion no one can any longer recollect but whose bite and wit are so clearly hers that they are treasured as "typical of Grandma." Do they resemble bits of wisdom available elsewhere? It does not matter; Grandma made them her own, giving them her own personal stamp and style.

No one is in the least disturbed by a lack of exact chronology in these stories, by a certain amount of repetition, or by the failure to get all the details straight. This is not a biography that is being researched but a family remembering its beloved founder. The memory of her makes her come alive again, just as the eating of the pumpkin pie prepared according to her secret recipe almost makes her appear in the kitchen door.

An observation of several families thus reminiscing about their grandmothers would yield an even greater stock of remarkably similar stories. Since grandmothers do tend to act alike in certain ways, cultural stereotypes of "typical grandmotherly" behavior develop. Sometimes it is hard to tell how much the shape of one family's very real memories of its grandmother may be affected by these larger cultural patterns. That their grandmother happened to fit several of these stereotypes, however, in no way diminishes their sense of her as real and singular in her presence to them.

Oral tradition of this sort has certain consistent tendencies. First, the specific details of time and place are rapidly lost, for the simple reason that they are largely irrelevant. What is important is the significant saying or deed, not the occasion; the point of the story is who the grandmother was and therefore who the family is. Second, and for the same reason, the punch line or decisive gesture is remembered far more clearly than the setup or situation in which it is now enclosed. Indeed, at times the situations almost appear to be interchangeable. Sometimes only the punch line is remembered and the family debates the appropriate setting. Third, the more often the stories are repeated, the shorter they get. They become more formulaic, tighter in focus, snappier. As a result, over time the stories tend to resemble each other more. The first time a story is told, it is filled with extraneous detail and subjective reactions; with frequent repetition it is reduced to the essentials.

The possibility of applying this analogy to the development of the memory of Jesus in the church seems clear. We have seen how ritual occasions and the need for community teaching stimulated the memory of Jesus among those who believed in him as risen Lord. We have also observed that the community's need for precedent and guidance gave this memory a definite shape, even as it shaped the community's identity.

The analogy also helps us see how a large number of stories about Jesus in the Gospels fall into stereotypical *forms*. However, there are limits to such an analysis. The first limit involves our analytic precision. Of course it is possible to divide the memories of Jesus into Things Said and Things Done, as it is possible to describe other subgroupings. But we must recognize that not only are forms combined (e.g., an exorcism story and a controversy story joined together into a literary whole, as in Mark 1:21-28) but also that some materials escape classification altogether. Second, care must be taken not to deduce too readily from the form of a story its life-setting or function within that setting. The real value in cataloguing these forms is twofold: it enables us to appreciate how the memory of Jesus was carried by means of short units rather than by complex discourses and narratives; and the description of a formal pattern enables us to detect deviations from it, which may prove helpful for the understanding of a particular story.

Among the sayings of Jesus, we find controversy stories, parables, aphorisms, and other looser discourses. Controversy stories (e.g., Mark 2:15—3:6; 7:1-23; 10:2-9; 12:13-17, 18-27, 28-34; pars.) have a regular sequence of elements: (1) an action by Jesus or his disciples (2) stimulates a challenge from opponents, which leads to (3) a pronouncement by Jesus. The pronouncement is often a well-formed statement of more general application than the particular situation that generated the controversy. In his parables, Jesus compares some readily observable natural or human phenomenon to the kingdom of God. Some parables are used for attack (Mark 3:23-27), others for defense (Luke 15:4-10); some attempt to enlighten (Matt. 13:24-30), others to mystify (Mark 4:3-8). They range from simple analogies (Matt. 13:44-46) to extended allegories (Mark 12:1-11), but all of them give a narrative form to metaphor.

In Jesus' aphorisms, we find single striking statements that can easily be separated from, or are only loosely attached to, their literary setting in the gospel story. Sometimes they are found joined together by the mnemonic device of catch-words (see, e.g., Mark 8:34-37). Other sayings material is less easily categorized. The apocalyptic discourse of Jesus in Mark 13, for example, can be broken down into individual parts (aphorisms, parables), but it also holds together as a sustained unit.

As with the controversy stories, other narratives about Jesus also reveal formal patterns. The most regular pattern is found in the healing and exorcism stories. In healing narratives, we find the following: (1) the notice of the sickness, (2) the action by Jesus, (3) the result, (4) the reaction of bystanders (see, e.g., Mark 1:30-31, 40-45; 2:1-12; 5:21-42; 7:31-37; 8:22-26; pars.). The pattern of exorcism narratives tends to be very similar: (1) the mention of the demoniac, (2) the dialogue between spirits and Jesus, (3) the command to depart, (4) the physical sign of departure, (5) the restored state of the exorcised person, (6) the reaction of bystanders (see, e.g., Mark 1:23-28; 5:1-13; 7:24-30; 9:17-29; pars.). Some stories about Jesus, such as his nature miracles (e.g., Mark 4:35-41; 6:45-52; pars.) and his feeding of the crowds (Mark 6:34-44; 8:1-10; pars.), do not fit as easily into set forms. Still other stories, like that of the transfiguration (Mark 9:2-8 pars.), resist categorization completely.

Two further literary remarks can be made about these patterns. First, the formal shape of many of the stories suggests that they were shortened and tightened with repetition, and thus grew to resemble each other; that they preserved the essential deed or saying more accurately than the circumstance; and that they had little concern for geography and chronology. Second, the stories about Jesus also resemble stories found in the broader cultural world of the first century. The form, if not the substance, of many of Jesus' sayings can be paralleled in parables told by rabbis, in *chreia* (short biographical vignettes with pronouncements) attributed to philosophers, and in controversy stories found in both traditions. The healings and exorcisms of Jesus can be paralleled by similar accounts in Hellenistic religious aretalogies and biographies.

The Memory of Jesus' Death and the Interpretation of Torah

Jesus' death on the cross became the most complex memory in the early church, requiring, therefore, the most interpretation. The shape and extent of that interpretation illustrate well the range of the church's creativity in transmitting Jesus' memory. I will begin with some general observations on the Passion narratives, which recount Jesus' last hours from his final supper with his disciples to his burial. Then I will raise questions concerning the origination of the accounts, before once more returning to the texts.

All four canonical Gospels have Passion narratives (Mark 14:1—15:47; Matt. 26:1—27:66; Luke 22:1—23:56; John 13:1—19:42). In each, the narrative is by far the most extensive segment in Jesus' story. This length is all the more impressive since the Passion narratives of each Gospel are coherent and sustained stories, rather than the sort of loose sequence of smaller units we find in the narratives concerning Jesus' ministry. Each is a narrative, moreover, that pays fastidious attention to detail. Notices of time and place elsewhere in the Gospels tend to be casual and vague; here they are specific. Elsewhere, long stretches of time can be indicated by "and then," whereas here we find virtually a minute-by-minute account.

The Passion narratives, furthermore, have a relatively high degree of agreement among them. The agreement is most striking between the Synoptic Gospels and the Gospel of John. The agreement of the Synoptics (Matthew, Mark, Luke) among themselves can to some extent be credited to their literary interdependence, but their accord with the Gospel of John requires a more complex explanation. Differences of detail and emphasis persist, to be sure; but by contrast to the rest of the story of Jesus, the Passion accounts show a remarkable unanimity. Even the relationship between the Passion narrative and the rest of the story of Jesus shows agreement as each Gospel meticulously prepares for the suffering and death of Jesus ahead of time, so that the course of the narrative as a whole points in the direction of Jesus' inevitable end. In the Synoptics, Jesus formally predicts his death three times (Mark 8:31; 9:31; 10:33-34; pars.). In John, repeated mention of Jesus' "hour," his "being lifted up," and his "being glorified" serve the same function of foreshadowing the cross (John 2:4; 3:14; 7:6, 39; 12:27-32).

These observations tend to support the conclusion that the Passion narratives are the earliest sustained accounts of Jesus' memory, indicating that the part of Jesus' life most requiring interpretation was its last hours. This is further supported by Paul's close agreement with a small segment of that narrative in his report of Jesus' words at the last supper, written some twenty years after the event (see 1 Cor. 11:23-25).

Paul's First Letter to the Corinthians also provides some insight into the reason it was necessary to crystallize this memory of Jesus so early in the church's life. When discussing the resurrection experience earlier, the kerygmatic tradition in 1 Cor. 15:3-8 was cited. Before Paul speaks of the resurrection "according to the Scriptures," he says that Jesus "died according to the Scriptures and was buried." He also insists that this is the message upon which their salvation rests—unless they believe in vain (1 Cor. 15:2). This insistence was necessary because the cross was the most difficult part of the message to accept. Everywhere in 1 Corinthians, we meet a congregation that was richly gifted with spiritual powers (1 Cor. 1:5, 7), understanding that this bestowal of power established them as leading members in God's kingdom (4:8). They were, therefore, less than eager to hear a part of the message that implied the need to suffer. Indeed, when Paul refers to his preaching to them, he says that the cross is foolishness to those who are perishing but "the power of God" to those being saved (1:18). He says further that the cross is "a stumbling block to the Jews and a folly to Gentiles." Why? "Because Jews demand signs and Gentiles seek wisdom" (1:22). But Paul's preaching did not meet those expectations: "we preach Christ crucified" (1:23; cf. Gal. 3:1). Paul here makes it plain that the preaching of the crucified Messiah reversed the expectations of his hearers' symbolic world. Not only were the expectations of outsiders overturned, but the expectations of insiders as well. The cross was the part of their experience of Jesus that demanded immediate and detailed interpretation.

By the standards of Hellenistic heroes, Jesus' end was obviously unimpressive. He had faced death not with apathetic calm but with fear and anguish; he had left his followers not with words of memorable grace but with a cry of utter desolation (Matthew and Mark); he had not embraced a dignified suicide but endured a grisly execution; he did not bypass death through elevation to divinity, escape it through sophistry, or use it as an opportunity to demonstrate virtue. He was simply executed as a common criminal. To Greeks, therefore, the cross was foolishness and weakness. Divine power (*dynamis*) did not work in this manner.

For those who lived within the symbols of Torah, Jesus' death was even harder to reconcile with the claim to have experienced the Holy Spirit through him. When they looked to Jesus for signs of messiahship, they were disappointed. He failed miserably and palpably by any zealot test of messiahship: he did not restore kingship, he bore only its mocking title on the tree. His death was particularly a "stumbling block" (see Rom. 9:33; 1 Pet. 2:8; cf. Luke 20:17, with reference to Isa. 8:14) for those Jews who had hoped for a religious messiah, one who would establish the rule of God's righteousness under Torah. Not only did he not fulfill in any visible or significant manner the recognized messianic texts (e.g., 2 Sam. 7:11-16; Psalms 45; 89; Isa. 9:2-7; 11:1-16; 49:8-13; 52:1-12; Amos 9:11; Micah 5:2-4; Mal. 3:1-4; 4:5), he was not even a recognizable martyr like those who resisted pagan pressure in the Maccabean accounts, thereby dying in defense of Torah (see esp. 2 Macc. 6:18-31 and 4 Macc. 5:1-7:23). Rather, from the beginning to the end he was a "sign of contradiction" (Luke 2:34), standing in complete opposition to their understanding of how God manifested his power and righteousness among his people. His life and death alike challenged the status of Torah as the absolute norm for life. In his manner of living, he was a sinner (2 Cor. 5:21), and in his manner of dying, he was one accursed by God. Torah could not, on this, be clearer: "Cursed be every man who hangs upon a tree" (Deut. 21:23). In the light of Jesus' death, this text must have been cited against the claims of the first Christians (see Gal. 3:13). Far from being the source of the Holy Spirit, Jesus was abandoned by God and his death proved it!

For those who believed in Jesus as risen Lord, the problem was no less severe. How could they ease the tension between their experience of the power of Jesus in their lives and the conviction they shared as hearers of Torah, that God did not work through sinners? Once more, we find the conflict between experience and symbolic world. And it is here we discover the impetus for interpretation: to defend their faith from outside attack and to support it against inner erosion and confusion.

Now we can return to Paul's puzzling statement that Jesus' death was "in accordance with the Scriptures." This was a bold claim, especially if Torah itself called his death a curse. Because of this contradiction, the first Christians turned again to the normative texts of their symbolic world. They reread Torah in search of meaning. This was an instinctive move. The same texts that condemned Jesus were the normative texts by which they understood their experience as well. But now they had to read them in the light of both the resurrection and the manner of Jesus' death. And this led them to texts they had never before considered messianic, causing them to read old texts in new ways. It was as though their eyes had been opened. Indeed, two Gospels make this aspect of the resurrection experience quite clear. In John's Gospel, it was when Jesus was raised from the dead that the disciples began to understand *both* what he had said and done *and* the Scripture (John 2:22; 12:16; 20:9). In Luke's appearance accounts, the risen Lord "opens the eyes" of the disciples to the real meaning of Torah: "Beginning with Moses and the Prophets, he interpreted to them in all the Scriptures the things concerning himself" (Luke 24:27; cf. 24:44-46).

Several key texts became newly visible as a result of the experience of the crucified and raised Messiah. In light of the resurrection, the first Christians appropriated the text that spoke of a king exalted to dominion but whose rule was not yet fully achieved (Ps. 110:1; cf. Mark 12:36; pars.; Acts 2:34; 1 Cor. 15:25; Heb. 1:3). In light of the suffering, they discovered texts that spoke not of a dominating king but of a lowly one (Zech. 9:9), and of a stone that was rejected by builders but had become the cornerstone (Ps. 118:22). Above all, they read with fresh eyes passages speaking of a just person who suffered at the hands of others not because of misdeeds but because of an allegiance to the Lord, hoping all the while for vindication from God for his fidelity (passages such as these they found in Psalms 69 and 22; cf. also Wis. 2:12—3:11; 4:7-18). In the Suffering Servant songs of Isaiah, they found almost the precise pattern of what, in fact, they had experienced in Jesus: a righteous one whose shameful death was in obedience to God and an offering for others (Isa. 42:1-4; 49:1-7; 50:4-11), the result of which led to his being "exalted and lifted up" by God (Isa. 52:13—53:12). In the encounter between Philip and the Ethiopian eunuch (Acts 8:29-40), the God-fearer who was reading Isa. 53:7-8 asked Philip of whom the prophet Isaiah spoke, himself or another. In answering, "Philip opened his mouth, and beginning with this Scripture, he told him the good news of Jesus" (Acts 8:35).

Such rereading and reinterpretation of the texts of Torah enabled Christians to place the experience of Jesus within their symbolic world. The way they read these texts would never find agreement among those Jews who did not share their experience or their conviction. But for them, the interpretive process was effective and convincing. They were not manipulating or distorting the texts; they were simply and truly seeing them in a new way.

These perceptions had to affect both the way they remembered the story of Jesus' last days and the manner in which they told that story. Now, the death of Jesus appeared to them not as accursed, but as a death in which he bore the curse of others (Gal. 3:13). Jesus was not a sinner but a righteous man (Luke 23:47; Acts 3:14), whose death was not a punishment but a sacrifice for others (Rom. 3:24-25; 1 Cor. 15:3). His death was not an accident but a fulfillment of God's will (Eph. 1:5-10). Rather than being the result of disobedience to Torah, his death was, in fact, the outcome of radical obedience to the God who revealed Torah (Phil. 2:8; Heb. 5:8), and, in light of it, Torah would now need to be reevaluated as the ultimate norm of righteousness. These convictions they found confirmed by Torah itself. The categories of interpretation became their categories of perception, and these progressively became the symbols by which they told the story itself.

In Jesus' Passion predictions, we find expressed the conviction that not only did Jesus know of his fate and accept it but that this fate was part of God's plan: "the son of man must [*dei*] suffer" (Mark 8:31; Luke 9:22; 17:25; cf. Luke 24:26; Acts 17:3). In the Passion narrative itself, Jesus tells his disciples at the meal that "the son of man goes as it is written of him" (Mark 14:21). As he gives them the cup of his blood, he says it is "for many" (Mark 14:24; cf. 10:45), words that directly recall the death of the servant "for many" in Isaiah 53:12. After the meal, Jesus himself cites the Scripture concerning his disciples' betrayal (Mark 14:27, citing Zech. 13:7):

> You will all fall away, for it is written, "I will strike the shepherd, and the sheep will be scattered." But after I am raised up, I will go before you to Galilee.

The impact of this rereading of Torah shows itself most emphatically in the description of Jesus' death. It was the moment of greatest scandal; it appears meaningless as fact. Yet, for the early believers, it was the meaningful revelation of "the power of God." In this scene, then, we find the very words of Torah shaping the story of Jesus' last moments. There is considerable variation between the Synoptics and John at this point. While John also uses the words of Torah to narrate the story, he utilizes entirely different texts to do so. I take notice only of Mark's account here.

In Mark's account, at the moment of his own death, Jesus cries, "My God, my God, why have you forsaken me?" Mark cites this in Hebrew and has the bystanders, ironically, misunderstand it. The readers hear it translated and understand. They recognize it as the beginning of the psalm of God's servant who suffers and is vindicated (Psalm 22), and they know the end of the story. A closer look at Mark 15:23-37 indicates that the words of Torah have provided more than a mere citation. Woven into the bare facts of the account are details that are shaped directly and unmistakably from the very words of the Psalms: Mark 15:23 = Ps. 69:21; Mark 15:24 = Ps. 22:18; Mark 15:29 = Pss. 22:7, 109:25; Mark 15:31 = Ps. 22:8; Mark 15:34 = Ps. 22:1; Mark 15:36 = Ps. 69:21). In this way, the Story of Jesus' Death is truly "according to Torah."

How did the continuing experience of Christians affect this memory of Jesus' death? They saw it from the other side of the resurrection and so remembered the death in the light of Jesus' power and the conviction that he was the Just One and God's Son. They saw it, further, in the light of their responses to Jewish counterclaims that Jesus' death was that of a sinner. Finally, in the process of recollection, they interpreted the death through their reading of Torah.

But did they invent or create this memory of Jesus' death? Precisely the need for interpretation—indeed, the problematic nature of that event—argues for its basic historicity. This community would not have invented a crucified messiah, since it showed itself so eager to escape the implications of that proposition. When we read the Passion narratives of the Gospels, therefore, we find a memory that, while unquestionably selected and shaped by the experience of the church, is equally a memory that itself shaped the church.

What we have discovered here can be applied, one suspects, with a somewhat lesser degree of certainty to the other memories of Jesus. Something happened, but the search for its meaning must recognize the element of interpretation that is always present. Indeed, only as interpreted could it be remembered at all.

Conclusion

In this chapter, I have attempted to provide a viable and defensible account of the generative experience that makes intelligible both the need to remember Jesus and the shape those memories took. Such an attempt must always be more suggestive than conclusive; perhaps that is its value. If the reader now turns to the individual writings of the NT with a sense that the process of their composition is somehow intelligible, the exercise is well rewarded.

And as the reader turns to these diverse writings, it should be with the following realizations: they are crystallizations of traditions that developed in complex and multiform contexts; they were written as witnesses and interpretations for other believers; they continue to engage, in their various literary forms, the symbolic world of first-century Judaism and Hellenism as they translate the story of Jesus for the continuing life of the church.

Study Questions

1. What were the major stages in the first geographical expansion of the earliest churches? What major regions are not covered in the book of Acts?

2. How did "teaching" reshape the memory of Jesus in the earliest churches?

3. What were the central "cultic" actions of the earliest churches?

4. What accounts for such extensive reflections on Jesus' death? How do the passion narratives in the Gospels reflect "cognitive dissonance"?

Bibliographical Note

This chapter's title is borrowed from the book by N. A. Dahl, *Jesus in the Memory of the Early Church* (Minneapolis: Augsburg Pub. House, 1976) wherein one can find his seminal article on *anamnēsis*. That essay, together with another significant piece, "The Crucified Messiah," is of fundamental importance for understanding the development of the gospel tradition (see the latter study and other of his essays in *Jesus the Christ: The Historical Origins of Christological Doctrine*, D. H. Juel [ed.] [Minneapolis: Fortress Press, 1991]).

For a sense of the Christian movement into the Greco-Roman world, see P. Brown, *Authority and the Sacred: Aspects of the Christianization of the Roman World* (Cambridge: Cambridge Univ. Press, 1995); A. Harnack, *The Mission and Expansion of Christianity in the First Three Centuries*, trans. J. Moffatt (New York: Harper & Brothers, 1961 [1908]); E. G. Hinson, *The Evangelization of the Roman Empire: Identity and Adaptability* (Macon, Ga.: Mercer Univ. Press, 1981); and R. MacMullen, *Christianizing the Roman Empire (A.D. 100–400)* (New Haven: Yale Univ. Press, 1984).

Various aspects of the social dimension of the earliest Christian movement are found in R. Banks, *Paul's Idea of Community: The Early House Churches in Their Historical Setting*, rev. ed. (Grand Rapids: Eerdmans, 1994); J. V. Hills (ed.), *Common Life in the Early Church* (Harrisburg, Penn.: Trinity Press Int'l, 1998); E. A. Judge, *The Social Pattern of Christian Groups in the First Century* (London: Tyndale Press, 1960); H. C. Kee, *Who Are the People of God? Early Christian Models of Community* (New Haven: Yale Univ. Press, 1995); G. Lohfink, *Jesus and Community: The Social Dimension of Christian Faith*, trans. J. P. Galvin (Philadelphia: Fortress Press, 1984); A. J. Malherbe, *Social Aspects of Early Christianity*, 2nd ed. (Philadelphia: Fortress Press, 1983); C. Osiek and D. L. Balch, *Families in the New Testament World: Households and House Churches* (Louisville: Westminster/John Knox Press, 1997); and L. E. Vaage & V. Wimbush (eds.), *Asceticism and the New Testament* (New York: Routledge, 1999). One of the best attempts to place the development of traditions within the social contexts of worship and controversy is C. F. D. Moule, *The Birth of the New Testament*, 3rd ed. (New York: Harper & Row, 1982).

On the speeches of Acts and their relation to the gospel tradition, see C. H. Dodd, *The Apostolic Preaching and Its Development* (New York: Harper & Row, 1964 [1935]). Less confident of the traditional nature of these speeches is M. Dibelius, "The Speeches of Acts and Ancient Historiography," in *Studies in the Acts of the Apostles*, trans. M. Ling (New York: Charles Scribner's Sons; London: SCM Press, 1956), 138–85. On early Christian tradition, see J. D. G. Dunn, "Jesus Tradition in Paul," in B. Chilton and C. A. Evans (eds.), *Studying the Historical Jesus: Evaluations of the State of Current Research* (NTTS, 19; Leiden: E. J. Brill, 1994), 155–78; J. I. H. MacDonald, *Kerygma and Didache: The Articulation and Structure of the Earliest Christian Message* (SNTSMS, 37; Cambridge: Cambridge Univ. Press, 1980); and G. N. Stanton, *Jesus of Nazareth in New Testament Preaching* (SNTSMS, 27; Cambridge: Cambridge Univ. Press, 1974).

On the Christian practice of preaching, see H. O. Old, *The Reading and Preaching of the Scriptures in the Worship of the Christian Church;* vol. 1: *The Biblical Period* (Grand Rapids: Eerdmans, 1998). For the apologetic function of the preaching, see B. Lindars, *New Testament Apologetic: The Doctrinal Significance of the Old Testament Quotations* (Philadelphia: Westminster Press, 1961); and, with an emphasis on the generative power of the Scripture, C. H. Dodd, *According to the Scriptures: The Substructure of New Testament Theology* (London: Nisbet & Co., 1952). The complicated question of getting from Christian prophets to the traditions about Jesus is thoroughly treated by M. E. Boring, *The Continuing Voice of Jesus: Christian Prophecy & the Gospel Tradition* (Louisville: Westminster/John Knox Press, 1991). On early Christian worship, see G. Delling, *Worship in the New Testament*, trans. P. Scott (Philadelphia: Westminster Press, 1962); F. Hahn, *The Worship of the Early Church*, trans. D. E. Green (Philadelphia: Fortress Press, 1973); J. Jeremias, *The Prayers of Jesus*, trans. J. Reumann and J. Bowden (Philadelphia: Fortress Press, 1967); idem, *The Eucharistic Words of Jesus*, trans. N. Perrin (Philadelphia: Fortress Press, 1966); R. P. Martin, *Worship in the Early Church*, rev. ed. (Grand Rapids: Eerdmans, 1974); idem, "Patterns of Worship in New Testament Churches," *JSNT* 37 (1989): 59–85; and É. Nodet and J. Taylor, *The Origins of Christianity: An Exploration* (Collegeville: Liturgical Press, 1998), a thorough study of Eucharist and Baptism in early Christianity.

On baptism, see L. Hartman, *"Into the Name of Jesus": Baptism in the Early Church* (Edinburgh: T. & T. Clark, 1997). The issue of the exclusion of messianists from the synagogue is treated by W. Horbury, "The Benediction of the Minim and Early Jewish-Christian Controversy," *JTS* 33 (1982): 19–61; R. Kimmelman, "*Birkat ha minim* and the Lack of Evidence for an Anti-Christian Jewish Prayer in Late Antiquity," in *JCS-D* 2:226–44; and S. G. Wilson, *Related Strangers: Jews and Christians 70–170 C.E.* (Minneapolis: Fortress Press, 1995), 169–94.

The middle section of this chapter represents an attempt to convey the valuable contributions of the discipline called *form criticism*, without getting caught in its semantic or historical tangles. For introductory treatments, see E. McKnight, *What Is Form Criticism?* (GBS; Philadelphia: Fortress Press, 1969); M. J. Buss, *Biblical Form Criticism in Its Context* (JSOTSup, 274; Sheffield: Sheffield Academic Press, 1998); and R. Bultmann and K. Kundsin, *Form Criticism*, trans. F. C. Grant (New York: Harper & Brothers, 1934). For a survey of the literature, see W. G. Doty, "The Discipline and Literature of New Testament Form Criticism," *ATR* 51(1969): 257–321. The classic early studies available in English are those of M. Dibelius, *From Tradition to Gospel*, trans. B. Woolf (New York: Charles Scribner's Sons, 1934); and R. Bultmann, *The History of the Synoptic Tradition*, trans. J. Marsh, rev. ed. (New York: Harper & Row, 1968). The tendency of early form criticism to postulate an excessively creative community was countered from the side of rabbinic practice by H. Riesenfeld, "The Gospel Tradition and Its Beginnings" in *The Gospel Tradition* (Philadelphia: Fortress Press, 1970), 1–29; and B. Gerhardssohn, *The Origins of the Gospel Traditions* (Philadelphia: Fortress Press, 1979); and from the side of Greek biographical techniques by G. Kennedy, "Classical and Christian Source Criticism," in W. O. Walker, Jr. (ed.), *The Relationships among the Gospels: An Interdisciplinary Dialogue* (Dallas: Trinity Univ. Press, 1978), 125–55. A systematic attack on the methodological soundness of traditional form criticism was made by E. Guttgemanns, *Candid Questions Concerning Gospel Form Criticism*, trans. W. G. Doty (Pittsburgh: Pickwick Press, 1979). For recent discussion of the form-critical criteria, with sound revisions, see J. P. Meier, *A Marginal Jew: Rethinking the Historical Jesus; Vol. 1: The Roots of the Problem and the Person* (New York: Doubleday, 1991), 167–95; and N. T. Wright, *The New Testament and the People of God* (Minneapolis: Fortress Press, 1992), 418–43.

More recent developments in NT scholarship have challenged the older form-critical views by emphasizing the greater interplay between orality and literacy in the creation of early Christian discourse (see W. Kelber, *The Oral and the Written Gospel: The Hermeneutics of Speaking and Writing in the Synoptic Tradition, Mark, Paul, and Q* [Philadelphia: Fortress Press, 1983]), and the significant contribution of ancient rhetoric to the formation of early Christian texts (see B. L. Mack and V. K. Robbins, *Patterns of Persuasion in the Gospels* [Sonoma, Calif.: Polebridge Press, 1989]). On the overall importance of orality in early Christianity, see P. J. Achtemeier, "*Omne Verbum Sonat*: The New Testament and the Oral Environment of Late Western Antiquity," *JBL* 109 (1990): 3–27.

Helpful comments on the shaping of forms can be found in V. Taylor, *The Formation of the Gospel Tradition* (London: Macmillan & Co., 1957). A survey of NT forms is available in J. L. Bailey and J. D. Vander Broek, *Literary Forms in the New Testament: A Handbook* (Louisville: Westminster/John Knox Press, 1992); D. Dormeyer, *The New Testament Among the Writings of Antiquity*, trans. R. Kossov (BS, 55; Sheffield: Sheffield Academic Press, 1998); and G. Strecker, *History of New Testament Literature*, trans. C. Katter (with H. J. Mollenhauer) (Harrisburg, Pa.: Trinity Press Int'l, 1997). For an example of cross-cultural form-critical work, see the essays in R. Tannehill (ed.), *Pronouncement Stories, Semeia* 20 (1981).

On the formation of the narrative and tradition of the death of Jesus in early Christianity, see W. H. Bellinger, Jr. and W. R. Farmer (eds.), *Jesus and the Suffering Servant: Isaiah 53 and Christian Origins* (Harrisburg, Pa.: Trinity Press Int'l, 1998); R. E. Brown, *The Death of the Messiah: From Gethsemane to the Grave*, 2 vols. (New York: Doubleday, 1994); J. T. Carroll and J. B. Green et al., *The Death of Jesus in Early Christianity* (Peabody, Mass.: Hendrickson Pubs., 1995); J. B. Green, *The Death of Jesus: Tradition and Interpretation in the Passion Narrative* (WUNT, 2/33; Tübingen: J. C. B. Mohr [Paul Siebeck], 1988); E. Lohse, *History of the Suffering and Death of Jesus Christ*, trans. M. O. Dietrich (Philadelphia: Fortress Press, 1967); D. Moo, *The Old Testament in the Gospel Passion Narratives* (Sheffield: Almond Press, 1983); E. Trocmé, *The Passion as Liturgy: A Study in the Origin of the Passion Narratives in the Four Gospels* (London: SCM Press, 1983); and S. K. Williams, *Jesus' Death as Saving Event: The Background and Origin of a Concept* (HDR, 2; Missoula, Mont.: Scholars Press, 1975).

The approach taken in this chapter should be contrasted with those scholars who postulate a high degree of creativity in the formation of the Passion account without giving much attention to a basis in prior tradition: see J. D. Crossan, *The Cross That Spoke: The Origins of the Passion Narrative* (San Francisco: Harper & Row, 1988); idem, *Who Killed Jesus? Exposing the Roots of Anti-Semitism in the Gospel Story of the Death of Jesus* (San Francisco: HarperCollins, 1995); and B. L. Mack, *A Myth of Innocence: Mark and Christian Origins* (Philadelphia: Fortress Press, 1988).

Houses and official buildings in first-century Jerusalem; this model is located at the Holyland Hotel, Jerusalem. (Photo by K. C. Hanson. Used by permission.)

PART THREE

The Synoptic Tradition

THE SYNOPTIC GOSPELS (Matthew, Mark, and Luke) are in many respects the most distinctive writings in the NT canon. They are not, however, the first composed. I treat them first because I am engaged not in a history of earliest Christianity or the development of its concepts, but rather in an interpretation of its writings. The point is made emphatically by discussing documents written between the years 60 and 90 C.E. (Gospels) *before* those written between 40 and 60 C.E. (Pauline letters). There is also the literary logic of building on the analysis of the previous chapter, by showing how the memory of Jesus is shaped into sustained narratives.

Why then only the Synoptics and not also the Gospel of John? The decision to treat the Fourth Gospel separately owes nothing to any judgment concerning the supposedly more ancient or reliable traditions found in the Synoptics. The Fourth Gospel is considered later simply because it is quite another sort of narrative about Jesus, best understood by being read with the other writings from the Johannine symbolic world (see "The Johannine Traditions," Part Six). I treat the Synoptics together because they share not only the same symbolic universe but also the same narrative framework, which includes a complex relationship of literary interdependence.

The Synoptic Problem

Determining the exact nature of the literary relationship among the Synoptic Gospels is not easy. There is a great amount of material shared by the three Synoptics that has nearly identical correspondence in the Greek language and in the ordering of the narratives. At the same time, in this shared material there are also significant variations in language and order. From the high degree of correspondence, there is no doubt that borrowing from one to another took place at some stage of written rather than oral

155

transmission. The striking and often minute differences over those same stretches, however, make the precise delineation of their relationship difficult. The designation "Synoptic Problem" is used to describe this complex phenomenon.

How can both similarity and diversity be explained? Most scholars think that Mark was written first and that Matthew and Luke followed Mark in the composition of their narratives, deriving from him the basic order of the story as well as much of their material. Matthew and Luke also used material not derived from Mark. Some of this non-Markan material shared by the other two evangelists is again so nearly identical in language that a written document—conventionally called "Q" (*Quelle*, i.e., "source")—primarily made up of sayings material (hence the designation "Sayings Source") is posited as their additional resource. As in the case of Markan usage, alongside the basic agreement there is also some significant variation in language and order in the Q material in Matthew and Luke, making a precise delineation of the "Sayings Source" difficult. Finally, Matthew and Luke each have distinctive material gathered from still other hypothetical sources designated "M" and "L" respectively. These designations represent what Matthew and Luke have as distinctive to their own Gospels, sharing the material neither with each other nor with Mark. Whether M and L are actually comprehensive sources, bits of free-floating oral and/or written material, or authorial invention, is a matter of debate.

Such is the "two-source" solution to the Synoptic tangle. A minority of scholars still resist it, claiming that the ancient tradition of Matthean priority is correct. They insist that the fact that Matthew and Luke share the same order of events as Mark need not entail their use of Mark; it could mean that Luke used Matthew and that Mark, in turn, utilized both Matthew and Luke, condensing the two. This is known as the "Griesbach Hypothesis." At the level of logic, it makes sense. But when one sits down with the Greek text in three columns and patiently sorts through the data, it is difficult to maintain this position. It is far easier to explain the acceptance of the ninety percent of Mark that the other two adopt and adapt to their purposes than it is to explain a Markan rejection of the juiciest parts of Matthew and Luke, together with the stylistic vulgarization of the remainder.

The two-source hypothesis covers most of the data simply, but some anomalies remain, reminding us that we have in our possession only a *hypothesis*. We need occasional reminding, for instance, that Q means only what is left out of Mark but shared by Matthew and Luke. In this case the difficulties in moving beyond the hypothetical to the real are enormous. Modern scholars have attempted, nonetheless, to reconstruct an alleged Q document, not only postulating the successive layers of material in the source, but reconstructing the actual community behind it. Despite the allure of such attempts, we do not possess enough information to allow us to move beyond Q's existence as a scholarly abstraction. It is difficult, for example, to reconstruct with any confidence an original text of the document. We can only speculate whether Matthew, Luke, or either, best represents an original wording and order in any given instance.

Moreover, once one moves from an abstraction to a real document, one must then entertain the possibility that some of the shared Markan material is in fact from Q rather than Mark, and that some M and L material represents Q material appropriated by one evangelist but not the other. Thus, the difficulties multiply the more one presses the point. Not only the problem of Q, but the possible influences from a continuing oral tradition—combined with liturgical and scribal harmonization—make the textual relations between these three Gospels even more complex than they might appear at first glance. Add to this the likely possibility of the existence and production of other gospel-like narratives and collections in circulation and interaction in early Christianity, and the possibilities for establishing the relationship of Mark, Matthew, and Luke become seemingly endless. We must therefore be modest in our literary judgments.

Among such judgments that the reader will simply find bracketed in the pages to follow are these: the possible prehistory of specific passages; the existence of successive layers of Q, if layers there be; and minute discriminations between an evangelist's traditions and the use he makes of them. I will periodically point out the differences between the three Gospels, based on the study of the parallels. The point of these observations is not to establish any literary or religious line of dependence but simply to sharpen our perception of each evangelist's method and message.

I consider the hypothesis of Markan priority to be correct and assume it in this book. My reading of each Gospel, however, *does not depend* on the correctness of that hypothesis. My approach is closer to that of literary criticism, and the analysis is based on the final form of the text. But the awareness that this final stage of composition resulted from a complex oral and written process makes us sensitive to the peculiar density of these texts, as well as more appreciative of the simplicity and coherence of their finished condition.

The Origins of the Gospels

A few preliminary words are in order concerning the nature of these writings and the possible reasons for their composition. The issue of genre does not require an elaborate discussion. The Gospels are obviously narratives about the life, death, and resurrection of Jesus. Despite occasional resemblance to Hellenistic legends and aretalogies, the form of the Gospels most closely resembles that of Hellenistic biographies. In tone they aspire to something more than entertainment or even edification: they retain something of the distinctive historical-mythical character of the church's primitive kerygma.

The reader is aware from the start of each of these narratives that the main character is not simply an admirable figure from the past, a teacher like Socrates or a wonderworker like Apollonius of Tyana. He is rather the one believed to be now alive and powerfully present in the community. The words and deeds of his past are given deep resonance by the sounding board of the readers' present experiences and convictions. Christian readers could not help finding something of their story in his, for with his resurrection, they saw him as active in their own lives.

But why were such narratives written in the first place? This question is not easy to answer. Some have found the motivation for writing in specific problems facing Christian communities. The evangelists are seen as responding to these situations by telling the story of Jesus in such a way as to give guidance to their own generation. Sometimes external problems, such as persecution or the delay of the second coming (the Parousia) are suggested. Other times the problems suggested are those arising from internal divisions created by disagreements over the nature of discipleship or even of Jesus himself. Problems like these certainly existed in early Christian communities. Traces of them can sometimes be discerned in the Gospel stories. But they were not new problems. Paul had already encountered all of them and had responded by sending delegates or writing letters. Such problems do not themselves explain why these early Christian teachers began to use the form of a written narration for their instruction, or why that narrative took the shape it did.

An older and simpler explanation may be more correct, namely the human desire to remember Jesus and preserve that memory accurately for the generations to follow. Such a desire is sufficiently universal to require no special defense in the case of aging eyewitnesses and ministers of the word, who shaped the story of Jesus for the ages to come. What is more interesting is that they fixed the tradition not in the form of propositions but in the form of realistic narratives. These lifelike portrayals of Jesus dominate the NT canon and provide the sharpest contrast to the literary productions of Gnosticism, which elevated the divine character of Jesus at the expense of his humanity. For the writers of the canonical Gospels, the story of the human being Jesus had continuing importance for the community that now confessed him as life-giving Spirit. The line from proclamation to the Gospel is extended by narrative. However realistic, the Gospels were not disinterested histories. They selected and shaped the story of Jesus for readers who already knew that story in some form, in accord with deliberate literary and religious purposes. In their witnessing, therefore, they interpreted, just as by their interpreting, the Gospels bore witness.

Study Questions

1. What are the meanings of the word "gospel" in the New Testament?

2. What factors prompted the writing of the Gospels?

3. Why are the Gospels not considered to be the compositions of eyewitnesses? What difference does it make?

4. What is the literary relationship among the Synoptic Gospels?

7. The Gospel of Mark

IN SOME WAYS, the shortest of the gospels is also the strangest and most difficult to grasp. This may account in part for its neglect in the history of interpretation. One could call the use of Mark by Matthew and Luke a sign of success, but in the process Mark was eclipsed by having its substance placed within the more open and easily intelligible narratives of the others.

Mark's Gospel was little read and less studied. This was partly due to the widespread opinion that he had only condensed Matthew's version, and partly due to the fact that his narrative met liturgical and catechetical needs less adequately than his Synoptic successors. No commentary on Mark appeared until the sixth century and not another until the ninth. Even the patristic writers who knew that Mark belonged in the canon could not agree on which of the allegorical beasts he should represent (see Irenaeus *Against Heresies* III.11.8 and Augustine *On the Harmony of the Evangelists* I.VI.9). What small attention patristic writers paid to Mark was due largely to his supposed role as Peter's translator and his thus having had a direct connection to the apostolic witness. This tradition went back at least as far as Papias (2nd cent. C.E.), perhaps based on the association of Mark with Peter in 1 Pet. 5:13. Even Papias felt it necessary to apologize for Mark's apparent lack of narrative order, assuring his readers that Mark had made no errors and had omitted nothing essential of what he had heard from Peter (Eusebius *Ecclesiastical History* III.39.15).

In sharp contrast, Mark has been the most popular of the Synoptics for scholars of the twentieth century. The first reason was the thought that Mark provided the earliest and most reliable historical source for those seeking to uncover the historical Jesus. When the Synoptic problem was solved in favor of Markan priority, Mark's Gospel was regarded as free from the dogmatic accretions found in Matthew and Luke, and therefore could be regarded as an unbiased witness. This hypothesis was first shaken by the discovery of the "messianic secret," Mark's peculiar way of at once revealing and hiding the significance of Jesus within the narrative (see 1:25, 34, 44; 3:12; 5:43; 7:36; 8:30; 9:9; cf. 5:19; 16:7). This pattern suggested something more than a guileless chronicle; in fact, it suggested a dogmatically motivated composition. Even more threatening to the perception of Mark as an untainted historical record was the work of the earliest form critics, who dismantled the narrative framework of Mark, saying that he was only an editor mechanically stitching together units of oral tradition.

The current favor accorded Mark began with pioneering literary-redactional studies. They showed that Mark's peculiar emphasis on Galilee (esp. 14:28; 15:41; 16:7) was a theological symbol. Likewise, Mark's anachronistic use of the term "gospel," *euangelion*, revealed a self-conscious awareness of the multilayered theological nature of his narrative (see 1:1, 14, 15; 8:35; 10:29; 13:10; 14:9). As a result, Mark's Gospel was seen less as a direct witness to the life of Jesus or to the period of oral transmission than as a witness to the Christian communities of Mark's day.

Two main preoccupations characterize the study of Mark's Gospel today. The first takes seriously Mark's ability to reveal something of the historical setting it addressed, and seeks to find within Mark's narrative clues for the deciphering of history. Such readers find in Mark's treatment of the disciples, for example, an allegorical attack on some specific group of heretics or ecclesiastical leaders in the Markan community. The second preoccupation has been generated by the enigmatic character of Mark's narrative. For many readers, Mark is not the simplest but the most sophisticated of the evangelists, whose compositional techniques appear remarkably contemporary. Mark is therefore the subject of purely literary studies, often carried out in conscious dialogue with contemporary models of literary criticism.

Approaching Mark's Narrative

Calling Mark a literary genius is undoubtedly excessive. On the other hand, it is proper to appreciate the decisive turning point his Gospel represented in the shaping of Christian traditions. We do not know who Mark really was or where he wrote. We do not know Mark's readers, although they were certainly already Christian and obviously read Greek. So far as we can tell, however, Mark was the first to connect the notion of "good news" *(Euangelion)*—first understood as what God had accomplished in the death and resurrection of the Messiah—to a narrative of what Jesus himself had said and done, calling it too, "good news" (1:1). It was a momentous decision with profound religious implications. By shaping Jesus' ministry so that it led inexorably to the Passion, Mark invited his readers to understand Jesus' words and deeds not as independent modes of revelation but as inextricably linked to that finale. And because Mark set out the traditions about Jesus in narrative form, the term "gospel" would henceforth have the sense of a literary medium as well as a message.

We can no longer reconstruct Mark's motivation for his writing or even determine when he did it. The absence of anachronism and sense of realism in his description of the temple's end (13:5-23) suggests a time before the end of the Roman War (67–70 c.e.); how long before, and whether connected to those tragic circumstances, we do not know.

Nor is it easy to find one's way into Mark's narrative itself. Even its beginning and end, as we shall see, have been debated. The more Mark's tale is pondered, the more it resists easy characterization. Apparently artless and straightforward at first reading, its reticence invites speculation from those who persist in questioning the text. Out of what silence did Mark's story emerge? What sources were available to him, and how did he use them? When his readers first heard Mark's narrative recited, did it challenge, correct, or confirm their previous understanding of Jesus' story? What did Mark himself want the narrative to accomplish? All these questions escape easy answers.

There are clues within the narrative itself that enable the contemporary reader to approach the heart of Mark's message. The first is the *literary structure of the Gospel*. Mark not only tells a story, he establishes deliberate and meaningful connections between parts of it, signaling those connections to the careful reader. The way a narrative is structured is often one of the most important clues to its significance.

A second sort of clue is the way Mark *delineates the characters* in his narrative. Most important is the figure of Jesus. Mark had several means of subtly shaping the literary presentation of Jesus. He could, for instance, employ various messianic titles in meaningful combinations, such as Christ, Teacher, Lord, Son of God, and Son of man. Likewise, Mark could describe Jesus' characteristic actions in terms that would suggest to his readers the images of great persons of the Hellenistic world, such as thaumaturges or sages. He could also use the language of Torah in order to connect the story of Jesus to earlier scriptural stories, thus creating deeper resonances in his narrative. We have already observed how Mark did this in the Passion narrative (see chap. 5, above).

Finally, Mark could delineate characters by portraying the interactions between them. There is, for example, the unseen but critical relationship between Jesus and the One whose will dominates the narrative and who speaks only to identify Jesus (1:11; 9:7), the one whom Jesus calls "Abba" (14:36) in his role as obedient son. Next, there is Jesus in conflict with opponents, above all with the scribes (see, e.g., 2:6; 3:22; 7:1; 8:31). Then there is the often elusive role played by those crowds among whom Jesus acts, whose own responses are variable. Finally, there is the interaction between Jesus and his chosen followers, the "disciples." In Mark's Gospel, it is this relationship that yields the most persuasive indications of Mark's religious purposes in writing. It is with the disciples that Mark's readers would most naturally identify, and through their characterization Mark could most directly instruct his readers.

In the sections that follow, I pursue some of these clues in Mark's text. First, I consider some of the specifically literary aspects of the narrative. Then, I review Mark's story as a whole, giving particular attention to the relationship between Jesus and the disciples.

Deciphering the Literary Clues

Style and Structure

By the high standards of Greek rhetoric, Mark's prose is unimpressive. Indeed, both Matthew and Luke find his Greek in constant need of correction and improvement.

Mark can be prolix and clumsy (see, e.g., 1:35; 9:3). His sentence structure is paratactic (that is, he joins clauses with "and" rather than by using relative pronouns and subordinate conjunctions), and this, together with his frequent use of the adverb "immediately" (*euthus*), gives his narrative an immediate, but also sometimes frenetic, quality. He is fond of slipping into the historical present in the middle of a story, thereby providing a sense of immediacy, although detracting from a more formal historical style (see, e.g., 5:35-43). Mark also helps his readers by translating Aramaic words into Greek (see 3:17; 5:41; 7:11; 15:22, 34) but sees no need to do so with Latin loanwords (see 5:9; 6:37; 12:15; 15:39), illustrating a lack of consistency.

Mark's compositional skills do not, at first glance, inspire much respect. Early form critics thought of him simply as an editor whose clusters of topically arranged materials, such as seed parables (4:3-32), controversy stories (2:15-3:6), and sayings on discipleship (8:34-37), were already organized in the process of oral transmission. They noted that Mark makes few real transitions, often being content to join vignettes by "and" or "immediately." Moreover, they argued that his chronological references are vague and unhelpful (see 9:2; 14:1; 15:42). Sometimes, he can follow the actions of Jesus hour by hour (1:21-38; 14:12—15:37); other times, he can summarize an indeterminate period of ministry with a single line (10:1). For those seeking in the Gospel a clean linear development like that in Luke-Acts, Mark is a disappointment.

But he is far from being a careless editor. He is, in fact, an author of considerable skill. The careful reader can find in his story signs of a very special compositional technique that makes his narrative less linear and more dialectical. Sometimes his narrative arrangement, which first appears to be repetitive and clumsy, actually provides important clues for understanding.

An illustration of Mark's way of making his reader look twice, and therefore more closely, can be found in the stories between 4:35 and 8:27. These stories occur in a series of matching sets: a miracle on water in 4:35-41 is mirrored by a second in 6:45-52; the healings of 5:21-42 correspond to that in 7:31-37; a multiplication of bread in 6:34-44 appears a second time in 8:1-10; a saying on the meaning of bread in 6:52 is matched by another in 8:14-21. This whole cycle of doublets helps move the story from the question asked by the disciples in 4:41, "Who is this man?" to the question put by Jesus to the disciples, "Who do you say that I am?" (8:29). In the paragraphs that follow, I will touch on some other examples of Mark's literary techniques.

Sets of Three

It has long been noted that Mark has a fondness for threefold patterns. He puts together three seed parables (4:3-32), three popular opinions about John (6:14-15), three popular opinions about Jesus (8:27-28), three predictions of the Passion (8:31; 9:31; 10:33-34), three failures of the disciples to stay awake in the garden (14:32-42), three denials of Jesus by Peter (14:66-72). This is more than simple fascination with a number or a law of folklore: for Mark, the triad becomes an architectonic principle.

This can be seen first in his frequent use of literary intercalation. In its smallest form, two fragments of one story frame a third passage in something of a sandwich arrangement. Mark's reader is forced to see the frame and the middle together, in tension. The central story is illuminated—or darkened—by its placement within the frame, whereas the outer story is given density by being filled in this fashion.

A striking example occurs early in Mark's narrative. In 3:21 we see Jesus' family members on their way to seize him since they think he is crazy ("beside himself"). We find them again in 3:31-35, knocking at the door of the house where Jesus is seated with his followers. They ask to see Jesus. He refuses to see them and identifies those in a circle about him as his real family: those who do the will of God. By itself this framing story would be a straightforward if negative account about the mutual rejection found in the family of the Messiah. Notice, however, that Mark inserts within this frame a controversy between Jesus and the scribes from Jerusalem (3:22-30). They accuse him of casting out demons by demonic power. He responds with a parable about a house divided! He also pronounces on the sin against the Holy Spirit that cannot be forgiven, because (Mark tells the reader) his opponents had said he had an unclean spirit. Given the connections between madness (3:21) and unclean spirits (3:30) in the ancient symbolic world, and given the pattern of rejection found in both frame and middle—that those who reject Jesus are themselves rejected—the composite appears as a powerful indictment. But of whom, exactly? The reader is left to wonder.

Mark also leaves the reader to puzzle out the connection between the healing of a twelve-year-old girl (5:22-24, 35-43) and the healing of a woman twelve years ill (5:25-34), which Mark inserts into that episode. Similarly, the prophetic shadow of John's beheading in 6:14-29 separates the sending of the Twelve on a mission in 6:7-12 and their return in 6:30. The transfiguration of Jesus (9:2-8), which reveals Jesus in splendor with Moses and Elijah, is placed between a saying about the kingdom's coming in power (9:1) and a question about the prior coming of Elijah (9:9-13) which that statement would logically have prompted. In a somewhat more alternating pattern, the fall of the temple is entwined in the fate of a fig tree: Mark has Jesus enter the temple (11:11); when departing, he seeks fruit from the tree, finds none, and curses it (11:12-14); he returns to cleanse the temple, which had failed its proper role (11:15-18); he departs the temple and finds the fig tree withered (11:20-25). Mark makes no comment on any of this. He leaves the reader to figure out the juxtapositions.

Mark's framing technique can be observed as well on a grander scale. He places larger portions of the narrative between compositional signals. In Mark's Gospel, for example, Jesus heals two blind men. The first is healed only gradually, since Jesus' first touch brings only hazy sight. This healing occurs immediately before the question is put to the disciples concerning Jesus' identity (8:22-26). The second man's healing is immediate, and leads to Bartimaeus following Jesus "on the way" (10:46-52). Between these healings—which symbolize the turn from blindness to sight and from sight to commitment—Mark has placed Jesus' most explicit instructions to his followers on his identity and their call.

Even the overall narrative of Mark can be seen to have a triadic structure. It has often been observed that a critical turning point in Mark's story occurs when Peter declares Jesus to be the Messiah (8:27-30). Before that point, the question, "Who is Jesus?" dominates. After Peter's confession, the journey to Jerusalem becomes the context for the Messiah's self-revelation to the disciples as the suffering Son of man. The transfiguration account is an essential part of this turning point in the story. When Jesus is shown to his closest followers as glorified, the voice from heaven identifies him, "This is my beloved son; listen to him" (9:7). The command "Listen" sets up the instructions on discipleship that follow (chaps. 9–10).

This announcement of Jesus as Son of God, however, is the middle one of three such declarations—leaving out the cries of demons. The first occurs at Jesus' baptism, when the voice from heaven tells Jesus alone, "You are my beloved son, in whom I am well pleased" (1:11). The last occurs at Jesus' death, when one of his executioners says, "Truly this was God's son" (15:39). This triad of declarations at critical points in the narrative establishes a frame for the reader's perception of Jesus as Son of God. The three aspects are held in a tension that is left unresolved: Jesus, the chosen servant of the Father; Jesus, the glorified Lord and revealer; Jesus, the executed criminal. It is within this tension that the reader understands Jesus' prayer to the Father ("Abba") in the garden (14:36), and his response to the high priest's question "Are you the Christ, the Son of the Blessed?" with a simple "I am" (14:61-62).

Later in this chapter, I will return to still another structural triptych, in the peculiar designation of Jesus as the stronger one (1:7): first in the Beelzebul controversy (3:23-27); last in the empty-tomb account (16:1-8); and in the middle, in the exorcism of the Gerasene demoniac (5:1-20).

The Open Ending

Typical of the difficulties with which Mark presents the reader is the end and the beginning of his Gospel. A consideration of each can lead us further into Mark's dense narrative and his particular shaping of the "good news."

The canonical text of Mark offers three different endings. The oldest and best manuscripts end at 16:8: the women who had come to the tomb to anoint Jesus fled, "and they said nothing to anyone, for they were afraid." Other manuscripts contain a series of appearance accounts (16:9-20). Still others insert a coda after 16:8, either as conclusion or as a bridge to the longer ending of 16:9-20. Which is the original Markan conclusion?

Some argue for the longer ending. They note that the Greek text of 16:8 ends with the conjunction "for" (*gar*), which appears to demand another clause. They think it odd to end a sentence, much less a whole book, so indeterminately. They add that 16:7, "There you will see him," calls out for the fulfillment that the longer ending supplies.

The arguments for the shorter ending are stronger. The basic rules of textual criticism state that the best-attested, shorter, and harder readings are generally to be preferred to readings that are longer, smoother, and less well-attested in manuscripts. Now, the ending in 16:8 certainly qualifies as the most difficult. Sentences and even whole books have been known to end with conjunctions, but Mark's ending is not for all that any less awkward. Next, the shorter ending is the best attested in the oldest and most reliable Greek manuscripts. Finally, it is much easier to explain the origin of the longer ending than it is to explain its loss: Mark 16:7, as we observed, opened a way for scribes to supply what they saw as the natural fulfillment of the prophecy, especially if these scribes knew the endings of Matthew and Luke. That this happened seems more likely since the longer ending weaves together traditions found in the other canonical Gospels (16:9 = John 20:11-18; 16:12 = Luke 24:13-35; 16:15 = Matt. 28:16-20; 16:19-20 = Acts 1:9-11). Finally, it seems likely that Matthew and Luke read Mark in this shorter version, since they both have an empty tomb account close to his but after that diverge dramatically in their appearance narratives.

The longer ending of Mark remains part of the canonical text, is read in the assembly as such, and contains a venerable tradition about the resurrection that is theologically significant in its own right. But the distinctive Markan witness to Jesus is seen more clearly when we work with the shorter ending.

And a puzzling finale it is. The women approach with amazement (16:5) and leave in fear (16:8). They do not pass on the message of a future appearance. The identity of the young man who delivers the message to them is left unstated (16:5). What are we to make of this? Mark obviously believes Jesus was raised from the dead; such is the presupposition of the book and of its readers. Indeed, such also is the burden of the young man's message: Jesus is not among the dead, but "goes before" the disciples. He will appear, but at his own choosing. But if Mark and his readers knew traditions of Jesus' having appeared—traditions, we have seen already, that are very old (see 1 Cor. 15:3-8)—then why didn't he narrate them?

We can only guess. Perhaps the stories of Jesus' appearance in the past to witnesses enabled early Christians to regard his lordship as a reassuring fact rather than as a demanding call to "follow after." Perhaps Mark wanted his readers to examine again the grounds of their experience of Jesus: was it in past visions or in present power and conviction? Because Mark declares Jesus to be alive and ready to appear but does not attach his appearing to any specific times and places in the past, he leaves open for his readers the imaginative possibility of new encounters with the risen one. He thereby reminds them that the one who rose did not simply take up again his former life but lives now as powerful Lord who continues to place their life in question.

In a way completely consonant with the rest of his narrative, Mark insists that as risen Lord, Jesus remains the Holy One of God (1:24), the alien strong man (3:27), the mystery of the Kingdom (4:11), who cannot be understood or controlled but only followed in fear and trembling (4:41; 5:15, 33; 9:32; 10:32). Mark's ending is really an opening. The "good news" about Jesus' resurrection does not reduce the mystery but heightens it. Readers are invited once more to wonder, Who is this man?

The Sudden Beginning

The beginning of Mark's narrative also suggests the special character of this Gospel. Before moving to this, however, another textual difficulty requires attention. The canonical version reads, "Beginning of the good news [*euangelion*] of Jesus Christ, Son of God" (1:1). Some manuscripts lack the phrase "Son of God," while others have it. Which should we read? Here is a case where the shorter ending is not the best. Not only do the best manuscripts support the inclusion of "Son of God," but this title also plays a significant thematic role in the narrative as a whole. I have already indicated its presence at the baptism, transfiguration, and crucifixion, as well as the repeated identification of Jesus as God's Son by demons (3:11; 5:7). The climax of Jesus' trial before the Sanhedrin is reached when he responds, " I am," to the high priest's question "Are you the Messiah, the Son of the Blessed One?" (14:62)—a question, we notice, that combines the two titles found in 1:1. The reading "Son of God" is thus probably correct.

What, then, does Mark mean by "beginning of the good news"? The question is made more difficult by the lack of clear syntactical connection to the verses that immediately follow and by the generally compressed character of Mark's first fifteen verses. Perhaps by "beginning," Mark means the chronological start of the ministry of John (see Acts 1:21-22; 10:37) or the theological rooting of John's ministry in the prophetic tradition (see the mixed citation from Exod. 23:20, Mal. 3:1, and Isa. 40:3 in Mark 1:2-3). Despite Mark's overall reticence regarding the citation of Torah, he begins his story with a literary cross-reference, alerting his readers to the fact that Jesus' story should be heard as the continuation of a longer one.

The "beginning of the good news" may also refer simply to the chronological start of what Jesus said and did, so that this verse forms a bracket with verse 15. In a still deeper but not impossible reading, the beginning (*archē*), with its almost unavoidable allusion to the *archē* in Gen. 1:1 (LXX), may have a specifically religious reference to the whole story of Jesus that Mark is about to relate: what happened in the words, deeds, death, and resurrection of Jesus is the absolute *archē*—both the beginning and continuing origin—of belief and discipleship. If the text can be read this closely, then 1:1 stands as a title for the Gospel as a whole. It marks off the narrative's major sections, the first ending with Peter's declaration of Jesus as Christ (8:29), the second with the declaration by the gentile centurion that Jesus was God's Son (15:39).

With whatever nuances, it is clear that the readers of this Gospel know from the beginning that Jesus is both Messiah and Son of God. Mark's *narrative* mystery—Jesus' being known at first only to demons, then vaguely to the disciples, then paradoxically to the soldier—is known already by the readers in 1:1. In the strictest sense, therefore, the Gospel as a whole is intensely ironic. The readers always know more than the characters in the story. This observation needs further development.

Apocalyptic and Irony

The symbolism of Mark's Gospel is fundamentally that of apocalyptic. The greatest concentration of it is found in Jesus' secret discourse to his closest followers (chap. 13) which is often called the "little apocalypse." In this chapter, we find private revelation (13:3) of things that are to happen (13:4) portrayed in terms of cosmic upheaval and conflict (13:7-8, 24-25), including persecution of the elect of God (13:9-13), causing apostasy from the true way (13:21-23). Those who persevere to the end will be saved (13:13). The end will be signaled by the coming of the Son of man, "with great power and glory" (13:26). These features are classically apocalyptic, with symbols that can be traced back to the Book of Daniel (see chap. 2, above, pp. 49–52).

If the discourse were straightforwardly apocalyptic, however, its function would be simply to comfort the hearers: they know the course of history, whereas the outsiders, the evil ones, do not. Indeed, the very reception of this sort of revelation would mark its hearers as insiders and the elect.

But Mark puts a twist on this apocalyptic theme. The insiders (Peter, James, John, and Andrew) are informed that they really do not know when all this is to happen but that they are to "take heed and watch" (13:32-33). More than that, Mark explicitly opens this "secret" discourse to all the readers. They are invited to overhear what Jesus says to the disciples and to understand it more clearly than his followers do: "Let the reader understand"(13:14). The readers of the Gospel are also warned: "And what I say to you I say to all: Watch!" (13:37). Apocalyptic is here. Apocalyptic aims at insiders and is understood by them, but here Mark works it into a literary irony. He warns his readers: "If you think you understand, if you think of yourself as an insider, beware, you may not be. If those insiders, the disciples, could find themselves on the outside, so could you."

Apocalyptic symbolism is scarcely confined to chapter 13. Mark's entire Gospel can be considered an apocalypse in narrative form, but one with a distinctive ironic element. The symbolism of apocalyptic enables us to understand how Jesus' ministry is one of conflict with cosmic forces. He is the stronger one who enters the house ruled by Satan, binds him, and releases his captives (3:27). Within this symbolic structure, we recognize how this conflict expresses the essential proclamation of Jesus, "The kingdom of God is at hand" (1:15), because Jesus himself is the content of that proclamation.

Mark's presentation of Jesus is not itself without ambiguity. From one point of view, Jesus is clearly a thaumaturge filled with the Spirit (1:10), whose works of healing and exorcism enable demons to recognize him as a "Holy One of God" (1:24), radiating an urgent power (5:30; 6:2). Yet, he cannot always use it (6:5). From another point of view, Jesus is a "teacher" (*didaskalos*). Mark has given him this designation more often, proportionately, than any other Gospel. Jesus is called *didaskalos* or *rabbi* by both friend and foe. But what a strange sort of teacher he is! He calls people to follow him with no preamble, and they do so with little apparent reason (1:17, 20). He demands of them complete renunciation (10:17-31) and promises in return only that they will face suffering (10:39). When he is questioned, he does not seek to persuade but issues abrupt pronouncements (2:1—3:6; 7:1-23). When he speaks in parables, he does not invite understanding but deflects it. Indeed, his parables might be called instruments of attack (see 3:23). He tells the disciples that the parables are "so that they may indeed see but not perceive" (4:12). Jesus' words in this Gospel are few and hard. So is his fate. He is obviously the one meant by the "Son of man" who will come in glory (8:38; 13:26; 14:62) and who now speaks with authority (2:10), yet this Son of man is above all one who must suffer and die (14:21, 41) and, before he does so, must experience the extremes of human anguish (14:33-34). It is no easier for the present-day reader than for Jesus' first disciples to comprehend fully this paradoxical Messiah.

Mysterious Revelation

Why is Mark's narrative so difficult and his presentation of Jesus so deflecting? The clue to this may be found in the explanation Jesus gives for speaking in parables (4:11). When the disciples ask him why he speaks in parables, he says that the parables are for those "outside." As for the disciples, they "have been given the mystery [*mystērion*] of the kingdom of God."

This statement is as important for what it does not say as for what it says. At first, it would appear that insiders and outsiders are distinguished on the basis of understanding or the lack of it. So we would expect the insiders, the disciples, to understand. But Jesus immediately asserts that they do not understand either: "Do you not understand this parable? How then will you understand all the parables?" (4:13). Knowledge or the lack of it does not by itself distinguish insiders and outsiders. But how can the insiders both be given the mystery and fail to understand it?

Here is a case where a comparison with Matthew's parallel passage helps us see what Mark intends. In Matthew, Jesus tells the disciples, "To you has been given to know the mysteries of the kingdom of heaven" (Matt. 13:11). We notice two important differences: the disciples "know," and they are given to know "mysteries" (in the plural). The word can justifiably be translated "secrets" (RSV). As we shall see later, it is important in Matthew's Gospel that the disciples understand and communicate the revelations of Jesus to others (see Matt. 28:20).

But Mark's point is different. The disciples are not given the gift to know, and what they have been given is in the singular, *mystērion*, not a secret but a mystery. This may well be the key word in Mark's narrative. One can scarcely miss the associations it suggests with the *mysterium tremendum ac fascinosum*. Jesus himself is the singular "mystery of the kingdom," and he is so as the Holy One. He is recognized fully only by God and other spiritual forces. He radiates an intense and fearful power. It is a power, furthermore, that at once attracts and repels, so that some are drawn to him and some reject him. Most of all, the *mystērion* resists understanding. It cannot be deciphered, controlled, or reduced to a formula. The mystery of the holy, *even when revealed*, remains beyond reach.

This presentation of Jesus as the Holy One helps us appreciate Mark's two-edged portrayal of the disciples. One side of the portrayal is positive: they are specially called by Jesus to be with him and share his work (3:14); they are given the mystery that is himself (4:11); to them is revealed his identity as suffering Son of man (8:31) and glorious Son of God (9:2-8); and they hear his secret discourse on the tribulation and triumph to follow (13:5-37). The other side of the portrayal is almost unrelievedly negative: they do not in fact understand (4:13, 41; 6:52; 7:18; 8:21); they reject a suffering messiah (8:32), seeking instead a place of honor in a glorious kingdom (9:34; 10:37); Judas betrays Jesus for money (14:10-11); Peter denies even knowing him (14:66-72); and none of them stays with him to the end—"They all fled" (14:50).

These literary observations suggest something of Mark's religious purpose in shaping the story of Jesus and the disciples in this fashion. Mark's readers would naturally, as we still do, identify themselves with the disciples. Mark therefore uses that relationship to teach his readers. The message is mainly one of warning against smugness and self-assurance. He seems to be saying "If you think you are an insider, you may not be; if you think you understand the mystery of the kingdom and even control it, watch out; it remains alive and fearful beyond your comprehension. If you think discipleship consists in power because of the presence of God, beware; you are called to follow the one who suffered and died. Your discipleship is defined by his messiahship, that is, in terms of obedience and service."

We do not need to postulate a distinct group of heretics or leaders in the Markan community at whom this message was aimed. Mark's sharp delineation of a paradoxical Jesus and an inadequate community of followers needed only readers who were human and, therefore, also with "spirit willing but flesh weak" (14:38). I turn, then, to a schematic reading of the Gospel, seeing in Mark an apocalyptic narrative in which the anticipated categories of insider and outsider are redefined in terms of response to the mystery of the kingdom that Jesus represents.

Following Jesus through the Story of Mark

The Prologue: 1:1-15

We see at once that this is no biography or history. No account is given of John's origins or Jesus' childhood. The narrative is dense and deeply allusive. John's baptism fulfills Torah's promise of a forerunner (1:2-3), but his message is reduced to a single announcement, "After me comes one stronger than I" (1:7). As we read, the full implications of this designation for Jesus will become clearer. But now we see that the one who is to baptize with the spirit (1:8) is himself baptized and declared God's beloved Son (1:11). The one who is to drive out demons is himself driven out (same Greek term is used in both instances) into the desert to grapple directly with Satan (1:12-13).

When Jesus returns from that testing, therefore, he comes as one who has already bound the strong one in single combat (see 3:27). There now remains for him only the emancipation of his captives. In Jesus' battle with cosmic forces, the outcome is not in doubt. Because the Stronger One has entered human history, the reign of evil is at an end. Jesus announces the effective rule of God—"The kingdom of God is at hand; repent and believe in the good news" (1:15)—which, in the rest of Mark's narrative, will be spelled out paradoxically.

In these opening verses, Mark's readers encounter the story of God's unique Son, who spins history on its axis and calls for conversion, a change of heart and mind. In the story of this man the mystery of God is at work.

Conflict and Selection: 1:16—3:34

Between Jesus' proclamation of the kingdom in 1:15 and his declaration in 3:35 that "whoever does the will of God is my brother, and sister, and mother," three patterns structure Mark's narrative. The first is the demonstration of Jesus' authority and power in healings and exorcisms (1:21-28, 29-34, 40-45; 2:1-12), which is summarized in 3:7-12. The second is a positive response to Jesus by those whom he calls (1:16-20; 2:13-14), which is brought to a head by the choosing of the Twelve in 3:13-19. The third is the rejection of Jesus by his opponents (2:1-12, 15-28), which reaches a climax in the Sabbath conflict that issues in the resolve of the Pharisees and Herodians to seek Jesus' death (3:1-6).

Mark weaves these patterns together artfully. At the level of human history, we see the Messiah beginning his career of open preaching and healing. His powerful message and presence cause some to follow him, and from among their growing number he chooses an inner group to be "with him" in a special fashion. But his assumption of authority also causes religious leaders to reject him and seek his death. While this is taking place at the historical level, Mark also shows his readers that at the level of cosmic conflict, "the Holy One of God" (1:24) is a mystery that at once attracts and repels.

Two paradigmatic stories illustrate the two levels of conflict. First, the cosmic conflict is illustrated by the exorcism in 1:21-28. Here is Jesus' first revelation of power. Mark characteristically fits the exorcism itself (vv. 23-26) into an account of Jesus' teaching in the synagogue (vv. 21-22, 27-28) by his intercalation technique. Jesus rebukes and expels the spirit who recognizes him as the Holy One, showing that in fact he is the Stronger One promised by John, through whom God's Spirit is at work binding Satan. The reaction of the crowd combines astonishment at both wonderworking and teaching: "What is this? A new teaching! With authority he commands even the unclean spirits and they obey him" (1:27). We see that for Mark, the essential teaching of Jesus is going to be connected to his personal presence. The second paradigmatic story is the synagogue controversy caused by Jesus' healing on the Sabbath (3:1-6). His opponents seek to accuse him of breaking Torah, just as they have challenged his practices in the previous stories. Although Jesus now once more silences them—just as he can silence demons—they leave with the intent to kill him. Thus early on, Mark foreshadows the eventual outcome of this conflict of the power "to do good or harm, to give life or to kill" (3:4).

The two levels of conflict are joined in the complex intercalation of 3:20-35 (see above, p. 163). Jesus has already chosen those who will be with him (3:13-19), from now on they will be his family (3:35). His natural family shows itself to be against him by seeking his arrest, and finds itself on the outside quite literally (3:21, 31-35). The scribes from Jerusalem, who accuse him of casting out demons by demonic collusion, show themselves as sinners against the Holy Spirit (3:22, 28-30). At the heart of this complex passage, Jesus' parable—the first he tells—interprets the cosmic implications of this human conflict: he is the Stronger One who has entered the house of the strong one and overcome him.

This opening plot sequence has established that Jesus' open preaching has already created a division between insiders and outsiders. Jesus prepares for a new mode of teaching by choosing a select audience to be with him. Those who have rejected his open speech and healing powers have put themselves on the outside, and Jesus has already begun to speak to them in parables!

Teaching in Parables: 4:1-41

Mark's peculiar use of parables becomes more intelligible in light of this plot sequence. In the Jewish wisdom tradition a parable (*mashal*) could be a dark and ambiguous saying like a riddle, but the dominant use of parables among contemporary Jewish teachers was as a means of clarifying scriptural difficulties. As an analogy in narrative form, it could lead someone from an understanding of the familiar to an understanding of the strange. This is also the dominant function of parables in both Matthew and Luke. In Mark, the case is different. Although the character of the parables themselves is no more difficult in this Gospel than in others, Mark exhibits a different use of them: he suggests that Jesus used parables to confound rather than to instruct.

If we have followed Mark's story, however, we see that it was because Jesus' open preaching caused a violent opposition and threat of death that he began to speak in a veiled way. Doing so, of course, accentuated further the distinction between insider and outsider. Now, to those outside, everything is in parables simply because they do not have the single necessary hermeneutical key: the acceptance of Jesus. So we find the parables of chapter 4 punctuated by apocalyptic warning signs: "Listen!" (4:3); "He who has ears to hear let him hear!" (4:9); "Whoever has ears to hear, let him hear" (4:23). There is, as well, talk about things that are now told in secret later being made manifest (4:21-25). To the outsiders the parables make obvious their previous failure to accept Jesus as the personification of the kingdom; the parable repels those who had already decided not to be attracted. These "may indeed hear but not understand, lest they should turn again and be forgiven" (4:12). If this stood as a comprehensive statement of Jesus' mission, it would show an extraordinarily harsh discrimination against the outsider. But it must be understood explicitly in light of the story Mark has already told; only in the face of massive rejection does Jesus turn to his inner group with language clear to them but repelling to outsiders. The parables here function like the coded insider language of apocalyptic.

In the light of Mark's plot development, the parable of the sower (4:3-8) is also easy to understand. For those, like the readers of the passage, who have just heard of Jesus' open preaching and its acceptance and rejection, the parable is a transparent commentary on that story. Like the parable of the vineyard at the end of Mark's Gospel, this parable calls out for an allegorical interpretation. The code is supplied by the previous narrative itself. As the seed sown meets various fates, so does the word preached by Jesus.

But now, Mark's irony begins to work. Those on the inside were supposed to understand the parables. The disciples were supposed to be insiders. But they do not understand; they seek an *interpretation* of the parable (4:10). When Jesus gives his interpretation, the commentary character becomes even more obvious, for the sower now sows "the Word" (see Mark 2:2; 4:16-17, 33; 8:32). But the disciples should not have needed this interpretation. They were given the hermeneutical key, the *mystērion* of the kingdom, who is Jesus himself.

As readers, we begin to suspect that those who were intended to be on the inside possibly were not. We recognize that when Mark says that "he did not speak to them without a parable, but privately to his own disciples he explained everything" (4:34), we are to understand by this not an absolute distinction but rather, various degrees of being outside. The disciples, we shall shortly see, grasp little more than others about Jesus.

Mark goes on to show his readers what kind of understanding Jesus demanded from his followers. It was the sort that came from the commitment of the heart, from being with Jesus in loyalty and fidelity. He shows us this with a parabolic story that concludes this chapter on parables (4:35-41). Jesus demonstrates his power privately before his disciples and in their behalf. He speaks to the raging winds as he did to the demons (4:39; compare 1:25). And like the demons, the winds are "bound" (4:39). Then, in the question Jesus puts to the fearful disciples, we discover what it is that Mark regards as the key to understanding the mystery of Jesus: the commitment of *faith*. The disciples' manifest lack of this loyalty is shown by their fear and by their question, which is programmatic for the next section of the narrative: "Who is this, then, that even the wind and sea obey him?" (4:41). The readers already know, and by now the disciples should know. By hearing those on the inside ask the same question asked earlier by those on the outside (see 1:27), the readers are instructed and warned.

To Caesarea Phillipi: 5:1—8:26

This part of Mark's narrative is given structure by its series of doublets (see above, p. 162). The story line, however, is carried by the various responses to Jesus' wonder-working. As intimated in the stilling of the storm, the positive response is that of faith; the negative, that of disbelief.

Mark had early established a connection between healing, the forgiveness of sins, and faith: "When Jesus saw their faith, he said to the paralytic, 'My son, your sins are forgiven'" (2:5). Now, the connection is made even more explicitly (5:21-43). Mark inserts the story of the healed woman into that of the raising of the young girl, so that the readers understand that the same power (5:30) and response were at work in both: "Daughter, your faith has made you well; go in peace and be healed of your disease" (5:34) and "Do not fear, only believe" (5:36). Likewise when Jesus is rejected in Nazareth by his townsfolk (6:1-6), "he could do no mighty work [*dynamis* = power, as in 5:30] there, except that he laid his hands on a few sick people and healed them; and he marveled because of their faithlessness" (6:5-6).

Jesus heals a wild demoniac (5:1-20), who then goes into gentile territory, "the Decapolis," to preach the word (5:20). Jesus also heals the daughter of a Greek woman from Syro-Phoenicia because of her bold faith (7:24-30) and a deaf mute in the region of the Decapolis (7:31-37). In short, ordinary needy people even from among the Gentiles recognize the power at work in Jesus and seek him out in faith (6:30-31; 7:35-36). In contrast, he is rejected by his townsfolk (6:1-6) and opposed by Pharisees and scribes (7:1-23). Only the reprobate Herod gives ironic testimony to the power that the reader—hearing the story from the perspective of Jesus' resurrection—could see at work in Jesus: "John the baptizer has been raised from the dead; that is why these powers are at work in him" (6:14).

All this time, however, the disciples remain dull and imperceptive. The ailing woman reaches out in faith to touch Jesus' garment, but the disciples around him say, "You see the crowd pressing about you and yet you ask, 'Who touched me?'" (5:31). After Jesus speaks with utter clarity on obedience to God rather than to human custom, the disciples ask for an explanation of "the parable" (7:17). Even plain speech is dark to them! Jesus responds, "Are you then also without understanding?" (7:18). After Jesus walks on the water (6:45-51), "they were utterly astounded, for they did not understand about the loaves because their hearts were hardened" (6:52). The passage of Isa. 6:9-10, which in 4:12 had been applied to outsiders, is here applied to the disciples. The application is made again, without equivocation, in the dialogue between

Jesus and the disciples after the second feeding, this one on gentile territory (8:1-10). Jesus asks them, "Do you not yet perceive or understand? Are your hearts hardened? Having eyes do you not see, and having ears do you not hear, and do you not remember? Do you not yet understand?" (8:17-21).

That harsh question is followed immediately by the healing of the blind man in two stages (8:22-26). This is one of the few Markan stories not taken over by Matthew and Luke, and it clearly serves a special symbolic role in Mark's narrative. It anticipates the progression of the disciples from a state of complete blindness to a state of feeble sight, which is to be shown in the succeeding narrative.

To Jerusalem: 8:27—10:52

Peter learned something from Jesus' multiplication of the loaves. He was able to recognize a messianic figure (see 2 Sam. 5:2; Ps. 23:1; Isa. 40:11; Ezek. 34:12; Zech. 10:2) from the sight of one who like a shepherd fed the sheep (6:34): "You are the Christ" (8:29). But like the vision of the man who saw humans walking about as trees (8:24), Peter's vision is still blurred. A messiah could mean many things in that world (see chap. 2, p. 48), and the working definition of the disciples, we quickly learn, has to do with power and prestige. Their sight needed correction, and Mark devotes the next section of his narrative to that task.

As Jesus moves inexorably toward Jerusalem and his own death, he reveals himself as the Son of man who is to be rejected, then suffer and die (8:31; 9:31; 10:33-34). After each of these announcements, his disciples betray a fundamental misunderstanding of his messiahship and therefore also of their discipleship (8:32; 9:33-34, 38; 10:35-37). In response to each misunderstanding, Jesus clarifies the nature of discipleship, making clear that it demands following after him in service even to death (8:34-38; 9:35-37, 39-41; 10:38-45).

The first instance is paradigmatic. Peter objects to Jesus' talk of suffering by "rebuking" him. The word used here is the same used when Jesus "rebukes" the demons; Peter seeks to "bind" Jesus as Jesus "bound" Satan. But Jesus now in turn rebukes Peter and identifies him as representing precisely the cosmic forces that resist God's rule; he calls Peter, simply, "Satan." Peter wants the mystery to match his own perceptions, but Jesus tells him, "You are not on the side of God but of men" (8:33), and reminds him of the proper place for a disciple, as a follower: "Get behind me."

Throughout the journey the disciples are not only fearful (9:6, 32; 10:32) and confused (9:28, 34, 38; 10:26, 37), they consistently try to tailor the mystery to their own measure. They do not want a suffering messiah (8:32). They use human standards of greatness (9:34). They divide the world easily into us and them (9:38); they want power over others in the kingdom (10:37). They do not perceive that the mystery of the kingdom *is* Jesus and that resisting his path toward death means resisting the kingdom of God.

Mark makes this teaching explicit. To be a disciple of Jesus, one must "take up the cross and follow" (8:34), be willing to lose one's life (8:35), be "last of all and servant of all" (9:35), allow others to perform wonders with no personal gain for oneself (9:39), be initiated into the death of Jesus, and live as slaves of all (10:39-44). In short, to learn from this teacher, that is, to be a disciple, one must walk in the way that Jesus is taking, following after him.

The transfiguration (9:2-8) alerts the readers to the proper understanding of this whole narrative sequence. The closest companions of Jesus see him proleptically in glory and they seek to preserve that condition. Peter says, "Lord, it is good for us to be here. Let us make three booths, one for you, one for Moses, one for Elijah" (9:5). Mark immediately lets the readers know that Peter's impetuous response is wrongheaded: "He did not know what to say, for they were exceedingly afraid" (9:5). Peter's error was twofold. First, he wanted to control and domesticate the mystery by reducing it to ritual expression (the tents). Second, he saw Jesus as just another "man of God" on an equal level with Moses and Elijah. The voice from the cloud pronounces correction to these errors, not only for the three disciples, but above all for Mark's readers. First, Jesus is not like other prophets and thaumaturges: "This is my beloved [or, unique] Son." Second, Jesus is the pattern for discipleship: "Listen to *him*." If we are to learn *how* Jesus is Christ and Son (1:1), Mark tells us, and if we are to learn what it means to be "with him" as a disciple, then we cannot listen to Peter and these others, who think just as we do. We must look to Jesus alone (9:8).

Jesus in Jerusalem: 11:1—13:37

While Mark has kept our attention focused on Jesus and the disciples, he has not let us forget entirely the opposition to Jesus from those who are truly outsiders, the Jewish leaders. Their opposition reaches a climax in the Jerusalem narrative, providing a dramatic prelude to the description of Jesus' death. Mark has another purpose in showing Jesus rebutting a whole series of Jewish opponents: through the teaching of Jesus, he situates his Christian readers with respect to Judaism and Torah.

We have seen how the active conflict between Jesus and Jewish leaders began in the series of controversies of 2:1-3:6, resulting in the resolve to kill Jesus. We have seen how scribes from Jerusalem accused Jesus of demonic possession (3:22-27), how scribes and Pharisees challenged him on purity regulations (7:1-13), and how Pharisees questioned him on divorce (10:2-9). In these last two cases, Jesus turns from a rebuttal of the opposition to private instruction of his followers (7:17-19; 10:10-12). For his followers he also corrects the scribal view of Elijah's return (9:11-13). Similarly, when the Pharisees ask for a sign from heaven after the multiplication of the loaves, he rebukes them (8:12), then warns his disciples, "Beware of the leaven of the Pharisees and the leaven of Herod" (8:15).

When Jesus enters Jerusalem publicly proclaimed as Messiah, the readers therefore know that he is entering the home of his enemies. The people who recognized the signs of a Davidic messiah in his feedings (6:34) and heard him called Son of David by blind Bartimaeus (10:52), now cheer him as he enters the city, shouting in exuberance: "the kingdom of our father David . . . is coming" (11:9-10). The leaders, however, do not cheer. They prepare themselves for the final conflict with Jesus.

We have already seen how Mark weaves together the fate of the fig tree and the temple (see above, p. 163). Neither the tree nor the temple yielded what God willed. Both will thus be rejected. So also, we are clearly to understand, will those who reject God's kingdom in Jesus. Indeed, the parable of the vineyard, placed in the middle of the Jerusalem sequence, plainly offers the reader this interpretation of events (12:1-11).

The temple from this point forward plays an important thematic role. Although Jesus predicts the temple's end in private discourse (13:2), it is the only charge made explicitly against him in the Sanhedrin trial (14:58). And when Jesus dies on the cross, "the curtain of the temple was torn in two, from top to bottom" (15:38). Mark thereby signals that the old separation between insider and outsider, between sacred and profane, is gone. Jesus is the place of the mystery where the holy is revealed. Mark anticipates Jesus' replacing the temple as focus of the cult for Christians by having Jesus prophetically cleanse it (11:15-17)—thus sealing his own fate (11:18)—and then using it as the scene for Jesus' final confrontation with his enemies (see 11:27).

Representative Jewish leaders approach Jesus as he teaches in the temple. Each asks a question appropriate to the group's concerns; and each in turn is bested by Jesus. Sanhedrin members question his authority (11:28-33); Pharisees and Herodians try to trap him on the issue of giving taxes to Caesar (12:13-17); and Sadducees challenge him on the resurrection life (12:18-27). The scribes have been Jesus' chief opponents throughout the narrative and the temple scene closes with Jesus' interaction with them. A scribe who identifies love of God and neighbor as the first commandments of Torah is said by Jesus to be "not far from the kingdom of God" (12:28-34). But the scribes who think the Messiah is nothing more than David's son (i.e., human) and not also Lord are said to be misguided (12:35-37). Jesus' last words in the temple form an attack on the rapacity of scribes who steal from widows (12:38-40), providing a sharp contrast to the widow who puts "all her living" into the poor fund of the temple (12:41-44).

Since the conflict with Jewish leaders took place in the temple precincts, the transition to Jesus' apocalyptic discourse is all the more striking. Here the contrast between insider and outsider is again expressed in spatial terms. Jesus withdraws from the temple, sits with his close companions on the mount facing the temple, and predicts the temple's fall (13:1-4). The insiders with Jesus are themselves in danger of becoming outsiders. The motif of taking heed and watching, which runs through this discourse, takes on a special poignancy at this place in the narrative, for we shall shortly see that those told to watch will prove incapable of doing so. Mark wants them to be a warn-

ing to his readers, for he closes the discourse with this opening to the readers, "What I
say to you I say to all, watch!" (13:37).

The Passion: 14:1—15:47

Mark's whole narrative has moved steadily toward Jesus' death. In the Passion narrative, the dialectic between the inner and outer becomes intensified, as Mark shifts the
readers back and forth from the outer plot to its inner meaning.

The outer plot shows Jesus caught up in the machinery of official rejection, condemnation, and death. The chief priests and scribes seek his death (14:1-2), arrest him
in the garden (14:43), try him (14:53-65), and as Jesus had predicted, hand him over
to Gentiles (15:1-15). And those who should have been with Jesus become part of the
apparatus of betrayal. Judas was chosen to be with Jesus, though even then Mark
warned the reader to expect betrayal by him (3:19). Now he conspires with Jesus' enemies (14:10-11) and leads them to him (14:44). The enormity of his betrayal is emphasized by the repetition of "one of the Twelve" in 14:10 and 14:43. Peter had always
resisted Jesus' suffering. Now, despite his foolish boasting (14:29), he denies Jesus three
times (14:66-72). When Jesus is arrested, "all forsook him and fled" (14:50). At this
point Mark adds a provocative statement, to which we will return: "And a young man
followed him [this is a suggestive phrase] with nothing but a linen cloth about his
body. And they seized him; but he left the linen cloth and ran away naked" (14:51-52).
Here is the real failure of the disciples: not lack of knowledge but lack of loyalty. They
were chosen simply to "be with him," to "follow," and in this they all failed.

While the outer plot unravels, Mark draws his readers into three scenes that reveal
its inner meaning: the anointing, the supper, and the garden. In the anointing (14:3-
9), an anonymous woman's action symbolizes Jesus' messiahship as inextricably
bound up with his death (14:8) and memorializes her "wherever the good news is
preached" (14:9). Typical of the women in this Gospel (cf. 5:28; 7:25), she shows more
insight into Jesus' identity than those with him. Only women stay anywhere near the
scene of Jesus' death, following and ministering to him (15:41). They did what the disciples were supposed to do—follow—and they did for the Messiah what he did for
others—minister. Women also witness the burial (15:47) and are the first entrusted
with the message of the resurrection (16:1-8). And although the shorter ending has
them flee in fear, telling no one, Mark's longer ending has Mary Magdalene report the
incident to the disciples (16:11), although they refuse to believe her.

At the supper (14:12-25), the mystery of the kingdom is revealed in ritual. The broken bread recalls the loaves shared on the mountains, and the body to be shattered on
the hill; Jesus is the body language of servanthood. The cup recalls the suffering
promised the disciples (10:39), which Jesus himself must now face (cf. 14:36). The
Passover meal is therefore transformed by his impending death "for many" (see 10:45).
But even here, the presence of his betrayer and of his denier renders the symbolism of

the bread ambiguous (14:17-21). Nevertheless, the supper points to a future beyond Jesus' betrayal and death: "I will drink it new in the kingdom of God" (14:25). And at the moment of entering the garden to face his agony, Jesus tells them, "You will all fall away, for it is written, 'I will strike the shepherd and the sheep will be scattered.' But after I am raised up, I will go before you to Galilee" (14:27-28).

In the garden, the mystery is not mediated by ritual but is exposed in the raw encounter of the Holy One alone and in fear. He asks that the cup be taken away, but the final words of his prayer reveal him to be truly both the obedient son and the pattern for discipleship: "Abba, . . . not my will but yours be done" (14:36). Even as Jesus thus prays, his closest companions whom he had asked to "watch with him" (14:34, 37; cf. 13:37) fall asleep three times, emphatically failing him, remaining outsiders to that lonely place where Jesus accepts the Father's will.

Having revealed in these three scenes the inner meaning beneath what appears to be a meaningless execution, Mark sweeps his readers back into the turmoil of the outer plot, moving them quickly through the arrest, hearing, trial, and at last, the crucifixion. How that climactic scene is made meaningful through scriptural midrash I have tried to demonstrate earlier (see chap. 6, pp. 145–49). But Mark does not thereby relieve the desolation of Jesus' death. Jesus is surrounded at the end by triumphant and mocking enemies. He is abandoned by his followers. Only the women from Galilee watch from afar, bearing witness (15:40-41). Jesus, the *mystērion* of the kingdom is at last alone before the still more awesome mystery of God. Only the Markan readers can recognize in the apparent cry of desolation "My God, my God, why have you forsaken me?" the faint anticipation of hope offered by Ps. 22:1. With consummate irony Mark chooses this moment to have the ultimate outsider, Jesus' executioner, become the only human character in the narrative to identify Jesus properly: "Truly this was God's son" (15:39). This is hidden revelation, indeed.

The Empty Tomb: 16:1-8

We return again to the ending, and this time, having followed Jesus all through Mark's narrative, find it surprisingly full of hope. The disciples who had abandoned Jesus will see him again "in Galilee" (see 14:28). Jesus is alive and goes before them; they are called once more to "follow after" him.

Now, we look more closely at the young man who delivers the message. He is dressed in a white robe. He sits at the right hand of the tomb. The white robe tells us that he has been transformed. But from what? Where have we seen this young man before? We remember him as the naked young man in the garden, who fled (14:51-52). And remembering this, we understand that those who fail can also be restored.

Hearing the young man's message, we are also moved to ponder again the meaning of this "Galilee" where they are to see Jesus. Where is it? For those who read now—and possibly for Mark's first readers—there remains only the Galilee of the text. The reader is therefore invited by the young man to follow Jesus in order "to see him there." The invitation is to read the story again with the "new eyes" one has been given.

When we read the text again, seeking the resurrected one in the story, we encounter another one who was "in the tombs" (5:2-5), the naked demoniac. He was so strong because of his demonic possession that no one could bind him. Yet he recognized the "Son of the most high God," and when he was freed from his self-alienation, he was found clothed, seated next to Jesus, and in his right mind (*sōphronounta*; 5:15). That man wanted to "be with" Jesus as his disciple (5:18), but Jesus did not allow him. Rather he was told to "go and tell all" what the Lord had done for him (5:19), just as these women at the tomb are told to "go and tell" by a young man, newly clothed, sitting at the right side of the tomb. The healed demoniac did not keep silence, but "went away and began to proclaim [*kēryssein* = preaching] in the Decapolis [= gentile territory] how much Jesus had done for him" (5:20).

Because Mark forces us to reconsider all his story by the openness of his ending, we discover that not fear and silence but proclamation of Jesus continued the gospel story, a proclamation announced by those who, however inadequate or even faithless, had come to be "in their right minds" by knowing that the Stronger One lives.

Study Questions

1. In Mark's Gospel, what role does apocalyptic symbolism play?

2. What roles do secrecy and irony play in Mark's Gospel?

3. How does the beginning of Mark's Gospel (1:1-15) establish different perceptions than Luke 1–2?

4. What are the important issues about the ending of Mark's Gospel? If you were publishing a translation of the New Testament, how would you deal with these issues in terms of printing and footnotes?

Bibliographical Note

The Synoptic Gospels

Evidence for the Synoptic Problem is displayed by B. H. Throckmorton Jr., *Gospel Parallels: A Comparison of the Synoptic Gospels*, 5th ed. (Nashville: Thomas Nelson Pubs., 1992). The classic argument for the two-source solution to the Synoptic problem was put forth by B. H. Streeter, *The Four Gospels: A Study of Origins* (London: Macmillan & Co., 1924); a more accessible treatment can be found in R. H. Stein, *The*

Synoptic Problem: An Introduction (Grand Rapids: Baker Books, 1987). Also see F. G. Downing, "Compositional Conventions and the Synoptic Problem," *JBL* 107 (1988): 69–85; and D. L. Dungan (ed.), *The Interrelations of the Gospels* (BETL, 95; Macon: Mercer Univ. Press, 1990). Matthew's priority is argued by B. C. Butler, *The Original-ity of St. Matthew* (Cambridge: Cambridge Univ. Press, 1951); and W. R. Farmer, *The Synoptic Problem: A Critical Analysis* (Dillsboro, N.C.: Western North Carolina Press, 1976 [1964]). For a critique of the Griesbach Hypothesis, see S. E. Johnson, *The Gries-bach Hypothesis and Redaction Criticism* (SBLMS, 41; Atlanta: Scholars Press, 1991); and C. M. Tuckett, *The Revival of the Griesbach Hypothesis: An Analysis and Appraisal* (SNTSMS, 44; Cambridge: Cambridge Univ. Press, 1983). For an argument of the primacy of oral tradition in the relationships among the Gospels, see J. M. Rist, *On the Independence of Matthew and Mark* (SNTSMS, 32: Cambridge: Cambridge Univ. Press, 1978).

On Q, see D. Catchpole, *The Quest for Q* (Edinburgh: T. & T. Clark, 1993); R. A. Edwards, *A Theology of Q: Eschatology, Prophecy, and Wisdom* (Philadelphia: Fortress Press, 1976); M. Goulder, "Is Q a Juggernaut?," *JBL* 115 (1996): 667–81; I. Havener, *Q: The Sayings of Jesus* (Collegeville, Minn.: The Liturgical Press, 1990 [1987]); A. D. Jacobson, *The First Gospel: An Introduction to Q* (Sonoma, Calif.: Polebridge Press, 1992); J. S. Kloppenborg, *The Formation of Q: Trajectories in Ancient Wisdom Collec-tions* (Philadelphia: Fortress Press, 1987); idem (ed.), *The Shape of Q: Signal Essays on the Sayings Gospel* (Minneapolis: Fortress Press, 1994); R. A. Piper (ed.), *The Gospel Behind the Gospels: Current Studies on Q* (NovTSup, 75; Leiden: E. J. Brill, 1995); and C. M. Tuckett, *Q and the History of Early Christianity* (Edinburgh: T. & T. Clark, 1996).

Popular introductions to the Synoptics as a whole are K. H. Nickle, *The Synoptic Gospels: An Introduction* (Atlanta: John Knox Press, 1980); and B. Reicke, *The Roots of the Synoptic Gospels* (Philadelphia: Fortress Press, 1986). For general issues, see J. B. Green et al. (eds.), *Dictionary of Jesus and the Gospels* (Downers Grove: InterVarsity Press, 1992). For a collection of essays on the three Gospels, see C. A. Evans and S. E. Porter (eds.), *The Synoptic Gospels: A Sheffield Reader* (Sheffield: Sheffield Academic Press, 1995); and P. Stuhlmacher (ed.), *The Gospel and the Gospels* (Grand Rapids: Eerdmans, 1991).

On the genre of the Gospels, see R. A. Burridge, *What Are the Gospels? A Compari-son with Graeco-Roman Biography* (SNTSMS, 70; Cambridge: Cambridge Univ. Press, 1992); C. H. Talbert, *What Is a Gospel? The Genre of the Canonical Gospels* (Philadel-phia: Fortress Press, 1977); and J. Z. Smith, "Good News Is No News: Aretalogy and Gospels," in his, *Map Is Not Territory: Studies in the History of Religions* (Chicago: Univ. of Chicago Press, 1993 [1978]), 190–207.

Treatments of the evangelists' purposes in writing (redaction criticism) can be found in S. Freyne, *The Twelve: Disciples and Apostles; A Study in the Theology of the First Three Gospels* (London: Sheed & Ward, 1968); N. Perrin, *What Is Redaction*

Criticism? (GBS; Philadelphia: Fortress Press, 1969); J. Reumann, *Jesus in the Church's Gospels: Modern Scholarship and the Earliest Sources* (Philadelphia: Fortress Press, 1968); and J. Rohde, *Rediscovering the Teaching of the Evangelists*, trans. D. M. Barton (Philadelphia: Westminster Press, 1968). Also see the collection of essays in R. Bauckham (ed.), *The Gospels for All Christians: Rethinking the Gospel Audiences* (Grand Rapids: Eerdmans, 1998).

The Gospel of Mark

Representative of early form critics' appreciation of Mark as an editor is R. Bultmann, *The History of the Synoptic Tradition*, trans. J. Marsh, rev. ed. (New York: Harper & Row, 1968), 337–51. Less complimentary is J. Meagher, *Clumsy Construction in Mark's Gospel: A Critique of Form and Redaktionsgeschichte* (New York: Edwin Mellen Press, 1979). More recent criticism of Mark's style can be found in D. W. Chapman, *The Orphan Gospel: Mark's Perspective on Jesus* (BS, 16; Sheffield: Sheffield Academic Press, 1993).

Mark's theological purposes were taken seriously in the pioneering study by R. H. Lightfoot, *History and Interpretation in the Gospels* (New York: Harper & Brothers, 1934). Of far greater influence was the study in redaction criticism by W. Marxsen, *Mark the Evangelist: Studies on Redaction History of the Gospel*, trans. J. Boyece et al. (Nashville: Abingdon Press, 1969). Also see, more recently, C. C. Black, *The Disciples According to Mark: Markan Redaction in Current Debate* (JSNTSup, 97; Sheffield: Sheffield Academic Press, 1989).

The community-crisis approach to Mark's Gospel is exemplified by W. Kelber, *The Kingdom in Mark: A New Place and a New Time* (Philadelphia: Fortress Press, 1974); E. Trocmé, *The Formation of the Gospel According to Mark*, trans. P. Gaughan (Philadelphia: Westminster Press, 1975); and T. Weeden, *Mark: Traditions in Conflict* (Philadelphia: Fortress Press, 1971). A fuller attempt to sketch the Markan community on the basis of the text is found in H. C. Kee, *Community of the New Age: Studies in Mark's Gospel* (Philadelphia: Westminster Press, 1977). A recent argument for taking the historical traditions of Mark seriously is made by M. Hengel, *Studies in the Gospel of Mark*, trans. J. Bowden (Philadelphia: Fortress Press, 1985). On the traditions surrounding Mark the evangelist, see C. C. Black, *Mark: Images of an Apostolic Interpreter* (Columbia: Univ. of South Carolina Press, 1994).

A thoroughly literary approach to Mark was pioneered by A. Farrer, *A Study in St. Mark* (Westminster: Dacre Press, 1951), and has become influential in recent scholarship, as represented by R. M. Fowler, *Let the Reader Understand: Reader-Response Criticism and the Gospel of Mark* (Minneapolis: Fortress Press, 1991); J. D. Kingsbury, *The Christology of Mark's Gospel* (Philadelphia: Fortress Press, 1983); E. S. Malbon, *Narrative Space and Mythic Meaning in Mark* (San Francisco: Harper & Row, 1986); D. Rhoads and D. Michie, *Mark as Story: An Introduction to the Narrative of a*

Gospel (Philadelphia: Fortress Press, 1982); S. H. Smith, *A Lion With Wings: A Narrative-Critical Approach to Mark's Gospel* (BS, 38; Sheffield: Sheffield Academic Press, 1996); R. C. Tannehill, "The Disciples in Mark: The Function of a Narrative Role," *JR* 57 (1977): 386–405; and M. A. Tolbert, *Sowing the Gospel: Mark's World in Literary-Historical Perspective* (Minneapolis: Fortress Press, 1989). For a variety of contemporary methodological approaches to Mark, see S. D. Anderson and J. C. Moore (eds.), *Mark & Method: New Approaches in Biblical Studies* (Minneapolis: Fortress Press, 1992).

For a general treatment of important themes and issues, see E. Best, *Mark: The Gospel as Story* (Edinburgh: T. & T. Clark, 1983); idem, "Mark's Narrative Technique," *JSNT* 37 (1989): 43–58; C. Bryan, *A Preface to Mark: Notes on the Gospel in its Literary and Cultural Settings* (New York: Oxford Univ. Press, 1993); R. Martin, *Mark: Evangelist and Theologian* (Grand Rapids: Zondervan, 1972); V. K. Robbins, *Jesus the Teacher: A Socio-Rhetorical Interpretation of Mark* (Philadelphia: Fortress Press, 1984); W. R. Telford (ed.), *The Interpretation of Mark*, 2nd ed. (IRT, 7; Edinburgh: T. & T. Clark, 1995); idem, *Mark* (Sheffield: Sheffield Academic Press, 1995); and A. Yarbro Collins, *The Beginning of the Gospel: Probings of Mark in Context* (Minneapolis: Fortress Press, 1992).

On the use of Torah in Mark, see H. Anderson, "The Old Testament in Mark's Gospel," in J. M. Efird (ed.), *The Use of the Old Testament in the New Testament and Other Essays* (Durham: Duke Univ. Press, 1972), 280–306; H. C. Kee, "The Function of Scriptural Quotations and Allusions in Mark 11–16," in E. E. Ellis and E. Grässer (eds.), *Jesus und Paulus* (Göttingen: Vandenhoeck & Ruprecht, 1975), 165–88; and J. Marcus, *The Way of the Lord: Christological Exegesis of the Old Testament in the Gospel of Mark* (Louisville: Westminster/John Knox Press, 1992).

Mark's peculiar use of secrecy was first explored by W. Wrede, *The Messianic Secret*, trans. J. C. Grieg (Cambridge: James Clark, 1971 [1901]). For more recent scholarship on the messianic secret, see H. Räisänen, *The "Messianic Secret" in Mark's Gospel*, trans. C. M. Tuckett (Edinburgh: T. & T. Clark, 1990); and C. M. Tuckett (ed.), *The Messianic Secret* (IRT, 1; Philadelphia: Fortress Press; London SPCK, 1983). On the use of the title "Son of man" in Mark, see D. R. A. Hare, *The Son of Man Tradition* (Minneapolis: Fortress Press, 1990); and M. D. Hooker, *The Son of Man in Mark* (Montreal: McGill Univ. Press, 1967).

On various aspects of the passion narrative, see E. Best, *The Temptation & the Passion: The Markan Soteriology*, 2nd ed. (SNTSMS, 2; Cambridge: Cambridge Univ. Press, 1990); E. K. Broadhead, *Prophet, Son, Messiah: Narrative Form and Function Mark 14–16* (JSNTSup, 97; Sheffield: Sheffield Academic Press, 1994); J. R. Donahue, *Are You the Christ? The Trial Narrative in the Gospel of Mark* (SBLDS, 10; Missoula, Mont.: Scholars Press, 1973); R. G. Hamerton-Kelly, "Sacred Violence and the Messiah: The Markan Passion Narrative as a Redefinition of Messianology," in J. H. Charlesworth (ed.), *The Messiah: Developments in Earliest Judaism and Christianity* (Minneapolis: Fortress Press 1992), 461–93; D. Juel, *Messiah and Temple: The Trial of*

Jesus in the Gospel of Mark (SBLDS, 31; Missoula, Mont.: Scholars Press, 1977); W. H. Kelber (ed.), *The Passion in Mark: Studies on Mark 14–16* (Philadelphia: Fortress Press, 1976); and F. J. Matera, *The Kingship of Jesus: Composition and Theology in Mark 15* (SBLDS, 66; Chico, Calif.: Scholars Press, 1982).

On discipleship, see S. C. Barton, *Discipleship and Family Ties in Mark and Matthew* (SNTSMS, 80; Cambridge: Cambridge Univ. Press, 1994); E. Best, *Disciples and Discipleship: Studies in the Gospel According to Mark* (Edinburgh: T. & T. Clark, 1986); idem, *Following Jesus: Discipleship in the Gospel of Mark* (JSNTSup, 4; Sheffield: Sheffield Academic Press, 1981); D. M. Rhoads, "Network for Mission: The Social System of the Jesus Movement as Depicted in the Narrative of the Gospel of Mark," *ANRW* II.26.2 (1995): 692–729; and W. T. Shiner, *Follow Me! Disciples in Markan Rhetoric* (SBLDS, 145; Atlanta: Scholars Press, 1995).

Among the studies that are congenial to the reading found in this chapter, see R. Meye, *Jesus and the Twelve* (Grand Rapids: Eerdmans, 1968); J. R. Donahue, *The Theology and Setting of Discipleship in the Gospel of Mark* (Milwaukee: Marquette Univ. Press, 1983); T. A. Burkill, *Mysterious Revelation* (Ithaca, N.Y.: Cornell Univ. Press, 1962); N. A. Dahl, "The Purpose of Mark's Gospel," in his *Jesus in the Memory of the Early Church* (Minneapolis: Augsburg, 1976), 52–65; F. Kermode, *The Genesis of Secrecy: On the Interpretation of Narrative* (Cambridge, Mass.: Harvard Univ. Press, 1979); D. M. Rhoads, "Losing Life for Others in the Face of Death: Mark's Standards of Judgment," *Int* 47 (1993): 358–69; J. M. Robinson, *The Problem of History in Mark and Other Marcan Studies* (Philadelphia: Fortress Press, 1982 [1957]); N. Perrin, *What Is Redaction Criticism?* (GBS; Philadelphia: Fortress Press, 1969), 40–57; idem, "The Interpretation of the Gospel of Mark," *Int* 30 (1976): 115–24; L. E. Keck, "The Introduction to Mark's Gospel," *NTS* 12 (1965–66): 352–70; H. C. Kee, "The Terminology of Mark's Exorcism Stories," *NTS* 14 (1967–68): 232–46; J. D. Crossan, "Mark and the Relatives of Jesus," *NovT* 15 (1973): 81–113; and G. H. Boobyer, "The Secrecy Motif in Mark's Gospel," *NTS* 6 (1959–60): 225–35. Mark as apocalyptic drama is found in N. Perrin, *The New Testament: An Introduction* (New York: Harcourt Brace Jovanovich, 1974), 143–67.

For other significant studies of themes and passages, see A. M. Ambrose, *The Hidden Kingdom: A Redaction-Critical Study of the References to Kingdom of God in Mark's Gospel* (CBQMS, 2; Washington: Catholic Biblical Assoc., 1972); G. R. Beasley-Murray, *Jesus and the Last Days: An Interpretation of the Olivet Discourse* (Peabody, Mass.: Hendrickson Pubs., 1993); M. A. Beavis, *Mark's Audience: The Literary and Social Setting of Mark 4.11–12* (JSNTSup, 33; Sheffield: Sheffield Academic Press, 1989); C. C. Black, "An Oration at Olivet: Some Rhetorical Dimensions of Mark 13," in D. F. Watson (ed.), *Persuasive Artistry* (JSNTSup, 50: Sheffield: Sheffield Academic Press, 1991), 66–92; R. P. Booth, *Jesus and the Laws of Purity: Tradition History and Legal History in Mark 7* (JSNTSup, 13; Sheffield: JSOT Press, 1986); M. J. Cook, *Mark's Treatment of the Jewish Leaders* (NovTSup, 51; Leiden: E. J. Brill, 1978); J. Dewey, *Markan Public Debate: Literary Technique, Concentric Structure and Theology in Mark 2:1—3:6* (SBLDS, 48;

Chico, Calif.: Scholars Press, 1980); S. E. Dowd, *Prayer, Power, and the Problem of Suffering: Mark 11:22–25 in the Context of Markan Theology* (SBLDS, 105; Atlanta: Scholars Press, 1988); T. Dwyer, *The Motif of Wonder in the Gospel of Mark* (JSNTSup, 128; Sheffield: Sheffield Academic Press, 1996); W. R. Farmer, *The Last Twelve Verses of Mark* (SNTSMS, 25; Cambridge: Cambridge Univ. Press, 1974); S. R. Garrett, *The Temptations of Jesus in Mark's Gospel* (Grand Rapids: Eerdmans, 1998); T. J. Geddert, *Watchwords: Mark 13 in Markan Eschatology* (JSNTSup, 26; Sheffield: Sheffield Academic Press, 1989); P. M. Head, *Christology and the Synoptic Problem: An Argument for Markan Priority* (SNTSMS, 94; Cambridge: Cambridge Univ. Press, 1997); B. W. Henaut, *Oral Tradition and the Gospels: The Problem of Mark 4* (JSNTSup, 82; Sheffield: Sheffield Academic Press, 1993); B. L. Mack, *A Myth of Innocence: Mark and Christian Origins* (Philadelphia: Fortress Press, 1988); J. Marcus, *The Mystery of the Kingdom of God* (SBLDS, 90; Atlanta: Scholars Press, 1986); C. D. Marshall, *Faith as a Theme in Mark's Narrative* (SNTSMS, 64; Cambridge: Cambridge Univ. Press, 1989); U. W. Mauser, *Christ in the Wilderness: The Wilderness Theme in the Second Gospel and Its Basis in the Biblical Tradition* (London: SCM Press, 1963); T. Shepherd, *Markan Sandwich Stories: Narration, Definition, and Function* (Berrien Springs, Mich.: Andrews Univ. Press, 1993); W. R. Stegner, *Narrative Theology in Early Jewish Christianity* (Louisville: Westminster/John Knox Press, 1989); W. R. Telford, *The Barren Temple and the Withered Tree* (JSNTSup, 1; Sheffield: JSOT Press, 1980); and J. F. Williams, *Other Followers of Jesus: Minor Characters as Major Figures in Mark's Gospel* (JSNTSup, 102; Sheffield: Sheffield Academic Press, 1994).

For studies treating the role of women in Mark and the rest of the Synoptics more generally, see K. L. Corley, *Private Women, Public Meals: Social Conflict in the Synoptic Tradition* (Peabody, Mass.: Hendrickson Pubs., 1993); R. S. Kraemer and M. R. D'Angelo (eds.), *Women and Christian Origins: A Reader* (New York: Oxford Univ. Press, 1999); L. Schottroff, *Lydia's Impatient Sisters: A Feminist Social History of Early Christianity*, trans. B. Rumscheidt and M. Rumscheidt (Louisville: Westminster/John Knox Press, 1995); E. Schüssler Fiorenza, *In Memory of Her: A Feminist Theological Reconstruction of Christian Origins* (New York: Crossroad, 1983), 103–59; B. Witherington, III, *Women in the Earliest Churches* (SNTSMS, 59; Cambridge: Cambridge Univ. Press, 1988), 158–74; and idem, *Women in the Ministry of Jesus* (SNTSMS, 51; Cambridge: Cambridge Univ. Press, 1984).

For more detailed, critical commentaries on Mark, see C. E. B. Cranfield, *The Gospel According to St. Mark*, 4th ed. (Cambridge: Cambridge Univ. Press, 1972); R. A. Guelich, *Mark 1—8:26* (WBC; Dallas: Word Books, 1989); and R. H. Gundry, *Mark: A Commentary on His Apology for the Cross* (Grand Rapids: Eerdmans, 1993). More straightforward guides are M. D. Hooker, *The Gospel According to St. Mark* (Peabody, Mass.: Hendrickson Pubs., 1991); L. W. Hurtado, *Mark*, 2nd ed. (Peabody, Mass.: Hendrickson Pubs., 1989); and E. Schweizer, *The Good News According to Mark* (Richmond: John Knox Press, 1970).

8. The Gospel of Matthew

MATTHEW IS THE GOSPEL of the church. Not only is it the only Gospel to use the term "church," *ekklēsia* (16:18; 18:17), but both its contents and structure indicate an interest in providing clear and coherent guidance to a community of believers. In contrast to the Gospel of Mark's rather marginal early existence, Matthew has been from the beginning the Gospel most used by the church in its worship, and in consequence, it has provided the text for the most preaching and commentary. Already quoted directly by Ignatius of Antioch (ca. 115), it was given a full-scale commentary by Origen (ca. 185–254). So far as ecclesial use is concerned, Matthew is the most successful edition of Mark's Gospel.

The patristic writers, moreover, regarded Matthew as the first of the Gospels to be written. Along with the Gospel's inherent excellence and usefulness, this putative priority gave Matthew a favored place. If Matthew was written first, and if its author was the apostle Matthew, then the earliest Gospel could claim apostolic and even eyewitness authority, a claim Mark obviously could not make. Papias is our earliest source for this traditional attribution. He says, "Matthew organized 'the sayings' [*ta logia*] in the Hebrew dialect, but everyone has translated them as best he could" (Eusebius *Ecclesiastical History* III.39, 16). It is not at all clear what "the sayings" really were, or what the "Hebrew dialect" was. It is not clear that Papias had any decent historical information at all. But Irenaeus (*Against Heresies* III.1.1) and Origen (*Eccl. Hist.* VI.25.3–6) understood that Matthew, one of Jesus' apostles, first wrote a Gospel in Hebrew that was later translated into Greek. Such also was the opinion of Jerome (*Commentary on Matthew*, pref. 5–7) and of Augustine (*On the Harmony of the Evangelists* I.II.4) who reduced Mark to the status of "a lackey and abbreviator" of Matthew (*Harmony* I.II.4).

Some internal evidence supports this tradition. The manuscripts of the Gospel uniformly bear the heading "According to Matthew" and twice in the text itself this name is supplied. The tax collector whom Mark calls Levi of Alphaeus, and Luke simply Levi, is named Matthew by this Gospel (9:9). More significant, in the list of the Twelve (10:3), he reappears as "Matthew the tax collector" (contrast Mark 3:18 and Luke 6:15). The conviction of Matthew's priority may also have influenced its consistent placement as first in the canonical collection.

Those who support Matthean priority today claim tradition as their ally and insist as well that their version of the Griesbach hypothesis (1787)—which updates Augustine by having Mark at once conflate and reduce *both* Matthew *and* Luke—simplifies the issue by eliminating needless constructs such as Q. But even if part of the prehistory of this Gospel goes back to an apostle, which is certainly possible, the present Greek text of Matthew does not suggest a direct translation from Hebrew or Aramaic. When compared with Mark, for example, Matthew shows a consistently clearer, more concise and correct, use of Greek. Matthew incorporates most of Mark and follows Mark's order for the most part, and when he does not, Luke does. When passage after passage is carefully compared, it remains far easier to explain the differences as Matthew's commentary on and correction of Mark than as Mark's clumsy omission of fifty percent of Matthew. Finally, the Jewish quality of Matthew's language is due not to Matthew's early date or original language but to the social context and symbolic world of the community within which it was composed.

Style and Structure

Matthew is much longer than Mark, and its length is especially impressive because of the considerable compression it has forced on the ninety percent of Mark it uses. Matthew shortens all of Mark's narratives, generally needing a third fewer words to tell a parallel story (cf., e.g., the story of the Gerasene demoniac, Mark 5:1-20 and Matt. 8:28-34). Additional length comes from the extension of the story line. Matthew includes a genealogy and birth narrative (chaps. 1–2), as well as resurrection appearance accounts (28:9-10, 16-20). Most of the additional bulk, however, comes from the rich collection of discourse material that Matthew includes.

The story line of Mark, therefore, gives Matthew its basic structure (see pp. 169–179) and Matthew does not fundamentally disagree with Mark's understanding of Jesus. The Passion narrative still holds the same prominent and climactic place; Matthew follows Mark particularly closely, making only minor changes. He does, however, provide additional structural elements in the rest of the narrative.

Four of those structural elements deserve mention. First, he uses stereotyped *summary transitions* between discourse material and narrative: "When Jesus had finished these words . . ." (7:28-29; 11:1; 13:53; 19:1; 26:1). These transitions accentuate the alternation between kinds of material. The effect is similar to saying "Now, to pick up the story again . . ." Second, Matthew uses two *temporal transitions*, which mark stages in Jesus' ministry: in 4:17, "From that time, Jesus began to preach . . . ," and in 16:21, "From that time, Jesus began to show his disciples . . ." Third, he introduces many of his direct quotations from Scripture with the stereotyped formula "This was to fulfill what was spoken . . ." (1:22; 2:5, 15, 17, 23; 4:14; 8:17; 12:17; 13:14, 35; 21:4; 27:9). These are conventionally called *formula citations*, and they offer an authorial commentary on the narrative. Fourth, Matthew also puts materials within literary brackets, using the technique called *inclusio*. The effect is less dramatic than in Mark, but provides the reader with important clues for reading the Gospel. The entire narrative, for example, is framed between the angelic announcement in 1:23, ". . . his name shall be called Immanuel, which means 'God with us,'" and the messianic announcement in 28:20, ". . . lo, I am with you always, to the close of the age."

Matthew's Gospel lacks Mark's dramatic force because of the way the evangelist has arranged the sayings of Jesus he found in Q and M. Although called "Teacher" proportionately less often in this Gospel than in Mark, Jesus here does much more teaching. Matthew collects the sayings of Jesus into the form of sermons or discourses, and inserts them block fashion into Mark's narrative structure. The result is a much slower, and sometimes less than dramatic plot development.

The sayings collections are by no means random. First, they tend to be grouped topically. Thus, we find separately treated the law (5:17-48), piety (6:1-18), demands of discipleship (10:1-42), parables of the kingdom (13:1-52), relations in the church (18:1-35), polemic against opponents (23:1-39), and eschatology (24:4-25:46). Second, Matthew uses similar formal elements within each discourse: parables in chapter 13, beatitudes and antitheses in chapter 5, and woes in chapter 23. Third, Matthew uses numerical groupings. He is even more fond of threefold structures than Mark. The genealogy has three sets of fourteen generations (1:1-17). There are three angelic messages for Joseph (1:20; 2:13, 19), three temptations of Jesus (4:1-11), three modes of piety (6:1-18), and more. He uses other numerical groupings as well, such as six (the antitheses, 5:21-48), seven (parables and woes, chaps. 13 and 23), and ten (miracles, chaps. 8–9).

The discourse material in Matthew is, in sum, characterized by fullness, order, and symmetry. Matthew is a systematizer. In the abstract, it is possible that Jesus spoke all his blessings in one sermon or all his woes in another. It is also possible that, as in the rabbinic tradition, sayings could be organized mnemonically during oral transmission. But when we observe the tendency to systematize not only in the sayings material but also in the narrative, it becomes more likely that it is owed to Matthew's literary technique.

Two major and meritorious proposals have been advanced for the overall structure of Matthew's Gospel. The first pays closest attention to the summary transitions between discourse and narrative, which establish a definite alternating pattern throughout the Gospel. A narrative of beginnings (chaps. 1–4) leads to the discourse called the Sermon on the Mount (chaps. 5–7). The narrative of messianic words and wonders (chaps. 8–9) precedes a discourse on mission and discipleship (chap. 10). The narrative telling of growing opposition to Jesus (chaps. 11–12) is followed by parabolic discourse (chap. 13). A narrative of miracles and predictions (chaps. 14–17) leads to the discourse on life in the community (chap. 18). The narrative of the Judean ministry (chaps. 19–23) is followed by a discourse on the coming kingdom (chaps. 24–25). The Gospel concludes with the narrative of the Passion, death, and resurrection (chap. 26–28).

On this reading, there are five discourses set off by the transition formulas, suggesting to some that Matthew has deliberately structured his Gospel in five books, corresponding to the five books of the Pentateuch, the heart of Torah. He seeks thereby to provide his community with the messianic equivalent of Torah. This has been an enormously popular hypothesis, and it has considerable strength. Matthew does give Jesus a Mosaic shading, and his Gospel definitely reflects dialogue with a developing Pharisaic Judaism for which Torah was the central symbol (see above, chap. 2, pp. 52–58). Taken alone, however, the analysis also has weaknesses. It effectively reduces the beginning and end of the narrative to prologue and epilogue; indeed, it neglects the narrative generally. More tellingly, the discourse of chapter 23 does not fit the pattern and can be accounted for by the hypothesis only if it is regarded more as instruction to the disciples, in the manner of the other discourses, than as polemic against opponents.

A second structural analysis places greater emphasis on the narrative, particularly on the temporal transitions of 4:17 and 16:21. These establish within the narrative, it is suggested, a three-stage presentation of Jesus as Messiah: the person of Jesus Messiah (1:1—4:16); the proclamation of God's kingdom by Jesus Messiah (4:17—16:20); and the revelation of Jesus Messiah to his disciples through his suffering, death, and resurrection (16:21—28:20). Such an analysis has the virtue of recognizing that 1:1—4:16 is an integral literary unit with a specific thematic development, and it respects the shifts in emphasis on Jesus' ministry that the transitions indicate. It is an analysis that also complements the five-book hypothesis above. Both summary transitions and temporal transitions provide the reader with clues to Matthew's purposes.

Setting

The massive amount of teaching material in this Gospel and the systematic way in which it is presented have suggested two ecclesial contexts for its composition. The first is broadly catechetical. Matthew provides instructions for missionaries, discipline in the community, and forms of piety in a way that anticipates later church writings called church orders, the earliest of which is the *Didache* (usually dated ca. 90). An even more specific setting has been suggested: such teaching was developed in something like a Christian "scribal school" where reflection on the words and deeds of Jesus included demonstrations of how they fulfilled Torah.

A second plausible church setting for the development of at least some of Matthew's materials is liturgical. It has long been noted how much more liturgical some of Matthew's renditions are when compared to Luke's (e.g., the Lord's Prayer in Matt. 6:9-13 and Luke 11:2-4), a reflection, perhaps, of use in worship. Some have suggested that the Matthean tradition developed as a form of homiletic expansion of Mark; others, that a specific kind of midrashic activity accounted for the shape of Matthew.

Both the catechetical and the liturgical settings could have helped influence the shape of this Gospel. Certainly the plausibility of those suggestions reminds the reader again of the community orientation of this Gospel. In the end, however, we must recognize that a work such as this one is never simply the product of a group, but also of the artistry and religious perceptions of an individual author.

Is there anything we can learn from Matthew about the larger social context within which it was composed? As always in the case of ancient writings whose precise provenance is unknown and that bear signs of conscious literary fashioning, we need to be cautious. Even so, the very shape of this Gospel and its obvious attention to community concerns, as well as the character of its symbolization, make such speculation more plausible than in the case of Mark. These factors suggest a community that was in contact with, and sought to define itself over against, a developing Pharisaic tradition within Judaism. We will see shortly many individual details in the text that support this suggestion. Matthew may not have been providing his church with a new Moses or a new Torah, but his Gospel does define Jesus and the church by using the symbols specifically associated with what in its later developed form is called rabbinic Judaism.

An imaginative extrapolation may help us reconstruct the situation that the Gospel's form seems to presuppose. In the Mesopotamian border city of Dura Europos (destroyed in 256 c.e.), archaeologists discovered a Christian house church and a synagogue side by side. Devotees attending each were close enough for mutual comparison and contrast. Matthew's Gospel seems to demand something like that sort of situation: the Christian sect not only was aware of the older and better-established Jewish tradition but also found itself required to explain and understand—first of all for itself—why it came to worship here and not in the synagogue down the street. Matthew's Gospel makes a great deal of sense if this pluralistic context is assumed, one in which rival and persuasive claims demand interpretation of one's own. In order to distinguish the story of Jesus and the church from that of Pharisaic Judaism, Matthew must appropriate the very symbols of that tradition. The movements of both separation and appropriation are evident in the text of the Gospel.

If Mark can be read as an apocalyptic narrative, Matthew's shaping of the story of Jesus owes most to the symbols of the rabbinic tradition. And if this suggested setting is accurate, the time and place of Matthew's final composition are easier to locate. Both the scribal quality of the Gospel and its knowledge of Pharisaic traditions suggest an urban setting, and nothing in the text disputes this. We cannot be sure which city, of course, though Antioch is the traditional favorite guess and remains so today. As for dating, we remember that the Pharisaic movement really emerged as dominant—eventually becoming normative—after the fall of the temple. Hostility between messianist and non-messianist Jews grew more fierce after that point and reached a crystallization in the *Birkat-ha-minim*, which brought curses on heretics and made it impossible for Christians to pray in synagogues from this point on. That benediction is usually, though not definitively, dated ca. 85 c.e. Further precision is not possible.

I am not suggesting that the Matthean church was necessarily Jewish-Christian demographically (although this is a possibility). It knows of the gentile mission and may itself be one of its fruits. But it is a church that must define itself in terms of a more dominant Jewish movement. This accounts both for the thoroughly Jewish (i.e., rabbinic) tone of the Gospel and for its intense hostility toward those who "sit on the seat of Moses" (23:2).

The interpretive remarks on Matthew that follow must be—because of the limits of space—only suggestive. The frame of the Markan narrative is presupposed, and I will not repeat here the parts of Matthew that are taken over from Mark without substantial alteration. Matthew's distinctive appropriation of Mark is often to be detected only in the cumulative effect of many minute additions and alterations, and thus a Synopsis should be consulted for analyzing the assertions that follow.

Who Is Jesus? Son of David, Son of God (1:1—4:16)

The opening of the Gospel shows how the Markan understanding of Jesus as Son of David and Son of God is, in Matthew, distinctively influenced by the reading of Torah and interaction with Pharisaic Judaism. For the sake of convenience I am here treating chapters 1–2 separately as an "infancy account." In fact, chapters 1–4 form a coherent literary unit. Matthew lacks the solemn transition to the ministry of John provided by Luke 3:1, and it is really only the fact that Mark begins with the Baptist that leads us to view Matthew's first chapters as a prologue.

The Infancy: Jesus as Son of David (chaps. 1–2)

The infancy narratives of Matthew and Luke have little in common beyond the characters of Jesus, Mary, and Joseph. Even here, however, there are differences: in contrast with Luke's account, Joseph is a more dominant character than Mary. Moreover, while the two Gospels interpret Torah midrashically, they do so in very different ways. They also use distinct literary devices and divergent geographical emphases. Each, in short, is fitted to the distinctive witness of the Gospel it begins.

Matthew's version is distinguished by its genealogy (1:1-17) and dense clustering of formula citations (1:23; 2:6, 15, 23). They help define the place of Jesus within traditional Jewish messianic expectation. For Christians in conversation with an aggressive Pharisaic movement (see 23:15), proclaiming Jesus as resurrected Messiah was insufficient; the credentials of a Davidic king required demonstration. For this, Jesus' dubious parentage and lowly place of origin were problematic (see John 1:46; 7:27). The formula citations prove that Jesus meets prophetic expectations, and the genealogy connects him to the royal line. Together, they answer—at least to this community's satisfaction—the questions of who Jesus is and whence he came.

The genealogy (1:1-17) fits Jesus into the literary forms and family lineage of Torah. By its arrangement into generations, furthermore, it shows his birth to be the "fulfill-ment of the times." He is immediately identified as "Messiah, son of David, son of Abraham" (1:1). As son of Abraham, he is connected to the people as a whole. This is an important link for other NT authors (esp. Paul), but Matthew does not exploit it (see only 3:9; 8:11; 22:32). The Davidic connection, stated first, is the more significant for Matthew since it establishes Jesus' messianic credentials "according to the flesh" (see Rom. 1:3) within Judaism: the stress in the genealogy falls on David the king in 1:6; Joseph is called son of David in 1:20; and the child's kingly status is made clear by 2:2, "Where is the king?" and 2:6, "For from you shall come a ruler" (Mic. 5:2).

Matthew's emphasis on this identification is found in many references to David not found in the text of Mark (see 9:27; 12:3, 23; 15:22; 20:30-31). It is made most explicit at Jesus' entry into Jerusalem. Matthew, with a formula citation from Zech. 9:9 that identifies Jesus as "your king," has Jesus awkwardly fulfill the letter of that citation by using both colt and ass in his procession (21:2, 7). The populace twice cries out: "Hosanna to the son of David" (21:9, 15). Precisely this stress makes more climactic the controversy—in Matthew, it is with the Pharisees—over whether the Messiah is David's son or Lord (22:41-45). As we shall see shortly, Jesus is definitely "Lord" for Matthew, but he is also assuredly a Davidic messiah.

The genealogy helps Matthew deal with Jesus' suspect parentage. Included among Jesus' ancestors are four women: Tamar (1:3), Rahab (1:5), Ruth (1:5), and Bathsheba ("wife of Uriah"; 1:6). All were outsiders to Israel; all were sexually suspect; and through all of them God had worked surprisingly for the salvation of the people. They prepare for the birth of a messiah by the virgin Mary.

Baptism and Testing: Jesus as Faithful Son of God (chaps. 3–4)

The formula citations of chapter 2 show that Jesus' hometown, as everyone knew, was Nazareth (2:23), but that his birthplace was the Davidic city of Bethlehem (2:5-6). Matthew draws his readers, however, into a deeper understanding of Jesus' origins and, therefore, his identity. Jesus is more than David's son, he is also Son of God. The strength of Matthew's use of the term is indicated by the citation of Isa. 7:14. Jesus is able to "save all the people" because he is Immanuel: he makes God truly present among them (1:23). Since 1:23 stands with 28:20 as an *inclusio* for the whole Gospel, a glance at that passage is appropriate here.

In this distinctively Matthean appearance account (28:16-20), Jesus shows himself to the disciples on a mount in Galilee, and they worship him (28:17). He claims "all authority" (28:18) and commissions them, "Go, make disciples of all nations, baptiz-ing them . . . teaching them to observe all that I have commanded you; and, Lo! I am with you always, to the close of the age" (28:19-20). Jesus continues to be present through his resurrection. More striking, though, is the suggestion that his presence will be mediated by the commandments he had taught. Because we know that Jesus makes God present (1:23) as his Son, the commandments of Jesus mediate God's presence as the Word of God. This perception of Jesus and his words has important implications for other Matthean motifs.

What Matthew means by "Son of God" in his Gospel owes a great deal to Torah. His understanding of the title is shown already in the formula citation of 2:15, "Out of Egypt I called my son" (cf. Exod. 4:22; Hos. 11:1). The prophet, of course, had referred to the people Israel in the exodus. By using this citation, Matthew not only interprets Jesus' journey, he identifies him as the faithful child whom God had desired in Israel. Matthew's image of Jesus as God's Son is therefore primarily relational. Jesus is the human being who is fully faithful and obedient to the will of God.

Several aspects of the infancy account, in fact, echo the exodus story in Torah and help create the image of Jesus as a Mosaic figure or one who represents the people of Israel. Jesus is miraculously born to "save his people" (cf. Exod. 3:10), he is saved from a wicked king (2:13-14; cf. Exod. 1:22—2:10), and he is "called out of Egypt" (2:15). Now, if we read straight on to Jesus' baptism (3:13-17), we cannot help noticing that it corresponds to the crossing of the people through the sea (see Exod. 14:21-25; cf. 1 Cor. 10:1-5). Here the heavens open and the voice proclaims, "This is my beloved Son, in whom I am well pleased" (3:17).

The allusion is by no means far-fetched. It is in fact confirmed by Matthew's version of Jesus' testing (4:1-11). Both he and Luke use Q material to expand Mark's terse account, thereby making the demonic temptations and Jesus' responses explicit. Matthew has Jesus led up to be tested just as Israel was in the desert. Israel's hardships, however, led to its "testing of the Lord" by rebellion and faithlessness (see Num. 11:1; 14:1; Deut. 1:26; Exod. 16:2; Pss. 95:8-11; 106:13-25). Jesus' testing will also determine his fidelity. The devil makes the issue explicit, saying twice, "If you are God's Son . . ." (4:3, 6). He holds out to Jesus the possibilities of pleasure, power, and divine protection. Jesus, however, answers with the very words of Torah: "It is written, 'Man shall not live by bread alone, but by every word that proceeds from the mouth of God'" (4:4; cf. Deut. 8:3; cf. also the citations for Deut. 6:13 and 6:16 in Matt. 4:7 and 4:10). Jesus is the faithful, obedient son of God. He represents the child God always wanted in Israel, and he perfectly fulfills the righteousness demanded by Torah (see 3:13-15).

Now his mission to Israel can begin. Those who hear his proclamation of the kingdom (4:17) and hear him teach from the mountain like Moses (5:1-2)—those at least who hear him in this narrative—recognize one who, like Israel, was called, passed through the water, and was tested in the wilderness.

A haunting echo of the temptation account occurs in Matthew's crucifixion scene. Though Matthew makes few alterations to Mark's Passion narrative, one he does make places blame for Jesus' death on the populace as a whole (27:25) and another has the passersby at the cross cry out to him derisively, "If you are the Son of God, come down from the cross" (27:40; cf. 27:43). Matthew here has the populace give voice to

"Satan's" perspective; in their taunt we hear an eerie reprise of Satan's "If you are Son of God, throw yourself down" (4:6). A Son of God, surely, was one who exercised power. But Jesus accepts his father's will (26:39), obedient to the end. When the centurion confirms, "Truly this was God's Son" (27:54), Matthew's readers understand that this is because of Jesus' fidelity and obedience. The centurion expresses the perception of Jesus already shaped by Matthew in the temptation scene.

Jesus as Teacher and Lord

Jesus' most prominent activity in Matthew's Gospel is teaching. As God's Son, he knows the Father's will in a unique way, and can reveal it to others (11:25-30). For the Matthean church, moreover, Jesus is now risen Lord, whose teachings mediate God's presence. By the resurrection, he has "all authority" granted by God (see 4:9). The readers of the Gospel hear the words of Jesus not as those of just another sage from the past but as the living words of the commanding Lord. For Matthew, Jesus is teacher precisely as Lord of the church.

Evidence for this observation—as well as an indication of how carefully Matthew adapts Mark—is found in Matthew's precise use of the terms "Teacher" (whether in the form of *rabbi* or *didaskalos*) and "Lord" (*kyrios*). We have seen (chap. 7, p. 168) that in Mark's Gospel everybody calls Jesus Teacher, whether opponents (Mark 12:14, 19, 32), those who encounter him but fail to follow (10:17-31), those who encounter him and believe (9:17), or the disciples (4:38; 9:38; 10:35; 13:1). On the other hand, Mark never has disciples or opponents call Jesus Lord; only the afflicted give him that title. Matthew's discrimination is finer. Who calls Jesus Teacher? Always outsiders, whether opponents such as the scribes (8:19; 12:38), Pharisees (12:38; 22:16, 36), Jewish tax collectors (17:24), Herodians (22:16), Sadducees (22:24), or those who encounter Jesus but do not follow, like the rich young man (19:16). Jesus is never called Teacher by the disciples, the afflicted, or those coming to faith in him. The disciples (8:25; 14:28; 16:22; 17:4; 18:21) and those coming to faith in Jesus (8:2, 6, 8; 9:28; 15:22, 25, 27; 17:15; 20:30) always call him Lord (but see 26:18).

If Matthew's community is, in truth, one that defines and defends itself against a Jewish scribal tradition, this distinction is dramatically effective. Those outside— remember the synagogue down the street—see Jesus as just another rabbi, whose opinions have only human authority. But those inside hear his words as those of the Lord, "God with us," filled with "all authority." The only apparent exception to this rule confirms it. The term "Lord" is never found on the lips of the betrayer, Judas. When Jesus predicts his betrayal at the last supper, the other disciples ask, "Is it I, Lord?" (26:22). Judas asks, "Is it I, Rabbi?" (26:25). And when he greets Jesus in the garden to arrest him, it is with these words, "Hail, Rabbi" (26:49). Matthew subtly but effectively portrays Judas as an outsider.

The Parables of Jesus in Matthew

Matthew's distinctive understanding of Jesus as teacher affects his presentation of Jesus as parable speaker. As in Mark, Jesus begins telling parables because his open preaching meets hostility and rejection. In chapters 8–9, Jesus works ten miracles, which are interpreted by a "servant" citation from Isa. 53:4: "He took our infirmities and bore our diseases" (8:17). In chapters 11–12, Jesus is rejected repeatedly by family and opponents, driving him to a more veiled mode of teaching. This is interpreted by a second servant citation from Isa. 42:2: "He will not wrangle or cry aloud, nor will anyone hear his voice in the streets" (12:19). When Jesus begins speaking in parables, this too is in fulfillment of the prophecy "I will open my mouth in parables" (Ps. 78:2, in 13:35).

In contrast to Mark, however, Matthew's parables are truly intelligible to the insiders. The disciples have been given "to know the mysteries of the kingdom of heaven" (13:11). Outsiders do not perceive; the prophecy of Isa. 6:9-10 about blindness and deafness applies to them, while the disciples do "see and hear" (13:16-17). The division between insiders and outsiders is here lacking irony. The role of knowledge, furthermore, is central for Matthew in a way it is not for Mark. This is indicated by the interpretation of the parable of the sower (13:18-23). In the parable itself, Matthew already made the seeds plural rather than singular, and the growth of the seed distributive, "some a hundredfold, some sixty, some thirty." These changes invite a more individualizing interpretation, which Matthew provides. Now, it is "anyone who hears" the word of the kingdom, and the point of differentiation is "understanding." The one who hears but "does not understand" has the word taken away (13:19). The one who "hears and understands" will yield fruit (13:23).

What is this proper understanding? It is the recognition that Jesus is not just another scribe but the Lord of the church. For Matthew as for Mark, understanding is fundamentally the commitment called faith. Such faith enables the disciples to grasp the significance of Jesus' teachings. Since Jesus' presence in the church is mediated by his words, it is also essential that those who hear them in faith understand, so they can pass them on to others. Thus, at the end of this first series of parables Jesus asks his disciples, "Have you understood all this?" They answer, "Yes." Then he tells them, "Therefore every scribe who has been trained for the kingdom of heaven is like a householder who brings out of his treasure what is new and what is old" (13:51-52). It is the disciples, we see, who are defined in terms of the rabbinic category of the scribe. They are to perform the scribal function for the messianic community, teaching the church what Jesus first taught them. They need, therefore, to understand.

As a consequence, the parables of Jesus in Matthew are more than defense weapons in his fight against opponents, and even more than the author's interpretation of the narrative. They are genuine instruments for teaching the church. Matthew includes some seventeen parables, many more than Mark. Three of them come from Mark, four from Q (the source shared with Luke), and ten from his own source, M. They fall into three clusters within the narrative. The first is the secret teaching of the disciples in chapter 13. The second occurs in the context of controversy in 18:23—22:14. The third is in the eschatological discourse to the disciples in 24:45—25:46.

The parables of Matthew 13 reveal "the mysteries of the kingdom" in a threefold fashion. They show that the kingdom is one that emerges suddenly and inexplicably in the world by God's will; this is expressed by the parables of growth: the mustard seed and the leaven (13:31-33). The kingdom demands a decision for or against it; this is expressed by the parables of decision: the pearl and the treasure (13:44-46). The kingdom involves judgment; depending on one's choice, there is reward or punishment. This is expressed by the parables of judgment: the weeds, and the net with the fishes (13:24-30 and 13:47-50). The parable of the sower is programmatic in that it combines all three elements of growth, decision, and judgment (13:3-9).

The parables in chapters 18–22 are dominated by the theme of acceptance and rejection, pointing to the destiny of Jesus and Israel. The parables of the two sons (21:28-30), the vineyard (21:33-43), and the wedding feast (22:1-14) all rather transparently indicate the rejection of those who reject Jesus and the transfer of the kingdom to others. But there is judgment for those within the church, as well, as is shown by the denouement of the wedding feast (22:11-14) and the parable of the wicked servant (18:23-35): "So also will my heavenly father do to each one of you, if you do not forgive your brother from the heart."

The parables in Jesus' eschatological discourse all center on the theme of judgment in some fashion: the wicked householder (24:45-51), the ten virgins (25:1-13), the talents (25:14-30), the sheep and the goats (25:31-46). Although these parables are intended for insiders and are understood by them, they by no means only comfort and confirm. They warn those already in the church that their decision for the kingdom requires constant renewal.

Jesus and Torah

The central religious symbol of the Pharisaic tradition was Torah (see chap. 2, pp. 43–44). It was the source of wisdom and the measure of righteousness, the reflection of the mind of God, the blueprint for creation, the ideal frame for humanity. Though revealed through Moses on Sinai, Torah was eternal; though dwelling among humans, it would live forever. Taking upon oneself the observance of Torah was to "take on the yoke of the kingdom of heaven."

Since the Matthean community interpreted its life in reference to this tradition, it was required both to separate itself from the actual synagogue and to reinterpret the symbols it shared with that tradition. Both aspects find their focus in Jesus. Because messianists confessed him as Christ and Lord, they were regarded as heretics (*minim*) by the synagogue. The figure of Jesus therefore also organizes the Christians' appropriation of the rabbinic symbolic structure. We can approach this dialectic in four stages: (1) Jesus as polemicist against scribes and Pharisees; (2) Jesus as the authentic interpreter of Torah; (3) Jesus as the fulfillment of Torah; (4) Jesus as the personification of Torah.

Polemic Against Scribes and Pharisees

The developing rabbinic tradition joined the religious ideals of the Pharisees to the legal expertise of the scribes. The groups here attacked by Jesus are the exact historical representatives of the Judaism Matthew's church confronted in its life. The polemic is not, consequently, an attack by Jesus on the Jewish people generally, much less an expression of anti-Semitism. It is, rather, an attack on the Jewish leaders of Matthew's own day. The polemic thus establishes distance and distinction between rivals who claim to be the authentic realization of Judaism, God's people. Some of the polemic, furthermore, such as the charge of saying but not doing (23:3, 13), is standard for disputes between ancient philosophical schools.

The attack is strategically placed within Matthew's narrative. It follows the series of Jerusalem controversy stories in 22:15-46 and precedes the eschatological instruction of the disciples in private (24:1—25:46). The placement dramatically expresses separation and distance. The discourse is given structure by its seven woes (23:13, 15, 16, 23, 25, 27, 29), which form a counterpart to the blessings spoken to the disciples in 5:3-12. The actual polemic is prefaced by an instruction to Jesus' disciples ("you") in 23:1-12: they are told what attitude to have toward the opponents and what view they should have toward their own leadership.

Valuable historical information on the Matthean setting can be gleaned from the polemic. We first notice the activities and preoccupations of the Pharisaic tradition: the title Rabbi for teachers (23:8), the aggressive missionary travels (23:15), the careful discrimination among commandments by means of midrash (23:16-22), the concern for tithing (23:23-24) and ritual purity (23:25-26). Apart from the honorific Rabbi, these match what we know of the early Pharisaic period from Paul and *Mishnah Demai* 2. The time period may be indicated by "your house left desolate" (23:38), although the reference to the temple is not certain. As for the Christians, they are being excluded from, and being persecuted in, the synagogues (23:34). This is precisely the sort of setting that makes the symbolic texture of Matthew intelligible.

The passage gathers together elements of polemic against scribes and Pharisees found in other places within the narrative, such as the polemics against swearing (23:16-22; cf. 5:33-37), neglect of mercy (23:23; cf. 9:13; 12:7), purity regulations (23:25-26; cf. 15:1-9), and hypocrisy (23:5-7, 28; 6:1-16).

The polemic against teachers is not an attack on Torah itself. The scribes and Pharisees, in fact, are condemned not for preaching but for not practicing what they preach (23:3), or practicing for people's approval (23:5-7) without a corresponding inner disposition (23:26, 27). Their casuistry distorts Torah by preferring lighter matters to the weightier ones of justice, mercy, and faith (23:23). Their midrash does not liberate but lays heavy burdens that keep people from the kingdom (23:4, 13). The allusion to "the yoke of the kingdom" cannot be missed here. Their real religious attitude is shown by their treatment of those who do follow God's word. They killed the prophets in the past (23:29-31); they persecute Christians today (23:34-37).

Christians, in turn, are to keep Torah ("Do as they say") but are not to imitate their behavior (23:3). Within the messianic community, therefore, no one is to bear the title of Rabbi, or Father. They have one father, God, and one teacher, the Messiah (23:10). The emphasis on God as father we will meet again shortly. As for the title Teacher given to the Messiah, it does not contradict Matthew's usage (i.e., "teacher" used for Jesus only by outsiders), for here only, he uses the term "master" (*kathēgētēs*). Authority within the messianic community is not expressed by honor and titles but by service (23:8-12). The Messiah is their teacher.

Jesus as Teacher of Torah

One form of messianic expectation within Judaism looked for the Messiah to interpret Torah definitively: "They shall not depart from any commandment of the law . . . until there should come a prophet and the Messiahs of Aaron and Israel" (1QS 9.9-11). Such an interpretation of Torah is one of the essential messianic functions given to Jesus in Matthew's Gospel. It is expressed programmatically in the Sermon on the Mount (chaps. 5–7). Matthew has prepared the reader to see in the one who speaks from the mountain a faithful representative of Israel, even a Mosaic figure. But Jesus is no new Moses and delivers no new law. He is God's Son who through Torah shows the real intent of God's word. He is a messianic interpreter.

The term "sermon" is a misnomer, for these chapters contain a collection of sayings material brought together by the evangelist. Some of it is paralleled in Luke's Sermon on the Plain (Luke 6:17-49; cf. Matt. 5:3-12, 38-48; 7:1-5, 15-20, 24-27). Other sayings are found within different contexts in Mark or Luke (see Matt. 5:13-16, 22-26, 31-32; 6:9-13, 19-23, 25-34; 7:7-11, 13-14). The rest is distinctively Matthean (5:17-20, 27-30, 33-37; 6:1-8, 16-18; 7:6). The sermonic turn Matthew gives these traditions is seen by comparing two of the shorter sayings to their parallels in Mark and Luke. The parallels both have, "Salt is good" (Mark 9:50; Luke 14:34), but Matthew adds, "You are the salt of the earth" (5:13). Mark 4:21 has, "Is a lamp brought in to be put under a bushel?" (cf. Luke 11:33-36). But in Matt. 5:14, Jesus says, "You are the light of the world." We find here direct teaching to the disciples. Messiah Jesus teaches the church, which hears his words as those of the powerful resurrected one.

The Beatitudes that open the sermon (5:3-12) establish the conditions of entry into the kingdom proclaimed by Jesus (4:17) and remind us again of the giving of the

Torah by Moses: it too was accompanied by blessings and curses (Deut. 27-28). In contrast to Luke's version (Luke 6:20-26), Matthew individualizes and interiorizes the Beatitudes. The kingdom is made up of those who are poor in spirit, lowly, sorrowing, meek, pure in heart, and persecuted. The Matthean community could certainly see itself in the last of these categories; and so its members were part of God's kingdom. Their inclusion, however, is less for their sake than for the world's. They are to be in the world like seasoning or like light, to the glory of their "father in heaven" (5:16). With this last phrase, we strike the essential note of the sermon: the kingdom is not Jesus' own or that brought about by human effort or demonic pretense (see 4:1-11); it is, rather, God's kingdom.

The phrase "father in heaven" runs throughout the sermon as the constant point of reference (5:16, 45, 48; 6:1, 4, 6, 14-15, 18, 26, 32; 7:11, 21). And if it is God's effective rule that Jesus announces, then God is the only adequate measure of it: "Be perfect as your father in heaven is perfect" (5:48). The words of Jesus, therefore, do not present a program capable of human fulfillment, but a measure for all Christian existence. A measure less ultimate than God would mean a kingdom less ultimate than God's. This is the essential framework for understanding the messianic interpretation of Torah by Jesus.

Jesus' statement in 5:17-20 is programmatic for all his words and deeds throughout Matthew's Gospel:

> Think not that I have come to abolish the law and the prophets; I have come not to abolish them but to fulfill them. For truly I say to you, till heaven and earth pass away, not an iota, not a dot, will pass away from the law until all is accomplished. Whoever then relaxes one of the least of these commandments and teaches men so, shall be called least in the kingdom of heaven; but he who does them and teaches them shall be called great in the kingdom of heaven. For I tell you, unless your righteousness exceeds that of the scribes and Pharisees, you will never enter the kingdom of heaven.

How has Jesus come to fulfill and accomplish Torah? Matthew has already shown us how Torah as witness is being brought to completion by the deeds and words of Jesus. But the term "fulfill" in this place also bears the sense of "reveal." By his teaching, Jesus will show the true and "full" meaning of God's Torah. The proper understanding of "these commandments" here is critical. The keeping of them will make people lesser or greater in the kingdom. We know that the kingdom in question is precisely that announced by Jesus. The phrase, "these commandments," then, does not refer to the Torah taken alone or to the Torah as interpreted by the Pharisaic tradition but *to the Torah as it is interpreted by Jesus Messiah.* Remember Jesus' final commission: "teaching them all that I have commanded you" (28:20).

These messianic teachings describe a "righteousness" that exceeds that of Pharisees and scribes (see 5:20). This is in direct contradiction to the Pharisaic claim to define "righteousness" (see chap. 2 above, pp. 54–58). But how do Jesus' teachings exceed those of the Pharisees? Certainly not in the multiplication of commands, for we are here presented with only a suggestive sample. The exceeding is to be found in the radical nature of Jesus' interpretation: radical in the sense of getting to the root. Jesus' interpretations assert God himself as the only adequate and ultimate norm for the kingdom (5:48). For the Matthean community, then, Torah meant the words of Scripture as interpreted by Jesus Messiah.

The six antithetical statements in 5:21-47 exemplify the messianic interpretation of Torah. Even in form, they show familiarity with the tradition they oppose. Jesus begins each with "You have heard it said," followed by a text of Torah. Then he responds, "But I say to you," and gives his interpretation. This pattern is formally similar to that relation of Mishnah to Gemara in the compilation of the halachic tradition, the Babylonian Talmud. In its finished state, the Talmud is centuries later than Matthew, but it only makes more formal a relation between text and interpretation that was much older. Matthew's use of this form is distinctive in two ways. First, he has Jesus quote Torah directly, rather than traditional oral teaching, although Matt. 5:43 does expand Lev. 19:18. Second, Jesus does not cite other authorities to support his own interpretation as the essential protocol in talmudic circles would dictate. He assumes a direct and unique authority to interpret: "Amen, I say to you." He claims direct knowledge of the original intent of Torah and, therefore, of God's mind.

How does the Messiah interpret Torah? He radicalizes it in three ways. In the case of murder and adultery (5:21-30), he demands an *interior disposition* corresponding to outer action. For the prohibitions of swearing and divorce (5:31-37), he demands an *absolute adherence* rather than a mitigating casuistry (though cf. 19:9). In matters of human relationships (5:38-47), he demands a *response that goes beyond* the letter of the commandment. These antitheses serve to assert Jesus' authority to interpret for the kingdom. They also provide directions for the understanding of Torah within God's kingdom. They do not provide a complete code of ethics and certainly not a full interpretation of Torah. The Sermon on the Mount remains a sketch, not a system.

Throughout the rest of his narrative, Matthew presents Jesus as the authoritative interpreter of Torah. In the controversy stories, Matthew characteristically refers to the proper understanding of Torah (see 8:4; 12:12; 15:1-9; Markan pars.). With some regularity, Jesus challenges his opponents' understanding of Torah, asking them rhetorically, "Have you not *read* in the Law (or Scripture) . . . ?" and following with a direct citation of Torah (see 12:5; 19:4; 21:16, 42; 22:31). The scribes and Pharisees, we are to infer, do not understand the very Torah to which they cling, for they do not recognize its full expression in the words and deeds of Jesus. They are told by him, "Go and learn what this means, 'I desire mercy and not sacrifice,' for I came not to call the righteous but sinners" (9:13; cf. 12:7 and Hos. 6:6).

Jesus the Fulfillment of Torah

Matthew makes the pattern of scriptural fulfillment far more explicit and prominent than Mark does. He cites Scripture directly some fifty-seven times, compared with Mark's thirty; his citations are also fuller and more deliberately arranged. This is found above all in his formula citations. By means of them, Matthew brings specific texts of Torah and specific moments in the Messiah's life together, so that they are mutually interpretive. From seeing Jesus, we understand the real meaning of Torah; by reading Torah, we discover the full meaning of Jesus' ministry.

From these citations alone, we learn a great deal about Matthew's understanding of Jesus and how he "fulfills" Torah: We learn that Jesus is Immanuel, God with us (1:23; cf. Isa. 7:14), and that he is God's Son (2:15; cf. Hos. 11:1). We understand that he is a Nazarene (2:23; cf. Judg. 13:5; Isa. 11:1?) but was born in Bethlehem as a ruler of the people (2:6; cf. Mic. 5:2). We glean that his kingship was made manifest at his entry into Jerusalem (21:5; cf. Zech. 9:9), and that he is also God's chosen servant who bears the ills of others (8:17; cf. Isa. 53:4), a hidden servant (12:18-21; cf. Isa. 42:1-4) who speaks in parables (13:35; cf. Ps. 78:2). We learn further that he is one betrayed by a companion, for money (27:9-10; cf. Jer. 18:1-3), and that his significance is not confined to Israel: he will proclaim justice to the Gentiles and in his name the Gentiles will hope (12:18, 21; cf. Isa. 42:1-4). For Galilee of the Gentiles, as for all nations (28:19), he is the great light that has dawned, to shine on those who dwell in darkness (4:15-16; cf. Isa. 9:1-2). The formula citations represent the explicit reflection of the "scribes of the kingdom" within Matthew's community on the messianic implications of Torah.

Jesus the Personification of Torah

We have seen Jesus as the focus both for the separation from the synagogue and for the appropriation of its symbolic system. Matthew shows Jesus to be interpreter and ful-filler of Torah. But does he go further in his shaping of the image of Jesus? Does he suggest that Jesus virtually personifies Torah—that he is, in effect, God's Word? This is more than a little likely, because of the way certain functions and attributes of Torah current in the Pharisaic tradition are suggested by Matthew's presentation of Jesus.

We find the personification of wisdom already in the Book of Proverbs, where Wisdom "calls out" in her own voice (8:4-20), claiming to be at once the first of God's creations present with him in the beginning (8:22-30) and the companion of humankind, "delighting in the sons of men" (8:31). In its praise of Sophia (Wisdom), the Wisdom of Solomon calls her the reflection and image of God. She passes from generation to generation into the souls of "holy people and prophets" (Wis. 7:25-27). The Book of Sirach explicitly connects this personified Wisdom to Torah: "All this is the book of the covenant of the Most High God, the law which Moses commanded us" (Sir. 24:23).

In the Pharisaic tradition, the identification of Wisdom with the study of Torah was well established. Those who studied Torah were wise men (*hakamim*), and those who did not were sinners. Haggadic speculation on Torah and its attributes led to the conclusion that Torah, like Wisdom, was from the beginning and had no end; that those who took its yoke upon them took on the yoke of the kingdom, which meant freedom and a share in God's rest; and that the study of Torah itself mediated God's presence by means of the *Shekinah* (see chap. 2 above, p. 57). These images provide a backdrop against which some of the statements that Matthew places in the mouth of Jesus become highly intriguing.

We have already seen the astounding authority claimed by Jesus when he says, "You have heard it said, but I say to you . . ." Such language asserts a virtual equality with Torah. In the midst of controversy with opponents, moreover, Jesus claims in turn to be greater than the temple (12:6), greater than Jonah (12:41), and greater than Solomon (12:42). Are these assertions of superiority chosen at random? Do the three things with which Jesus compares himself stand only for themselves? Or do they stand for the three parts of Torah: Law, Prophets, and Writings?

That such a suggestion cannot be entirely dismissed is shown by Jesus' statement "I came not to call the righteous but sinners" (9:13). As Wisdom called to life, so does he. And as Wisdom "delighted in the sons of men," so do we find Jesus defending himself when attacked for consorting with undesirables: "Wisdom is justified by her deeds" (11:19). And in his own voice, Jesus says, "I will send out prophets and wise men and scribes" (23:34). We know from 5:48 that the Father is the measure of what is perfect; but Jesus tells the rich man who wanted eternal life (19:16) first to "keep the commandments" (19:17). When the man says he has done this, Jesus tells him, "If you want to be perfect, sell all you possess and come, follow me" (19:21). In 5:18, Jesus says of Torah, "Until heaven and earth pass away, not an iota, not a dot, will pass from the law until all is accomplished"; but in 24:35, he says of his own words, "Heaven and earth will pass away, but my words will not pass away." Finally, he commissions his disciples to teach all nations "all that I have commanded you. Lo, I am with you till the close of the age" (28:20).

The foregoing examples are suggestive and only that; it would be impossible to make a case from them alone. In the following passages, however, there is no mistaking the equation of Jesus and Torah. Jesus had attacked the scribes and Pharisees for placing heavy burdens on people (23:4). In 11:28-30, after declaring his unique capacity to reveal the Father, Jesus says:

> Come to me all who labor and are heavily burdened and I will give you rest. Take my yoke upon you, and learn from me, for I am gentle and lowly in heart, and you will find rest for your souls; for my yoke is easy and my burden light.

Several points require comment in this extraordinarily rich passage. First, because he is gentle and lowly, Jesus personifies membership in God's kingdom (cf. 5:3-5). Second, as Torah revealed God's will, so Jesus reveals the Father to whomever he wishes (11:27). Third, in contrast to scribes and Pharisees—the "wise" from whom the revelation is hidden (11:25)—Jesus gives a light burden. Fourth, his "yoke" corresponds exactly to the symbol of Torah as "yoke of the kingdom of God." Fifth, as the Pharisees looked to Torah to learn God's ways, so those whom Jesus calls are to "learn from me." Sixth, the commandment that, above all, defined Jews in society was the Sabbath observance, which was regarded as participation in God's own Sabbath rest; here, learning from Jesus brings rest for the soul.

Finally, the *Shekinah* was said to dwell among even two or three who studied Torah together. We hear Jesus tell his community in 18:20: "Where two or three are gathered in my name, there I am in the midst of them." In Matthew's Gospel, Jesus is teacher of Torah, fulfillment of Torah, and the very personification of Torah.

The Church of the Messiah

I have mentioned that Matthew is the only Gospel to use the term "church" (*ekklēsia*; 16:18; 18:17) and that this Gospel shows a constant concern for the identity and integrity of the messianic community. This focus makes more intelligible the Gospel's hostility toward Jewish leaders. Jesus' polemic gives voice to a community's struggle to define itself against an older, more powerful, and antagonistic tradition.

Jew and Gentile

The struggle for self-definition was all the harder for the Matthean community, since it was caught in a tension between particularity and universality. In what way were they part of Judaism and in what way were they from among the Gentiles? Part of the community's traditions made it clear that the mission of Jesus and his first disciples had been intended only for Israel (2:6; 9:36; 10:5-6, 23; 19:28). Twice, however, a strange phrase is used to express this. Jesus tells the Syro-Phoenician woman that "I was sent only to the *lost sheep* of the house of Israel" (15:24), and he tells the Twelve whom he sends out, "Go nowhere among the Gentiles . . . but go rather to the *lost sheep* of the house of Israel" (10:5-6).

The sayings material in this Gospel also reveals a pronounced animus toward Gentiles. They are like dogs and swine (7:6). Their manner of pleasure (6:32), power (20:25), prayer (6:7), and hospitality (5:47) are all criticized. Furthermore, as Jesus was handed over to the Gentiles (20:19) so would the disciples give testimony before all nations (10:18), even though they would be hated by them (24:9). Perhaps the most revealing instance of how this community appropriated to itself the symbolic structure of Judaism is this remark concerning a community troublemaker: "If he refuses to listen to the *church*, let him be to you as a Gentile and tax collector" (18:17).

At the same time, the community knew that its Messiah had been rejected by the Jewish leadership and the populace of Jerusalem (27:25), and that he continued to be rejected by those who worshiped in the synagogue down the street. The community remembered the moral of the parable of the two sons, that tax collectors and sinners entered the kingdom first (21:28-32), as well as the words of Jesus, "Many will come from the east and west and sit at the table . . . while the sons of the kingdom will be thrown into outer darkness" (8:11-12). It recalled how the parable of the vineyard made this point: "The Kingdom of God will be taken away from you and given to a nation producing the fruits of it" (21:43). And it recalled how in the parable of the wedding feast, "the king was angry and he sent his troops and destroyed those murderers and burned their city" (22:7), and that Jesus had told the scribes and Pharisees, "Behold your house is forsaken and desolate" (23:38).

The community scribes had also pondered the texts of Torah that spoke of the Messiah as a servant who would be a hope and a light to Gentiles (4:15-16; 12:18-21). They hinted at the Messiah's universal significance already in his birth narratives (2:2). And the community knew stories of Gentiles who had shown faith in the Messiah when Jews had not. "I have not seen such faith in Israel," said Jesus of the centurion (8:10), and he told the Syro-Phoenician woman, "O woman, great is your faith" (15:28). The community knew above all that Jesus' promise of the gospel's being preached to all nations (24:14) so that all nations might come before him in judgment (25:32) had been given as an express command in the words of the risen Lord to the Eleven, "Go, make disciples of all nations" (28:19). That commission had begun to be fulfilled; that this church included Gentiles in its membership is a virtual certainty. But it was also a community that was forced to work out its particular identity—perhaps as the lost sheep of the house of Israel—in confrontation with a developing Pharisaic Judaism, and that so thoroughly appropriated the symbols of Judaism to itself that it called those outside the messianic community, simply, Gentiles (18:17).

The Disciples in Matthew

Matthew treats the disciples—he is fond of the term "the twelve disciples" (10:1; 11:1; 20:17; 26:20)—far more favorably than Mark does. We have already seen the reason: the disciples must pass on the words of the Lord to others; they cannot be totally faithless and unintelligent. We know that they understand and both "see and hear" (13:10-17; 51-52). Matthew by no means hides the hard facts about Jesus' first followers: they all still abandon him (26:56), and even at his resurrection appearance "some doubted" (28:17; cf. 14:31). But Matthew consistently softens Mark's harsher portrait in scenes such as the stilling of the storm (8:23-27), the hemorrhaging woman (9:18-26), the transfiguration (17:1-8), and the second passion prediction, where the disciples are not "afraid," as in Mark, but only "greatly distressed" (17:23). Matthew defines their problem as one of having little faith (17:20), and the phrase "men of little faith" is effectively his epithet for the disciples (6:30; 8:26; 14:31; 16:8).

Matthew's treatment of the disciples is most noteworthy for the prominent role played by Peter. Much more than in Mark, Peter here emerges as the representative of the other disciples. In the story of the walking on the water, a whole section is devoted to his individual response (14:28-31). Jesus' prediction of twelve thrones for the twelve disciples within Israel is given in response to a question from Peter (19:27-30). In the garden of Gethsemane, it is twice emphasized that Peter (not "Simon," as in Mark) was sleeping (26:37, 40).

The positive and negative sides of Peter's prominence are exemplified by his confession of Jesus and his denial of him. Peter's recognition of Jesus at Caesarea Philippi is fuller than in Mark: "You are the Christ, the Son of the living God" (16:16). Jesus responds in kind with a blessing specifically directed to Peter. He is the rock of the church, and in a community of scribes, he has the power to "bind and loose," that is, he has decision-making authority. The scribes and Pharisees "lock up" the kingdom, but Peter is given "the keys to the kingdom" (16:19). Since the whole community is also said to "bind and loose" in 18:18, Peter's authority is not isolated from that of the community, but articulates it. He is once more a representative figure. And Matthew shows immediately that the greatness of his confession is matched by the depth of his resistance to God's will. When he hears of Jesus' suffering, he says, "God forbid, Lord!" (16:22), and Jesus calls him "a stumbling block" (16:23).

With a small but telling detail, Matthew also heightens the enormity of Peter's denial of Jesus (26:69-75). Peter denies him three times, as in Mark, but in two of his denials he takes a curse upon himself and swears (26:72, 74). By this, Matthew shows that Peter denied not only Jesus but also his teachings (see 5:34). Peter thus represents the disciples at their best and worst.

Instructions to the Church

In one sense, all of Jesus' words in this Gospel instruct the church. In chapters 10 and 18, however, there is a more obvious focus on the life and activity of the community. Jesus sends the Twelve out on a mission in 10:1-42. Matthew, like Mark, allows the shadow of rejection and persecution to fall over this enterprise by placing the discourse in a part of the narrative where Jesus is being rejected (see chaps. 8–9, 11–12). Thus they too are to expect rejection, persecution (10:14-25), and division within their households because of him (10:34-36). In these circumstances, however, they are not to fear (10:26-33). Not only do they bear the authority to carry out the tasks of the Messiah (10:1, 7-8), as his representatives they make him present. They can therefore expect the same reception and rejection that were his (10:40-42). In Matthew's scribal context, this saying would be heard distinctly: "A disciple is not above his teacher, nor a servant his master; it is enough for the disciple to be like his teacher, and the servant his master" (10:24-25).

Chapter 18 addresses the inner life of the church. There is a remarkable concentration on humility and service. Rebuke, correction, even excommunication may be necessary for the messianic community, as they are for other communities. But this is not a community that defines itself first of all in terms of power. Greatness is measured by smallness, and the model for receiving the kingdom is a child (18:1-4). In similar fashion, the community as a whole is to show an active concern for "the little ones," They are to be received (18:5) and not scandalized (18:6-9) or despised (18:10). They are to be searched out and saved: "It is not the will of my father that one of these little ones should perish" (18:12-14). As so often in Matthew, the note of forgiveness becomes the characteristic attitude of those in the church (18:21-35; cf. 6:12-15; 9:2-6).

If discipline and forgiveness are necessary, this means Matthew does not regard the church as an assembly of the perfect. The parable of the weeds, with its interpretation (13:24-30, 37-43), the parable of the net and fishes (13:47-50), and the parable of the wedding feast (22:1-14) have already made clear that continual reform and response are required, even for those in the church. No parable makes plainer how the community stands under judgment than that of the sheep and goats (25:31-46). It states unmistakably that the criterion for reward or punishment will be what one has done "for one of these least of my brethren" (25:40, 45). The Torah of Jesus demands "mercy, not sacrifice" (12:7).

Study Questions

1. Why is Matthew's Gospel appropriately called "the gospel of the church"?

2. What role do the infancy narratives play in Matthew's Gospel?

3. How does Matthew's Gospel portray Jesus in chapters 5–7 (the Sermon on the Mount)?

4. What are the basic differences in the portrayals of Jesus in Mark and Matthew?

5. How is Torah central to the symbolism of Matthew's Gospel?

Bibliographical Note

Discussions of Matthean priority can be found in the bibliographical note to chap. 7. The five-book hypothesis for Matthew was developed most fully by B. W. Bacon,

Studies in Matthew (New York: Henry Holt, 1930). For an analysis based on the temporal transitions, see J. D. Kingsbury, *Matthew: Structure, Christology, Kingdom* (Philadelphia: Fortress Press, 1975). Aspects of Matthew's literary technique can be found in D. R. Bauer, *The Structure of Matthew's Gospel: A Study in Literary Design* (JSNTSup, 31; Sheffield: Sheffield Academic Press, 1988); C. H. Lohr, "Oral Techniques in the Gospel of Matthew," *CBQ* 23 (1961): 403–35; and C. R. Smith, "Literary Evidences of a Fivefold Structure in the Gospel of Matthew," *NTS* 43 (1997): 540–51.

On Matthew's subsequent influence, see U. Luz, *Matthew in History: Interpretation, Influence, and Effects* (Minneapolis: Fortress Press, 1994); and É. Massaux, *The Influence of the Gospel of Saint Matthew on Christian Literature before Saint Irenaeus*, trans. N. J. Belval and S. Hecht, 3 vols. (Macon: Mercer Univ. Press; Leuven: Peters Press, 1990–93). On the Matthean community and setting, see S. H. Brooks, *Matthew's Community: The Evidence of His Special Sayings Material* (JSNTSup, 16; Sheffield: Sheffield Academic Press, 1987); J. A. Overman, *Matthew's Gospel and Formative Judaism: The Social World of the Matthean Community* (Minneapolis: Fortress Press, 1990); and A. J. Saldarini, *Matthew's Christian-Jewish Community* (Chicago: Univ. of Chicago Press, 1994). On discipleship, see S. C. Barton, *Discipleship and Family Ties in Mark and Matthew* (SNTSMS, 80; Cambridge: Cambridge Univ. Press, 1994); W. Carter, *Households and Discipleship: A Study of Matthew 19–20* (JSNTSup, 103; Sheffield: Sheffield Academic Press, 1994); and M. J. Wilkins, *Discipleship in the Ancient World and in Matthew's Gospel*, 2nd ed. (Grand Rapids: Baker Books, 1995). On general issues and themes, see R. T. France, *Matthew: Evangelist and Teacher* (Grand Rapids: Zondervan, 1987), and J. P. Meier, *The Vision of Matthew: Christ, Church, and Morality in the First Gospel* (New York: Crossroad, 1991 [1979]). For a survey of modern interpretation, see G. N. Stanton, "The Origin and Purpose of Matthew's Gospel: Matthean Scholarship from 1945–1980," *ANRW* II.25.3 (1980): 1889–1951.

Matthew's systematic use of Scripture is examined by R. H. Gundry, *The Use of the Old Testament in St. Matthew's Gospel* (NovTSup, 18; Leiden: E. J. Brill, 1967); and K. Stendahl, *The School of St. Matthew and Its Use of the Old Testament* (Philadelphia: Fortress Press, 1968), who suggests a school context for this exegetical enterprise. The way Matthew's use of Torah can shape and influence narration and theology is shown by D. C. Allison, Jr., *The New Moses: A Matthean Typology* (Minneapolis: Fortress Press, 1993); T. L. Donaldson, *Jesus on the Mountain: A Study in Matthean Theology* (JSNTSup, 8; Sheffield: JSOT Press, 1985); M. Knowles, *Jeremiah in Matthew's Gospel: The Rejected Prophet Motif in Matthean Redaction* (JSNTSup, 68; Sheffield: Sheffield Academic Press, 1993); and J. H. Neyrey, "The Thematic Use of Isaiah 42:1-4 in Matthew 12," *Bib* 63 (1982): 457–73 (also see Gundry's commentary below). The liturgical context of Matthew is stressed by G. D. Kilpatrick, *The Origins of the Gospel According to St. Matthew* (Oxford: Clarendon Press, 1946); and M. D. Goulder, *Midrash and Lection in Matthew* (London: SPCK, 1974). On teaching in Matthew, see S. Byrskog, *Jesus the Only Teacher: Didactic Authority and Transmission in Ancient Israel,*

Ancient Judaism, and the Matthean Community (ConBNT, 24; Stockholm: Almqvist & Wiksell, 1994). On the apocalyptic dimensions, see D. C. Sim, *Apocalyptic Eschatology in the Gospel of Matthew* (SNTSMS, 88; Cambridge: Cambridge Univ. Press, 1996).

On Matthew's first chapters, see R. E. Brown, *The Birth of the Messiah*, enl. ed. (Garden City, N.Y.: Doubleday & Co., 1993); R. Pesch, "'He Will Be Called a 'Nazorean': Messianic Exegesis in Matthew 1–2," in C. A. Evans and W. R. Stegner (eds.), *The Gospels and the Scriptures of Israel* (JSNTSup, 104; Sheffield: Sheffield Academic Press, 1994), 129–78; and K. Stendahl, "'Quis et Unde?' An Analysis of Mt 1–2," in *Meanings: The Bible as Document and as Guide* (Philadelphia: Fortress Press, 1984), 71–83. On the passion narrative, see D. Senior, *The Passion of Jesus in the Gospel of Matthew* (Wilmington: Michael Glazier, 1985); and idem, *The Passion Narrative According to Matthew: A Redactional Study* (BETL, 34; Leuven: Leuven Univ. Press, 1975). Matthew's special use of the titles of Jesus is studied by J. D. Kingsbury, "The Title 'Son of David' in Matthew's Gospel," *JBL* 95 (1976): 591–602; idem, "The Title 'Kyrios' in Matthew's Gospel," *JBL* 94 (1975): 246–55; and B. J. Malina and J. H. Neyrey, *Calling Jesus Names: The Social Value of Labels in Matthew* (Sonoma, Calif.: Polebridge Press, 1988).

For the parables generally, see C. Blomberg, *Interpreting the Parables* (Downers Grove: InterVarsity Press, 1990); M. Boucher, *The Mysterious Parable: A Literary Study* (CBQMS, 6; Washington, D.C.: Catholic Biblical Assn., 1977); C. Carlston, *The Parables of the Triple Tradition* (Philadelphia: Fortress Press, 1975); J. Jeremias, *The Parables of Jesus*, trans. S. Hooke, rev. ed. (New York: Charles Scribner's Sons, 1963); B. B. Scott, *Hear then the Parable: A Commentary on the Parables of Jesus* (Minneapolis: Fortress Press, 1989); and M. A. Tolbert, *Perspectives on the Parables: An Approach to Multiple Interpretations* (Philadelphia: Fortress Press, 1979). For the Matthean use of parables, see J. D. Kingsbury, *The Parables of Jesus in Matthew 13* (Richmond: John Knox Press, 1969).

For attempts at deciphering the Matthean context from the polemic in chapter 23, see D. R. A. Hare, *The Theme of Jewish Persecution of Christians in the Gospel According to Matthew* (SNTSMS, 6; Cambridge: At the Univ. Press, 1967); S. Van Tilburg, *The Jewish Leaders in Matthew* (Leiden: E. J. Brill, 1972); O. L. Cope, *A Scribe Trained for the Kingdom of Heaven* (CBQMS, 5; Washington, D. C.: Catholic Biblical Assn., 1976); D. E. Garland, *The Intention of Matthew 23* (NovTSup, 52; Leiden: E. J. Brill, 1979); and K. G. C. Newport, *The Sources and Sitz im Leben of Matthew 23* (JSNTSup, 117; Sheffield: Sheffield Academic Press, 1995). The polemical intention of chapter 7 is examined by D. Hill, "False Prophets and Charismatics: Structure and Interpretation in Matthew 7:15-23," *Bib* 57 (1976): 327–48. On Matthean polemic in general, see F. W. Danker, Matthew: A Patriot's Gospel," in *The Gospels and the Scriptures of Israel*, 94–115; and S. McKnight, "A Loyal Critic: Matthew's Polemic with Judaism in Theological Perspective," in C. A. Evans and D. A. Hagner (eds.), *Anti-Semitism and Early Christianity: Issues of Polemic and Faith* (Minneapolis: Fortress Press, 1993), 55–79. On polemic in early Christianity as a whole, see L. T. Johnson, "The New Testament's

Anti-Jewish Slander and the Conventions of Ancient Rhetoric," *JBL* 108 (1989): 419–41.

No section of Matthew has received more attention than chapters 5–7. For various aspects, see H. D. Betz, *Essays on the Sermon on the Mount*, trans. L. L. Welborn (Philadelphia: Fortress Press, 1985); idem, *The Sermon on the Mount*, ed. A. Yarbro Collins (Hermeneia; Minneapolis: Fortress Press, 1995); W. D. Davies, *The Setting of the Sermon on the Mount* (BJS, 186; Atlanta: Scholars Press, 1989 [1963]); R. Guelich, *The Sermon on the Mount* (Dallas: Word Books, 1982); J. Meier, *Law and History in Matthew's Gospel: A Redactional Study of 5:17–48* (Rome: Biblical Inst. Press, 1976); and B. Przybylski, *Righteousness in Matthew and His World of Thought* (SNTSMS, 41; Cambridge: Cambridge Univ. Press, 1980).

The literary relationship between Torah, Wisdom, and Jesus in Matthew is explored by C. M. Deutsch, *Lady Wisdom, Jesus, and the Sages: Metaphor and Social Context in Matthew's Gospel* (Valley Forge, Pa.: Trinity Press Int'l, 1996); J. M. Gibbs, "The Son of God as Torah Incarnate in Matthew," *SE* 4/*TU* 102 (1968): 38–46; and M. J. Suggs, *Wisdom, Christology, and Law in Matthew's Gospel* (Cambridge, Mass.: Harvard Univ. Press, 1970). The special role played by Peter among the disciples is examined in R. Brown et al. (eds.), *Peter in the New Testament* (Minneapolis: Augsburg Pub. House, 1973).

Collections of essays touching on a number of Matthean themes include D. L. Balch (ed.), *Social History of the Matthean Community: Cross-Disciplinary Approaches* (Minneapolis: Fortress Press, 1991); D. R. Bauer and M. A. Powell (eds.), *Treasures New and Old: Contributions to Matthean Studies* (SBLSS, 1; Atlanta: Scholars Press, 1996); G. Bornkamm et al., *Tradition and Interpretation in Matthew*, trans. P. Scott (Philadelphia: Westminster Press, 1963); G. N. Stanton, *A Gospel for a New People: Studies in Matthew* (Edinburgh: T. & T. Clark, 1992); and idem, (ed.), *The Interpretation of Matthew*, 2nd ed. (IRT, 3; Edinburgh: T. & T. Clark, 1995).

For narrative readings of Matthew, see R. A. Edwards, *Matthew's Story of Jesus* (Philadelphia: Fortress Press, 1985); idem, *Matthew's Narrative Portrait of Disciples: How the Text-Connoted Reader Is Informed* (Harrisburg, Pa.: Trinity Press Int'l, 1997); J. P. Heil, "The Narrative Role of the Women in Matthew's Genealogy," *Bib* 72 (1991): 538–45; J. D. Kingsbury, "The Developing Conflict Between Jesus and the Jewish Leaders in Matthew's Gospel: A Literary Critical Approach," *CBQ* 49 (1987): 57–73; idem, *Matthew as Story*, 2nd ed. (Philadelphia: Fortress Press, 1988); and idem, "The Rhetoric of Comprehension in the Gospel of Matthew," *NTS* 41 (1995): 358–77.

For technical commentaries, see W. D. Davies and D. C. Allison, Jr., *A Critical and Exegetical Commentary on the Gospel According to Saint Matthew*, 3 vols. (ICC; Edinburgh: T. & T. Clark, 1988–97); R. H. Gundry, *Matthew: A Commentary on His Handbook for a Mixed Church Under Persecution*, 2nd ed. (Grand Rapids: Eerdmans, 1994); D. Hagner, *Matthew*, 2 vols. (WBC; Dallas: Word Books, 1993, 1995); and U. Luz, *Matthew 1–7*, trans. W. C. Linss (Minneapolis: Fortress Press, 1989). For more general guides, see F. W. Beare, *The Gospel According to Matthew* (San Francisco: Harper & Row, 1981); D. J. Harrington, *The Gospel of Matthew* (SP; Collegeville, Minn.: The Liturgical Press, 1991); D. Hill, *The Gospel of Matthew* (NCB; Grand Rapids: Eerdmans, 1972); J. A. Overman, *Church and Community in Crisis: The Gospel According to Matthew* (Valley Forge, Pa.: Trinity Press Int'l, 1996); and E. Schweizer, *The Gospel of According to Matthew* (Atlanta: John Knox Press, 1975).

9. Luke-Acts

LUKE-ACTS IS a conventional abbreviation for the Gospel of Luke and the Acts of the Apostles. The hyphenated title calls attention to the conviction that the two documents, separated in the canon by the Fourth Gospel, are two volumes of a single literary project.

The separation must have taken place early. We have no manuscripts in which they appear joined, and the patristic writers, who know of their common authorship, treated them separately. Reasons for their separation may have been straightforward. The first volume fits well among the other Gospels, but Acts looks unlike any of the other NT writings. On the other hand, Acts provides a fine introduction to the letters of Paul. We notice that Acts ends with Paul in Rome, and the Pauline collection ordinarily began with his Letter to the Romans. Acts also presents a portrait of Paul that emphasizes his place within the larger mission of the church. Thus, Luke and Acts, from early on, may have performed different functions, thereby causing a separation of the two according to their respective foci: Luke as Gospel and Acts as introduction to the Pauline literature.

Character of the Writing

The literary unity of the work is indicated by the prologue to each volume. The Gospel prologue (Luke 1:1-4) is longer and offers valuable clues to the author's intentions:

> Inasmuch as many have undertaken to compile a narrative [*diēgēsis*] of the things that have been accomplished [or, fulfilled: *plērophoreō*] among us, just as they were delivered to us by those who from the beginning were eyewitnesses and ministers of the word [*logos*], it seemed good to me also, having followed all things closely for some time past, to write an orderly account [*kathexēs*] for you, Most Excellent Theophilus, that you may know the truth [or, that you may know security: *asphaleia*] concerning the things of which you have been informed [or, instructed: *katēcheō*].

The prologue to Acts (1:1-2) follows convention by providing only a short summation of the first volume:

> In the first book [*logos*], O Theophilus, I have dealt with all the things that
> Jesus began to do and teach, until the day when he was taken up, after he had
> given commandment by the Holy Spirit to the apostles whom he had chosen.

In addition to the clear evidence of the prologues, a variety of structural, stylistic, and thematic elements coalesce to convince nearly all contemporary scholars that Luke-Acts is a united witness within the NT canon. The implications of that recognition for interpreting Luke-Acts, however, are seldom fully developed.

A composition dedicated to an individual would ordinarily bear his or her name. Luke-Acts, then, would be called *Ad Theophilum*, "To Theophilus." A formal prologue also often indicated formal publication, with the addressee being the sponsor. The identity of this "God lover" (the meaning of "Theophilus") is unknown to us; we are not even sure whether he was an individual or the symbol for Luke's readers. The implication of "the things of which you have been informed" (Luke 1:4) is that the reader knows of the Christian movement. If translated more stringently as "the things in which you have been instructed," the phrase suggests that the reader is a member of the Christian movement, one prominent enough to merit the honorific title of "Excellent" and wealthy enough to sponsor publication.

According to the superscription of the Gospel and the consensus of tradition, the author is someone called Luke. Ancient authorities identified him with the physician Luke, Paul's co-worker (see Phlm. 24; Col. 4:14; 2 Tim. 4:11). The Pauline connection seems strengthened by the fact that substantial portions of Acts dealing with Paul are written in the first-person plural, thus suggesting the presence of an eyewitness (see Acts 16:10-18; 20:5—21:18; 27:1—28:16). The traditional attribution is often challenged because of the perception that Luke-Acts is a second-generation writing (see esp. Luke 1:2; Acts 20:17-35). A designation such as "second-generation," however, does not lead to precise dating, nor does it automatically preclude authorship by a Pauline companion. The traditional attribution may be correct. It is not significantly supported, however, by supposed textual evidence of a physician's insight or vocabulary. The data adduced for such claims show only that Luke shared an educated vocabulary in no way unusual for his time, not that he used the technical language of a physicians' guild. In any case, the question of authorship does not help us greatly in interpreting the work.

We have then a two-volume work by an otherwise unknown Christian to an otherwise unknown patron sometime in the latter part of the first century. It is later than Mark, for it uses that Gospel as a source. How much later is impossible to determine. The readers were in all likelihood Christian. They could understand a significantly higher level of Greek than that found in most other early Christian writings. We assume that they appreciated Luke's often somewhat subtle stylistic touches and literary allusions. Beyond these general conclusions, we have only the text itself to guide our investigation into its destination and intentions.

We notice first its length. Though by classical standards not a writing of great proportions, it is by far the longest in the NT collection, with its fifty-two chapters occupying a full quarter of the canon. The length is not due to verbosity: Luke's Greek style is spare and effective. He has aroused deserved admiration as a teller of short stories who in a few words can evoke a whole world. Luke-Acts is studded with vivid vignettes. They range in Acts from the humorous portrayal of Rhoda dithering at the door (12:12-17) to the irony of the secret and frightened Sanhedrin session (5:33-39); from the polish of Paul's preaching to the philosophers (17:16-34) to the simple humanity of the story of Eutyches' fall from a window (20:7-12). In the Gospel are the parables of compassion and mercy, the prodigal son (15:11-24) and the good Samaritan (10:30-35). The sense of satisfying fullness given by these stories arises not from length but from artistry.

The length of Luke-Acts is due to the scope of Luke's vision. He writes "an orderly account" of "the things that have been fulfilled," and his narrative reaches back to the very beginning of humanity: while Matthew's genealogy begins with Abraham, Luke's starts with Adam (3:23-38). Luke tells us more than Matthew about Jesus' birth and childhood (see esp. 2:39–51), and much more about his resurrection appearances (24:1-53). The "things fulfilled" do not even stop there. They reach up to Luke's own day: "among us."

Here is Luke's decisive contribution to the development of early Christian literature. He tells as the one story of God's fulfilling his promises to Israel *both* the life, death, and resurrection of Jesus *and* the birth and spread of the church. Herein also is the real significance of hearing Luke-Acts as a single witness. In a single vision, Luke grasps the meaning of Jesus and the church for the world, and he tells that story so that what happens with Jesus foreshadows the church's experience and what happens in the church finds meaning as the continuation of Jesus' story.

It witnesses to Luke's literary skill that for two millennia people thought he told the story just the way it happened, indeed, had to have happened. The story of the church's beginnings need not, however, have been told at all. It might also have been told very differently. That we read it as a continuation of Jesus' story is the accomplishment of Luke.

Over the two volumes, his narrative covers some sixty years. The text gives an initial impression of completeness and consecutiveness. The impression owes more to literary skill than to an abundance of materials. In the first seven chapters of Acts, for example, Luke has only a handful of specific stories with which to work: the election of Matthias, Pentecost, the healing of a lame man, the death of Ananias and Sapphira, the gift of Barnabas, an early Christian community dispute, and the stoning of Stephen. Likewise, in the ministry of Paul recounted in chapters 15–18 of Acts, Luke has available only a few anecdotes beyond a bare-bones itinerary. When we read these sections, however, we gain a sense of detailed amplitude. How does he do it? He fills out his few specific stories by means of summaries that amplify and generalize the details of the accounts. And he extends dramatic moments with speeches that comment upon and interpret the events recounted in the narrative.

Genre and Purposes

If Luke is a storyteller, is he then simply and straightforwardly a maker of fiction? Or is he in some sense what he was so long considered, a historian? This question leads to a consideration of his composition's genre and purposes.

Traditionally, it was held that Luke was a historian and intended to be one; the discussion would then move to the issue of whether he was a good or bad historian. There are reasons for taking this position seriously: (1) His prologue tells us that he is writing an "orderly account." Historians of his age used such language to describe their work. He refers as well to oral and written sources, and he knew that others had written narratives before him. He had sources, therefore, and we have every reason to believe that he regarded them as such, and he used them critically. (2) He tries to relate his story to the broader historical context. He does this first by providing chronological references for pivotal events (see Luke 1:5; 2:1-2; 3:1-2; Acts 18:12). In addition, he identifies power blocs and governing agents, not only in Palestine (Acts 12:20-22) but in Asia Minor (Acts 19:31) and Europe (Acts 18:12-17) as well. (3) Above all, Luke has the historian's instinct for chronology and causality: he makes connections between events, so that a thread of purpose runs through his narrative.

If Luke is a historian, what kind is he, and how good? These questions are clearly related. To a considerable extent, a historian is dependent on his or her sources. Luke tells us he had some reports from eyewitnesses (Luke 1:2). Perhaps his unusually good information on Herod's household came from such a source (8:3). The "we" source in Acts could also have been based on an eyewitness, whether the author or another. Since the first-person plural could be used conventionally in travel narratives, however, we cannot be certain. Luke also had written sources (Luke 1:1). In the Gospel, he used Mark, materials from Q, and other distinctive materials designated L. We can check his use of a source in the case of Mark with the most assurance.

Luke uses Mark differently from the way Matthew does. When he follows Mark's order, he does so more closely, although he tends to eliminate blatant doublets, such as the feeding stories—unlike Matthew, who multiplies them. Instead of inserting blocks of discourse material into the narrative framework, he alternates narrative and sayings more subtly. Jesus' sayings in Luke have an air of biographical plausibility (see, e.g., chaps. 9–19). So far as we can tell, then, he is faithful to his Gospel source. But that is the real problem: telling where there *is* a source. If Matthew and Mark were not both extant and available for comparison, I doubt we could be really sure, even in the Gospel, just where Luke was using a source. Like many ancient historians, he rewrote as he borrowed from his sources. He even adjusted the Greek of Mark, bringing it closer to his own.

The real problem in discovering Luke's sources is his capacity of writing convincingly in a variety of styles. Taking the Greek of the Gospel prologue and contrasting it with that of the infancy account, then adding to the mix Peter's Pentecost sermon and Paul's defense speeches from Acts, one could easily be convinced that they come from different books and different writers. Luke follows the ancient rhetorical ideal of "writing in character" (*prosōpopoiia*), which fits style to character and occasion. In the infancy account of the Gospel, for example, his Greek has a Semitic coloration. Some have concluded he was using Hebrew or Aramaic sources. Was he? When we observe other places where he shows a flair and fascination for a biblical or, more accurately, septuagintal style, the distinguishing between source and literary artistry becomes extremely difficult.

In Acts, the search for Luke's sources is even more frustrating since we have no way to check his usage. It appears that he had fewer written sources and more literary control in Acts than in the Gospel. Apart from the "we" sections—which are otherwise stylistically consistent with the material around them—we cannot identify any particular sources with certainty. Attempts to identify a Jerusalem or an Antiochean source for the first fifteen chapters of Acts have proved in the main to be needlessly complex.

How reliable is Luke as a historian? Taking into account his fidelity to the one source we can check, his general accuracy in matters we know about from archaeological or documentary sources, and the overall agreement between his description of Paul's movements and the descriptions in the Pauline letters, we conclude that Luke is accurate in what he tells us. The phrase "what he tells us" is critical because Luke writes selectively. In Acts, Luke either does not know some things or chooses to ignore or minimize them. He describes neither a Galilean mission of the church (only 9:31; notice the conspicuous absence in Acts 1:8 and 15:3) nor any rural evangelization; the cities are his focus. Of the first missionaries, he concentrates on Peter and Paul to the virtual neglect of all others. Although Paul's arrival in Rome is the climax of Acts, Luke never bothers, for example, to inform us when the Christian movement itself reached there (see Acts 28:14-16).

Luke so concentrates on Jesus and on a few of his followers that some consider him less of a historian and more of a biographer. It has been shown that the biographies of some Hellenistic philosophers, such as those found in Diogenes Laertius, fall into a twofold form similar to that of Luke-Acts. First, the life of the founder is considered, together with an account of his deeds and teachings; then a succession narrative tells of the deeds and teachings of his students. This attractive hypothesis accounts for some features of Luke's work. It omits consideration, however, of one of the most important "characters" in that work: the people Israel. Because Luke shows a constant concern through both volumes for the fate of this historic people, his writing is properly—if roughly—categorized as a form of history.

This pushes us closer to a consideration of what kind of historian Luke might be. He was obviously not a disinterested observer, and he was not attempting to set down a comprehensive record of the Christian past. The possibility of open publication suggested by the prologue, however, may indicate some interest in influencing the outside, non-Christian world. Perhaps Luke-Acts is the first example of Christian *apologetic* literature?

Noting Luke's positive view of Gentiles generally—he entirely lacks Matthew's xenophobia—and of Roman officials in particular, some have concluded that Luke was writing an apology for the Christian movement. In this view, he sought to demonstrate the political harmlessness of the movement so that magistrates might give Christians the same freedom enjoyed by "other Jews." In this light, Luke's description of Christianity as rooted in Judaism makes an important political point. The proconsul Gallio's decision in Acts 18:14-15 is therefore exemplary: in matters of dispute among Jews, magistrates need not meddle.

Others have noted the abrupt ending of Acts with Paul under house arrest (Acts 28:30-31) and have considered Luke-Acts to be an apology for Paul, perhaps even a defense brief for use in his trial. Certainly Luke's concentration on Paul and his defense requires explanation. But the rest of his long narrative would ill fit such a narrow role. Luke-Acts has been considered an apology for Paul in yet another way. To appease a significant and theologically vocal minority of Jewish believers within the Christian community, it is suggested, Luke presents Paul not as one opposed to Torah but as a true teacher of Israel. Once again, however, that undoubted emphasis does not help us grasp the purposes of Luke-Acts as a whole. The problem with these suggestions concerning the apologetic character of Luke-Acts is that they understand apologetic literature itself too narrowly.

We remember that Jewish apologetic literature had a double function (see chap. 3, above). Outwardly, it defended Jews against attack and misunderstanding. But it also had a function for the community of Jews. It reinterpreted the tradition within a pluralistic context. Luke-Acts has a similar double-edged function. It presents the Christian movement to a hypothetical outside reader as enlightened, harmless, and beneficent. Its more immediate and important function, however, points inward, to the reinterpretation of the gospel within the context of a pluralistic environment composed of both Jews and Gentiles. To see this, another and closer look at the prologue of the Gospel is required.

The Gospel prologue (Luke 1:1-4) shows that although it may have been published and therefore available to outside readers, Luke-Acts is addressed first of all to the Christian community. Theophilus has already been "instructed" in the Christian story. Why, then, does Luke write still another version for him? Luke writes to give him "security" in his knowledge of "things brought to fulfillment among us." Not only the distant past, therefore, but also present circumstances require interpretation: the "among us" reaches to Luke's own day. The expression "fulfilled" is in the passive voice. In the biblical idiom, this means "realities that *God* brought to fulfillment." The narrative, we begin to see, is about the fulfillment of God's promises, right up to the present. But why is security (*asphaleia*) required? And how will a narrative written "in sequence" provide it?

The text of Luke-Acts seems to suggest that Luke's audience was almost entirely Gentile. There may still have been Jewish members of his churches, but the Jewish mission, which Acts shows us so repeatedly failing, appears to be less than vigorous. In contrast, the closing statement regarding the Gentiles is "they will listen" (Acts 28:28). And for Luke's readers, that statement has come true. But precisely these two facts of Gentile acceptance and Jewish rejection of the Gospel message create a severe "uncertainty" for thoughtful gentile Christians.

God's promises, after all, had been made to the people Israel, through Abraham (Gen. 12:1-3). If that historical people was not *now* in possession of the promised blessings, and someone else was, what did that signify for God's reliability? Did God keep his word, or did he utterly betray Israel? And what were the implications for *gentile* believers in this God? Could they rely on "the things fulfilled among them" any more than the Jews could? If God's word failed Israel, could it not fail the Gentiles as well?

The problem addressed by Luke's narrative is precisely and properly one of *theodicy*, that is, of defending God's work in history. By telling how each thing happened "in order," he wants to show that God in fact did *first* fulfill his promises to Israel and *then* extended the blessings to the gentile world. Therefore, the word that had reached the Gentiles was trustworthy. Here we see the importance of the "in order," or consecutiveness, of Luke's narrative: the fulfillment of the promises to Israel was required precisely for the security of gentile faith.

Luke is therefore a historian, but of a special kind. He is required to write the continuation of the biblical narrative. By showing the story of Jesus to be rooted in that of Israel and by demonstrating how God's promises were realized in a restored Israel, Luke assures gentile Christians that they can trust the "good news" that has reached them. Luke's purposes are not determined by a momentary crisis or a fleeting misunderstanding. They are generated by the fundamental mystery posed by a messianic sect's existence among gentile peoples. So successful was Luke that his narrative has become the etiological or foundational myth of gentile Christianity.

Many of the distinctive literary features of Luke's work, furthermore, can be best appreciated when seen as serving his overall purpose: his emphasis on the fulfillment of OT prophecy, his characterization of the early Christians as spirit-inspired prophets, his development of a prophetic Christology and model of authority, and his use of the story of Moses for the structuring of the two volumes. It is to these literary dimensions of Luke-Acts that we now turn.

Literary Structure and Interpretation

Luke-Acts so clearly bears the marks of literary skill and intentionality that attempts to isolate its dominant literary patterns have not been lacking. Among them are studies that emphasize the cyclical structure of the work: events in Acts clearly parallel those of the Gospel. Mary, for example, appears at the beginning of each volume; the apostles work wonders remarkably similar to those of Jesus; Paul's final journey to suffering resembles Jesus' journey to suffering. Intricate analyses of these correspondences, however, lack plausibility when raised to the level of a central organizing principle. The cyclical patterns in Luke-Acts are placed within a story that is essentially and intentionally linear. Things really change in Luke-Acts: the story begins in the OT priesthood and ends in a Roman apartment. Luke tells us that he is writing a narrative "in order"; thus, for the understanding of Luke-Acts, *where* something occurs in the narrative is almost as important as *what* occurs.

Geographical Structure

Luke uses geography as a literary and theological instrument. The center of his story is the city of Jerusalem. The whole movement of the Gospel is *toward* Jerusalem. Thus, the infancy account leads to the presentation of Jesus in the temple (Luke 2:22) and to his discovery there after being lost (2:41-51). The Lukan temptation account reverses Matthew's order for the last two temptations, so the climax is reached in Jerusalem (4:9). The transfiguration at the end of the Galilean ministry explicitly prepares for the journey to Jerusalem and Jesus' death (9:31). The journey itself begins with a solemn announcement (9:51), followed by multiple references, during the journey, to Jesus' destination (13:22, 33-34; 17:11; 18:31; 19:11, 28). After Jesus' resurrection, all his appearances take place in the environs of Jerusalem, the last of them ending with his instruction "Stay in the city" (24:1-49).

The movement of Acts is *away from* Jerusalem. Jesus says in Acts 1:8, "You shall be my witnesses in Jerusalem and in all Judea and Samaria and to the end of the earth." This is fulfilled by the narrative: the ministry centered in Jerusalem (chaps. 1–7) is followed by the evangelization of Judea and Samaria (chaps. 8–12), then Asia Minor and Europe (chaps. 13–28). Each outward movement, in turn, circles back to Jerusalem before reaching out still further (see Acts 12:25; 15:2; 18:22; 19:21; 20:16; 21:13; 25:1).

Jerusalem is therefore the *center* of the narrative. The middle twelve chapters of Luke-Acts narrate events in and around the city. Why is Jerusalem so central? The city and its temple were obviously of historical importance for Judaism, and the city was also historically important for the Christian movement—after all, it is where Jesus was killed and the church was born. The importance of Jerusalem for the church is abundantly noted by Paul (1 Thess. 2:14-15; Gal. 1:17-2:1; Rom. 15:19, 26-28). But more than historical recollection is at work for Luke. The city and the temple, for him virtually identical, symbolize the people of Israel. The death of Jesus and the birth of the church in that place are the paradigmatic expression of the Jewish people's acceptance or rejection of God's prophet. Jerusalem is the pivotal place in the story of the prophet and the people. This brings us to the second major literary pattern.

Prophecy as Literary Device

We have seen that proof from prophecy was a standard element in early Christian apologetic. Matthew used a highly developed form of it in his formula citations. Luke expands and refines the notion of prophetic fulfillment. Not only the events of Jesus' ministry, death, and resurrection fulfill the Scripture, but also stages of the church's life and mission are among the things "fulfilled among us" (Acts 3:24; 13:40; 15:15; 28:25-27). Unlike Matthew, Luke does not mechanically align texts and events. His references are more general and inclusive. He often uses the phrase "it is necessary" (*dei*) of various situations, indicating how outcomes were determined by prophecies: the suffering and glorification of the Messiah (Luke 9:22; 17:25; 24:7; Acts 3:21; 17:3), the apostasy of Judas and the election of Matthias (Acts 1:16-22), the sufferings of Paul (Acts 9:16) and those of all Christians (Acts 14:22).

Specifically Lukan is the use of literary prophecy. Things predicted by characters within the story are later shown to be fulfilled explicitly in the narrative. Only Luke combines with Jesus' three Passion predictions (Luke 9:22, 44; 18:32) the clear announcement of their fulfillment in the resurrection accounts (24:6-8, 44). Jesus' prediction of the tribulations of his witnesses (Luke 21:12-19) is literally fulfilled in the narrative of Acts (4:3-5, 14; 5:17-42). His instruction about proper responses to unbelieving cities (Luke 9:5; 10:11) is carried out by the missionaries in Acts (13:51). Jesus says the Twelve are to be judges over Israel (Luke 22:30), and later we find them exercising judgment among the people in Acts (5:1-11). The prophet Agabus predicts sufferings for Paul (Acts 21:10-14), which speedily come true (21:30-35).

Of particular importance for interpreting Luke's narrative are his programmatic prophecies. These are spoken by characters at critical junctures within the narrative and provide an interpretation of the narrative that follows. The reader understands that the plot development fulfills the prophecy. We have seen already how Jesus' commission in Acts 1:8 functions as a guide to the whole book of Acts. I have also suggested that the final announcement of Acts 28:28, "This salvation of God has been sent to the Gentiles; they will listen," is understood as having been fulfilled among Luke's readers. The prophecies at the end and beginning of the Gospel are equally important. Jesus' promise of a "power from on high" (Luke 24:49) enables the reader to perceive the "ascension" (Luke 24:50-53; Acts 1:9-11) not as an absolute departure but as a transformation of presence, and to understand the outpouring of the Holy Spirit in Acts 2:1-4 as the fulfillment of Jesus' saying, "I will send the promise of my father upon you." Likewise, the prophecy of Simeon at the start of the Gospel, "This child is set for the fall and rising of many in Israel and for a sign that is spoken against" (Luke 2:34), prepares the reader to understand the subsequent Gospel narrative as the story of a prophet whose ministry creates a division among the people.

A similar fulfillment pattern is found within smaller units. Luke arranges speech and narrative so that a story immediately following upon a saying fulfills the saying, often ironically. Here are some examples: Jesus declares that a prophet is not acceptable in his own country, and his own townspeople reject him (Luke 4:16-30). After Jesus declared that sinners accepted God but the Pharisees rejected God's plan, and after quoting the charge that he was a friend of tax collectors and sinners, Jesus is accepted by a woman who is a sinner and subsequently rejected by a Pharisee (Luke 7:36-50). Stephen, who we know is a prophet filled with the Holy Spirit, accuses the Jewish leadership of rejecting prophets and the Holy Spirit; after which they reject him (Acts 7:51-60). Upon Paul warning the Jews of Antioch in Pisidia not to reject the gospel lest they be rejected and it be given to others, they do reject it and it goes to Gentiles (13:40-48). Speech and narrative are often mutually interpretive in Luke-Acts. That Luke uses speeches in Acts as a means of interpreting the narrative (Acts 2:14-36; 3:11-26; 17:22-31) has long been recognized. But Luke uses this technique of the Hellenistic historian in his Gospel narrative as well.

Interpreting the Gospel Through Acts

The prophetic structuring of Luke's work is seen in the relationship between his two volumes. That observation requires considerable development, but the essential points can be made at once. First, the Book of Acts both continues the story of the Gospel and fulfills/confirms it. What is found only by way of implication in the story of Jesus is made explicit in the story of the apostles. The pertinence of this for the reader is that, in Acts, Luke provides the first, authoritative *interpretation* of his Gospel. For understanding the specific shape of Luke's Gospel, the perspective given by Acts is even more important than that given by Synoptic comparison. Second, the two volumes are parts of a two-stage prophetic model. Here I will argue these points in order, moving from a consideration of the prophetic image of the main characters in Acts to the implications of the theme of a "prophet like Moses."

Acts has been appropriately called the Book of the Holy Spirit. The Holy Spirit is an active power intervening in the progress of the mission, both impelling and guiding it (Acts 8:29, 39; 10:19; 11:15; 13:2; 15:28; 16:6; 20:22). There are five separate accounts of an "outpouring" of this power on believers (2:1-4; 4:28-31; 8:15-17; 10:44; 19:6). Although for Luke all Christians definitely "have" the Holy Spirit, he describes his important characters as 'men of the Spirit" in a special way. Although he never calls them by the title, he describes them as *prophets*.

Scholars have noticed the similarity between Peter and Paul in Acts. They preach the same sort of message (chaps. 2 and 13); they perform similar miracles (3:1-7; 14:8-11). Less often has it been remarked that *all* the characters in Acts who advance the plot in significant ways are described in stereotypical terms. Whether Peter and John, Philip and Stephen, or Barnabas and Paul, they share all, or nearly all, of certain characteristics. They are "filled with the Holy Spirit" (4:8; 5:32; 6:3; 7:55; 11:24; 13:9) and are bold (*parrēsia*) in their proclamation (4:13; 13:46; 28:31). What they proclaim is "good news" (5:42; 8:4, 12, 25, 40; 11:20; 13:32; 14:7; 15:35) or the Word of God (4:29; 8:14; 13:5). They are witnesses (2:32; 10:41; 13:31; 22:20) who work signs and wonders (*sēmeia kai terata*; 4:30; 6:8; 8:6; 14:3; 15:12), which they preach and perform among the people (*laos*), that is, the Jewish populace considered as God's people (3:12; 4:1; 6:8; 13:15). Because of their activity, they create a division among the people; some accept their message, others do not (4:1-4; 6:1-11; 8:6; 13:40-50). Those characteristics, taken together, reflect a particular image within the biblical tradition: the prophet. The witnesses to Jesus' resurrection are portrayed, in Acts, as prophets among the people Israel.

In Peter's speech at Pentecost, where he interprets the first outpouring of the Spirit for his listeners (and Luke's readers), he cites the prophecy of Joel 2:28-32 about the Spirit's being poured out on all flesh (Acts 2:17-21). Luke makes three significant alterations in this citation. By changing Joel's "after these things" to "in the last days," he indicates that this outpouring of the Spirit is an eschatological event. By adding the words "and they shall prophesy" to verse 17, he accentuates the prophetic character of this Spirit already suggested by the citation. By adding the phrase "and signs on the earth below" in verse 19, he forms the combination "signs and wonders." He has, therefore, brought together three elements—an eschatological prophetic spirit manifested by signs and wonders—that suggest a very specific image in the biblical tradition, that of Moses, the first and greatest of prophets (see, e.g., Ps. 78:11-12, 32, 43). Messianic expectation for a "prophet like Moses" was not unknown in first century Judaism (cf. 4Q *Testimonia*, 1–5) and was based on texts such as Deut. 34:10-12:

> There has not *arisen a prophet* since in Israel like Moses, whom the Lord knew face to face. He was unequaled in all the *signs and wonders* which the Lord sent him to do in the land of Egypt . . . and in all the mighty power and in all the great and terrible deeds which Moses wrought in the sight of *all Israel*.

We notice at once the potential of a phrase such as "a prophet arisen" for the interpretation of a resurrected Messiah. And immediately after the Joel citation, Peter describes Jesus in terms that explicitly recall the prophet Moses (Acts 2:22-24):

> Jesus of Nazareth, a man attested to you by God with *mighty works and wonders and signs* which God did *through him in your midst* . . . this Jesus you crucified . . . but God *raised him up*.

Jesus is described in terms that explicitly recall the prophet Moses.

As we read further, we find it repeated that the Spirit that is active in the prophetic witnesses is the Spirit of Jesus (Acts 2:33; 3:13; 4:10, 30, 33). The rejection of these witnesses by the people was also anticipated by Jesus, as shown by the kerygmatic passages that recall his rejection by humans and his vindication by God in the resurrection

(2:23, 36; 10:39). The longest of these kerygmatic statements (3:13-15a) says that the people were not entirely to blame because they were ignorant: they were not fully aware of what they were doing when they killed Jesus (3:17). In the offer of repentance extended to them, Peter draws an explicit connection between Moses and Jesus (Acts 3:22-23; cf. Deut. 18:18-19):

> Moses said, "The Lord God will *raise up a prophet* among your brethren as he raised me up. You shall listen to him in whatever he tells you. And it shall be that every soul that *does not listen* to that prophet *shall be destroyed from the people.*

Both Jesus and the apostles are described in terms reminiscent of Moses. The connection, moreover, is made even firmer in the description of Moses found in Stephen's speech (Acts 7:17-44). His discourse at first sight appears to be a straightforward retelling of the biblical version. Closer examination shows that Luke has selected and structured the Moses story so that it matches exactly the story of Jesus and his witnesses.

Moses' story falls into three stages. At the time when the promises to Abraham were about to be fulfilled (Acts 7:17), Moses is sent by God to "visit" the people (i.e., to "save" them). They are "ignorant" of his identity and role, so they reject him a first time and he must flee into exile (7:23-29). While in exile, Moses is empowered by God and sent back to the people a second time. He leads them out of Egypt and through the desert with "signs and wonders." But they reject him and his words a second time, preferring an idol made with their own hands. As a result, those who reject him this time are themselves rejected (7:39-43).

Here we have two sendings by God, the first with Moses in weakness, the second with him in power. Here are two offers of salvation made to the people. The first is rejected out of ignorance, and so leads to a second chance; when this is refused in full knowledge of the signs and wonders, God rejects the people. This is striking enough, but the connection between Jesus and Moses is made absolutely clear. At the heart of the Moses story we find the same sort of kerygmatic statement made elsewhere about Jesus (Acts 7:35-37):

> This Moses, whom they refused, saying, "Who made you ruler and judge?" God sent as both ruler and deliverer by the hand of the angel that appeared to him in the bush. He led them out, having performed wonders and signs in Egypt and at the Red Sea and in the wilderness for forty years. This is the Moses who said to the Israelites, "God will raise up for you a prophet from your brethren as he raised me up."

Some implications of these observations can now be spelled out. We cannot be sure whether Luke's perception of Jesus' death and resurrection affected his portrayal of

Moses, or if the influence moved in the opposite direction. It is clear, however, that the story of Moses, as Luke understood it, illustrates the "necessity" of a prophet's suffering before glory (see Luke 13:33-34; 24:25-26, 44-46). The Moses connection also reveals the typology and succession of spiritual authority important for Luke. Moses provides the type of prophetic authority and Jesus is the prophet like Moses. But Jesus has not only been "raised up" in the sense of "elected," he is also "raised up" by the resurrection as Lord (Ps. 110:1; Acts 2:34-36). As Moses "received the living words and gave them" to the people in the desert (7:38), so Jesus received from God the Holy Spirit and poured it out on his witnesses (2:33). In their testimony, the message of Jesus is filled with power. The offer of salvation now bears with it an equally great threat: those who do not listen to the voice of "this prophet" will be "cut off from the people" (3:23).

The pattern of the Moses story provides the fundamental structure for Luke's two-volume work. In the Gospel, we read the story of God's first sending of the prophet Jesus to "visit" his people for their "salvation" (Luke 1:68; 7:16; 19:44); of their initial rejection of the salvation, out of ignorance; and of Jesus' being "raised up" from death. In Acts, we find his establishment in power signified by the outpouring of the Holy Spirit, the sending of his witnesses filled with that Spirit, and the second offer to Israel of salvation "in his name" (Acts 4:12; 5:31). This time, the cost of a refusal is separation from God's people. The pattern also shows us the precise reason the Jerusalem narrative is so dominant and critical: it is in Jerusalem that the first rejection, the empowerment, the second offer, and either acceptance or rejection by the people all occur.

Luke clearly had more freedom to craft this image in Acts. But if Acts gives us Luke's interpretation of his Gospel narrative, then we can expect to find in his Gospel, with stricter constraints, the same understanding of Jesus as a prophet like Moses. Only a full reading could make this plausible, but three small details can be anticipated here. First, when Jesus raises a widow's son from the dead (Luke 7:11-15), the story concludes (7:16):

> Fear seized them all, and they glorified God, saying, "A great *prophet has arisen among us!*" And, "God has *visited* his people!"

The alert reader hears definite echoes of that identification when reading Acts 3 and 7. Second, at the conclusion of the transfiguration story, the voice from heaven identifies Jesus as Son, and says, "Listen to him" (Luke 9:35). Commentators on Matthew and Mark see here a possible allusion to Deut. 18:19 and the prophet like Moses. In the light of Acts 3:22, the allusion is clearly certain and deliberate in Luke. Third, Gospel readers hear the disciples on the road to Emmaus (Luke 24:19) describe "Jesus of Nazareth, who was *a prophet mighty in deed and word* before God and *all the people.*" When they hear in Acts of the "prophet whom God has raised up," they will realize how accurate that description was. Thus, the shape of Luke's story in Acts enables us to detect subtle shadings in his Gospel narrative.

We can now turn to a fuller consideration of Luke's first volume, presupposing once more the basic Markan story line and paying close attention to the Lukan redaction.

The Gospel Narrative

The Infancy Stories

Luke's infancy account (chaps. 1–2) is a form of haggadic midrash: his language evokes both specific texts from Torah and the general atmosphere of the biblical world. After the elegant Greek of the prologue (1:1-4), the reader is plunged suddenly into the world of Judges and Ruth by the septuagintal style of 1:5. The speech of both angels and humans resonates with passages of OT Scripture. Gabriel's annunciation to Mary (1:28-33) recalls at once the annunciation in Judges 13:2-5, the oracles of Zeph. 3:14 and Zech. 2:10, and the prophecy of 2 Sam. 7:12-16. Mary's Canticle (Luke 1:46-55) adapts and alters the Song of Hannah from 1 Sam. 2:1-10. The very description of characters suggests the piety associated with the "poor of Yahweh" in Zeph. 3:11-16 and Psalms 34 and 40 (cf. 1:6; 2:25, 36-37). The infancy account, in short, roots the story of Jesus in the longer story of Israel. At the same time it points forward to the ministry of Jesus and beyond, by establishing motifs that are later developed by means of programmatic prophecies.

The infancy account has a complex internal structure. It contains two sets of contrasting narratives. The annunciation to Zechariah (Luke 1:8-23) is contrasted to the one made to Mary (1:26-38), and the birth of John (1:57-67) is placed against that of Jesus (2:1-21). The first set of narratives is followed by the visitation of Mary to Elizabeth (1:39-45) and the Canticle of Mary, the Magnificat (1:47-55). The second is flanked on one side by the Canticle of Zechariah, the Benedictus (1:67-79), and on the other by the purification, the Canticle, and the prophecy of Simeon (2:22-35) and the praise of the prophetess Anna (2:36-38). The narrative reaches a climax with the discovery of Jesus in the temple (2:41-51). Short panels describing the growth of John (1:80) and Jesus (2:52) point the reader to their future roles. As always in Luke, the geographical movement centers on Jerusalem, both beginning (1:8) and ending (2:42) there.

From the prophetic announcements and canticles we learn of the significance of John and Jesus. They are both prophetic figures. John will "go before him in the spirit and power of Elijah . . . to prepare a people for the Lord" (1:17). Luke does not later need to make an explicit connection between John and Elijah after the transfiguration (cf. Luke 9:36 with Matt. 17:11-13) because he has already made it here. In his canticle, Zechariah says of John, "You, child, will be called prophet of the most high, for you will go before the Lord to prepare his ways, to give knowledge of salvation to his people in the forgiveness of their sins" (1:76-77). John, we see, will be "great before the

Lord" (1:15). But Jesus "will be great and will be called Son of the Most High" (1:32). John and Jesus both stand in the line of prophets, but Jesus is Messiah, Son, and Lord, while John remains precursor (see also 7:24-35).

Luke makes clear that Jesus is also a Davidic messiah. The oracle of 2 Sam. 7:12-16 is applied directly to him by Gabriel: Jesus will be given "the throne of his father David" (Luke 1:32-33). The Davidic link is forged securely by 2:4 ("city of David . . . lineage of David") and 2:11 ("born this day in the city of David"). In Luke's genealogy, too, Jesus is son of David (3:31); later, Luke will incorporate the other Son-of-David passages from Mark (Luke 6:3; 18:38-39), in addition to exploiting this lineage in Acts 2:25; 13:22-23; 15:16. Like Matthew, however, Luke stresses that Jesus is more than David's son; he is also Lord (Luke 20:41-44; cf. 7:13; 10:1; 17:6; 18:6; 19:8—and much more frequently in Acts, after the resurrection). Because Mary is overshadowed by the Holy Spirit, Jesus is also Son of God (Luke 1:35; 3:22; cf. 4:3; 8:28; 10:22; 22:70—but in Acts, only 9:20; 13:33).

Luke's characteristic preoccupation is with the meaning of John and Jesus *for Israel*. John, we have seen, will "prepare a people for the Lord." In the Benedictus, Zechariah praises God for his "visitation" of his people for their redemption in fulfillment of the promises to Abraham (1:68-69; cf. Acts 7:17). The story of Jesus now brings to completion the ancient and fundamental promises of God that gave birth to a people. The figure of Abraham and the fulfillment of the promises to him play a more central role in Luke-Acts than in the other Gospels (see, e.g., Luke 16:22-31; 19:9; Acts 3:25; 7:2-8; 13:26), precisely because Luke is concerned to connect the church's story to Israel. And it is a story of salvation. The language of "God's visitation" here is echoed later (Luke 7:16; 19:44; Acts 7:23; 15:14): it is God's intervention to save his people. In Mary's canticle, this action of God reverses the fortunes of rich and poor, powerful and weak; the birth of the Messiah transforms the measure of the world even as it brings the promises to Abraham to their completion (1:55).

The significance of Jesus for the people goes far beyond that of John. In Jesus is the dawn of *salvation*. Zechariah praises God for "raising up a horn of salvation for us in the house of his servant David" (1:68-69), and at Jesus' birth the angels announce "a savior who is Christ the Lord" (2:11). The understanding of Jesus as one who brings salvation is a specifically Lukan emphasis. By it he makes explicit a conviction found already in Mark, which is shared also by Matthew. Luke uses the vocabulary of "saving" with great frequency. In the Gospel, he increases Mark and Matthew's thirteen uses of the verb "to save" to seventeen, adding thirteen more in Acts. He is also fond of substantives for "salvation," using *sōtēria* in four times in Luke (1:69, 71, 77; 19:9) and six time in Acts (4:12; 7:25; 13:26, 47; 16:17; 27:34), while reserving *sōtērion* for the critical passages of Luke 2:30 and 3:6, and Acts 28:28. This last is the prophecy with which Acts ends: the Gentiles will listen to "this salvation from God."

Luke also gives the title Savior (*sōtēr*) to Jesus in Luke 2:11 and Acts 5:31; 13:23. As Moses went to visit his people (Acts 7:23) to bring them "salvation" (Acts 7:25), so God visits the people Israel in the offer of salvation made through Jesus. However, in contrast to the salvation and redemption of old, which was a freeing from slavery and an inheritance of a land, this salvation is a redemption from sins, leading to the capacity of worshiping God "without fear," because of the inheritance of the Holy Spirit (Luke 1:73-77; Acts 2:38-39).

Jesus' ambiguous relationship to his people is suggested by his presentation in the temple. The "righteous and devout" Simeon had been awaiting the "consolation of Israel." When he takes the child Jesus in his arms, he praises God for allowing his eyes "to have seen thy salvation." This salvation will be "a light of revelation unto the Gentiles and for glory to thy people Israel" (2:29-32). The reader is here prepared for the spread of the word to the Gentile world (Acts 13:47), but Luke's primary interest is the fate of Israel. The salvation brought by Jesus is to be its "glory." But there is more. In the prophecy made to the child's parents, Simeon predicts a division within the people caused by Jesus (2:34). This programmatic prophecy interprets the subsequent narrative. The pattern of the prophet like Moses would lead us to expect a complete rejection of the prophet sent by God, and there are elements of that in Luke. But his most consistent presentation is of a division within the people of God. Some accept the prophet, and some do not.

Luke's infancy account is also noteworthy for the important role played by Mary. Luke is generally observant and appreciative of the life and activity of women. Most of his male characters have a female counterpart (see, e.g., Luke 1:6-7; 2:36-38; 4:25, 38; 7:11-15, 36-50; 8:1-3, 19-21, 43-56; 10:38-42; 11:27; 13:10-17; 15:8-10; 17:29-32; 18:1-8; 23:28-31, 49, 55-56; 24:1-11, 22-24; Acts 1:14; 2:17-18; 5:1-11, 14; 6:1-2; 8:12; 9:36-43; 12:12-17; 13:50; 16:1, 11-18, 40; 17:12, 34; 18:1-4, 18, 26; 21:5, 8-9; 22:4; 23:16; 24:24-25; 25:13; 26:30). Mary is far more than a representative woman, however; she also represents the faithful people of Israel. The reversal of her condition symbolizes the great reversal that God's visitation will bring upon the whole people (cf. 6:20; 7:22). As a woman she was lowly and an outcast, a member of the poor in a patriarchal society, and as a virgin she was further marginalized by her lack of valued offspring. But God "raised her up" by choosing her to be the one filled with grace, just as he lifted up the poor; and by overshadowing her with the Holy Spirit, God showed that out of apparent powerlessness comes strength, for "nothing is impossible with God" (1:37; cf. 18:27). Mary also represents Israel in her anguish. For just as Jesus will be a sign of contradiction, causing a division within the people; so Mary will have "a sword pierce her soul" (2:35) as she grieves Israel's final rejection of her son. Finally, Mary represents the restored Israel, for she is present at the definitive outpouring of the Holy Spirit at Pentecost (see Acts 1:14). With other women, she is among the daughters and women servants who prophesy (Acts 2:17-18).

Mary is also an individual person of faith. She identifies herself as a "servant of the Lord" (Luke 1:38). By saying, "Let it be done to me according to your word," she demonstrates a response to God structurally identical to that of Jesus (see Luke 22:42).

She is a model of the faithful acceptance of God's will. Elizabeth cries out to her, "Blessed is she who believed there would be a fulfillment of what was spoken to her by the Lord" (1:45). Jesus later identifies as "blessed" and as his "mother and brothers" those "who hear the word of God and keep it" (8:19-21; 11:27-28). Last but surely not least, Luke shows Mary to be one who reflected on the Word of God, turning it over in her heart (1:29; 2:19, 51), and one who was able to interpret the new experience of God through the symbols of God's word in Torah (1:47-55).

The Prophetic Messiah

The relationship between John and Jesus continues into the ministry narrative. John's prophetic role is immediately made clear: "The word of the Lord came to John" (3:2). From this point forward, "the word of God" is thematic in Luke-Acts. The phrase contains an explicit theological significance that is also given to the speeches of John, Jesus, and Jesus' followers, linking them together in a succession of prophetic authority. In Luke's parable of the seed, "the seed is the word of God" (8:11; cf. 5:1; 8:21; 11:28). In Acts, "the word of God" is virtually a synonym for the Christian mission: "So the word of God grew and prevailed mightily" (Acts 19:20; cf. 4:31; 6:2, 7).

Jesus' baptism by John also suggests a prophetic anointing. Luke gently removes John from the actual scene in order to show that it is God who bestows the Spirit on Jesus (Luke 3:21-22). The reality of the bestowal is signified by the bodily descent of the dove. The Spirit descends, furthermore, while Jesus is praying (3:21), just as the disciples pray when the Spirit is bestowed at Pentecost (Acts 1:14). Indeed, Jesus prays in this Gospel at every critical turn in his ministry (see Luke 6:12; 9:18, 28-29; 10:21; 11:1; 22:32, 41-46; 23:46). We understand by this that Jesus' sonship to God is above all a matter of faithful obedience. In Acts, Jesus' followers also pray for guidance and for power (Acts 1:14, 24; 2:42; 3:1; 4:24; 6:6; 8:15; 10:9; 12:12; 13:3; 14:23; 16:25; 20:36; 28:8).

That Jesus is a prophetic messiah is shown clearly in the story of his rejection in Nazareth (Luke 4:16-30). Luke moved this story from the later position it holds in Mark (and Matthew) to the very beginning of the ministry. He has also expanded it into a programmatic statement on the nature of Jesus' mission. The reader has learned already that Jesus received the Spirit bodily (3:22) and that, "full of the Holy Spirit," he was led by the Spirit into the wilderness for forty days (4:1). After his testing, Jesus began preaching "in the power of the Spirit" (4:14). Now, in Nazareth, he reads from Isaiah, "The Spirit of the Lord is upon me because he has anointed me to preach good news to the poor (Luke 4:18; cf. Isa. 58:6; 61:1-2). He then announces, "Today this Scripture has been fulfilled in your hearing" (4:21). Luke understands the title Messiah (anointed) literally: Jesus is Christ, "the anointed," because he has been anointed *by the Holy Spirit* (see also Acts 4:27; 10:38). The nature of his messiahship is to proclaim deliverance to the outcast and afflicted, bringing to completion (or, fulfillment) the prophetic ministry of the Isaianic herald. Jesus is a prophetic messiah.

The story points as well to the second aspect of this prophetic ministry. His townspeople at first hear him gladly, but they turn against him when he compares himself to Elijah and Elisha (Luke 4:25-27). The reason is that they were prophets through whom God worked salvation for those *outside* the historical people of Israel. The townspeople represent those Jews who do not accept a prophet who offers God's "visitation" to any but themselves. In seeking to kill him, they illustrate one of Luke's main themes: this prophet's preaching creates a division within the people, revealing "the designs of many hearts" (2:35).

The next section of the Gospel showing intensive Lukan redaction continues the prophetic motif. In Luke's Sermon on the Plain (6:17-49), Jesus proclaims both blessings and woes (6:20-26). The programmatic prophecy of 4:18 is here fulfilled as the Messiah brings "good news" to the poor, the hungry, those who weep, and those who are persecuted. In contrast, he pronounces woes for those who are rich, well fed, joyful, and approved by others. These "have their consolation now" (6:24) and do not need the "consolation of Israel" brought by Jesus (Luke 2:25). The rich are sent away empty and the powerful brought low, while the poor are lifted up. Luke's blessing of the poor fits within this pattern of messianic reversal established earlier in the Magnificat. He does not prescribe a "spiritual attitude" for his followers but announces that God is upsetting the measure of the world: those considered outcast and excluded from the "consolation" of full membership in God's people are accepted by God. The "good news" to them is that the standards of humans are not those of God: "Yours is the kingdom of God."

Luke similarly has Jesus signal this nature of his messiahship in 7:21-22, when he sends word to John of his messianic deeds, the listing of which culminates in Jesus stating that "the poor have the good news preached to them." In the parable of the great banquet, Jesus likewise suggests that those preoccupied with possessions could not respond to the kingdom invitation and therefore were rejected, so that the call went out to the poor, maimed, blind, and lame (14:21; cf. 14:13). Finally, the Lukan parable of the rich man and Lazarus brings the theme to completion. In language that deliberately echoes that of the Beatitudes, this parable reverses fortunes: he who was rich is lost; he who was poor is received "in the bosom of Abraham" (16:22-23).

Although Luke is concerned throughout his work with the role of material possessions in symbolizing one's response to the call of God (see, e.g., Luke 12:13-40; 14:26-33; 16:1-13; 17:22-35; 18:18-30; Acts 2:41-47; 4:32-37; 20:17-35), the language of the "rich and poor" does not serve primarily such a teaching function. It functions first of all to demonstrate that Jesus is a prophetic messiah who proclaims "good news" to the outcast among the people, and that he, in turn, is a prophet rejected by the well-established and powerful. In the narrative, the role of the poor is played by sinners and tax collectors, and the role of the rich by the Pharisees and lawyers. Because in his ministry the visitation of God to his people is effective, those who reject him are rejected from the people; those who accept him are accepted by God.

Jesus had compared himself to Elijah and Elisha in Luke 4:25-27. In 7:1-16, he imitates them. Elisha had healed the Syrian general Naaman through the intercession of a young Jewish girl (2 Kings 5:1-14). In Luke 7:1-10, Jesus heals the slave of a gentile centurion through the intercession of Jewish elders. Just as the prophet Elijah had raised to life the son of the widow of Sarephath (1 Kings 17:17-24), the prophet Jesus raises the son of the widow of Naim from the dead (Luke 7:11-15). Luke makes the connection clear by using the same phrase in 7:15 that appears in 1 Kings 17:23 (LXX): ". . . and he gave him to his mother." The people recognize the identification, for they proclaim Jesus as a great prophet and praise God for visiting his people (Luke 7:16). This is the point where John seeks confirmation that Jesus is the awaited one; Jesus responds: "The poor have good news proclaimed to them" (7:22). As with Elijah and Elisha before him, Jesus reaches out to the lowly of society, and in this the Messiah's mission is realized.

The discourse and narrative that follow this scene sharpen our understanding of the division within the people created by the prophet. Jesus praises John as a prophet and as more than a prophet (7:26). But John had been accepted as such only by "the people and the tax collectors." In contrast, the Pharisees and lawyers ("lawyers" is Luke's term for scribes) had "rejected the purpose of God for themselves, not having been baptized by him" (7:29-30). They rejected John as a prophet on the charge that he had a demon. Now quite a different sort of prophet appears in Jesus. He is no ascetic. But he too is rejected because "he is a friend of tax collectors and sinners" (7:34). Immediately after this, Jesus is accepted by a woman who is a sinner, and her sins are forgiven; but he is rejected by a Pharisee who cannot recognize in him a prophet sent by God (7:36-50). These parallels between Jesus and John help clarify this theme of division.

The division in Israel is between two groups. On the one hand, there are the ordinary people of the land—in particular those made marginal or outcast by ritual law: the poor, lame, blind, maimed, and women (and in Acts, eunuchs, Samaritans, and Gentiles). These accept this prophet and are thereby accepted into the people God is forming. On the other hand, there are the leaders of the people—the rich, the powerful, and the arrogant, who seek "to justify themselves" (see Luke 16:15; 18:9). These already had their consolation in their power and prestige, did not accept either John or Jesus, and would not later accept Jesus' emissaries.

The Formation of the People

Already in the Gospel's first eight chapters we catch glimpses of the people of God forming around Jesus. He calls disciples who are sinners (5:1-11) and tax collectors (5:27), who leave all to follow him (18:28-30). From among them, he chooses twelve who are explicitly called apostles (6:13; the term is very frequent throughout Luke-Acts: see, e.g., 9:10; 11:49; 17:5; 22:14; 24:10; Acts 1:2; 1:26). After the story of the sinful woman, we begin to see the nucleus of the people gathering: Jesus and the Twelve are preaching in Galilee. With them is a group of women, who support them (8:1-3). Here is the core of the restored Israel, merely a small band of followers from Galilee.

Beginning in Luke 9:1, Jesus prepares a foundation for authority within the people to replace the Jewish leaders who reject the prophet. He sends out the Twelve with "power and authority" to preach the kingdom and to heal (9:2)—to engage, that is, in precisely the activities of Jesus himself (see, e.g., 9:11). When they return, Jesus has them distribute food to feed the five thousand (9:10-17). Luke thereby establishes a connection, which he consistently makes, between authority among the people and service at table fellowship. That these Twelve will take over the leadership of Israel is suggested in the Lukan parables of the pounds (19:11-27) and the vineyard (20:9-18). At the last supper, Jesus explicitly bestows authority (*basileia*) on the Twelve to judge the twelve tribes of Israel (22:30), which is fulfilled in their exercise of leadership in the Jerusalem community (Acts 2:41-47; 4:32—5:11).

In the meantime, we are shown the people itself in process of formation, particularly in that distinctive section of Luke's Gospel called the journey narrative (9:51—19:44). It is called this because the movement toward Jerusalem dominates the section. At the transfiguration, Jesus converses with Elijah and Moses about the *exodus* (literally "his going out," but also a play on the Mosaic exodus of the OT) he was going to accomplish in Jerusalem (9:31). His turn toward the city is solemnly announced in 9:51: "When the days drew near for him to be received up, he set his face to go to Jerusalem." Some seventeen times in the succeeding chapters we are told that Jesus is "on his way." This travel motif gives the entire section a dynamic quality and renders more dramatic the calls to discipleship (see 9:57-62).

What is taking place here is more than a simple journey—even one toward suffering and death (Luke 9:22; 18:31). Luke places within the journey's framework the largest portion of his sayings material. Jesus is always speaking. As he travels, furthermore, he is surrounded by three groups. There are the amorphous crowds (*ochloi*), his opponents (above all the Pharisees in this section), and his disciples (*mathētēs* occurs twenty-two times in chaps. 9–19, compared with sixteen in the rest of the Gospel). Luke makes considerable effort to note, moreover, exactly what Jesus says to whom in these sayings.

As for the substance of the sayings, the words addressed to each group have a distinctive character. To the crowds Jesus issues warnings of judgment and calls to discipleship. To his opponents he tells parables that warn of their rejection. To the disciples he gives specific instructions on prayer, hospitality, suffering, and possessions. Luke arranges these sayings in an alternating pattern: Jesus turns from one group to another as he journeys. A short review of one section—13:18 to 17:10—will indicate the pattern.

Jesus speaks parables to the crowd on the growth of the kingdom and the reality of selection and judgment in the kingdom (13:18-30). Then he turns to the Pharisees. To them he speaks a lament over Jerusalem and its rejection of prophets (13:31-35); while at dinner with them he rebukes their seeking of honor and prestige (14:1-14) and tells the parable of the great banquet (14:15-24), which suggests their rejection of God's invitation and the consequent call to the outcast. Jesus turns immediately again to the crowd and, in terms that resonate with the parable, calls them to discipleship and spells out its demands (14:25-35). Next, he tells the Pharisees the three parables of the lost (sheep, coin, son) because they had objected to his attracting sinners and tax collectors (15:1-32). Turning to the disciples, Jesus gives instructions on the use of possessions in almsgiving, telling the story of the unjust steward, with its appended morals (16:1-13). The Pharisees, who are called lovers of money and those who justify themselves (16:14-15), reject this teaching on discipleship. Jesus then tells them the parable of the rich man and Lazarus (16:19-31), with its clear threat of rejection for those who heed neither the demands of the Torah on almsgiving nor the voice of the prophet: "They will not be convinced if someone should rise from the dead" (16:31). Finally, Jesus turns again to the disciples with teaching on scandal and faith (17:1-10).

A subtle but effective point is made by this alternating pattern of sayings. On the way to Jerusalem to face his rejection and death at the hands of the leaders, the prophet Jesus is forming the true people of God around himself. The crowds are being called to repentance, and those who respond are being instructed in the nature of discipleship. But those who reject the prophet are being warned of their own rejection by God. When the Pharisees ask him when the kingdom of God will come, Jesus answers, "The kingdom of God is in the midst of you" (Luke 17:21). In this context, his answer can be taken literally: the people obedient to the prophet's call are being formed all around the Pharisees; they alone cannot see the signs of what is happening.

The journey reaches an end with Jesus' triumphant entry into Jerusalem. The small band of followers we spotted in Luke 8:1-3 has now swelled, so that "the whole multitude of disciples" (19:37) greets Jesus as king. The Pharisees, in contrast, tell Jesus, "Rebuke your disciples" (19:39). Jesus then voices a solemn lament over the city of Jerusalem. It will face destruction because it did not recognize the "time of its visitation" (19:44). The Lukan parable of the pounds (19:12-27), which is told just before the entry into the city, interprets the larger narrative: the one who is king will reward his faithful followers with authority in the kingdom, but those who resisted his kingship will be utterly cut off.

The Passion Narrative

While Matthew follows Mark's Passion narrative closely, Luke significantly alters his Markan source. He deletes the anointing at Bethany (7:36-50 is another story altogether) and the shepherd citation from Zechariah. He shifts two elements of the

Passion to Acts: the death of Judas (see Acts 1:16-20) and the false witnesses who accuse Jesus of speech against the temple (see Stephen in Acts 6:11-14). Luke also adds significant materials. He attributes Judas' betrayal to Satan's entering his heart (22:3). He expands the last-supper sayings to include a discourse on leadership as service within the community (22:24-38). He also includes a separate hearing before Herod (23:6-12). Moreover, the entire crucifixion scene is richer, with Jesus addressing both the crowds around him as he carries his cross (23:28-31) and the two criminals crucified with him (23:39-43). The cry of abandonment from the cross found in both Mark and Matthew becomes in Luke a prayer of acceptance (23:46), and it is preceded by words of forgiveness (23:34) and promise (23:43).

These alterations make Luke's Passion narrative the closest of the Synoptics to John's Passion account. Two emphases emerge, however, that are distinctively Lukan: the image of Jesus as *sophos*, and the role of the populace in his death.

Luke does not deny the scandal of the cross, but he shades the image of Jesus to more closely resemble the *sophos* (wise man/sage) of Hellenistic moral ideals, whose self-control, freedom from fear, and courage are a model for his followers. At the last supper, Jesus disposes of his heritage: as he had received authority (*basileia*) from God, so he bequeaths it to the Twelve (22:29-30). Jesus also provides them with a model for this authority: "I am among you as one who serves" (22:27). He instructs his disciples and prepares them for the future (22:35-38). In the Garden of Gethsemane, he tells them to pray lest they fall into temptation (22:40; cf. 8:13). When he withdraws from them to pray, he is not overcome with sorrow (*lupē*), but the disciples are—a sign of their weakness and lack of courage (22:45). Jesus is comforted by an angel in his bloody sweat (22:43; although note textual problem here), which reworks a theme from the temptation account (4:9-13; cf. Mark 1:13). When Peter strikes the high priest's servant, Jesus heals the man's ear (22:51). At the end he is not powerless but goes willingly to do his father's will (22:42). His self-control is further shown by his words of comfort and warning to the women of Jerusalem (23:28-31) and his offer of a place in paradise to the thief (23:39-43). Jesus is thus portrayed as confronting death with a courage, resoluteness, and dignity befitting the great individuals of the ancient world.

The *sophos* is also one who is just (*dikaios*). That Jesus is innocent of any crime deserving death is emphasized by Pilate's threefold declaration of his innocence (23:4, 14, 22), a verdict confirmed by Herod as well (23:15). Jesus' "righteousness" is demonstrated by the forgiveness he extends to his executioners (23:34) and the entrusting of his life to God: "Father, into your hands I commit my spirit" (23:46). The image of Jesus as the Just One is confirmed by the statement of the centurion at the cross. Rather than identify Jesus as God's Son (as in Matthew and Mark), he declares, "Truly, this man was righteous" (23:47). The term "righteous" (*dikaios*) is often translated "innocent" in this place. Although that agrees with one of Luke's emphases, it is too weak to capture the full significance of Jesus as the Righteous One. Throughout his

Gospel, Luke shows that righteousness is found in the total devotion to God demonstrated by Jesus (see Luke 1:6, 17; 2:25; 16:15; 18:9, 14; 20:21; 23:50), and Jesus is three times given the title "the Just One" in Acts (3:14; 7:52; 22:14).

Luke's sharpest contrast with Matthew's Passion narrative concerns the role of the populace in the death of Jesus. Matthew explicitly involves all the people of Jerusalem: "His blood be upon us and upon our children" (Matt. 27:25). Luke also knows traditions that implicate "all the people" (Acts 3:14), but in the narrative itself he does all he can to minimize the participation of the people as such in the rejection and death of Jesus. In the Passion narrative, the split between the ordinary people and the leaders, now represented by the Sanhedrin, Sadducees, and priestly classes, is sharply delineated. The rejection of Jesus thus falls squarely on the shoulders of the Jewish leadership in Jerusalem.

The post-resurrection declaration of the travelers on the road to Emmaus accurately summarizes Luke's view of this division (Luke 24:20-21):

> . . . how our *chief priests* and *rulers* delivered him up to be condemned to death, and crucified him. But *we* had hoped that he was the one to redeem Israel.

In only one instance in the narrative does one find the "people" listed together with the "chief priests" and "rulers" (23:13). So anomalous is the appearance of the people here that some scholars seek the desperate remedy of an emendation to "rulers *of* the people." The solution is wrong, but the fact that it was needed points to the way Luke otherwise removes the people from the proceedings.

To accomplish that removal, he makes many small alterations in Mark's text. After Jesus cleanses the temple (19:45-46), the "priests and scribes and leaders of the people" try to destroy him, but the common people hang onto his words (Luke 19:47-48). Jesus is in the temple teaching "the people" when the leaders begin their attack (20:1-2). In 21:38, again, "the people" come early in the morning to the temple to hear him teach. The leaders, by contrast, must be circumspect in their plot against Jesus, "for they feared the people" (22:2). Judas must carry out his betrayal "in the absence of the multitude" (22:6). The crowd that comes to arrest Jesus is made up not of the general population but entirely of chief priests, captains, and elders (22:47, 52). It is they who take Jesus to trial (23:1) and accuse him before Pilate (23:2). On the way to the crucifixion, women lament over him and a great crowd follows him (23:27). At the cross, only the *rulers* mock him (23:35), whereas in Mark (15:29) and Matthew (27:39) *all* the passers-by revile Jesus. At the point of Jesus' death, Luke pays particular attention to the common people. They had come as though witnesses to a spectacle, but now, they turn away, "beating their breasts" (23:48). With this sign of distress and remorse, Luke suggests a preparation for the repentance of the people in Acts. They will become part of the restored people of God.

The Resurrection and Ascension

Just as Moses was vindicated by God after his first rejection and was sent back with new power (Acts 7:34-38), so now Jesus is vindicated by his resurrection, becoming the "prophet whom God raised up" in power (Acts 2:24; 3:13-15). Luke-Acts has a rich and complex presentation of Jesus' resurrection, which by no means is confined to the empty-tomb and appearance accounts of the first volume.

Unique to Luke is the ascension motif (Luke 24:50-51; Acts 1:9-11; cf. Luke 9:31, 51). According to Acts 1:3, the ascension occurred after forty days of appearances to "witnesses." According to Peter's speech in Acts 10:40-41, "God raised him up on the third day and made him manifest; not to all the people, but to us who were chosen by God as witnesses, who ate and drank with him after he rose from the dead." At first the ascension appears to be a temporary withdrawal: "This Jesus, who was taken up from you into heaven, will come in the same way as you saw him go into heaven" (Acts 1:11). But it does not in the least make him absent in the narrative of Acts. He is seen by Stephen "standing at the right hand of God" (7:55-56) and by Paul in a blinding light (9:1-9). These are appearances of the resurrected one to his chosen witnesses. Ananias told Paul, "The God of our fathers has appointed you to know his will, to see the Just One, and to hear a voice from his mouth" (Acts 22:14). More significant, Jesus' presence continues palpably through the words and deeds of his witnesses. The power of the Holy Spirit operative in them comes from him, so that they preach and heal "in the name of Jesus" (Acts 3:6, 16; 4:10, 29-31; 5:28; 10:43; 16:18; 19:13). Indeed, Jesus is even more powerfully present—through the signs and wonders worked by them "among all the people"—than he was during his earthly ministry.

The ascension, therefore, does not signal a removal of Jesus from the story, but symbolizes his presence in a new mode. The ascension accounts provide a bridge between the appearances to witnesses and Jesus' presence in the community through the Holy Spirit. The reader can hardly miss the prophetic typology at work in this spiritual empowerment. Elijah, too, was carried up into heaven by a whirlwind (2 Kings 2:1-12). Before he left, his disciple Elisha asked to inherit a double share of his prophetic spirit (2:9). Because Elisha was able to see Elijah depart in the chariot of fire, it was granted to him (2:11-12). He then performed a miracle fully as impressive as Elijah's (or Moses' for that matter): he parted the waters (2:13-14). The response of those who witnessed his power was that "the spirit of Elijah rests on Elisha" (2:15). In a similar manner, upon watching Jesus taken up to heaven, the disciples receive a share of Jesus' spirit, moving quickly to evidence this newly inherited power through signs and wonders.

As for Luke's appearance accounts, they have several distinct characteristics. I have already mentioned their geographical concentration in Jerusalem. The women at the tomb are not told, "Go to Galilee," but "Remember how he told you in Galilee" (Luke 24:6). The disciples are told to "remain in the city" for the bestowal of power (24:47-

49). Luke also makes the fulfillment-of-prophecy motif more explicit. Jesus' Passion predictions are fulfilled (24:6), as are "all the Scriptures" (24:25-26, 44). The content of these Scriptures was that "the Christ must suffer first before entering his glory" (Luke 24:26, 46; cf. Acts 3:18; 17:3).

Luke's appearance accounts combine matter-of-factness with mystery. On one side, the reality of Jesus' bodily resurrection is stressed, above all in 24:39. This is one of the functions of his eating and drinking with the disciples (24:30, 41-43; Acts 1:4; 10:41). Another is to suggest the way in which Jesus continues to be present for the Christian assembly "in the breaking of the bread" (24:35). On the other side, although the one who appears to the disciples is the same Jesus—"It is I myself"—he is difficult to recognize. He is mistaken for a stranger on the road (24:13-35); reports of his appearance are met with incredulity (24:11, 24). Even his palpable appearance causes them to "disbelieve for joy" (24:41). By a subtle interweaving of experience and mutual witnessing, Luke shows how the community is formed into a people as it gains a shared narrative of Jesus' resurrection.

Finally, the appearances point forward to the story's continuation in Acts. In Jesus' last Gospel appearance (24:47-49), the basic plot of Acts is sketched:

> Repentance and forgiveness of sins should be preached in his name to all nations, beginning from Jerusalem. You are witnesses of these things.

The period of the church is a period not of Jesus' absence but of his presence in a new and more powerful way. Through his apostles, the offer of salvation will be made once more to Israel (Luke 24:49):

> Behold, I send the promise of my father upon you. But stay in the city until you are clothed with power from on high.

The Acts Narrative

The Restored Israel in Jerusalem

Luke's Gospel presents the reader with a prophet like Moses who is rejected despite his offer of salvation. His preaching creates division within the people. At the end of this first volume, the people are ready for repentance, and the leaders prepared by Jesus await the power that will make them ministers of the word and authorities over Israel.

The next part of the story is most critical. In the Jerusalem narrative of Acts (chaps. 1–8), Luke must answer the fundamental question of God's fidelity to his promises, so that his readers will find assurance (*asphaleia*). He must show that God kept his promise to Israel and can be trusted to keep his word to the Gentiles who now believe in him. To do this, Luke must demonstrate that there was a restored Israel, which received the blessings God had promised to Abraham, blessings that reached the gentile world as well. His story must make clear the identity of the authentic people, the nature of the leadership over it, and how the Gospel was transferred with essential continuity from Jew to gentile believer.

Luke's concern for the church as the restored Israel is made clear at once by the account of Matthias's election (Acts 1:15-26). Luke has steadily built up an expectation for the outpouring of the Spirit: "I send the promise of my Father upon you" (Luke 24:49); "Wait for the promise of the father" (Acts 1:4); and "You will receive power when the Holy Spirit comes upon you" (Acts 1:8). Luke's natural tendency is to have fulfillment follow prophecy as rapidly as possible. The delay of this particular fulfillment is significant. It tells us that Judas' betrayal of Jesus was not simply a personal failure; it was a defection from the ranks of the apostolic office. It is necessary to replace Judas before the gift of the Spirit is given. Why? Because the Twelve, as we have already learned in Luke 22:30, are to rule over Israel, and themselves symbolize the Twelve Tribes of the restored Israel. They are the nucleus of the people that is to be empowered by the Holy Spirit. When the circle is filled, the leadership of the people is in place. Then all those who had come up from Galilee and devoted themselves to prayer (Acts 1:13-14) could welcome the long-awaited promise of the Spirit.

The People Restored

The Pentecost story uses external symbols to describe the witnesses' internal transformation (Acts 2:1-4). The mighty wind and tongues of fire signal the presence of God (see, e.g., Exod. 19:18; 24:17; 1 Kings 18:38; 19:11-13). The essential work of this Spirit is transforming eyewitnesses into "ministers of the word" (Luke 1:2): "They began to speak in other tongues as the Spirit gave them utterance" (Acts 2:4). Already in fact they are "witnesses to the end of the earth" (1:8), since Jews from all over the Diaspora had gathered in the city for the feast and hear them proclaim "the mighty acts of God."

The many languages at Babel were a consequence of human arrogance and had resulted in the dispersion of people into nations and confusion (Gen. 11:1-9). Because of that scattering, God had selected one man—Abraham—from whom he would make a people for himself (Gen. 12:1-3). Now, in this gift of the Holy Spirit, the promise to Abraham was finally fulfilled, and those who heard, in their own tongues, the praise of God, were drawn together (Acts 2:11). But even in this highly charged symbolic moment, Luke does not fail to note the mixed reception: some of those who heard marveled, but others simply mocked (2:12-13). Without interpretation, experience is ambiguous and witness obscure.

Peter's speech (Acts 2:14-36) interprets the event and makes the witness explicit. The Joel citation shows that the outpouring of the Spirit is one of eschatological prophecy exercised by all the faithful. The "prophet whom God raised up" is now more powerfully present than before. The conclusion of Peter's speech is particularly important. It illustrates Luke's understanding of the first messianic community. After demonstrating that the messianic texts of Pss. 16:8-11, 110:1, and 132:11 applied not to David but to Jesus, Peter declares (Acts 2:36):

> Let all the *house of Israel* therefore know assuredly that God has made him both Christ and Lord, this Jesus whom you crucified.

The focus is on Israel. They had rejected the prophet, and now they are called to repentance. This is their second offer of salvation, "Save yourselves from this crooked generation" (2:40), now issued by the prophetic word of the Messiah's witness. And as the people had responded to the prophet John by asking, "What shall we do?" (Luke 3:10), so also do they respond to Peter's prophetic proclamation with "What shall we do?" (Acts 2:37).

Peter's response makes Luke's perception of the first community clear. If the people repent and are baptized, they also will receive the Holy Spirit (Acts 2:38). And what is this Spirit? It is "the promise" (2:39). Here the visitation of God according to the promises made to Abraham is brought to fulfillment for "you" and "your children"; that is, for the Jewish population of Jerusalem and "their descendants." But for them only? No: "And to all that are far off, every one whom the Lord God calls to him" (2:39; cf. 2:21). Those who respond make up the restored people of God.

In his idyllic picture of the first community (Acts 2:41-47), Luke stresses its Jewish character. The believers attend the temple together and enjoy favor with all the people. Their beginning number of three thousand steadily increases. In principle, therefore, the people of God within the historical Israel has been restored. Indeed, it already has a universal character, since it includes Jews from all over the Diaspora. For some of his purposes, Luke could have stopped his story at this point, for part of the problem had been solved: God in fact did keep his promise to Abraham, and the Jewish people enjoyed the blessings of the Spirit. But still another issue must be resolved: Who are the real leaders over this people? The infant community is devoted to the apostles' teaching (2:42), but will the Jewish leadership that opposed Jesus and had him put to death allow his prophetic successors to succeed where he did not? The story takes up that point next.

Leadership Over the People

Peter's speech after his healing of a lame man (Acts 3:11-26) interprets the next part of the narrative. The healing, Peter tells us, was done "in the name of Jesus" (3:6, 16). We see that the signs and wonders worked by the witnesses are evidence that the prophet's power is active among the people (see 2:43). Peter's speech ends with a promise and a warning. These provide the reader with a programmatic prophecy for understanding the succeeding narrative. The promise is that those who join the messianic movement will participate in the "times of refreshment" (3:19) within the restored people of God (Acts 3:25-26):

> You are the sons of the prophets, sons of the covenant which God gave to our fathers, saying to Abraham, "And in your posterity shall all the families of the earth be blessed." God, having raised up his servant, sent him to you first.

The warning is that those who reject this final proclamation will be separated definitively from God's people (3:22-23):

> Moses said, "The Lord God will raise up a prophet from among your brethren as he raised me up. You shall listen to him in whatever he tells you. And it shall be that every soul that does not listen to that prophet shall be destroyed from the people."

The narrative following this programmatic prophecy focuses squarely on the apostolic witnesses. From the outside, their authority over the restored people is threatened by opposition from the Sanhedrin. Twice they are brought to trial (4:1-22; 5:17-42). Within the community, however, they are established in power and rule over Israel (4:23—5:16). The progression deserves closer examination.

The people who heard Peter's speech are divided between leaders and populace. Many who heard are converted (Acts 4:4), but the leaders arrest the apostles and put them in prison (4:1-3). At this first hearing, the apostles directly accuse the leaders of responsibility for Jesus' death: "This is the stone which *you* the builders rejected" (4:11; cf. Luke 20:17). The Sanhedrin are still very much in charge. Thus, while they find no way to contradict the healing (Acts 4:14), they nevertheless threaten the apostles (4:21). They unwittingly testify, however, to the slipperiness of their hold over the people in their statement, "in order that it may spread no further among the people" (4:17). Will the official warning stop Jesus' witnesses or lessen their authority over the people?

The answer is given in Acts 4:23—5:12. The apostles pray for power, and another gift of the Spirit is given (4:23-31). This further solidifies their role as authorities within the community of goods. All who sell their possessions "lay them at the feet of the apostles" (4:35, 37; 5:2), and the apostles make distribution according to their perception of need (4:35). Their prophetic spirit and authority are forcibly brought home for the whole church (Luke's first use of the term "church" occurs in 5:11) when Ananias and Sapphira, counterfeiting the sharing of Spirit symbolized by the sharing of possessions, are prophetically tested by Peter and fall dead "at his feet" (5:1-11). They have not obeyed the prophet's voice and have been—literally—cut off from the people (see 3:22-23). Now, the power of the apostles is greatly extended (5:12-16). The healing deeds performed by Jesus are performed by his witnesses (5:16), just as their boldness in speech had made their association with him evident (4:13).

When the Sanhedrin try to stop the apostles a second time, a great reversal has taken place. They are now "jealous" of the apostles' success among the people (Acts 5:17). They cannot hold them in prison, for an angel frees them (5:19). They fear using coercion to bring them to trial, "for they were afraid of being stoned by the people," and they are reduced to inviting them to a hearing (5:26). With delicate irony, Luke has a Pharisee, one of those who had opposed every deed of Jesus, interpret the narrative. He gives a fine theological explication: if the movement is from God, nothing can stop it; if merely human, it will collapse. What is ironic about this interpretation is that the reader already knows the movement is from God, and knows as well that Peter's challenge at the hearing—heard by Gamaliel—was not a theological reflection but a plea for conversion. Gamaliel thus proves he does not have "the Holy Spirit whom God gives to those who obey him" (5:32).

Despite receiving a beating, therefore, the apostles continue to preach Jesus as the Messiah (Acts 5:42). Luke has made his essential point clear: whatever political manipulations might still be available to the Sanhedrin, effective religious authority over Israel, considered as God's people, has passed to the apostles. They rule over the Twelve Tribes of the restored Israel in Jerusalem.

Luke could once again have stopped there. But another question still required an answer. Granted that God had remembered Israel and had established the Twelve as leaders over the people, how did that blessing reach the gentile world? Was the community represented by Theophilus *in continuity with* Israel or was it a new thing altogether, and therefore only artificially connected to the story of Abraham? As he has done twice before, Luke first prepares a leadership for the transfer of the Gospel to the Gentiles, to show that there was continuity between the Twelve and those who preached to pagans. He uses a fragmentary tradition about a dispute in the Jerusalem community over the feeding of widows to make this point. The seven chosen by the community and ratified by the apostles to serve over the distribution of goods (6:1-6) were those who, themselves filled with the prophetic spirit, preach the word to Hellenists in Jerusalem and to the pagan world. As the apostles had their spiritual authority symbolized by their function of feeding the people (see Luke 9:10-17; 12:42-48; 22:25-30; Acts 4:32-37), so the seven have their spiritual authority for the Hellenistic mission signified by their charge to feed the Hellenistic widows.

The arrest, trial, and murder of Stephen, which combine elements of mob action with a judicial proceeding, close the Jerusalem narrative. With his death, the missionaries, except for the Twelve, are scattered, and as a consequence the word spreads beyond the city. As we have seen repeatedly, Stephen's speech offers an interpretation of Luke's entire narrative structure. But its conclusion also contains a startling and effective element of irony. Here is Stephen, who we know is filled with the Spirit and who works signs and wonders among the people. He preaches about Moses who worked signs and wonders and was twice rejected. In closing, he attacks the leaders— those whom he addresses at his "trial"—for always rejecting the prophets, opposing the Holy Spirit, and for killing Jesus, the Just One. At that moment, he is filled with the Holy Spirit and sees Jesus at the right hand of God. And at that moment, he is killed.

The Gentile Mission

God had always willed in principle that Israel's blessing should be extended to the Gentiles as well. Such is the clear implication of the allusion to Isa. 42:6 in Simeon's canticle, when he calls the salvation brought by Jesus a light for revelation to the Gentiles (Luke 2:32). So also is the import of the full citation from Isa. 40:5 (only in Luke) that introduces John's ministry: "All flesh shall see the salvation of God" (Luke 3:6). John himself warned his hearers that God could raise children to Abraham out of stones (Luke 3:8). Jesus had compared himself to prophets whose work had reached outside Israel (4:25-27). In his journey to Jerusalem, Luke alone has Jesus send out a second group of seventy (-two) before him; given Luke's avoidance of doublets, the additional mission suggests an anticipation of the later sending out of missionaries— "two by two"—to the Gentiles (Luke 10:1-12; cf. Acts 13:1-3). The resurrected Jesus told his disciples that repentance would be preached in his name "to all nations" (Luke 24:47) and that they would be his witnesses "to the end of the earth" (Acts 1:8).

In the narrative of Acts, however, the gentile mission proceeds in a more haphazard and human fashion than these intimations might suggest. Gentiles are preached to in the first place because of Jewish rejection of the gospel. That rejection is never total; some Jews, even in the Diaspora, convert to the messianic sect. What is most striking about Luke's perception is that believing Jews and Gentiles together make up the authentic Israel, the people of God.

Stephen had already debated Hellenistic Jews in Jerusalem (Acts 6:9). After his execution, a persecution drove all but the Twelve from the city (8:1). Philip, who carried the gospel to Samaria, working signs and wonders there (8:13) as well as in Gaza (8:26-40), had his mission confirmed by representatives from Jerusalem (8:14-24). Luke thereby shows that the mission maintained continuity with Jerusalem. This is important because for him, the primitive Jerusalem church is the restored people of Israel. Continuity with it is critical if the gentile church is to be rooted in the Israel of the promise.

The gospel is carried to Antioch on the Orontes and preached to Greeks by those who were scattered because of the Stephen persecution (11:19-26). Barnabas, who had shown himself doubly submissive to the authority of the Twelve (he had placed his possessions at their feet and had received a new name from them, 4:37), is sent to confirm the Antiochean mission (11:22), a certification all the more important because Paul will come from that church. In the meantime, Peter works wonders in the coast towns of Lydda and Joppa (9:32-43), ending up in Caesarea. In his conversion of the centurion Cornelius (chap. 10), we have the first *narrative* description of gentile conversion and its consequences.

It is from within this context that Luke's hero Paul emerges. Glimpsed first as a collaborator at the death of Stephen (Acts 8:1) and as a rabid persecutor of the church, he encounters the risen Lord on the road to Damascus (9:1-9). After being baptized and instructed by Ananias, he preaches Jesus in Damascus, is persecuted there, is given access to the Jerusalem community through the influence of Barnabas (9:27), debates and is persecuted there, and is sent off to Tarsus (9:30). From there, Barnabas recruits him to work with the church in Antioch (11:25)and they carry a collection to the Jerusalem community (11:30). After they complete that task (12:25), they are sent by the Antiochean church on a mission (13:1-3). (It should be noted that this summary is culled from a considerably more complex narrative in which the emergence of Paul is intermixed with the mission of Philip, Peter, and John in Samaria and Judea, the conversion of Cornelius, the trouble that causes, and the imprisonment of Peter.)

Both literary art and theological purpose are here interwoven. Peter, Barnabas, and Paul appear and reappear as central figures. The complexity of their movements not only reinforces the impression of fullness in Luke's narrative but also places Paul squarely within the overall missionary effort of the church. So carefully has Luke crafted this account that it undoubtedly serves to make two apologetic points concerning Paul. The first is that his mission to the Gentiles is not idiosyncratic but part of the Spirit's guidance of the entire church. The second is that his mission is intimately connected—the role of Barnabas is crucial here—to the believing community in Jerusalem, and therefore to the restored Israel.

Luke's continuing concern for Israel is demonstrated further by the first missionary tour of Barnabas and Paul. They do not intend to convert Gentiles. Only when their message is rejected in Antioch of Pisidia do they turn away from the Jews of that place. Paul's sermon there is remarkably like Peter's at Pentecost, with its emphasis on the promise to the Jewish people carried by Jesus (Acts 13:32):

> We bring you the good news that what God promised to the fathers, this he has fulfilled to us their children by raising Jesus.

When the offer is rejected, Barnabas and Paul turn to the Gentiles. At this point, Luke explicitly applies to Paul the phrase from Isaiah 49:6, "light of the Gentiles" (Acts 13:44-48; cf. 26:17; Luke 2:32). In Iconium and Lystra, the pattern is repeated (Acts 14:1-21): the Jews' failure to accept the gospel drives the missionaries to the more receptive Gentiles. Paul and Barnabas therefore return to Antioch with the report of how God "had opened a door of faith to the Gentiles" (14:27).

Before describing Paul's distinctive and far-ranging mission to the Gentiles, however, Luke first must address the issue of the legitimacy of gentile inclusion within the messianic community. God had willed their salvation, and the Spirit had guided the proclamation of the gospel to them, but what were the implications for the church's identity as the people of God? The Council of Jerusalem (15:1-35) takes up that issue. It also forms a watershed in the Acts narrative. Before it, all the apostles were at least ostensibly in view. After it, Paul's work totally dominates. The council brings Peter back into the narrative for the last time. James is the chief spokesperson for the Jerusalem church during the council, and he only reappears once more, to confirm its decision and confront Paul (21:18). The narrative of the council itself forms the climax of a complicated plot development that has quietly been providing the background for Paul's emergence. Acts 15 is unintelligible unless read continuously from the conversion of Cornelius. In this narrative, Luke shows how the decision to recognize the full status of Gentiles within the messianic community resulted from a complex interaction of divine intervention and human obedience.

Peter had preached to Cornelius' household in the first place only because his own deeply ambiguous personal vision received clarification from the experience of the gentile Cornelius as it was reported to him (Acts 10:1-28). When he preached about Jesus, the Holy Spirit fell on the whole household (10:34-44). The witnesses of the event, who included Jewish believers, recognized that the same gift given to them in the beginning was now shared by these Gentiles. Because God had acted, so could the church: the Gentiles were baptized (10:44-48). The decision is immediately challenged by the Jerusalem leadership. Peter's defense of his action consists—in the narrative simply "in order" (*kathexēs*; as in Luke 1:1-4)—of his experience and that of Cornelius, showing how they had led him into a deeper understanding of his own vision and indeed of the very words of Jesus (Luke 11:15; cf. Acts 1:5).

The Jerusalem leadership ratifies the decision (Acts 11:18). But the issue is not fully settled. Even if Gentiles are accepted into this church, the question of fellowship is not thereby decided. This was critical above all for Jewish believers. They already belonged to God's special people, and symbolized that by circumcision and the observance of laws of ritual purity and diet. Are Gentiles also fully equal members of this people of God?

The members of the Pharisaic party of believers from Jerusalem attack the very foundations of the gentile membership in the church, claiming that one cannot be saved except by observance of Torah (15:1-2). This attack coincides with Barnabas and Paul's return to Antioch with the news of how God had done great deeds through them among the Gentiles (14:27-28). Luke effectively draws his main characters from their diverse missions to this one critical point. The reader already knows God's will in the matter; will the church ratify God's action by its decision?

In the end, yes. No further burden is placed on gentile believers beyond the norms known to them already through the diffusion of Mosaic values in the Diaspora (Acts 15:19-21). More significantly, these regulations were not conditions of membership in the people but were intended to enable table fellowship with Jewish believers. The decision was made by the assembly as a whole and was communicated to the church in Antioch. It was a decision of fundamental importance as it opened the way for a law-free gentile mission. In the narrative of Acts, it also clears the path for a full concentration on the missionary work of Paul.

We note in passing the consistent viewpoint Luke brings to his description of this great decision. The narrative of the experience of God within the assembly enables the community to discern the working of the Spirit. The experience also gives the community's members deeper insight into the meaning of Scripture. The text of the prophet Amos is said to agree with the experience of God among them, rather than the experience being made to conform to their previous understanding of the prophet (15:15-18). And the gentile mission itself is understood as a restoration of Israel. The words of James resonate with many individual notes within Luke's story (15:14-18; cf. Amos 9:11-12):

> Simeon has related how God first visited the Gentiles, to take out of them a people for his name. And with this the words of the prophets agree, as it is written, "After this I will return, and I will rebuild the dwelling of David which has fallen; I will rebuild its ruins, and I will set it up, that the rest of men may seek the Lord, and all the Gentiles who are called by my name, says the Lord, who has made these things known from of old."

Finally, Luke suggests that the experience of God's free gift of the Spirit among the Gentiles led even these Jewish witnesses to a new understanding of their own salvation (Acts 15:11):

> We believe that we shall be saved through the grace of the Lord Jesus, just as they will.

The Picture of Paul in Acts

The last thirteen chapters (16–28) of Acts are devoted to Paul. Since Acts gives us the only sustained narrative account of Paul's ministry, critical questions inevitably arise concerning its reliability. I made the point earlier Luke is generally reliable, as in the movements of Paul checked against his letters. More must be said on this subject, in order to sharpen our perception of *Luke's* presentation of Paul.

Considered as historical evidence, Acts is a secondhand primary source for the life and thought of Paul. It is also a later source. Even if it relies at least in part on eyewitnesses, it looks back on Paul's career as past history (see esp. 20:17-35). How much distance is involved is impossible to determine. Acts is also a source that, apart from some speeches that reflect distinctively Lukan concerns, focuses almost entirely on Paul's actions.

In contrast, the letters of Paul, leaving aside for the moment the issue of which are authentic, are firsthand primary sources. They are also obviously contemporary to the events they describe. Paul speaks at greater or lesser length on his past and present activities in 1 Thessalonians, 1 and 2 Corinthians, Galatians, Romans, Philippians, and 2 Timothy. These letters would ordinarily have much greater value as historical sources. Two considerations, however, must temper enthusiasm about their objectivity. First, Paul was less obsessive about biographical accuracy—with the possible exception of Galatians, where he takes an oath on some points—than he was about the development of his argument and the instruction of his community. Second, Paul also has biases. He was often under attack, and many of his autobiographical remarks—as in Galatians—have an apologetic if not polemical edge to them. Nevertheless, his letters must be given great weight, particularly in disputed cases.

If the sources agreed completely about what Paul did, said, and thought, there would, of course, be no problem. In fact, however, there among the sources three major divergences—chronology, apostolic style, and theology—that force the reader to make difficult choices.

Chronology

Only because of a fortuitous correlation between Acts 18:12, telling us that Gallio was proconsul of Achaia when Paul encountered him in Corinth, and an inscription found at Delphi, telling us that Gallio was proconsul of Achaia in 50–51 C.E., can we work toward an absolute and not just a relative chronology for the Pauline mission. In at least that sense, Acts is the indispensable starting point for a Pauline chronology, despite some scholars' protestations that they use only the letters. The attempt to erect even a relative chronology on the letters alone is futile, for their internal evidence is insufficient to support supposed lines of development. However little acknowledged, it is only the narrative of Acts 16–19 that enables us to date with reasonable accuracy 1 Thessalonians, 1 and 2 Corinthians, and Romans.

How wide is the disparity between Acts and the letters concerning what happened when and in what sequence? We have already seen part of Acts' version. Paul's conversion (Acts 9:1-9) is followed by his preaching in Damascus (9:10-25), a first visit to Jerusalem with Barnabas (9:26-27), and work in Jerusalem, Cilicia, and Antioch (9:28-30; 11:25-26). After being recruited by Barnabas, Paul carried a collection to Jerusalem with him from the Antioch church (11:29-30; 12:25). Then Barnabas and he were commissioned by the Antioch community for a first "missionary journey" (chaps. 13–14). A third visit to Jerusalem was for the Jerusalem Council (15:1-29), which was followed by a second "missionary journey" with Silas (15:36—18:21) overland through Asia Minor into Europe. He made a fourth trip to Jerusalem to "greet the church" in 18:22. He then went on a third "missionary journey" from Antioch, once more through Asia Minor to Europe (18:23—21:14). His fifth visit to Jerusalem led to his arrest, a transfer to Caesarea for a two-year imprisonment, a long sea voyage to Rome, and a final two-year (and upwards) house arrest there (21:15—28:31). From this account, we have the picture of an apostle who goes on well-structured missionary journeys. At the end of each, he touches base with the Jerusalem church, making five visits there in all. Jerusalem is the center of his missionary work as it was for all the apostles.

The information in the Pauline letters is more scanty. Paul's call as an apostle (Gal. 1:15-16) was not followed by a journey to Jerusalem, but by a three-year period of ministry in Syria and Arabia (Gal. 1:17), which was then followed by a short trip to Jerusalem (Gal. 1:18-20). Next Paul spent some eleven years in missionary activity "in the regions of Syria and Cilicia" (Gal. 1:21). Then came a second journey to Jerusalem—the "after fourteen years" of Gal. 2:1 is variously computed—for a meeting with the "pillars" of that community (Gal. 2:1-10). This was followed by activity in Galatia, Asia Minor, Macedonia, Achaia, and possibly Dalmatia, as indicated by his cryptic references to his movements in Galatians, 1 and 2 Corinthians, and Romans. He planned to visit Jerusalem a final time to bring a collection he had taken up from his churches (Rom. 15:25-32); then he wanted to visit Rome and use it as the base for a ministry to the West.

Paul stresses his independence from Jerusalem with regard to his own status as an apostle of God (Gal. 1:11-12; 2:5-11), although his visits there—he mentions three—also bear testimony to the importance he accorded that community. From his letters it is difficult to detect journeys of the sort suggested by Acts. Rather, Paul seemed to use various urban centers for greater or lesser periods as the base of his missionary operations (Acts 18:11 and 19:10 give some support for this impression). Still, the disparity between the sources, measured against other ancient historical writings, is not remarkable and confirms more than it calls into doubt. Even so, two critical cases point us to some deeper difficulties.

Was there an apostolic council? If so, who took part? When was it? Paul (Gal. 2) says a meeting took place after fourteen years of missionary work; Acts, at least on the face of it, would suggest a much shorter period before the conference. In Acts, Barnabas and Paul are sent to Jerusalem as part of a community delegation; in Galatians, Paul's companion is Titus, and he goes up in response to a revelation (Gal. 2:1-2). Was this a full gathering of the church (Acts) or was it a private meeting between peers? More critically, did it come before or after the encounter between Peter and Paul in Antioch, as recounted in Gal. 2:11-14? Galatians could be construed either way. If it came after, then Paul and Acts might agree that the meeting in Jerusalem resolved differences caused by an Antiochean dispute. But if before, then the meeting settled nothing about fellowship that did not remain troublesome. Did the meeting issue a decree concerning dietary regulations (Acts), or only an agreement about areas of missionary work (Galatians)? If there was a decree, why didn't Paul refer to it when discussing idol meat in 1 Cor. 8–10? These historical questions have proved incapable of sure resolution.

A second difficulty concerns the collection of money organized by Paul for the Jerusalem church. According to his letters, the collection was a major task of the latter part of his ministry (Gal. 2:10; 1 Cor. 16:1-4; 2 Cor. 8-9; Rom. 15). But the Acts account of Paul's fateful last journey to Jerusalem mentions nothing of such a collection. Acts does say that Paul was accompanied by delegates from the very places where the collection was taken up (Acts 20:4-5) and that Paul was taking with him a large amount of money (24:17, 26). Paul saw the collection as an act of reconciliation and fellowship between Gentile and Jewish churches. But Acts has James suggest to Paul at his arrival in the city quite another gesture of reconciliation (21:23-25). On the other hand, Luke has both Paul and Barnabas take part in a collection for the Jerusalem church, sponsored by the Antiochean community, at the very beginning of Paul's career (11:29-30). Again, it is extremely difficult to put these versions together.

The limited value of Acts and the letters in establishing a sequence of Paul's actions carries over into the sequence of the letters as well. Certain letters—such as 1 and 2 Thessalonians, 1 and 2 Corinthians, and Romans—fit well within the Acts narrative. But those written from captivity—Colossians, Philemon, Philippians, Ephesians, and 2 Timothy—could come from Paul's imprisonment in Caesarea (Acts 24:27) or in Rome (Acts 28:30), or even from some detention not mentioned in Acts (see 2 Cor. 11:23-27). Still other letters—Galatians, 1 Timothy, Titus—are virtually impossible to place with any confidence within the framework of Acts.

All this implies that both the letters and Acts are concerned with things other than biography. A more telling point is that in all the narrative of Acts, Paul is never said to have written a single letter. Paul the preacher and founder of churches is the subject of Acts. And this brings us to the next point of difference.

The Apostolic Style

Differences between Acts and the letters in the presentation of Paul's apostolic style have often been noted. In his letters, Paul confesses to little eloquence (2 Cor. 11:6). In Acts, he is a masterful talker in every situation, whether speaking before Jews in the synagogue (13:16-40), to sophisticated philosophers in Athens (17:22-31), or before rulers in his own defense (24:10-21). Although in the letters Paul acknowledges his ability to work signs and wonders as certifications of his power (2 Cor. 12:12; Rom. 15:19), he downplays such displays in favor of preaching the cross (1 Cor. 2:1-5). In Acts, however, Paul works signs and wonders, performing both healings and exorcisms (Acts 19:11-20; 20:7-12; 28:1-10), and shows himself clever and resourceful in crisis (16:25-30; 27:21-25). Acts stresses Paul's relationship to, and even his dependence on, Jerusalem; Paul in the letters minimizes both. In Acts, Paul is portrayed as an observant Jew, taking a vow (18:18), purifying himself in the temple (21:24-27), even having his close follower Timothy circumcised (16:3). In his letters, Paul says he is a "Jew to the Jews" (1 Cor. 9:20-23), but he also refuses to circumcise Titus when that act might be construed as a submission to the demands of Torah (Gal. 2:3).

These are significant differences. They should be placed, however, within the intentions and literary conventions of the respective sources. Luke-Acts sees Paul as part of the prophetic tradition that emphasizes both the manifestation of God's work through the display of signs and wonders, and the speaking of God's word through boldness. It therefore stresses Paul's rhetoric and wonders. Paul in his letters contrasts his suffering ministry to the arrogance of the "superapostles" who oppose him. He is therefore concerned to minimize rhetoric and miracles in favor of a paradoxical weakness.

Theology

Luke-Acts contains little of what is distinctively Pauline theology. It is easy, in fact, to contrast individual points within Acts and the letters, such as the treatment of natural law in Acts 17:27 and in Romans 1:18-32, or the powerful presentation of righteousness by faith in Galatians and the mild echo of that argument in Acts 13:39: "By him everyone that believes is freed from everything from which you could not be freed by the law of Moses." Such point-by-point comparisons are almost meaningless. The Paul of Acts, like the Peter and Stephen of Acts, does not speak in his own voice. He gives expression in his speeches to the religious perceptions—the theology—of Luke. Through the speeches of his characters, Luke interprets the story for his readers. Differences can be accounted for through Luke's use of *prosōpopoiia*: his characters are given speeches appropriate to their circumstances. Paul before the philosophers sounds more like Dio Chrysostom, whereas Paul in the synagogue sounds more like Peter. Given the prophetic typology with which Luke works, which demands the minimizing of individual characteristics in favor of a common literary presentation, the small element of the distinctively Pauline that does emerge within Acts is all the more remarkable.

The Lukan Presentation of Paul

We have been trying to sharpen our perception of Luke's understanding of Paul. At each point of comparison, we find that divergence results from specifically Lukan literary and religious concerns that affect Luke's treatment not only of Paul but of all his major characteristics: the connection to Jerusalem and to Judaism; the powerful works and rhetoric; the stereotypical teaching.

What, then, is Luke's positive appreciation of Paul? He calls him an apostle together with Barnabas (14:4) and—more tellingly for him—a witness (22:15; 26:16). Like the other major figures of the church's mission, Paul is described in specifically prophetic terms (14:3). The prophetic imagery is made sharper when Paul is called a chosen instrument (9:15; cf. Jer. 1:5 and Gal. 1:15) and a light to the Gentiles (13:47; cf. Isa. 49:6; Luke 2:32).

Paul was not alone in bringing the "good news" to the Gentiles, nor even the first. For Luke, however, he was preeminent in that mission. It was a ministry, furthermore, carried out in obedience to Jesus' command, which is emphasized in Luke's three versions of Paul's apostolic call. The first is found in direct narrative (Acts 9:1-9), the others in Paul's speeches of defense (22:6-21; 26:12-23). All three versions tell the same story, with some variations: his companions, for example, hear the voice but see nothing in 9:7, while in 22:9 they see the light but are deaf to the voice. The element of shining light is constant in all three accounts and is connected to his commission to be a light to the Gentiles. The climax of each version is reached with the command to go to the Gentiles (9:15; 22:21; 26:23). In the defense speeches, this creates a negative response (22:22; 26:24). As with the rejection of Jesus in Nazareth, the Jewish refusal of the prophet's message has something to do with its universal scope.

Yet, Paul's preaching in Acts is by no means exclusively to Gentiles. As we have seen, he turns to them only upon repeated rejection in the synagogue. The first time it happens, Paul solemnly announces a redirection of his efforts to Gentiles (Acts 13:46); but we still see him preaching to Jews and converting some. Two more times he declares a turn to the Gentiles (18:6; 28:23-29), but even the last and most somber of these pronouncements is made in the face of less than total rejection, since some Jews believe (Acts 28:24-25). Indeed, throughout Paul's ministry in the Diaspora, Luke shows us a division within the people: some accept the gospel, others do not (see 17:11; 18:4; 19:9-10). The emphasis in Paul's ministry is definitely on those who do not. This is indicated linguistically by the overwhelming dominance of the term "the Jews" in the narrative devoted to Paul. It is used, except in titles, only once in the Gospel (Luke 7:3) and nine times in Acts apart from Paul. But in reference to those who oppose Paul, the word "Jew" (*Ioudaios*) occurs some seventy times.

The Paul of Acts never sees his mission as separated from God's concern for Israel. In the defense speeches above all, Paul defines himself in terms of Jewish messianic expectation, specifically the Pharisaic hope in the resurrection, which he insists has come to fulfillment in the resurrection of Jesus (see 22:3-4; 23:6; 24:14-21; 26:4-11). To the Jewish leaders in Rome, this apostle of the Gentiles declares (Acts 28:20):

> For this reason, therefore, I have asked to see you and speak to you, since it is because of the hope of Israel that I am bound with this chain.

However much Paul carried the gospel to "the end of the earth," he remained for Luke the teacher of Israel.

That the gospel reached the gentile world through the ministry of Paul is made plain by Luke's literary mastery. Just as surely as he took his readers back into the world of ancient Israel by the style of his infancy account, so he leads them here, bit by bit, into the world of Greek religious and philosophical perceptions. This is not a matter of sources but of Luke's writing appropriately to the circumstances of his characters.

Down to the minutiae of style, his Greek becomes less biblical and more secular in the vignettes that show us the gospel's impact on pagans.

Such scenes are among the most lively in the two-volume work. When Paul heals a cripple in Lystra (Acts 14:8-18), the pagan population thinks "the gods have come down to us in the likeness of men." They call Barnabas Zeus, since he is the leader and possibly more striking in appearance, and Paul, Hermes, since he is the speaker. They try to offer them sacrifice and are barely restrained. Paul tells them that the message he and Barnabas bring is precisely that pagans should turn "from these vain things to a living God" (see also 1 Thess. 1:9). This scene would fit comfortably within Apuleius' *Golden Ass*: the wandering sages have such impressive thaumaturgy that they are regarded as immortals and need to teach their would-be worshipers the true nature of piety and the divine.

In a similar vein, the turbulence at Ephesus caused by the success of Paul's mission there (Acts 19:11-40) could have sprung from the pages of Philostratus' *Life of Apollonius of Tyana*. Paul's thaumaturgic powers are extraordinarily active. Demons come to prefer being exorcised by him to being exorcised by rival Jewish exorcists (19:11-15). The defeated magicians burn their books, acknowledging the superiority of this new power abroad: "So the Word of God grew and prevailed mightily" (19:20).

The carefully crafted scene of Paul preaching at the Areopagus in Athens (Acts 17:16-34) shows the gospel fully clothed for the gentile world. Luke accurately evokes the world of the wandering philosopher or sophist like Dio Chrysostom, who builds on the native piety of his listeners to create a higher understanding of the one divine power (see Dio *Oration* 12). Here are the Epicureans and Stoics with their characteristic Greek interest in barbaric deities, novelty, and debate, just as we find them in the pages of Lucian (see *The Eunuch* 1–13). In Paul's preaching we hear not only a rhetorically effective use of pagan images for the divine (17:26-29) but quite possibly an authentic echo of the sort of gentile preaching carried out by Paul and his companions (17:30-31; cf. 1 Thess. 1:9-10; Heb. 6:1-2):

> The time of ignorance God overlooked but now he commands all men everywhere to repent because he has fixed a day on which he will judge the world in righteousness by a man whom he has appointed, and of this he has given assurance by raising him from the dead.

Luke also indicates in this scene that Gentiles as well as Jews could refuse God's invitation and turn away in mockery (17:32). But some do believe, and from among them, as from among believing Jews, God fashions "a people for his name" (15:14).

In Luke's treatment of Paul, then, as in his Gospel story of Jesus and his account of the earliest Jerusalem community, we find the same consistent religious preoccupation. Luke's story, from beginning to end, concerns God's fidelity to his promises worked out in the intricate and often opaque events of history. Through the prophets

God never stops calling the people, offering fulfillment of the promises of liberty from captivity and of freedom to serve God "without fear, in holiness and righteousness" (Luke 3:74-75).

Study Questions

1. What does it mean to say, "Acts is the first and most important interpretation of Luke's Gospel"?

2. How would you describe the geographical structure of Luke-Acts?

3. Why is the retelling of the Moses story in Acts 7:17-44 important for grasping the structure of Luke-Acts as a whole?

4. What are the elements of Luke's portrayal of his leading characters as prophets?

5. How does Luke describe the disciples of Jesus differently from Mark?

6. How and why are the infancy narratives in Luke different from those in Matthew?

7. In Luke's passion narrative, is the Judean responsibility for Jesus' death expanded or minimized when compared to Matthew's version?

8. Why is the choice of Matthias in Acts 1:15 (and following) so important to Luke's story?

9. What is the importance of the baptism of Cornelius and his family (Acts 10) for Luke's story?

10. Why does Luke retell the "call" of Saul/Paul three times in the narrative of Acts? Are different aspects emphasized in each?

Bibliographical Note

Still a classic introduction to Luke-Acts as a literary unity is H. J. Cadbury, *The Making of Luke-Acts* (New York: Macmillan Co., 1927). For a whole battery of critical issues, combined with commentary, see F. J. Foakes-Jackson and K. Lake (eds.), *The Beginnings of Christianity: The Acts of the Apostles*, 5 vols. (London: Macmillan & Co., 1920–27). The pioneering redactional study of Luke that initiated serious discussion of its theology was H. Conzelmann, *The Theology of St. Luke*, trans. G. Buswell (Philadelphia: Fortress Press, 1982 [1961]). The best collection of essays devoted to the two volumes remains L. Keck and J. L. Martyn (eds.), *Studies in Luke-Acts* (Philadelphia: Fortress Press, 1980 [1966]), although one should also consult R. J. Cassidy and P. J. Scharper (eds.), *Political Issues in Luke-Acts* (Maryknoll: Orbis Books, 1983); J. H. Neyrey, *The Social-World of Luke-Acts: Models for Interpretation* (Peabody, Mass.: Hendrickson Pubs., 1991); E. Richard (ed.), *New Views on Luke-Acts* (Collegeville, Minn.: The Liturgical Press, 1990); C. H. Talbert (ed.), *Luke-Acts: New Perspectives from the Society of Biblical Literature Seminar* (New York: Crossroad, 1984); idem (ed.), *Perspectives on Luke-Acts* (Danville, Va.: Assn. of Baptist Professors of Religion, 1978); C. M. Tuckett (ed.), *Luke's Literary Achievement: Collected Essays* (JSNTSup, 116; Sheffield: Sheffield Academic Press, 1995); and B. Witherington III (ed.), *History, Literature and Society in the Book of Acts* (Cambridge: Cambridge Univ. Press, 1996). One should also consult B. W. Winter (ed.), *The Book of Acts in Its First Century Setting*, 6 vols. (Carlisle: The Paternoster Press; Grand Rapids: Eerdmans, 1993–97) for numerous essays dealing with the historical, cultural, literary, and theological contexts of Acts. On Luke-Acts scholarship, see F. Bovon, *Luke the Theologian: Thirty-Three Years of Research (1950–1983)*, trans. K. McKinney (Allison Park, Pa.: Pickwick Pubs., 1987); W. W. Gasque, *A History of the Interpretation of the Acts of the Apostles* (Peabody, Mass.: Hendrickson Pubs., 1989 [1975]); and the brief survey by E. Richard, "Luke—Writer, Theologian, Historian: Research and Orientation of the 70's," *BTB* 13 (1983): 3–15. For further bibliography see J. B. Green and M. C. McKeever, *Luke-Acts & New Testament Historiography* (Grand Rapids: Baker Books, 1994).

Luke-Acts as a historical writing is discussed by D. L. Balch, "Comments on the Genre and a Political Theme of Luke-Acts: A Preliminary Comparison of Two Hellenistic Historians," *SBLSP* 28 (1989): 343–61; H. Cancik, "The History of Culture, Religion, and Institutions in Ancient Historiography: Philological Observations Concerning Luke's History," *JBL* 116 (1997): 673–95; F. F. Bruce, "The Acts of the Apostles: Historical Record or Theological Reconstruction," *ANRW* II.25.3 (1980): 2569–2603; C. Hemer, *The Book of Acts in the Setting of Hellenistic Historiography* (WUNT, 49; Tübingen: J. C. B. Mohr [Siebeck], 1989); M. Hengel, *Acts and the History of Earliest Christianity* (Philadelphia: Fortress Press, 1979); I. H. Marshall, *Luke: Historian and Theologian* (Grand Rapids: Zondervan Pub. House, 1970); and G. E. Sterling, *Historiography & Self-Definition: Josephos, Luke-Acts & Ancient Apologetic Historiography* (NovTSup, 64; Leiden: E. J. Brill, 1992).

For Luke-Acts as a form of biography, see C. H. Talbert, *Literary Patterns, Theological Themes, and the Genre of Luke-Acts* (SBLMS, 20; Missoula, Mont.: Scholars Press, 1974); as an ancient novel, and the critical issues involved, see R. I. Pervo, *Profit with Delight: The Literary Genre of the Acts of the Apostles* (Philadelphia: Fortress Press, 1987); and M. C. Parsons and R. I. Pervo, *Rethinking the Unity of Luke and Acts* (Minneapolis: Fortress Press, 1993); as a type of rewritten Scripture, see C. A. Evans, "Luke and the Rewritten Bible: Aspects of Lukan Hagiography," in J. H. Charlesworth and C. A. Evans (eds.), *The Pseudepigrapha and Early Biblical Interpretation* (JSPSS, 14;

Sheffield: Sheffield Academic Press, 1993), 170–201. For an interesting study relating Luke-Acts to the Jewish writer Josephus and the Greek novelist Chariton, see D. R. Edwards, *Religion & Power: Pagans, Jews, and Christians in the Greek East* (New York: Oxford Univ. Press, 1996).

For the importance of the Gospel prologue for understanding Luke-Acts as a whole, see R. J. Dillon, "Previewing Luke's Project from His Prologue," *CBQ* 43 (1981): 205–27; and F. Ó Fearghail, *The Introduction to Luke-Acts: A Study of the Role of Lk 1,1–4,44 in the Composition of Luke's Two Volume Work* (AnB, 126; Rome: Biblical Inst. Press, 1991). On the prefaces more generally, see L. Alexander, *The Preface to Luke's Gospel: Literary Convention and Social Context in Luke 1.1–4 and Acts 1.1* (SNTSMS, 78; Cambridge: Cambridge Univ. Press, 1993). For the use of Scripture, see R. L. Brawley, *Text to Text Pours Forth Speech: Voices of Scripture in Luke-Acts* (Bloomington: Indiana Univ. Press, 1995); J. Drury, *Tradition and Design in Luke's Gospel: A Study in Early Christian Historiography* (Atlanta: John Knox Press, 1976); C. A. Evans and J. A. Sanders, *Luke and Scripture: The Function of Sacred Traditions in Luke-Acts* (Minneapolis: Fortress Press, 1993); and J. R. Wagner, "Psalm 118 in Luke-Acts: Tracing a Narrative Thread," in C. A. Evans and J. A. Sanders (eds.), *Early Christian Interpretation of the Scriptures of Israel: Investigations and Proposals* (JSNTSup, 148; Sheffield: Sheffield Academic Press, 1997), 154–78.

For various issues related to the writing of Acts, see L. R. Donelson, "Cult Histories and the Sources of Acts," *Bib* 69 (1987): 1–21; J. Dupont, *The Sources of the Acts*, trans. K. Pond (New York: Herder & Herder, 1964); M. Dibelius, *Studies in the Acts of the Apostles*, trans. H. Greeven (New York: Charles Scribner's Sons; London: SCM Press, 1956); W. S. Kurz, "Intertextual Use of Sirach 48.1–16 in Plotting Luke-Acts," in C. A. Evans and W. R. Stegner (eds.), *The Gospels and the Scriptures of Israel* (JSNTSup, 104; Sheffield: Sheffield Academic Press, 1994), 308–22; J. Reumann, "The 'Itinerary' as a Form in Classical Literature and the Acts of the Apostles," in M. P. Horgan and P. J. Kobelski (eds.), *To Touch the Text* (New York: Crossroad, 1989), 335–57; and M. L. Soards, *The Speeches in Acts: Their Content, Context, and Concerns* (Louisville: Westminster/John Knox Press, 1994).

On the purposes for writing Luke-Acts, including a treatment of apologetic, see P. F. Esler, *Community and Gospel in Luke-Acts: The Social and Political Motivations of Lucan Theology* (SNTSMS, 57; Cambridge: Cambridge Univ. Press, 1987); R. Maddox, *The Purpose of Luke-Acts*, ed. J. Riches (Edinburgh: T. & T. Clark, 1982); and D. L. Tiede, *Prophecy and History in Luke-Acts* (Philadelphia: Fortress Press, 1980). For essays that take seriously the Lukan attempt at intra-Jewish dialogue, see J. Jervell, *Luke and the People of God: A New Look at Luke-Acts* (Minneapolis: Augsburg Pub. House, 1972); and idem, *The Unknown Paul: Essays on Luke-Acts and Early Christian History* (Minneapolis: Augsburg Pub. House, 1984).

On Luke's infancy account, see R. E. Brown, *The Birth of the Messiah*, enl. ed. (Garden City, N.Y.: Doubleday & Co., 1993). For aspects of the travel narrative and Moses typology, see D. P. Moessner, *Lord of the Banquet: The Literary and Theological Signifi-cance of the Lukan Travel Narrative* (Minneapolis: Fortress Press, 1989). On the passion account, see J. H. Neyrey, *The Passion According to Luke: A Redaction Study of Luke's Soteriology* (New York: Paulist Press, 1985); and R. J. Karris, *Luke-Artist and Theolo-gian: Luke's Passion Narrative as Literature* (New York: Paulist Press, 1985). For the res-urrection accounts as they relate to the whole narrative, see P. Schubert, "The Structure and Significance of Luke 24," *Neutestamentliche Studien für R. Bultmann* (BZNW, 21; Berlin: Töpelmann, 1954), 165–86; and R. J. Dillon, *From Eyewitnesses to Ministers of the Word* (AnB, 82; Rome: Biblical Inst. Press, 1978). On the ascension narrative(s), see M. C. Parsons, *The Departure of Jesus in Luke-Acts: The Ascension Narratives in Context* (JSNTSup, 21; Sheffield: Sheffield Academic Press, 1987).

For narrative readings, see J. A. Darr, *On Character Building: The Reader and the Rhetoric of Characterization in Luke-Acts* (Louisville: Westminster/John Knox Press, 1992); J. M. Dawsey, *The Lukan Voice: Confusion and Irony in the Gospel of Luke* (Macon: Mercer Univ. Press, 1986); J. D. Kingsbury, *Conflict in Luke: Jesus, Authorities, Disciples* (Minneapolis: Fortress Press, 1991); and R. C. Tannehill, *The Narrative Unity of Luke-Acts: A Literary Interpretation*, 2 vols. (Philadelphia: Fortress Press, 1986, 1990).

On Lukan theological emphases and themes, see O. W. Allen, Jr., *The Death of Herod: The Narrative and Theological Function of Retribution in Luke-Acts* (SBLDS, 158; Atlanta: Scholars Press, 1997); W. Braun, *Feasting and Social Rhetoric in Luke 14* (SNTSMS, 85; Cambridge: Cambridge Univ. Press, 1985); S. Brown, *Apostasy and Perseverance in the Theology of Luke* (AnB, 36; Rome: Biblical Inst. Press, 1969); R. J. Cassidy, *Society and Politics in the Acts of the Apostles* (Maryknoll: Orbis Books, 1987); J. A. Fitzmyer, *Luke the Theologian: Aspects of His Teaching* (New York: Paulist Press, 1989); C. H. T. Fletcher-Louis, *Luke-Acts: Angels, Christology and Soteriology* (WUNT, 2.94; Tübingen: J. C. B. Mohr [Siebeck], 1997); E. Franklin, *Luke: Interpreter of Paul, Critic of Matthew* (JSNTSup, 92; Sheffield: Sheffield Academic Press, 1994); S. Garrett, *The Demise of the Devil: Magic and the Demonic in Luke's Writings* (Minneapolis: Fortress Press, 1989); J. B. Green, *The Theology of the Gospel of Luke* (Cambridge: Cam-bridge Univ. Press, 1995); J. Jervell, *The Theology of the Acts of the Apostles* (Cambridge: Cambridge Univ. Press, 1996); L. T. Johnson, The *Literary Function of Possessions in Luke-Acts* (SBLDS, 39; Missoula, Mont.: Scholars Press, 1977); I. H. Marshall and D. Peterson (eds.), *Witness to the World: The Theology of Acts* (Grand Rapids: Eerdmans, 1998); P. K. Nelson, *Leadership and Discipleship: A Study of Luke 22:24–30* (SBLDS, 138; Atlanta: Scholars Press, 1994); J. T. Squire, *The Plan of God in Luke-Acts* (SNTSMS, 76; Cambridge: Cambridge Univ. Press, 1993); C. H. Talbert, "Discipleship in Luke-Acts," in F. Segovia (ed.), *Discipleship in the New Testament* (Philadelphia: Fortress Press, 1985), 62–75; and J. B. Tyson, *Luke-Acts and the Jewish-People: Eight Critical Per-spectives* (Minneapolis: Augsburg Pub. House, 1988). On the Spirit in Luke-Acts, see J. D. G. Dunn, *Baptism in the Holy Spirit* (London: SCM, 1970); idem, *Jesus and the Spirit: A Study of the Religious and Charismatic Experience of Jesus and the First Christians as*

Reflected in the New Testament (Philadelphia: Westminster Press, 1975); R. P. Menzies, *The Development of Early Christian Pneumatology with Special Reference to Luke-Acts* (JSNTSup, 54; Sheffield: Sheffield Academic Press, 1991); and W. H. Shepherd Jr., *The Narrative Function of the Holy Spirit as a Character in Luke-Acts* (SBLDS, 147; Atlanta: Scholars Press, 1994).

On Stephen and the Hellenists, see C. C. Hill, *Hebrews and Hellenists: Reappraising Division within the Earliest Church* (Minneapolis: Fortress Press, 1992). The gentile mission in Luke-Acts is treated by J. Dupont, *The Salvation of the Gentiles*, trans. J. Keating (New York: Paulist Press, 1979); and S. G. Wilson, *The Gentiles and the Gentile Mission in Luke-Acts* (SNTSMS, 23; Cambridge: Cambridge Univ. Press, 1973). On the apostolic council, see S. G. Wilson, *Luke and the Law* (SNTSMS, 50; Cambridge: Cambridge Univ. Press, 1983). On Luke's treatment of Paul, see J. C. Lentz, Jr., *Luke's Portrait of Paul* (SNTSMS, 77; Cambridge: Cambridge Univ. Press, 1993); R. I. Pervo, *Luke's Story of Paul* (Minneapolis: Fortress Press, 1990); and D. R. Schwartz, "The End of the Line: Paul in the Canonical Book of Acts," in W. S. Babcock (ed.), *Paul and the Legacies of Paul* (Dallas: Southern Methodist Univ. Press, 1990), 3–24, 307–24. For issues of Pauline chronology, see the bibliography in chapter 10.

On women in Luke-Acts, see J. M. Arlandson, *Women, Class, and Society in Early Christianity: Models from Luke-Acts* (Peabody, Mass.: Hendrickson Pubs., 1997); R. M. Price, *The Widow Traditions in Luke-Acts: A Feminist-Critical Scrutiny* (SBLDS, 155; Atlanta: Scholars Press, 1997); I. Richter Reimer, *Women in the Acts of the Apostles: A Feminist Liberation Perspective*, trans. L. M. Maloney (Minneapolis: Fortress Press, 1995); T. Karlsen Seim, *The Double Message: Patterns of Gender in Luke & Acts* (Nashville: Abingdon Press, 1994); and B. Witherington III, *Women in the Earliest Churches* (SNTSMS, 59; Cambridge: Cambridge Univ. Press, 1988), 128–57.

For critical commentaries and rich bibliography on Luke, see J. A. Fitzmyer, *The Gospel According to Luke*, 2 vols. (AB; New York: Doubleday, 1981, 1985); J. Green, *The Gospel of Luke* (NICNT; Grand Rapids: Eerdmans, 1997); I. H. Marshall, *The Gospel of Luke* (NIGTC; Grand Rapids: Eerdmans, 1978); and J. Nolland, *Luke*, 3 vols. (WBC; Dallas: Word Books, 1989–93). For Acts, see C. K. Barrett, *A Critical and Exegetical Commentary on The Acts of the Apostles: 1–14* (ICC; Edinburgh: T. & T. Clark, 1994); F. F. Bruce, *The Acts of the Apostles: Greek Text with Introduction and Commentary*, 3rd ed. (Grand Rapids: Eerdmans, 1990); E. Haenchen, *The Acts of the Apostles: A Commentary*, trans. B. Noble et al. (Philadelphia: Westminster Press, 1971); and B. Witherington III, *The Acts of the Apostles: A Socio-Rhetorical Commentary* (Grand Rapids: Eerdmans, 1997). For more general treatments, on Luke, see F. W. Danker, *Jesus and the New Age: A Commentary on Luke's Gospel*, rev. ed. (Philadelphia: Fortress Press, 1988); E. E. Ellis, *The Gospel of Luke*, 2nd ed. (NCB; Grand Rapids: Eerdmans, 1974); L. T. Johnson, *The Gospel of Luke* (SP; Collegeville, Minn.: The Liturgical Press, 1991); and J. Knight, *Luke's Gospel* (New York: Routledge, 1998). For Acts, see J. D. G. Dunn, *The Acts of the Apostles* (Valley Forge, Pa.: Trinity Press Int'l, 1996);

J. A. Fitzmyer, *The Acts of the Apostles* (AB; New York: Doubleday & Co., 1998); L. T. Johnson, *The Acts of the Apostles* (SP; Collegeville, Minn.: The Liturgical Press, 1992); H. C. Kee, *To Every Nation Under Heaven: The Acts of the Apostles* (Harrisburg, Pa.: Trinity Press Int'l, 1997); and F. S. Spencer, *Acts* (Sheffield: Sheffield Academic Press, 1997).

An early manuscript fragment of Romans (Rom 8:27-35) from the Chester Beatty Papyri

PART FOUR

Pauline Traditions

THE CHRISTIAN MOVEMENT found its first and most vivid voice in the letters of the apostle Paul. The evangelists remained anonymous behind their shaping of Jesus' story. Paul's letters, by contrast, reveal a human personality so forcibly yet with such great complexity that, for some, coming to grips with Christianity means first of all coming to grips with Paul.

Paul's personality appears at first to be full of contradictory elements. He can be gentle (2 Cor. 10:1) and also harsh (1 Cor. 4:21). He is full of restless energy (2 Cor. 2:12-13) yet also of firm resolution (2 Cor. 1:17). He claims to be weak rather than strong (2 Cor. 12:5) even as he boasts of power (2 Cor. 12:11). He is sublime in the expression of ideals (Rom. 12:14) but very human in his lack of them (Gal. 5:12). So frequent and even violent do the shifts of his moods sometimes appear that some have thought him mentally unbalanced. This first impression of a volatile and perhaps unhinged ego, however, requires qualification by some other observations.

Paul had remarkable organizing ability. His missionary work did not result from impulsive gestures but from sustained and coordinated expeditions. He worked side by side with other missionaries, male and female, during the rapid spread of the Christian movement in its first thirty years. His letters do show something of Paul's heart and mind. But close examination also reveals that the letters are scarcely the result of raw, unprocessed emotion. To the contrary, they are composed with considerable art, often in cooperation with fellow workers. There is certainly as much rhetoric as ego to be found in them. The Hellenistic world did not exalt self-expression as an ideal of style but rather valued the capacity to address circumstances appropriately through a variety of "selves."

An equal caution must be applied to characterizations of Paul's thought. It is sometimes called radical. There is no doubt he is fond of the either/or, and he develops antitheses such as death/life, sin/righteousness, flesh/spirit, law/grace, works/faith, wisdom/folly, power/weakness. At the same time, however, more than any other NT writer Paul seeks to reconcile opposites: in his letters we find the reconciliation of God/world, Jew/Greek, female/male, slave/free, rich/poor.

Much of the history of the interpretation of Paul has consisted in construing one part of his multifaceted literary presentation as the whole. More often than not, this results from treating him as a thinker or theologian who had a center to his system. But Paul was first of all a founder and pastor of churches. His thought was forged on anvils of various controversies and needs, some personal, some communal; and his thought was given expression in his letters through a complex process of composition.

Every construal of Paul requires decisions on certain basic questions. The first is: Where is the real Paul? Some decision must be made from the beginning concerning the weight to be accorded the treatment of Paul in Acts and in the letters. And once that is done, a harder issue still remains: Which of the letters traditionally attributed to Paul are written by him and which by his followers? Deciding between authentic and inauthentic letters is not possible, however, on purely objective grounds; it requires some prior sense of who the "real" Paul is. Furthermore, even those letters acknowledged as authentic look quite different, depending on how they are read: in continuity with the presentation of Acts and the Pastorals; or in isolation from the developments of the Pauline tradition, often regarded largely as a betrayal of Paul himself.

A second major issue concerns Paul's historical importance for earliest Christianity. Does the dominance given him in the NT canon reflect historical reality or a theological decision? Was Paul the most important of the missionaries to the Gentiles, or only the one whose writings happened to be preserved? Did his influence die out quickly, or was it still active in radical and conservative forms throughout the second century? Decisions concerning the authentic and inauthentic letters, and the way to understand a Pauline "school," are obviously important for that discussion.

A third issue concerns Paul's religious significance. What is the relation between Jesus and Paul? Is Paul a solitary religious genius, the second founder of Christianity, or is he a man of tradition, the heir to, and transmitter of, a communal understanding? Does Paul fundamentally pervert the message of Jesus, or does he faithfully interpret it for changed circumstances? Is Paul the heart of the NT canon? If so, why? And if so, *which* Paul?

All such questions are about Paul's place in history. They are sufficiently compelling to draw attention away from the individual literary documents that alone can provide answers. In this book, however, our concern will be Paul's *letters* as witnesses to and interpretations of the experience of the crucified and raised Messiah Jesus in the continuing life of the church. No attempt is made here to decide on the shape of a Pauline theology or to reconstruct Paul's place in earliest Christianity. These issues are discussed only as they are necessary for an intelligent reading of the letters themselves.

Preliminary to that reading, some general remarks should be made on the overall pattern of Paul's ministry and the ways he communicated with his churches.

10. Paul's Ministry and Letters

OF PAUL'S EARLY LIFE we know very little. He is called a young man (*neanios*) at the death of Stephen (Acts 7:58) and refers to himself as an old man (*presbytēs*) in one of his letters (Phlm. 9). According to consistent tradition, he was martyred under Nero (54–68 C.E.). Correlating these points of reference with his encounter with Gallio (ca. 50–52) in Corinth, we can place his date of birth about 5–15 C.E. According to Acts, he was born in Tarsus of Cilicia (22:3), which truly was "no mean city" (21:39). It was a center for Hellenistic culture. Popular philosophers and rhetoricians preached in its streets (Dio *Oration* 33.3–4), and important Stoic teachers such as Athenadoras, the tutor of Caesar Augustus, lived and taught there (see Lucian *Octogenarians*; Plutarch *On Stoic Contradictions* 1033D). Mystery cults were also known to have flourished there. In Tarsus, Paul the Jew could breathe the same Hellenistic air as his older contemporary Philo Judaeus could in Alexandria.

Paul had a particularly impressive Jewish heritage, in which he took considerable pride: "I was circumcised on the eighth day, of the people of Israel and the tribe of Benjamin, a Hebrew of Hebrew origins" (Phil. 3:5; cf. Rom. 11:1). He grew defensive if his pedigree was challenged: "Are they Hebrews? So am I! Are they Israelites? So am I! Are they descendants of Abraham? So am I!" (2 Cor. 11:22). And he never relinquished his sense of identification with his "kinspeople according to the flesh" (Rom. 9:3).

According to Acts 22:28, Paul was born with Roman citizenship, a fact that enabled him to appeal to Caesar (25:11-12) and that astonished his jailer, who had to purchase his own citizenship (22:28). Citizenship in the city of Rome was extended considerably in the first century, but for provincial Jews to have this privilege for at least two generations suggests that Paul's family was socially prominent. His original social status may give some edge to his awareness of all he gave up for the Messiah (Phil. 3:8) and to his complaints about his manual labor (1 Cor. 4:12; 1 Thess. 4:11; 2 Thess. 3:7-9). During his ministry, he probably worked as a tentmaker (Acts 18:3). Such manual labor was practiced by Pharisees as well as by Cynic philosophers who did not want to take payment for preaching. It enabled Paul to be self-sufficient (Phil. 4:11) and to share with others (Acts 20:34-35).

Paul's specific religious commitment was to Pharisaism: "as to the law a Pharisee, . . . as to righteousness under the law, blameless" (Phil. 3:5-6). His dedication to that strict brotherhood was intense, even fanatical: "I advanced in Judaism beyond many of my own age among my people, so extremely zealous was I for the traditions of my fathers" (Gal. 1:14). The importance of Paul's Pharisaism cannot be overestimated: it involved an understanding not only that observance of Torah was the absolute measure of righteousness before God but also that the study of Torah was the way to wisdom. Paul was a scholar in the symbolic world of Torah. Of all first-generation Christians, he was the most aware of the issues a crucified Messiah posed for the Jewish symbolic world.

It was possible to be a Pharisee in the Diaspora, but the movement was centered in Judea. This raises the question of the place where Paul was reared and educated. According to tradition, he came to Jerusalem as a young man and received technical scribal training there. This is noted in Acts 22:3:

> I am a Jew, born in Tarsus of Cilicia, but I was brought up in this city [Jerusalem]. Here I sat at the feet of Gamaliel and was educated strictly in the laws of our fathers.

Some scholars think that Gal. 1:22-23 argues decisively against this since they find it difficult to believe that, if Paul were from Judea, the early Christians would not know him:

> I was still not known by sight to the churches of Christ in Judea; they only heard it said, "He who once persecuted us is now preaching the faith he once tried to destroy."

But even Judea is large and populous enough for a former Pharisaic student and persecutor, however notorious, to be unknown by sight to small messianic communities. If we take all the evidence seriously—Acts' general agreement with the letters on Paul's background; the precise biographical language in Acts 22:3; the indications of Paul's having some relatives in the city (Acts 23:16); and the greater probability of scribal training, evidenced by Paul in his letters, being available in Jerusalem than in the Diaspora—it suggests that Paul went to Jerusalem as a young man, was educated in the study of Torah, and there first encountered and persecuted the deviant messianic sect.

Paul's place of upbringing and education has usually been considered important because it would seem to determine the relative strength of cultural influences on his thought. Those who understand Paul in terms of apocalyptic or rabbinic categories would like to place his roots in Palestine. Those who view Paul as being influenced predominantly by Greek thought exploit the Tarsus connection, interpreting him from the standpoint of Hellenistic philosophy (Stoicism, Cynicism, Epicureanism) or religion (the mystery religions). We have already seen, however, that geographical and symbolic worlds do not neatly coincide in the first-century Hellenistic world (see p. 73, above). In Paul, as in Philo, we find creative reshaping of a complex symbolic world by a single thinker responding to the multiform needs of a Diaspora community. No single aspect of that symbolic world will completely explain Paul, for his creativity consists precisely in his realignment of that world's elements. Far more important in the process is the personal religious experience that distinguishes Paul among all the first witnesses: he was a persecutor of the church and was then called by the risen Lord to be an apostle. Paul is paradigmatic for understanding the way a religious experience can re-create a symbolic world.

Paul's persecution of the church is emphasized both in his letters and in Acts: "You know how I persecuted the church of God violently and tried to destroy it" (Gal. 1:13; cf. Phil. 3:6). Even after twenty years his call still seemed remarkable to him: "I am the least of the apostles; unfit to be called an apostle because I persecuted the church of God" (1 Cor. 15:9). Paul contrasts the mercy shown him in his call to Christian service with his former behavior as the chief of sinners: "I formerly blasphemed and persecuted and insulted him, but I received mercy because I acted ignorantly in unbelief" (1 Tim. 1:13). According to Acts, Paul colluded in the stoning of Stephen (7:58), persecuted the Christians in Jerusalem (8:3), and was traveling to Damascus to continue his persecution of "the way" (9:1) when he encountered Jesus.

Why did Paul seek to extirpate the messianic sect? Our best clues are his self-designation as one zealous for the law, together with his subsequent polemic against the ultimacy of Torah (see esp. Gal. 3:10—4:10, 5:1-4). By the norms of Torah, Jesus could not be righteous, much less Messiah, since he was a sinner and cursed by God (see Deut. 21:23). If God was truly at work through Jesus, the whole symbolic framework of Judaism was threatened; Torah could not be the ultimate norm of righteousness. In Paul's messianic theology, the same either/or is carried through consistently, only in reverse. If Jesus is Messiah and Son of God, then Torah cannot be regarded as the ultimate norm of God's activity for righteousness, for Jesus does not fit. Before Paul's call and after, the categories remain the same, they are simply transvalued. It is no wonder that his theology is markedly dialectical, and that his habitual contrast is between the then and the now; for such was his own life.

The experience that turned him from persecutor to apostle was both a prophetic call and a direct encounter with Jesus. It happened, according to Gal. 1:15-16,

> when he who had set me apart before I was born and had called me through his grace, was pleased to reveal his son to me [or, in me] in order that I might preach him among the Gentiles.

Paul stresses that his call did not come from human beings, but directly from Jesus: "by revelation from [or, of] Jesus Christ" (Gal. 1:12). Formally, the experience was a resurrection appearance: "Last of all, as to one untimely born, he appeared also to me" (1 Cor. 15:8); "Am I not free? Am I not an apostle? *Have I not seen* Jesus our Lord?"

(1 Cor. 9:1; cf. 2 Cor. 12:1-3). The experience almost certainly provides the context for the remarkable statement in 2 Cor. 4:6:

> It is the God who said, "Let light shine out of darkness," who has shone in our hearts to give the light of the knowledge of the glory of God in the face of Christ.

The Acts narratives of Paul's call also emphasize the personal encounter with Jesus. They indicate that the call was not a result of logical deduction but of an unexpected and shattering collision. It reversed Paul literally in mid-stride. The identification of the risen Jesus with the community persecuted by Paul is made clear. Both Acts and the letters see the experience less as a conversion—though as a radical turning it is properly so designated—than as a resurrection experience issuing in a command to be apostle to the Gentiles (Acts 9:15; 22:21; 26:23; Gal. 1:15). For the Pharisee Paul, to be assigned this specific task was a tremendous paradox in his life, but it was an assignment he gladly accepted, spending his life carrying out the task (see Rom. 1:5; 11:13; 15:16; Eph. 3:1; 1 Tim. 2:7; 2 Tim. 4:17).

The direct impact of Paul's experience is obvious: it impelled him on the mission of proclaiming Jesus as Messiah. But the experience also indirectly affected his interpretation of that proclamation. Paul's starting point is never the memory of Jesus' deeds or words but the transforming experience of the risen Lord: "Even if we once knew Christ according to the flesh, we no longer so know him" (2 Cor. 5:16). For Paul, Jesus is not so much the past founder of a messianic community as the present source of its life and power (2 Cor. 3:17-18):

> Now the Lord is the Spirit, and where the Spirit of the Lord is, there is freedom. And we all, with unveiled face, beholding the glory of the Lord, are being changed into his likeness from one degree of glory to another; for this comes from the Lord who is the Spirit.

Because the Lord is its life force, the community is the Messiah's "body" (1 Cor. 12:12-27; Eph. 4:12-16), "the fullness of him who fills all in all" (Eph. 1:23). It is also the "temple of the Lord," sanctified by the presence of his Holy Spirit (1 Cor. 3:16; 2 Cor. 6:16; Eph. 2:21).

Because Paul was plunged, in a moment, from hostility toward a false messiah to belief in a risen Lord, his thought is dominated by the turning of the ages. What he and his fellow Jews had hoped and longed for was now accomplished in the resurrected Jesus. But the fulfillment was far more profound and paradoxical than could ever have been expected. Jesus did not inaugurate an age of righteousness and messianic rule within Israel alone. Through his resurrection, God inaugurated a renewal of humanity and of the world itself, with Jesus as the firstborn from the dead and the new Adam:

"If any one is in Christ, there is a new creation; the old has passed away, behold, the new has come" (2 Cor. 5:17; cf. Rom. 5:12-21; 1 Cor. 15:42-50; Eph. 1:9-10; Col. 3:10-11). And since Paul was a Jew zealous for Torah, he had, above all, to resolve the cognitive dissonance between belief in a crucified, cursed Messiah as Lord, and in the words of Torah, which were "holy, just, and good" (Rom. 7:12).

Paul's Ministry

The difficulties presented by the sources for reconstructing Paul's ministry have already been recounted (see chap. 9). Even when the biases of the sources have been taken into account, much of what we would like to know they simply cannot tell us. Neither Acts nor the letters say much about the important years before Paul began his collaboration with Barnabas. Neither source is helpful on his method of actually founding communities. Acts is preoccupied with patterns of preaching and with Paul's turning from Jew to Gentile; the letters are written to communities already established and thus much is tacitly assumed. We do not learn what first steps Paul took to establish the movement in a new place. Did he, as Acts suggests, always begin in the synagogue, or is that just a reflection of Luke's apologetic interest? Paul does retain some of the "Jew first, then Gentile" perspective on the mission (see Rom. 1:16; 11:11-12), but we cannot know whether this stemmed from or affected his missionary practice.

The sources do, however, agree on some important patterns in his ministry. Paul's mission was almost entirely an urban one. He tended to use the most important city of a territory as his base of operations, accepting financial support for the work of evangelization from churches of that city. That Antioch on the Orontes was the sponsor of his first venture to the West is stated in Acts (13:1-3). From the letters, we know that Philippi, his first European community, was active in his support (Phil. 4:15-16; 2 Cor. 11:8-9) and that Paul hoped to find the Roman church an equally committed sponsor of his mission to Spain (Rom. 1:13; 15:28—16:2). Paul worked with his hands to support himself, but his mission required considerable financial assistance. Travel and lodging, particularly for an entourage, were expensive.

The sources show clearly that Paul did not work alone but as the head of a team. Acts lists these significant associates in the mission of Paul: Barnabas (13:2), John-Mark (13:5; 15:37), Silas (15:40), Timothy (16:3), Priscilla and Aquila (18:2-4), Apollos (18:24-28), Erastus (19:22), Sopater, Aristarchus, Secundus, Gaius, Tychichus, and Trophimus (20:4)—fourteen people. In his letters, Paul also makes frequent mention of associates and co-workers. In the Roman church, which he had never seen, he could greet twenty-six people by name—ten of them explicitly designated as workers for the gospel—and pass on greetings from nine others with him (Rom. 16:1-23). The Corinthian congregations could recognize references to these workers for the mission: Cephas (1 Cor. 1:12; 9:5), Apollos (1 Cor. 1:12; 3:6; 16:12), Barnabas (1 Cor. 9:6),

Sosthenes (1 Cor. 1:1), Timothy (1 Cor. 16:10), Aquila and Priscilla (1 Cor. 16:19), Titus (2 Cor. 8:16) as well as other local workers (1 Cor. 16:15-17; 2 Cor. 8:23). The Philippians knew the fellow workers Euodia, Syntyche, Clement, and Epaphroditus (Phil. 4:2-3, 18). At Colossae, we find Epaphras (Col. 1:7), Luke and Demas (Col. 4:14), Tychichus and Onesimus (Col. 4:7-9), Aristarchus (Col. 4:10), Nympha (Col. 4:15), and Archippus (Col. 4:17). Second Timothy adds Onesiphorus (1:16) and Crescens (4:10), while Titus contributes Artemas and Zenas (Titus 3:12-13). This list contains only field agents, not local leaders, although it is difficult to distinguish between them accurately. The list is therefore a rough one but must also, given the random nature of this evidence, be considered conservative. We can estimate that the Pauline mission involved at least forty persons, female and male.

The effort and organization required to mobilize and coordinate these co-workers must have been considerable. Paul's daily care for the churches was not an insignificant entry in his catalogue of sufferings (2 Cor. 11:28). A consequence of this complex network is that Paul could not do everything himself. Some tasks needed to be delegated. His letters show how Paul frequently used delegates to handle important and delicate missions when he himself could not make a visit (1 Cor. 4:17; 2 Cor. 8:23; Eph. 6:21; Phil. 2:19, 25; Col. 4:7-8; 1 Thess. 3:2; 1 Tim. 1:3; Titus 1:5). His letters were another way of maintaining contact in place of a personal visit.

A precise chronology of Paul's ministry is impossible to determine. Acts and the letters sufficiently overlap to allow us a plausible insertion of some of the epistles into the Acts narrative. Because of the coincidence of Paul's stay at Corinth from the winter of 50 to spring of 52 and of Acts' close attention to his movements before and after, these letters can be dated between 50 and 58, and in a reasonable sequence: 1 and 2 Thessalonians, 1 and 2 Corinthians, and Romans. Those are, however, only five letters out of thirteen. The letters written from captivity could have come from a Caesarean (Acts 24:27) or a Roman (Acts 28:30) imprisonment, or from some earlier detention about which Acts is silent. It is therefore impossible to give a definite date and sequence to Philemon, Colossians, Ephesians, Philippians, and 2 Timothy. The three remaining letters (Galatians, 1 Timothy, and Titus) presuppose Paul's active ministry but contain too little circumstantial information to place them in the framework of Acts. Informed guesses are possible, but they remain guesses. The largest portion of Paul's correspondence, in sum, cannot be placed with certainty during what we know of his career!

There is not sufficient evidence, therefore, to trace accurately the development of Paul's thought within the corpus of his extant letters. There are two reasons for this. (1) Our first letter from Paul was written some twelve years after he began his missionary work; in all likelihood, his basic ideas were already well established. (2) Apart from the letters that fall within an eight-year range, we cannot fix the date of the remaining letters. There may have been some development or change in thought or in attitude—old age and imprisonment and discouragement have left their mark on the writings of others. But our evidence is not such as would allow us to make such determinations with confidence. Other factors, as we shall see, were even more important for the process of composition than Paul's personal development.

Since Paul worked for many years before writing the first of the letters still in our possession, he had available to him the community traditions of his own and other churches, both Palestinian and Diaspora. As a leader in an extensive and complex missionary endeavor, Paul could not be, and does not show himself to be, purely charismatic and idiosyncratic. The customs and traditions of the churches were important to him, since lack of order and peace were dangerous. In choices between spontaneity and structure, Paul chose structure with surprising frequency (see, e.g., 1 Cor. 5:1-5; 7:17; 11:16; 14:33-36; 2 Cor. 6:14—7:1; Gal. 6:7-10; Titus 1:3).

The Pauline Correspondence

In the NT canon, Paul's letters are arranged in order of length, from Romans to Philemon. Several conventional categories are used to group these epistles. "Travel Letters" are those written during Paul's active ministry. They include 1 and 2 Thessalonians, 1 and 2 Corinthians, Galatians, and Romans; 1 Timothy and Titus also fit into this category. "Captivity Letters" are those written from prison: Philippians, Philemon, Colossians, Ephesians, and 2 Timothy. 1 and 2 Timothy and Titus are also called "Pastoral Letters," though a better designation would be "Letters to Delegates." The term "Great Letters" is sometimes used for Romans, 1 and 2 Corinthians, and Galatians, especially by those scholars who regard Paul's teaching on freedom and justification by faith as the heart of his theology; but it is obviously a value-laden designation.

Paul's correspondence was carried out in a cultural setting that both valued and had highly developed the art of writing letters (*epistulae*). Philosophers and statesmen and poets alike used the epistle as a literary vehicle for moral and aesthetic exposition (cf. Horace, Seneca, Cicero). Such epistles were often self-consciously literary and aimed at a readership beyond the addressee; posterity was as much in mind as the correspondent. Not just the learned used letters. Archaeologists have uncovered thousands of letters from the Hellenistic period scrawled on papyri or even shards of clay—genuine correspondence dealing with business and personal affairs. Employing a rather rigid distinction between literary and non-literary letters, and assuming a sociological distance between the writers of each, many have considered Paul's correspondence a collection of the non-literary type. As a result, the literary features of his correspondence were for a long time neglected. This classification of Paul's correspondence also supported the picture of the low social standing of the first Christians.

The distinction between literary and non-literary letters is helpful but overly sharp. Even popular letters followed the norms appropriate to literary types, which were later described in considerable detail in rhetorical handbooks. Such handbooks give examples of how certain epistolary types should be written: the friendly letter, the parenetic letter, the protreptic letter—each had its appropriate conventions and stylized expressions. Such epistolary forms provide valuable guidance to the reader of Paul's letters.

In the ancient world, letters were composed for a variety of purposes. Epicurean and Jewish communities used letters both to instruct and to propagandize. Christians inherited from Diaspora Jews the custom of writing letters of commendation between communities (see 2 Cor. 3:1), examples of which survive in the NT (see Romans 16; Philemon, 3 John). Perhaps the only universal function was that of making one who was absent, present; in a real sense, the letter was viewed as bearing the presence of the sender.

The Pauline correspondence is marked by great variety. Philemon is essentially a personal note, and 1 and 2 Timothy and Titus are personal letters to delegates in the field. In contrast, Ephesians is the most public sort of letter, an encyclical. Colossians and Romans were written to churches founded by others that Paul does not know firsthand. In contrast, Philippians is a letter of friendship to Paul's dearest and closest community. Galatians is a letter of rebuke and argument. The Thessalonian and Corinthian letters probably come closest to being genuinely pastoral letters, whose contents and shape are determined above all by the current needs of the addressees.

Despite their variety, the Pauline letters have some shared characteristics. All are marked by a degree of occasionality: they were written not for publication or posterity but for the contemporary addressees. In this sense, they are genuine letters. For all that, however, even the shortest of them does not lack literary artistry. All of them show care in their composition. Paul's letters also have an official character. He never writes simply as a friend or colleague but always as Paul the apostle. With the possible exception of Philemon and the Pastorals, furthermore, all his letters were intended to be read aloud to the community (see 1 Thess. 5:27; 2 Thess. 2:2, 15) and even to be exchanged between communities (see Col. 4:16). Finally, it is clear that Paul wrote letters not as a hobby or pleasant diversion but out of a sense of need, especially when he could not attend to a problem in person. The more we can recover the occasion for a letter, therefore, the more we are aided in understanding Paul's purpose in writing. This is not to say, however, that the meaning of a letter can always be reduced to such purposes.

Epistolary Structure

The Hellenistic letter had a simple structure. The addressee's name was usually written on the outside of the papyrus roll. A greeting opened the letter. Its normal form was "From A to B, greetings [*chairein*]" (see 1 Macc. 10:25; 11:30; 12:6; Acts 15:23; 23:26). The body of the letter followed, and then a short farewell, normally consisting of a wish for health or good fortune. Paul's letters follow this basic structure, with each of the elements characteristically expanded.

1. In the *greeting*, for example, Paul changes the secular *chairein* to *charis*, "grace," and adds the normal Jewish greeting *eirēnē*, "peace." In effect, the letter begins with a prayer as well as a greeting. Paul also sometimes expands any one of the three basic elements of the greeting, giving further information about the senders (Rom. 1:1-6; Gal. 1:1-2; 1 Tim. 1:1; 2 Tim. 1:1; Titus 1:1-3), the recipients (1 Cor. 1:2; 2 Cor. 1:1; Phlm. 2), or the wish he has for the recipients (Gal. 1:3-5). Such expansions can provide important clues to later developments in the letter.

2. Paul follows the greeting with a *prayer*. He ordinarily uses a thanksgiving formula: "I give thanks," *eucharistō* (Rom. 1:8; 1 Cor. 1:4; Phil. 1:3; Col. 1:3; 1 Thess. 1:2; 2 Thess. 1:3; 1 Tim. 1:12; 2 Tim. 1:3; Phlm. 4). Twice he uses the familiar Jewish blessing formula, "Blessed be God," *eulogētos ho theos*; (2 Cor. 1:3 and Eph. 1:3). In only two letters (Gal. 1:6; Titus 1:5) does Paul omit the prayer, and the alteration is striking. The prayer often anticipates themes developed later in the body of the letter, thus also functioning as instruction and persuasion. There is considerable variation in the length of the prayer, and to a lesser degree in its placement as well: the prayer in 1 Thessalonians takes up much of the first three chapters; in 2 Thessalonians, there are two formal thanksgivings (1:3-4; 2:13-17), and in 1 Timothy, the prayer follows a preliminary exhortation.

3. In the *body* of the letter, Paul either addresses the specific difficulties of the community or begins to develop his argument. The body is introduced with one of a variety of transitional formulas, including "I exhort you" (1 Cor. 1:10; 1 Thess. 4:1; 1 Tim. 1:3; 2:1; Phlm. 9), "We ask you" (2 Thess. 2:1), "I do not want you ignorant" (2 Cor. 1:8), "I want you to know" (Phil. 1:12), and "On this account . . ." (Eph. 1:15; Col. 1:9; 2 Tim. 1:6; Titus 1:5). Similar formulas often introduce new topics within the body of the letter or mark a transition from one topic to another (see, e.g., 1 Cor. 7:1; 8:1; 10:1; 12:1; 15:1; 16:1).

4. The body of the Pauline letter eases imperceptibly into the *final greetings* and *farewell*. The greetings are often fairly extensive, showing us the complex and communal nature of Paul's mission. The letters characteristically close with a prayer formula, wishing grace from God on the readers (see Rom. 15:33; 16:25-27; 1 Cor. 16:23-24; 2 Cor. 13:13; Gal. 6:18; Eph. 6:23-24; Phil. 4:23; Col. 4:18; 1 Thess. 5:28; 2 Thess. 3:18; 1 Tim. 6:21; 2 Tim. 4:22; Titus 3:15; Phlm. 25).

Within this basic structure, the Pauline letters contain numerous variations that are important for interpretation.

Elements of Composition

The composition of Paul's letters involved a complex process, which affects how we understand his authorship of the various epistles ascribed to him. Paul "authors" all his letters, in the broad sense that they were composed under his authority and direction. But it is sometimes difficult to determine the exact nature of his role in the writing process. There are several considerations.

Since writing on parchment or papyrus was awkward and physically tedious, particularly in the case of letters as long as Paul's, the job of writing was often given to a trained secretary (*amanuensis*). Cicero, for example, often dictated his letters to Atticus (see, e.g., VII.13a; VIII.13; X.3a; XI.24; XIII.25). We know that Paul also used a secretary for at least some of his letters. The scribe appears explicitly in Romans, "I Tertius, the writer of this letter, greet you in the Lord" (Rom. 16:22). At other times, Paul indicates that he is penning the greeting in his own hand, which indicates that he had dictated the rest (see 1 Cor. 16:21; Col. 4:18; 2 Thess. 3:17; and possibly Gal. 6:11). In fact, only in Philemon does Paul explicitly state that "I, Paul, am writing with my own hand" (Phlm. 19). This phenomenon is important to note because skilled and trusted secretaries were sometimes given considerable latitude in the actual composition of letters. Given the main point to be made, they could work up an appropriate treatment consonant with the author's thought and often his style as well. We have no direct evidence for this happening in Paul's correspondence, but the wide variety of styles within the Pauline corpus forces us at least to consider the possibility seriously.

Many of Paul's letters were also cosponsored. He did not write in his name alone, but also in the name of Timothy (2 Cor. 1:1; Phil. 1:1; Col. 1:1; Phlm. 1), of Silas and Timothy (1 Thess. 1:1; 2 Thess. 1:1), of Sosthenes (1 Cor. 1:1), and of the "brethren with him" (Gal. 1:2). Only Romans, Ephesians, and the three letters to his delegates Timothy and Titus are sent out in Paul's name alone. How seriously should this be treated? Was cosponsorship merely a formal matter, or did the cosponsor contribute to the thought or style of the letter?

The question becomes sharper when we consider the social setting presupposed by some passages in Paul's letters. Scholars have long recognized elements of an oral-diatribal style in parts of Paul's letters, notably in Romans and the Corinthian correspondence. This style is highly dialogical, with the readers being addressed directly and with frequent use of apostrophe and rhetorical questions. It uses stock examples for illustration, citation of written authorities, and stereotypical moral commonplaces, such as virtue and vice lists, tables of household responsibilities, and polemics against opponents.

Until recently, this style was associated with public preaching. More recent study has shown its primary social setting to be the classroom—diatribe is above all a style of teaching. Elements of diatribe in Paul's letters therefore represent a literary transposition of the vivid dialogical exchanges between teacher and student in a communal activity of study. At the workbench, in the lecture hall, or in a local house church, Paul would have had opportunity to instruct associates like Timothy, Titus, Sosthenes, and Silas.

Other portions of his letters contain elaborate midrashim (see esp. Gal. 3–4; Rom. 9–11; Eph. 2) in which scriptural texts are carefully expounded within a sometimes highly technical argument. For the Pharisaic tradition in which Paul was schooled, midrash was always a communal activity. It was how teacher and students engaged the text of Torah. There is the strong probability, therefore, that in these parts of the letters, we find set pieces worked out by Paul and his co-workers in their communal midrashic study.

These literary forms and the evidence from the nature of the composition of the letters, combined with the presumed social contexts for such activity, together suggest the existence of a "Pauline school," a form of intentional and prolonged contact between master and students. Paul's "school" was operative in the production of his letters even during his lifetime. Although Paul authorized each of the letters that bore his name, it is highly probable that many hands and minds contributed to their final composition. The social setting for the Pauline correspondence is as complex as for his ministry.

The composition of his letters, furthermore, involved the use of traditional materials. By a kind of literary inertia, these materials affect the style and vocabulary of the contexts within which they are found. They also affect the argument, since Paul comments and elaborates upon them. In some of his letters (e.g., Romans, 1 and 2 Corinthians, Galatians), Paul makes extensive use of explicit citations from Torah. In others (Ephesians, Philippians, Colossians, 1 and 2 Thessalonians, 1 and 2 Timothy, Titus, and Philemon), he scarcely uses Torah at all. Paul also uses confessional formulas (Rom. 10:9; 1 Cor. 12:3), kerygmatic statements (Rom. 4:24-25; 1 Cor. 15:3-8; 1 Thess. 1:9-10; Titus 3:4-7), hymns (Phil. 2:6-11; Col. 1:15-20; 1 Tim. 3:16; 2 Tim. 2:11-13), liturgical formulas (1 Cor. 6:11; Gal. 3:28; 4:6; Eph. 5:14), and even—occasionally—the words of Jesus (1 Cor. 7:10; 9:14; 11:24-25; 1 Thess. 4:15; 1 Tim. 5:18). These elements also indicate his profound involvement in the wider Christian movement into which he himself had been baptized and instructed, since he adopts and reinforces shared symbols.

Authentic and Inauthentic Letters

Since the eighteenth century, the authenticity of certain Pauline letters has been debated. At one time or another, the authenticity of virtually all thirteen letters has been doubted by critics. As a result of these debates, a broad consensus has developed. Nearly all critical scholars accept seven letters as written by Paul: Romans, 1 and 2 Corinthians, Galatians, Philippians, 1 Thessalonians, and Philemon. There is almost equal unanimity in rejecting 1 and 2 Timothy and Titus. Serious debate can occasionally be found concerning 2 Thessalonians, Colossians, and Ephesians, but the clear and growing scholarly consensus considers them to be non-Pauline.

If some of the letters do not stem from Paul, then who wrote them? The consensus view of the Pauline corpus argues that a radical and embattled Paul wrote the seven undisputed letters, but after his death, his followers—sometimes called the "Pauline school"—continued to write in his name. Colossians is written soon after his death, pushing Paul's thought in a cosmic, even mystical, direction. Ephesians is written later, perhaps on the basis of Colossians. At a considerably later time, perhaps in the second century, more conservative admirers of Paul perpetuate his tradition in 2 Thessalonians and the Pastorals, combating Gnosticism and misunderstandings of Paul. Thus, almost half the Pauline corpus is to be regarded as pseudonymous literature. It may have been written in the spirit and tradition of Paul, but it cannot be taken into account when assessing his ministry or his thought. It is of value primarily for showing the permutations of the Pauline tradition through succeeding generations.

A variety of criteria are used for determining authenticity and inauthenticity within the Pauline corpus. The first is style. This includes not only vocabulary but also sentence length and structure. It can be extended to include variations in epistolary form, modes of argumentation, and density of scriptural use. The second criterion is broadly theological and concerns consistency in content. This is usually measured by certain standard categories, including view of the law, eschatology, and Christology. Another important content consideration is the view of the church reflected in the letter—particularly the role of structure and authority—as well as the relation of the church to Christ and to the world. Yet another subcategory is ethics, determining whether the epistle is defined by radical freedom tempered by service or by the fulfilling of household responsibilities. The third major criterion is the fit within Paul's ministry, focusing on whether there is a place for the composition of this letter within the narrative of Acts or Paul's other letters.

A full discussion of the issue of authenticity is too complex to serve our present needs. Some methodological remarks, however, are in order. They are especially appropriate since I do not agree with the consensus opinion in this matter, and the reader deserves to know why.

Of the above criteria, only the last is really verifiable by the evidence. If we had a full biography of Paul and there would simply be no place for the writing of a particular letter, then the criterion would be decisive. In fact, however, a full biography is exactly what we lack! We cannot pin down with precision most of Paul's letters. The sources leave us just as ignorant of the circumstances surrounding Galatians as they do in the case of Titus. Yet if Paul wrote Galatians to north Galatia rather than to the churches Acts says he founded in south Galatia (cf. Acts 14:1-21; 16:1-6; 18:23), it is never, on that account, considered inauthentic. And properly so, for our sources do not come close to telling us everything about Paul's activities. The other criteria are therefore more determinative.

They are also much more debatable. Both the style and the content criteria presuppose a fixed center of consistency as a norm for measuring deviance. But precisely such a center does not exist! Even in the seven unquestioned letters there is great variety in both style and content. If 1 Thessalonians were held to the same standards as the Pastorals, it would be judged equally inauthentic: it is not diatribal, it lacks Scripture citations, it has no significant teaching on sin, grace, faith, righteousness, or Torah, and it has a suspiciously un-Pauline anthropology. But its place within Paul's career is magnificently confirmed by Acts, so the criteria of style and content are waived.

Since there is a significant range of style and content even within the undoubted letters, clearly the criteria are largely subjective: they appeal to the reader's sense of what constitutes acceptable deviance from a presumed norm. Statistical analyses, sometimes invoked as support for this appeal, are completely unreliable, since the sample is too small and cannot take into account the most critical factors determining style in ancient writing: genre, topic, audience, and occasion.

The discussion of authenticity has thus been distorted by doubtful premises. Even within the *undoubted* letters it has yet to deal satisfactorily with the complexity of the composition process, a complexity that suggests the activity of a "school" during Paul's lifetime. It has also failed to reckon with the great variety of style and theme within the undoubted letters. Moreover, it seldom notes that the very act of isolating three similar documents—for example, the Pastorals—then comparing them together against the corpus as a whole, already predetermines the result. Indeed they are different. But the differences are magnified because the three are compared not with all the letters but with an already reduced "authentic" core. The result might be quite different if, for example, 2 Timothy were compared with Philippians, or 1 Timothy with 1 Corinthians. Ephesians, likewise, is rarely compared with the other twelve letters to test its style, but with the seven already determined to be authentic. If 1 and 2 Thessalonians were isolated and compared as a set with the remaining corpus, they would be found inauthentic on stylistic and content grounds—even though on its own 1 Thessalonians is considered authentic. In other words, prior formulations of epistolary relationships skew the results, predetermining—in effect—the conclusions.

In the present treatment of Paul's letters, issues pertaining to the authenticity of each letter will be treated only briefly, since our purpose is to understand them in their literary integrity, not to reconstruct Paul's career or theology. The issue of authenticity will always remain secondary. The reader may be surprised at my bias for the authenticity of all the letters. It is based on the persuasiveness of their literary self-presentation, the ability to find plausible places for them in Paul's career, and a conviction that the whole Pauline corpus is one that Paul "authored" but did not necessarily write.

Study Questions

1. How might Paul's background as a Pharisee have affected his understanding of Christ and the Torah?

2. On what grounds could Paul's authority as an apostle be challenged?

3. Compare Acts 15 and Galatians 1. What points of discrepancy about Paul's career do you find?

4. Why are stylistic criteria for judging the authenticity of Paul's letters problematic?

5. What does it mean to say that Paul's letters are "occasional"?

6. Why is attention to form and rhetoric in Paul's letters important?

Bibliographical Note

For a convenient treatment of Paul, combining primary texts with critical notes and essays, see W. A. Meeks (ed.), *The Writings of St. Paul* (New York: W. W. Norton & Co., 1973). For the history of Pauline interpretation, see E. E. Ellis, *Paul and His Recent Interpreters* (Grand Rapids: Eerdmans, 1961); V. P. Furnish, "The Jesus-Paul Debate: From Baur to Bultmann," in A. J. M. Wedderburn (ed.), *Paul and Jesus: Collected Essays* (JSNTSup, 37; Sheffield: Sheffield Academic Press, 1989), 17–50; R. B. Matlock, *Unveiling the Apocalyptic Paul: Paul's Interpreters and the Rhetoric of Criticism* (JSNTSup, 127; Sheffield: Sheffield Academic Press, 1996); B. S. Rosner, *Understanding Paul's Ethics: Twentieth-Century Approaches* (Grand Rapids: Eerdmans, 1995); A. Schweitzer, *Paul and His Interpreters*, trans. W. Montgomery (New York: Macmillan Co., 1912); and S. Westerholm, *Israel's Law and the Church's Faith: Paul and His Recent Interpreters* (Grand Rapids: Eerdmans, 1988). Also see the annotated bibliography by G. L. Borchert, *Paul and His Interpreters* (Madison: InterVarsity Press, 1985).

On Pauline chronology, see R. Jewett, *A Chronology of Paul's Life* (Philadelphia: Fortress Press, 1979); G. Luedemann, *Paul, Apostle to the Gentiles: Studies in Chronology*, trans. F. S. Jones (Philadelphia: Fortress Press, 1984); J. Murphy-O'Connor, *Paul: A Critical Life* (Oxford: Oxford Univ. Press, 1996); R. Riesner, *Paul's Early Period: Chronology, Mission Strategy, and Theology* (Grand Rapids: Eerdmans, 1997); and D. Slingerland, "Acts 18:1–18, the Gallio Inscription, and Absolute Pauline Chronology," *JBL* 110 (1991): 439–49. For helpful introductions to various issues, see G. F. Hawthorne et al. (eds.), *Dictionary of Paul and His Letters* (Downers Grove: InterVarsity Press, 1993).

Among the classic appreciations of Paul's life and work, see A. Deissman, *Paul: A Study in Social and Religious History*, 2nd ed. (New York: Harper & Row, 1927); G. Bornkamm, *Paul*, trans. D. M. G. Stalker (New York: Harper & Row, 1971); J. Munck, *Paul and the Salvation of Mankind*, trans. R. Clarke (Richmond: John Knox Press, 1959); K. Stendahl, *Paul among Jews and Gentiles* (Philadelphia: Fortress Press, 1976); N. A. Dahl, *Studies in Paul* (Minneapolis: Augsburg Pub. House, 1977); and E. Käsemann, *Perspectives on Paul*, trans. M. Kohl (Philadelphia: Fortress Press, 1971). On Paul's life and larger cultural context, see M. Hengel (with R. Deines), *The Pre-Christian Paul*, trans. J. Bowden (London: SCM Press; Philadelphia: Trinity Press Int'l, 1991); M. Hengel and A. M. Schwemer, *Paul Between Damascus and Antioch: The*

Unknown Years, trans. J. Bowden (Louisville: Westminster John Knox, 1997); R. A. Horsley (ed.), *Paul and Empire: Religion and Power in Roman Imperial Society* (Harrisburg, Pa.: Trinity Press Int'l, 1997); R. N. Longenecker (ed.), *The Road from Damascus: The Impact of Paul's Conversion on His Life, Thought, and Ministry* (Grand Rapids: Eerdmans, 1997); G. Lyons, *Pauline Autobiography: Toward a New Understanding* (SBLDS, 73; Atlanta: Scholars Press, 1985); B. J. Malina and J. H. Neyrey, *Portraits of Paul: An Archaeology of Ancient Personality* (Louisville: Westminster/John Knox, 1996); J. H. Neyrey, *Paul, In Other Words: A Cultural Reading of His Letters* (Louisville: Westminster/John Knox, 1990); C. J. Roetzel, *Paul: The Man and the Myth* (Columbia: Univ. of South Carolina Press, 1998; Minneapolis: Fortress Press, 1999); and A. F. Segal, *Paul the Convert: The Apostolate and Apostasy of Saul the Pharisee* (New Haven: Yale Univ. Press, 1990).

For the influence of the Hellenistic world on Paul, see C. E. Glad, *Paul & Philodemus: Adaptability in Epicurean & Early Christian Pyschagogy* (NovTSup, 81; Leiden: E. J. Brill, 1995); T. Engberg-Pedersen (ed.), *Paul in His Hellenistic Context* (Minneapolis: Fortress Press, 1995); J. L. Jaquette, *Discerning What Counts: The Function of the Adiaphora Topos in Paul's Letters* (SBLDS, 146; Atlanta: Scholars Press, 1995); W. L. Knox, *St. Paul and the Church of the Gentiles* (Cambridge: Cambridge Univ. Press, 1961 [1939]); A. J. Malherbe, *Paul and the Popular Philosophers* (Minneapolis: Fortress Press, 1989); H.-J. Schoeps, *Paul: The Theology of the Apostle in the Light of Jewish Religious History*, trans. H. Knight (Philadelphia: Westminster Press, 1961); R. Wallace and W. Williams, *The Three Worlds of Paul of Tarsus* (New York: Routledge, 1998); and B. W. Winter, *Paul and Philo among the Sophists* (SNTSMS, 96; Cambridge: Cambridge Univ. Press, 1997). The importance of apocalyptic categories is exploited by J. C. Beker, *Paul the Apostle: The Triumph of God in Life and Thought* (Philadelphia: Fortress Press, 1980). Paul's Jewish background is highlighted by W. D. Davies, *Paul and Rabbinic Judaism: Some Rabbinic Elements in Pauline Theology*, 4th ed. (Philadelphia: Fortress Press, 1980 [1948]); J. Murphy-O'Connor and J. H. Charlesworth (eds.), *Paul and the Dead Sea Scrolls* (New York: Crossroad, 1990); and E. P Sanders, *Paul and Palestinian Judaism: A Comparison of Patterns of Religion* (Philadelphia: Fortress Press, 1977).

For the social dynamics in Paul's ministry and in his congregations, see R. S. Ascough, *What Are They Saying about the Formation of the Pauline Churches?* (Mahwah, N.J.: Paulist Press, 1997); R. Banks, *Paul's Idea of Community*, rev. ed. (Peabody, Mass.: Hendrickson Pubs., 1994); E. Best, *Paul and His Converts* (Edinburgh: T. & T. Clark, 1988); F. G. Downing, *Cynics, Paul and the Pauline Churches* (New York: Routledge, 1998); R. Hock, *The Social Context of Paul's Ministry: Tentmaking and Apostleship* (Philadelphia: Fortress Press, 1980); B. Holmberg, *Paul and Power: The Structure of Authority in the Primitive Church as Reflected in the Pauline Epistles* (Philadelphia: Fortress Press, 1978); E. A. Judge, "The Early Christians as a Scholastic Community," *JRH* 1 (1960–61): 4–15, 125–37; J. S. Kloppenborg, "Edwin Hatch, Churches, and *Col-*

legia," in B. H. McLean (ed.), *Origins and Method: Towards a New Understanding of Judaism and Christianity* (JSNTSup, 86; Sheffield: Sheffield Academic Press, 1993), 212–38; M. Y. MacDonald, *The Pauline Churches: A Socio-Historical Study of the Institutionalization in the Pauline and Deutero-Pauline Writings* (SNTSMS, 60; Cambridge: Cambridge Univ. Press, 1988); A. J. Malherbe, *Social Aspects of Early Christianity*, 2nd ed. (Philadelphia: Fortress Press, 1983); W. A. Meeks, *The First Urban Christians: The Social World of the Apostle Paul* (New Haven: Yale Univ. Press, 1983); J. Meggitt, *Paul, Poverty and Survival* (Edinburgh: T. & T. Clark, 1998); and B. W. Winter, *Seek the Welfare of the City: Christians as Benefactors and Citizens* (Carlisle: The Paternoster Press; Grand Rapids: Eerdmans, 1994). On women in Pauline perspective, see M. Y. MacDonald, *Early Christian Women and Pagan Opinion: The Power of the Hysterical Woman* (Cambridge: Cambridge Univ. Press, 1996), 127–82; E. Schüssler Fiorenza, *In Memory of Her: A Feminist Theological Reconstruction of Christian Origins* (New York: Crossroad, 1983), 160–284; and B. Witherington III, *Women in the Earliest Churches* (SNTSMS, 59; Cambridge: Cambridge Univ. Press, 1988), 24–127.

On Pauline theology in general, see C. K. Barrett, *From the First Adam to Last: A Study in Pauline Theology* (New York: Charles Scribner's Sons, 1962); idem, *Paul: An Introduction to His Thought* (Louisville: Westminster/John Knox, 1994); D. Boyarin, *A Radical Jew: Paul and the Politics of Identity* (Berkeley: Univ. of California Press, 1994); F. F. Bruce, *Paul: Apostle of the Heart Set Free* (Grand Rapids: Eerdmans, 1977); T. L. Donaldson, *Paul and the Gentiles: Remapping the Apostle's Convictional World* (Minneapolis: Fortress Press, 1997); J. D. G. Dunn, *The Theology of Paul the Apostle* (Grand Rapids: Eerdmans, 1998); J. Fitzmyer, *Pauline Theology: A Brief Sketch*, 2nd ed. (Englewood Cliffs, N.J.: Prentice-Hall, 1989); S. Kim, *The Origin of Paul's Gospel* (Grand Rapids: Eerdmans, 1981); T. Laato, *Paul and Judaism: An Anthropological Approach*, trans. T. McElwain (SFSHJ, 115; Atlanta: Scholars Press, 1995); J. L. Martyn, *Theological Issues in the Letters of Paul* (Nashville: Abingdon Press, 1997); R. Penna, *Paul the Apostle*, trans. T. P. Wahl, 2 vols. (Collegeville, Minn.: The Liturgical Press, 1996); and D. Wenham, *Paul: Follower of Jesus or Founder of Christianity?* (Grand Rapids: Eerdmans, 1995). For a full exposition of Pauline theology, the first volume of R. Bultmann, *Theology of the New Testament*, trans. K. Grobel (New York: Charles Scribner's Sons, 1951), remains fundamental.

On specific themes, see the bibliography in subsequent chapters, as well as M. N. A. Bockmuehl, *Revelation and Mystery in Ancient Judaism and Pauline Christianity* (Grand Rapids: Eerdmans, 1997 [1990]); E. A. Castelli, *Imitating Paul: A Discourse of Power* (Louisville: Westminster/John Knox Press, 1991); G. D. Fee, *God's Empowering Presence: The Holy Spirit in the Letters of Paul* (Peabody, Mass.: Hendrickson Pubs., 1994); L. A. Jervis and P. Richardson (eds.), *Gospel in Paul* (JSNTSup, 108; Sheffield: Sheffield Academic Press, 1994); R. K. Jewett, *Paul's Anthropological Terms: A Study of Their Use in Conflict Settings* (AGJU, 10; Leiden: E. J. Brill, 1971); C. B. Kittredge, *Community and Authority: The Rhetoric of Obedience in the Pauline Tradition* (Harrisburg,

Penn.: Trinity Press Int'l, 1998); L. J. Kreitzer, *Jesus and God in Paul's Eschatology* (JSNTSup, 19; Sheffield: Sheffield Academic Press, 1987); A. T. Lincoln, *Paradise Now and Not Yet: Studies in the Role of the Heavenly Dimension in Paul's Thought with Special Reference to His Eschatology* (SNTSMS, 43; Cambridge: Cambridge Univ. Press, 1981); D. B. Martin, *Slavery as Salvation: The Metaphor of Slavery in Pauline Christianity* (New Haven: Yale Univ. Press, 1990); R. P. Martin, *Reconciliation: A Study of Paul's Theology*, rev. ed. (Grand Rapids: Zondervan, 1989); P. Richardson, *Israel in the Apostolic Church* (SNTSMS, 10; Cambridge: Cambridge Univ. Press, 1969), 70–158; R. Scroggs, *The Last Adam: A Study in Pauline Anthropology* (Philadelphia: Fortress Press, 1966); A. J. M. Wedderburn, *Baptism and Resurrection: Studies in Pauline Theology Against Its Graeco-Roman Background* (WUNT, 44; Tübingen: J. C. B. Mohr [Siebeck], 1987); N. T. Wright, *The Climax of the Covenant: Christ and the Law in Pauline Theology* (Minneapolis: Fortress Press, 1991); and J. A. Ziesler, *The Meaning of Righteousness in Paul: A Linguistic and Theological Enquiry* (SNTSMS, 20; Cambridge: Cambridge Univ. Press, 1972). Also see the useful collection of essays in S. E. Porter and C. A. Evans (eds.), *The Pauline Writings: A Sheffield Reader* (Sheffield: Sheffield Academic Press, 1995); R. T. Fortna and B. R. Gaventa (eds.), *The Conversation Continues: Studies in Paul and John* (Nashville: Abingdon Press, 1990); M. D. Hooker and S. G. Wilson (eds.), *Paul and Paulinism* (London: SPCK, 1982); and E. E. Johnson and D. M. Hay (eds.), *Pauline Theology, Vol. 4: Looking Back, Pressing On* (SBLSS,4; Atlanta: Scholars Press, 1997).

On the formation of the Pauline corpus, see the older study by C. L. Mitton, *The Formation of the Pauline Corpus of Letters* (London: Epworth Press, 1955), and the more recent introduction by D. Trobisch, *Paul's Letter Collection: Tracing the Origins* (Minneapolis: Fortress Press, 1994). For a general picture of the early Christian context of reading and writing, see H. Y. Gamble, *Books and Readers in the Early Church: A History of Early Christian Text* (New Haven: Yale Univ. Press, 1995). On the disputed Pauline letters, see R. F. Collins, *Letters That Paul Did Not Write: The Epistle to the Hebrews and the Pauline Pseudepigrapha* (Wilmington: Michael Glazier, 1988); and on the larger issue of Christian pseudonymity, see K. Aland, "The Problem of Anonymity and Pseudonymity in Christian Literature of the First Two Centuries," *JTS* 12 (1961): 39–49; D. G. Meade, *Pseudonymity and Canon: An Investigation into the Relationship of Authorship and Authority in Jewish and Earliest Christian Tradition* (Grand Rapids: Eerdmans, 1986); and B. M. Metzger, "Literary Forgeries and Canonical Pseudepigrapha," *JBL* 91 (1972): 3–24. On the role of the secretary in Paul's letters, see E. R. Richards, *The Secretary in the Letters of Paul* (WUNT, 2/42; Tübingen: J.C.B. Mohr [Siebeck], 1991). On the literary features of the ancient letter, see W. G. Doty, *Letters in Primitive Christianity*, 2nd ed. (Philadelphia: Fortress Press, 1973); A. J. Malherbe, *Ancient Epistolary Theorists* (Atlanta: Scholars Press, 1988); S. K. Stowers, *Letter Writing in Greco-Roman Antiquity* (Philadelphia: Westminster Press, 1986); J. L. White, *The Body of the Greek Letter* (SBLDS, 2; Missoula,

Mont.: Scholars Press, 1972); and idem, *Light from Ancient Letters* (Philadelphia: Fortress Press, 1986).

On Paul's letters in particular, see P. Schubert, *The Form and Function of the Pauline Thanksgiving* (Berlin: Töpelmann, 1939); P. T. O'Brien, *Introductory Thanksgivings in the Letters of Paul* (NovTSup, 49; Leiden: E. J. Brill, 1977); S. E. Porter, "Paul and His Letters," in S. E. Porter (ed.), *Handbook of Classical Rhetoric in the Hellenistic Period 300 B.C.–A.D. 400* (Leiden: E. J. Brill, 1997), 533–85; A. B. Spencer, *Paul's Literary Style* (Jackson: Evangelical Theological Society, 1984); J. L. White, "Apostolic Mission and Apostolic Message: Congruence in Paul's Epistolary Rhetoric, Structure and Imagery," in B. H. McLean (ed.), *Origins and Method: Towards a New Understanding of Judaism and Christianity* (JSNTSup, 86; Sheffield: Sheffield Academic Press, 1993), 145–61; and G. P. Wiles, *Paul's Intercessory Prayers: The Significance of the Intercessory Prayer Passages in the Letters of Paul* (SNTSMS, 24; Cambridge: Cambridge Univ. Press, 1974). On the function of Paul's letters as mediating his presence, see the classic article by R. Funk, "The Apostolic Presence: Paul," in *Parables and Presence* (Philadelphia: Fortress Press, 1982), 81–102. For Scripture and tradition in Paul's writings, see E. E. Ellis, *Paul's Use of the Old Testament* (Grand Rapids: Baker Book House, 1981 [1957]); C. A. Evans and J. A. Sanders (eds.), *Paul and the Scriptures of Israel* (JSNTSup, 83; Sheffield: Sheffield Academic Press, 1993); A. T. Hanson, *Studies in Paul's Technique and Theology* (Grand Rapids: Eerdmans, 1974); and R. B. Hays, *Echoes of Scripture in the Letters of Paul* (New Haven: Yale Univ. Press, 1989). A useful tool for the study of the formal aspects of Paul's letters is F. Francis and J. P. Sampley (eds.), *Pauline Parallels*, rev. ed. (Philadelphia: Fortress Press, 1988).

11. 1 and 2 Thessalonians

THE THESSALONIAN correspondence marks the probable beginning of Christian literature. In these two short letters we already find characteristic features of the Pauline mission and correspondence. Paul's overriding concern is the identity and integrity of the community. He writes because he is not personally able to visit the church and his delegate's work needs further support. He needs to clarify misunderstanding or confront disaffection. We also find in this young community what we discover elsewhere in churches founded by Paul: that an enthusiastic reception of his message did not necessarily mean a thorough grasp of it.

Acts paints a fairly full picture of the events preceding the letters. Paul was imprisoned in Philippi at the start of his first European campaign (Acts 16:19-24; 1 Thess. 2:1-2). He then went to Thessalonica, the capital city of Macedonia, and in the synagogue proclaimed Jesus as Messiah (Acts 17:1-3). Some Jews were converted, along with even more God-fearing (*sebomenoi*) Greeks and "not a few" of the city's prominent women (17:4). This success stirred other Jews of the city to a jealous rage; though seeking Paul, they hauled the convert Jason and some others before the city magistrates, charging Paul with treason in absentia because he said, "Jesus is a king" (17:7). Paul was then sent by the Christians of Thessalonica to Beroea (17:10). There, he enjoyed further success until the enraged Jews from Thessalonica came and again interfered (17:13). Paul left Timothy and Silas there and went on to Athens (17:14-15). After a mixed reception in that city, he went to Corinth, which became his new center of operations (18:1-4; see esp. 18:11).

During his stay in Corinth, Silas and Timothy join him from Macedonia (Acts 18:5). According to 1 Thess. 3:2-6, Paul had sent them to the Thessalonians because of his anxiety for that community. The sending of delegates in this situation shows us the function of Paul's emissaries. Timothy was sent "to establish you in your faith and to exhort you" (3:2). These are exactly the goals Paul also hopes to accomplish by his letter (see 3:13; 4:1). Because of the persecution being experienced by this young church, Paul had feared that the tempter would seize the opportunity to sway them (3:5). Timothy's report gave Paul some reassurance, and he thanks God, "for we now live, if you stand fast in the Lord" (3:8). The real issue, we see, is stability in the face of oppression. Paul does not write his first Thessalonian letter in response to an acute crisis but wants to give support to the work already done by Timothy, exhorting the Thessalonians "to live and please God just as you are doing" (4:1). Such support is all the more necessary since harsh persecution can shake the convictions of a young, immature community. Since the agreement between the sources is far greater than the disagreement, the authenticity of 1 Thessalonians has been free from serious challenge.

The makeup of the church at Thessalonica is a major point of confusion in the sources. Acts tells us there were Greek converts but says the church contained Jews as well. Paul's conversion language in 1 Thess. 1:9-10 suggests a pagan, not Jewish, background: ". . . turning from idols to the living and true God." The Jews in 2:14 are spoken of in a manner suggesting that they are completely outsiders. The precise identity of the persecutors is also obscure. Acts makes it clear they are Jews. But 1 Thess. 2:14 says that the Thessalonians are suffering at the hands of their own countrymen (*tōn idiōn symphuletōn*). This could mean Jews if there were Jewish members in the Christian community. But it could also mean Greeks, or simply fellow Macedonians. A decision would rest on whether or not one wanted to see a parallel in 1 Thess. 2:14 between "your own countrymen" and "the Jews" (in Judea) as a contrast. The internal evidence strongly suggests a gentile majority in the community, with at best a Jewish minority. The issue is clouded by Acts' consistent concern to portray some success among the Jews in the Diaspora mission of the church (see chap. 9, above).

First Thessalonians

The letter's structure is simple. A short, classic greeting (1:1) is followed by an extended thanksgiving (1:2—3:13). The thanksgiving passage is actually transformed into a long recollection of Paul's first preaching to this community and its response (1:6), returning to explicit prayer again only in 3:11-13. A series of moral exhortations (4:1—5:22) concludes with a prayer (5:23-24). The final greetings are general (5:25-27), and the farewell is short (5:28).

First Thessalonians has features resembling the Hellenistic epistolary form called the parenetic letter, though less impressively than 2 Timothy. The term "parenesis" refers to traditional "moral exhortation." It is sometimes used broadly of loosely arranged moral maxims. In a narrower sense, parenesis involves the interplay of three elements, which can be variously combined: memory, model, and maxims. Moral instruction was thought to be best accomplished by imitation of an example. The model was brought to life by memory, but since it was only an outline, it required filling out by means of maxims. These are often arranged antithetically, as in 1 Thess. 5:21-22: "Hold fast to what is good, abstain from every form of evil." The specific moral instructions begin in 4:1, but the elements of memory and model appear already in the first three chapters.

The Self-Presentation of Paul

First Thessalonians is remarkable for its reminiscence of Paul's first preaching to the community. He reminds the Thessalonians of their beginnings in order to strengthen their sense of identity. He recalls not only his manner of preaching but also their mode of response. In both, the distinctive Christian reshaping of symbols can be found.

Paul recalls his sojourn among the Thessalonians in terms similar to the self-characterization of wandering Hellenistic philosophers (e.g., Dio *Orations* 32.8–11, 35.8). He first contrasts himself to charlatans. Unlike them, he did not teach error, nor did he speak out of impure motives or guile (2:3). He was not out to flatter people, to steal their money, or to win their praise (2:5). He thus claims freedom from the three classic vices of charlatans: love of pleasure, love of possessions, and love of glory. Instead, Paul belonged to the tradition of philosophers who preached because of a divine call (see Dio *Orations* 13.9–10, 32.12), "not to please men but to please God who tests the hearts" (2:4). Paul also characterizes himself positively. He was "gentle as a nurse" among them (2:7). This phrase has two important aspects. The image of nurse coincides with the frequent understanding of philosophy as a spiritual medicine: healthy teaching cures the illness of the soul, which is vice (see chap. 1, above). Second, Paul's gentleness places him in a tradition that contrasts itself with the harsh "surgical" methods of some philosophers, whose vituperative methods called people to reform by reviling them. He was one who taught by positive example and instruction (see Dio *Oration* 77/78.38-45; Lucian *Demonax*).

Paul also calls himself a father to this church (2:11). He thereby establishes the accustomed social relationship for parenesis: the moral teacher takes the place of a father with his children. Paul asserts this claim to special authority with other churches as well (e.g., 1 Cor. 4:15). Finally, he presents himself as a model to the community: they are to imitate him (1:6). This has nothing to do with arrogance; such imitation is the normal mode of moral education in Paul's world. The Thessalonians also imitate the churches in Judea, insofar as they suffer like them (2:14). And they have become, in turn, examples to all the communities in Macedonia and Achaia because of the way they accepted the gospel (1:7).

The message of Paul, Silas, and Timothy was not, however, simply another form of moral instruction; it was the word of God in power. They brought a message from God and about God (see the use of the phrase "gospel of God" in 2:2; 2:8; 2:9). Their proclamation did not simply express an abstract ideal; it had the power to transform its hearers. It came to them "not only in word but also in power and in the Holy Spirit and with full conviction" (1:5). Paul rejoices that the Thessalonians recognized and accepted the gospel "not as the word of men, but as it really is, the word of God which is at work in you believers" (2:13). Paul and his fellow workers are therefore more than sophists and philosophers; they are "apostles of Christ" (2:7).

The Call of the Church

The "good news" from God is first of all that he has "called" these people "into his kingdom and glory" (2:12; cf. 4:7; 5:24). By his call, they have become part of God's people: "He has chosen you" (1:4). The call of God demands a "turning" from their former way of life (4:7) to one appropriate to a world ruled by God. Before, they had been "those who do not know God" (4:5), those "without hope" (4:13), "sons of darkness who sleep in the day and are drunk at night" (5:7). Now, as the assembly of God (*ekklēsia tou theou*; 1:1; 2:14), they must "lead a life worthy of God" (2:12). Furthermore, since God is holy, they too are to be "established in holiness before God" (3:13), for "this is the will of God, your sanctification" (4:3). To be holy is to be different. God's holiness is marked by his complete difference from the world. The task of the Thessalonians is to express their "differentness" through their behavior, while remaining very much part of the larger world.

The norm is set by their first conversion, which established them as a community (1:9-10):

> You turned to God from idols, to serve a living and true God, and to wait for his Son from heaven, whom he raised from the dead, Jesus who delivers us from the wrath to come.

The kerygmatic statement establishes the framework for all of Paul's parenesis in this letter. The Thessalonians had turned their lives toward a "true" and "living" God, so their behavior must be measured by God's own life. A share in this had in fact been given to them by the power of the Holy Spirit: the gospel had been proclaimed in the power of this Holy Spirit (1:5) and had been received in the joy of the Holy Spirit (1:6). Whoever in the community chooses not to live by this norm of holiness "disregards not man but God, who gives his Holy Spirit to you" (4:8). Their lives are to manifest this life and power, not stifling the work of the Spirit (5:19).

Living by such a measure inevitably involves affliction (*thlipsis*). Obedience to God is difficult; the turn from death to life is painful. But more than that, in a world of falsehood and death, allegiance to a transcendent truth and life is threatening, leading almost inevitably to rejection and persecution: "You received the word in much affliction" (1:6). The Thessalonians suffered at the hands of their neighbors just as the Judean churches were persecuted by "the Jews" (2:14). One should note that Paul uses the distancing term "Jews" only in this context; ordinarily he avoids such usage (but cf. 1 Cor. 1:22-23; 2 Cor. 11:24; Gal. 2:13). Paul warned them from the beginning that this would happen: "We told you beforehand that we were to suffer affliction, just as it has come to pass, and as you know" (3:4). In this, too, they have an example in Paul (2:15-16) and above all "in the Lord Jesus and the prophets," who were killed for speaking God's word (2:15).

Life Between Times

The Thessalonians' suffering stemmed in part from the tension created by the distance between their convictions and their circumstances. They knew that they were beloved by God and chosen by him (1:4). They knew that Jesus was raised from the dead and would deliver them from the wrath to come (1:10). But the deliverance had not visibly occurred, and the wrath seemed to be very much upon them (2:16). They seemed to be more under the promise than the fulfillment (5:9-10):

> God has not destined us for wrath but to obtain salvation through our Lord Jesus Christ, so that whether we wake or sleep we live with him.

The last part of this conviction—that awake or asleep they lived with Christ—was exactly what those in the Thessalonian church did not grasp. Paul must therefore pay particular attention to their shaken confidence in the triumph of God, caused by the death of some community members.

Paul's initial preaching may, as in other cases, have helped create the problem. On the evidence, this was a young community, only recently turned from paganism. When Paul mentioned that they were now waiting "for his son from heaven" (1:10), they apparently understood that this climactic triumph would happen *very soon*, surely in their lifetime. But now, some in the community had died, perhaps even killed in the persecution. This raises the question of whether or not they have missed out on the full realization of the kingdom. It would seem so, especially if the revelation of God's power was for the future only, and not already revealed in the present. Because those who died apparently missed out on the "not yet," the members of the community mourned, forgetting their more significant participation in the "already" of God.

Paul responds to the problem at three levels. First, he sketches a picture of the end time (4:16-18), clarifying that those already dead will not in any way be disadvantaged at the coming of the Lord. Second, he warns that the time of this coming is not a matter of timetables or calculations but is in God's hands (5:1-3). But Paul's third point is the most important for him: the crisis in the community arose only because its members had forgotten a fundamental part of their identity. The essential victory over death and evil had *already* been won in the resurrection of Jesus. In it, God already showed himself triumphant. The God who raised Jesus to life is not a powerless projection of human desires, like idols, but a "living and true God" (1:9-10). The God preached by Paul lives. The members' mourning for the dead is therefore both a loss of hope and a fall from faith.

The Christian identity of the Thessalonian assembly was shaken, since they were responding like those outsiders who do not understand the distinctive view of God gained by the resurrection of Jesus. Those who "did not know God" in this way lived in the world "with no hope," for their gods were dead. But those who had come to know the God who raised Jesus from the dead had hope rooted in reality. They knew that just as he had raised Jesus, so could he also raise them to life: "God will bring with him those who have fallen asleep" (4:14). The timing may be uncertain, but the outcome is sure: "We shall always be with the Lord" (4:17).

Paul does not use eschatological language for its own sake but to serve as a support for exhortation. He wants the Thessalonians to live appropriately within this in-between time. Their lives should be filled with alertness and watchfulness (5:5-10). They are not to be on the lookout for an external event—like trying to spy a thief creeping up in the night (5:2)—but are to be attentive to the transcendental measure of their existence as people called by God. In a series of contrasts stereotypical both of moral and of eschatological discourse, Paul opposes the life symbolized by darkness, night, sleep, and drunkenness—a life of oblivion and forgetfulness—to the life symbolized by light, day, wakefulness, and sobriety—a life lived on the eschatological edge (5:4-9). This contrast, in turn, points to the reciprocity established by God in the death and resurrection of Jesus, "who died for us, so that whether we wake or sleep, we might live with him" (5:10). This reversal was possible, finally, only because the power that accomplishes all of this is not of human projection but from the living God (1:9-10).

But what does Christian existence look like during this in-between time? How is watchfulness expressed through behavior? Perhaps surprisingly, Paul's moral exhortations are not in the least innovative. He explicitly calls them traditions in which the Thessalonians have already been instructed (4:1-2, 11). We may have here, indeed, elements of an early Christian catechism. Moreover, the exhortations that spell out the implications of holiness clearly resemble the moral standards of Hellenistic Judaism. This is hardly surprising, since the primitive Christian communities existed in exactly the same Diaspora context. They too had to work out the meaning of being God's chosen people in a pluralistic setting, determining how to live within worldly structures without being utterly defined by them.

Paul exhorts the Thessalonian assembly to abstain from sexual immorality. As they had turned from idols to the living God, so must their behavior also turn from the "passion of lust like heathen who do not know God" (4:5). The proper context for sexual activity is a chaste marriage; adultery wrongs a fellow Christian and breaks covenant with the believers (4:6). This sexual ethic is not extraordinary. What is striking is the way Paul invokes divine retribution: the community lives under the judgment of God (4:6-8).

Since they have turned away from the ethos of the outside world, they require strong positive attitudes toward other members of the church. Paul praises them for their brotherly love (*philadelphia*), which they have been taught by God (4:9-10). We may have here (as in 4:15) a memory of the teaching of Jesus. Paul also gives advice that was advanced by other philosophers of his age, notably the Epicureans, when he tells the Thessalonians to "live quietly, mind your own affairs, and work with your hands" (4:11). Avoidance of political activity in part strengthens the cohesion of the community and assures outsiders that they have nothing to fear from the church (4:12). Paul emphasizes the need for mutual edification: "Comfort one another with these words" (4:18), and "Encourage one another, and build one another up, just as you are doing" (5:11; cf. 5:14). Although in terms of Paul's symbolic world the Thessalonian community is "called by God," the congregation is also what sociologists would call an "intentional community," a group not supported by the bonds of natural kinship and therefore in need of maintaining itself by mutual commitment. As such an intentional community, the church lives by mutual confirmation of its shared knowledge and convictions: leaders are to be esteemed (5:12) and the community is to live at peace (5:13).

The same tone of sobriety and reason governs Paul's remarks on the working of the Spirit in prayer and prophecy. The Spirit is not to be quenched and prophecy is not to be despised, but everything is to be tested (5:21). The pertinence of this will be apparent when we turn to 2 Thessalonians. The community is responsible to God for its life during the "in-between time," that period between the "already" and the "not yet": the "already" of God's essential victory over sin and death in the resurrection of Jesus, leading to his present power in the life of the community, and the "not yet" of the coming establishment of the full rule of his kingdom. This eschatological tension should lead not to an obsessive reading of signs but to a calm community life. Within the period between Jesus' resurrection and the final triumph of God, this people still needs to "hold fast to what is good and abstain from every form of evil" (5:21-22).

Second Thessalonians

Second Thessalonians is sometimes considered inauthentic, although it is difficult to make this case convincing. There is no problem placing the letter in Paul's career; the internal evidence presupposes a situation naturally following upon that of the first letter. The style is so close to that of 1 Thessalonians that the argument against authenticity must claim a direct and deliberate imitation of that letter. Moreover, 2 Thessalonians explicitly bears the personal signature of Paul as a mark of authenticity (3:17), an emphasis understandable in its context (see 2:2). Those otherwise convinced of the letter's pseudonymous character, of course, see this validation as a sign of forgery. Furthermore, some skeptics have argued that Paul is out of character in 2 Thessalonians, as he is quite harsh toward opponents (2 Thess. 1:6-9; 2:10-12). He is, however, equally harsh in some other letters (cf. 1 Thess. 2:15-16).

The only real difficulty, then, concerns consistency in content. The description of the end time in 2 Thessalonians is thought by some to contradict that found in 1 Thess. 4:13-5:3, especially since it seems to imply a schedule of events whereas 1 Thessalonians explicitly eschews any set sequence. There is unquestionably some difference between the two eschatological accounts. They are best understood, however, as successive responses by a pastor to stages in a community's panic, rather than the eschatological formulations of two different individuals.

The structure of 2 Thessalonians is not unusual. The short, unadorned greeting (1:1-2) is followed by an equally short thanksgiving (1:3-4), which, as in 1 Thessalonians, shifts imperceptibly into the body of the letter (1:5—2:12). A second thanksgiving passage (2:13-17) becomes a request for mutual prayer and support (3:1-5). A series of rather sharp exhortations (3:6-15) concludes with a prayer (3:16), the signature (3:17), and a farewell (3:18).

The Crisis

The tone of 2 Thessalonians is definitely sharper than that of the first letter. The persecution is spoken of in more explicit terms (1:3-5). The judgment awaiting the persecutors is more dramatic (1:6-9). People in the community who have left their normal occupations are severely rebuked: "If anyone will not work, let him not eat" (3:10). Disobedience to the letter's instructions make one liable to shunning by other community members, so that the deviant might be made to conform (3:14-15). The letter indeed appears to be responding to a crisis.

The nature of the crisis is suggested by 2 Thess. 2:1-2:

> Now concerning the coming of our Lord Jesus Christ and our assembling to meet him, we beg you, brethren, not to be quickly shaken in mind or excited, either by spirit or word, or by letter purporting to be from us, to the effect that the day of the Lord has come.

The church is in a state of panic, thinking that the end time is upon them. Some have ceased working altogether, devoting themselves to waiting for the arrival of Jesus, an event they apparently expect very soon. But why should they have thought the end so imminent? Three things have contributed to shaping the crisis: the immaturity of the community, Paul's instructions in 1 Thessalonians, and the classic apocalyptic scenario of the end-time. To this already volatile mixture was added an intensification of the church's suffering through persecution, catalyzing the crisis.

Paul, we remember, had used the term "affliction" (*thlipsis*) in reference to the persecution the Thessalonians were enduring (1 Thess. 1:6; 3:3-4, 7). He also associates the term "wrath" (*orgē*) with their suffering (1 Thess. 1:10; 2:16; 5:9). Both terms were part of the apocalyptic end-time scenario. The Day of Affliction was sometimes thought to be a time of cataclysmic suffering by the saints that would usher in the definitive intervention of God (see, e.g., Dan. 12:1; *1 Enoch* 45.2; 48.8; 50.2; Matt. 24:21, 29; Mark 13:19, 24). The suffering is combined with persecution (*diōgmos*) in Matt. 13:21 and Mark 4:17 (see also Rom. 2:9, 8:35; Rev. 1:9; 2:9-10; 7:14). The term "wrath" could likewise point to the coming of God for judgment, as Paul elsewhere employs it (Rom. 2:5; 5:9; cf. Rev. 6:17; 14:10). For those already confused concerning when "the Son from heaven" would come to relieve their suffering and bring them salvation (1 Thess. 1:10), the temptation would be great to see in every increment of persecution the final progress toward that climactic moment when God would intervene.

The advice Paul gave in 1 Thessalonians would not have turned them definitively from that temptation. In his brief sketch of the Lord's coming (1 Thess. 4:13—5:3), he assured them that all Christians would be saved, attempting to allay their concern for their dead. But when he refused to give a timetable for the end, calling only for alertness and watchfulness, he fed a preoccupation that apparently was already well established. What Paul meant by watchfulness, as we have seen, was a steady attentiveness to life in the community according to the measure of God's holiness. But the members of the community could easily have heard it as an encouragement for an increased obsession with the time of the "thief's coming." No sleep or rest for them, no ordinary toil of life to distract them; they would give up all their activity and devote themselves to just this one thing.

If we imagine a group seized with such a conviction gathered together in an assembly where there is prophetic utterance, it is easy to see how a "word of the Lord" or even a "spirit letter" from Paul could precipitate a panic with the pronouncement "The end is upon us; the affliction has reached its outermost extreme; the Son of man is coming on the clouds." Just such a catalyst seems presupposed by Paul's reference to their being shaken "by spirit or word or by letter purporting to be from us" (2 Thess. 2:2). The effect of the pronouncement was to throw this fragile church into an even deeper crisis than that posed by the death of its members.

The Time Before the End

Once more, Paul responds to the crisis in three steps. First, he reaffirms a basic understanding that he shares with the community's members: this intense affliction will lead to their salvation and to the punishment of their oppressors (1:6-10). But Paul subtly alters their perception of this reality. He shows them that the affliction is not simply an external force to be endured but is a positive factor in the strengthening of their identity. It enables them to grow in faith and love (1:3), in steadfastness and endurance (1:4; cf. Rom. 5:1-5). They suffer for the kingdom of God (1:5), and the affliction makes them worthy of that kingdom (1:5, 11). Their experience leads to the goal that "the name of Jesus Christ might be glorified in you, *and you in him*" (1:12). As in his first letter, Paul calls them back to a sense of their identity. He insists that the in-between period is not "wasted time" but is a period during which the work of God is being manifested in their lives: they are glorifying God and preparing for his coming rule already in their present existence.

Second, Paul corrects the narrowness of the Thessalonians' vision. Their local affliction is not necessarily the climax to world history. More is at stake in God's work than
their mere experience—a point, Paul reminds them, that he had already touched on
when he was with them (2:5). They are thus freed from preoccupation about the coming of the end, for its advent will be unmistakable. Paul does not really provide a
schedule for the end. Rather, he describes features from traditional apocalyptic expectation that must be in place before the grand reversal will occur: the reign of lawless-
ness will be personified in a "son of perdition" who, as a minion of Satan (2:9), will
claim divine status and seek a place in the temple (2:4). By working signs and wonders
(2:9) he will lead all the wicked astray (2:10-12), eventually being destroyed himself by
the coming of the Lord (2:8). The effect of this panoply is simple: the end will be more
cosmic in scope than the persecution of a single Thessalonian church.

Now according to Paul, since the general period of the lawless one's dominance has
begun (2:7), the congregation should consider itself as being in the general period of
the end-time. It is not, however, at its climax. Indeed, Paul refers in 2:7 to a person or
thing that is keeping the whole process in check: the restrainer (*ho katechōn*). Nothing
is murkier than the language of apocalyptic, and this passage is no exception. We no
longer know what some of Paul's terms meant or to what events or persons he alluded.
Some have suggested that the restrainer was the Roman Empire; others that it was
God; still others that Paul's own ministry was conceived by him as holding back the
final retribution. Without further information, we will not know. The pastoral intent
of the passage, on the other hand, seems clear: Paul wants to move the Thessalonians
away from self-preoccupation and obsession about the end. Far from giving them further signs to discern, he deflects them from this enterprise by suggesting that an indefinite period of time must be endured before the eschaton arrives.

Third, Paul tries to direct their attention away from apocalyptic scenarios to their
own lives. He suggests, in two prayers, what their proper focus should be. In the first,
he asks ". . . that God may fulfill every good resolve and work of faith by his power"
(1:11), and in the second, he prays, "May our Lord . . . comfort your hearts and establish them in every good work and word" (2:17). Paul also expresses hopeful "confidence in the Lord about you, that you are doing, and will do, the things which we command" (3:4). Thus, Paul requires that the members of the assembly attend to their own
identity: "May the Lord direct your hearts to the love of God and the steadfastness of
Christ" (3:5). To this end, Paul sharply rebukes those who have given up their worldly
occupations, telling them to get back to work (3:6-12). And he warns others to avoid
people who have ceased normal, daily activity, lest they be influenced to do the same.
In his exhortation to work, therefore, Paul presents himself as a model of one working
with his hands: "It was not because we did not have that right [i.e., to receive support
from the community] but to give you in your conduct an example to imitate" (3:9).

As in his first letter, Paul views the time between the resurrection and the second
coming not as a period of meaningless anticipation but as a time enriched by the

presence of the Lord through the Holy Spirit, shaped by his call to holiness (2:13). His harsh demands for obedience and for community pressure on deviance (2:3; 3:6, 14-15) stem from a fear that the very identity of this immature community is threatened by external oppression and internal misunderstanding. Paul reminds them, as he had done before, that even though they are a part of the great eschatological drama, their call is simple: "Brethren, do not weary in well-doing" (3:13).

Study Questions

1. Why was the issue of the "end-time" so critical to the Thessalonian church?

2. How and why are Paul's instructions to the Thessalonians concerning the "end-time" different in the two letters to that church?

3. Why was Paul so harsh toward those in Thessalonica who had stopped working?

4. What metaphors does Paul use to describe himself to the Thessalonian church? Why might he have chosen these particular metaphors?

5. How can "edification" fairly be called the central concern of Paul in these two letters?

Bibliographical Note

The most useful studies of 1 Thessalonians as a parenetic letter are A. J. Malherbe, "Gentle as a Nurse: The Cynic Background to 1 Thessalonians 2" and "Exhortation in 1 Thessalonians" in his *Paul and the Popular Philosophers* (Minneapolis: Fortress Press, 1989), 35–48, 49–66. On parenesis in general, see L. G. Perdue, "The Social Character of Paraenesis and Paraenetic Literature," *Semeia* 50 (1990): 5–39. Formal elements of the letter are discussed in H. Koester, "I Thessalonians—Experiment in Christian Writing," in *Continuity and Discontinuity in Church History* (Leiden: E. J. Brill, 1979), 33–44; and H. Boers, "The Form-Critical Study of Paul's Letters: 1 Thessalonians as a Test Case," *NTS* 22 (1975): 140–58. For an analysis of 1 Thessalonians as a letter of consolation, see J. Chapa, "Is First Thessalonians a Letter of Consolation?" *NTS* 40 (1994): 150–60; and A. Smith, *Comfort One Another: Reconstructing the Rhetoric and Audience of 1 Thessalonians* (Louisville: Westminster/John Knox, 1995).

Interpolation of the anti-Jewish sentiment in 2:13-16 is argued by B. A. Pearson, "1 Thessalonians 2:13-16: A Deutero-Pauline Interpolation," in his *The Emergence of the Christian Religion: Essays on Early Christianity* (Harrisburg, Pa.: Trinity Press Int'l, 1997), 58–74; D. Schmidt, "I Thess 2:13–16: Linguistic Evidence for an Interpolation,"

JBL 102 (1983): 269–79; and J. A. Weatherly, "The Authenticity of 1 Thessalonians 2.13–16: Additional Evidence," *JSNT* 42 (1991): 79–98. Further fragmentation of the letter is undertaken by W. Schmithals, *Paul and the Gnostics*, trans. J. Steely (Nashville: Abingdon Press, 1972), 123–218. On this issue, see R. F. Collins, "Apropos the Integrity of 1 Thess.," *ETL* 55 (1979): 65–106.

Not surprisingly, the eschatology of 1 Thessalonians receives a disproportionate amount of attention. Useful discussions are found in C. L. Mearns, "Early Eschatological Development in Paul: The Evidence of First and Second Thessalonians," *NTS* 27 (1980): 137–57; R. N. Longenecker, "The Nature of Paul's Early Eschatology," *NTS* 31(1985): 85–95; B. N. Kaye, "Eschatology and Ethics in First and Second Thessalonians," *NovT* 17 (1975): 47–57; J. H. Neyrey, "Eschatology in I Thess.: The Theological Factor in 1:9–10; 2:4–5; 3:11–13; 4:6; and 4:13–18," *SBLSP* 19 (1980): 219–31; C. E. D. Moule, "The Influence of Circumstances on Paul's Eschatology," *JTS* 15 (1964): 1–15; J. Plevnik, *Paul and the Parousia: An Exegetical and Theological Investigation* (Peabody, Mass.: Hendrickson Pubs., 1997), 65–121; J. Gillman, "Signals of Transformation in 1 Thessalonians 4:13–18," *CBQ* 47 (1985): 263–81; and W. A. Meeks, "Social Functions of Apocalyptic Language in Pauline Christianity," in D. Hellholm (ed.), *Apocalypticism in the Mediterranean World and the Near East* (Tübingen: J. C. B. Mohr [Paul Siebeck], 1983), 687–705.

On Paul's relationship with the Thessalonian community, see J. M. G. Barclay, "Thessalonica and Corinth: Social Contrasts in Pauline Christianity," *JSNT* 47 (1992): 49–74; D. Lührmann, "The Beginnings of the Church at Thessalonica," in D. L. Balch et al. (eds.), *Greeks, Romans, and Christians* (Minneapolis: Fortress Press, 1990), 237–49; and A. J. Malherbe, *Paul and the Thessalonians: The Philosophic Tradition of Pastoral Care* (Philadelphia: Fortress Press, 1987). On the context of the church, see K. P. Donfried, "Cults of Thessalonica and the Thessalonian Correspondence," *NTS* 31 (1985): 336–56; idem, "2 Thessalonians and the Church of Thessalonica," in B. H. McLean (ed.), *Origins and Method: Towards a New Understanding of Judaism and Christianity* (JSNTSup, 86; Sheffield: Sheffield Academic Press, 1993), 128–44; and P. Perkins, "1 Thessalonians and Hellenistic Religious Practices," in M. P. Horgan and P. J. Kobelski (eds.), *To Touch the Text* (New York: Crossroad, 1989), 325–34.

Other features of 1 Thessalonians are treated by R. F. Collins, *Studies on the First Letter to the Thessalonians* (BETL, 66; Leuven: Leuven Univ. Press, 1984); D. A. deSilva, "'Worthy of his Kingdom': Honor Discourse and Social Engineering in 1 Thessalonians," *JSNT* 64 (1996): 49–79; K. P. Donfried, "The Theology of 1 Thessalonians as a Reflection of Its Purpose," *To Touch the Text*, 243–60; L. Fatum, "Brotherhood in Christ: A Gender Hermeneutical Reading of 1 Thessalonians," in H. Moxnes (ed.), *Constructing Early Christian Families: Family as Social Reality and Metaphor* (New York: Routledge, 1997), 183–97; I. H. Marshall, "Pauline Theology in the Thessalonian Correspondence," in M. D. Hooker and S. G. Wilson (eds.), *Paul and Paulinism* (London: SPCK, 1982), 173–83; J. Munck, "I Thess 1:9–10 and the Missionary Preaching of

Paul," *NTS* 9 (1962–63): 95–110; T. H. Olbricht, "An Aristotelian Rhetorical Analysis of 1 Thessalonians," in D. L. Balch et al. (eds.), *Greeks, Romans, and Christians* (Minneapolis: Fortress Press, 1990), 216–36; D. M. Stanley, "'Become Imitators of Me': The Pauline Conception of Apostolic Tradition," *Bib* 40 (1959): 859–77; and J. A. D. Weima, "An Apology for the Apologetic Function of 1 Thessalonians 2.1–12," *JSNT* 68 (1997): 73–99.

A representative discussion of the inauthenticity of 2 Thessalonians can be found in J. A. Bailey, "Who Wrote II Thessalonians?" *NTS* 25 (1978–79): 131–45. The peculiar problems presented by its eschatology are treated by J. M. Bassler, "The Enigmatic Sign: 2 Thessalonians 1:5," *CBQ* 46 (1984): 496–510; J. M. Barclay, "Conflict in Thessalonica," *CBQ* 55 (1993): 512–30; C. H. Giblin, *The Threat to Faith: An Exegetical and Theological Re–Examination of II Thess. 2* (AnB, 31; Rome: Biblical Inst. Press, 1967); and J. Townsend, "II Thessalonians 2:3–12," *SBLSP* 19 (1980): 233–46.

For some of the background to Paul's statements on manual labor, see R. E Hock, "The Workshop as a Social Setting for Paul's Missionary Preaching," *CBQ* 41(1979): 438–50. The most positive use made of 2 Thessalonians for the construal of Paul's theology and his understanding of his mission is that found in J. Munck, *Paul and the Salvation of Mankind*, trans. F. Clarke (Richmond: John Knox Press, 1959), 36–68. For a recent rhetorical analysis, see F. W. Hughes, *Early Christian Rhetoric and 2 Thessalonians* (JSNTSup, 30; Sheffield: Sheffield Academic Press, 1989). Also see G. S. Holland, *The Tradition That You Received from Us: 2 Thessalonians in the Pauline Tradition* (Tübingen: J. C. B. Mohr [Siebeck], 1988).

For recent analysis of the theology of 1 and 2 Thessalonians, as well as comparison with other early Pauline letters, see the relevant essays in J. Bassler (ed.), *Pauline Theology, Vol. 1: Thessalonians, Philippians, Galatians, Philemon* (Minneapolis: Fortress Press, 1991). Also see the collection of essays in R. F. Collins (ed.), *The Thessalonian Correspondence* (BETL, 87; Leuven: Leuven Univ. Press, 1990). For a thorough study of the entire correspondence, see R. Jewett, *The Thessalonian Correspondence: Pauline Rhetoric and Millenarian Piety* (Philadelphia: Fortress Press, 1986).

For critical commentary on the Thessalonian letters, see F. F. Bruce, *1 & 2 Thessalonians* (WBC; Waco: Word Books, 1982); and C. A. Wanamaker, *The Epistles to the Thessalonians: A Commentary on the Greek Text* (NIGTC; Grand Rapids: Eerdmans, 1990). Also see the more general treatments of E. Best, *The First and Second Epistles to the Thessalonians* (HNTC; New York: Harper & Row, 1972); and I. H. Marshall, *1 and 2 Thessalonians* (NCB; Grand Rapids: Eerdmans, 1983).

12. The Corinthian Correspondence

OUR KNOWLEDGE OF earliest Christianity would be considerably diminished without Paul's two Letters to the Corinthians. We find in them a portrait of a community whose life together was a mixture of confusion, pettiness, and ambition, combined with enthusiasm and fervor. The community struggled to define its identity as the church of God in a complex and sophisticated urban setting. The letters also reveal Paul's relationship with a beloved but stubborn community founded by him, a tie that forced him to delineate his full understanding of his mission, his apostleship, and the implications of these for his authority. We thus meet here Paul the pastor and the father of a community.

The Corinthians were the first to face the problems that have proved to be perennial for all Christian communities: how to live in holiness and freedom within the very real structures of a given social world. They confronted these issues in culturally conditioned cases—for example, eating meat offered to idols, women wearing veils while prophesying—that provide structural analogies to situations faced by churches in every generation. In this correspondence, we discover the difficulty of defining an identity within a pluralistic context. Rather than the specific solutions offered by Paul, it is his way of thinking about these issues and the principles he invokes that remain of contemporary interest.

The Church and the Correspondence

The restored city of Corinth, a port city with harbors to the east and to the north, was the capital of the province of Achaia. It hosted a large transient population, which typically brought its trades as well as its cults to the city. The diversity that developed out of this phenomenon is attested by archaeology, which confirms the presence of both synagogue and Isis shrine in the same city. As one would expect, numerous problems accompanied such an influx of peoples into the region. For instance, like most ancient ports, Corinth enjoyed a reputation for sexual immorality. And with the constant movement of people in and out of the city, attachment to particular pagan rituals and clubs became a necessary means of maintaining some form of social stability, a practice that would become a particular problem for early Christians.

Paul established the first Christian community in Corinth (1 Cor. 4:15). The evidence of Acts is generally confirmed by that of the letters. Paul came to Corinth from Athens and met Aquila and Priscilla (see 1 Cor. 16:19), who had recently been expelled from Rome with other Jews by Claudius (Acts 18:2). Paul joined them in tentmaking, and began preaching in the synagogue. Rejected there (18:6) and rejoined by his Macedonian delegates (1 Thess. 3:6), Paul moved next door to the house of Titus Justus (Acts 18:7). He converted Crispus, the ruler of the synagogue (18:8; cf. 1 Cor. 1:14), and stayed in Corinth some eighteen months (18:11). During that time, he was brought before the proconsul Gallio (18:12). When Gallio dismissed the case, the Jews beat Sosthenes, whom Acts refers to as a "ruler of the synagogue" (18:17) and who appears as Paul's "brother" and co-writer in 1 Cor. 1:1.

When Paul left Corinth to return to Antioch, he took Aquila and Priscilla with him as far as Ephesus (18:18-21). In his absence, they encounter the charismatic Apollos, instruct him, and support his journey to the province of Achaia (18:24-28). Thus Apollos worked in Corinth after Paul (19:1). Acts gives special attention to Apollo's eloquence (18:24), and it is evident that he played a significant role in the life of the Corinthian church (1 Cor. 1:12; 3:4-7, 21-23; 4:6; 16:12).

In Acts 19:21-22, we find Paul planning to return to Macedonia and Achaia before going to Jerusalem and then Rome (1 Cor. 16:5; 2 Cor. 1:15). One of his delegates at that point is Erastus, identified in Rom. 16:23 as the treasurer of the city (cf. 2 Tim. 4:20). Paul then spends three months in Achaia before departing for Macedonia (Acts 20:3). Paul's letters basically agree with this sketch, but fill it out considerably with reference to frequent visits by Paul and his delegates Timothy and Titus (1 Cor. 2:1; 4:19; 16:3-10; 2 Cor. 1:15; 8:6; 9:3; 12:14). Paul also wrote the letters to the Thessalonians and Romans from Corinth.

The church had members from both Jewish and gentile backgrounds. The issues treated in the first letter highlight the difficulties of former pagans, but the overarching symbolism by which the whole community understood itself came from Torah (see esp. 1 Cor. 10:1-13). The community also had a mixed social background. Paul says, "Not many of you were of noble birth" (1 Cor. 1:26), but some enjoyed a more prominent status than others, such as Erastus (Rom. 16:23) and the heads of households where the community assembled (1 Cor. 1:11, 16; 16:15-17). One cause of strife in the young church came from the diverse social origins, expectations, and perspectives that were carried over from their world into the assembly of God.

The Corinthians' faults came from over-enthusiasm, not tepidity. Impressed by the powers given them by the Spirit (1:5-7), they were less concerned with understanding these powers (2:12) than with using them. They were fascinated by the specious and the spectacular. Although a difficult community for Paul to deal with, they were, nonetheless, very much a Pauline church, even if they tended to reduce the distinctive elements of his gospel to slogans and catchwords (see 6:12-13; 7:1; 8:1; 10:23; 14:22). Paul had the uncomfortable task of reaffirming his premises while trying to lead them to better conclusions.

Stemming from their overenthusiasm for the powers of the Spirit, a form of spiritual elitism infected the community. Some were so awed by their new knowledge and freedom and capacities for ecstatic speech that they considered themselves fully mature and perfect (2:6—3:4). They tended to judge each other and even their mentors (4:1-5) while at the same time neglecting the moral demands of their calling (5:1—6:20). These tendencies seem to have been rooted in an understanding of the resurrection that stressed its present power within them but denied its completion in a future life; they had no need of transformation, for they enjoyed the life of glory now. They collapsed the delicate tension between the "already" and the "not yet" by regarding themselves as already rich and ruling in God's kingdom (4:8). Such attitudes are also found in varieties of Gnosticism, which became a recognizable Christian option in the second century C.E. Ideas like those of the Corinthians were developed in later gnostic texts. Congregations like this one, indeed, may have provided the connection between an earlier diffused dualistic outlook and later more fully developed Gnosticism. We find here, however, only the possible first seeds of that astonishing many-branched growth.

Spiritual elitism led to factionalism. The Corinthians tended to define themselves by their differences rather than by their common life. From the beginning of 1 Corinthians, we find groups identifying themselves by their allegiance to a particular apostle—"I belong to Paul," "I belong to Apollos," "I belong to Cephas"—or claiming the need of no teacher at all: "I belong to Christ" (1:12). Much scholarship has treated these groups as representatives of competing factions within earliest Christianity, construing the lines as Jewish-Christian against Gentile-Christian, for example. Little in the letters supports such hypotheses. Not even in 2 Corinthians, where disputes between teachers become explicit, does any teaching show a clear delineation of disparate factions. Paul certainly does not align himself with a Pauline group, and rejects entirely even the idea of such groups, asserting his role as teacher of the whole community (4:14-21). The factions, in fact, were, if not generated, at least made more explicit by the circumstances leading to the first letter: the Corinthians' own concerns regarding their conduct in the church and the world.

The canonical collection contains two Letters to the Corinthians. Paul's correspondence with this church, however, was considerably more extensive. It involved five letters, possibly more: (1) Paul alludes in 1 Cor. 5:9 to an earlier letter, now either lost or, as some think, found in 2 Cor. 6:14-7:1. (2) In 1 Cor. 7:1, Paul refers to a letter full of questions written to him by the Corinthians. (3) He writes 1 Corinthians—the unity of this letter is sometimes questioned, though without cause—in response to their questions and other problems in the church. (4) Paul mentions in 2 Cor. 2:4 a "letter in tears," now either lost, found in 2 Corinthians 10–13, or simply to be identified with 1 Corinthians. (5) Paul wrote 2 Corinthians, which may be not a literary unity but an edited composite of several notes. The most significant aspect of this sequence is the testimony it offers—confirmed by the frequent personal visits of Paul and his delegates—to Paul's close and careful concern for his communities. It is no accident that the Corinthian correspondence is extraordinarily lively, for the relationship that generated it was genuinely alive.

The First Letter to the Corinthians

After Paul left Corinth, problems developed concerning the maintenance of community boundaries: some in the church thought they could continue in their former associations and practices. Even after Paul wrote a first note warning them not to associate with immoral people (1 Cor. 5:9), the situation was not resolved. Relations within the community were strained because of the diverse approaches to moral behavior. At this point, some wanted to ask Paul's advice (see 7:1). This suggestion, however, did not meet with unanimous approval. Why should they turn to Paul? What authority did he possess? Was he an original apostle like Cephas (1:12; 9:5) or a great preacher like Apollos (1:12; 2:1)? Why not turn to them for guidance? The need for definitive advice brought already latent allegiances and disaffections into the open.

At least some in the community decided to send Paul a letter asking his advice on the disputed issues. It may have been delivered by Stephanus, Fortunatus, and Achaichus (16:17), or by the domestic servants of Chloe (1:11). "Chloe's people" in any case brought Paul news of further developments: how some were flagrantly sinning, some were initiating lawsuits against others in the community, and others questioning Paul's authority to teach them. So, if he hoped to instruct them and correct their distorted perceptions, Paul first had to reestablish his credibility as the father of this community.

The outline of the letter corresponds to this sequence of events. After the greeting (1:1-3) and thanksgiving (1:4-9), Paul immediately turns to the divisions within the community, reminding its members forcefully of his own authority to teach them (chaps. 1–4). Next, he deals with the problems reported to him orally: sexual immorality and litigation in pagan courts (chaps. 5–6). Paul then treats the questions posed by their letter, dealing in turn with virginity and marriage (chap. 7), food offered to idols (chaps. 8–10), and problems in worship (chaps. 11–14). In chapter 15, he provides the theological teaching on the resurrection, which undergirds his treatment of specific issues. Finally, Paul raises his personal project, the collection of money for the saints in Jerusalem (16:1-4).

The Church of God (1 Corinthians 1–4)

Paul anticipates his basic message to the Corinthians already in the greeting: they are "sanctified in Christ Jesus [*hēgiasmenoi*]," but they are also "called to be saints [*klētoi hagioi*]" (1:2). Throughout the letter, Paul affirms their gifts but insists that these gifts contain a mandate: the Holy Spirit, which enlivens the Corinthians, must also lead to their behavioral transformation. Likewise, in the thanksgiving, Paul acknowledges that they have been "enriched" with every spiritual mode of speech and knowledge. He then prays that the gift that has been made "secure" among them might remain protected and "blameless" until the end (or, until they become perfect) "in the day of our Lord Jesus Christ" (1:4-8).

The eschatological reference is deliberate: Because God's kingdom has not yet been fully achieved, they cannot yet be perfect. When Paul tells them in 4:8, "Already you have been filled, already you are rich, already apart from us you have come into your kingdom," he is being sarcastic—their "rule" is illusory. The last verse of the thanksgiving sets the proper perspective. They have been called into fellowship with Jesus, but neither the call nor the growth is their own doing. Both are the work of God, who is faithful (1:9). Fellowship with Jesus means conformity to his measure; and the place where this happens is the church of God.

Although they were called into a fellowship (*koinōnia*) with Jesus, they are in fact destroying that unity by their factiousness. Paul exhorts them therefore to have the same mind (*nous*) and judgment (*gnōmē*) among themselves (1:10). By this he means more than mere unanimity. The same mind they should have is that formed by the one with whom they have been joined: they should have the "mind of Christ" (2:16). Their party spirit has "divided Christ" (1:13). Factions and rivalries are characteristic of human gatherings in which people define themselves by their knowledge, power, or prestige. In God's church, such measurements do not apply.

Their calling is not an invitation to a club or a cultic association, which would demand of them allegiance to their patron or mystagogue (see 1:13-14). Those are the perceptions of the world and not of the gospel. The Corinthians have been called into God's convocation (*ekklēsia*), through an invitation and command apart from natural abilities or predilections. God's call transcends human status (1:26), exceeds human strength (1:25), and confounds human wisdom (1:18). It is a call that reverses all human norms, for it is based not on the persuasiveness of human rhetoric but on the preaching of the cross (1:17). The identity of the church is indelibly marked by the one who remains a scandal to the Jews and a fool to the Gentiles (1:18-23), Jesus Christ. To accept this invitation means to regard the measure of the world as an inadequate measure for one who is "the power of God, the wisdom of God" (1:24).

Life in the church therefore demands measuring all of reality in a new way: not by the "wisdom of this age" (2:6) but by the "secret and hidden wisdom of God" (2:7). This wisdom is not the revelation of esoteric cosmic realities but a profound initiation into the ways of the Spirit's working among the people (2:12). Those who use spiritual realities as a means of self-aggrandizement are not really spiritual people but immature (3:1). Those who truly have "the mind of Christ" (2:16) and know the depths of God (2:10) have learned to use these gifts appropriately for the building up of God's community in the world.

So, far from being rivals, Paul and Apollos together provide an example of the attitudes the Corinthians should have toward their own community (4:6). Paul and Apollos have each been given a separate function by the Lord, but both regard themselves as servants (3:5) and fellow workers (3:9) who cooperate in their efforts, knowing that "God gives the growth" (3:6). The Corinthians, too, should not "be puffed up in favor of one against another" (4:6) lest they forget that everything they have comes as a gift (4:7). If they treat the church as though it were simply a human institution, they profane and destroy the temple of God, because this community lives not by mutual contract but by the life-breath of the Holy Spirit (3:16-17). Paul therefore concludes (3:21-23):

> Let no one boast of men. For all things are yours, whether Paul or Apollos or Cephas or the world, or life or death or the present or the future, all are yours; and you are Christ's; and Christ is God's.

Although Paul is only a servant and worker, he has been given a special role in the Corinthian community: it was his task to "plant" (3:6) and to "lay the foundation" (3:10). He is more than a pedagogue, since he gave this community its birth through the preaching of the gospel, and thus deserves to be regarded as its father (4:15). And as a father, it is his responsibility to instruct the community in morals. He will therefore, despite the Corinthians' reluctance, teach them both by his words and by his deeds: "I urge you, then, be imitators of me" (4:16).

The Church in the World (1 Corinthians 5–10)

The "mind of Christ" must be applied to the very real problems of life in a pluralistic society. Like Jews of the Diaspora, the Corinthians are pulled between the movements of separation and assimilation. Paul insists on the need for separation from the world's values; there must be real boundaries between the inside and the outside. But he denies the need to withdraw from society altogether, a lesson he had previously to teach the Thessalonian church. The church is to be holy, otherwise it is not God's people but just another part of the world. The church's holiness, however, is found not in flight from, but rather in a quality of life within, the structures of the world. Paul leaves much ambiguous at the level of directive, for he wants the Corinthians to learn to think for themselves; they must "understand their gifts" (2:12) within the context of their society and their community.

Paul's advice must move in a delicate space between two extremes in the congregation. Both extremes wanted to avoid ambiguity by reducing norms to slogans. Some pushed Paul's gospel of freedom to a virtual antinomianism: "All things are lawful for me" (6:12). For them, spiritual identity is secure and unassailable; material and social realities are strictly irrelevant: "Food for the stomach, the stomach for food" (6:13).

They place great store in their knowledge—"All of us possess knowledge" (8:1)—and consider their spiritual state to be sufficiently secure to enable them to engage the world indiscriminately. Paul calls them "the strong" (4:10; 10:22); they tended to be arrogant and contemptuous of those who worried about behavioral norms as a safeguard for identity, namely the people Paul calls "the weak" (8:7-10). "The weak" were convinced that Christian identity was fragile, requiring definite social practices different from those of society. Sexual activity should be distinctive and radical: "It is good not to touch a woman" (7:1). Food and drink could contaminate; thus it was better to maintain a more rigid diet, avoiding contact with pagan practices (10:28).

Paul agrees intellectually with the position of the strong; his bias is always for freedom. But his understanding of this freedom or power (*exousia*) is different. If one's identity is secure, it is because it is based in God (1:6), not in one's own accomplishments. It is not that the Christians have come to know God but that God has known them, and this is what has given them freedom (8:1-3; 13:12). In that sense, "food will not commend us to God" (8:8). But the strong are naive about the social dimensions of human existence; spiritual life does involve physical entanglements. In fact, their vaunted freedom and knowledge have led to a neglect of others. They have become spiritual solipsists, forgetting they are part of a community. And Paul's focus is always the community: the primary gift of the Spirit is love (13:1-13); its main manifestation is the building up (*oikodomē*) of others in faith and understanding (8:1, 10; 10:23; 14:3, 12). Therefore, rather than boast of their superiority, "the strong" should build up "the weak."

THE HOLINESS OF THE CHURCH (5:1—6:20)

When Paul turns to the problems reported by Chloe's people, his basic principle is clear: the church must maintain its integrity. Since the people have been "washed . . . sanctified . . . justified in the name of the Lord Jesus Christ and in the Spirit of our God" (6:11b), they can no longer live by their former standards (6:9-11a). But unless they are to go out of the world altogether—an option Paul does not recommend—they must continue to associate with those who do not share their perceptions (5:9-10). The community must therefore exercise discernment in its internal life. Its task is not judging apostles (4:3-5) or outsiders; that sort of judgment is God's work (5:13). They must judge themselves and the quality of their life together (5:12). While they had been evaluating everyone else, they had let slide their own critical awareness of themselves as a community (6:2-5).

According to Paul, the community was failing precisely because boundaries between the world and the church were collapsing. For instance, members sued each other in pagan courts (6:1-5). Such litigiousness was not only contrary to community spirit—better to suffer fraud than to defraud others (6:1-7)—it also indicated an abdication of responsibility for judging within the community. Such matters should be settled among themselves (6:2). Another instance involved an acceptance of sexual immorality. Boundaries had been virtually destroyed by the community's willingness to allow a man committing incest to remain in communion (5:1-2). The Corinthian church allowed behavior even pagans detested (5:1). Since the community failed to exercise even a rudimentary self-discipline, Paul orders it to excommunicate the wrongdoer (5:2), both for his own sake (5:5) and for the sake of the community's integrity: "Cleanse out the old leaven" (5:7). A church that so ill-maintained its separation from the world's standards, Paul says, is indeed presumptuous and arrogant when it judges apostles (5:2).

Freedom within the Christian church is therefore limited in several ways. The first limit regards the appropriateness of the exercise of freedom. Freedom that leads to the slavery of sin is not from the Lord (6:12). Another limitation is placed on freedom by particular features of bodily existence. The disposition of the body creates new spiritual combinations that must be taken seriously. Sex is not like food, for it demands a deeper level of human intentionality. Sexual intercourse with a prostitute, therefore, is wrong not because it is physically contaminating but because by it one becomes "one flesh" without the commitment of the spirit, counterfeiting the physical and spiritual exchange that is at the heart of the sexual relationship.

For Paul, Christian freedom is determined most of all by relationship to the Lord. Christians are already united to the Lord through the Spirit (6:17), therefore they must orient their bodies in a manner fitting to that relationship. They are not "their own" but live by the gift of another (6:20). When Paul tells them that their bodies are "the temple of the Holy Spirit," he establishes the two fundamental coordinates for Christian behavior: the primary relationship with the Lord, by whom the Christian lives by the gift of the Spirit, and the network of relationships that constitutes the community (6:19). Far from regarding physical existence as irrelevant for the spiritual life, Paul gives it a positive function: "Glorify God in your body" (6:20). This can be understood in two ways, which are mutually reinforcing: "Glorify God in your individual bodily lives," and "Glorify God within this body that is your community."

MARRIAGE AND CELIBACY AS GOD'S GIFTS (7:1-40)

In Paul's treatment of the community's questions, he must do what those who formulated the slogans probably least want: he must make distinctions. He starts with their slogan "It is good not to touch a woman (7:1). He agrees with it at one level, but for reasons other than those of the Corinthians: to express separation by a celibate lifestyle. Paul's partial agreement derives from the eschatological perspective he gives to the entire discussion. When he says that "the frame of this world is passing away" (7:31), he is making a temporal statement that the end is coming soon, and establishing a axiom that all created things are contingent and therefore transitory. Christians must live as people both engaged with, and detached from, worldly structures. They cannot flee from them, but neither can they treat them as though they were permanent or ultimate. They are to live within them "as though not" (7:29-31), a difficult feat for anyone, and particularly for people attracted to simple solutions. But Paul refuses simple answers. He forces his readers to move through a serious reflection on the meaning of sexual existence in the kingdom of God.

His first and most important step is to distinguish between the call of God and different states of life (7:17-24). Since all human beings are called by God, no station in life can either impede or aid one's response. Male and female, Jew and Greek, slave and free, all are called to a life of righteousness. Therefore, neither sexual, social, nor ethnic divisions matter before God. In the church, then, stations in life are properly *adiaphora*—that is, they are not essential and can be understood as matters of free choice. Paul thinks of them as gifts consonant with each one's dispositions and capacities. Like all gifts, they are intended not for self-gratification but for the good of the entire community. Marriage and celibacy are both such gifts from God, contributing to the common welfare: "Each one has his special gift from the Lord, one of one kind, and one of another" (7:7).

Paul's personal preference for celibacy does not reflect a dualistic distaste for the physical or procreation. Celibacy is not advanced as an intrinsically superior mode of life. It is appropriate because of the situation of the church in the world. In a period of tribulation and the anxiety that results, Paul considers married people to be torn between their legitimate care for spouses and children and their service for the Lord in mission. In such a setting, celibacy has a functional superiority: it frees a person for the service of the whole community.

But not everyone has the gift of celibacy, so marriage is to be valued equally. In particular, Paul suggests that two types of people are helped by marriage: those celibate people who are susceptible to sexual immorality (7:2) and those Christians who, because of a lack of self-control, are so preoccupied with the opposite sex that they are "aflame with passion" (7:9). For these, celibacy has lost its purpose. Alongside this rather negative construal, Paul also takes time to portray the marriage relationship more positively. The bodies of husband and wife belong to each other (see 6:19; 7:4), and abstinence should be only temporary in order to give one's attention to prayer (7:5). Just as sexual relations with a prostitute had negative spiritual implications (6:16), the sexual bonding of husband and wife has positive spiritual implications: they can sanctify each other and their children (7:14). Marriage is a covenant; there is no divorce (7:10). The only exception is the separation—with freedom—that results from a fundamental spiritual estrangement when one is a Christian and the other a pagan, making it impossible for a man and woman to live at peace (7:15).

Paul carefully notes the authority he invokes for each stage of his discussion. The prohibition against divorce in 7:10, for example, is backed by a command of the Lord (Mark 10:11; Matt. 5:32; 19:9; Luke 16:18), whereas the questions pertaining to mixed marriages are answered with Paul's own counsel (7:12). Paul has no command for the unmarried, only counsel (7:25). And for the widows he offers no command, only the advice of one who also has "the Spirit of God" (7:39-40).

CONSCIENCE AND FREEDOM: THE ISSUE OF IDOL FOOD (8:1—11:1)

Meat was not a staple in the diet of ordinary first-century people. For those who could afford it, the most accessible source was the meat market connected to pagan temples. In idol shrines, one could also enjoy a festive meal involving meat dishes. But the Christian conversion was from "idols to the living and true God" (see 1 Thess. 1:9). How could the Corinthians have any further contact with idolatry? On the other hand, how could they avoid it? For the wealthier and more socially active members of the congregation, there could be serious disadvantages if they avoided shrine meals, since these often had much more serious civic rather than sacred connotations. Here we meet again the problem of separation and assimilation. Must Christians abstain from meat to the same rigorous degree that they abstain from immorality? Or must they operate their own meat markets to ensure purity from idolatrous contaminations?

Some of the "strong" Corinthians claim that since idols were not real, no harm was done by participation in these purely social contacts. But the "weak" are not convinced that the contacts are innocuous. They see them as collusion in idolatry. Beneath this conflict lies the issue of the legitimacy of plurality in Christian community practice and the relative importance of right knowledge and love. There are four major stages to Paul's argument.

Stage One: Initial Distinctions (8:1-13). Paul distinguishes immediately between a knowledge that "puffs up" (synonymous with "boasts"; see 4:6, 18, 19; 5:2; 13:4) and a love that "builds up" (8:1). This distinction controls his whole argument. For Paul, being theoretically correct without community sensitivity is useless. Conceptually, he agrees with "the strong": there is no ultimate power in the world but the one God (8:4-6); idols are nothing but human projections. This knowledge, however, is of no value to the one who cannot be convinced of it. Thus, Paul insists on the primacy of the individual conscience in moral choice. If some in the church think that idols are real and that eating idol meat acknowledges this reality, then for them, such eating is wrong. Their conscience is defiled if they act on what they truly consider wrong.

What obligation does this place on "the strong"? Paul again agrees with their basic understanding: eating and drinking are not by themselves determinative of our relation with God (8:8)—even though this position was distorted by some (see 6:13). But the liberty (or, power: *exousia*) this knowledge grants must not be used in a way that is a "stumbling block" (1:23) to "the weak" (8:9). Christ identified himself with strong and weak alike (8:11-12); "the strong", therefore, must limit their freedom for the sake of others. Willingly giving up a position of strength for one of weakness is the pattern of exchange that becomes shorthand for the gospel of the crucified Messiah (see 1:17-25), a pattern Paul himself exemplifies (8:13).

Stage Two: The Apostolic Example (9:1-27). Paul shows how the pattern is operative in his apostolic style. He, too, has *exousia*: he has seen Jesus; he is an apostle (9:1-2). He has a "right" to be supplied food and drink, a wife as a companion, and support for his ministry (9:3-7). Such rights are specified by Torah (9:8-11), the custom of Israel

(9:13), and Jesus himself: "Those who proclaim the gospel should get their living by the gospel" (9:14; cf. Matt. 10:10; Luke 10:7; 1 Tim. 5:18). But Paul does not use this *exousia*, lest he place an obstacle to the proclamation of the "good news" (9:12-18). His freedom will not become a stumbling block (*scandalon*) to others. He is an example of power emptied out in service to others. He extends this to being available to all people, "that I might by all means save some" (9:22). He views his ministry as a "life for others," and therefore their life together should be one of mutual service rather than of competition and dissension. Paul teaches them by example (see 4:16).

Stage Three: The Warning of Torah (10:1-13). The Corinthians should consider another example, one pertinent to more than this single issue. In a midrash on the exodus and wilderness narratives from Torah (see Exodus 14–34; Numbers 11–20), Paul compares the Christians in Corinth to Israel in the desert. He wants them to consider the earlier story as part of their own. That earlier generation had also been gifted by God (10:1-5) just like the Corinthians (cf. 1:5-7). In spite of its great gifts, however, the desert generation was overthrown (10:5). Paul says they are a warning: what happened to them is a *type* (10:6) of the dangers facing the present Corinthian generation. The stories were written, indeed, to provide such examples (10:11). Israel fell from God's favor despite its gifts precisely because it was not faithful to its call; it did not live appropriately to its identity. Those people were idolaters (Exod. 32:6) and sexually immoral (Num. 25:1-3). They tested the Lord (Num. 21:5) and grumbled (Num. 14:2). There is a lesson here for both strong and weak. To "the strong", a warning: "Let anyone who thinks he stands take warning, lest he fall" (10:12). To "the weak", a consolation: "With the temptation [God] will also provide the way of escape" (10:13).

Stage Four: Freedom Is for Edification (10:14—11:1). Paul now turns to the subject of fellowship meals at idol shrines. Those having knowledge are warned to "shun the worship of idols" (10:14), since they may be involving themselves in ways they cannot anticipate or control. Paul insists that even mere bodily participation can lead to spiritual entanglement. His argument runs thus: just as sharing in the Eucharist involves a participation in the body and blood of Jesus (10:16-17), so consuming food at the table of idols can involve participation in those malevolent spiritual forces associated with pagan practices. Idols may not be real, but the spiritual atmosphere of distortion characteristic of idolatry (cf. Rom. 1:18-32) is real and dangerous. Participants in fellowship meals at idol shrines may thus find themselves unwittingly the partner of demons (10:20-21).

Paul again asserts the essential freedom of "the strong" conscience: no one should be governed utterly by another's perceptions, but one should be governed by one's own informed judgment (10:25-27, 29-30). And if circumstances allow, one must act on that judgment. But if the good of a neighbor is involved, one's freedom is conditioned: "Let no one seek his own good, but the good of his neighbor" (10:24). Such service is not a denial of one's rights, but a self-emptying for the sake of a weak brother or sister (10:28-29) in order to "build them up" (10:23). Paul closes his argument with the simple exhortation to do all for the glory of God (10:31; cf. 6:20), which is shown most clearly by seeking the advantage of others rather than oneself. In Paul, the Corinthians can find both an example of this and a pointer toward a still more fundamental model: "Be imitators of me, as I am of Christ" (11:1).

The World in the Church (1 Corinthians 11–14)

The attitudes that divide the Corinthians in their dealings with the world also affect their common worship when the members "come together as church" (11:18). A community's identity is expressed by its communal activities. In the worship of the spiritual (*pneumatikoi*), their fleshly (*sarkikoi*) attitudes are revealed (see 3:1-3).

The structure and circumstances of the Corinthian assemblies are difficult to reconstruct. We know that the Corinthian Christians came together at least on the first day of the week (16:2), probably in a large room of a household (see 11:22, 34). They celebrated a ritual meal called the Lord's Supper (*kyriakon deipnon*; 11:20). Its cup of blessing and bread of breaking were regarded as a participation (*koinōnia*) in the body and blood of the Messiah (10:16). The meal contained a recital of Jesus' words at the last supper (11:23-25). We don't know how this cultic action was connected to the meals that provided the occasion for abuse (11:21, 33-34). Still less are we able to determine the circumstances of other liturgical activities involving various forms of speech: teaching (14:26), prophesying (14:1), speaking in tongues (14:2), interpretation of tongues (14:13), hymns, revelations, and prayers (14:14, 26).

It is obvious that the congregation was extraordinarily active and perhaps even spectacularly successful in its cultivation of spiritual utterances. Paul admits that it lacks no gift of knowledge or speech (1:5-7). The Corinthians' use of the gifts, however, is as a means of self-aggrandizement rather than as a means of building up (*oikodomē*) community identity. The attitudes of the world have infected the assembly of God. Its members have "gifts of the spirit" but they do not show the deeper wisdom of the "mind of Christ" (2:12-16), which teaches that gifts are for sharing.

They act as though they are blind to the implications of their liturgical behavior for others in the community, for outsiders, and for the identity of the church as a whole. We find in these discussions a tension between individualism and community consciousness, and between enthusiasm and tradition. Paul invokes the tradition of the churches four times in order to correct the Corinthians (11:16, 23; 14:33-36; 15:1-3). His appeal to tradition is especially striking because some of the Corinthians' perceptions undoubtedly came from him. Once again, he must assert the intrinsic value of an activity (e.g., the speaking in tongues, 14:18) while shifting the perception of it from an individual to a communal level. Not the prestige of this person or that but the health of the whole body is Paul's preoccupation. The integrity of the church as church is his concern. This also accounts for his attention to the impression outsiders have of the community (14:20-25; cf. 1 Thess. 4:12). Good order in the assembly is important because the continued stability of the community depends on it, and an untrammeled spontaneity can lead to the subtle enslavement of spiritual manipulation. But it is even more important because the source of all the spiritual gifts is "not a God of confusion, but of peace" (14:33).

THE PRAYER AND PROPHECY OF WOMEN (11:2-16)

The extraordinary complexity and confusion of this passage is itself the most important clue to its interpretation. Paul begins to commend the Corinthians for holding to traditions (11:2) but then launches into ways they do not, beginning with one that apparently bothered him emotionally: the way women were prophesying and praying in the assembly. This is obviously something that is happening, for no one would struggle as grimly as Paul does here against a mere hypothesis. Nor is there any doubt that ecstatic utterance is at issue. In 14:34-36, Paul says that women are to be silent in the assembly, but that passage suggests a context of teaching, an activity culturally associated with males, particularly in Judaism. Here, it is not teaching but the charismatic gifts of prayer and prophecy that are at issue. Paul has no problem with women doing these things; the gifts, after all, come from the Spirit. But the manner of their performance upsets him.

Unfortunately, like so much in this passage, the precise nature of their offense is not clear. Did they pray or prophesy without veils over their heads? Or did they, like mantic prophetesses, unbraid their hair and let it fly freely while they spoke? We cannot tell. In Paul's eyes, however, a fundamental line of social decency has been crossed. His position was difficult. He was convinced, as they were, that in Christ, there is neither female nor male (Gal. 3:28), and he was not eager to set external constraints on prophets (14:32). But whether or not the lack of a veil suggested insubordination, or the unbraiding of the hair implied pagan prophecy, Paul is disturbed.

Paul wants to establish order and decency in the liturgical assembly. Like everybody in his age, he understood social order as intimately connected to cosmic order. As a male in a hierarchically structured society, therefore, he invokes a series of arguments: the cosmic hierarchy of female-male-Christ (11:3); the order of creation, with male first and female second (11:7-8); an obscure reference to the angelic role in worship (11:10); and Hellenistic social sensitivities (11:5, 14-15).

The intrinsic weakness of Paul's position is indicated by the number of arguments he must invoke and his constant need to qualify them. He does not really believe, for example, that in Christ women are fundamentally subordinate to men (cf. 11:11). He is for once unable to argue from first principles to social behavior, for the very good reason in this case that the social norm has nothing to do with Christian first principles. It is just a matter of custom and customary perceptions. Paul at last recognizes that this is the only argument left to him: "If anyone is disposed to be contentious, we recognize no other practice, nor do the churches of God" (11:16).

ABUSES AT THE LORD'S SUPPER (11:17-34)

Once more, the exact nature of the problem is not completely clear. Because "each one goes ahead with his own meal," Paul says that some are filled while others go hungry (11:21). Are people bringing their own food and proceeding without waiting for the ritual actions that join them together? Are their uneven resources being selfishly and privately consumed, so that not everyone has enough? Or are those who provide the meal taking larger portions for themselves and their clients, like patrons of clubs and cults? We cannot be sure. This much, though, is clear: Paul perceives that the Christian sacred meal is being infiltrated by the attitudes of the world (11:20). Divisions between people on the basis of wealth or position threaten the common identity of the church. Paul berates those responsible for "humiliating those who have nothing," and by so doing, "despising the church of God" (11:22). Their party spirit is contrary to the very notion of church.

Paul responds with his most extensive and explicit citation of Jesus' words, introduced by the technical language of scribal tradition: "I received . . . what I also delivered to you" (11:23). The words are close to the Synoptic version of Jesus' last supper, providing an important clue to the development of the gospel traditions. Paul agrees with Luke 22:19 by including the command "Do this in memory of me," but he attaches it to both loaf and cup (11:24-25). He also makes explicit the connection of this broken bread to the crucifixion: "You proclaim the Lord's death until he comes" (11:26). By the words "until he comes," he reminds them that the ritual life of the church is framed by the "already" of the death and resurrection and the "not yet" of the Parousia. In such a context, the liturgical cry with which he ends the letter would have been most natural: "Lord, come [*maranatha*]" (16:22).

Paul draws a direct theological and behavioral inference from the tradition (11:27). By sharing loaf and cup Christians participate in the body and blood of the Lord; this is axiomatic (see 10:16). And if that sharing establishes them as "the body of the Lord" (10:17), those who are contemptuous of other members of the assembly also profane "the body and blood of the Lord" (11:27). Everyone, therefore, should "discern the body," lest eating and drinking lead to judgment (11:28-29). The consequences Paul draws for failure to do this are obscure (11:30-32), but his main point is clear: when the Corinthians "come together as church" they do not eat a worldly meal (they can eat that at home [11:22, 34]), but they enter into a ritual fellowship meal that establishes the community as "the body of the Lord." The worldly attitudes of self-aggrandizement and rivalry are not only inappropriate, they destroy the church and call down God's judgment upon the perpetrators (11:34).

THE SPIRITUAL GIFTS (12:1—14:40)

In the Corinthians' use of their gifts of speech, the attitudes of elitism, rivalry, and individualism are painfully present. To grasp Paul's concern and argument, it is necessary to appreciate how active the pneumatic phenomena were in the congregation, as well as how highly esteemed such forms of ecstasy were in the Hellenistic world. The form of prophecy called mantic was particularly favored. It was thought to result from a direct inspiration, a virtual possession of the psyche by the divine Spirit, leading to *enthusiasmos*. Rapt in ecstasy, the prophetess or prophet cried out in unintelligible speech, which required translation and interpretation (see above, chap. 1).

Just this form of spiritual utterance seems to be what the Corinthians called "tongues." And consonant with the views of the ancient world, they considered such ecstatic babbling to be the highest manifestation of the Spirit. Teaching and the rational discourse Paul calls prophecy seem to have been regarded lightly by them. With their characteristic capacity for making gifts into badges of their own worth, the Corinthians ranked the gifts, declaring that the sign of a truly spiritual person (*pneumatikos*) was the manifestation of tongues (see 14:22). Paul does not challenge the divine origin of this gift, and claims to possess it himself (14:18). But he wants the Corinthians to begin to "understand the gifts given them by God" (2:12) within the context of their community function.

He warns them first that not all "spiritual powers" are necessarily good. When they had been pagans, they also had been caught up in rapture (*agomai*), but this had only resulted in their alienation (*apagomai*; 12:2). He wants them to understand, therefore, that he is not talking about spiritual realities (*ta pneumatika*; 12:1), but gifts from God (*ta charismata*; 12:4). The first work of God's Holy Spirit is to bring a human being into relationship with the Lord, enabling him or her to say, "Jesus is Lord." Any impulse that denies that relationship cannot be from God (12:3).

Since the Spirit they have received comes from the God who called them into community, the diverse manifestations of this Spirit serve functions within that community. Paul insists on two reciprocal aspects of this community context. First, since all the gifts come from the same God, there is a fundamental unity and equality between them (12:4-11). All the gifts have been given for the common good (12:7; cf. 6:12), not by the random selection of an impersonal force but by the direction of a personal spirit, the activity of the living God (12:11). Second, within this unity there is a proper diversity of function within the church, which Paul here explicitly identifies as the "body of Christ." As eating the same loaf and drinking the same cup made them "one body" (10:16-17), so here the drinking of one spirit in baptism makes them one body (12:13). The parts of a human body exist in mutual interdependence (12:14-26), and therefore so should the members of the church: "You are the body of Christ and individually members of it" (12:27). All the functions are required for the body to be complete; there is no place for comparison or conflict among them.

Chapter 13 is not a digression but serves the parenetic function of presenting Paul as a model of "seeking the higher gifts" (12:31; cf. 9:1-27). The highest expression of the Spirit is self-sacrificing love (*agapē*). In contrast to passionate love (*eros*), a drive that seeks the other in order to fulfill the self, this *agapē* means having the disposition toward others that God had first toward them. It transcends all differentiating gifts; they represent the partial whereas it is the perfection (13:10). This is because *agapē* is the essential articulation of the life of the Spirit, which is to say, the life of God. The gifts of speech are transitory; only *agape⁻* will be the bond between God and humans in the life to come, when "we shall know even as we have been known" (13:12). Without *agapē*, the other gifts are meaningless (13:1-3). With it, the other gifts are ordered toward mutual edification, and life together can become "life for the other" (13:4-7). This is the "more excellent way" that Paul demonstrates in his apostolic ministry (13:1).

In Paul's discussion of the separate gifts, he concentrates only on tongues and prophecy. His preference for prophecy is plain. An utterance in tongues is ecstatic and unintelligible, requiring interpretation. As a mode of prayer, it can glorify God and "build up" the one who prays (14:4), but it can also become self-absorbing and meaningless: the church is not built up by it. Prophecy, in contrast, is a rational mode of speech that, even when a revelation, is intelligible to all by the way it addresses the community with the demands of the gospel. Paul prefers prophecy because it engages the mind (14:14) and edifies the community (14:4). In fact, he reverses the slogan of the elitists who had claimed tongues as a sign of believers. With a midrash on Isa. 28:11-12 ("By mean of foreign tongues and by the lips of foreigners will I speak to this people and even then they will not listen to me"), Paul shows that tongues can actually be a sign of unbelief (14:21-22). That such was the case with the Corinthian elitists is clearly implied.

Prophecy, however, is a sign that calls people to belief, and builds on the foundation of Christ first laid by the apostolic preaching (see 3:10-15; 12:28). If outsiders come to the assembly and hear only tongues they would naturally identify the church as one more form of a Hellenistic cult involving mantic prophecy; they would say, "You are raving [*mainesthe*]." But if they hear prophecy, they would be moved to say, "God is among you" (14:25). Paul therefore demands responsibility, maturity, and thought (14:20) from the Corinthians. Even in the context of spiritual worship, the whole community must exercise judgment: "Let all discern" (14:29). The prophets should control their utterances (14:32), speech should be orderly and in turn (14:26-31), and women should not teach publicly (14:34-36). Everything should be done with an eye to edification (14:26) but also "decently and in order" (14:40).

The Church and the Kingdom (1 Corinthians 15)

Paul's long and carefully constructed treatment of the resurrection is neither an afterthought nor unconnected to the Corinthian problems. In it, he provides the theological underpinning for his practical directions throughout the letter. The arrogance and self-aggrandizement of some of the Corinthians are based on the conviction that they are already in full possession of God's life. They know God (8:2; 13:12); they have all the spiritual gifts (1:5-7); they are mature (2:6; 14:20) and "spiritual people" (3:1); they are strong (10:12); they are already filled, rich, and reigning in the kingdom (4:8).

From that perception comes their contempt for others who appear to be less well endowed, and their neglect of their own human entanglements. Because they are already perfect, there is no need for discernment in their behavior.

When Paul reminds them of the "fundamental" (15:3) message of the resurrection, he does more than recall historical facts. He reminds them of the structure of their existence "by which you are *being saved* if you hold it fast" (15:2), making that salvation both progressive and conditional. He needs to remind them of the pattern of the Spirit's work, which they see in Jesus. Jesus first died, then rose to a new life (15:3-4), becoming in fact "life-giving Spirit" (15:45). Just as with Jesus there was first the sowing of the mortal body, *then* the spiritual (*to pneumatikon*; 15:44), so with them: the full reality of the spiritual life is not now in the flesh but only in their resurrection.

More significant still, Jesus' resurrection and the outpouring of his spirit are not yet the fulfillment of God's work. The Corinthians are still in the in-between period. Jesus is only the first fruits from the dead (15:20); death must still be overcome for all others (15:21). Everything has not yet been brought into subjection to the Lord (15:28), and therefore Jesus cannot at this time hand the kingdom over to the Father. Only then "comes the end" (15:24). The point of this is clear: the Corinthians cannot be now "ruling" (4:8), for there is as yet no kingdom of God. They are like fools sitting on fantasy thrones.

Paul orients them fully toward the future. If the present were already the fulfillment, then they would be the most miserable of creatures. Their grandeur is self-deceptive made possible only by ignoring the fact of death. Indeed, people in the community continue to die (11:30). If there is no future resurrection, if the present were all there was, then they would be fools to suffer for their faith (15:29-32). Paul now reverses the argument: if Jesus is the pattern of their life before God (2:16; 11:1) and if there is no final resurrection for all Christians, then, by implication Jesus did not rise from the dead (15:13-16). And if he did not rise, then he could not be the life-giving Spirit: all their gifts would be absent and their faith a delusion (15:14). And if that were so, then they would still be in their sins (15:17) and those who have already died would be utterly lost (15:18). There is a sharp point being made here: they have negated in their lives the very gospel they hold so dear in words. Paul suggests that precisely their neglect of the future and their selfish grasping after their present gifts leaves them open to such sin: "Come to your right mind, and sin no more. For some have no knowledge of God. I say this to your shame" (15:34).

When Paul speaks of the future life, he must shift to metaphor (15:35-49), since these matters are also unknown to him (cf. 13:12). His message is nevertheless clear: "Flesh and blood cannot inherit the kingdom of God" (15:50). We are reminded of his other "kingdom" formulation: "The unrighteous will not inherit the kingdom of God" (6:9). For Paul, there is an infinite qualitative difference between the existence of all created beings, however sanctified, and the Holy God. Although the Corinthians share in the Spirit, they are still merely human. The kingdom, however, necessitates their sharing in God's glory (15:42-43, 49), and for this they must be radically changed: "We shall not all sleep, but we shall all be changed" (15:51). The required transformation, furthermore, is not only metaphysical but moral as well (15:34, 58). The future kingdom will be glorious (15:51-58), but the Corinthians are not yet there. Indeed, this is precisely the function of the Spirit's work among them: to change them in preparation for their sharing in God's glory.

The Second Letter to the Corinthians

Second Corinthians has many major historical and literary problems, making the reconstruction of the situation faced by Paul more difficult than in the case of 1 Corinthians.

It is difficult, first of all, to piece together what transpired between the writing of the two letters. Although Paul's relations with the community were strained, he had planned to visit it after passing through Macedonia (1 Cor. 16:5), in order to pick up the collection on the way to Jerusalem (1 Cor. 16:3). In the meantime, he had anticipated sending Timothy, expecting his early return (1 Cor. 16:10-11; cf. 4:17).

There is no lack of biographical data in 2 Corinthians, but the sequence of events remains elusive. In 1:8, Paul refers to an "affliction" he had experienced in Asia, which threatened his life (1:9). Was this in any way connected to his "fighting the beasts in Ephesus" (1 Cor. 15:32)? In 1:16, he speaks of a visit that he had planned to make to the Corinthians in connection with his trip to Macedonia (the same itinerary as in 1 Cor. 16:3-5) but that he had called off since he did not wish another "painful visit" (2:1). But what visit is this? He then speaks of a "letter written out of much affliction and anguish of heart and with many tears" (2:4). Is this 1 Corinthians or another letter? It certainly caused considerable distress (2 Cor. 2:5-11; 7:8-13).

In 2 Cor. 2:12, Paul begins to relate his actual movements rather than his plans. He had gone to Macedonia not through Corinth but by way of Troas. Not finding his delegate Titus in Troas, he did not linger but went straight on to Macedonia. Here the travelogue stops momentarily. It is resumed in 7:5, where we find Paul recounting the comfort he had received in Macedonia by the arrival there of Titus, who bore Paul news of the Corinthians' zeal for him (7:7). At this point, therefore, he appears reconciled with them (7:6-16).

In 8:6, Paul says that Titus had already begun work for the collection among them, and in 8:16-18, he writes that he is about to send Titus and "another brother" to complete that work. There is, however, a slight but troubling shift in 9:3-5, where Paul indicates that he is sending "brethren" for the collection. Is he simply collapsing together Titus and the "brethren" (cf. 8:23)? Things get even murkier when we find in 12:18 that Paul had already sent Titus and "the brother" to Corinth to work for the collection. Is this a reference to the earlier (8:6) or the later (8:16-18) visit of the delegate? Finally,

Paul says in 12:14, "Here for a third time I am ready to come to you," whereas we would have expected this to be only his second visit.

It is not impossible to establish a sequence, although some filling in of spaces is required. Specifically, we must postulate a second "painful" visit to the community (2:1), and correlate it with at least three other factors: the excommunication of an erring member of the community, Paul's collection plans, and the popularity of other teachers. We remember that already in 1 Corinthians Paul threatened to come "with a rod," if the community did not heed him (1 Cor. 4:21). That threat immediately preceded his command to excommunicate the brother living in incest (1 Cor. 5:1-5). It is plausible to suppose that Paul did come to the community, did demand obedience in this matter, and was rebuffed. This would obviously be a "painful visit." He could then have returned to Ephesus and penned the "letter in tears," which once more demanded obedience. The letter, probably delivered by Titus who went to Corinth on business for the collection, worked. It caused resentment, however, precisely because Paul had been forced to exert his authority so blatantly. The growing estrangement between Paul and the community cannot have been decreased by the demand for money made by Titus. And Paul's authority over this church was still more tenuous because the Corinthians were increasingly fascinated with other apostles, whether those they had known earlier (see 1 Cor. 1:12) or newer visitors who were more impressive than Paul and were viewed as being straightforward in their demands for support, not "devious" like him. Paul therefore writes this letter at a point when he wants the Corinthians to cooperate in his great effort of reconciliation, while he himself is uncertain of his reconciliation with them!

This historical reconstruction must remain tentative because of the serious reservations that are held by many scholars concerning the literary integrity of 2 Corinthians. They surmise that our canonical document is not a single composition but an edited composite of several notes by Paul written at various times. No manuscript evidence supports this hypothesis, but a number of seams in the letter appear to some readers incompatible with its being a unitary composition. These scholars detect a striking difference in tone, for example, between chapters 1–9, which are irenic and conciliatory, and chapters 10–13, which are polemical and defensive. Chapters 10–13, in fact, are sometimes thought to be the "letter written in tears" sent to the Corinthians *before* chapters 1–9. But since that letter dealt with an act of discipline, whereas 2 Corinthians 10–13 makes no mention of any disciplinary action, the suggestion is not convincing.

Even within the first nine chapters, moreover, there seem to be gaps. The detailed itinerary of 1:15—2:13, for example, breaks off without warning, only to be picked up in 7:5 as though nothing had intervened. The small segment 6:14—7:1, furthermore, appears to contain non-Pauline vocabulary and thought patterns, as well as a break in the coherence and natural sequence of 6:13—7:2. Is this a pre-Pauline or even anti-Pauline fragment interpolated by a later editor? Finally, chapters 8 and 9 deal with the collection, but chapter 9 begins with such an independent thought—"Now it is superfluous for me to write to you about the offering for the saints" (9:1)—that it seems difficult to regard this as a continuation of the argument of chapter 8. That has led some to see in these two chapters separate notes on the collection.

Second Corinthians is therefore commonly regarded as an edited collection of Pauline letter fragments. The case is not, however, absolutely conclusive. The shift in tone between chapters 9 and 10 can be accounted for on rhetorical rather than editorial grounds. The disparity between chapters 8 and 9 is not so great as it first appears. The broken itinerary is difficult but not impossible to explain. Even in what appears to be a clear instance of interpolation (6:14-7:1), the insertion may have been done by Paul himself or, at least under his supervision. (In light of the great cost of writing materials and the effort involved, it would not have been unusual for an author to make an insertion into a letter rather than rewrite it.) If, in fact, he wrote something like this in his "lost letter" to the Corinthians, warning them to avoid immoral associations (see 1 Cor. 5:9), it is not impossible that he used it again here to make a definite point: if the Corinthians reject him in favor of other teachers, it is tantamount to "yoking themselves with Belial."

Still, in view of the literary complexity of the writing, it is prudent not to insist on a sequential development of argument. Nor is such a linear reading required in order to make good sense of the occasion for the letter. Whatever the precise historical situation, this much is clear: Paul's relationship with the Corinthians is shaky. They are more attracted to other teachers than to him. The apostolic work of the collection has only exacerbated the tension, making the Corinthians think Paul is defrauding them. Whether Paul wrote one or a series of letters, he is clearly a man trying to build a bridge across a rapidly widening gulf. His task is therefore one of reconciliation. Even as he seeks to advance his own great project of reconciliation with the Jerusalem church (in the collection), he must try to reestablish peace with his own community.

For Paul, to think about reconciliation means thinking about the nature and style of his apostleship. It is possible, then, to see the three major sections of this letter as addressing that issue from slightly different angles: apostleship negatively defined, in his self-defense (10–13); apostleship positively defined, in the ministry of the new covenant (2:14—7:4); and apostleship symbolized in the collection (8–9).

Apostleship Negatively Defined: Paul and the Superapostles (2 Corinthians 10–13)

It may finally be impossible to determine the historical identity of Paul's rivals in Corinth. Were they representatives from Jerusalem claiming superior apostolic credentials and fidelity to the commands of Jesus? Was their teaching significantly different from his? Our knowledge comes only from Paul's self-defense, which is impassioned and polemical. Where Paul claims a plus we may be tempted to attribute a minus in the rivals and thus construct a portrait through mirror reading. In the end, however, it will be a portrait only of Paul's presentation, which is not necessarily fair or accurate. There is no reason to regard his rivals as representing an organized Jewish-Christian resistance to Paul's ministry, for the issue of observance of Torah never enters the discussion. Nor is it certain that they had a distinct Christology, which construed Jesus as a Divine Man in the tradition of a Hellenistic "wonder-worker," although Paul does say, in 11:4,

> If someone comes and preaches another Jesus than the one we preached, or if you receive a different spirit from the one you received, or if you accept a different gospel from the one you accepted, you submit to it readily enough.

It is not at all clear how much of this is rhetoric and how much reflects reality.

The major issue in the debate is apostolic style and rival claims to authority over the Corinthians. Paul insists on a direct connection between his style of ministry and the kerygma he proclaims. We cannot assume that the rivals make the same connection. Indeed, it is somewhat misleading to think of them as opponents, since Paul does not directly attack them, except in the slander of 11:13-15. His anger and frustration are directed more at the Corinthian congregation, which is so easily led from sobriety and stability by the attraction of the spectacular. Paul's perception of his rivals is important mostly for leading us to his perception of his own ministry as an apostle.

Paul says his rivals claim to be apostles of Christ, as he is. He dismisses this claim with direct slander: they are in reality "false apostles, deceitful workers, disguising themselves as apostles of Christ" (11:13). But he begrudgingly admits their surface plausibility, for he calls them superapostles (*hyperapostoloi*; 11:5, 12:11). They claim a Jewish pedigree sufficiently impressive to arouse Paul's defenses (11:22). They engage in self-commendation and measure themselves over against others (10:12). They also travel with letters of recommendation from churches to validate their authority (3:1). They claim to work on the same basis Paul does, preaching the gospel for free (11:12), but they accept money for their preaching (11:7-10). They are peddlers of God's word (2:17), and they tamper with it (4:2). They are, in short, apostles of churches, not of Christ.

Some other characteristics of his rivals may be guessed from the emphases of Paul's self-presentation—the things he feels the need to stress in his comparison with them. They seem to have been rhetorically gifted, placing great stock in their knowledge and speech (10:10; 11:6). They are able to work miracles to back up their claims (12:12). They have mystical experiences (12:1-5). They are spiritual athletes who have endured great hardships as "servants of Christ" (11:23-27). In all these things, they "boast" (11:21).

In response, Paul first matches them boast for boast. Everything they claim, he is and has. He does not need letters from churches, for the Corinthians are a letter "written by the spirit in the heart" (3:2-3). Or at least they should be. In fact, Paul knows they are turning away from him, and he rebukes them for forcing him to sing his own praises: "I ought to have been commended by you" (12:11). Ultimately, however, Paul and his co-workers do not need certification from any human source. Their competence comes from God (3:5). Paul's authority comes not from humans but from God (10:8, 18); he "belongs to Christ" (10:7). He is weak in speech but not deficient in knowledge (11:6). As they can testify, he has worked among them the signs of an apostle: wonders and mighty works (12:12). His Jewish background is better than any his rivals can claim (11:22). His visions are more impressive, for he has "heard things that cannot be told, which a person may not utter" (12:1-5). And if they boast of hardships endured for God, he has an unparalleled catalogue of sufferings. He is truly a "servant of Christ" (11:23-27).

Paul is well aware of the delicate position in which this boasting puts him. In his theological lexicon, boasting is a mode of self-assertion he everywhere condemns as the epitome of "fleshly" behavior (see 1 Cor. 1:29; 3:21; 4:7; 5:6; 13:3). By so exposing his "divine jealousy" for the Corinthians to see, Paul appears "foolish" (11:1, 16-18). But he does not stop boasting. This is because he is really boasting of the work of God in him, rather than of his own human capacities. He repeats here his principle from 1 Cor. 1:31: "Let him who boasts boast in the Lord, for it is not the person who commends their self who is accepted, but the individual whom the Lord commends" (10:17-18; cf. Jer. 9:24). And God has commended Paul, so that his boasting is in effect a praise of God. To deny his qualifications would be to deny God's work. This, indeed, is what so upsets Paul about the Corinthians' fascination with other teachers: if they dismiss Paul, they also dismiss the adequacy of their experience of God, which Paul mediated to them. They reject their own past by choosing a Christianity of show rather than of service. And because his gospel is one of service, Paul's greatest boast is in his weakness: "If I must boast, I will boast in the things that show my weakness" (11:30; 12:5, 9-10).

Paul stresses his weakness to show that it is really God's power at work, not human prowess. He attaches this perception directly to his Christology in 13:3-4:

> Since you desire proof that Christ is speaking in me, he is not weak in dealing with you, but is powerful in you. For he was crucified in weakness but lives by the power of God. For we are weak in him, but in dealing with you we shall live with him by the power of God.

In 1 Corinthians, Paul taught that the pattern of exchange between wisdom and foolishness, strength and weakness, was the way of living together according to the "mind of Christ." Now, he demonstrates that pattern in his apostolic style: "We are glad when we are weak and you are strong" (13:9).

Apostleship Positively Defined: Treasure in Earthen Vessels
(2 Corinthians 2:14—7:4)

This long section of the letter, which bears some marks of having been worked out separately either as a distinct letter or as a midrashic argument, describes the apostolic ministry of Paul and his co-workers. It is dominated by the contrast between the glory of the message and the inadequacy of the messengers.

The ministry itself comes directly from God, according to 1:21-22:

> It is God who establishes us with you in Christ, and has commissioned us; he has put his seal upon us and given us his Spirit in our hearts as a guarantee.

The mission can therefore be described in terms of glory and power. It is like a triumphant march of conquerors (see also 1 Cor. 4:9). The apostles, however, do not lead the procession. It is God in Christ "leading us in triumph" (2:14). The images here are difficult to sort out, but the essential point is that the gospel is a message that calls for a decision with life-and-death consequences (2:15-16).

In Paul's insistence that an apostle is commissioned by God rather than by human assemblies with their "letters of recommendation" (3:1), his language moves toward his major metaphor of the ministry: Paul does not have letters "written on tablets of stone" but ones written "with the spirit of the living God . . . on tablets of human hearts" (3:3). The opposition in 3:6 between spirit and writing, and in 3:3 between stone and heart, becomes a contrast between covenants, perhaps suggested by the same sort of contrast in Jer. 31:31-34. According to 3:6,

> [God] has made us competent to be ministers of a new covenant, not in a *written code*, but in the *spirit*; for the written code *kills*, but the spirit *gives life*.

For Paul, as we shall see again in Galatians, the code kills because by it Jesus is condemned, and the Spirit gives life because by it Jesus was raised. In a complex midrash on Exod. 34:29-35, Paul opposes the glory of this new covenant in Christ to the old covenant under Moses. "Glory" in this passage obviously bears the connotation of "radiance," as well as that of "presence" (3:7-11). The revelation of God in Christ is so much more powerful than in Torah, that only in its light can Torah itself be understood (3:12-16). Only by "turning to the Lord," that is, to Jesus, can the veil of blindness be removed and the "dispensation of condemnation" become a figure for the "dispensation of righteousness" (3:9). Paul does not speak idly when he calls his midrash on Exodus "bold" (3:12), for it makes him the superior of Moses. Moses had to veil his face to hide from the Israelites the fading glory (3:13; but cf. Exod. 34:35). Such is not the case for Paul and his co-workers, who (3:18) with unveiled face, beholding the glory of the Lord, are being changed into his likeness from one degree of glory to another. For this comes from the Lord, who is Spirit.

The glory of Paul's gospel, therefore, comes not from rhetoric or worldly wisdom but from the presence of God's power working through it. The Spirit of the Lord is working to reveal "the glory of Christ, who is the likeness of God" (4:4). The same God who called light out of darkness (Gen. 1:3) "has shone in our hearts to give the light of the glory of God in the face of Christ" (4:6).

Paul does not deduce from the glory of the message that the messenger should also be glorified. Indeed, he draws an absolute distinction between the power of the gospel and the dignity of the minister: "What we preach is not ourselves, but Jesus Christ as Lord, with ourselves as your servants for Jesus' sake" (4:5). The message is powerful, the messengers are not: "Who is sufficient for these things?" (2:16). The messenger's weakness serves to illustrate that it is God at work and not simply human skill. The apostles are like clay pots, through whose cracks the divine light shines to enlighten others (4:7). And like such disposable pots, they are rejected and afflicted (4:8-9). In them is the paradox of Jesus' death and resurrection found in a new bodily expression (4:10-11): "Death is at work in us, but life in you" (4:12).

The apostles hope for a future glory; they do not enjoy it now. They know that "he who raised the Lord Jesus will raise us also with Jesus and bring us with you into his presence" (4:14). And they are convinced that the present suffering is meaningful for that future (4:17). But in the meantime, they feel the anguish of being pulled between the desire for God and the need to serve others (5:1-10). The apostles find their lives defined by those two relationships. Because of the gift of love given them by God in Christ, they pour themselves out for their brethren: "It is all for your sake" (4:15). In doing this, they replicate the pattern of Jesus' life and death for others (5:14-15):

> For the love of Christ controls us, because we are convinced that one has died for all; therefore all have died. And he died for all, that those who live might live no longer for themselves but for him who for their sake died and was raised.

So revolutionary is this new life given by the Spirit that it amounts to more than a new covenant; it is a "new creation" (5:17), which demands viewing human life in an altogether different way. The Spirit shapes them into the likeness of Jesus (3:18) who himself reveals the image of God (4:4). No longer is life to be defined by individual happiness and fulfillment, but by service; no longer by individual rights leading to alienation, but by self-emptying leading to reconciliation. The model for this is as follows: "In Christ, God was reconciling the world to himself" (5:19), and it is manifested thus: "For our sake he made him to be sin who knew no sin, so that by him we might become the righteousness of God" (5:21).

Paul's style of ministry is therefore based on the pattern of God's reconciling work. The crucified and raised Messiah is the paradigm for ministry, which embodies in the world its paradoxical revelation of God's power. When Paul characterizes that style (6:1-10), he falls naturally into the same pattern of exchange (6:9-10):

> ... dying, and behold we live; as punished and yet not killed; as sorrowful, yet always rejoicing; as poor, yet making many rich; as having nothing, and yet possessing everything.

The Apostolic Fellowship: The Collection (2 Corinthians 8–9)

Paul's fund-raising project for the Jerusalem church was a major preoccupation of his ministry (see Rom. 15:25-29; 1 Cor. 16:1-4; Gal. 2:10). Despite the fact that his asking the Corinthians for money exacerbated the alienation between them, he continued to seek their cooperation. The Corinthians saw his collection as a surreptitious way of exploiting them for personal gain. Despite his care to avoid misunderstanding (8:20-24), his sending of delegates for money was misconstrued (12:16-18). His rivals may well have seized on Paul's "inconsistent" monetary policy as a sign of his lacking proper apostolic credentials. Even Paul's boast of preaching to them freely (1 Cor. 9:15-18) is now twisted to appear as a lack of love for this church (2 Cor. 11:7-11). It is more than a little ironic that as Paul tried to establish a worldwide reconciliation, he was stymied by a local alienation. The importance of this project for Paul is indicated by his persistence in it even in the face of opposition and rejection.

The collection was so important in part simply because it was a response to need (Gal. 2:10). For the first Christians, as for other Jews, the mandate of sharing possessions with the needy was binding on all (9:12). But Paul also wanted the collection to serve a symbolic function: to establish a reconciliation between his gentile communities and the Jerusalem church. This reconciliation was now the more needed, since Paul's ministry had stirred considerable hostility. Paul does not stand on his "rights" as an apostle to the Gentiles, but "empties himself out" in this complicated, arduous, and thankless enterprise. He asks his Gentile communities to do the same.

If the Corinthian church participated in the collection, they would return thanks to God for all that they had been given by him (9:12; cf. 4:15). They would also fulfill the Hellenistic ideals of friendship by establishing a fellowship (*koinēnia*) with the Jerusalem church (8:4; 9:13) and an equality (*isotēs*) that is reciprocal in nature (8:14). This reciprocity is expressed more fully in Romans: the Gentiles had received spiritual things (*ta pneumatika*) from the Jewish Christians; now they owed them material things (*ta sarkika*) in return (Rom. 15:27). The same principle is found in 1 Cor. 9:11: "If we have sown spiritual things [*ta pneumatika*] among you, is it too much to reap your material things [*ta sarkika*]?" Here, the material generosity of the Corinthians is answered by the Jewish Christians' prayer for them (1 Cor. 9:14).

Paul does not call for a structured sharing of possessions. He does not demand a contribution as an obligation or "temple tax" (8:12; 9:5). He has, however, engaged in some competitive rhetoric that now threatens to embarrass him. He had told the Macedonians that the Corinthians were extremely generous in their pledges (9:2), just as he now boasts of the Macedonians' generosity in order to stimulate the Corinthians (8:2-5). The Macedonians have fulfilled their pledges, but the Corinthians have not, and Paul might appear a liar (9:3-4).

More than his personal embarrassment is at stake. Paul sees giving as a demand of the Christian life. Sharing is an act of obedience to the gospel (9:13). The reason is that when Christians "give out of poverty" (8:2), they express with the body language of material possessions the pattern of "life for others" that Paul has been trying to engender among them. They have the opportunity to show toward other communities the attitudes he has been urging them to have toward each other: gifts are not for clinging and boasting but for sharing freely to build up others. The pattern for this is again found ultimately in the "mind of Christ" (2 Cor. 8:9):

> For you know the grace (or, gift: *charis*) of our Lord Jesus Christ, that though he was rich, yet for your sake he became poor, so that by his poverty you might become rich.

Did the Corinthians reconcile with Paul and respond? We have two signs that they did. First, when writing to the Romans, Paul later reports: "For Macedonia *and Achaia* have been pleased to make some contribution for the poor among the saints in Jerusalem" (Rom. 15:26). Second, they preserved his letters.

Study Questions

1. What factors created divisions in the church at Corinth?

2. What was the perspective of those Paul calls "the strong"?

3. What point does Paul make with his metaphor of "the body of Christ" in 1 Corinthians 12?

4. In 1 Corinthians 8–12, what is the issue Paul addresses, and how does he resolve it?

5. How does Paul correct the abuses of the Lord's Supper in the Corinthian church?

6. Why can 2 Corinthians properly be called "a letter of reconciliation"?

7. Why do many scholars think of a 2 Corinthians as an "edited composite"?

8. How does the Corinthian correspondence show us the importance of the "Jerusalem collection" for Paul?

Bibliographical Note

On the city of Corinth, see D. Engels, *Roman Corinth: An Alternative Model for the Classical City* (Chicago: Chicago Univ. Press, 1990); and J. Murphy-O'Connor, *St. Paul's Corinth: Texts and Archaeology* (Collegeville, Minn.: The Liturgical Press, 1983). Helpful for the historical, social, and literary setting are J. K. Chow, *Patronage and Power: A Study of Social Networks in Corinth* (JSNTSup, 75; Sheffield: Sheffield Academic Press, 1992); D. G. Horrell, *The Social Ethos of the Corinthian Correspondence: Interests and Ideology from 1 Corinthians to 1 Clement* (Edinburgh: T. & T. Clark, 1996); A. J. Malherbe, *Social Aspects of Early Christianity*, 2nd ed. (Philadelphia: Fortress Press, 1983), 71–91; P. Marshall, *Enmity in Corinth: Social Conventions in Paul's Relations with the Corinthians* (WUNT, 2/23; Tübingen: J. C. B. Mohr [Siebeck], 1987); W. A. Meeks, *The First Urban Christians: The Social World of the Apostle Paul* (New Haven: Yale Univ. Press, 1983); and G. Theissen, *The Social Setting of Pauline Christianity: Essays on Corinth*, trans. J. H. Schultz (Philadelphia: Fortress Press, 1981).

On the multiple profiles of the community and its outlook, see D. J. Doughty, "The Presence and Future of Salvation in Corinth," *ZNW* 66 (1975): 61–90; R. A. Horsley, "'How Can Some of You Say There Is No Resurrection of the Dead?' Spiritual Elitism in Corinth," *NovT* 20 (1978): 203–40; D. B. Martin, *The Corinthian Body* (New Haven: Yale Univ. Press, 1995); B. A. Pearson, *The Pneumatikos-Psychikos Terminology in I Corinthians* (SBLDS, 12; Missoula, Mont.: Scholars Press, 1973); W. Schmithals, *Gnosticism in Corinth*, trans. J. Steely (Nashville: Abingdon Press, 1971); and A. C. Thiselton, "Realized Eschatology in Corinth," *NTS* 24 (1977–78): 520–26.

For the immediate occasion of 1 Corinthians, see N. A. Dahl, "Paul and the Church at Corinth According to I Corinthians 1:10–4:21," in his *Studies in Paul* (Minneapolis: Augsburg Pub. House, 1977), 40–61; J. C. Hurd, Jr., *The Origin of I Corinthians* (London: SPCK, 1965); M. M. Mitchell, *Paul and the Rhetoric of Reconciliation: An Exegetical Investigation of the Language and Composition of 1 Corinthians* (Louisville: Westminster/John Knox Press, 1991); and S. M. Pogoloff, *Logos and Sophia: The Rhetorical Situation of 1 Corinthians* (SBLDS, 134; Atlanta: Scholars Press, 1992).

Consideration of special issues in the first letter can be found in M. de. Boer, "The Composition of 1 Corinthians," *NTS* 40 (1994): 229–45; A. R. Brown, *The Cross & Human Transformation: Paul's Apocalyptic Word in 1 Corinthians* (Minneapolis: Fortress Press, 1995); W. Deming, *Paul on Marriage and Celibacy: The Hellenistic Background of 1 Corinthians 7* (SNTSMS, 83; Cambridge: Cambridge Univ. Press, 1995); B.

Fiore, "'Covert Allusion' in I Corinthians 1–4," *CBQ* 47 (1985): 85–102; C. Forbes, *Prophecy and Inspired Speech in Early Christianity and Its Hellenistic Environment* (WUNT, 2/75; Tübingen: J. C. B. Mohr [Siebeck], 1995); T. W. Gillespie, *The First Christian Theologians: A Study in Early Christian Prophecy* (Grand Rapids: Eerdmans, 1994); P. D. Gooch, *Dangerous Food: 1 Corinthians 8–10 in Its Context* (Waterloo, Ont.: Wilfrid Laurier Univ. Press, 1993); C. R. Holladay, "1 Corinthians 13: Paul as Apostolic Paradigm," in D. L. Balch et al. (eds.), *Greeks, Romans, and Christians* (Minneapolis: Fortress Press, 1990), 80–98; R. A. Horsley, "Gnosis in Corinth: 1 Cor 8:1–6," *NTS* 27 (1980): 32–51; A. R. Hunt, *The Inspired Body: Paul, the Corinthians, and Divine Inspiration* (Macon: Mercer Univ. Press, 1996); D. W. Kuck, *Judgment and Community Conflict* (NovTSup, 66; Leiden: E. J. Brill, 1992); J. Lambrecht, "Paul's Christological Use of Scripture in I Cor 15:20–28," NTS 28 (1982): 502–27; D. Litfin, *St. Paul's Theology of Proclamation: 1 Corinthians 1–4 and Greco-Roman Rhetoric* (SNTSMS, 79; Cambridge: Cambridge Univ. Press, 1994); J. Murphy-O'Connor, "The Non-Pauline Character of 1 Cor 11:2-16?" *JBL* 95 (1976): 615–21; R. A. Ramsaran, *Liberating Words: Paul's Use of Rhetorical Maxims in 1 Corinthians 1–10* (Valley Forge, Pa.: Trinity Press Int'l, 1996); R. Scroggs, "Paul and the Eschatological Woman," *JAAR* 40 (1972): 283–303; S. K. Stowers, "Paul on the Use and Abuse of Reason," in D. L. Balch et al. (eds.), *Greeks, Romans, and Christians* (Minneapolis: Fortress Press, 1990), 253–86; W. L. Willis, *Idol Meat in Corinth: The Pauline Argument in 1 Corinthians 8 and 10* (SBLDS, 68; Chico: Scholars Press, 1985); V. L. Wimbush, *Paul the Worldly Ascetic: Response to the World and Self-Understanding according to 1 Corinthians 7* (Macon: Mercer Univ. Press, 1987); and A. Clark Wire, *The Corinthian Women Prophets: A Reconstruction through Paul's Rhetoric* (Minneapolis: Fortress Press, 1990).

For a series of penetrating essays on both epistles, but particularly on Paul's rivals, see C. K. Barrett, *Essays on Paul* (Philadelphia: Westminster Press, 1982), 1–117. On the correspondence as a whole, also see L. L. Welborn, *Politics and Rhetoric in the Corinthian Epistles* (Macon: Mercer Univ. Press, 1997). On the theology of the Corinthian letters, see the collection of essays in D. M. Hay (ed.), *Pauline Theology, Vol. 2: 1 and 2 Corinthians* (Minneapolis: Fortress Press, 1993). Also see the collection of essays in R. Bieringer (ed.), *The Corinthian Correspondence* (BETL, 125; Leuven: Leuven Univ. Press, 1996).

The issue of the integrity of 2 Corinthians always means a discussion of interpolations. For two views, cf. H. D. Betz, "2 Cor 6:14—7:1: An Anti-Pauline Fragment," *JBL* 92 (1973): 88–108; idem, *2 Corinthians 8 and 9: A Commentary on Two Administrative Letters of the Apostle Paul*, ed. G. W. MacRae (Hermeneia; Philadelphia: Fortress Press, 1985); and N. A. Dahl, "A Fragment and Its Context: II Cor 6:14—7:1," in *Studies in Paul*, 62–69. On the wider question of literary unity, see W. H. Bates, "The Integrity of II Corinthians," *NTS* 12 (1965–66): 56–69; and D. A. DeSilva, "Measuring Penultimate against Ultimate Reality: An Investigation of the Integrity and Argumentation of 2 Corinthians," *JSNT* 52 (1993): 41–70.

On the issue of Paul's opponents in 2 Corinthians, see the highly influential study by D. Georgi, *The Opponents of Paul in 2 Corinthians: A Study of Religious Propaganda in Late Antiquity*, rev. ed. (Philadelphia: Fortress Press, 1985); as well as A. B. Kolenkow, "Paul and His Opponents in 2 Cor 10–13: THEIOI ANDRES and Spiritual Guides," in L. Borman et al. (eds.), *Religious Propaganda & Missionary Competition in the New Testament World* (NovTSup, 74; Leiden: E. J. Brill, 1994), 351–74; J. P. Sampley, "Paul, His Opponents in 2 Corinthians 10–13, and the Rhetorical Handbooks," in J. Neusner et al. (eds.), *The Social World of Formative Christianity and Judaism* (Philadelphia: Fortress Press, 1988), 162–77; and J. L. Sumney, *Identifying Paul's Opponents: The Question of Method in 2 Corinthians* (JSNTSup, 40; Sheffield: Sheffield Academic Press, 1990). For Paul's defense of his apostleship in the Corinthian Correspondence in general, see J. H. Schütz, *Paul and the Anatomy of Apostolic Authority* (Cambridge: Cambridge Univ. Press, 1975); J. T. Fitzgerald, *Cracks in an Earthen Vessel: An Examination of the Catalogues of Hardship in the Corinthian Correspondence* (SBLDS, 99; Atlanta: Scholars Press, 1988); and in 2 Corinthians in particular, G. G. O'Collins, "Power Made Perfect in Weakness: II Cor 12:9-10," *CBQ* 33 (1971): 528–37; and S. J. Hafemann, *Suffering & Ministry in the Spirit: Paul's Defense of His Ministry in II Corinthians 2:14—3:3* (Grand Rapids: Eerdmans, 1990).

On Paul's midrash on Moses, see L. L. Belleville, *Reflections of Glory: Paul's Polemical Use of Moses-Doxa Tradition in 2 Corinthians 3.1-18* (JSNTSup, 53: Sheffield: Sheffield Academic Press, 1991); S. J. Hafemann, *Paul, Moses, and the History of Israel: The Letter/Spirit Contrast and the Argument from Scripture in 2 Corinthians 3* (Peabody, Mass.: Hendrickson Pubs., 1996 [1995]); and H. Marks, "Pauline Typology and Revisionary Criticism," *JAAR* 52 (1984): 71–92. On Paul's collection for the church in Jerusalem, see D. Georgi, *Remembering the Poor: The History of Paul's Collection for Jerusalem* (Nashville: Abingdon Press, 1992); and K. F. Nickle, *The Collection: A Study in Paul's Strategy* (London: SCM Press, 1966).

On some specific issues, see F. W. Danker, "Paul's Debt to the *De Corona* of Demosthenes: A Study of Rhetorical Technique in Second Corinthians," in D. Watson (ed.), *Persuasive Artistry* (JSNTSup, 50; Sheffield: Sheffield Academic Press, 1991), 262–80; J. F. Fitzgerald, "Paul, the Ancient Epistolary Theorists, and 2 Corinthians 10–13," in D. L. Balch et al. (eds.), *Greeks, Romans, and Christians* (Minneapolis: Fortress Press, 1990), 190–200; and S. R. Garrett, "The God of This World and the Affliction of Paul: 2 Cor 4:1-12," in D. L. Balch et al. (eds.), *Greeks, Romans, and Christians* (Minneapolis: Fortress Press, 1990), 99–117. Also see the general studies by A. E. Harvey, *Renewal through Suffering: A Study of 2 Corinthians* (Edinburgh: T. & T. Clark, 1996); L. J. Kreitzer, *2 Corinthians* (Sheffield: Sheffield Academic Press, 1996); and F. Young and D. F. Ford, *Meaning and Truth in 2 Corinthians* (Grand Rapids: Wm. B. Eerdmans, 1987); as well as the important collection of essays in R. Bieringer and J. Lambrecht (eds.), *Studies on 2 Corinthians* (BETL, 112; Leuven: Leuven Univ. Press, 1994).

For commentary on the Corinthian Correspondence as a whole, see C. H. Talbert, *Reading Corinthians: A Literary and Theological Commentary on 1 and 2 Corinthians* (New York: Crossroad, 1987); and B. Witherington III, *Conflict & Community in Corinth: A Socio-Rhetorical Commentary on 1 and 2 Corinthians* (Grand Rapids: Eerdmans, 1995).

For critical commentary on 1 Corinthians, see H. Conzelmann, *1 Corinthians*, trans. J. W. Leitch (Hermeneia; Philadelphia: Fortress Press, 1975); and G. D. Fee, *The First Epistle to the Corinthians* (NICNT; Grand Rapids: Eerdmans, 1987). More accessible yet careful guides through the text are C. K. Barrett, *A Commentary on the First Epistle to the Corinthians* (HNTC; New York: Harper & Row, 1968); and C. R. Holladay, *The First Letter of Paul to the Corinthians* (Austin: Sweet Co., 1979).

For critical commentary on 2 Corinthians, see P. Barnett, *The Second Epistle to the Corinthians* (NICNT; Grand Rapids; Eerdmans, 1997); R. Bultmann, *The Second Letter to the Corinthians*, ed. E. Dinkler, trans. R. A. Harrisville (Minneapolis: Augsburg Pub., 1985); V. P. Furnish, *II Corinthians* (AB; Garden City: Doubleday, 1984); R. P. Martin, *2 Corinthians* (WBC; Waco: Word Books, 1986); and M. E. Thrall, *A Critical and Exegetical Commentary on the Second Epistle to the Corinthians: 1–7* (Edinburgh: T. & T. Clark, 1994). Helpful again is the readable commentary by C. K. Barrett, *A Commentary on the Second Epistle to the Corinthians* (HNTC; New York: Harper and Row, 1973).

13. The Letter to the Galatians

IN PAUL'S LETTER to the Galatians we find the apostle at his most difficult and exhilarating. In the face of opposition and rejection, he pushes the scandalous implications of the gospel to their limits, leaving Christianity its "charter of freedom." Here he moves beyond an apparently narrow parochial problem to the deepest questions concerning life before God. In the process, he allows his own and the community's personal religious experience to reshape their shared symbolic world in a radical way.

The interpretation of the letter is difficult not only because of the density of Paul's arguments but also because the circumstances to which he was responding are not entirely clear. We have only the information of the letter itself, and are reminded again just how helpful Acts is in other cases. Paul is writing to a group of churches (Gal. 1:2) whose members he can call Galatians (3:1). They could either be descendants of Celtic tribes who inhabited the territory of northern Asia Minor and whose major city was Ancyra, or people who lived in the southern part known as the Roman province of Galatia. The cities of Iconium, Lystra, and Derbe, evangelized by Paul and Barnabas (Acts 14:1-21), were in that province, though Luke does not identify it by its proper name. When he does speak of Galatia, he joins it with Phrygia. He has Paul make a short trip through this territory, without mentioning the foundation of any churches (Acts 16:6). Later, Paul swings through both territories again to visit churches there (Acts 18:23; cf. 20:4). Thus, Acts just does not provide enough information on this point. And it is doubtful we would be much helped even if we could decide where the addressees of Paul's letter lived, since the specific historical and cultural context would still be difficult to ascertain.

The dating of the letter is equally uncertain. Paul says the troubles there began "so quickly" (Gal. 1:6) and he recalls his first visit to them (4:13-14; cf. 1 Thess. 2:1-16); these might be indications of an early date. Some, however, place Galatians later because of its thematic resemblance to Romans. In the end, it could have been written any time during Paul's active career.

The tone of the letter is distinctive. Its rhetoric is emotional and polemical from its beginning, "Paul an apostle not from men but from God" (1:1), to its end, "Henceforth let no man bother me, for I bear on my body the marks of Christ" (6:17). Paul drops his characteristic thanksgiving section, and replaces it with "I am astonished! [*thaumazō*]" (1:6). Against those who are causing trouble he twice levels a curse (*anathema*; 1:8, 9). He accuses the congregation of stupidity (3:1) and is anguished by its fickleness: "I am afraid I have labored over you in vain" (4:11); "You were running so well, who has hindered you from obeying the truth?" (5:7). He is openly hostile toward the troublemakers: "I wish those who upset you would castrate themselves" (5:12). Equally sharp is the opposition Paul establishes in this letter between slavery and freedom, between spirit and flesh, between law and faith, and between death and life. The theological vocabulary that in Romans is placed within the frame of a magisterial statement is here forged in combat and is all the sharper because of it. Yet this letter is by no means simply an outpouring of raw emotion. Its polemic is not random but carefully aimed, and the largest part of Galatians is a carefully constructed argument. Both the polemic and the thought of Galatians can best be appreciated when, within the limits of the text itself, we try to reconstruct the situation Paul addressed.

The Occasion and the Issues

In spite of a physical weakness, Paul had founded these churches: "You know that it was because of a bodily ailment that I preached the gospel to you at first; and though my condition was a trial to you, you did not scorn or despise me, but received me as an angel of God, as Christ Jesus" (4:13-14). The term "angel of God" may also be rendered "messenger from God" and shows us again how Paul appropriated the sort of self-designation Hellenistic philosophers also used (see Epictetus *Diss.* III.22.49, 63, 72). There may be implied in this term as well a contrast to other messengers (see 1:8; 3:19). When the Galatians received him "as Christ Jesus," they recognized an intimate, even mystical, identity between the Messiah and his emissary. Paul's mystical bonding with Jesus is distinctive in this letter (see 1:16; 2:20; 6:14, 17), though not unique to it (cf. 2 Cor. 5:16-21).

In order to grasp the problem and Paul's response, it is crucial to understand that the Galatians were converted directly from paganism (2:8, 14; 3:8, 14; 4:8-9; 6:13). They probably first heard of Torah through Paul's preaching; certainly they had not lived by it (3:2; 4:21; 5:4). When Paul preached a crucified Messiah to them (3:1) and they accepted this message as "good news" in faith, they received a palpable outpouring of the Holy Spirit, manifested in wondrous deeds (3:2-5). They had thereby come "to know God, or rather to be known by God" (4:9). Their "life in the Spirit" (5:25) had come about precisely through the preaching of the cross (3:1). The community, however, did not have a mature grasp of this identity "in Christ," and events in the churches since their conversion and his departure have made Paul anxious: "My little children, with whom I am again in travail, until Christ be formed in you! I wish I could be present with you now and change my tone, for I am perplexed about you" (4:19-20). What has happened to make these churches, which formerly would "pluck out their eyes" for Paul (4:15), now doubt both him and his message?

Paul is not at all certain who is responsible for their "turning to another gospel" (1:6). He asks them, "Who has bewitched you?" (3:1), and "Who hindered you from obeying the truth?" (5:7). He is certain that at stake is the "truth of the gospel" (2:5, 14; 4:16; 5:7). Since Paul is vague, and perhaps even ignorant, concerning the troublemakers' identity, we have no definite knowledge of them either. The methodological problems of identifying the rivals in Corinth face us here as well. There are real people whom Paul opposes, but we do not know *their* understanding, only Paul's perception of it. Many suggestions about the opponents in Galatia have been made. Were they representatives of the "James party" from Jerusalem (2:12), or "Gnostics" (4:9)?

The problem is made more complex because the real difficulty seems to lie within the community. A stimulus may have come from the outside ("They make much of you," 4:17), but individuals within the church are promoting a different version of the gospel ("those being circumcised," 5:3). Although Paul is against those who "compel you to be circumcised" (6:12-13), he may himself not know whether they are insiders or outsiders. Consequently his energy is directed at those likely to be seduced, the "foolish Galatians" themselves. From ancient times, the deviance Paul struggles to correct has been called "Judaizing" (from "to live like a Jew," 2:14), a term appropriate not for Jews but for Gentiles who wish to imitate them. It indicates in broad terms the question agitating the young gentile communities: Did they need Torah as well as Christ?

The agitators have two interrelated complaints. First, like the rivals in Corinth, they question Paul's apostolic credentials. Paul is not one of the original apostles but is dependent on Jerusalem. He is inconsistent in his teaching and practice, trying to please people rather than God; indeed, he has even circumcised one of his closest delegates, Titus (2:3). But second, just as Paul's apostolic credentials are deficient, so is his "good news." He has preached only of God's work in the crucified Messiah. He therefore delivers to the Galatians an incomplete, inadequate form of Christianity. In order to be truly righteous—to be in a proper covenantal relationship with God—it is necessary as well to observe the commandments of Torah.

The Messiah is, after all (we can hear them say), a Jewish savior. Being "in the Messiah" therefore demands becoming part of the historic people, the "Israel of God" (6:16) as well. Circumcision is the ritual symbol for "taking on the yoke of Torah" (see 5:1), which initiates one into this people. Paul deceived the Galatians by foisting on them merely the ritual washing of baptism. Like commitment to Christ, it is a beginning, but more is required for full maturity. Obedience to the gospel without obedience to Torah's commandments is, according to Paul's opponents, a superficial and distorted version of Judaism. The ultimate norm for God's righteousness, and therefore for human righteousness, is now—as always—Torah. If they are circumcised, the Galatians signal their willingness to advance to this more mature position within the people of God (5:2). Such an argument would have made excellent sense to those who converted directly from paganism, for multiple initiations signaling stages of introduction into a mystery were a standard feature of Greco-Roman religions (see Apuleius, *Golden Ass* XI), and even Philo can speak in terms of being initiated into the "holy mysteries" of Moses (*On the Cherubim* 42, 48–49).

This much of their argument seems clear. Some details are hard to pin down, because we do not know whether they or Paul injected them into the debate. Did they, for example, make a point of the angels' role in the giving of Torah, or did Paul (3:19)? Did they advocate obeisance to angelic forces, the "elements of the universe," or did Paul draw that polemical equation (4:3, 9)? Did they or he make the connection between the observance of "days and months and seasons and years" and the observance of Torah (4:10)?

In any case, the religious issues raised by this dispute over circumcision go far beyond proper ritual procedure. They touch on the adequacy of the experience of God in Jesus, and on whether Torah or "the law of Christ" is the ultimate norm for Christian existence. These questions lead in turn to the relationship between God and humans: Is it established by human effort or always by God's gift? Is God constrained by human ways of measuring his consistency, or must humans measure themselves by the ways God shows himself to be consistent?

Paul perceives such questions as implicit within the seemingly innocuous Gentile desire for "something more" than Christ. By their desire for more, the Gentiles will lose what they already have (5:2-4). Paul's defense of his apostolic office is intimately connected to his defense of the adequacy of his gospel; the "truth" of the Galatians' experience of God rests on both.

Much in Paul's response is difficult to understand, not only because we hear only one side of the conversation but also because the symbols presupposed by both parties, and their modes of argumentation, are sometimes obscure. But Paul's basic theological method is clear. He begins with his personal experience (1:1, 4, 11-12, 15; 2:11-20; 4:12; 6:14, 17) and the personal experience of the Galatian Christians (1:4; 3:1-5; 4:12-15; 5:24-25). Then, in the light of these mutually confirming experiences, he reinterprets the very Torah that is the point of disputation (3:6—4:31). In Paul's manner of presentation, therefore, the basic question is already answered: the experience of God in Jesus Messiah is the ultimate norm for life before God; even Torah itself must henceforth be understood in the light of this new experience of God.

Apostolic Apologia

Against insinuations that his apostleship is derived and dependent, Paul insists that it came about by a direct call (1:1) and election (1:15) from God, who, in a revelation of Jesus Messiah (1:12), turned Paul's life around. He was not then and is not now dependent on the leaders of the Jerusalem community. He did not confer with them after his call (1:16). His only meeting was a private one three years after the start of his ministry

(1:18-20). When he had a full meeting with the "pillars" of that church fourteen years later, he was recognized by them as their full equal. They agreed to divide the mission between him and Peter (2:9); Titus was not required to be circumcised (2:2-3); and their only request concerned a matter he had already begun in his collection: the care for the poor (2:10). All this took place despite the "false brethren" who had tried to "spy out our freedom" (2:4). Paul wants the Galatians to grasp this analogy to their present situation. He had not then submitted to the false brethren, "so that the truth of the gospel might be preserved for you" (2:5). So now, he wants them to resist any threat to their freedom.

The final evidence for both Paul's independence and the consistency of his preaching is his confrontation with Cephas. When even Paul's partner Barnabas (see 2:1) had capitulated to the pressure exerted by "certain men from James" (2:12) and stopped eating with Gentiles in Antioch, Paul opposed Cephas to his face (2:11), because Cephas, Barnabas, and all the Jews had not been "straightforward about the truth of the gospel" (2:14). Paul's consistency is also shown by the opposition he had to face in the past and continues to face: "If I were still pleasing men, I would not be a slave of Christ" (1:10). The sign of the servant is suffering and rejection: "But if I, brethren, still preach circumcision, why am I still persecuted?" (5:11); "I bear on my body the marks of Jesus" (6:17).

Paul turns the charge of insincerity back on his opponents (2:13). Those upsetting the Galatians are like the "false brethren" who had bothered him in both Jerusalem and Antioch (2:4, 12). They are deceivers: "They make much of you, but for no good purpose; they want to shut you out, so that you may make much of them" (4:17). In a pointed statement, Paul suggests in 6:12-13 that their real motivation is not only to gain prestige but to avoid persecution from the Jews:

> It is those who want to make a good showing in the flesh that would compel you to be circumcised, and only in order that they may not be persecuted for the cross of Christ. For even those who receive circumcision do not themselves keep the law, but they desire to have you circumcised that they may glory in your flesh.

What stake did community members have in circumcision? According to Paul, it made them appear to be normal members of Israel rather than candidates for persecution and martyrdom, a persecution that was brought about precisely because the crucified Messiah was a stumbling block to those who saw Torah as the ultimate norm of righteousness (3:13)—a point illustrated by Paul's own past experience (1:13-14). While it may be difficult to contextualize these statements in the life of the Galatian church—since we know so little about their experience—it is clear that, in Paul's eyes, the choice of circumcision was both cowardly and a rejection of the experience of God through the preaching of the crucified Messiah (3:1). Paul himself utterly rejects that choice (6:14):

But far be it from me to glory except in the cross of our Lord, Jesus Christ, by which the world has been crucified to me, and I to the world.

The Galatians outrage and puzzle (4:15) Paul all the more because of their willingness to deny their own experience, something he refuses to do. In their hearing of the gospel, they had already experienced the Holy Spirit powerfully (3:2-5). In their baptism, they had already been joined to the Messiah as children of God and heirs of the kingdom (3:26-27), calling God "Father" (4:6-7). To seek now another form of initiation is to denigrate the first. To seek righteousness by the norm of Torah means denying the righteousness they received from the faith of the Messiah. The Galatians resemble healthily breathing people who are told the only way to breathe is by means of an artificial respirator. No one can deny the efficiency of a respirator for those who cannot breathe for themselves. But if the Galatians are now breathing by the life of the Spirit, to choose a respirator is to choose slavery.

The Gospel in Outline

Paul's defense of the gospel is so dense and elliptical that it is helpful to review some of his presuppositions, such as we are able to pick out from his argument here as well as from the fuller exposition in Romans.

A person is established in a right relationship with God not by external observance of commandments but by a fundamental response of faith (2:16; 3:11). Such faith means a turning away from idolatry, a position that negates God's claim on human existence in exchange for the acceptance of lesser and more easily managed powers (4:8-9). God calls all human beings to this form of righteousness. In whatever circumstances God becomes manifest, the human being must respond. In Torah, Paul finds the primordial pattern of this dialogue: God promised a blessing to Abraham and his descendants, which elicited faith (3:8, 16-18), and that promise has come to fulfillment in Jesus (3:16b, 22, 26, 29).

But whose faith is now at work? There is great dispute over Paul's view here because of the ambiguity of his language, particularly in the cryptic expression *pistis christou*. The expression can be translated either "faith *in* Christ" or "faith *of* Christ" (i.e., Christ's own faith). What makes the case difficult is that Paul seems to mean both at different times. He can speak clearly about the Christians' "faith in Christ" (cf. Col. 1:4). This kind of faith is confessional: those who have faith in Christ acknowledge that God has manifested himself in Jesus the Messiah, and commit themselves to that revelation. But Paul also uses faith language with God as the object, as in "Abraham believed God" (3:6). The difficult question is whether he speaks of Jesus' responding in this way to God—whether he speaks of the "faith *of* Christ"—and if so, what the significance of that response is. In almost all contemporary translations and commentaries, there is a clear bias toward only one understanding, that of "faith *in* Christ." If this is correct, then Paul sets in juxtaposition two principles of salvation: that which seeks to win God's favor by observance of Torah, and that which responds to God by "faith in Christ."

I am convinced, however, that in this case the majority opinion is incorrect: Paul frequently uses the expression *pistis christou* to refer to the human response of the man Jesus to God: the "faith of the Messiah." This response of Jesus, furthermore, is part of the salvific act. What Paul means by it is the faithful *obedience* that Jesus showed to the Father in his life and death (see Phil. 2:6-11; Rom. 5:18-19). The "faith of Jesus" is Jesus' human response to God, which enables others to "have faith" and to "be made righteous by faith." In other words, God established the fundamental gift of righteousness through Jesus' obedience on the cross; humans appropriate that gift by trusting and obeying it the same way Jesus did.

That is the sense in which Paul speaks of faith in 2:20 (against the RSV): "I live by the faith of the Son of God who loved me and gave himself for me." Throughout this letter, he emphasizes that in accordance with the will of God (1:4) Jesus is active in the bestowal of this gift of faith to humans. If this faith of Jesus establishes righteousness, those who accept the gospel accept such righteousness in obedience and trust, receiving as a result the Holy Spirit (3:2, 5; 4:6, 29; 5:5). In this, the promise to Abraham is fulfilled for both Jews and Gentiles (3:8, 28).

Since this Spirit is the very life and power of God, it brings freedom from death, slavery, flesh, and the law (4:1-7, 31; 5:1, 13). The source of life determines the shape of life. If persons live by the Spirit of God, then their existence is given its norm by the same Spirit. Both power and norm, the Spirit relativizes the ultimacy of Torah as the measure of life before God (5:16-18, 25; 6:8). Nor is the work of the Spirit random. It replicates in individual human lives the pattern of life for others that is found in Jesus. This pattern is "the law of the Messiah" (6:2; cf. 2:20; 4:6-7, 19; 5:24; 6:14). God's life has come to the Galatians entirely unmediated by Torah.

What, then, is the status of Torah? It is both *annulled* and *fulfilled* by the Messiah. It is annulled as an absolute norm for God's activity and human righteousness. If the only measure of righteousness is Torah, then Jesus cannot be the source of God's life. This is because Jesus is unrighteous according to that norm: He is a "sinner," one "cursed by God" because he "hangs on a tree" (Deut. 21:23). The cross is therefore pivotal, for Torah rejects a crucified messiah. But if the Galatians have come to know, or be known by, God through Jesus, something has to give: Torah can no longer be ultimate.

The necessary choice between Jesus and Torah as the *ultimate* norm for life shows why Paul calls the desire for circumcision apostasy from Christ (5:4) and an attempt to avoid persecution for the cross (6:12). When Paul declares that "Christ redeemed us from the curse of the law, having become a curse for us" (3:13), the corollary is that Torah's power is annulled. Jesus cannot be their righteousness and cursed by God at the same time. But Paul goes further: those baptized into the Messiah have also "died to the law" (2:19) since their life comes from the spirit of the resurrected Jesus. Paul therefore can conclude: "I do not nullify the grace of God, for if righteousness were through the law, then Christ died to no purpose" (2:21).

Because it was always more than law—being God's revelation and wisdom—Torah is also fulfilled in the Messiah. Paul cannot even speak of righteousness without using Torah's narratives and prophecies. Only in Romans does he more fully state Torah's function as witness to the Messiah (see Rom. 3:21), but even here, we see that the problem is less with Torah than with the claim that it is a source of life (Gal. 3:12). Torah as the definitive norm of God's work is superseded. God did something new in Jesus' death: he revealed righteousness outside the norm of Torah. This calls for a new response of faith, which shows that Torah as the bearer of promise is also fulfilled. Before Jesus, one could think of Torah as ultimate, as Paul himself did when he persecuted the church of God (1:13). But it never gave life (3:21). Paul cannot understand Jesus without the symbols of Torah; but neither can he rightly understand the symbols of Torah without Jesus.

Before the Messiah, Torah had two functions. It helped reveal the slavery to sin under which all humans labored before the heir came (3:19). It also functioned as a pedagogue, holding humans under the restraint of minimal moral observance until faith was revealed (3:23). But in the light of God's revelation in the cross and resurrection of Jesus, "circumcision means nothing, uncircumcision means nothing, but [there is] a new creation" (6:15).

The Argument of Gal. 2:15—4:31

Some observations can now be made on the stages of Paul's argument. Paul's use of midrash in the heart of this letter is technical and complex. His Pharisaic teachers would applaud his methods, although they would be appalled by his conclusions. His argument is not convincing unless one agrees with his starting point, the experience of God's life through Jesus.

The argument comes directly and without transition on the heels of his apologetic narration. He begins with a series of dialectical assertions much like those of 5:2-6, which recapitulate the argument. Paul insists on the opposition between the faith that comes through the Messiah and observance of the law as principles of righteousness (2:15-16). This does not mean, however, that the one who chooses faith is a sinner (2:17-18), because Paul and other Christians are mystically united to the Messiah and live through him (2:19-21). This is not yet explained, though we later learn that baptism is an initiation into the Messiah's life (3:27). At this stage, Paul stresses the connection between the present life of Christians, its origin in God, and its mediation through the cross of Jesus.

The appeal to experience (3:1-5) is critical to his argument—if the Galatians agree, then his argument is cogent; if they disagree, they deny their own experience. The experience is that they have been given life through the Holy Spirit, mediated through the preaching of the cross and received in faith. Thus, life did not come to them through observance of the law.

If the experience is granted, then Paul can begin to reinterpret Torah in the light of it. His first appeal to Scripture takes the form of a balanced series of propositions. He uses two statements about Abraham in Genesis: that all nations would be blessed in him (Gen. 12:3) and that his righteousness came by faith (Gen. 15:6). On this basis, Paul can conclude that all nations (that is, Gentiles) who have faith are also children of Abraham, sharing in his blessing (Gal. 3:6-9). The value of Torah as a witness is implicitly asserted here, but its meaning is only unlocked by the present experience mediated through the Spirit; in the narrative of the promise the Galatians find the beginning of their own story.

Paul's second appeal to Scripture (3:10-14) forms a well-constructed midrash on Torah. Paul uses the midrashic rule that when two texts of Scripture contradict each other, a third text can resolve them. Here, we see that the prophet Habakkuk says that life comes from the righteousness of faith (Hab. 2:4). But Leviticus 18:5 claims that life comes by observing the commands of law. Paul sharpens the contradiction by citing in favor of Leviticus the text of Deut. 27:26, which levies a curse (the opposite of life) on those who do not keep the commandments. But then he says that this curse was redeemed by Jesus. This happens in two stages. First, his death was one accursed—according to Deut. 21:23—since he was left hanging on a tree. Second, however, Jesus' crucifixion did not lead to a curse but to a blessing, did not end in death but led to life: Jesus above all *lives*! It follows, therefore, that in this conflict between texts, the one stands that says, "The righteous one will live by *his* faith" (Hab. 2:4), and it is fulfilled first in the faithful death and resurrection of Jesus Messiah. This is a midrash on Torah that operates out of explicitly Christian assumptions and experiences.

Paul's third appeal to Scripture (3:16-18) is a midrash on the promise to Abraham in Gen. 12:3-7. It is complicated and depends on the technique of reading a collective noun (*sperma*, "seed" or "offspring") as a singular, referring not to all of Abraham's descendants but to a single individual—the Messiah (see also 2 Sam. 7:14)—and then subsequently moving out to those who belong to him. Paul has thereby shown that the Messiah is the ratification of the essential covenant (*diathēkē*, also "will") between God and humans, thus sidestepping the Mosaic covenant as though it were only a digression in God's larger plan.

But was the Mosaic covenant simply a mistake? Only in its claims, not in its purposes. Torah was not eternal but only a temporary agreement; it was not given directly by God but only through the mediation of Moses, and angels; it did not, above all, lead to life (3:21). It could reveal transgression and teach morality, but it could not empower or transform. The law did not contradict, but neither did it fulfill the promise (3:21-22). Only in the Messiah's faith is the promise fulfilled (3:22). And Christians are joined to the Messiah by the response of faith and by the ritual of baptism; they become thereby "one in Christ Jesus . . . heirs according to the promise" (3:28-29).

Paul now moves to the contrast between slavery and freedom. Both Jews and Gentiles were like slaves before the coming of the Messiah. As children under the guardianship of the law, the Jews were no better off than the pagans who were subject to cosmic forces (4:1-4, 8-9). Only the Son can give them both a "share in the inheritance" that is his by nature and that will enable them to enjoy the freedom of the children of God (4:6-7):

> And because you are sons, God has sent the Spirit of his son into our hearts crying, Abba, Father! So through God you are no longer a slave but a son, and if a son, then an heir.

The same contrast between slavery and freedom provides the perspective for Paul's fourth appeal to Scripture, addressed by way of a rebuke to those who "wish to be under the law" (4:21-31). In an allegorical interpretation worthy of his contemporary Philo Judaeus, Paul reads Genesis 16 and 21, together with Isaiah 54, out of the conviction that Christians as the "children of Abraham" enjoy the freedom of children, whereas the Jews are still enslaved. As Isaac was formerly persecuted by Ishmael, so are the present children of the free woman being persecuted by the Jews (4:29). In a very bold move, Paul says (4:30; cf. Gen. 21:10):

> But what does the Scripture say? "Cast out the slave and her son; for the son of a slave shall not inherit with the son of the free woman."

Jews persecuted Christians because of the cross. But the cross brought the Christians life and freedom, making them children of the promise. They can therefore "cast out" those in their midst who advocate a flight from the cross to circumcision. In an intriguing series of reversals, Paul switches the position of Jews and Christians, thereby ousting from the Christian community those who would be as Jews.

In Gal. 5:2-6, Paul presents a summation of the argument. Those who seek circumcision deny their experience of God and turn away from Christ. Within the community of the Messiah, distinctions between Jew and Gentile are meaningless, "for in Christ Jesus, neither circumcision nor uncircumcision is of any avail, but faith working through love" (5:6).

One should not lose sight of the fact that in all of this Paul has been addressing gentile converts from paganism. That is to say, Paul's statements should be placed in this context: the specific arguments serve the purpose of keeping the Galatian gentile Christians from circumcising. These arguments should not be construed as Paul's declaration on Judaism as such.

Life According to the Spirit

The Spirit is both the power and the norm for life before God (5:25). Rejection of Torah as an ultimate norm for righteousness does not entail its rejection as a moral guide, much less an opening to antinomianism. Self-aggrandizement—"living according to the flesh"—is always part of the human predicament before God's rule is finally established (5:21). The impulse of the flesh, based on rivalry and competition, leads to boasting in one's own accomplishments and contempt of others. Such an attitude is not foreign to those wishing to impose Torah observance and circumcision as a measurement of righteousness: "If you bite and devour one another, take heed that you are not consumed by each other" (5:15). But those who are given the Spirit are called to conform their behavior to *its* impulses rather than to the impulses that arise from self-seeking.

Like the Corinthian elitists, the Judaizers must be reminded of the community context of their lives. The gift of God's Spirit enables them to live by the "law of the Messiah," which requires a life lived for others rather than oneself: "Bear one another's burdens and so fulfill the law of Christ" (6:2). Although each person must answer to God individually (6:4-5), care and compassion are demanded collectively (6:1). Christians are to "do good to all, especially to those who are of the household of faith" (6:10).

The flesh leads to rivalry, dissension, and factionalism; it wages war against the Spirit (5:19-21). The Spirit's work, in contrast, is manifested in attitudes that promote the building up of community, beginning with love (*agapē*): "Against these, there is no law" (5:23). The Galatians, by God's gift, have been freed from the power of the flesh even as they continue to resist it (5:13). And they are enabled by the Spirit to have the disposition to overcome it: "Those who belong to Christ Jesus have crucified the flesh with its passions and desires" (5:24).

The full meaning of Torah, then, is found only in Jesus. Torah never ceases to provide a norm for Christian existence. But it does so only as interpreted through the pattern of Jesus' life for others: "Through love be servants of one another. For the whole law is fulfilled in one word: 'You shall love your neighbor as yourself'" (5:13-14; cf. Lev. 19:18). Those who "walk by this norm" are the true "Israel of God," and upon them—by the gift of the Spirit—comes peace (6:16).

Study Questions

1. Why is the term "the Torah" better than "the Law" in a discussion of first-century Judaism?

2. What is the deeper significance of the battle over circumcision?

3. Who was advocating the conformity to the Mosaic regulations in Paul's churches?

4. What strategies does Paul use in Galatians to defend his role as apostle?

5. How is Paul's experience and that of the Galatians critical to Paul's argument?

Bibliographical Note

Valuable historical, cultural, social, and religious information on the region of Galatia—including a discussion of Paul's letter itself—can be found in S. Mitchell, *Anatolia: Land, Men, and Gods in Asia Minor*, 2 vols. (New York: Clarendon Press, 1993).

Despite our lack of real information about the Galatian churches, there have been many attempts to reconstruct the situation faced by Paul. For a sample, see W. Schmithals, *Paul and the Gnostics*, trans. J. Steely (Nashville: Abingdon Press, 1972), 13–64; R. Jewett, "The Agitators and the Galatian Community," *NTS* 17 (1970): 198–212; and G. Luedemann, *Opposition to Paul in Jewish Christianity*, trans. M. E. Boring (Minneapolis: Fortress Press, 1989), 97–103. The most convincing rendering is J. Munck, "The Judaizing Gentile Christians," in *Paul and the Salvation of Mankind*, trans. E Clarke (Richmond: John Knox Press, 1959), 87–134.

The most thorough attempt to deal with Galatians within the canons of ancient epistolary rhetoric has been made by H. D. Betz, "The Literary Composition and Function of Paul's Letter to the Galatians," *NTS* 21(1974–75): 353–73; see also J. D. Hester, "The Rhetorical Structure of Galatians 1:11—2:14," *JBL* 103 (1984): 223–33; K. A. Morland, *The Rhetoric of Curse in Galatians: Paul Confronts Another Gospel* (Atlanta: Scholars Press, 1995), 111–38; and J. Smit, "The Letter of Paul to the Galatians: A Deliberative Speech," *NTS* 35 (1989): 1–26. For the Jerusalem visit, see M. Hengel and A. M. Schwemer, *Paul Between Damascus and Antioch: The Unknown Years*, trans. J. Bowden (Louisville: Westminster John Knox Press, 1997); and J. P. Sampley, "Societas Christi: Roman Law and Paul's Conception of the Christian Community," in J. J. Jervell and W. A. Meeks (eds.), *God's Christ and His People* (Oslo: Universitetsforlaget, 1977), 158–74.

The basic lines of Paul's position are sketched by M. Barth, "The Kerygma of Galatians," *Int* 21 (1967): 131–46. Also see the discussion of the larger themes of Galatians and Romans in H. Boers, *The Justification of the Gentiles: Paul's Letters to the Galatians and Romans* (Peabody, Mass.: Hendrickson Pubs., 1994).

The complexities of Paul's scriptural argument are touched on by T. Callan, "Pauline Midrash: The Exegetical Background of Gal. 3:19b," *JBL* 99 (1980): 549–67; N. A. Dahl, "Contradictions in Scripture," in his *Studies in Paul* (Minneapolis: Augsburg Pub. House, 1977), 159–77; idem, "The Atonement: An Adequate Reward for the Akedah?" in *Jesus the Christ: The Historical Origins of Christological Doctrine* (Minneapolis: Fortress Press, 1991), 137–51; R. B. Hays, *Echoes of Scripture in the Letters of Paul* (New Haven: Yale Univ. Press, 1989); and S. K. Williams, "Promise in Galatians: A Reading of Paul's Reading of Scripture," *JBL* 107 (1988): 709–20. On Paul's use of Abraham, see G. W. Hanson, *Abraham in Galatians: Epistolary and Rhetorical Contexts* (JSNTSup, 29; Sheffield: Sheffield Academic Press, 1989); and J. S. Siker, *Disinheriting the Jews: Abraham in Early Christian Controversy* (Louisville: Westminster/John Knox Press, 1991), 28–76. On the significance of the Galatian experience for Paul's argument, see D. J. Lull, *The Spirit in Galatia* (SBLDS, 49; Chico, Calif.: Scholars Press, 1980).

The "faith in/of Christ" issue is discussed from the traditional standpoint by A. Hultgren, "The Pistis Christou Formulations in Paul," *NovT* 22 (1980): 248–63. My treatment here agrees more with the position of G. Howard, *Paul: Crisis in Galatia* (SNTSMS, 35; Cambridge: Cambridge Univ. Press, 1979); and esp. R. B. Hays, *The Faith of Jesus* (SBLDS, 56; Chico, Calif.: Scholars Press, 1983). On this, see also D. A. Campbell, "Romans 1:17—A *Crux Interpretum* for the *Pistis Christou* Debate," *JBL* 113 (1994): 265–85; idem, "False Presuppositions in the *PISTIS CHRISTOU* Debate," *JBL* 116 (1997): 713–19; and the relevant essays in E. E. Johnson and D. M. Hay, *Pauline Theology, Vol. 4: Looking Back, Pressing On* (SBLSS, 4; Atlanta: Scholars Press, 1997), 35–92.

On other specific issues in the interpretation of Galatians, see J. M. G. Barclay, *Obeying the Truth: Paul's Ethics in Galatians* (Minneapolis: Fortress Press, 1988); H. Boers, "We Who Are by Inheritance Jews; not from the Gentiles, Sinners," *JBL* 111 (1992): 273–81; B. H. Brinsmead, *Galatians—Dialogical Response to Opponents* (SBLDS, 65; Chico, Calf.: Scholars Press, 1982); J. D. G. Dunn, *The Theology of Paul's Letter to the Galatians* (Cambridge: Cambridge Univ. Press, 1993); P. F. Esler, "Family Imagery and Christian Identity in Gal 5:13 to 6:10," in H. Moxnes (ed.), *Constructing Early Christian Families: Family as Social Reality and Metaphor* (New York: Routledge, 1997), 121–49; R. G. Hall, "Arguing like an Apocalypse: Galatians and an Ancient *Topos* outside the Greco-Roman Rhetorical Tradition," *NTS* 42 (1996): 434–53; idem, "Historical Inference and Rhetorical Effect: Another Look at Galatians 1 and 2," in D. Watson (ed.), *Persuasive Artistry* (JSNTSup, 50; Sheffield: Sheffield Academic Press, 1991), 308–20; R. B. Hays, "Christology and Ethics in Galatians: The Law of Christ," *CBQ* 49 (1987): 268–90; L. W. Hurtado, "The Jerusalem Collection and the Book of Galatians," *JSNT* 5 (1979): 46–62; B. C. Lategan, "Is Paul Developing a Specifically Christian Ethics in Galatians?" in D. L. Balch et al. (eds.), *Greeks, Romans, and Christians* (Minneapolis: Fortress Press, 1990), 318–28; B. Longenecker, *The Triumph of God: The Transformation of Identity in Galatians* (Nashville: Abingdon Press, 1998); and T. W. Martin, "Apostasy to Paganism: The Rhetorical Stasis of the Galatian Controversy," *JBL* 114 (1995): 437–61. Also see the relevant essays in J. Bassler (ed.), *Pauline Theology, Vol. 1: Thessalonians, Philippians, Galatians, Philemon* (Minneapolis: Fortress Press, 1991).

One of the fundamental issues that dominates Paul's discussion in Galatians (and Romans) is Torah/Law. For assessments that reflect a diversity of angles on the subject, see J. D. G. Dunn (ed.), *Paul and the Mosaic Law* (Tübingen: J. C. B. Mohr [Siebeck]. 1996); L. Gaston, *Paul and the Torah* (Vancouver: Univ. of British Columbia Press, 1987); H. Hübner, *Law in Paul's Thought: A Contribution to the Development of Pauline Theology*, trans. J. C. G. Greig (Edinburgh: T. & T. Clark, 1984); H. Räisänen, *Jesus, Paul and Torah: Collected Essays*, trans. D. E. Orton (JSNTSup, 43; Sheffield: Sheffield Academic Press, 1992), 15–126; idem, *Paul and the Law* (Philadelphia: Fortress Press, 1983); E. P. Sanders, "On the Question of Fulfilling the Law in Paul and Rabbinic Judaism," in E. Bammel et al. (eds.), *Donum Gentilicum* (Oxford: Clarendon Press, 1978), 103–26; idem, *Paul, the Law, and the Jewish People* (Philadelphia: Fortress Press, 1983); E. J. Schnabel, *Law and Wisdom from Ben Sira to Paul: A Traditional Historical Enquiry into the Relation of Law, Wisdom, and Ethics* (WUNT, 2/16; J. C. B. Mohr [Siebeck], 1985); P. J. Tomson, *Paul and the Jewish Law: Halakha in the Letters of the Apostle to the Gentiles* (CRINT, 3.1; Assen: Van Gorcum; Minneapolis: Fortress Press, 1990); and M. Winger, *By What Law? The Meaning of Nomos in the Letters of Paul* (SBLDS, 128; Atlanta: Scholars Press, 1992). For a survey of the issues, see C. J. Roetzel, "Paul and the Law: Whence and Whither?," *CR:BS* 3 (1995): 249–75. For the issues in each of Paul's letters, see F. Thielman, *Paul and the Law: A Contextual Approach* (Downers Grove: InterVarsity Press, 1994).

For critical commentary with full bibliography and careful attention to literary form, see H. D. Betz, *Galatians: A Commentary on Paul's Letter to the Churches in Galatia* (Hermeneia; Philadelphia: Fortress Press, 1979); as well as F. F. Bruce, *Commentary on Galatians* (NIGTC; Grand Rapids: Eerdmans, 1982); R. N. Longenecker, *Galatians* (WBC; Waco: Word Books, 1990); and J. L. Martyn, *Galatians* (AB; New York: Doubleday, 1998). For a more general treatment, see D. Lührmann, *Galatians*, trans. O. C. Dean (Minneapolis: Fortress Press, 1992); and B. Witherington III, *Grace in Galatia: A Commentary on Paul's Letter to the Galatians* (Grand Rapids: Eerdmans, 1998).

14. The Letter to the Romans

ROMANS IS GENERALLY considered the central writing of the Pauline corpus for its subject matter as well as its length, power, and clarity of argument. Unlike those letters in which Paul responds to specific problems in virtual shorthand, Romans is an epistle both ample and magisterial. It is unmistakably scholastic, with an air of detachment that challenges the simplistic identification of purpose and meaning. Paul's reasons for writing Romans are not obscure, but there is a great gap between his prosaic purpose and the power of the instrument he crafted to meet it.

Paul had neither established (see Acts 28:14-15) nor ever met the Roman churches (Rom. 1:10-13). He does not write in response to a crisis within the community. His treatment of differences between the "strong" and the "weak" (14:1-15:6) is general. There may have been differences in practice within—or between—the Roman assemblies, but Paul's knowledge of them does not appear either detailed or intimate—there is no urgency to his discussion, unlike the situation in Galatians. He is careful throughout the letter not to assert the same role he thought he could assume with the Corinthians (1 Cor. 4:15), since he was neither a founder nor a father. He qualifies his desire to "impart some spiritual gift to them," for example, by adding quickly, "that is, that we may be mutually encouraged by each other's faith, yours and mine" (1:12). Although he wrote "on some points very boldly by way of reminder" (15:15), he does not suggest that the Romans deserve rebuke for any deficiency: "I myself am satisfied about you, my brethren, that you yourselves are full of goodness, filled with all knowledge, and are able to instruct one another" (15:14; cf. 16:17-20).

Paul's purpose in writing is practical and has to do with the future of his mission. In the thanksgiving section, he says he had wanted to visit the Romans for a long time but had been delayed (1:10-11, 13). He explains at the end of the letter why he had not come earlier (15:22): he had been preaching throughout the East, "from Jerusalem to Illyricum" (15:19), always in places no one else had gone (15:20). Now he has completed that circuit and hopes to begin a mission to the West, toward Spain (15:24), using Rome as his point of departure (15:24). Before he can do that, however, Paul plans to complete delivery of his collection from the gentile churches to Jerusalem (1 5:25-29). He is not sure of success and thus requests prayer for his mission there, and that the gift might be accepted (15:30-31).

Paul is at a juncture in his ministry marked by the completion of his attempt at the reconciliation of Jew and Gentile through the collection. With the symbolism of that enterprise in his mind, he writes to the Romans, preparing the way for them to become his new base of operations in the West, as Philippi had been for his Macedonian and Achaian mission (Phil. 4:15; 2 Cor. 11:9). He hints at his financial expectations in the thanksgiving: he had wanted to visit earlier "to reap some harvest among you as well as the rest of the Gentiles" (1:13). He had wanted, in other words, to include the Romans in the collection effort. Now he offers them another chance to provide support, as he makes plain at the end of the letter: he hopes "to be sped on my journey there [to Spain] once I have enjoyed your company for a little" (15:24). The term "be sped on my journey" (*propempō*) is used technically for outfitting expeditions (cf. 3 John 6). His expectation to be refreshed (*synanapauomai*) among them also suggests monetary support (15:32; cf. the use of "refreshed," *anapauō*, in Phlm. 7).

This expectation enables us to make good sense of Romans 16, which at first sight seems a strange appendix; indeed, some scholars have questioned whether it originally belonged to Romans. But the chapter admirably serves Paul's purpose: the greetings demonstrate Paul's extensive contacts within the community, thus serving to recommend him. More pertinently, Paul recommends to the Romans the deacon of the church at Cenchrae, Phoebe (16:1-3). Paul says that "she has been a helper of many and of myself as well." The term "helper" (*prostatis*) is often used of financial patrons. Paul now expects the Romans in turn "to help her in whatever she may require from you." His language unmistakably refers to financial matters. Phoebe has helped support Paul's mission in the East, and he now sends her to Rome to organize and prepare for his expedition to the West. In effect, Romans 16 functions as a commendation of Phoebe to the Roman church.

But if Paul's purpose is so practical, why did he write so long and elaborate a letter? Since he was known to this church only by name, his understanding of the gospel and of his mission needed to be expounded in detail. Before he could ask a new community to support his mission financially, he had to let it know what it would be backing. Romans is, therefore, Paul's letter of recommendation *for Paul*. It is true he had claimed no need of such letters from local churches before (cf. 2 Cor. 3:2), but that was when he had founded such communities. On the other hand, who could recommend a "servant of Jesus Christ," one "called to be an apostle, set apart for the gospel of God" (1:1), except the apostle himself, through his teaching? For Paul to recommend his ministry is to recommend the gospel in which he "boasts" (1:16).

Romans is by no means a systematic summary of Paul's theology. Many of his distinctive ideas about Jesus, the end time, wisdom, and reconciliation are at best only touched on. Instead, the letter brings to mature expression Paul's religious interpretation of his work of evangelization and reconciliation among the gentile churches of the East. The teaching on justification by faith, shaped by the polemic of Galatians, is here developed on a more explicit anthropological basis, being made the principle for interpreting the relations between Jew and Gentile in history. The pastoral response to community conflicts in Corinth is likewise here placed within the same overarching framework.

The epistolary structure of Romans is unexceptional. In terms of content, however, the letter at first appears to be divided between a theological argument devoted to justification by faith (chaps. 1–8) and an appendix devoted to scriptural midrash (chaps. 9–11), with general ethical teaching tacked on (chaps. 12–15). In fact, however, chapters 9–11 are not an appended afterthought but the climax to the opening argument, and chapters 12–15 are integral to the overall thesis of the letter. There is, furthermore, thematic unity in the three discernible sections of the letter. Paul first demonstrates God's way of making humans righteous; the premise underlying his argument is the lack of partiality in God (chaps. 1–8). He then shows God's righteousness being worked out in the history of Jews and Gentiles. The principle here is the same: there is no partiality in God (chaps. 9–11). He then applies that same principle as a paradigm for life together in any Christian community (chaps. 12–15), arguing that life in the Christian community must reflect who God is and what he has done for his people (15:1-9). The argument of Romans is therefore theological in the proper sense: it describes and praises the work of the one from whom, and through whom, and to whom are all things (11:36).

Romans as Scholastic Diatribe

The affinity between Romans and the Hellenistic rhetorical style known as the diatribe has long been observed. A vivid, dialogical form of discourse, the diatribe uses many of the stylistic devices that are detectable in Romans: apostrophe (2:1, 3, 17); rhetorical questions (2:3-4, 21-23; 7:1; 8:31-35; 9:19-21, 30; 10:14-15; 11:34-35); questions answered by abrupt answers like "By no means" (3:2-9; 6:1-2, 15; 7:7, 13; 11:1, 11); hyperbole (8:37-39; 9:3); vice lists (1:29-31); exemplars from the past (4:1-25); and citation of written texts as authorities (9:1—11:36). All these devices help place the reader in the context of a literary dialogue between a speaker and an imagined "interlocutor" (a person or group) to whom the speaker responds, enabling the argument to develop its own internal momentum, logic and clarity. The concentration of these elements outside Romans is strongest in the *Discourses* of Epictetus, but the elements are found in other philosophers and rhetoricians as well.

Because of the oral character of the diatribe, it was long thought to be a style of public preaching such as that carried out by Cynic philosophers on street corners. By analogy, Romans would then be a sample of Paul's oral preaching, but sent to the Romans in epistolary form. Recent investigation has shown, however, that the life setting for the diatribe was not public preaching but the classroom. Epictetus, for example, ran a school for would-be philosophers, in which he trained his followers in the techniques and message of his philosophy. By analogy, then, Romans is a sample of

Paul's teaching within his school of delegates and fellow workers. The diatribe is not a formless rant but a structured form of argument with the following features: (1) a statement of the thesis (e.g., "Every good person is free"); (2) a demonstration by means of antithesis (e.g., vice leads to slavery); (3) a restatement of the thesis; (4) a demonstration of the thesis by example (e.g., Heracles was free because of his virtue even though he was a slave); (5) an exposition of the thesis; (6) an answering of objections to the thesis (e.g., to the objection "Are there not virtuous people who are prisoners?"). These components are not always found together, but they are combined often enough to support the suggestion that Romans is such a scholastic argument, worked out by the Pauline school and sent to the Roman church as a commendation of Paul's gospel.

The pattern of argumentation also provides the key to reading Romans. Paul states his thesis in 1:16-17 and follows immediately with its antithesis in 1:18—3:20. He then restates the thesis in 3:21-31 and demonstrates it by example in 4:1-25, before completing his exposition in 5:1-21. Objections to the thesis are raised as early as 3:1-8, but are not picked up and answered systematically until 6:1—11:3.

The "Good News" of God's Righteousness

Romans 1–11

The letter's greeting already commends Paul and anticipates important elements of his teaching: he is an apostle of God (1:1); the gospel was promised in the prophetic writings (1:2; cf. 10:14-21); what he preaches fundamentally agrees with the traditions of the churches, as illustrated by the traditional kerygmatic formula of Jesus as the Davidic messiah raised as Son of God by the Spirit of holiness (1:3-4); Paul's distinctive missionary call is to evangelize the Gentiles, among whom he includes the Romans (1:5-6); the gospel demands a response Paul calls "the obedience of faith" (1:5). This last phrase is both difficult and critical to Paul's thought (see 5:12-21; 16:26). It makes "faith" and "obedience" mutually defining terms: "the obedience that is faith" and "the faith that is obedience."

Announcement of Thesis (1:16-17)

> For I am not ashamed of the gospel: it is the power for salvation to every one who has faith, to the Jew first, and also to the Greek. For in it, the righteousness of God is revealed through faith for faith [*ek pisteōs eis pistin*]; as it is written, "The righteous by faith shall live."

The thesis is properly dense. Paul purposely understates for effect when he says that he is "not ashamed," since the "good news" is actually his basis for *boasting*, in contrast to any basis in human accomplishment (3:27; 5:2-3; cf. 1 Cor. 1:31; 2 Cor. 10:17; Gal. 6:13-14). The "good news" is not merely verbal. It is a power (*dynamis*) for salvation (see 1 Cor. 1:18-21; 2 Cor. 2:15) at work universally: among both Jew and Greek (see chaps. 9–11). In this "good news," God's righteousness (or, "justice," *dikaiosynē*) is revealed. The phrase is polyvalent. It refers both to a quality of God (he is just) and to God's activity (he establishes humans in right relationship with him; see esp. 3:26). That God is righteous was axiomatic in Judaism; that humans could be righteous before him was equally assumed. The edge of Paul's thesis comes in the assertion that these propositions are "revealed in the good news" by free gift (3:24; 5:15), being appropriated by the response of faith.

The revelation of righteousness itself is qualified by the elliptical phrase *ek pisteōs eis pistin*, literally, "out of faith to faith." The phrase might simply be adverbial: "thoroughly faithfully," or "beginning and ending in faith." It might also specify the dynamic of gift and response: the revelation of righteousness begins in God's faithfulness to humans and is answered by their obedient acceptance. A third possibility is even more specific and quite likely correct: God's righteousness is revealed *out of the faith of Jesus and leads to the faith of Christians*. In this way the ambiguity in the Habakkuk citation—"the righteous by faith shall live"—intentionally denotes both Christ (the righteous one who lives by faith) and the believer (the one made righteous by faith and who lives as a result). If the "faith of the Messiah" is thus an essential part of the free gift from God—and Paul explicitly says it is (3:25-26; 5:12-21)—then the text of Hab. 2:4 refers first of all to Jesus. He is the one who through faithful obedience unto death is righteous and lives by the resurrection (see above, 1:4). The faith of Christ toward God, in turn, initiates the faith of the believer, which is specified by the confession of Jesus as Lord (10:9) and expressed through faithful obedience toward the One who raised Jesus from the dead. This is the compressed statement Paul will develop throughout the letter.

The Antithesis: Faithless Humanity and the Power of Sin (1:18—3:20)

By means of the antithesis, Paul seeks to show the logical need for his thesis: since God's righteousness comes by gift, every form of human grasping misses the mark.

He begins with an attack on idolatry taken over from Hellenistic Judaism (see Wisdom of Solomon 13–19), giving it (in 2:17-24) a distinctive twist. Paul is also much harsher than the Wisdom of Solomon, which made allowance for the seductive beauty of created things. For Paul, "there is no excuse" (1:20; 2:1); idolatry is rebellion.

If the gospel "reveals" righteousness, the "revelation of God's wrath" comes through sin (1:18). "God's wrath" (*orgē tou theou*) is not a description of God's emotions but a symbol for the retribution that comes upon humans because of their willful rejection of God (2:5; 3:5; 4:15; 5:9; 12:19; 1 Thess. 1:10; 2:16; 5:9; also Isa. 51:17; Jer. 6:11; 25:15; Hos. 13:11; Zeph. 1:15); for those alienated from God, even the face of mercy is looked upon in hate. The retribution here results from the distortion of their God-given existence.

That God can be known from the shape of creation is axiomatic (1:19; Wis. 13:1). But humans can refuse to acknowledge that reality, negating its claim on their lives. Idolatry begins in the refusal to "glorify God as God" (1:21, 28), exchanging the truth of his rule for the lie of human supremacy—a rejection of contingency and dependence on God.

In this way idolatry systematically distorts and corrupts social life. The great lie—that God can be reduced to human impulses and experiences—is itself a "suppression of the truth" (1:18) and leads to progressive deterioration of the capacity to know truth (1:25). Sight itself becomes crooked ("Their senseless minds became darkened," 1:21); they begin to see the world according to the way they have constructed it (1:21-22). Each stage of degradation is marked by the phrase "God handed them over" (1:24, 26, 28), but it is clear that the process results from the misuse of human freedom: "They receive in their own person the due penalty for their error" (1:27). The polemic ends with the vice list in 1:29-31, which is remarkable especially for its number of anti-social, hostile vices. Paul essentially asserts again the lesson of the Fall: rupture of the relationship with God through rebellion leads to the rupture of relations between humans through the reign of envy and murder (as the story of Cain and Abel aptly illustrates). Jewish listeners would ordinarily be cheered by such a stock attack on pagan vice, thinking that as worshipers of the true God, they were exempt from its sting. Paul will shortly challenge that assumption.

Before turning to his self-confident Jewish hearer (real or imagined), Paul argues in 2:1-16 that God is utterly fair in his judgment. We meet here the first enunciation of the principle that "there is no partiality in God" (2:11). The axiom is rooted in Israel's ancient legal procedures: those who sat at the gate as judges between rival claims were not to be "respecters of persons," that is, they were not to take "appearances" into account but were to consider only the merits of the case. They were not, in short, to take bribes of any kind, as Lev. 19:15 makes clear: "You shall do no injustice in judgment; you shall not be partial to the poor or defer to the great; but in righteousness shall you judge your neighbor." If God is such a fair judge (2:5), then all people must be held to the same standard: the response of the human heart to God. Using common pious vocabulary rather than the language of disputation, Paul speaks here of "works" (2:6), meaning that humans are judged by God not on the basis of their origin or ritual allegiances, but on the basis of what they in fact do (2:9-11):

> There will be tribulation and distress for every human being who does evil, the Jew first and also the Greek, but glory and honor and peace *for every one* who does good, the Jew first and also the Greek. For God shows no partiality.

 And if this is so, it means that a positive response to God is also possible for pagans and that God accepts such a response. This is just what Paul argues: neither membership in a nation nor ritual observance—only the response of the heart in obedience—establishes humans before God; whether they have Torah or not, the same response is required of all (2:12-16).

Paul now turns this leveling principle on any who might be smug because they possessed Torah. The Jews enjoyed tremendous privileges because of Torah (2:17-20), but if these became simply a means of measuring themselves over against others, of demarcating their cultural boundaries, or of self-assertion (boasting, 2:23), while they themselves did not observe the law's commandments, the privileges did not matter at all (2:25-28). According to 2:29, the Jew is that person

> who is one inwardly, and real circumcision is a matter of the heart, spiritual and not literal. His praise is not from humans but from God.

Paul does not deny the advantages given to the Jews by Torah (3:1; cf. 9:4-5). His point is that these do not fundamentally give them an advantage with regard to their relationship with God (i.e., righteousness). Even though they have Torah, they are as much under the power of sin as pagans (3:9)—an assertion supported midrashically by a chain of verses from Torah (Rom. 3:10-18; cf. in sequence Pss. 14:2-3; 53:1-2; 5:9; 140:3; 10:7; Isa. 59:7-8; Ps. 36:1 which demonstrate that "none is righteous, no not one; no one understands, no one seeks for God" (3:10; Ps. 14:2-3). The texts of Torah are addressed to those who have the "advantage" of Torah, so "that every mouth may be stopped" (3:19). The antithesis concludes in 3:20 with a paradox for Jewish understanding that will only be resolved in 7:7-12:

> For no human being will be justified in his sight by works of the law, since through the law comes knowledge of sin.

The argument of the antithesis has been so compressed that some interpretive remarks might enable the reader to follow the next steps of Paul's argument more securely. Sin, as Paul speaks of it, is not first of all a moral category but a religious one. He does not suggest that every pagan and Jew is locked in vice. He would grant—if pushed to it—that both Jews and Greeks could be virtuous. Immorality is a sign and consequence of sin, but it is not itself sin. The opposite of sin is not virtue but faith. Thus, sin and faith are the two fundamental responses of a human being to God: "Whatever does not proceed from faith is sin" (14:23). In such contrasts, Paul speaks of sin in the singular, because it is a rebellion found not in multiple acts of moral failure, but in a basic disposition, or orientation, of human freedom. It is a turning away from God.

At root, sin is the disposition that strives to establish one's own existence and value apart from the claims of the Creator God. It is a refusal to acknowledge contingency and dependency on an absolute other; it is idolatry. This disposition is what Paul terms "life according to the flesh," for it measures reality apart from the transcendence of the spirit. He calls it boasting, for it involves a self-aggrandizement that asserts the value of the self at the expense of others. Refusing that side of contingency that is the gift of being from another, idolaters seek to construct life and worth out of their own effort, in effect establishing themselves as the god of their own lives. This requires such ceaseless toil and vigilance that, combined with the darkening of the mind that results, it leads to slavery. If the human person is locked in this orientation, then morality, virtue, and even the observance of Torah's commandments can be an expression of sin. They all can articulate the human attempt to establish life and worth on one's own terms. Virtue can therefore be a source of boasting over another person who is immoral. But such judgment is itself a hostile expression of the flesh, and an expression of sin (2:1-3). Likewise, observance of God's commandments can become a form of boasting (2:23), as one attempts to achieve righteousness apart from God's granting of it.

Through all this Paul virtually makes *sin* into a personified entity, giving it at times an almost mythical coloration (see 5:12-14). This is because he views human freedom as being inevitably in allegiance with, and in service to, some greater spiritual force, either the spiritual systems of idolatry or of the one true God (6:15-23). But the capacity for choice remains as a potential, even when the human being is "enslaved" by the "power of sin." If liberated by the gift of knowledge and love from the Other who was once refused, the human being can be made truly free in faith.

The Thesis Restated (3:21-31)

The human efforts at self-assertion that "fall short of the glory of God" (3:23) are now reversed by "God's way of making humans righteous" (3:21), which is, in short, through the gift of faith in Jesus (3:24-26). Paul's language here is again extraordinarily dense, and I should stress that my reading of the Greek differs considerably from that of many translators. God put forward Jesus as a sacrifice to establish unity between himself and humans (cf. Lev. 16:12-16) "by his blood" (3:25). The death of Jesus, however, was not a mechanical offering but the faithful death of a living human being: it was an act of obedience to God. Thus it was an act "through faith" (3:25). Since Jesus is God's son, in him the gift was at once given from God and received by humans. In the body language and freedom of a single human being, God has acted on behalf of all (3:22). Both God's nature (righteousness) and God's activity for humans (making others righteous, 3:26) are evidenced.

God makes all humans righteous on the same basis. The gift is for all who will have it, both Jews and Greeks; there is no distinction between them (3:22). There is one basis for judgment (2:11); there is one gift; and there is one mode of acceptance, "by faith." On the cross, Jesus relinquished any claim to life or worth apart from God's gift. Thus, he is the "righteous one by faith," and therefore "lives" by virtue of his resurrection (see Rom. 1:17; Hab. 2:4). Those who have been empowered by the Spirit that comes from him to have "the faith of Jesus" (reading 3:26 as "the one who has faith *like* Jesus" rather than "*in* Jesus") are established in right relationship with God. They do not seek to assert their own life and worth but accept in obedience the "free gift" of God in Jesus.

God's revelation of his righteousness in the body and freedom of a crucified Messiah has taken place apart from, and even against, the norm of Torah. But this does not make Torah totally irrelevant. It is a witness to God's way of making humans righteous (3:21). Paul will next show how, but first he makes three rapid assertions. First, all human boasting is now excluded; one can glory (or, boast) only in the gift of God. No human achievement, not even the observance of God's commandments, can place a claim on God (3:27-28). Second, Jews do not have privileged access to God's gifts or to righteousness (3:29-30). Such partiality would contradict God's very being, and would reduce the one God of heaven and earth to the level of a tribal deity. If God is Lord of all creation and if God is fair, then there must be one principle by which all humans can be righteous before him. It is in fact the principle of faithful obedience. Known already in Torah, the principle was obstructed by the power of sin. But now it has been made powerfully available through the faithful death and life-giving resurrection of Jesus. Third, Torah itself is therefore properly established in its true status as a witness to God's righteousness when it is read as evidencing its basis in faithful obedience (3:31). To that demonstration, Paul now turns.

The Example of Abraham (4:1-25)

Paul uses Abraham as his example in the diatribal argument and as proof that Torah is "established" on the principle of faith. He does this through a midrash on Gen. 15:6: "Abraham believed God and it was reckoned to him as righteousness." In contrast to what he did in Gal. 3:6-18, Paul here concentrates on Abraham himself and the structure of his faith. His presentation relies on two midrashic premises: (1) The textual sequence of events is significant; thus, Abraham was called righteous in Gen. 15:6 *before* he was circumcised in Gen. 17:11. (2) The meaning of a term in Torah can be clarified by use of the same term elsewhere in Scripture (the term "reckon," used in both Gen. 15:6 and Ps. 32:1, shows that God is not a passive "keeper of the book" but one who "makes righteous" even the ungodly). Paul's presentation of Abraham as the father of everyone who believes (4:11) is all the more striking because of the praise of Abraham within contemporary Judaism as one whose righteousness was proved by his "works" (see, e.g., *Aboth de Rabbi Nathan* 7, 33; James 2:18-26).

First, Paul argues that Abraham was called righteous not because of his accomplishments but because of his faith (4:1-12). He did nothing that could give him reason to boast (4:2) or that earned God's obligation (4:4-5). His righteousness was a gift of God received by faith; God makes humans righteous (4:5, 6-8). That he was declared righteous before his circumcision demonstrates that his righteousness derived from his obedient response to the promise. He thus manifested the principle of faith for all, becoming the "father" of both Gentiles—"who believe without being circumcised and who thus have righteousness attributed to them"—and Jews—"the circumcised who are not merely circumcised but also follow the example of the faith of Abraham" (4:11-12).

Second, Paul asserts that the law played no role in making humans righteous (4:13-15). He deliberately twists the implication of 3:31 that the principle of faith would destroy (*katargeō*) Torah. Here, Paul asserts that if law were the principle of righteousness, *faith* would be empty (*kenos*) and destroyed (*katargeō*; 4:14).

Third, Paul declares that the structure of Abraham's faith is the same for Christians, involving trust, hope, and obedience. Despite all the appearances of death (his age, Sarah's "dead" womb—*nekrōsis*, 4:19), Abraham had faith in the God "who gives life to the dead and calls into existence things that do not exist" (4:17; cf. 1 Cor. 1:28). Abraham was not an idolater who refused to glorify God (1:21); for he grew strong in faith, giving "glory to God" (4:20). In this way, the structure of Christian faith is specified, not by the birth of Isaac from the dead womb of Sarah but by the resurrection of Jesus from the dead. Indeed, Christians have placed their trust in a God who consistently illustrates this pattern in his activity—he continually "raises from the dead"—the prime example for which was the raising of "the dead Jesus our Lord; who was put to death for our transgressions and was raised for our righteousness" (4:24-25).

The Consequence of the Gift: Peace and Reconciliation (5:1-21)

Paul's presentation hinges on 5:1-21, wherein he concludes the exposition of the thesis that began in 3:21 and sets up the objections that will come to the fore in 6:1. The consequences of righteousness are stated in 5:1-11 as being peace and reconciliation with God. In 5:12-21, the thesis of 3:21-31 (that humans are made righteous through the faithful death of Jesus) is reargued, now explicitly in terms of *obedience*. Paul uses the *qal we chomer* argument (light and heavy) borrowed by Jewish scribes from Hellenistic philosophy ("from the lesser to the greater"). Thus, in 5:9, 15, and 17, the expression "how much more" contrasts a previous state with the present one. For the argument to work, one must grant more than a purely symbolic function to representative figures in history. For Paul, they are persons whose actions determine, or at least fundamentally condition, the existence of others. The contrast in this case is absolute: between the first human being, Adam, and Jesus, the firstborn of a new creation (cf. 1 Cor. 15:20-22). Their respective responses to God provide a range of possibility for those who follow them.

In Rom. 5:1-11, the objective nature of the gift is stated: once made "righteous," humans are "reconciled with God" (5:10-11; cf. 2 Cor. 5:16-21). God's gift is real; justification is not simply a decree, but a transforming action—"God's love poured into our hearts through the Holy Spirit which has been given to us" (5:5). The gift is all the more astonishing because it is given to those alienated from (5:8), and hostile toward (5:10), God. Because God has in Jesus reached across that space of alienation, he has brought about a state of covenantal "peace" (5:1) in which humans have free access to the gift (5:2). Now they can indeed "boast," not on the grounds of their accomplishment, but on the basis of God's love, making boasting itself praise of God (5:2, 11)!

Paul now describes the way the gift has come to humans through the faith of Jesus. Because of Adam's transgression, people lived under the power of sin and experienced death as alienation from God (5:12-14). But the free gift has destroyed the reign of sin and death, being infinitely more powerful in its effects (5:15-21), as Paul demonstrates in a series of five antithetical contrasts. (1) Although many died because of Adam, even more will live because of the free gift "of the one man Jesus Christ" (5:15). (2) The judgment of God, after the trespass, led to condemnation; the free gift brings a decree of righteousness (5:16). (3) One man's trespass allowed death to rule, but now those made righteous "through the one man Jesus Christ" reign in life (5:17). (4) One man's trespass led to condemnation for all, but one man's "act of righteousness" led to acquittal and life for all (or, to the acquittal that is life: *dikaiōma zoēs*; 5:18). (5) One man's disobedience "established" all humans as sinners; Jesus' obedience leads to the possibility and reality ("they will be established") of being righteous (5:19).

The formal parallelism between 5:12-21 and 3:21-26 makes clear that the gift of righteousness is brought about by the "faith of Jesus" considered as obedience to God. The "righteous one who by his faith will live" is first of all Jesus. His faith established the possibility for others to be righteous through faith, since his life has been given to them by the Spirit (5:5). A new power rules in the world, "so that as sin reigned through death, grace also might reign through righteousness to eternal life through Jesus Christ our Lord" (5:21).

Implications of the Gift (6:1-23)

Paul must now answer objections to his thesis. He begins with the question raised first in 3:8, "Are we to continue in sin, that grace may abound?" (6:1) and shifts slightly in 6:15 to "Are we to sin since we are not under the law but grace?" His emphasis on the free gift that has "exceeded" human sin has obviously left him open to charges of being antinomian or "lawless." Paul regards these accusations, however, as essentially trivial, because they misconstrue completely the point he has been making: the gift is real and effective; it changes things. Grace is not an external judgment about humans but a gift of knowledge and love from God that transforms them. To suggest that sin is compatible with this new life and empowerment is to err fundamentally.

Paul reminds his readers of the implications of their baptism (6:2-14). In it, they were identified with Christ's death, so that they might "rise" to a new form of life (6:3-4). Since they now live by the spirit of the resurrected Jesus, they must, in their behavior, "die" to sin (6:6-7), so that, like Jesus, they might be "alive to God" (6:11). The logical outcome is clear: having been brought from "death to life" there is no returning to the former "life of the flesh"—giving sin "dominion" and "obeying the passions" (6:12)—but there is now only a life lived as "instruments of righteousness" (6:13).

The mention of law in 6:14 shifts Paul's language from the contrast between death and life to that between slavery and freedom. To continue in sin is to forget that it is slavery. When Paul's readers considered themselves "free" from God's claim on them, they were self-deluded: their own compulsions imprisoned them (6:20-21). Now that, through faith, they are "obedient from the heart" to God (6:17; cf. 2:15, 29), they are "slaves of righteousness, having been set free from sin" (6:18). Obedience to the Lord of all, the source of all, is actually true freedom, for in it creatures are established in "right relationship" with their Creator. Each form of obedience brings a reward. Slavery to sin accrues wages of death (cf. 4:4); but obedience to God (faith) enabled by "the free gift in Christ Jesus our Lord," receives eternal life (6:22-23). Something has happened to them, reversing their lives; to turn back to any other power, or to measure their lives by any norm other than the gift, is to lose it.

The Problem of the Law (7:1-25)

Paul has spoken of this change in terms of death and life in 6:1-14 and in terms of slavery and freedom in 6:15-23. He now shifts explicitly, albeit awkwardly, to the contrast between law and freedom. He does this by means of a tangled analogy: just as a marriage contract is broken by the death of a partner, so has "a death" broken the Christian's obligation to any contract with the law (7:1-3). However tortuous, the example illustrates that Christian identification in baptism with the death of Christ has made the believer (with him) "dead" to the claims—and curse—of Torah (6:6; cf. Gal. 2:19; 3:13). Christians live by his new resurrection life and are free from the claims of the law on their lives (7:4). They are no longer under an "old written code" but serve God in the "new life of the Spirit" (7:6; cf. esp. 2 Cor. 3:7-18). Paul frames the problem of the Torah, therefore, in terms of a contrast between written prescription and power.

Throughout the letter, Paul has hinted at a collusion between sin and law: "Through the law comes knowledge of sin" (3:20); "For the law brings wrath, but where there is no law, there is no transgression" (4:15); "Sin is not counted where there is no law" (5:13); "Law came in to increase trespass" (5:20); and "Sin will have no dominion over you, since you are not under the law but under grace" (6:14). These statements, in turn, remind us of others Paul has made elsewhere: above all, "Why the law? It was added because of transgressions" (Gal. 3:19) and "The sting of death is sin and the power of sin is the law" (1 Cor. 15:56). The climactic assertion of 7:5, "While we were living in the flesh, our sinful passions, aroused by the law, were at work in our members to bear fruit for death," demands a more comprehensive explanation, and it is to this that Paul turns.

It is necessary to stress, if we are to understand this discussion of Torah, that Paul is not describing the situation of those who have the "new life of the Spirit" (7:6). His whole point, after all, is that grace has changed things. Rather, he speaks here of the perplexity faced by those "living in the flesh" (7:5). At the same time, there is no reason to detect in these remarks an autobiographical account of Paul's preconversion struggles. Paul never suggests that he had trouble keeping the commandments, and insists that he is, by the measure of Torah, righteous (see Phil. 3:6). He addresses here the state of humanity enslaved by the power of sin, and above all the inability of Torah to change that state by itself. He argues for the distinction between the prescription of codes and the empowerment to maintain them. We have here, then, no portrayal of an existential battle within humanity, but an objective description of the human relationship with law. Paul is not being introspective, but uses internal language to describe external realities.

Paul insists that Torah is good (7:13) and reveals God's will for humans (7:7). As God's word it is by definition spiritual (7:14): "so the law is holy and the commandment is holy and just and good" (7:12). Indeed, the commandments reveal wrongdoing precisely as sin. They show that wickedness is not just "immorality" but a rupture of the relationship with God through transgression (7:7, 9, 13). An analogy can help. A child may feel an irresistible urge to tease the cat. Only when her mother says, "Don't tease the cat," however, does the child know the deed as transgression of a command. Now, teasing the cat is not only wrong but disobedience as well.

Paradoxically, by making sin and disobedience clear and evident, commands also inadvertently increase sin and disobedience since humans become fully aware of potentials that were otherwise unknown to them; and knowing creates a desire for doing, according to Paul (7:7-8). Going back to the previous analogy, suppose we have a child who never thought about teasing the cat, yet when told by her mother "don't tease the cat"—simply as a warning should the child ever decide to do so. Now the child is aware of a potential sin that was otherwise unknown to her, and indeed may start teasing the cat or at least have the desire created within her to do so. This all goes back to Paul's understanding of humanity in 1:18-32: humans are fundamentally disobedient; they know God but choose to rebel. The commands of Torah simply provide humans with more opportunity to do just that, and the power of sin will ensure that the desire is created to motivate people toward that end.

Thus, Paul sees the commands of Torah as only verbal. They cannot empower new behavior in a person and counter the impulse toward the old: "I am in the flesh, sold under sin" (7:14). The power of sin (7:8, 9, 11) continues to drive human actions. The commandment, therefore, is really powerless to change a person and in fact exacerbates the situation. Torah as revelation is good, but if it pretends to give life, it is deceitful (7:10; cf. Lev. 18:5) and can in fact kill precisely because it does not give life (7:11). As in the case of one critically ill, having a doctor's diagnosis or even a script for medicine does not help: one needs medicine.

The conflict of 7:15-25 is between the perception of the good made available through Torah, and the inability to do it because of the self-aggrandizing power of sin. The tension is there, we should note, *even when the commandments are observed.* This point is essential to Paul's argument—though it becomes evident only in 9:32—10:4: the Jews could reject obedience to God precisely because they regarded Torah as the only norm for God's action as well as their own. The conflict is stated succinctly: "I serve the law of God with my mind, but with my flesh I serve the law of sin" (7:25; cf. 8:7). What is needed is a power from the outside, a gift that can create the capacity for freedom from the power of sin and death (7:24). That such a gift has in fact been given moves Paul to praise (7:25).

The Fruit of Righteousness: Life in the Spirit (8:1-39)

Paul now picks up the programmatic statement of 7:6—"We serve in the new life of the Spirit"—to develop more fully the meaning of the righteous life. What humans could not accomplish, God has accomplished (8:3). Because of the gift of life by the Spirit, human behavior can now reflect the new empowerment, "in order that the just requirement of the law might be fulfilled in us who walk not according to the flesh but according to the Spirit" (8:4; cf. Gal. 5:25). In his description of this new direction of life, Paul expounds more fully the two options available to Christians: the way of sin and death and the way of righteousness and life (8:5-10). He makes it clear that because of the reality of the new power that has come to persons from the resurrected one (8:11), they must in their behavior also "put to death the deeds of the body" (8:13). And this is truly possible because they have been freed from the power of sin. God's Spirit is not one of "slavery" but of Sonship, enabling them to greet God as Jesus did with the filial cry "Abba, Father!" (8:15).

Paul reminds his readers as well, however, that just as the gift is real, for "the love of God has been poured into their hearts" (5:5), so also its full realization is not yet manifest. They still live in the in-between time. The Spirit, then, is a "pledge" of their future redemption (8:23). Their human suffering is not eliminated by the resurrection life, but it is transformed, since they are sustained in it by the Spirit (8:17-21). And since the Spirit is at work in the world to bring about a radical renewal of all creation, there is genuine hope for the future (8:22-25). Thus Christians live like Abraham, who, despite the signs of death, hoped in the one who calls into being the things that are not. Although the evidence looks like death, Christians should see the suffering of this world as birth pangs for the new world (8:21). And this is possible because even now the Spirit is at work transforming their lives (8:12-14) into "the image of his son that he might be the firstborn of many" (8:29), and even in their suffering the Spirit prays for them "according to the will of God" (8:12-14). It is not blind optimism but the paradox of hope in suffering that enables Paul to declare that there is meaning even in the reversals of history, even in blindness and hurt. Only on the basis of their own deeply ambiguous experience can Paul's readers assert: "We know that in everything, God works for good with those who love him" (8:28).

Abraham had shown faithful obedience to God by being willing to offer his only son Isaac in sacrifice (Gen. 22:12-13). God, in return, has shown himself faithful to Abraham and his "offspring": measure for measure, he too, "did not spare his own Son but gave him up for us all" (8:32). In praise of this gift, Paul's argument reaches its first conclusion: "If God is for us, who is against us?" (8:31). Since it is God who has acted for us, the gift is final and absolute; nothing can threaten it, nothing can "separate us from the love of God in Christ Jesus our Lord" (8:39).

God's Plan for the Salvation of Jew and Greek (9:1—11:33)

Paul has asserted that God works for the good of those who love him (8:28) and also that his call to humans has been effective: "Those whom he called he justified, and those he justified he also glorified" (8:30). But when those assertions are taken together with the principle that God has made no distinction between Jew and Gentile (2:9; 3:22, 29), Paul is forced to defend the working out of God's will in history. Paul therefore provides the messianic community its first "history of salvation" in a sustained midrash on some thirty texts from Torah. Paul reinterprets Torah from the perspective of messianic belief: Jesus is the Messiah. The questions raised earlier are now treated in turn: 9:4 = 3:1-4; 9:6 = 3:3; 9:14 = 3:5; 10:12 = 3:22; 11:26 = 3:29; 11:32 = 3:19-26.

Despite the invitation these chapters appear to offer for discussions concerning free will and predestination, Paul's concern here is not with the ultimate fate of any individual before God, still less with philosophical issues of fate versus freedom. Paul rather praises God's work in the history of peoples, as he can trace it in the stories of his own tradition. His engagement with biblical history is governed by the contemporary Jewish rejection of the "good news" about Jesus as Messiah and Lord, and the acceptance of that same proclamation by contemporary Gentiles. These events, in which Paul's mission itself plays the most pivotal role, raise difficult questions: What is the meaning of "God's people"? Has God been faithful to his word? Is Israel as a people rejected, and if so, can God be trusted?

These are far from abstract considerations for Paul. He is filled with anguish for his people (9:2). In a striking contrast to "Nothing can cut us off from the love of God" (8:39), Paul declares that he would wish to be "accursed and cut off from Christ" (9:3) for their sake, taking on the role of Moses for the people, "if you will forgive their sin—and if not, blot me out of the book you have written" (Exod. 32:32).

Paul outlines at the beginning the blessings of the Jews, which include the Messiah (9:4-5). But these great blessings of God only make the present situation of the Jews more critical and puzzling. The question must be raised whether God's word has failed (3:3; 9:6). Paul's reinterpretation of Torah is therefore a defense of God's word and work in history, and is ultimately praise for God's actions.

He first distinguishes between the "people of God" and historical Israel (9:6-13). Israel as a people was never simply conterminous with the Jews as an ethnic or national group. In the stories of the patriarchs, it is God's election that establishes the line through which the promises are fulfilled (9:6-9). Election has everything to do with God's gift and nothing to do with human accomplishment (9:11). Paul has little patience for the objection that such choices are arbitrary and make God an unjust despot (9:14-23). To think of God's justice in terms of human concepts of fairness shows little grasp of the infinite distance between Creator and creature, a distance measurable only in terms of the Creator's mercy, not the creature's standards of justice. Everything comes from God, and there is no independent standpoint from which the critic can question God (9:19-21). Paul also insists that however ambiguous particular cases appear, the face God shows toward the world is always one of mercy rather than wrath.

But it is all God's doing. For the second time he asserts, "It depends not on man's will or exertion but upon God's mercy" (9:16; cf. 9:11). The prophets show God's mercy reaching out to people who were not part of the historical nation; already in Torah, God calls into being a people from among the nations (9:24). The prophets also show that many of the Jews were stubborn, failing to heed God's call to repentance. Israel as a religious reality was both larger and smaller than the nation: it was a remnant defined by faith (9:25-29).

The critical part of Paul's argument is its middle (9:30—10:21), where he must account for the contemporary rejection of the Jews and the call of the Gentiles. Now the argument of chapters 1 through 8 appears pertinent. The Gentiles have become part of the righteous people on the basis of faith (9:30). That is easy enough (see 3:30; 4:11). But so many Jews have fallen away precisely because they treated righteousness as a matter of accomplishment, not as a gift. By so doing, they failed to "fulfill Torah" (9:32). Paul can say this only on the basis of the rejection of Jesus by the Jews. Here is the case above all where God's call has come outside (and even against) the norms of Torah, in a crucified Messiah. For many Jews, the cross remains a stumbling block rather than the cornerstone of belief (9:32). In the present choice between God's unexpected call through Jesus and the precedents of Torah, they choose Torah as a supposed safe and sure norm for righteousness. Their zeal for God has not slackened, but it is blind (10:2). They have tragically made their understanding of God's consistency in Israelite history the measure of their own consistency toward Torah. By so doing, they have failed to grant God the freedom to speak in new ways (10:3-4):

> Being ignorant of the righteousness that comes from God, and seeking to establish their own, they did not submit to God's righteousness. For Christ is the end of the law, that everyone who has faith may be justified.

In a stunning midrashic move, Paul now collapses the historical distance between the time of Torah and the present. He reads Torah as a fully messianic text.

First, the claim of Moses that righteousness by law will give life (10:5; Lev. 18:5) is opposed by reading Deut. 30:12-13 messianically: the word that God placed close to the people was the word of faith concerning Christ; what Torah intended from the beginning was the Messiah (10:6-9). He is the Lord (cf. 2 Cor. 3:17-18) who, when called upon, saves (10:13). All humans can therefore have equal access to God (10:12):

> For there is no distinction between Jew and Greek; the same Lord is the Lord of all and bestows his riches upon all who call upon him.

Second, Paul says that the rejection of the Messiah is found already in the prophet Isaiah. When Paul says, "They have not all obeyed the good news" (10:16), he does not mean only the Jews of his own generation, for the "good news" was also proclaimed by the prophets: "How beautiful are the feet of those who preach good news" (Isa. 52:7). Paul has insisted from the beginning of this letter that the "good news" was "announced ahead of time (*proepangellomai*) by the prophets in the holy writings" (1:2). He also asserted that it was "witnessed to by the law and the prophets" (3:21).

The prophet that Paul particularly had in mind is Isaiah. Throughout this letter, full citations or allusions to the latter part of that prophet play an important thematic role. It is clear that Paul has pondered his ministry in the light of a careful reading of Isaiah 49–60: Isa. 49:18/Rom. 14:11; Isa. 50:8/Rom. 8:33; Isa. 51:1/Rom. 9:31; Isa. 51:5/Rom. 1:17, 3:21; Isa. 51:7/Rom. 2:15; Isa. 51:5/Rom. 1:17; Isa. 52:5/Rom. 2:24; Isa. 52:7/Rom. 10:15; Isa. 52:15/Rom. 15:21; Isa. 53:1/Rom. 10:16; Isa. 53:5/Rom. 4:25; Isa. 53:11/Rom. 5:19; Isa. 53:12/Rom. 4:24; Isa. 54:16/Rom. 9:22; Isa. 59:7-8/Rom. 3:15-17; Isa. 59:20-21/Rom. 11:26.

Now when he quotes Isa. 53:1, "Lord who has believed what he has heard from us?" (10:16), we know that Paul has in mind precisely the proclamation of Christ in Isa. 52:13—53:12, the Song of the Suffering Servant. It is an allusion too obvious for his readers to miss. There in the text of Isaiah is proclaimed one who died for others, becoming the source of their righteousness (Isa. 53:11):

> By his knowledge shall the righteous one my servant make many to be accounted righteous; and he shall bear their iniquities.

Even before Jesus, therefore, the Jews had heard the "good news." They should have recognized from their reading of Torah that one who was "numbered with transgressors" (Isa. 53:12) could be God's righteous servant. They could have recognized in Jesus, even on the basis of Torah, not one cursed by God but one who made others righteous through his faithful obedience. In this sense Isaiah fairly says, "All day long I have held out my hands to a disobedient and contrary people" (10:21; Isa. 65:2).

The third part of Paul's argument shows that, despite Jewish rejection of the gospel, God has not rejected his people. Indeed, Paul and his fellow Jewish messianists are proof that there is, even now, a believing remnant within Judaism (11:5-6):

> So too at the present time there is a remnant chosen by grace; but if it is by grace, it is no longer on the basis of works; otherwise grace would no longer be grace.

As for the Jews of the present who reject Jesus, their blindness is only temporary and serves God's larger purpose in history (11:7-10). Indeed, God wants all Israel to be saved (11:26), and will bring this about dialectically. The "good news" was preached to the Gentiles only because of Jewish rejection (11:11-12). In like manner, the conversion of the Gentiles—and Paul's own ministry!—has as its main purpose the stimulation of the Jews to envy, so that they too will "turn to the Lord" (11:13-14). Gentiles therefore should not boast. Their inclusion had nothing to do with their relative merits before God. They can even more easily be cut off and the Jews restored, for the Jews were there from the beginning (11:17-24). Paul makes the Jewish priority plain (11:28-29):

> As regards the gospel they are enemies of God for your sake; but as regards election, they are beloved for the sake of their forefathers. For the gifts and the call of God are irrevocable.

God's word has not failed, but neither has it finished. The Gentiles are called to recognize, as their contemporary Jews had failed to, that God's working is mysterious and never ending. They must remain open to new and surprising manifestations of his will in the world. All that is sure is the fidelity and mercy of God, which have been shown in all his works, even those that appear most harsh: "For God has consigned all people to disobedience in order to have mercy on all" (11:30).

In his prayer of praise, Paul again asserts the infinite distance between human knowledge and God's action. Humans do not counsel God; they can only struggle to follow after the traces of God's thoughts (11:33-34): there is an infinite gulf between human effort and divine gift. At the end Paul alludes to Job 41:11: "Who has ever given a gift to [God] in order to receive a gift in return?" (11:35). God is not a human judge who can be bribed. God is always and everywhere the source of all being and beauty, "for from [God], and through [God], and to [God] are all things." So the argument concludes with a call to the obedience of faith, not idolatry (cf. 1:21).

It becomes apparent after Paul concludes Romans 9–11 that the problem with the Jews is *not* fundamentally that they tried to earn God's favor or that they based their claim to salvation on a "work-righteousness." Paul's argument has often been construed in this manner, but it is an inadequate understanding of Paul's own description of his theology and mission. Some elements of this construal do enter into Paul's logic of argumentation on the issue of the inadequacy of Torah, as he attempts to demonstrate why this measure of righteousness cannot be upheld *for Gentiles*. But these arguments must be understood in precisely that context: Paul's justification of why

Gentiles are not—and indeed cannot be—saved on the basis of Torah. In the process, Paul does clarify what his fundamental problem is with his fellow Jews, and it is simply this: because they so exclusively defined themselves by the traditional interpretation of Torah—reading Torah non-messianically—they could not be open to God's new work both in Christ and, subsequently, among the Gentiles.

Life in the Christian Community

Romans 12–15

Paul's practical directives in Romans 12–13 appear at first to have no connection to the preceding magnificent theological argument, for they are thoroughly commonplace and traditional in their treatment of gifts in the community (12:3-8), attitudes of reciprocity (12:9-21), submission toward ruling authorities (13:1-7), the law of love (13:8-10), and the eschatological dimension of Christian existence (13:11-14). This collection of parenetic materials shows the Roman church that if it supports Paul's mission, it will not be sponsoring a renegade or idiosyncratic version of the Christian life. Moreover, it implicitly elaborates on the nature of his gospel, which he detailed in Romans 1–11. In general, Paul now denotes what "faith of/in Christ" entails for those who accept the claim of God upon their lives, and, in particular, he develops more fully the basic premises of Romans 6–8: the nature of the transformed life in the Spirit.

Although there is much in this parenesis that could be found in both pagan and Jewish moralists, there are also some distinctive emphases. The injunction to be "lowly" (12:16), for example, could only be considered a virtue in light of a Messiah who was "lowly" and a slave; for pagan moralists, this attitude was a vice, not a virtue. Likewise in 12:10 (cf. 1 Thess. 4:9) the Romans are told to have brotherly love (*philadelphia*) rather than love for humanity (*philanthrōpia*). We notice as well the emphasis on hospitality and contributing to the needs of the saints (12:13). All in all, however, the classic parenetic summary works here as well: "Avoid evil, cling to what is good" (12:9).

Paul does not, however, leave the parenesis entirely without his distinctive touch. He begins (12:1-2) with a call for a transformation of the mind that will enable one to test what is good (see also 1 Cor. 2:12-16). The gift of the Spirit empowers one's capacity to measure reality differently than by the measures of the world, and to discern in concrete circumstances the appropriate response through which God will be praised (12:1). At the end of this section, Paul also tells his readers to "put on the Lord Jesus Christ, and make no provision for the flesh" (13:14; cf. Gal. 5:13). They are to put on their Christian identity symbolized by the new clothing of their initiation into Christ (cf. 6:1-14) in such manner that their behavior reflects their new identity as "slaves of righteousness" (6:15-23). They are to live by the pattern of the Messiah's "life for others" rather than by the pattern of the flesh's self-seeking. And the pattern of the Messiah is found already in Torah (13:8-10):

> The one who loves the neighbor has fulfilled the law. The commandments, "You shall not commit adultery, you shall not kill, you shall not steal, you shall not covet, and any other commandment are summed up in this sentence, "You shall love your neighbor as yourself." Love does no wrong to a neighbor; therefore love is the fulfilling of the law.

There is a deliberate echo of 10:4 here: "Christ is the end of the law, that everyone who has faith may be justified."

In Rom. 14:1-15:13, Paul calls for this measure of discernment and love in the tensions that naturally result in a community with a pluralism of practices. The situation resembles that of 1 Corinthians 8–10, but with much less detail. The "weak in faith" (14:1) find it necessary to have stricter observance in matters of diet (14:20) as well as calendar (14:5). They judge those who are less observant. Those who are "strong," on the other hand, despise "the weak" (14:3).

Paul agrees with "the strong" that the kingdom of God is not a matter of observance (14:17; cf. 1 Cor. 8:8), but he also allows for diversity of practice within the same community. The important thing is that God be given praise (14:6). God alone is master and Lord; all humans must answer to God alone (14:4, 10-12). There is, therefore, no place among them for either condemnation or contempt (14:3-4, 10, 13). Freedom of conscience stands as the norm for individual decisions (14:14, 20), but service to one another is the superior norm. Whenever values conflict, life lived in service to the other should prevail (14:15, 20).

Paul provides specific theological backing for these guidelines and by so doing establishes a connection to his earlier argument. Christians should accept one another in their diversity, because God has accepted all of them, Jew and Greek alike: all humans have been accepted in Christ (14:3). They were accepted through Christ because the Messiah died and lived again, so that he might be Lord of all, and so that whether they lived or died, they would belong to him (14:7-8). Christ died for all, and this must be the pattern of their life together: "Do not let what you eat cause the ruin of one for whom Christ died" (14:15). Christ is therefore the effective cause of their being accepted by God (15:8-9) and the model (15:2-6) of how they are to accept one another in mutual service: "Welcome one another, then, as Christ has welcomed you, for the glory of God" (15:7).

Now Paul returns to the argument of chapters 9–11. God's work in history should guide Christians' actions toward one another. The Messiah became a servant to the circumcised in order to reveal God's truth (*alētheia*), so that the promises to the patriarchs might be secured (15:8). And the mission to the Gentiles in Christ's name (15:9-13) is precisely so that Gentiles might glorify God for his mercy (*eleos*; 15:9). Paul has here brought together the very attributes of God. The expression "truth and mercy" translates the Hebrew *emeth we chesed*, the attributes of the Lord revealed to Moses (Exod. 34:6): "The Lord, the Lord, a God merciful and gracious, slow to anger, and abounding in steadfast love and faithfulness." But "truth" and "mercy" can also be translated as "faith" (*pistis*) and "love" (*agapē*). Paul suggests three closely connected truths in this allusion. First, in the realm of history, humans come to know God as he really is, a God of fidelity and loving kindness. Second, the perfect expression of the nature of God is found in Messiah Jesus, whose faithful obedience to God was expressed in his loving service to humans. Third, the pattern of life for all who belong to the Messiah is such that their faith in God is also expressed in their mutual love and acceptance of one another, "that together you may give glory [cf. 1:21] to the God and Father of our Lord, Jesus Christ" (15:6).

Study Questions

1. What issues do Romans and Galatians share? What is the difference in how they are handled in the two letters?

2. How do Abraham, Sarah, and Hagar figure in Paul's argumentation in Romans and Galatians? Why would Paul have chosen these three figures in dealing with the issues he addresses?

3. What does Paul mean by "faith" and "the faith of the Messiah"? What difference is made by translating the Greek phrase *pistis christou* as "the faith of the messiah"?

4. How has the issue of "Christ and Torah" affected all of Christian history?

5. What does Romans share with the classical rhetorical style of "diatribe"? How does that affect the interpretation of the letter?

6. What conclusions can you draw from the names mentioned in Romans 16? Which of these names appear in other letters of Paul and Acts?

Bibliographical Note

For the history of the interpretation of Romans, see J. D. Godsey, "The Interpretation of Romans in the History of the Christian Faith," *Int* 34 (1980): 3-16; and R. Jewett, "Major Impacts in the Theological Interpretation of Romans Since Barth," *Int* 34 (1980): 17–31.

On various issues related to the study of Romans, see A. J. Guerra, *Romans and the Apologetic Tradition: The Purpose, Genre and Audience of Paul's Letter* (SNTSMS, 81; Cambridge: Cambridge Univ. Press, 1995); P. Minear, *Obedience of Faith: The Purposes of Paul in the Epistle to the Romans* (London: SCM Press, 1971); A. J. M. Wedderburn, *The Reasons for Romans* (Minneapolis: Fortress Press, 1991); and the essays in K. P. Donfried (ed.), *The Romans Debate*, rev. ed. (Peabody, Mass.: Hendrickson Pubs., 1991). On Romans 16, see H. A. Gamble Jr., *The Textual History of the Letter to the Romans: A Study in Textual and Literary Criticism* (Grand Rapids: Eerdmans, 1977); R. Jewett, "Paul, Phoebe, and the Spanish Mission," in J. Neusner et al. (eds.), *The Social World of Formative Christianity and Judaism* (Philadelphia: Fortress Press, 1988), 142–61; and N. R. Petersen, "On the Ending(s) to Paul's Letter to Rome," in L. M. White and O. L. Yarbrough (eds.), *The Social World of the First Christians* (Minneapolis: Fortress Press, 1995), 337–47.

On Romans as a scholastic diatribe, the indispensable study is S. K. Stowers, *The Diatribe and Paul's Letter to the Romans* (SBLDS, 57; Chico, Calif.: Scholars Press, 1981). For Paul's overall argument, see J. D. G. Dunn, "Paul's Epistle to the Romans: An Analysis of Structure and Argument," *ANRW* II.25.4 (1987): 2842–90. Also useful for critical stages in Paul's argument are the following: G. N. Davies, *Faith and Obedience: A Study in Romans 1–4* (JSNTSup, 39; Sheffield: Sheffield Academic Press, 1990); C. L. Porter, "Romans 1:18-32: Its Role in the Developing Argument," *NTS* 40 (1994): 210–28; B. J. Brooten, *Love Between Women: Early Christian Responses to Female Homoeroticism* (Chicago: Univ. of Chicago Press, 1996), 189–302 [intriguing study of Rom. 1:18-32]; K. R. Snodgrass, "Justification by Grace—to the Doers: An Analysis of the Place of Romans 2 in the Theology of Paul," *NTS* 32 (1986): 72–93; N. A. Dahl, "Romans 3:9: Text and Meaning," in M. D. Hooker and S. G. Wilson (eds.), *Paul and Paulinism* (London: SPCK, 1982), 184–204; L. E. Keck, "The Function of Rom. 3:10-18: Observations and Suggestions," in J. J. Jervell and W. A. Meeks (eds.), *God's Christ and His People* (Oslo: Universitetsforlaget, 1977), 141–57; R. B. Hays, "Psalm 143 and the Logic of Romans 3," *JBL* 99 (1980): 107–15; L. T. Johnson, "Romans 3:21–26 and the Faith of Jesus," *CBQ* 44 (1982): 77–90; S. K. Stowers, "*ek pisteōs* and *dia tēs pisteōs* in Romans 3:30," *JBL* 108 (1989): 665–74; R. B. Hays, "*Pistis* and Paul's Christology: What Is at Stake?," *SBLSP* 30 (1991): 714–29; C. T. Rhyne, *Faith Establishes the Law* (SBLDS, 55; Chico, Calif.: Scholars Press, 1981); M. Barth, "Abraham in Romans 4: The Father of All Who Believe," *NTS* 41 (1995): 71–88; R. B. Hays, "'Have We Found Abraham to Be Our Forefather According to the Flesh?' A Reconsideration of Rom. 4:1," *NovT* 27 (1985): 76–97; C. C. Black, "Pauline Perspectives on Death in Romans 5–8," *JBL* 103 (1984): 413–33; B. Byrne, "Living Out the Righteousness of God: The Contribution of Rom 6:1—8:13 to an Understanding of Paul's Ethical Presuppositions," *CBQ* 43 (1981): 557–81; H. D. Betz, "Transferring a Ritual: Paul's Interpretation of Baptism in Romans 6," in T. Engberg-Pedersen (ed.), *Paul in His Hellenistic Context* (Minneapolis: Fortress Press, 1995), 84–118; P. W.

Meyer, "The Worm at the Core of the Apple," in R. T. Fortna and B. R. Gaventa (eds.), *The Conversation Continues* (Nashville: Abingdon Press, 1990), 62–84; K. Stendahl, "The Apostle Paul and the Introspective Conscience of the West," in his *Paul Among Jews and Gentiles* (Philadelphia: Fortress Press, 1976 [1963]), 78–96; S. K. Stowers, "Romans 7:7-25 as Speech-in-Character (prosōpopoiia)," in T. Engberg-Pedersen (ed.), *Paul in His Hellenistic Context* (Minneapolis: Fortress Press, 1995), 180–202; J. W. Aageson, "Scripture and Structure in the Development of the Argument of Romans 9–11," *CBQ* 48 (1986): 265–89; E. E. Johnson, *The Function of Apocalyptic and Wisdom Traditions in Romans 9–11* (SBLDS, 109; Atlanta: Scholars Press, 1989); R. Räisänen, "Paul, God, and Israel: Romans 9–11 in Recent Research," in J. Neusner et al. (eds.), *The Social World of Formative Christianity and Judaism* (Philadelphia: Fortress Press, 1988), 178–206; N. A. Dahl, "The Future of Israel," in his *Studies in Paul* (Minneapolis: Augsburg Pub. House, 1977), 137–58; C. K. Barrett, "Romans 9:30—10:21: Call and Responsibility of Israel," in his *Essays on Paul* (Philadelphia: Westminster Press, 1982), 132–53; R. Badenas, *Christ the End of the Law: Romans 10.4 in Pauline Perspective* (JSNTSup, 10; Sheffield: Sheffield Academic Press, 1985); S. R. Bechter, "Christ the *telos* of the Law: The Goal of Romans 10:4," *CBQ* 56 (1994): 288–308; R. Hvalvik, "A 'Sonderweg' for Israel: A Critical Examination of a Current Interpretation of Romans 11.25-27," *JSNT* 38 (1990): 87–107; J. Moiser, "Rethinking Romans 12–15," *NTS* 36 (1990): 571–82; M. Thompson, *Clothed with Christ: The Example and Teaching of Jesus in Romans 12.1—15.13* (JSNTSup, 59; Sheffield: Sheffield Academic Press, 1991); M. B. Thompson, "Romans 12.1-2 and Paul's Vision of Worship," in M. Bockmuehl and M. B. Thompson (eds.), *A Vision for the Church: Studies in Early Christian Ecclesiology* (Edinburgh: T. & T. Clark, 1997), 121–32; G. Smiga, "Romans 12:1-2 and 15:30–32 and the Occasion of the Letter to the Romans," *CBQ* 53 (1991): 257–73; W. T. Wilson, *Love without Pretense: Romans 12.9-21 and Hellenistic-Jewish Wisdom Literature* (WUNT, 2/49; Tübingen: J. C. B. Mohr, 1991); E. Käsemann, "Principles of Interpretation of Romans 13," in his *New Testament Questions of Today* (Philadelphia: Fortress Press, 1969), 196–216; J. P. Sampley, "The Weak and the Strong: Paul's Careful and Crafty Rhetorical Strategy in Romans 14:1–14:13," in L. M. White and O. L. Yarbrough (eds.), *The Social World of the First Christians* (Minneapolis: Fortress Press, 1995), 40–52; R. B. Hays, "Christ Prays the Psalm," in W. A. Meeks and A. J. Malherbe (eds.), *The Future of Christology* (Minneapolis: Fortress Press, 1993), 122–36; J. R. Wagner, "The Christ, Servant of Jew and Gentile: A Fresh Approach to Romans 15:8-9," *JBL* 116 (1997): 473–85; and R. Jewett, "The Rhetorical Function of Numerical Sequences in Romans," in D. Watson (ed.), *Persuasive Artistry* (JSNTSup, 50; Sheffield: Sheffield Academic Press, 1991), 227–45.

Interpreting Romans inevitably involves a treatment of Paul's theology. For an opening statement, see R. P. Martin, "The Kerygma of Romans," *Int* 25 (1971): 303–28. For a range of issues, see the following: J. Bassler, *Divine Impartiality: Paul and a Theological Axiom* (SBLDS, 59; Chico, Calif.: Scholars Press, 1981); R. Bultmann, *Theology of the New Testament* (New York: Charles Scribner's Sons, 1953), 1:288–306; N. A. Dahl, "The Missionary Theology in the Epistle to the Romans," in his *Studies in Paul*, 70–94; W. D. Davies, "Paul and the Law: Pitfalls in Interpretation," in his *Jewish and Pauline Studies* (Philadelphia: Fortress Press, 1984), 91–122; N. Elliott, *The Rhetoric of Romans: Argumentative Constraint and Strategy and Paul's Dialogue with Judaism* (JSNTSup, 45; Sheffield: Sheffield Academic Press, 1990); D. B. Garlington, *Faith, Obedience, and Perseverance: Aspects of Paul's Letter to the Romans* (WUNT, 79; J. C. B. Mohr [Siebeck], 1994); L. E. Keck, "'Jesus' in Romans," *JBL* 108 (1989): 443–60; R. Morgan, *Romans* (Sheffield: Sheffield Academic Press, 1997); H. Moxnes, *Theology in Conflict: Studies of Paul's Understanding of God in Romans* (NovTSup, 53; Leiden: E. J. Brill, 1980); idem, "Honor, Shame, and the Outside World in Paul's Letter to the Romans," in J. Neusner et al. (eds.), *The Social World of Formative Christianity and Judaism* (Philadelphia: Fortress Press, 1988), 207–18; M. D. Nanos, *The Mystery of Romans: The Jewish Context of Paul's Letter* (Minneapolis: Fortress Press, 1996); R. Scroggs, "Paul as Rhetorician: Two Homilies in Romans 1–11," in R. Hamerton-Kelly and R. Scroggs (eds.), *Jews, Greeks and Christians: Religious Cultures in Late Antiquity* (SJLA, 21; Leiden: E. J. Brill, 1976), 271–98; S. K. Stowers, *A Re-Reading of Romans: Justice, Jews, and Gentiles* (New Haven: Yale Univ. Press, 1994); J. C. Walters, *Ethnic Issues in Paul's Letter to the Romans: Changing Self-Definitions in Earliest Roman Christianity* (Valley Forge, Pa.: Trinity Press Int'l, 1993); F. Watson, *Paul, Judaism, and the Gentiles: A Sociological Approach* (SNTSMS, 56; Cambridge: Cambridge Univ. Press, 1986); and S. K. Williams, "The Righteousness of God in Romans," *JBL* 99 (1980): 241–90. Also see the collection of essays in D. M. Hay and E. E. Johnson (eds.), *Pauline Theology, Vol. 3: Romans* (Minneapolis: Fortress Press, 1995).

For a commentary in the tradition of classic Lutheran interpretation of Paul, see E. Käsemann, *Commentary on Romans*, trans. G. W. Bromiley (Grand Rapids: Eerdmans, 1980). Also see the major critical commentaries: J. D. G. Dunn, *Romans*, 2 vols. (WBC; Waco: Word Books, 1988); J. A Fitzmyer, *Romans* (AB; New York: Doubleday, 1993); and D. Moo, *The Epistle to the Romans* (NICNT; Grand Rapids: Eerdmans, 1996). For nontechnical treatments, see M. Black, *Romans*, 2nd ed. (NCB; Grand Rapids: Eerdmans, 1989); B. Byrne, *Romans* (SP; Collegeville, Minn.: Liturgical Press, 1996); and L. T. Johnson, *Reading Romans: A Literary and Theological Commentary* (New York: Crossroad, 1997).

15. The Letter to the Philippians

THE CHURCH Paul founded at the Roman colony of Philippi was his first in Europe (Acts 16:12-40; Phil. 4:15). The community stood behind Paul's work by financially supporting his mission (4:15-16; cf. 2 Cor. 11:7). The gentle tone of the letter conveys the special relationship between Paul and the community. When Paul wrote the letter (with Timothy, 1:1), he was in prison (1:12-14), but the work of the ministry continued—if not entirely to his satisfaction (1:15-17; 4:2-3)—and Paul fully expected to be released (1:19; 2:24). This much is clear. There is less unanimity among scholars concerning Paul's location, the situation he addressed, or even the literary integrity of the letter.

It is impossible to decide from which of Paul's several imprisonments he wrote the letter. Mention of the whole praetorium (1:13) and those of Caesar's household (4:22) would naturally if not necessarily suggest captivity in Rome or Caesarea (Acts 24:26-27; 28:30). Those who question the letter's unity and see it as an edited version of several letter fragments add the observation that there is communication between Paul and his readers by means of delegates (2:19-30; 4:18). They conclude that Ephesus would be an appropriate place for the letter's provenance simply on the basis of its geographical proximity to Philippi. They therefore postulate a Pauline imprisonment in this city. If the literary unity is not in doubt, however, then a hypothetical imprisonment in Ephesus is not required.

The authenticity of Philippians is not seriously challenged, but the presence of apparent editorial seams, changes of tone within the letter, and conflicting information lead some to doubt its literary integrity. As for the matter of the seams, the letter appears to have several endings, since Paul twice uses the phrase "finally" (*to loipon*)—an expression that usually signals a conclusion—without actually ending the letter but moving on, instead, to another section (3:1; 4:8). The shift in tone is found only in one place, when Paul moves from an encouragement to rejoice in the Lord (3:1) to a warning against "the dogs" (3:2). As for conflicting details, in 2:25-28 Paul says he plans to send Epaphroditus, the Philippians' emissary, back to them after he had been sick to the point of death; but when he mentions Epaphroditus' delivery of their monetary gift in 4:18, no mention is made of a lengthy stay. Some also consider Paul's not thanking them for their gift until 4:10-20 to be unconscionable, whereas if this were a separate letter (beginning in 4:10), Paul's thanks would be direct and his comments on Epaphroditus more consistent.

Such literary observations are joined to a reconstruction of the Philippian situation that emphasizes the role of the "opponents" (1:28). Paul says that some preach the gospel out of envy and rivalry (1:15-17), that there is murmuring and grumbling in the community (2:14), and that some of the mission workers are not getting along (4:2-3). He also mentions some who are "enemies of the cross" (3:18); and refers to certain "dogs" and "evil workers" who put their pride in circumcision (3:2-4). The conclusion is reached that the fragments of Philippians reveal stages of a conflict developing in the community generated by Pauline opponents and answered by Paul in a series of notes.

On this reading, three separate letter fragments are later sewn together, which accounts for the unevenness in the final version. The first is 4:10-20, a note thanking the Philippians for their gift of money. The second warns against divisions in the church (1:1—3:1; 4:4-7, 21-23). The third sharply attacks the false teachers who have fomented dissension (3:2—4:3; 4:8-9). The history of the community troubles follows the same progression. There is no hint of trouble in the first letter. In the second, there is rivalry and grumbling, which Paul thinks he can contain by exhortation. The third letter reveals a situation more dangerous than he had supposed, requiring a direct rebuttal of the opponents.

This hypothesis is needlessly complex and not required by the evidence of the text itself. The literary breaks in the letter are not so severe as those in 2 Corinthians. Paul's thanks for the money in 4:10-20, for example, is clearly anticipated by the language of the epistolary thanksgiving (1:3-11). The "outbreak" of 3:2—4:3 has been foreshadowed in 1:15-17, 28 and 2:21-22. This supposed polemic, furthermore, is bracketed on both sides by exhortations to "rejoice" (3:1; 4:4), which suggests deliberate framing rather than clumsy editing. The discrepancy regarding Epaphroditus is only apparent: Paul has no need to refer back to his long period of illness at this point in the letter. There is no reason, therefore, to treat Philippians as a composite of three letters.

The attempt to reconstruct a historical sequence is even more hazardous. Even if there were a series of letters, the progression could have gone in the opposite direction, from severe trouble to moderate grumbling to fellowship and the sharing of money. Going on the little information we possess, any construal is possible. In the final analysis, atomizing the letter distracts the reader from discovering the way the writing works as a text. Is the section 3:2—4:3 really a polemic, or does it have another literary function? Is there a coherent thematic and structural pattern being followed in chapters 2 and 3? Unless the text is read as a single composition written with some degree of literary integrity, such questions cannot be asked, let alone answered.

The Character of Philippians

Philippians challenges any oversimplified rendering of the Pauline corpus. It contains—side by side and sometimes intertwined—elements that are often considered logically opposite. Its authenticity is not seriously questioned, yet it has a surprising number of features ordinarily associated only with inauthentic letters. Stylistically, for example, it is "flatter," without the dialogical vigor of the diatribe; it lacks any scriptural citations; and it has some expressions found elsewhere only in other captivity letters (see, e.g., "the praise of glory," Phil. 1:11 and Eph. 1:6, 12, 14). Substantively, Paul here calls Jesus, Savior (3:20), a title otherwise found in the so-called "non-genuine" letters (Eph. 5:23; 2 Tim. 1:10; Titus 2:13; 3:6). The perception of his sufferings in Phil. 1:16-18 finds its clearest echo in 2 Tim. 1:8-12; 2:9. The emphasis on the cosmic implications of Christ's resurrection (Phil. 2:6-11; 3:21) is matched most closely by Col. 1:15-20 and Eph. 1:19-23.

Alone of the so-called "genuine" letters, Philippians mentions bishops and deacons in a manner suggesting an office or position (1:1). The term "overseer" (*episkopos*) is elsewhere found in the Pauline corpus only in 1 Tim. 3:2 and Titus 1:7 (and only in the singular). The term "deacon" or "servant" (*diakonos*), on the other hand, is used often with reference to his own ministry (1 Cor. 3:5; 2 Cor. 3:6; Eph. 3:7); and to the service of others—Phoebe (Rom. 16:1), Apollos (1 Cor. 3:5), Tychichus (Eph. 6:21), Epaphras (Col. 1:7), and possibly Timothy (cf. the variant readings in 1 Thess. 3:2 and 1 Tim. 4:6)—but never, it seems, suggesting a particular position or church office. For designating the function of members of a local community *diakonos* is used only here and in 1 Tim. 3:8, 12 and 4:6, although Paul often refers to the local leaders of churches without the use of any precise designation (see 1 Thess. 5:12; Gal. 6:6; 1 Cor. 6:5-6; 12:28; 16:15-17; Rom. 12:8; Phlm. 1-2). One should not overlook the significance of this, since the presence of church offices has been one of the reasons for considering the Pastorals as "inauthentic" Pauline letters (i.e., offices are thought to reflect a later development in the Pauline churches) despite the presence of such terminology in the "genuine" letter to the Philippians.

The eschatology of Philippians is also complex. Paul expresses a definite future expectation like that found in 1 Thess. 4:13—5:3 (Phil. 1:10; 2:16; 3:11, 20-21); and he even gives such expectation a similar note of urgency: "The Lord is near" (4:5). On the other hand, should he die, he expects to experience a union with Jesus before "the day of the Lord" (1:6). He will then "be with" Christ (1:21-23), a hope that more closely resembles what he expressed in 2 Cor. 5:1-5. Paul also sees the Christians' "homeland" in spatial rather than temporal terms: it is "in heaven" (3:20; as also in 2 Cor. 5:1-2; Eph. 6:9; Col. 1:5; 4:1). The Christology of this letter places equal stress on the "cosmic Christ" (2:5-11; 3:21; cf. above), on "Christ the righteousness from God that depends on faith" (3:9; cf. Rom. 3:22; 1 Cor. 1:30; 2 Cor. 5:21), and on Christ the exemplar of faith (2:5; cf. 1 Cor. 11:1; 2 Tim. 2:8-13).

Philippians also contains diverse aspects of Paul's self-understanding as an apostle. Suffering is a sign of genuine ministry (1:15-25; 2:17; 3:8-10), as it is of all Christian existence (1:29-30). Paul presents himself as a model (*typos*) for the community to imitate (3:17; cf. 1 Cor. 4:16; 11:1; 1 Thess. 1:6; 2 Thess. 3:9; 1 Tim. 1:16; 2 Tim. 1:13). His delegate Timothy is "like a son" and is "genuinely concerned" for the members of the community as he labors with Paul for the gospel (2:19-24; cf. 1 Cor. 4:17; 1 Tim.

1:2; 2 Tim. 3:10). In contrast to his usual claim of independence from community financial support (2 Thess. 3:6-9; 1 Cor. 9:15-18; 2 Cor. 11:7-12), Paul here gladly admits that from "the beginning of the gospel" he has been in a relationship of "giving and receiving" with this church (4:14-15). At the same time, he emphasizes his personal contentment or self-sufficiency (*autarkeia*) with respect to possessions (4:11-13). That he accepts financial support from this community is a symbol of the fellowship he enjoys with them.

Philippian's emotional warmth is often and justly remarked. One does not find here the outrage and anger of Galatians, only the warmth of affection and tenderness, even of sweetness. Positive expressions of feeling abound: "I hold you in my heart" (1:7); "I yearn for you with all the affection of Christ Jesus" (1:8); "I am glad and rejoice with you all; likewise you should be glad and rejoice with me" (2:18); "My brethren whom I love and long for, my joy and my crown" (4:1); "It was kind of you to share my trouble" (4:14). Above all, a quality of quiet joy pervades the letter (1:4, 19; 2:2, 17-18, 19, 28, 29; 3:1; 4:1, 4, 10), a joy deriving from special fellowship (1:5; 2:1; 3:10; 4:15). This leads us to the most distinctive thematic element in Philippians, as well as its organizing principle: it is a letter of friendship.

In calling Philippians a letter of friendship, I do not suggest that it precisely follows the letter form for the "friendly letter" (*epistolē philikē*) as attested in the rhetorical handbooks (cf. Pseudo-Demetrius). I mean, rather, that Paul uses the rhetoric of friendship to evoke appropriate responses in his readers. To appreciate the force of his language, it is necessary to remember how the topic of friendship fascinated Greek moralists, finding distillation in a series of proverbs universally used and endlessly expounded. Friendship could be defined simply as fellowship (*koinōnia*). Everyone agreed that "friends hold all things in common [*tois philois panta koina*]." Such sharing included both material and spiritual goods. Friendship was a form of equality (*isotēs*). So close was the spiritual unity between friends that a friend was "another self." Friends were one soul (*mia psychē*), sharing a common frame of mind (*to auto phronein*). Friendship language employed many compound words using the prefix "with" (*syn-*), since fellowship always involved some sort of "life together." The proverbs are so well known that they are reversible. To speak of being one soul or holding all in common automatically implied as well equality, friendship, and fellowship (for a condensed treatment, see Aristotle *Nicomachean Ethics* 8–9).

The friendship language of Philippians is easily observed in the Greek, though it is less obvious in English translation. Paul uses forms of the term "fellowship" (*koinōnia*) in 1:5; 2:1; 3:10; and 4:15. These occur, it will be noted, in all four "fragments" of the letter. The same distribution applies to Paul's frequent use of the *syn-* prefix. He attaches the prefix to verbs such as "struggle" (1:27; 4:3), "rejoice" (2:17, 18), "be formed" (3:10), "receive" (4:3), and "share" (*synkoinōneō*; 4:14); and to nouns like "sharer" (*koinōnos*; 1:5); "soul" (2:2); "worker" (2:25; 4:3); "soldier" (2:25); "imitator" (3:17); "form" (3:21); and "yoke" (4:3). If one consistently translated each instance with "fellow," the repetitive force of the Greek would be evident. Paul also uses variations on the motif of unity, writing of having one soul (*mia psychē*; 1:27); and one spirit (1:27), and thinking the same thing (2:2). He also utilizes variants on expressions for "the same thing" *(to auto*; 1:6, 30; 2:2, 18). Finally, he mentions equality (*isos*) once with reference to Jesus (2:6), and another with reference to Timothy (2:20).

The power of this friendship language for a community that was from the beginning of Paul's ministry a "fellow sharer" with him in the work of the gospel is obvious. It evokes the positive connotations of the relationship between the community and himself. More significantly, it serves a real rhetorical function for a community experiencing dissension because of envy and rivalry (1:15). Quite apart from the possible influence of outside agitators—whose presence is not certain—the Philippians have among them some who are grumbling and bickering (2:14; 4:2-3). With its emphasis on equality and unity, friendship language counters the impulses of self-assertion. Paul's rhetoric is even more powerful, however, because he has made fellowship the organizing principle of the letter.

Fellowship in the Gospel

The fellowship binding the Christian community is not, as with a Hellenistic club or benevolent association, based on like interests or mutual material benefits. Nor is it, as in some Hellenistic schools of philosophy, based on shared convictions concerning a particular philosophical outlook (for example, later Pythagoreans based the value of friendship on their belief in the metaphysical unity of all beings). Like such schools, the Christians are committed to the principles of "having one mind" (1:27); and "sharing their possessions" (4:15), but the "spirit" joining them together is the Holy Spirit of God: theirs is a "fellowship of the Spirit" (2:1). They "stand in the one Spirit" (1:27); and they worship God "in spirit" (3:3). This spirit is not theirs by nature but by gift (4:23). It is "the Spirit of Jesus Christ," who is at work both in Paul and in them (1:19).

Since the Spirit came to them through the hearing of the "good news," theirs is also a "fellowship in the gospel" (1:5). The "good news" has bound them together from the beginning (4:15). They have supported it financially (4:10-20), have labored together in its proclamation (2:22; 4:3), and have suffering together in its defense (1:7, 12, 16, 29-30; 3:10). If they are "one soul" it is because they "struggle together in faith for the gospel" (1:27). That "good news," furthermore, demands from them a response consonant with the gift: "Let your life be worthy of the gospel of Christ" (1:27).

Envy is a vice in which one seeks one's own good at the expense of others. For Paul, it is unthinkable that rivalry, envy, and competition should arise over the preaching of the gospel (1:15), when that is precisely the focus of Christian unity. In his use of the language of fellowship, Paul therefore rebukes those members of the community who abandon the common good, seeking their own self-interest. If they are grumbling and complaining against each other (2:14), they will no longer "shine like lights in the world" (2:14), missing the real reason why God has called this fellowship into existence: "God is at work in you, both to will and to work for his good pleasure" (2:13).

The Form of Fellowship Is Service

Philippians 2:1-4:3 is an extended demonstration of how Christian fellowship should shape the community's identity. A statement of principle (2:1-4) is followed by a series of examples that illustrate it: Jesus (2:6-11), Paul (2:17), Timothy (2:19-24), Epaphroditus (2:25-30), and Paul again, this time in contrast to self-seekers (3:2-16). A call for the imitation of these examples (3:17-21) is followed by the specific application to individual disputants (4:2-3).

Paul begins with a rich compilation of terms evoking friendship (2:1-2): the members of the community are to be "like-souled," to "think the same thing," and "have the same love." Because their fellowship is based on their being "of the spirit" and "in Christ," the form of that fellowship is provided by the way the Spirit works through the Messiah. Paul contrasts this ideal paradigm with its opposite, then explicates the proper attitude. Their fellowship cannot be based on party spirit or conceit, which are forms of self-seeking. They are, rather, to have toward each other an attitude of humble- or lowly-mindedness (*tapeinophrosynē*). They should count or reckon (*hēgeomai*) others above themselves. Notice Paul does not call for a denial of the self as in the ascetic ideal, but for a functional "reckoning" that relativizes individual interests for the sake of others—the same communal consciousness, in short, that he advocates for the Corinthians. Paul spells this out when he says, "Let each one of you look not only to his own interests but also [or, "even more so"] to the interests of others" (2:4).

Three examples illustrate the proper attitude. The first and most important is that of Jesus. Paul's language in 2:6-11 is dense and rhythmic, possibly indicating reliance on a traditional Christian hymn about Jesus. The correspondence in structure and language to the rest of this section is so close that it is also possible that Paul himself wrote the hymn or, at the very least, that he conformed his language in the surrounding text to match the vocabulary of the poem. Certainly of greater significance is the content of the hymn, and how it functions for Paul as part of his larger argument in Philippians. Playing off Paul's previous use of friendship language—particularly in association with the use of possessions—the hymn establishes a model for Christian imitation in terms of possessing and dispossessing positions of power. Paul writes of Jesus (2:6-11),

> . . . who, though he was in the form of God, did not count equality with God a thing to be grasped, but emptied himself, taking the form of a slave, being born in the likeness of humanity. And being found in human form he humbled himself and became obedient unto death, even death on a cross. Therefore God has highly exalted him and bestowed on him the name which is above every name, that at the name of Jesus every knee should bow, in heaven

and on earth and under the earth, and every tongue confess that Jesus Christ is Lord, to the glory of God the Father.

Here is one who was in the form of God (*morphē tou theou*) but did not reckon or count (*hēgeomai*) himself above God, and therefore did not seize the position of equality (*isos*) with God as one would take possession of something (*hapargmon* suggests "booty"). Rather, he "emptied himself" and took on the form of a slave (*morphē doulou*). This is the essential exchange.

Then, being found (*heuretheis*) in the form of a human being, he humbled himself further (*etapeinōsen*) by his obedience that led to his death on the cross (2:8). The cross is the ultimate symbol of self-emptying and of the obedience that is faith precisely because it was the human symbol—in Paul's day—for ultimate rejection, scorn, and degradation. The hymn has thus moved downward, toward "dispossession." It also clearly corresponds to the command for community members to "reckon" and "be humble" (2:3): Jesus illustrates—indeed actualizes—these principles in his own life.

Now, the movement is reversed. The one who did not "grasp at" equality with God has been honored by God (2:9) and exalted as Lord. He is greeted and worshiped as Lord by all creation (2:10-11). The pattern is therefore clear: precisely because (*dio*, "therefore," in 2:9 is emphatic) Jesus gave up his "legitimate interest" of equality with God, he was honored with exaltation. In a marvelous line of reversals, the one who *dispossesses* all—indeed coming to the point of being *dispossessed* himself—comes to *possess*, in the end, all things as Lord. This principle had a strong impact on early Christian teaching (cf. Mark 9:33-35; 10:35-45; Matt. 23:11-12; Luke 9:46-48; 22:24-27), particularly in the sense that Paul uses it here: as a model not only for Christian fellowship in general, but for Christian leadership in particular.

Scholars debate whether the pattern describes the mythological descent and ascent of the incarnation: the preexistent Christ "emptied himself out" of his divine status by becoming human only to receive it back in the resurrection. This would not be foreign to Paul, who is fond of cosmic exchanges (cf. 2 Cor. 5:21; 8:9; Gal. 4:4-7). Others argue that the focus is less on the incarnation than on the manner of Jesus' messianic activity. They claim that Paul here interprets the story of Jesus through a meditation on Isaiah 52–53—the Song of the Suffering Servant—showing how in his lifetime Jesus refused the status of claiming equality with God and consistently "emptied himself out" in service. This reading too is intelligible and corresponds to Paul's sensitivity to the faith of Jesus as the cause and shape of Christian identity. There is no real need to choose between the options. For Paul, both the gift of God that was the coming of the Messiah and the "Messiah's faith" that was spelled out in obedience take the form of "self-emptying for others."

Jesus is a model to the Philippians of how they should not "grasp after equality" by seeking their own interests, but "empty themselves" in service to one another, with the expectation that, like Jesus, they will be honored and glorified by God. The work of the spirit in them replicates the pattern of its work in Jesus. This is why Paul introduces the hymn in this manner: "You have this mind in you which is yours in Christ Jesus" (2:5). The ambiguity of the Greek should not go unnoticed, as it can be read both indicatively ("you do have") and imperatively ("you must have"). They have this mind already because of the Spirit (cf. 1 Cor. 2:16); but they must strive to live it out in imitation of Jesus. The hymn concludes then with the following: "Therefore my beloved, as you have always obeyed, so now" (2:12); otherwise, Paul's work among them has been in vain (2:16). God's work among them (2:13) should not lead to divisiveness (2:14) but to mutual service.

Moving along to his next example (in 2:17), Paul utilizes himself as a model by referring to his own work for, and among, the Philippians: "Even if I am to be poured out as a libation upon the sacrifice and offering of your faith, I am glad and rejoice with you all." He rejoices *with* them because he spends his life *for* them (note the striking similarity between "poured out" [2:17] and "emptied out" [2:7]). They should, therefore, respond in kind: "You also rejoice the same [*to auto*] and rejoice with me [*synchairein*]" (2:18). In other words, if they "pour out" themselves for each other they will be honoring Paul for his own work on their behalf. The ancient notion of reciprocity is clearly evident here: I have given (myself on your behalf) therefore you must give (to each other on my behalf). And it is precisely this "pouring out" for each other that constitutes "rejoicing with" Paul.

Timothy also is an example of the proper "mind of Christ." He is "equal minded" with Paul (2:20) because he is "genuinely anxious" for the welfare of the Philippians. His service is defined by their needs, not his desires (2:21-22):

> They all look after their own interests, not those of Christ Jesus [cf. 2:4]. But Timothy's worth you know, how he served [or, "slaved," *edouleusen*; cf. 2:7] with me in the gospel.

As Jesus was a slave (2:7), so Paul and Timothy have slaved not for their own glory, but for the good of the Philippians in the gospel. Thus they imitate the slave Jesus and can themselves therefore bear the title of "slave" (cf. 1:1).

Epaphroditus, too, is an example of life lived for others (2:25-30). He is Paul's fellow worker and fellow soldier (2:25). He was sent by the Philippians as a supplier (or, "servant"/"offering," *leitourgos*; cf. 2:17) of Paul's needs. Because his illness was so serious, he was almost literally "obedient unto death," since he "risked his life to complete your service to me" (2:30). Again, the theme is clear: the pattern of Christ is imitated by his followers, whose self-sacrifice flows out of their "friendship" with other believers.

In 3:2-16, Paul again presents himself as an example of the same attitude. The literary function of this section, which is so often considered a polemic against false teachers, is actually that of a counter example, used to highlight the positive model of Paul. One reason the historical delineation of Paul's opponents in Philippians is so difficult is that they may not be *his* opponents at all. The only explicit mention of opponents in the letter refers to those standing against the Philippians themselves (1:28). Paul's descriptions here lack specificity. He writes of "dogs" and "evil workers" (3:2; cf. 2 Cor. 11:13) who "mutilate the flesh" (*katatomē*—a play on *peritomē*, "circumcision"). Using stereotypical slander, he says, "their end is destruction, their god is their belly, their glory is their shame" (3:19; cf. Rom. 16:18). Otherwise, they are simply "enemies of the cross" (3:18). In Gal. 6:12, similar language is used to refer to those who choose circumcision in order to avoid persecution as a Christian. That is also possible here. But in the light of 2:6-11, the cross also stands as a symbol of self-emptying obedience and service, in contrast to those who glory in their own accomplishments and status; and this is the real point of Paul's argument.

Paul does not directly attack these opponents or argue against them. He simply tells the Philippians to look at (*blepete*) them. The term *blepete* can be used as "beware of," but it can also mean simply "observe" (cf. 1 Cor. 1:26; 3:10; 10:18). They are to "consider" those who glory in the flesh as the contrasting image of Paul's positive example. When 3:2-16 is read according to the pattern of the Christ hymn in 2:6-11, the parallelism is patent, and Paul's parenetic use of the counter example becomes clear.

The hymn contrasted a status once held "by right" with a new status as a slave, brought about by obedience. So also does Paul contrast his former and his present status. In every respect, he had reason for "confidence" in his Jewish background. He was, indeed, "as to righteousness under the law, blameless" (3:6). In his portrayal of the reversal, he again uses the language of possessions (cf. 2:6), and states (3:7-8):

> Whatever gain I had, I counted [*hēgeomai*] as loss, for the sake of Christ. Indeed, I count [*hēgeomai*] everything as loss because of the surpassing worth of knowing Christ Jesus my Lord.

His obedience to the Messiah involved the same sort of loss of status and paradoxical gain as in the case of Jesus (3:8):

> I have suffered the loss of all things for his sake, and count [*hēgeomai*] them as refuse [lit. "manure"] in order that I might gain Christ.

Paul wants to be found (*heurethō*) in him, just as Jesus was found (*heuretheis*) in the form of a human being (3:9; cf. 2:8). Because he is so found in Jesus, he also is honored by God (3:9),

> not having a righteousness of my own based on law, but that which is through the faith of Christ, the righteousness from God which depends on faith.

Now Paul demonstrates how the pattern is empowered and manifested (3:10): because he "knows the power of the resurrection," he experiences the Spirit that comes from the risen Lord. That Spirit works in him, however, so that he "might share in his sufferings, becoming like him in his death, that if possible I might attain the resurrection from the dead." The term "being like him" is stronger in the Greek: "formed together into his death" explicitly draws on the language of form [*morphē*] from 2:6-8. For Paul, the imitation of Jesus' model is to be taken quite literally.

Paul has therefore allowed the form of Christ's self-emptying to become the form of his own existence. Unlike those who preach circumcision, he does not cling to a status of which he can boast but receives the gift of righteousness that comes by Jesus' faith. So also should the Philippians regard themselves (3:15-16). The process has not yet been completed in Paul; he still must struggle as an athlete (3:12-14); he has not reached the resurrection glory. He is still being conformed to the suffering of Christ. This is their call as well, since "Christ Jesus has made [them] his own" (3:12-14).

Paul calls them to imitation in 3:17-21. They can look to Jesus, Paul, Timothy, and Epaphroditus as examples of the mind of Christ: ". . . join in imitating me, and observe those who so live according to the example you have in us." As often in parenesis, Paul contrasts this positive command with its negative opposite—those opponents of the cross whose minds are set on earthly things (3:18-19)—before picking up the language of the hymn once more and drawing his readers with him into the Spirit's work of transformation (3:20-21):

> Our commonwealth is in heaven, and from it we await a savior, the Lord Jesus Christ, who will change [*metaskēmatizō*] our lowly body [*sōma tapeinōseōs*] to be like [or, formed with: *symmorphē*] the body of his glory, by the power which enables him to subject all things to himself.

Paul at last turns this demonstration to its practical end, making clear that the discussion in chapters 2–3 has been occasioned, at least in part, by the issues Paul now addresses in chapter 4. (Notice how the double *parakalō* in 4:2, with the *paraklēsis* of 2:1, brackets the entire section of chaps. 2–3.) He exhorts his "fellow laborers" Euodia and Syntyche to "think the same thing in the Lord" (4:2). There is now no doubt what this "one thing" is: the fellowship of the Christian community rests not in the assertion of rights but in the relativization of those rights for the sake of others. As Paul says in 3:15-16:

> Let those of us who are mature be thus minded; and if in anything you are other minded, God will also reveal this to you. Only let us hold true to what we have attained.

In fact, Paul finds in the relationship between the Philippian community and himself just such a living fellowship. We see, as further evidence for the literary unity of this letter, that the central argument of chapters 2:1—4:3 is framed by the same pattern of "life for others." In the beginning of the letter (1:21-26), Paul shows how he gave up the gain that would be his by dying—going to "be with Christ"—for the sake of the Philippians' "progress and joy in the faith." Likewise, at the end of the letter, the Philippians themselves have "thought on behalf of Paul" (4:10, with the Greek rendered literally); and have "shared his affliction" (4:14): they sacrifice financially for his mission. Paul thus wants the Philippian Christians to treat each other both the way he has been and continues to be toward them and the way they show themselves to be toward him.

Throughout this letter, then, we see a compelling progression. Paul starts off with the language of friendship from the Greco-Roman cultural context and uses it to develop a particularly Christian understanding of friendship. The fellowship of Christians is a unity that issues forth from the Holy Spirit, being expressed through self-sacrifice and self-emptying love toward the other. The friendship of Jesus with God, of Jesus with humans, of Paul with the Philippians, of Timothy and Epaphroditus with Paul, and, finally, even of the Philippians with Paul, all illustrate this same pattern: not counting oneself above the other leads to service for others. Because of the paradigm of Christ reflected in the pattern of the hymn, the standards of the world have here been reversed.

Study Questions

1. What characteristics have suggested to some scholars that Philippians has been pieced together from multiple letters of Paul?

2. What image of Jesus emerges from the "hymn" in Phil. 2:6-11? What gets left out of this characterization?

3. How would you describe Paul's notion of community based on Philippians?

4. In what ways does Paul portray himself as an example for the Philippian church?

Bibliographical Note

On the cultural and religious context of ancient Philippi, with emphasis on the experience of women, see V. A. Abrahamsen, *Women and Worship at Philippi: Diana/Artemis and Other Cults in the Early Christian Era* (Portland: Astarte Shell, 1995); and L. Portefaix, *Sisters Rejoice: Paul's Letter to the Philippians and Luke-Acts as Received by First-Century Philippian Women* (ConBNT, 20; Stockholm: Almqvist & Wiksell, 1988). Also see C. Bakirtzis & H. Koester (eds.), *Philippi at the Time of Paul and after His Death* (Harrisburg, Penn.: Trinity Press Int'l, 1998); and L. M. White, "Visualizing the 'Real' World of Acts 16: Toward the Construction of a Social Index," in L. M. White and O. L. Yarbrough (eds.), *The Social World of the First Christians* (Minneapolis: Fortress Press, 1995), 234–61.

For the place of Philippians in Paul's career, as well as the issue of literary integrity, see, among many, L. Alexander, "Hellenistic Letter-Forms and the Structure of Philippians," *JSNT* 37 (1989): 87–101; W. J. Dalton, "The Integrity of Phil," *Bib* 60 (1979): 97–102; R. Jewett, "The Epistolary Thanksgiving and the Integrity of Philippians," *NovT* 12 (1970): 40–53; T. E. Pollard, "The Integrity of Philippians," *NTS* 13 (1966–67): 57–66; J. T. Reed, *A Discourse Analysis of Philippians: Method and Rhetoric in the Debate over Literary Integrity* (JSNTSup, 136; Sheffield: Sheffield Academic Press, 1997); J. Reumann, "Philippians 3:20-21—A Hymnic Fragment?" *NTS* 30 (1984): 593–609; and W. Schmithals, *Paul and the Gnostics*, trans. J. Steely (Nashville: Abingdon Press, 1972), 65–122. On the opponents, alongside Schmithals, see R. Jewett, "Conflicting Movements in the Early Church as Reflected in Philippians," *NovT* 12 (1970): 361–90; A. F. J. Klijn, "Paul's Opponents in Phil. 3," *NovT* 7 (1964–65): 278–84; H. Koester, "The Purpose of the Polemic of a Pauline Fragment," *NTS* 8 (1961): 317–32; G. Luedemann, *Opposition to Paul in Jewish Christianity*, trans. M. E. Boring (Minneapolis: Fortress Press, 1989), 103–9; M. Tellbe, "The Sociological Factors Behind Philippians 3.1-11 and the Conflict at Philippi," *JSNT* 55 (1994): 97–121.

For the Christ hymn in 2:6-11, besides the standard treatment by R. P. Martin, *Carmen Christi: Philippians 2:5-11 in Recent Interpretation and in the Setting of Early Christian Worship*, rev. ed. (Grand Rapids: Eerdmans, 1983 [1967]), the following are representative: C. Basevi and J. Chapa, "Philippians 2.6-11: The Rhetorical Function of a Pauline 'Hymn'," in S. E. Porter and T. H. Olbricht (eds.), *Rhetoric and the New Testament* (JSNTSup, 90; Sheffield: Sheffield Academic Press, 1993), 338–56; G. Bornkamm, "On Understanding the Christ-Hymn, Phil 2:6-11," in his *Early Christian Experience* (New York: Harper & Row, 1969), 112–22; G. Howard, "Phil 2:6-11 and the Human Christ," *CBQ* 40 (1978): 368–87; C. F. D. Moule, "Further Reflections on Phil 2:5-11," in W. Gasque and R. P. Martin (eds.), *Apostolic History and the Gospel* (Grand Rapids: Wm. B. Eerdmans, 1970), 264–76; J. Murphy O'Connor, "Christological Anthropology in Phil II, 6-11," *RB* 83 (1976): 25–50; and C. H. Talbert, "The Problem of Pre-Existence in Phil 2:6-11," *JBL* 86 (1967): 141–53. Most of these studies isolate the hymn from its literary context; an exception is the analysis of M. D. Hooker, "Philippians 2:6-11," in E. E. Ellis and E. Grasser (eds.), *Jesus und Paulus* (Göttingen: Vandenhoeck & Ruprecht, 1975), 151–64. On the hermeneutical problem of the language see S. Briggs, "Can an Enslaved God Liberate? Hermeneutical Reflections on Philippians 2:6-11," *Semeia* 47 (1989): 137–53.

For discussion of Philippians 1, see D. W. Palmer, "To Die Is Gain (Phil 1:21)," *NovT* 17 (1975): 203–18; and V. J. De Vogel, "Reflections on Philippians 1:23-24," *NovT* 19 (1977): 262–74. For other aspects of the letter, see L. G. Bloomquist, *The Function of Suffering in Philippians* (JSNTSup, 78; Sheffield: Sheffield Academic Press, 1993); N. A. Dahl, "Euodia and Syntyche and Paul's Letter to the Philippians," in L. M. White and O. L. Yarbrough (eds.), *The Social World of the First Christians* (Minneapolis: Fortress Press, 1995), 3–15; T. Engberg-Pedersen, "Stoicism in Philippians," in T. Engberg-

Pedersen (ed.), *Paul in His Hellenistic Context* (Minneapolis: Fortress Press, 1995), 256–90; E. M. Krentz, "Military Language and Metaphors in Philippians," in B. H. McLean (ed.), *Origins and Method: Towards a New Understanding of Judaism and Christianity* (JSNTSup, 86; Sheffield: Sheffield Academic Press, 1993), 105–27; J. W. Marshall, "Paul's Ethical Appeal in Philippians," in S. E. Porter and T. H. Olbricht (eds.), *Rhetoric and the New Testament* (JSNTSup, 90; Sheffield: Sheffield Academic Press, 1993), 357–74; R. P. Martin and B. J. Dodd (eds.), *Where Christology Began: Essays on Philippians 2* (Louisville: Westminster John Knox Press, 1998). D. Peterlin, *Paul's Letter to the Philippians in the Light of Disunity in the Church* (NovTSup, 79; Leiden: E. J. Brill, 1995); G. W. Peterman, *Paul's Gift from Philippi* (SNTSMS, 92; Cambridge: Cambridge Univ. Press, 1997); J. Reumann, "Contributions of the Philippian Community to the Paul and to Earliest Christianity," *NTS* 39 (1993): 438–57; and F. W. Weidmann, "An (Un)Accomplished Model: Paul and the Rhetorical Strategy of Philippians 3:3-17," in V. Miles et al. (eds.), *Putting Body & Soul Together* (Valley Forge, Pa.: Trinity Press Int'l, 1997), 245–57. On the influence of Paul's imprisonment on the writing of his letters, see C. S. Wansink, *Chained in Christ: The Experience and Rhetoric of Paul's Imprisonments* (JSNTSup, 130; Sheffield: Sheffield Academic Press, 1996). On the theology of Philippians, see the relevant essays in J. Bassler (ed.), *Pauline Theology, Vol. 1: Thessalonians, Philippians, Galatians, Philemon* (Minneapolis: Fortress Press, 1991).

On friendship in antiquity, see D. Konstan, *Friendship in the Classical World* (Cambridge: Cambridge Univ. Press, 1997); and J. T. Fitzgerald (ed.), *Greco-Roman Perspectives on Friendship* (Atlanta: Scholars Press, 1997). For another collection of essays, see J. T. Fitzgerald (ed.), *Friendship, Flattery, and Frankness of Speech: Studies on Friendship in the New Testament World* (NovTSup, 82; Leiden: E. J. Brill, 1996), particularly: J. Reumann, "Philippians, Especially Chapter 4, as a 'Letter of Friendship': Observations on a Checkered History of Scholarship"; K. L. Berry, "The Function of Friendship Language in Philippians 4:10-20"; A. J. Malherbe, "Paul's Self-Sufficiency (4:11)"; and J. T. Fitzgerald, "Philippians in the Light of Some Ancient Discussions of Friendship."

My reading of the central section of Philippians owes much to W. Kurz, "Kenotic Imitation of Paul and Christ in Phil. 2 and 3," in F. Segovia (ed.), *Discipleship in the New Testament* (Philadelphia: Fortress Press, 1985), 103–26. For a different approach to this language, see J. P. Sampley, "Societas Christi: Roman Law and Paul's Conception of the Christian Community," in J. Jervell and W. A. Meeks (eds.), *God's Christ and His People* (Oslo: Universitetsforlaget, 1977), 158–74; and *Pauline Partnership in Christ: Christian Community and Commitment in Light of Roman Law* (Philadelphia: Fortress Press, 1980).

For critical commentary with extensive bibliography, see G. D. Fee, *Paul's Letter to the Philippians* (NICNT; Grand Rapids: Eerdmans, 1995); G. F. Hawthorne, *Philippians* (WBC; Waco: Word Books, 1983); and P. T. O'Brien, *The Epistle to the Philippians: A Commentary on the Greek Text* (NIGTC; Grand Rapids: Eerdmans, 1991). For a more general treatment, see B. Witherington III, *Friendship and Finances in Philippi: The Letter of Paul to the Philippians* (Valley Forge, Pa.: Trinity Press Int'l, 1994).

16. The Letter to Philemon

THE SHORTEST OF Paul's letters possesses an importance beyond itself as a factor in deciphering a larger part of the Pauline collection. While its own authenticity is unquestioned, Philemon has literary links to Colossians and Ephesians, whose authenticity is much discussed and frequently rejected. A consideration of each of these three writings will be helped by a preliminary display of the connections between them and a discussion of the ways in which scholars have construed the relationship. Such historical detection does not bear on the literary merit or religious message of the writings, but the issues raised help sharpen the literary character and religious dimensions of these Pauline traditions.

Connections and Construals

Connections

The three letters share several features. Each claims to be written by Paul from captivity (Phlm. 1; Col. 4:10, 18; Eph. 3:1; 4:1; 6:20). Philemon is cosponsored by Timothy (v. 1), and Paul writes at least part of the letter in his own hand (v. 19). Colossians also claims to come from Paul and Timothy (1:1), with Paul adding at least the final greeting himself (4:18). Ephesians makes no mention of an amanuensis or cosponsorship (1:1).

There is a considerable overlap in the names mentioned in each letter. In prison with Paul, according to Philemon, is Epaphras, his "fellow prisoner," and Mark, Aristarchus, Demas, and Luke (vv. 23-24). Paul is sending the slave Onesimus back to his owner, Philemon (v. 10). In the assembly that meets in Philemon's household, Paul greets his "sister" Apphia and his "fellow soldier" Archippus (v. 2). In Colossians we meet the some of the same cast, plus others. Paul says he is sending Tychichus (4:7-9) and Onesimus (4:9) to report to the community about him. Paul's fellow prisoners are Aristarchus, Mark, Jesus Justus (4:10-11), Luke, Demas (4:14), and Epaphras, "one of yourselves" (4:12). With the exception of Tychichus and Jesus Justus, the names match exactly. Among those in the church at Colossae, Paul has a message only for Archippus: "See that you fulfill the ministry that you have received in the Lord" (4:17). He greets his fellow Christians at Laodicea, including "Nympha and the church at her house" (4:15). Moreover, he expects the Colossians and Laodiceans to exchange letters (4:16), demonstrating Paul's view that the communities of Hierapolis, Colossae, and Laodicea form part of a circuit of churches bound by communication (4:13). The coincidence of names suggests that these letters were written at the same time from the same place by the same person. Ephesians lacks any personal references, except in 6:21-22:

> Now that you may also know how I am and what I am doing, Tychichus, the beloved brother and faithful minister in the Lord will tell you everything. I have sent him to you for this very purpose, that you may know how we are, and that he may encourage your hearts.

As the one who delivers personal information about Paul, Tychichus thus links Colossians and Ephesians. This chain of names matches what we know from other NT writings. Mark, the cousin of Barnabas, was a companion of Paul for a time (Acts 15:37-39), as were Tychichus (Acts 20:4; 2 Tim. 4:12; Titus 3:12), Aristarchus (Acts 19:29; 27:2), Demas (2 Tim. 4:10), and Luke (2 Tim. 4:11). The local personalities Epaphras and Onesimus, in contrast, are attested only in Philemon and Colossians. Paul's companion Jesus Justus is found solely in Colossians. Philemon is mentioned only in the letter bearing his name.

The letter to Philemon is so short that not a great deal can be advanced regarding its style. Colossians and Ephesians, however, share much common vocabulary and have similar sentence structures and thematic emphases. Their similarities can be overdrawn, for their shared terms often occur in different contexts and with distinct nuances. But when the documents are viewed side by side, one could easily conclude that some literary relationship, though not necessarily one of dependence, connects the two letters.

The three letters differ most in their intended audiences and function. Philemon is basically a personal note. It greets others in the church but is written throughout in the second-person singular. The letter also has a very personal purpose: Paul wants Philemon to receive back his runaway slave Onesimus. The injunction "Receive him as you would me" (Phlm. 17) makes this note, in effect, a letter of recommendation. Onesimus is no longer simply property, he is a brother in the faith and should be received as such.

Colossians is written not to an individual but to a community. Paul writes to a church founded by his fellow prisoner Epaphras (Col. 1:7). He responds to misconstruals and misunderstandings of the Christian faith that have arisen in the young community. These appear to resemble the problems in Galatia, except that fewer details are known or revealed in this case and Paul must instruct a church that he has never met personally (Col. 2:1).

In Ephesians, the community and situation are much more difficult to reconstruct because of the lack of personal information and the seeming paucity of direct references to conflict. Here, the themes and images of Colossians are placed within the framework of a theological exposition concerning God's reconciling work in the world.

The relation of Ephesians to Colossians is almost precisely that of Romans to Galatians: the issues forged in controversy are elevated to the level of a general, more sustained statement. Ephesians, however, is even more general in its teaching than Romans.

Each letter raises its own distinct problem, whether taken individually or together with the others. The authenticity of Philemon is not seriously challenged. But why would such a personal note, and one with so little apparent general appeal, be preserved and made part of a collection? Was it perhaps not sent by itself, but as part of a larger collection of letters intended for wider circulation? Colossians is obviously related to Philemon, but because its authenticity is often challenged on other grounds, the network of names becomes a possible indication of pseudepigraphy. In that view, a later author used the names found in Philemon to give the impression that Colossians was written by Paul. Although some ancient pseudepigraphy made use of biographical information, it is difficult to understand how details from a short note like Philemon, which clearly must have had limited circulation, could have given Colossians an air of Pauline authenticity. Better to have drawn on the people mentioned in 1 Corinthians or Romans 16.

The authenticity of Ephesians is most often challenged on the grounds of its style and theology. Some think it represents a Pauline understanding as filtered through a mystical, possibly even gnostic, framework. Many also argue that Ephesians reflects a later form of Pauline thought. It is maintained, for example, that in Paul's time one could not speak of the reconciliation between Jew and Greek as an accomplished reality in the church. Moreover, it is believed that Paul's ethics could never have been as domesticated in his own day as the lists of household duties seem to suggest. Furthermore, many find it difficult to believe that Paul could have written to a church so well known to him in such an impersonal and distant fashion.

One solution to this problem—particularly the seeming incompatibility of Paul's manner of writing elsewhere, with the general nature of the teaching found in Ephesians—is the position of the second-century radical Pauline interpreter Marcion, who identified this letter as the one written to the Laodiceans (cf. Col. 4:16), of which otherwise no trace exists. Marcion's solution is unlikely, but the fact that he suggested it shows that from early on the precise destination of this letter was in doubt or confusion. The manuscript evidence supports this: some good, early manuscripts lack the name Ephesians in the title, having only "to the saints" (1:1). The omission is all the more striking, since the form of the Greek sentence calls out for a place name: "to the saints at _____." The absence of the place name hardly seems like an accidental occurrence, and therefore must have a function.

When these observations are taken together, it is not surprising that many scholars consider that Ephesians was not written to a specific community, but was a circular letter to be delivered to several communities, with the name of the community being added as the letter was read aloud by the person who delivered it. This would explain why the material in Ephesians is so general in nature: Paul was not addressing the situation of one particular community, but was writing in a manner that would give the letter pertinence beyond any immediate context.

Construals

Scholars construe these three letters in several different ways. First, some consider all three letters to be an elaborate literary hoax, much as some regard the Pastorals. But there is no reason to doubt the genuineness of Philemon. Second, either Colossians or Ephesians is regarded as inauthentic, and the literary relations among the letters explained on the basis of copying and imitation. Finally, all three are seen as genuine, and their differences explained on the basis of their audience, form, and function. Since the present discussion serves simply to place Philemon within a specific epistolary context, I leave aside further consideration of the authenticity of Colossians and Ephesians in this chapter.

If, as a number of scholars still think, Colossians is authentic, the situation is clarified considerably. If Colossians and Philemon were sent together by Paul to Colossae, the preservation of Philemon is explained, and only the production of Ephesians needs an explanation. One suggestion is that Onesimus, upon reading Colossians, undertook, after Paul's death, the collection of all his letters. Having read those he collected, he borrowed liberally from their substance if not their style and, in an act of filial loyalty to Paul, undertook the composition of Ephesians. He intended it to be a compendium of Paul's theology and to act as an introduction to the Pauline collection. This is an ingenious theory. It solves the issue of pseudonymity and the literary relation to Colossians: Onesimus simply lifted portions of Colossians when writing Ephesians. However, the hypothesis lacks any manuscript evidence that Ephesians headed up the collection, and it greatly oversimplifies the stylistic similarities between Colossians and Ephesians. Moreover, there is little evidence or inherent reason to connect the writing of Ephesians to the individual Onesimus.

On one level, however, this theory has more value than the one that challenges the authenticity of both Colossians and Ephesians. The latter must account for both the similarities of the two letters (Were they written by the same individual?) and their distinctive elements (Why is it deemed necessary in Colossians to authenticate the letter with personal names of Pauline companions, but not in Ephesians?). Moreover, attributing the letters to two separate writers does not solve the problem. Rather, it creates the odd situation of a later Pauline writer copying the style of an earlier copier of Paul—and this raises numerous problems of its own. What all these solutions—inadequate as they may be—suggest, however, is the need to account for the unique relationship that exists between Colossians and Ephesians.

If Colossians and Ephesians are not written by different individuals, then the best solution is to regard all three letters as authentically Pauline in the sense used in this book: they are all written in Paul's lifetime and under his supervision. The major difficulty with this hypothesis is not stylistic but thematic, and the cases of Colossians and Ephesians will each require separate discussion. But if a Pauline sponsorship in the broad sense can be granted, then the literary relationship of the three letters is clear, and the figure that emerges as a key to the correspondence is Tychichus.

Here is a possible reconstruction. Paul is in prison with the founder of the Colossian community, Epaphras. He is joined by the runaway slave Onesimus. The slave or someone else brings news to Paul and Epaphras of a crisis regarding the Christian faith in the Colossian church. Epaphras asks Paul to support his ministry there by writing a letter to the troubled community. Paul obliges. He also writes a letter of support for Onesimus, and uses the occasion of sending the slave back to his master to have the Colossian letter delivered. The critical link here is this: Philemon's congregation is among the house churches of Colossae, so it is only natural that the letters of Philemon and Colossians should have been connected—they arrived together—and this ensures the preservation of the personal letter to Philemon.

At the same time, Paul composes a circular letter employing many of the themes of Colossians but recasting them in a distinctive and more general format, expounding God's work in the church as a whole. He wants this letter to be delivered to the circle of gentile churches associated with his mission though not necessarily founded by him. Tychichus, Onesimus' companion, carries three or four letters: the letter of recommendation for Onesimus; the letter to the Colossian church, which Paul expects will be read aloud at the assembly; another possible letter, perhaps for the local assembly at Laodicea; and the circular letter, Ephesians, which Tychichus will deliver to Hierapolis, Ephesus, and other cities in Asia Minor. At the same time, he brings to these churches personal information concerning Paul's condition in prison.

The close proximity of Ephesus, Colossae, and Laodicea makes this thesis especially appealing, regardless of where Paul is imprisoned at the time. Moreover, the fact that Paul requests that the Colossians exchange their letter with the Laodiceans (Col. 4:16) provides evidence—in this very collection of letters—for the type of thing I am suggesting here for Ephesians. Furthermore, we know that Paul used his co-workers in this manner, and this scenario recreates one of the plausible sociological situations for the people connected with Paul's missionary school: they acted as his emissaries to various Gentile congregations throughout the Roman world. This is the simplest of the hypotheses, and it covers the data well. It is the imaginative picture I have when I read these three letters.

The Letter

In spite of its brevity, Philemon is a carefully crafted witness to an emerging Christian ethos, showing both its power to transform symbols and attitudes and its struggle to transcend social forms. It also reveals a Paul who is unexpectedly diplomatic, urbane, and even witty. Within its classic epistolary form—opening greeting (vv. 1-3), thanks-giving (vv. 4-7), body (vv. 8-20), closing greetings (vv. 21-24), and farewell (v. 25)—the letter is a masterpiece of subtle suggestion.

Paul needs considerable diplomatic skill for his situation is awkward. Philemon, the slave owner, has the Roman law on his side, and since Paul is the cause of Onesimus' defection, he is legally to blame. But he is also convinced that Onesimus—now that he is a Christian—cannot be considered simply property. He is an equal before the Lord and a "brother." By accepting Onesimus among his companions, Paul has brought some financial harm to Philemon, which he promises to repay (v. 18). At the same time, Paul is Philemon's benefactor: through the Pauline mission, Philemon has been given life, so that Paul can say to him, "You owe me even yourself" (v. 19). Paul may owe Philemon monetary recompensation, but Philemon owes Paul much more. Paul thus trumps Philemon in the hierarchy of obligation.

The situation is even more complex: Paul does not want to lose the assistance of Onesimus, so he would like Philemon to send Onesimus back. Although Paul's posi-tion may be tenuous from a legal standpoint, he states that "in Christ" he can indeed command Philemon's compliance (v. 8). One of the great examples of Paul's power of suggestion is that after stating this, he goes on to say that he will not demand Phile-mon's submission on the issue but will "appeal" to him on the "basis of love" (v. 9). Yet, Paul's remarks about his being "an old man" (or, "ambassador") and "a prisoner of Christ Jesus" should be read as his subtle—perhaps not so subtle—manipulation of the "appeal on the basis of love." Actually, in the realm of the Christian *oikomene* (which includes not only Philemon's immediate household, but all the Christian households in the larger Pauline communities), Paul possesses the authority of a "head." This means, in effect, that Paul has authority over Philemon's own household, including Onesimus, thus trumping the Greco-Roman social hierarchy of obligation. Clearly Paul wants Philemon to read between the lines and follow his wishes, but he has also left him little choice in the matter. Paul does, however, provide a way out of the situation that will also bring honor to Philemon.

The letter contains a number of elegant puns. The Greek name Onesimus means "useful." Paul tells Philemon that Onesimus had formerly been "useless" (*achrestos*) to him but now had become "useful" (*euchrestos*) (v. 11), since he had been "begotten" by Paul as a son in the faith (v. 10). The pun is actually double, since the Greek *chrēstos* suggests "Christ" (*Christos*). So, before his conversion, Onesimus was useless (*achrestos*) because he was "without Christ" (*a-Chrestos*) but now he is useful (*euchrestos*) because he is a "good Christian" (*eu-Chrestos*). Onesimus, in other words, found his true identity in the gospel, as did Philemon himself (v. 19).

A second pun is suggested in the thanksgiving. Paul remembers how Philemon had "refreshed the hearts [*ta splanchna*] of the saints" (v. 7). The expression undoubtedly refers to the hospitality and financial support Philemon had made available to fellow Christians from the resources of his household (see, e.g., v. 22). But when Paul speaks of returning Onesimus to him, he virtually sighs, "I am sending my very heart" (the same term in Greek; v. 12). The two levels of the pun are intertwined in v. 20. Paul tells Philemon, "Yes brother, I want some benefit [a play on Onesimus' name again] from you in the Lord; refresh my heart in Christ." The pun here rests on the reciprocal relationship between patron and client in ancient benefaction. Philemon is first honored as a patron for his benefaction of the Christian movement. Paul then subtly reverses the situation so that his returning of Onesimus becomes a form of benefaction for Philemon—as noted above, Paul is Philemon's patron and "head" in the Christian household, so he did not have to return the runaway slave. But while Philemon is now the recipient of Paul's benefaction, he can again become the great benefactor of Paul's mission by "giving" him back Onesimus. No wonder Paul can add, "Confident of your obedience, I write to you, knowing that you will do even more than I say" (v. 21): Paul has utilized the full weight of the social practice of reciprocity, knowing that his own "giving" will necessitate the "giving" of Philemon.

The Letter to Philemon opens a small but light-filled window on the Pauline mission. It shows us the close network of fellow workers (vv. 2, 23-24), the importance of benefaction (v. 7) and of hospitality (v. 22), the leadership role of women (v. 2), the understanding of the community as "the holy ones" (vv. 4, 7), and the prominence of the households as the place of Christian meeting (v. 2). We find the fellowship (*koinōnia*) of the Christian community to be one of faith that is active in sharing (v. 6), service (v. 13), and reciprocity (v. 17). The fellowship "in Christ" (vv. 8, 20) and "in the Lord" (v. 16) transcends natural kinship relationships and social stratification. Paul is a "father" to Onesimus because he converted him to the "good news" (v. 10), and that new status makes the slave now also a "beloved brother" to his master (v. 16). We begin to see how this new sort of fellowship—the Christian household—will strain ever more urgently against the framework of ancient social structures, so that not even tact and diplomacy will resolve the tension between these statements: "There is neither slave nor free" and "Slaves be submissive." And at last we see again the paradox of Paul, who, while in chains (vv. 1, 10), is giving freedom to both slaves and masters through the "good news."

Study Questions

1. What word-plays does Paul use in the letter to Philemon?

2. How would you describe the relationships between Paul, Philemon, and Onesimus?

3. What situation prompts Paul's writing of this letter? What has changed in Onesimus' circumstances?

4. How can Philemon fairly be called a "letter of commendation"?

Bibliographical Note

Understandably, Philemon by itself has not enjoyed a great deal of scholarly attention. Concerning its role in the Pauline corpus, see P. N. Harrison, "Onesimus and Philemon," *ATR* 32 (1950): 268–94. Above all, see J. Knox, "Philemon and the Authenticity of Colossians," *JR* 18 (1938): 144–60; and idem, *Philemon Among the Letters of Paul*, rev. ed. (Nashville: Abingdon Press, 1959). The role of Onesimus in the composition of Ephesians is also proposed by E. J. Goodspeed, *The Meaning of Ephesians* (Chicago: Univ. of Chicago Press, 1933); and is taken up by C. L. Mitton, *The Formation of the Pauline Corpus of Letters* (London: Epworth Press, 1955). See also C. P. Anderson, "Who Wrote the Letter from Laodicea?" *JBL* 85(1966): 436–40, who argues that it was Epaphras. F. C. Baur showed his usual consistency by stating that the authenticity of all three rose or fell together, then rejecting all of them as inauthentic, calling Philemon "a Christian romance serving to convey a genuine Christian idea." See his *Paul the Apostle*, trans. R. A. Menzies (London: Williams & Norgate, 1875), 2:1–44, 80–84.

In contrast, Philemon is used as a key to Paul's world in N. R. Petersen, *Rediscovering Paul: Philemon and the Sociology of Paul's Narrative World* (Philadelphia: Fortress Press, 1985). See also D. J. M. Derrett, "The Functions of the Epistle to Philemon," *ZNW* 79 (1988): 63–91; J. H. Elliott, "Philemon and House Churches," *The Bible Today* 22/23 (1984): 145–50; and S. C. Winter, "Paul's Letter to Philemon," *NTS* 33 (1987): 1–15. For a rhetorical analysis, see F. F. Church, "Rhetorical Structure and Design in Paul's Letter to Philemon," *HTR* 71(1978): 17–33. On various aspects of the letter, see J. M. G. Barclay, "Paul, Philemon and the Dilemma of Christian Slave-Ownership," *NTS* 37 (1991): 161–86; R. F. Hock, "A Support for His Old Age: Paul's Plea on Behalf of Onesimus," in L. M. White and O. L. Yarbrough (eds.), *The Social World of the First Christians* (Minneapolis: Fortress Press, 1995), 67–81; L. L. Lewis, "An African American Appraisal of the Philemon-Paul-Onesimus Triangle," in C. H. Felder, *Stony the Road We Trod: African American Biblical Interpretation* (Minneapolis: Fortress Press, 1991), 232–46; C. J. Martin, "The Rhetorical Function of Commercial Language in Paul's Letter to Philemon (Verse 18)," in D. Watson (ed.), *Persuasive Artistry* (JSNTSup, 50; Sheffield: Sheffield Academic Press, 1991), 321–37; J. G. Nordling, "Onesimus Fugitivus: A Defense of the Runaway Slave Hypothesis in Philemon," *JSNT* 41 (1991): 97–119; H. Riesenfeld, "Faith and Love Promoting Hope: An Interpretation of Philemon v. 6," in M. D. Hooker and S. G. Wilson (eds.), *Paul and Paulinism* (London: SPCK, 1982), 251–57; and K. O. Sandnes, "Equality within Patriarchal Structures: Some New Testament Perspectives on the Christian Fellowship as a Brother- or Sisterhood and a Family," in H. Moxnes (ed.), *Constructing Early Christian Families: Family as Social Reality and Metaphor* (New York: Routledge, 1997), 150–65.

In commentaries, Philemon is most often teamed with Colossians. On both letters, see J. D. G. Dunn, *The Epistles to the Colossians and to Philemon* (NIGTC; Grand Rapids: Eerdmans, 1996); E. Lohse, *Colossians and Philemon*, trans. W. R. Poehlmann and R. J. Karris (Hermeneia; Philadelphia: Fortress Press, 1971); P. T. O'Brien, *Colossians, Philemon* (WBC; Waco: Word Books, 1982); and C. F. D. Moule, *The Epistles of Paul the Apostle to the Colossians and to Philemon* (Cambridge: Cambridge Univ. Press, 1962). On Philemon alone, see A. D. Callahan, *Embassy of Onesimus: The Letter of Paul to Philemon* (Valley Forge, Pa.: Trinity Press Int'l, 1997).

17. The Letter to the Colossians

THE SITUATION PRESUPPOSED by Colossians is clear. Paul is a prisoner (1:24; 4:3, 18) with Epaphras (4:12), who founded the Colossian community (1:7) as part of Paul's larger mission among the Gentiles (1:23-24). Paul does not know the community personally (2:1). He and Epaphras hear of problems caused in the young church by troublemakers. Paul takes the occasion of the return of Onesimus to his owner Philemon (4:7-9) to have Tychichus report to the Colossians and Laodiceans on his condition (2:1; 4:13), delivering this letter to be read aloud (4:16) to the troubled assembly in Colossae.

The Issue of Authenticity

Although a significant number of scholars think Colossians is authentic, a growing majority consider it inauthentic. As a result, it is often neglected in serious discussions of Paul's mission and thought, being treated instead as a witness to traditions developing after the apostle's death. Sometimes appeal is made to the widespread practice of pseudonymity in the Hellenistic world or to the first Christians' lack of interest in distinguishing between the sources and origins of spiritual teaching.

Those observations are without either general or specific pertinence. Pseudonymity was practiced, but most often as a transparent fiction employing the name of a person long dead and known to be so (e.g., Enoch in Apocalypses or Socrates in the Cynic letters). Here, in contrast, we have a school producing a letter shortly after Paul's death, deliberately using signals—his autograph, the network of names—that make the enterprise much more like a deliberate forgery. The first generations of Christians, furthermore, were very much concerned with the sources of spiritual teaching and with distinguishing between true and false teachers; they did not live in a charismatic fog (see 1 Cor. 7:10-12; 14:29; 2 Cor. 11:13-15; 2 Thess. 2:2).

The style of the letter is not much help on this question. The Greek is well within the range Paul displays elsewhere, especially if the sample of comparison includes the Captivity Letters. As in Philippians and Philemon, he does not cite Torah. As in Philippians and 2 Timothy, he uses hymnic material (see 1:15-20). Much of his vocabulary is affected by the use of liturgical traditions, above all those associated with Baptism (see 2:20; 3:1-5, 9-12).

Colossians presupposes no elaborate or hierarchical church order. The governing image for the church is that of the body of Christ (1:18, 22, 24; 2:17, 19; 3:15). The similarity to 1 Cor. 12:12-27 is strong, although in Colossians, as in Eph. 4:4-16, Christ is depicted as the head of the body. Colossians makes no reference to authority in the community, apart from calling Epaphras a slave (4:12), commanding Archippus to fulfill his ministry (*diakonia*; 4:17), and greeting Nympha, the head of a household where the assembly meets (4:15).

One of the main arguments for regarding Colossians as inauthentic is that ethics in the letter lack the typical Pauline eschatological edge. The table of household ethics in 3:18—4:6 is offered in evidence. The use of this stereotypical teaching, however, has less to do with the passage of time and the "routinization of charism" than it does with Paul's audience. He is writing to a community that does not know him personally. As in Rom. 12:1—13:7, therefore, and Eph. 5:21—6:9, his moral exhortations fall into the general framework of household ethics, the variations on which we will note later. His other ethical admonitions depend in large part on the baptismal traditions shared by gentile churches (3:1-17; cf. Rom. 6:1-14; 1 Cor. 6:9-11).

The argument that the theology of Colossians deviates dramatically from the recognizably Pauline is also unconvincing. Paul calls himself an apostle (1:1); and a servant (1:25). His suffering is on behalf of the church (1:24). His preaching is based on the revelation of a "mystery" hidden in the past but now made known (1:26; 4:3; cf. Rom. 11:25; 16:25-26). His work is above all among the Gentiles (1:27), and his goal is to present people as mature in Christ (*teleios*; 1:28; cf. 1 Cor. 2:6; 14:20; Phil. 3:15). Paul understands Jesus as the source of wisdom and understanding (2:3). Moreover, because of his resurrection, Christ rules over angelic forces (2:10,15; cf. Phil. 2:10-11); and he was operative in creation (1:15-16; cf. 1 Cor. 8:6). Furthermore, the instrument of salvation is the cross and Jesus' redemptive blood (1:14, 20, 22; 2:14). The Pauline character of these points is self-evident.

The most serious charge of inconsistency is leveled at the eschatology of Colossians. On the basis of 2:12 ("you were buried with him in baptism, in which you were also raised with him through faith in the working of God"), 2:13 ("You were made alive in him") and 3:1 ("If then you have been raised with Christ"), it has been suggested that Colossians has a "realized eschatology" that destroys the delicate tension between the "already" and the "not yet" typical of Paul's statements elsewhere. Apart from the issue of how much latitude an author has before he reaches self-inconsistency, and apart from the rather obvious shifts in eschatological emphasis in the undisputed letters, this charge simply misreads these sections of Colossians. It is clear from 2:20 and 3:1-4 that the "death" to sin in baptism leads to a "resurrection life" not of glory but of faith, which requires of the Colossians a conversion of their behavior. Their "life" indeed is "hid with God in Christ"; only at the end, "when Christ our life appears," will they themselves be in a state of "glory" (3:4). The language is slightly different, but the thought is virtually identical to that found in Rom. 6:1-14. And though the language underscores the transformation of human character that has occurred through faith and baptism—one has died to the old and been raised to new life—it should not be taken as a statement on eschatology as such.

Neither the stylistic nor the substantive reasons for doubting the authenticity of Colossians are convincing. Given the lack of evidence to the contrary, it is likely that Paul himself wrote Colossians, at least in the sense used elsewhere in this book: Paul, as head of a missionary school, commissioned and supervised the production of the letter. The similarity to Paul's thought in the "genuine" letters is unmistakable.

The Crisis in Colossae

Colossae was in Phrygia, a region renowned in the ancient world for its fascination with all things magical and mysterious. From Phrygia came the cult of the mother goddess Cybele, as well as the later enthusiastic version of Christianity known as Montanism. We can understand how a recently founded community, the cult of the Christ, having lost its founding figure—Epaphras—to imprisonment, was placed in the difficult and vulnerable position of making comparisons with other cults and re-evaluating its own teaching in this light. Fascinated by the charms of those who could offer them more, these newly converted gentile Christians were easy prey to the offer of a greater perfection (or, maturity: *teleios*) than that available in their own cult.

Hints of Paul's concern are subtly suggested even in his praise of the Colossians. Using the metaphor of plant maturity, Paul acknowledges that the "good news" is "bearing fruit and growing" among them (1:6), but immediately he prays that they "might bear fruit in every good work and increase in the *knowledge* [*epignōsis*] of God" (1:10; cf. 2:2). The significance of "knowledge" will be evident shortly. At the very end of the letter, Epaphras also prays that "they stand mature [*teleios*] and fully assured in all the will of God" (4:12). Furthermore, Paul wants them to be "stable in the good news" (1:23) and to be "mature [*teleios*] in Christ" (1:28), and he rejoices because of their good order and the "firmness of the faith in Christ" (2:5). The issue that begins to emerge from these hints concerns the nature of perfection (maturity) before God, particularly its character and basis.

Paul's fundamental position is clear even from these first hints. He wants the Colossians to be mature "in Christ" (1:28). Their further growth and perfection will come through an ever-deepening recognition of what they already have been given and who they already are. Thus Paul prays that they have "recognition of the gift [grace] of God in truth" (1:6) and follows this immediately with, "just as you learned it from Epaphras" (1:7). Paul wants them to have recognition (*epignōsis*) of "Christ the mystery of God" (2:2) as a protection against the wiles of false teaching (2:4). The crisis in Colossae was one of confidence or assurance (4:12): is what they have been given in Christ enough for perfection, or do they require more for maturity? It is exacerbated, however, by troublemakers.

Once more we meet the problem of identifying the "opponents" and their influence in Paul's mission. Are they visitors from the outside? Are they local representatives of rival cults? Or are members of the church itself—perhaps the reprimanded Archippus—agitating for alliances after the forced departure of Epaphras? We cannot know for certain, since we are totally dependent on Paul's secondhand information. His characterizations tend to be general: he calls their teaching a "philosophy" based on human traditions according to "the elemental spirits of the universe" and not Christ (2:8). This "philosophy" generates a desire to observe festivals and a special diet (2:16). It also involves an admiration for physical asceticism (2:20-22). This philosophy in fact would appear to be some variety of Judaism, since the role of Torah (2:14) and of circumcision (2:11) figure in Paul's response. The most problematic piece of the puzzle is provided by the troublesome text in 2:18:

> Let no one disqualify you, insisting on self-abasement [or, humility: *tapeinōphrosynē*] and worship of [or, with] angels, [for such opponents are] taking a stand on visions, being puffed up without reason by a sensuous mind.

The pieces have been put together in various ways. Some scholars have detected advocates of pagan mysteries, others an esoteric and rigorous form of Judaism, such as the Essene type. Still others have found Judaizing Gentiles, as in Galatia (see Gal. 3:19; 4:3, 9). The mention of visions, however, suggests Jewish mystics of the Merkabah variety. These were fond of esoteric traditions and demanded strict observance of Torah and sexual asceticism as prerequisites for their flights of prayer to the heavenly throne chariot (*merkabah*) where they "worshiped with angels" (cf. 2 Cor. 12:1-5; Ezek. 1).

More important than their specific identity is the way the agitators understood perfection or maturity before God, and the attitude they adopted toward others in the Colossian community. They saw perfection as the achievement of new levels of spiritual status, marked by observance of law, sexual asceticism, and, above all, initiation into the higher mysteries of visionary experiences. By such marks, they could identify who was "fleshly" and who was "spiritual." Christ was for them only a beginning; to be fully mature before God meant taking on more elaborate and visible forms of religious observance, including the experience of higher planes of ecstasy. On the basis of their greater spiritual maturity, furthermore, they could "judge" others (2:16) and even seek to "disqualify" them (2:18, suggesting disqualification from a race).

Such attitudes outrage Paul. The spiritual athleticism and theosophy of these people only show them to be "puffed up without reason in their sensuous mind" (2:18; cf. 1 Cor. 8:1). Their "love of wisdom" is nothing of the sort, only a cover for fleshly behavior (2:23), for as we learned in 1 Cor. 3:1-3, the "flesh" above all means the hostile judgment of others. This self-regard and contempt of others is the exact opposite of genuine spiritual maturity, which has to do not with the cultivation of the human psyche, but with obedience to God's Spirit, expressing itself in love and mutual support. Paul will not debate these spiritual dilettantes; his concern is for the faith of those whom they are corrupting. He wants to remind these that what they have already been given—the "gift of God"—provides the only real basis for Christian maturity.

Paul treats the troublemakers with contempt, characterizing them as self-deluded charlatans. In Christ, the Colossians already have "all the treasures of wisdom and knowledge" (2:3), even though these riches are hidden. The seducers, in contrast, dangle before their eyes shiny coins, seeking to "defraud" them (2:4) and, if they succeed, the Colossians will become their booty (2:8). The monetary metaphor running through this section is unmistakable in the Greek. Paul's point is that the Colossians have the true wealth that comes from God; they should not be taken in by counterfeit coinage. To illustrate how the attempt to achieve spiritual maturity on the basis of human accomplishment is illusory, Paul uses another metaphor: it is like reaching after a "shadow" when the "body" (*sōma*) that casts that shadow is present (2:17). This image is very similar to Plato's famous cave metaphor, in which people settle for the shadows on the wall when the ideal and real is just outside the cave opening. For Paul, the shadow is the Colossian quest; the body (or, reality) is Christ. Their growth, therefore, is also illusory. In 2:19, Paul indicates that this is

> because they do not hold fast to the head, from whom the whole body is nourished and knit together through its joints and ligaments, and grows with a growth that is from God.

That the "growth comes from God" is critical and reminds us of Phil. 1:6: "I am confident that he who began a good work in you will bring it to completion at the day of Jesus Christ" (cf. Gal. 3:1-5).

Following this line of thought, Paul uses yet another mixed metaphor of growth (2:6-7):

> As therefore you received Christ Jesus the Lord, so live in him, rooted and built up in him and established in faith, just as you were taught, abounding in thanksgiving.

The sentence is carefully constructed. As (that is, in the manner) they received Christ, so (again, in that manner) are they to grow. The phrase "just as you were taught" echoes 1:7: ". . . just as you learned from Epaphras." Paul reminds them that maturity will come not by taking on esoteric lore and rituals but by increasing in awareness (*epignōsis*) of the gift already given by God in Christ (cf. 1 Cor. 1:12), "to recognize the grace of God in truth" (1:6; cf. 1:9, 10; 2:2; 3:10).

The Gift of God in Truth

The Colossian congregation is to learn that because they are "in Christ" they are also "in God." When they meet Jesus, they encounter the ultimate power in the universe. By way of demonstration, Paul cites the christological hymn of 1:15-20. Possibly liturgical in origin, it reworks the traditions associated with the preexistent wisdom of God (Prov. 8:22-31; Wis. 7:22-8:1) and with Adam as the "image and likeness of God" (Gen. 1:26-27; 2 Cor. 4:4), in light of the conviction that in the "beloved son," Jesus, ultimate reality came into existence and continues to be transformed. So he is the "image of the unseen God" (1:15), and all things both came into existence through his agency (1:16)—even those angelic powers with whom they would like to worship!—and are sustained by his power (1:17). Indeed, in him "all the fullness of God was pleased to dwell" (1:19). This means, of course, that when Jesus acts, God is at work. Through him, therefore, God reconciles the world to himself (cf. 2 Cor. 5:16-21) "making peace by the blood of his cross" (1:20; cf. Rom. 5:1). This ultimate power, moreover, is still active in the world, for "he is the head of the body, the church" (1:18). Those who are incorporated into the church, then, are in touch with the power of God. The pretensions of the spiritual adepts are hollow, for "they do not cling to the head from whom the whole body . . . grows with a growth that is from God" (2:19). They only chase after shadows (cf. 2:17), neglecting both the beginning, source, and *telos* of all reality as well as the head of the Christian body.

Paul is talking not about abstract convictions but about present experience. Through initiation into the church in baptism, Christians have passed over into God's kingdom. Paul thus frames the hymn by these two statements:

> He has delivered us from the realm of darkness into the kingdom of his beloved Son, in whom we have redemption and forgiveness of sins, (1:13)

and

> You who were once estranged and hostile in mind . . . he has now reconciled in his body of flesh by his death. (1:21)

The crossing over and reconciliation are real because they were established by God. Now Paul's readers know why they should not allow anyone to "judge" them (2:16) or "disqualify" them (2:18) on the basis of human knowledge, for God has already "qualified" them to "share in the inheritance of the saints in light" (1:12). In other words, the false notions being propagated among the Colossians have nothing to do with the full knowledge available in Christ, but reflect human wisdom and understanding, which, for Paul, are inadequate measures.

The Colossians do not need another ritual of initiation such as circumcision, since, in their baptism, they have been initiated into the ultimate "mystery," into the very "working of God" (2:12). The triumph of Jesus' death and resurrection, together with his annulment of the power of law exercised by the inimical spiritual powers (2:14-15), has been made available to them in a powerful way (2:12):

> You were buried with him in baptism, in which you were also raised with him through faith in the working of God who raised him from the dead.

Such is the basis of their confidence that enables them to "grow and bear fruit, to continue in the faith, stable and steadfast, not shifting from the hope of the gospel which you heard" (1:23); it is their insight into the "knowledge of God's mystery in Christ" (2:2), the mystery for which Paul himself is in prison (4:3). For in Christ, Paul says (2:9-10),

> the whole fullness of deity dwells bodily, and you have come to fullness of life in him, who is the head of every rule and authority.

They need only to realize their new identity and translate it into appropriate behavior within the community.

Paul has taken some of the key concepts of "higher" knowledge in the ancient world and recast them in an explicitly Christian framework. He uses the notions of "mystery," "fullness of experience," "higher forms of knowledge," "special initiations," and "realized eschatology" to make the argument that all these things are realized "in Christ." As Christ is the ground of all reality, those that transfer—through baptism—into the Christian community with Christ as its head have access to everything in its fullness. It is precisely because of Paul's appropriation of the Greco-Roman "mystery" language, however, that so many scholars have misconstrued his real argument, which rests not in the language itself, but in its use.

A New Form of Humanity

Despite his reassurance concerning how they have been "planted," Paul is quite clear that the Colossians have not yet attained full maturity, as demonstrated by their present conduct. According to Paul, they have "died to the elemental powers of the universe" (2:20) and live by the power of a new life (2:13), and are therefore called to shape their behavior in accordance with that identity. This does not entail new rules for asceticism or flights of mystic ecstasy. Their growth in God is one that comes through their way of living together in community.

The images Paul uses to remind them of their identity come from the ritual of Baptism, which was their initiation into the "messianic body." It is within that body that their growth will come. As baptism was a "dying and rising" with Christ, so are they to "put to death" their former practices (3:5) and "seek the things that are above where Christ is" (3:1). Baptism signified a change of identity through enacting a dying and rising with Christ. Paul reminds them (3:10) to "put off" their old self with its attitudes so they can "put on the new nature that is being renewed in knowledge [*epignōsis*] after the image of its creator" (3:10). Their call, therefore, is to abandon the actions and attitudes "in which they once lived" (3:7) and to adopt new attitudes and behavior.

Since they have come to know "the gift of God in truth" (1:6), which came to them through "the word of truth, the gospel" (1:5), they can transcend human ways of thinking and behavior, accepting, instead, the manner of life that comes from knowledge of God. Thus, they are able to speak the truth to one another, rather than lie (3:9). They also should no longer discriminate on the basis of origin or status (3:11):

> Here there cannot be Greek and Jew, circumcised and uncircumcised, barbarian, Scythian, slave, free man, but Christ is all, and in all.

Moreover, since they have been brought into contact with the ultimate power of the world, they no longer ought to be governed by the forces of idolatry that bring upon them God's wrath (3:5-6), but should be compassionate and forgiving toward others (3:12-13). Indeed, the very thing the Colossians have been seeking outside—"new humanity"—is being created and shaped in the community itself. Here, then, is the goal of Christian maturity: not the self-assertion and pride of the ascetic or mystic, which leads to the judging of others, but the patience of love that leads to service for others (3:14-15). This is not a spectacular phenomenon; indeed, their life is "hidden in Christ" (3:3), just as all the treasures of God are "hidden" in him (2:3). But just as "the fullness of God dwelt in Christ bodily" (2:9), so will this manner of life "in the body" allow the "word of Christ to dwell in them richly" (3:16) and make of all their lives a praise of God (3:17).

The Colossians do not live "above, where Christ is" (3:1), but only anticipate the "hope laid up for them in heaven" (1:5). They must live in the very real social structures of the world, which never correspond precisely to the shape of God's kingdom. When Paul, then, turns to the mutual duties owed by members of a household (3:18-4:6), he by no means proposes a revealed Christian social order. Rather, he reminds the Colossians that "maturity in Christ" does not mean fleeing the world in visions or in alternative social structures of a purely "religious" character, but in coming to grips with the real and resistant structures of the world. He takes for granted the societal framework of the Hellenistic world, which had as its basic unit the extended patriarchal household, with lines of authority running from the *paterfamilias* at the top to the slaves and clients at the bottom, all held together by the submission of each level to the one above it. Paul could no more have envisaged another kinship system than he could have proposed a Jeffersonian democracy in place of the Roman Empire.

To this structure of the household Paul applies the best available philosophical teaching, specifying the duties and obligations expected of each tier in the hierarchical power structure. The Pauline version is noteworthy, however, for its emphasis on reciprocity between the various levels. Wives are to be submissive to their husbands (not to all males), but husbands are to "love" their wives. The term means not simply erotic affection but *agape**, the self-sacrificing love that empties itself into service for others (3:18-19). Children are to obey both parents, but fathers, who are responsible for discipline, are to show them understanding in return (3:20-21). Paul gives most attention to the relations between slaves and masters, undoubtedly because of the circumstances in which the letter was written: it accompanied Onesimus back to his master, Philemon, and no doubt the larger community of masters and slaves was aware of the problem. Thus, Paul emphasizes that singleness of heart is expected of the slave, but masters are to show justice and also equality (*isotēs*) toward slaves. This means more than simply "justly" and "fairly." It is a recognition that subtly subverts the social stratification itself (3:22-4:1) by utilizing the language of "fellowship" and "friendship" (*koinōnia*)—terms reminiscent of Philippians—to describe a relationship that was anything but *koinōnia* in the ancient world.

Indeed, Paul relativizes the entire social system by placing it within the critical framework of the "good news" from God. First, this implies that any form of stratification will be in tension with the community ideal of "neither slave nor free, neither Jew nor Greek" (3:11) and "neither male nor female" (Gal. 3:28). Second, Paul also brings the principle of transcendence to bear on the social arrangements and attitudes themselves. Submission is conditioned by the measure of what is "fitting in the Lord" (3:18). For instance, obedience to parents pleases the Lord (3:20). Moreover, slaves are to serve as those "fearing the Lord" (3:22) and as though they are "serving the Lord rather than humans" (3:23), because they are, in fact, "serving the Lord Christ" (3:24). They can know that every wrongdoer, including a master, will receive just retribution, "for there is no partiality" with God (3:25): masters, too, have a "master in heaven" to whom they are held accountable (4:1).

Each of these expressions can be—and has been—taken as legitimizing the social structure itself and as strengthening the response of submission. But this interpretation contradicts Paul's clear intention. By placing all these relations "in the Lord," he demands of all an allegiance and obedience first and foremost to God. Any submission that would oppose or distort the more fundamental obedience owed to God must be resisted. The phrase "in the Lord," therefore, places this social structure itself, as well as all social structures, under the critical judgment of the gospel.

A tension, of course, remains and will always remain, for the gospel is incapable of being translated into any specific social arrangement. At the same time, some sort of social structure will always prove necessary, for Christians must go on living in the world no less than other people. So Paul wants them to act—in the assembly of faith and in their households—in a manner appropriate with respect to God, with love toward their fellow Christians, and "wisely toward outsiders," knowing that as they share in the riches of Christ, they can in fact make the most of their remaining time in the world (4:5).

It is one of the intriguing features of Colossians that a letter, which sets out utilizing so many cosmic themes should be so grounded—at the end—in the specific setting of the ancient household. But this illustrates Paul's point made throughout: instead of seeking the "extra" or "higher" things, Christians should look to their own community and their present experience of God, for there they will find the manifestation of everything they so fervently desire. This re-orientation of the Colossians' faith transforms, in the process, human ways of understanding, the behavior of the flesh, and worldly social structures as they embrace the true knowledge of God, the present experience of the Spirit, and the fullness of life in Christ.

Study Questions

1. What are the reasons some scholars have proposed that Paul did not write this letter? What do you conclude after reading the letter for yourself?

2. What does Colossians share in common with Ephesians in terms of vocabulary and themes?

3. What clues are in this letter about the opponents of Paul in Colossae? How does Paul describe the problems he had with them?

4. What role does baptism play in this letter?

5. How do the instructions concerning household relations (3:18—4:1) fit within Colossians' overall moral teaching?

Bibliographical Note

Arguments against the authenticity of Colossians are marshaled from the side of literary connections by E. P. Sanders, "Literary Dependence in Colossians," *JBL* 85 (1966): 28–45; and from the standpoint of theological consistency by E. Lohse, "Pauline Theology in the Letter to the Colossians," *NTS* 15 (1969): 211–20. For a fuller treatment, see M. Kiley, *Colossians as Pseudepigraphy* (Sheffield: JSOT Press, 1986). An extensive and positive position on authenticity is argued by G. E. Cannon, *The Use of Traditional Materials in Colossians* (Macon, Ga.: Mercer Univ. Press, 1983). On the relationship with Ephesians, see E. Best, "Who Used Whom? The Relationship of Ephesians and Colossians," *NTS* 43 (1997): 72–96.

The crisis in Colossae has been variously interpreted. For a fine collection of essays representing various hypotheses, see W. A. Meeks and F. O. Francis (eds.), *Conflict at Colossae*, rev. ed. (SBS, 4; Missoula, Mont.: Scholars Press, 1975). The essay by F. O. Francis, "Humility and Angelic Worship in Col 2:18," *Studia Theologica* 16 (1963): 109–34, covers the data well. For various other treatments on the opponents and the nature of the heresy, see C. E. Arnold, *The Colossian Syncretism: The Interface between Christianity and Folk Belief at Colossae*, rpr. (Grand Rapids: Baker Books, 1996 [1995]); H. W. Attridge, "On Becoming an Angel: Rival Baptismal Theologies at Colossae," in L. Bormann et al. (eds.), *Religious Propaganda & Missionary Competition in the New Testament World* (NovTSup, 74; Leiden: E. J. Brill, 1994), 481–98; R. E. DeMaris, *The Colossian Controversy: Wisdom and Dispute at Colossae* (JSNTSup, 96; Sheffield: Sheffield Academic Press, 1994); J. D. G. Dunn, "The Colossian Philosophy: A Confident Jewish Apologia," *Bib* 76 (1995): 153–81; C. A. Evans, "The Colossian Mystics," *Bib* 63 (1982): 188–205; M. D. Hooker, "Were there False Teachers in Colossae?" in B. Lindars and S. S. Smalley (eds.), *Christ and Spirit in the New Testament* (Cambridge: Cambridge Univ. Press, 1973), 315–31; L. T. Johnson, "Ritual Imprinting and the Politics of Perfection," in *Aspects of Religious Experience in Early Christianity* (Minneapolis: Fortress Press, 1998); T. W. Martin, *By Philosophy and Empty Deceit: Colossians as Response to Cynic Critique* (JSNTSup, 118; Sheffield: Sheffield Academic Press, 1996); and J. Sumney, "Those Who 'Pass Judgment': The Identity of the Opponents in Colossians," *Bib* 74 (1993): 220–43.

Various aspects of the letter are covered by J. M. G. Barclay, *Colossians and Philemon* (Sheffield: Sheffield Academic Press, 1997); N. A. Dahl, "Christ, Creation, and the Church," in *Jesus in the Memory of the Early Church* (Minneapolis: Augsburg Pub. House, 1976), 120–40; F. O. Francis, "The Christological Argument of Colossians," in W A. Meeks and J. Jervell (eds.), *God's Christ and His People* (Oslo: Universitetsforlaget, 1977), 192–208; A. T. Hanson, "The Conquest of the Powers," in his *Studies in Paul's Technique and Theology* (Grand Rapids: Eerdmans; London: SPCK, 1974), 1–12; B. Hollenbach, "Col 2:23: 'Which Things Lead to the Fulfillment of the Flesh'" *NTS* 25 (1978–79): 254–61; E. Käsemann, "A Primitive Christian Baptismal Liturgy," in his *Essays on New Testament Themes* (Philadelphia: Fortress Press; London: SCM Press, 1964), 149–68; J. C. O'Neill, "The Source of the Christology in Colossians," *NTS* 26 (1979–80): 87–100; B. Vawter, "The Colossian Hymn and the Principle of Redaction," *CBQ* 33 (1971): 62–81; H. Weiss, "The Law in the Epistle to the Colossians," *CBQ* 34 (1972): 294–314; W. Wink, "The Hymn of the Cosmic Christ," in R. T. Fortna and B. R. Gaventa (eds.), *The Conversation Continues* (Nashville: Abingdon Press, 1990), 235–45; W. T. Wilson, *The Hope of Glory: Education and Exhortation in the Epistle to the Colossians* (Leiden: E. J. Brill, 1997); N. T. Wright, "Poetry and Theology in Colossians 1:15-20," *NTS* 36 (1990): 444–68; and R. Yates, "A Reappraisal of Colossians," *Irish Theological Quarterly* 58 (1992): 95–117.

For the household ethics, see J. E. Crouch, *The Origin and Intention of the Colossian Haustafel* (Göttingen: Vandenhoeck & Ruprecht, 1972); L. Hartman, "Code and Context: A Few Remarks on the Parenesis of Col. 3:6—4:1," in G. F. Hawthorne and O. Betz (eds.), *Tradition and Interpretation in the New Testament* (Grand Rapids: Eerdmans, 1987), 237–47; C. J. Martin, "The *Haustafeln* (Household Codes) in African American Biblical Interpretation: 'Free Slaves' and 'Subordinate Women'," in C. H. Felder, *Stony the Road We Trod: African American Biblical Interpretation* (Minneapolis: Fortress Press, 1991), 206–31; and E. Schweizer, "Traditional Ethical Patterns in the Pauline and Post-Pauline Letters and Their Development (Lists of Vices and House-Tables)," in E. Best and R. McL. Wilson (eds.), *Text and Interpretation* (Cambridge: Cambridge Univ. Press, 1979), 195–209. For a more extensive treatment of the Hellenistic background, see D. Balch, *Let Wives Be Submissive: The Domestic Code in I Peter* (SBLMS, 26; Chico, Calif.: Scholars Press, 1981).

In addition to the commentaries listed in chapter 16 (Philemon), see also M. Barth and H. Blanke, *Colossians*, trans. A. B. Beck (AB; New York: Doubleday, 1994); P. Pokorny, *Colossians: A Commentary*, trans. S. S. Schatzmann (Peabody, Mass.: Hendrickson Pubs., 1991); and E. Schweizer, *The Letter to the Colossians: A Commentary*, trans. A. Chester (Minneapolis: Augsburg Pub., 1982).

18. The Letter to the Ephesians

EPHESIANS IS THE least personal of Paul's letters. The standard epistolary elements of opening greeting (1:1-2), blessing (1:3-14), thanksgiving (1:15-23), body (2:1—6:20), and final greeting (6:23-24) are all formal. The letter is almost devoid of references to the circumstances of either the writer or the readers. About Paul, we learn only that he is a prisoner (3:1-13; 4:1; 6:19-20). He does not know the community firsthand but has only heard of its "faith in the Lord Jesus and love toward all the saints" (1:15). No community crisis seems to have motivated the writing of the letter; its two brief references to false teaching (4:14; 5:6) serve as warnings against the possibility, rather than actuality, of deviance. The only person mentioned by name is Tychichus who appears, as in Colossians, to be the one delivering personal news from Paul (6:21-22).

This would indeed be a strange document if written by Paul to a church where, according to Acts, he had spent over two years (19:10). If written pseudonymously, the author in this case failed to create a plausible impression of intimacy between Paul and a church he apparently knew so well. As noted earlier in the discussion of Philemon and Colossians, however, important early manuscripts lack the name Ephesians in the greeting (1:1). The evidence suggests that Ephesians is a letter generated not by the immediate circumstances of Paul or a specific community crisis, but by the desire to communicate the implications of his mission to a wider circle of gentile churches. Ephesians should thus be viewed as a circular letter. But since the authenticity of Ephesians is so widely rejected, we must ask whether the evidence of the text itself forces us to see in it not the work of Paul but that of a devoted follower writing sometime after Paul's death.

The Issue of Authenticity

If the authorship of Paul's letters is understood in the manner outlined earlier—a production by Paul *and* his fellow workers—then the criterion of style is by itself less pertinent than if we were comparing a sample of writings produced totally by a single hand. Still, a short discussion of stylistic factors helps define the character of this writing.

Ephesians is stylistically closest to Colossians, except that it is even more expansive, with a tendency to heap substantives for effect (see, e.g., 1:19; 3:7). Some phrases are almost identical in the two writings (Eph. 1:4/Col. 1:22; Eph. 1:15/Col. 1:4; Eph. 2:13/Col. 1:20; Eph. 4:2-3/Col. 3:12-13; Eph. 6:21-22/Col. 4:7-8). More often, similar terms are used in slightly different ways or in slightly different combinations (cf. Eph. 1:18/Col. 1:9; Eph. 2:15/Col. 2:14; Eph. 3:2/Col. 1:25; Eph. 3:16/Col. 1:11). A good example is Eph. 5:19, which has the same words in the same order as Col. 3:16 ("psalms," "hymns," "spiritual songs," "singing in your hearts to the Lord/God"), yet with quite a different effect, since the context of the series is in each case distinctive.

Some expressions characteristic of Ephesians are found in both Colossians and other Pauline writings, although not necessarily in the same concentration. The expression "powers and principalities" (*archai kai exousiai*) is used as a term for cosmic forces several times in Ephesians (1:21; 3:10; 6:12) and in Colossians (1:16; 2:10, 15), and is also found in Rom. 8:38 (possibly in 1 Cor. 15:24 as well, depending on the textual variant). A similarly obscure designation, "the elemental powers of the universe" (*stoicheia tou kosmou*), is found in Col. 2:8, 20, as well as in Gal. 4:3, 9—though it is not in Ephesians. The term "surpass" (*hyperballō*) an important concept for Ephesians (1:19; 2:7; 3:19), does not occur in Colossians, but is found in 2 Corinthians in even greater concentration (1:8; 3:10; 4:7, 17; 9:14; 11:23; and 12:7). Likewise, the phrase "praise of glory" (Eph. 1:6, 12, 14) occurs, in a variant form, in Phil. 1:11.

Ephesians at first glance seems to be unusually rich in language about knowledge and enlightenment, but a closer look reveals that the concentration is not remarkable for a Pauline letter. "Knowledge" (gnōsis) is used once (3:19), and is found throughout the Pauline corpus (cf. Rom. 15:14; 1 Cor. 1:5; 2 Cor. 4:6; Phil. 3:8; Col. 2:3). "Recognition" (epignōsis) (Eph. 1:17; 4:13) is a favorite expression in Colossians (1:9, 10; 2:2; 3:10), and is used similarly in Rom. 10:2; Phil. 1:9; 1 Tim. 2:4; 2 Tim. 2:25 and Phlm. 6. The expression "to be enlightened" (phōtizō) occurs twice (Eph. 1:18; 3:9), and is found also in 1 Cor. 4:5 and 2 Tim. 1:10. "Light" (phōs) as a metaphor for revelation (5:8-9, 13) is found also in Rom. 13:12; 2 Cor. 4:6; 6:14; Col. 1:12; 1 Thess. 5:5; 1 Tim. 6:16.

In summary: the vocabulary and syntax of Ephesians does not reflect a later period of Christian thought, and the knowledge language is a key element in most of Paul's major letters. Moreover, the stylistic idiosyncrasies of Ephesians decrease when the letter is compared with all the captivity letters (Philippians, Colossians, 2 Timothy, and Philemon) or with those parts of the travel letters that are specifically devoted to prayer (e.g., Rom. 16:25-27; 2 Cor. 1:3-7).

Trying to decide authorship on the basis of style is always tenuous, as the endless disputes concerning the real Shakespeare attest. Subjective judgments are inevitable, particularly on issues such as how much range an author is allowed or what circumstantial factors are to be considered. For instance, is the *Laws* of Plato to be considered as authentic as *The Republic*, even though the dialogical form is almost nonexistent and the style flat? We are fortunate that we are not called on to decide the genuineness of Lucian's *On the Writing of History*, having as a standard of comparison only his more scurrilous dialogues and tales. One factor often left out of this discussion is that ancient rhetorical training cultivated using and adapting a wide range of styles to match particular rhetorical occasions. Handbooks for speeches, such as Hermogenes *On Types of Style* and those associated with the epistolary theorists, clarify this issue: the style and character of a text is determined mostly by the occasion that gives rise to it, the type of material treated, the particular persona the writer chooses to adopt, and the writer's specific relationship with the reader. One only need compare Galatians with Philemon, or Romans with 1 Corinthians, to see how this plays itself out in the Pauline corpus.

Following the other line of argument for the moment, if the style of Ephesians is regarded as too far from Paul's own to allow for authenticity, how can one account for its production? If Colossians is thought to be authentic, then a later Pauline pseudepigrapher lifted parts of that letter to convince his readers that it was Paul writing Ephesians, while at the same time he enriched the vocabulary by extensive excavation of the language of other genuine letters. The relation between Ephesians and Colossians would then be much like the perceived connection between 1 and 2 Thessalonians. Thus, in an odd reversal of the logic used to establish Pauline authorship of the "genuine" letters, the very similarity of style between the two letters would argue against the authenticity of the one already suspect on other grounds.

This account, however, has two major weaknesses. First, it is difficult to believe that a later writer who followed Colossians so assiduously would use the shared vocabulary in such different ways. The whole idea behind pseudepigraphy is to replicate the thought and style of the exemplar as closely as possible. Second, it would seem to follow that if the forger had available other genuine letters, he would have used them in a more effective and convincing manner than they are in Ephesians. For instance, a more extensive list of Pauline co-workers might have been given, based on the pattern of the genuine epistles.

A second option for those who reject the Pauline authorship of Ephesians is to challenge the authenticity of Colossians. This, of course, calls for a rather complex formulation of the data. First, Colossians must be viewed as a deliberate forgery, using the information derived only from Philemon to certify its authenticity, even though Philemon is a private note. Then, Ephesians must be thought of as written by the same pseudepigrapher in a style very similar, but not identical, to that of Colossians—except that the impulse to certify authenticity by using personal references would have been mysteriously neglected. This is altogether too clumsy. The only possible modification of this thesis would be to view both Colossians and Ephesians as pseudepigraphy written by different authors, with the forger of Ephesians being dependent on the forger of Colossians. But dependency is a problem for this theory because the chronological time frame required is too great. Moreover, if they are not written by the same writer, what reason can be given for the writer of Ephesians so slavishly following key elements in Colossians while borrowing freely, but less assiduously, from other Pauline texts? One might suggest that the writer of Ephesians is deliberately trying to modify the theology of Colossians, but there is no real evidence for this in Ephesians, and only our modern mis-readings of Colossians make this necessary in the first place.

If the style of Ephesians is not so diverse as to demand authorship by another writer than those available in the Pauline circle during Paul's life (that is, in the school of Paul active in his ministry), then the relation to Colossians obviously strengthens rather than weakens the case for authenticity: they were both written under Paul's supervision. Moreover, the shared relationship to the rest of the Pauline corpus is accounted for by their shared authorship: the same mind and heart authorized and directed their production. Finally, if Colossians and Ephesians were written at the same time—and likely by the same person(s)—then the similarity of language, expression, and material is easily explained, and the differences are accounted for by their different audiences and functions.

What was said about Colossians with regard to church structure and ethics applies equally to Ephesians. There is no attention to church order apart from the list of apostles, prophets, evangelists, pastors, and teachers (4:11). The gifts of the spirit articulate the expression of community life (4:11-12), and behavior derives from the transforming power of the Holy Spirit (4:15-16, 23-24). Moreover, while Ephesians has a distinctive twist on the Pauline imitation motif (4:20-21; 5:1-2)—be imitators of Christ and God—and devotes much of its treatment of household responsibilities (5:21—6:9) to the marriage relationship, none of this demands a period after Paul's death. It simply illustrates the range any author has in adapting language to a specific occasion.

The real challenge to Ephesian authenticity comes—or ought to come— from its distinctive theological perspective: it is sufficiently different on a number of points so that legitimate questions can be raised as to whose mind is at work. For example, Paul does not often talk about the kingdom of God, but when he does, it is always "God's kingdom" (Rom. 14:17; 1 Cor. 4:20; 6:9; 15:50; Gal. 5:21; Col. 4:11; 1 Thess. 2:12; 2 Thess. 1:5). Yet in Eph. 5:5 it is "the kingdom of Christ and God" (although cf. Col. 1:13: "the kingdom of his beloved Son"). It is true that in 1 Cor. 15:24 Paul states that Christ will rule until he hands over the kingdom to his father, and that Ps. 8:6, "He has put all things under his feet," is used in a remarkably similar way in both 1 Cor. 15:27 and Eph. 1:22, but there is still a slight difference in the particular theological formulations of the kingdom in Ephesians. Likewise, it is certainly Pauline to call the church the "body of Christ." In Eph. 1:23 and 4:16, however, Christ is said to be the head of this body from which it derives growth, an anatomical specification not detailed in 1 Cor. 12:27 (but, again, cf. Col. 1:18). In Eph. 5:23, furthermore, Christ is called the Savior of the body, using a title found only in 3:20 of Philippians, one of the undisputed letters.

In a similar vein, the author of Ephesians uses the term "mystery" (3:3-4; 6:19) to refer to the relationship between Jews and Gentiles in God's plan, which is certainly Pauline (Col. 1:27; Rom. 11:25; 16:25). But he also applies the word "mystery" to marriage (5:32), giving that relationship a positive connotation only implicit in 1 Cor. 7

and seemingly lacking elsewhere in Paul. When the author of Ephesians refers to the "dispensation"/"commission" (*oikonomia*) of God's will (1:10; 3:2, 9), he uses the term "dispensation," found otherwise only in Col. 1:25, 1 Cor. 9:17, and 1 Tim. 1:4 though Paul can refer to himself elsewhere as a dispenser (*oikonomos*) of the mysteries of God (1 Cor. 4:1-2). In Eph. 2:8-9, the expressions "saved through faith" and "not by works" have an unmistakable Pauline resonance but lack Pauline distinctiveness. Nowhere else in the Pauline corpus is there reference to being "*saved* through faith"; it is always "*justified* through faith." Moreover, Paul generally uses "works of the law" in Romans and Galatians, rather than just "works" (indeed, Eph. 2:8-9 could be construed as an over-simplified reading of Rom. 3:27-28; but cf. 2 Tim. 1:9; Titus 3:5). Along similar lines, the statement in 2:15, "he has abolished the law," is stronger than any made in either Romans or Galatians, and indeed seems to contradict Rom. 3:31. Thus, Ephesians seems to lack the distinctive Pauline nuance on law and faith found elsewhere in the genuine letters.

More troublesome are differences in perspective that would at first appear to derive from a lapse in time between the career of Paul and the writing of this letter. Paul, for example, ordinarily uses the term "church" (ekkle‾sia)—often in the plural—to refer to local communities (Rom. 16:4, 16; 1 Cor. 1:2; 4:17; 2 Cor. 8:1; Gal. 1:2; Phil. 4:15; 1 Thess. 2:14). In the singular, he uses it of the assembly as such (1 Cor. 11:18; 12:28) or when he refers to his persecution of the "church" before his call to be an apostle (1 Cor. 15:9; Phil. 3:6). But in Ephesians, only the singular usage is found, and here with reference not to the local assembly but to the whole association of Christians, as in "Christ is the head of the church" (5:23; cf. 1:22; 3:10; 21; 5:23-32). Only Col. 1:18 and 1:24 are close to this. Does the difference reveal the perspective of a Pauline successor who looked back to the joining of many local assemblies into a self-consciously worldwide movement? Or was the perspective available as well to the Paul who engaged in a collection precisely to engender such a sense of church as something more than a local congregation?

A similar question is raised by the treatment of Jews and Gentiles (2:11-22). As we shall see, the exposition is in some respects remarkably close to Romans 9–11. In Romans, however, the reconciliation of Jew and Greek is dialectical and spoken of as a future hope. By contrast, Ephesians appears to depict it as a present reality. This shift could be explained as the result of a change in *temporal* perspective (i.e., realities in the post-Pauline church), except that there is little evidence to suggest a growing state of harmony between Jews and Gentiles after Paul's death. One could also understand it as a shift in *focus*: Romans addresses the larger historical relationship between Jews and Gentiles, while Ephesians focuses on a realized harmony within the actual Pauline communities. Or the difference could derive from a new *function*, so that Ephesians portrays something in the indicative as a way of formulating an imperative statement on how the relationship ought to be. Despite the range of solutions, this is still a problematic point.

Finally, Ephesians speaks of the church as a temple (*naos*; 2:19-22)—certainly a Pauline designation (cf. 1 Cor. 3:16; 2 Cor. 6:16)—and of individuals as "members of a household" (*oikeioi*; 2:19; cf. Gal. 6:10). But when it describes this temple as "built up on the foundation of the apostles and prophets, with the cornerstone being Christ Jesus" (2:20), this seems to represent a metaphoric shift from 1 Cor. 3:11, which says that "no other foundation can be laid except that which has been laid, Jesus Christ." Does the reference to apostles and prophets represent a backward look to an "apostolic age" by someone who was not a member of it? Or does the language address not Paul's own apostolic role but the whole missionary enterprise of the church, so that here (as in 1 Cor. 12:28 and Eph. 4:11!) the author can say unequivocally that "God has placed in the church first apostles, second prophets, third teachers"?

The decision concerning the authenticity of Ephesians is much more difficult than that concerning the authenticity of Colossians. But there is nothing in it that cannot be accounted for by the special circumstances and purpose of the letter. Ephesians could be regarded—even more so than Romans—as a summary of Paul's *gospel*. Thus, themes from other letters are developed, but also economized, as Paul sets forth various emphases that have arisen during the course of his ministry. If read in this light— Ephesians as a circular letter written under the authorization of the captive Paul to Gentile communities—then the lack of personal references, the distinctive stylistic traits, the use of tradition, and the perspective on the church are not only all intelligible but virtually necessary as well.

The Character of Ephesians

If not written by Paul or under his direct supervision, Ephesians is the work of Paul's best disciple, one whose religious perceptions and theological vision are equal to Paul's own. In Ephesians we find a masterly statement on the work of God in the world and church, expressed not by the passion of polemic or the logic of argumentation but by prayerful meditation. Ephesians has variously been described as a homily or a sapiential discourse. But it is the pervasive atmosphere of prayer that is its most distinctive feature. The peculiar effusiveness of its Greek derives not from a mindless enthusiasm but from the traditional rhythms of liturgical prayer. The best analogies are the *berakoth* and *tefilloth* of synagogue worship (see chap. 2, pp. 59–60); and the Christian eucharistic prayers (*anaphora*). In Ephesians, theology informs prayer, and prayer itself is the vehicle for theology.

In this letter are found distinctive elements of the Pauline gospel in a symbolic framework only suggested in other Pauline writings. We find the Pauline emphasis on justification by God's free gift (grace) accepted by humans through faith (1:13; 2:5, 8-9); the conviction that the gift came above all through the cross of Jesus (2:15-16), whose sacrificial death brought redemption (1:7). We find the Pauline perception of the Holy Spirit as a transforming (1:13-14; 4:17-5:2) and reconciling (2:17-18) power, which manifests itself in the community by diverse gifts (4:1-13); the Pauline emphasis on the relation between Jew and Gentile in God's plan (1:12-13; 2:11-12; 3:6) expressed from the point of view of one who is himself a Jew (1:12; 2:11-14; 3:1). Finally, we find Paul's conviction that his ministry to preach the "good news" to the Gentiles (3:3-5) came about through a revelation from God (3:7-8).

In contrast to other Pauline letters, however, the "good news" is placed within the framework of a cosmic battle in which the conflict between truth and falsehood, good and evil, light and darkness is represented by spiritual powers active in the world (see 6:10-18). These "powers and principalities" appear as superior to humans, yet interconnected with the dispositions of the human heart (see 1:21; 2:2; 3:10). Such a symbolization of religious reality was not infrequent in the Hellenistic world. It is impossible, therefore, to determine whether the author tapped specific sources that fed groups like the Sectarians at Qumran, or simply gives sharper definition to elements drawn from the broadly apocalyptic framework widely attested in early Christian traditions (cf., e.g., 2 Cor. 6:14—7:1; 1 Thess. 5:6-11). More important than the origin of the symbols is their use in Ephesians: human freedom is situated in the context of a struggle for the cosmos. Human alienation from God is expressed as enslavement to forces fighting God, and manifested in hostility toward, and alienation from, fellow human beings. The prime example of this hostility is the division of humanity into "two races," the historical competition between Jew and Gentile.

The "good news" in Ephesians announces God's work as a reversal of this state of cosmic-historical hostility. God has revealed his mysterious plan to reconcile all reality, bringing about harmony between God and humans and therefore establishing the possibility of unity among humans themselves. The agent of this reconciliation is the Messiah, whose paradoxical death heals the rupture between God and humanity, eradicates the cosmic forces that have enslaved humans to captivity, and reveals the possibility of a new way of being human, one that is not divided by hostility but united in peace.

The sign of this reconciliation is the unity of Jew and Greek in the church. In the messianic community, the one Spirit gives all humans equal access to God, drawing them into a humanity that is based on the pattern of the Messiah. Such is the gift that creates the church. Such also, however, is its mandate: if the church is to be the sign of God's reconciling power at work in the world, then it must actually manifest that unity in its life. The church is "the fullness of him who fills all things" (1:23). The church is therefore the central focus of Ephesians (see 1:22; 2:21; 3:5-6) precisely because it is, as a living community, the revelation to the world and to the cosmic powers of God's work in the world (3:10):

> that through the church the manifold wisdom of God might now be made known to the principalities and powers in the heavenly places.

The Gift: The Church as the Place of Reconciliation
Ephesians 1–3

The special emphasis of Ephesians is laid out in the opening to the epistle. Unlike other Pauline letters (except for 2 Cor. 1:3-7), Ephesians opens not with a thanksgiving section but with a prayer of blessing (1:3-14). This prayer resembles the Jewish *berakah* formula and shares its threefold structure: blessing God (1:3); recounting the reasons for this blessing; and interjecting periodic response of praise (1:6, 12, 14). In this prayer Paul announces the major themes of the letter: the "mystery" (1:9) that God is working out in history according to his purpose and will (1:5, 9, 11) through the redemptive death of his son Jesus (1:7), and that he made available to humans by free gift (1:6). This "mystery" is the plan to re-unify all reality with God (1:10). The first sign (seal) of its realization is the Holy Spirit (1:13), whose present activity among Christians guarantees their future inheritance (1:14). The gift, furthermore, has been made available not only to those Jews who had awaited the Messiah but also to the Gentiles, who had more recently come to believe in him (1:12-13). The opening prayer is, in effect, an expansion of the condensed praise of God's purpose in Rom. 8:28-30.

In the thanksgiving passage that follows (1:15-23), Paul reminds his readers of the reality of this gift, so that they might come to a deeper understanding of what is being accomplished among them (1:17-18). They should become aware not only of what lies before them—the "hope to which they have been called" and their eventual "inheritance among the saints" (1:18)—but above all, of their present reality: "the immeasurable greatness of God's power in us who believe." It is the actuality and ultimacy of God's power among them—"the working of his great might" (1:19)—that Paul wants them to appreciate. It is the same power by which God raised Jesus from the dead and established him above all spiritual beings (1:20-21). It is precisely this power that is at work in their experience within the community (1:22-23):

> He has put all things under his feet and has made him head over all things for the church, which is his body, the fullness of him who fills all in all.

The thanksgiving passage moves imperceptibly into the theological exposition (2:1-22) that forms the heart of the letter. In it Paul continues to describe the effect of the gift for humans, first in their relationship with God (2:1-10), then in their relations with one another (2:11-22). The argument worked out by diatribe in Romans is here presented by epitome. In 2:1-2, Paul briefly sketches the state of humanity as being subject to the power of evil (cf. Rom. 1:18—3:20). Here, the spiritual alienation is expressed in terms of subjection to spiritual forces: "the prince of the power of the air, the spirit that is now at work among the sons of disobedience" (2:2). But Paul does not exclude from the power of sin those who possess Torah (cf. Rom. 2:17—3:20), for "we," the Jews, were in the same state of alienation (2:3): "We were by nature children of wrath [cf. Rom. 1:18] like the rest of humanity." Paul argued in Rom. 3:21—5:21 that God had reversed the state of alienation by bringing about reconciliation and peace through the faithful death of Jesus; now in Eph. 2:4-10 he similarly states that God brought those who were "dead" in sin (2:1, 5) to life through the resurrection of Jesus (2:5). Again, there is an emphasis on the cosmic implications of the reconciliation (2:6-7), but the human response is unmistakably Pauline (2:8-9):

> For by grace you have been saved by faith, and this is not your own doing, it is the gift of God—not because of works, lest any person should boast.

The cosmic alienation of humanity from God is manifested through human "trespasses and sins" (2:1). The alienation between humans is expressed by the perversion of religious symbols through the division of Jew and Greek. We come now to the densest and most difficult part of the letter. In a daring haggadic midrash, Paul reworks the argument of Romans 9–11 by combining the images of Torah and temple. He suggests that, although these gifts from God were the basis of Jewish claims for distinctive access to God (cf. Rom. 9:4-5), they were thereby a sign of the power of sin, since they separated rather than united humans. The imagery here is complex. It depends on the physical arrangement of the Jerusalem temple, which had a wall dividing the court of the Gentiles from the Holy Place with a sign threatening death to any Gentile who transgressed the boundaries. Since the Holy Place promised "access" to God, this physical arrangement symbolized at once both the wall dividing humans and the cosmic wall separating God from humanity. Because those who were circumcised and who observed Torah could enter into the Holy Place, they could suppose that they had special access to God, whereas those who did not share these symbols were excluded. The problem lay not with Torah or temple as such, but with the human hostility that perverted even the gracious gifts of God into signs of self-aggrandizement, rivalry, and boasting—all the signs, in short, of hostility (2:14).

Paul drastically restructures these symbols through the figure of the crucified Messiah. By his death on the cross, he "brought the hostility to an end," namely the enmity between God and humans and between Jew and Greek. The blood of the rejected one becomes the new bond of unity for all (2:13, 15-16), in the process reshaping the entire Jewish symbolic structure (2:14-15):

> He is our peace who has made us both one, and has broken down the dividing wall of hostility, by abolishing in his flesh the law of commandments and ordinances.

Paul asserts that in Jesus there is not only the revelation of God's gift but also the basis for a new humanity. Jew and Greek both find in him a new way of access to God (2:15-16),

> that he might create in himself one new individual in place of the two, so making peace, and might reconcile us both to God in one body through the cross.

What Torah and temple offered only to Jews, Jesus gives to all humans by God's free gift (2:17-18):

> And he came and preached peace to you who were far off and to those who were near; for through him, we both have access in one spirit to the father.

Paul now moves on to reappropriate the symbolism of the temple for the messianic community. The church is founded on the "cornerstone" of Jesus. But since he is the living Lord and "head of the church," it is a living entity, "joined together and growing into a holy temple of the Lord." Therefore, the church is the place of reconciliation in the world, carrying on the process begun by the death of Jesus. Those who were once "without God and hope in the world" (2:12) are no longer "sojourners and strangers" but "fellow citizens with the saints and members of the household of God" (2:19). Jews and Greeks together form the living community of united worship "for a dwelling place of God in the Spirit" (2:22).

Paul interprets his own call and ministry (3:1-3, 7-8) along similar symbolic lines: his message—and indeed his imprisonment—is directly related to God's revelation of this "mystery" to him and to Paul's own proclamation of this "mystery" to the Gentiles. Paul's ministry, in fact, is characterized by the affirmation that the church is the place where God's reconciling will for the world is made manifest. Such is his special insight (3:4) into the "mystery of the Messiah": Gentiles (3:6) were

> fellow heirs, members of the same body, and partakers of the promise in Christ Jesus through the gospel.

The church, therefore, has both a salvific and a revelatory function in and for the world. It is to be the place where the world can see reconciliation as a reality (3:10),

> that through the church, the manifold wisdom of God might now be made known to the principalities and powers in the heavenly places.

When people in the world see the possibility for a humanity based not in rivalry and boasting (enmity) but in the gift of God (reconciliation), they will be drawn into the community of peace. The church does not, in Ephesians, exist for itself, but as a sacrament for the world: it offers to the world both a sign and a realization of the world's own future possibility, so that in the church, God might be "glorified," that is, his presence in the world might truly be acknowledged (3:20-21).

The Mandate: Living a Reconciled Life
Ephesians 4–6

The moral exhortation of Ephesians is closely tied to its theological exposition and makes clear that the letter's emphasis on the "realized" victory of Jesus over the cosmic forces (2:5-8) does not imply that members of the messianic community are free from further struggle. In Christ, there is the possibility of a new form of humanity (2:15). And the same Spirit that works to give humans access to God through him (2:18) is active also in transforming them, so that their behavior will be consistent with their new identity:

> Be renewed in the spirit of your minds, and put on the new nature, created after the likeness of God in true righteousness and holiness. (4:23-24)

This call goes out not only to individuals but to the whole church: the community as a whole is to "grow up in every way into him who is the head, into Christ," by love (4:15-16). Since the gift given by the Spirit is one of peace and unity, we are not surprised to find that the list of the Spirit's gifts in 4:1-13 emphasizes the unity that underlies their diversity, and that this harmony is based ultimately in the oneness of the Gift-Giver, the "one God and Father of all, who is above all and through all and in all" (4:6). This view of the organic unity of the Christian community motivates Paul's ensuing discussion.

If the church is to manifest God's work in the world and reveal the mystery to the principalities and powers (3:10), it must also do battle against those forces in the world that continue to resist truth and light and that lead to dissension and disunity. The transformation from the old life to the new is fundamentally a movement from discord to unity, and thus Paul consistently emphasizes those aspects of Christian behavior that lead to the building up of a peaceful and harmonious community body. It is only through a life in unity that the church stands as a witness to the world—in sharp contrast to the cosmic powers. Its members, therefore, require all the "armor" of God if they are to stand "against the devil" in this cosmic battle (6:10-18). Above all, they require the power of the Spirit (6:17-18), enabling them to "live in a way worthy" of their call (4:1).

The power at work in them is the Spirit, but the measure of their transformation is Jesus himself. The whole life of the community, therefore, is to be based on those attitudes of "lowliness, meekness, patience" (4:2) that they learned from the Messiah Jesus. On his pattern, they will be able to "forbear one another in love, eager to maintain the unity of the Spirit in the bond of peace" (4:3). In this way, they are to attain to a state of mature humanity, which, while being created after the likeness of God (4:24), is "the measure of the stature of the fullness of Christ" (4:13). For this reason, Paul, using baptismal imagery, tells them to "cast off" all their hostile attitudes and actions that formerly characterized them when "they were darkened in their understanding, alienated from the life of God, because of their ignorance" (4:18), and to live by the new measure of the Messiah: if they no longer live in the darkness but in the light, they will act accordingly (5:6-14).

Thus, when Paul speaks of their former ways, he explains "You did not learn Christ in this way" (4:20-21), and then follows this up with a programmatic statement and a series of contrasting commands. They are to give up falsehood (4:25), hostility (4:26), stealing (4:28), evil talk (4:29), bitterness, wrath, anger, and malice (4:31), all fundamentally antisocial behaviors. In exchange, they are to speak the truth because they are—according to the body analogy of 4:15-16—members of each other (4:25). Moreover, they are to do honest work so that they can share their possessions with each other (4:28); they are to speak so as to build one another up in their identity (4:29); and they are to be kind and forgiving to everyone (4:32). The desired result of this is manifest in 5:1-2:

> Therefore be imitators of God as beloved children, and walk in love, as Christ loved us and gave himself up for us, a fragrant offering and sacrifice to God.

Households, too, should engender the same sort of attitudes in their members. In the Ephesian table of household duties (5:21—6:9), we find the same notes of reciprocity and relativization as in Col. 3:18—4:6, but the attitudes of submissiveness are here broadly generalized. Thus, when Paul begins with "Be subject to one another out of reverence for Christ" (5:21), he deliberately echoes his earlier statement "Walk in love as Christ loved us and gave himself for us" (5:2), clarifying the self-sacrificial nature of this Christian submission. These are the very attitudes by which the assembly itself is to live; by carrying them into the forms of social life, they begin to "reveal" the mystery of God in the world in a concrete manner. The household codes, therefore, give a practical edge to Paul's argument here in Ephesians.

The most remarkable feature of this household ethic is the lengthy and positive attention given to marriage. Although the wife is plainly told to be submissive to her husband, the strongest admonitions are given to the "higher" member of the relationship, the husband. He is called to leave all other ties (5:31) in order to "love his wife as Christ loved the church and gave himself up for her" (5:25). Paul states in effect that the pattern revealed in Jesus—strength becoming weak and love being manifest in submission to the needs of others—is above all incumbent on the "higher" members on the social scale. Paul's language must be taken seriously here; he does not say the husband is to "love" his wife only in the sense of having erotic or affectionate feelings for her; he is to "love" her with *agapē*, the self-emptying disposition that God revealed in Jesus. Although Paul is clearly indebted to his own cultural world for his understanding of the hierarchical relationship, his theological twist illustrates that he has much more invested in this description than the concern over proper order: the marriage relationship is a paradigm for the way God works in the world.

This connection is what enables Paul to conclude the treatment of marriage with a remarkable statement (5:32):

> This mystery is a profound one, and I am saying that it refers to Christ and the church.

We remember that Paul's "mystery" is that Jews and Greeks are reconciled and made one in the church. The relationship between husband and wife, therefore, symbolizes the mystery of unity in plurality and makes that mystery present within the community. This completes the Pauline perception of "neither Jew nor Greek, neither male nor female." It also suggests that, as the church is the sacrament (i.e., the effective sign) of the world's possibility as a place of peace and reconciliation, so is marriage a sacrament to the church of what it should progressively become. As male and female submit to each other in mutual respect, love, and service, finding unity and peace not in a merging of identities but in a pluralistic unity, so should Jew and Greek celebrate their unity in service to each other, so that God's purpose might be fulfilled, "to unite all things in him, things in heaven and things on earth" (1:10).

It is fitting, then, that Paul should close off his letter with this emphasis on marriage as an analogy for the unity of Jew and Greek. Paul's stress throughout has been on expounding the significance of the organic unity of the Christian body for the church's self-understanding. This unity stands as a witness against cosmic discord and chaos, testifying to the world through both the unity of Jew and Greek and the harmony in the community and household. The theme that community and ethnic unity manifest the fullness of God's purposes in history is probably one of the finest summaries of Paul's theology found anywhere in his epistolary corpus. Here we see the strands of Romans and Galatians coalescing with Philemon, Philippians, and 1 Corinthians. It is not difficult to believe that Paul himself was behind this formulation in Ephesians, as it clearly reaches to the core of his theology and self-understanding.

Study Questions

1. How does Ephesians differ from letters such as Romans and Philippians?

2. What roles do the themes of alienation and reconciliation play in Ephesians?

3. What did Jesus' death accomplish according to Ephesians? How does that fit in with other concerns of Paul?

4. What behaviors does the author encourage should be eradicated from the life of the church?

5. According to Ephesians, what is the basic task of the church?

Bibliographical Note

On the city of Ephesus and the surrounding region, see H. Koester (ed.), *Ephesos—Metropolis of Asia: An Interdisciplinary Approach to its Archaeology, Religion, and Culture* (HTS, 41; Valley Forge, Pa.: Trinity Press Int'l, 1995); and E. M. Yamauchi, *New Testament Cities in Western Asia Minor* (Grand Rapids: Baker Book House, 1980).

A classic expression of the difficulties posed by Ephesians is H. J. Cadbury's "The Dilemma of Ephesians," *NTS* 5 (1958): 91–102. The case against authenticity is argued in various ways by E. J. Goodspeed, *The Meaning of Ephesians* (Chicago: Univ. of Chicago Press, 1933); J. Coutts, "The Relationship of Ephesians and Colossians," *NTS* 4 (1957–58): 201–7; idem, "Ephesians 1:3-14 and I Peter 1:3-12," *NTS* 3 (1956–57): 115–27; J. A. Allen, "The 'In Christ' Formulations in Ephesians," *NTS* 5 (1958–59): 54–62; and E. Käsemann, "Ephesians and Acts," in L. Keck and J. Martyn (eds.), *Studies in Luke-Acts* (Philadelphia: Fortress Press, 1980 [1966]), 288–97. The most sustained treatment in favor of authenticity is A. Van Roon, *The Authenticity of Ephesians* (NovTSup, 39; Leiden: E. J. Brill, 1974). On the relationship with Colossians, see E. Best, "Who Used Whom? The Relationship of Ephesians and Colossians," *NTS* 43 (1997): 72–96.

For the textual problem in 1:1, see M. Santer, "The Text of Ephesians 1:1," *NTS* 15 (1968–69): 247–48; R. Batey, "The Destination of Ephesians," *JBL* 82 (1963): 101; and E. Best, "Recipients and Title of the Letter to the Ephesians: Why and When the Designation 'Ephesians'?," *ANRW* II.25.4 (1987): 3247–79.

Aspects of Ephesians' liturgical tone are touched on in P. T. O'Brien, "Ephesians 1: An Unusual Introduction to a New Testament Letter," *NTS* 25 (1978–79): 504–16; and J. C. Kirby, *Ephesians, Baptism, and Pentecost: An Inquiry into the Structure and Purpose of the Epistle to the Ephesians* (London: SPCK, 1968).

The specific symbolic structure of Ephesians is discussed in N. A. Dahl, "Cosmic Dimensions and Religious Knowledge," in E. E. Ellis and E. Grässer (eds.), *Jesus und Paulus* (Göttingen: Vandenhoeck & Ruprecht, 1975), 57–75; and F. Mussner, "Contributions Made by Qumran to the Understanding of the Epistle to the Ephesians," in J. Murphy-O'Connor (ed.), *Paul and the Dead Sea Scrolls* (New York: Crossroad, 1990 [1968]), 159–78. The background and identity of the cosmic forces so important for both Colossians and Ephesians are discussed by G. B. Caird, *Principalities and Powers: A Study in Pauline Theology* (Oxford: Clarendon Press, 1956); H. Schlier, *Principalities and Powers in the New Testament* (New York: Herder & Herder, 1961); and W. Wink,

Naming the Powers: The Language of Power in the New Testament (Philadelphia: Fortress Press, 1984). Other thematic elements in the letter are treated in C. E. Arnold, *Ephesians: Power and Magic; The Concept of Power in Ephesians in Light of Its Historical Setting* (Grand Rapids: Baker Book House, 1992 [1989]); M. Barth, "Traditions in Ephesians," *NTS* 30 (1984): 3–25; idem, "Conversion and Conversation: Israel and the Church in Paul's Epistle to the Ephesians," *Int* 17 (1963): 3–24; C. C. Caragounis, *The Ephesian Mysterion: Meaning and Content* (ConBNT, 8; Lund: CWK Gleerup, 1977); L. Cerfaux, "The Revelation of the Mystery of Christ," in his *Christ in the Theology of St. Paul* (New York: Herder & Herder, 1959), 402–38; W. H. Harris III, *The Descent of Christ: Ephesians 4:7–11 and Traditional Hebrew Imagery* (Grand Rapids: Baker Book House, 1998 [1996]); K. G. Kuhn, "The Epistle to the Ephesians in the Light of the Qumran Texts," in *Paul and the Dead Sea Scrolls*, 115–31; A. T. Lincoln, "The Use of the OT in Ephesians," *JSNT* 14 (1982): 16–57; idem, "Ephesians 2:8-10: A Summary of Paul's Gospel?" *CBQ* 45(1983): 617–30; W. A. Meeks, "In One Body: The Unity of Humanity in Colossians and Ephesians," in W. A. Meeks and J. Jervell (eds.), *God's Christ and His People* (Oslo: Universitetsforlaget, 1977), 209–21; J. P. Sampley, *"And the Two Shall Become One Flesh": A Study of Tradition in Eph. 5:21-23* (SNTSMS, 16; Cambridge: Cambridge Univ. Press, 1971); R. A. Wild, "The Warrior and the Prisoner: Some Reflections on Ephesians 6:10-20," *CBQ* 46 (1984): 284–98; and idem, "'Be Imitators of God': Discipleship in the Letter to the Ephesians," in F. Segovia (ed.), *Discipleship in the New Testament* (Philadelphia: Fortress Press, 1985), 127–43. Also see the collection of studies in E. Best, *Essays on Ephesians* (Edinburgh: T. & T. Clark, 1997).

For critical commentary, see M. Barth, *Ephesians*, 2 vols. (AB; Garden City, N.Y.: Doubleday & Co., 1974); E. Best, *A Critical and Exegetical Commentary on the Epistle to the Ephesians* (ICC; Edinburgh: T. & T. Clark, 1998); A. T. Lincoln, *Ephesians* (WBC; Dallas: Word Books, 1990); and R. Schnackenburg, *The Epistle to the Ephesians: A Commentary*, trans. H. Heron (Edinburgh: T. & T. Clark, 1991).

19. Pastoral Letters:
1 Timothy, 2 Timothy, Titus

PAUL'S LETTERS TO Timothy and Titus have been designated the "Pastoral Letters" since the eighteenth century. They were accepted and cited as genuinely Pauline by early Christian writers, but for two hundred years scholars have debated their authenticity. Lately the debate has ebbed, with the great majority of scholars thinking the issue has been decided: all three are considered inauthentic, at best a later and derivative testimony to genuine Pauline theology. Some scholars persist in thinking that conclusion to be somewhat hasty. Even those who are not absolutely convinced that the letters come directly from Paul find unconvincing many of the reasons given for assigning their composition to a later Pauline forger.

Since these are letters and not narratives, a decision concerning their authenticity affects our picture of Paul's ministry, our understanding of the development of Paulinism, and, most importantly, our reading of the letters themselves. Even though this debate already dominates scholarship on these writings and threatens to obscure their distinctive and individual witness to early Christian experience and interpretation, a consideration of the issues can nevertheless lead to an appreciation of the special character of these canonical writings.

There are strong tendencies in the debate, and it is helpful to note them at the outset. The first tendency derives from the primary and positive place most scholars accord Paul among NT writers. He is, after all, "*the* apostle." Scholars often want to find in him that which confirms their perceptions of "genuine" Christianity, and consider inauthentic those elements that contradict these perceptions. Those who regard the heart of Paul, if not of the whole NT, to be the teaching of righteousness through faith tend to reject the Pastorals as moralizing. On the other hand, those committed to traditions within which doctrine, church structure, and the inspiration of Scripture are important, tend to find these elements in the undisputed as well as the Pastoral letters. They are, consequently, inclined to regard the latter as genuine also. Thus, the issue of authenticity is directly correlated with the reconstruction of the "authentic" Paul: scholarship is not fully determined by bias, but we do tend to read Paul in our own image and out of our own particular theological context.

A second tendency also derives from Paul's place as the earliest and most prominent Christian writer. A judgment against authenticity of any letter means for some a judgment on its value as well. They implicitly measure the worth of a writing by its authorship, rather than by its content or its place within the community's canon. The tendency is found on both sides of the debate. Some fight the authenticity of the Pastorals, thinking such a recognition would inevitably mean as well an acceptance of their teaching. Others defend their authenticity for the same reason. These tendencies complicate the making of good literary and historical judgments.

A third tendency in the debate does not come from bias but is an inevitable result of categorization: the three letters are invariably treated together as a group. Characterizations of "the Pastorals" are typically drawn from all three letters coalesced into a whole, while the individual characteristics of the respective letters are overlooked. The Pastorals are often said, for example, to contain an elaborate ecclesial structure. But 2 Timothy lacks any reference to order at all, and Titus contains only a trace. Reference is also made to "the opponents in the Pastorals," even though there is a distinct profile in each of the letters. Such generalizing dulls the perception of the individual letters, heightening a sense of their isolation from the rest of the Pauline corpus. A similar effect would result from treating the Thessalonian correspondence as a separate group without ever referring them to other Pauline writings. But if Titus is read with other travel letters, or 2 Timothy with other captivity letters, their otherness is greatly diminished.

Even when such tendencies are taken into account, the Letters to Timothy and Titus raise unique and difficult questions for every reader. No one denies that they represent a strain of Paulinism. They are written in his name, and seek to communicate teaching which is recognizably Pauline. But in each letter there is also just enough divergence from any reader's instinctive perception of what is Pauline, that even those most sympathetic to their authenticity must wonder at this blend of the familiar and the strange so erratically distributed over three documents.

Factors To Be Considered

Since the issues are so complex, a full discussion is impossible, but each criterion for determining genuineness is touched upon in what follows. The first issue is their placement in the scheme of early Christian history and the Pauline mission. Although the letters lack obvious anachronisms, some find it difficult to fit them into Paul's career such as it can be reconstructed from Acts and the other letters. First Timothy and Titus presuppose Paul's active ministry among his churches. In 1 Timothy, Paul has left his delegate in Ephesus for a time while he goes to Macedonia (1 Tim. 1:3); Timothy is to attend to affairs until Paul's return within a short period (3:14). In principle, such a letter could have been written any time during Paul's lengthy Aegean ministry. Titus is written to Paul's delegate in Crete (Titus 1:5). Paul's whereabouts are not revealed. He plans to winter in Nicopolis (3:12), which could be any of several cities of that name.

That there should be a church in Crete is not surprising. The account in Acts, however, places Paul there only tangentially, and then as a prisoner (Acts 27:7-15). Could he have had the opportunity to found churches or to commission a delegate to found them? The phrase "I left you in Crete" is also ambiguous. Did Paul take his leave of Titus there? Or did Paul leave Titus in an assignment?

Second Timothy is written from (probably a Roman) captivity (1:16-17). But does Paul's reference to a first defense (4:16) indicate that this is a second imprisonment, since he was released from the first (4:17)? In contrast to 1 Timothy and Titus, 2 Timothy contains information about fifteen of Paul's helpers (4:9-21). Nothing in their movements directly contradicts the little we know of them elsewhere, although some scholars have great difficulty with the apparent discrepancy between Acts 21:29 and 2 Tim. 4:20 in the matter of Trophimus. Other information is startlingly confirming, such as the short remark "Erastus remained in Corinth" (4:20; cf. Rom. 16:23).

The problem is rendered more difficult by the attempt to place all the letters in the same time frame. The following options are possible. Some think the letters are pseudonymous and written at the same time after Paul's death. The biographical information in this case only serves the interest of pseudonymity and is thus irrelevant. A second option invokes the ancient tradition (cf. *1 Clem.* 5.7) that Paul was released from a first Roman imprisonment and preached in Spain before again becoming a captive and finally being put to death. Supporters argue for a period of active work between the two imprisonments, such as is reflected in these letters. A third option is to regard the letters as genuinely Pauline and to try to fit them into Paul's ministry as we know it from Acts and the other letters. This is not impossible, although it requires considerable ingenuity.

A fourth option is the best, though rarely chosen. It admits that neither Acts nor the letters give us a full chronology of Paul: Acts gives us only a selective and highly stylized rendering of Paul's travels, while the letters provide only fragmentary bits and pieces of information. Thus, while the Pastorals do not by themselves account for their placement in his life, they may give us important information about incidents in Paul's career and captivity that the other sources do not. Just as 2 Corinthians tells us of imprisonments we would otherwise not suspect, so do these letters tell us of Pauline missionary endeavors—in Crete and Dalmatia—that, aside from the tantalizing reference to Illyricum in Rom. 15:19, would otherwise be unknown to us.

The criterion of style is difficult to apply to the Pastorals. They obviously contain a large number of words not found in other Pauline letters and share other terms not otherwise attested in the NT. But there are also real differences among the three letters. On the whole, 2 Timothy has a vocabulary remarkably close to that of other Pauline epistles, whereas the terminology in 1 Timothy and Titus varies more significantly. How much of this special vocabulary is due to the nature of the letters, the character of the addressees, and the subject matter is difficult to determine. Unlike the genuine Pauline letters, there is no indication that the letters were dictated to a scribe, although the use of an amanuensis cannot be ruled out. Since a large amount of the vocabulary of 1 Timothy and Titus is found in the NT elsewhere only in Luke-Acts, Luke has been proposed as the amanuensis (2 Tim. 4:11) or even the author of the letters.

More than vocabulary is involved in stylistic analysis. The syntax of the Pastorals is generally smoother than in letters like Galatians and Romans. Sentences are longer and more regular; the use of particles is less varied and rich. Yet, one must ask how much the style of Romans and Galatians is itself affected by the adoption of the diatribal mode in those letters. If the Pastorals are compared to 1 Thessalonians or Philippians, the differences are less extreme. The issue of style is further complicated by the fact that the Pastorals do not reveal a consistent "hand," as do Colossians and Ephesians. Rather, the mixture of vocabulary and sentence structure is complex and varied. Some have even suggested that the Pastorals may contain fragments of authentic Pauline notes, worked up later into new pseudonymous compositions. But the close correlation of "non-Pauline" passages with the subject matters unique to the Pastorals has largely gone unnoticed. This is a significant oversight since it is precisely the difference in subject matter that most clearly separates these three letters from the rest of the Pauline corpus. Finally, on the issue of style, one should also recall the significance of "writing in character" (see chap. 10): the style of a letter is adapted to the persona a writer adopts for the sake of creating persuasive letters. This rhetorical phenomenon further complicates the reading of the evidence.

One of the early reasons for questioning the genuineness of the Pastorals was the nature of the opponents or heresy they attack. It was thought to be a form of "gnosis" (see 1 Tim. 6:20)—unknown until the second century—that believed the resurrection life had already been accomplished (2 Tim. 2:17-18), scorned marriage, advocated physical asceticism (1 Tim. 4:3, 8), and was interested in the practice of Jewish law (1 Tim. 1:7; Titus 3:9). This picture is of course a composite of the three letters. Even as such it does not preclude Pauline authorship, for there is nothing in this mix not already encountered in the undisputed letters (cf., e.g., 1 Cor. 8:1-3; 15:17-19; Gal. 4:8-10; 1 Cor 7:1; cf. Col. 2:20-22). The composite sketch, however, ignores the real differences between the letters themselves, each of which is internally consistent and need not be read in light of the others. Some object further that the manner of responding to the opponents is typically un-Pauline, since it relies on polemic rather than on refutation. This is slightly inaccurate, since 1 Timothy does clarify theological points several times (1:8; 4:3-5, 7-8; 6:5-10), and the genuine Paul is not immune from the use of slander against rival teachers (cf. 2 Cor. 11:13-15; Gal. 5:12; 6:13; Phil. 3:2). What is distinctive in the Pastorals is the amount of polemic, its largely stereotypical character, and the literary function it performs in 1 and 2 Timothy.

A major challenge to the authenticity of the letters is made on the basis of church organization. Here, it is claimed, there is not merely a shift in emphasis, such as making Christ the head of the body (as in Colossians) but an entirely different outlook. The organic sense of the church is lost, replaced by an organization—the "household of God"—that has a hierarchical ministry of bishops, presbyters, and deacons, together with orders of deaconesses and widows. Such attention to structure, it is thought, results from a "routinization of charism" when eschatological expectations diminish and the church grows accustomed to being in the world and adapts to its ways. Others see here a defensive reaction against a popular Paulinism that was more radically egalitarian, such as one finds in the *Acts of Paul and Thecla*. The Pastorals, on this reading, arise from a situation like that found in the letters of Ignatius of Antioch (ca. 115) in which a monarchical episcopate and hierarchical order are understood to be essential for the well-being of the church (see Ign. *Eph.* 2.2; *Magn.* 3.1; *Trall.* 2.2; 3.1).

Such conclusions move well beyond the evidence of the letters themselves. First, it is inaccurate to speak of the church order of the Pastorals, since there is none in 2 Timothy, and the little found in Titus does not match precisely the fuller account in 1 Timothy. Second, what organization is spoken of is not elaborate. It corresponds rather well, in fact, to what we know of the synagogal structure of Diaspora Judaism in the first century, as well as to the structure of the religious and social associations prevalent in the ancient Greco-Roman world. Early Christianity did not develop in a vacuum; it naturally adopted and adapted pre-existing institutions. Third, the organizational structure is not legitimated in these letters, that is, it is neither theologically defended nor interpreted, unlike the case in the Ignatian letters. Fourth, the letters do not prescribe a particular order but presuppose it; they contain not job descriptions for new positions but moral and mental qualifications for those who are to fill established places in the church. Fifth, sociological studies of intentional communities in every era suggest that they do not survive for decades without strong structures for decision making and social control: a great time lapse between the birth of a community and the establishment of structure is thus counterintuitive: structure and charism frequently coexist. Sixth, the undisputed letters of Paul not only refer by title to the offices found in the Pastorals (bishops and deacons, Phil. 1:1; woman deacon, Rom. 16:1), but explicitly recognize the role of authority figures in specific communities (cf. 1 Cor. 16:15-17; Gal. 6:6; Col. 4:17; 1 Thess. 5:12). Seventh, the attention that is given to organizational matters in two of these letters owes a great deal to the nature of the writings and the identity of the addressees.

The most telling objection to the authenticity of the Pastorals is the criterion of theology and ethics. Even when full credit is given to Paul's wide range in these areas, some elements in the Pastorals appear to be marginal. Common Pauline terms such as "faith," "law," and "righteousness" occur, but all with slightly different nuances. "Law" appears as something that can be used "lawfully" (1 Tim. 1:8), "faith" seems less an obedient response to God than the common body of conviction and commitment (Titus 1:1; 1 Tim. 5:8) or, simply, a virtue (2 Tim. 2:22). "Righteousness" (*dikaiosynē*) does not signify a state of right relation with God but denotes a virtue in the Greek sense of "justice" (1 Tim. 6:11; 2 Tim. 2:22). Tradition is a deposit of truth that is to be protected (1 Tim. 6:20; 2 Tim. 1:12-14) rather than a process of transmission (1 Cor. 11:2, 23; 15:3). Christology emphasizes the role of Jesus as Savior (2 Tim. 1:10; Titus 1:4; 3:6) and his coming "appearance" (1 Tim. 6:14; 2 Tim. 1:10). It must be said that each one of these elements can be found somewhere in the undisputed letters, but never in this concentrated combination. Therein lies the difference and the problem.

A similar point can be made about ethical teaching. There is certainly nothing explicitly like Paul's command in 1 Corinthians 7 to live in the world "as though not." Here, the attitudes and aptitudes of household members are appropriate as well to the life of the community as a whole. The Pauline note of conscience (syneidēsis) appears, not in terms of weak and strong (cf. 1 Cor. 8:7-12) but of "good" (1 Tim. 1:5, 19) and "pure" (1 Tim. 3:9; 2 Tim. 1:3) in contrast to "soiled" (Titus 1:15) and "cauterized" (1 Tim. 4:2). Here, too, is the contrast between "healthy teaching" (1 Tim. 1:10; 6:3; 2 Tim. 1:13; 4:3; Titus 1:9; 2:1) and "sickness" (2 Tim. 2:17; 1 Tim. 4:2), expressing itself in a life of virtue (1 Tim. 1:10; 3:2-4, 11; 4:13; 2 Tim. 2:22, 24; 3:10; Titus 1:7-9; 2:7) and vice (1 Tim. 1:8-10; 2 Tim. 3:2-5; Titus 3:3).

Listing these elements is easy; evaluating them is more difficult. Appeal to the outlook of an aging apostle is of little help, and an assumed shift to a second generation of Paulinist Christians seems inadequate. The issue is complicated by the supposition of uniformity in Pauline Christianity: one must be careful about assuming that every Pauline church looked the same; clearly each community would have had a unique context that shaped its experience and expression. Take the question of subject matter. The "household" theme, for example, is prevalent in Paul, but takes on a variety of forms and nuances depending on the community Paul addresses. Even appeals to the character of the language itself provide ambiguous evidence. These letters do have a more Greek and less "biblical" mode of presentation. Yet, before drawing conclusions, it is good to remember that the "biblical" style of Paul in Galatians and Romans is no more natural than his "Greek" style in 1 Thessalonians or Philippians. His style is affected by his subject matter, his audience, and the traditions upon which he was reliant.

In fact, one of the solutions to the problem may rest precisely in these differences. Titus and Timothy, we recall, both have at least a partial Greek background, and both are portrayed in the role of teachers. These factors may help us locate the kind of language used in the letters addressed to them, particularly if we ask how Paul might have spoken and written to his more educated Hellenistic associates. The polished Greek, the moralizing tone, the specific subject matter treated, and the general tone and function of the letter may be determined less by the passage of time and more by the specific character and role of the delegates to whom Paul wrote.

Accounting for the Correspondence

Most scholars see the Pastorals as the production of a "Pauline school" long after Paul's death, perhaps as late as the mid-second century. Rather than real letters, the Pastorals are considered a single literary composition in the form of fictitious correspondence in which biographical elements serve only to provide an air of plausibility. In this view the three letters together represent the beginning of church orders, a genre of documents that regulated church worship and ministry (e.g., the *Didache*, the *Didascalia Apostolorum*, and the *Apostolic Constitutions*). They were written as part of a conservative reaction within Paulinism, possibly reacting against the use of Paul by heretics who radically extended Paul's ascetic tendencies. It has even been suggested that Polycarp of Smyrna wrote them as a weapon in his fight against Marcionism. Another suggested stimulus was the growing egalitarianism, especially among women, that threatened the stability of communities.

The author of the Pastorals therefore sought to adapt the Pauline message for a new generation, emphasizing structure and order, while resisting ascetic and egalitarian excess. In the process, certain elements seem presupposed: a diminished eschatological expectation, a growth in church structure, and an increased accommodation to the world. In this view, the Paulinism of the Pastorals is refracted through the prism of second and third-generation concerns. Paul is a legendary hero whose authentic genius is diminished, reduced to being part of the "deposit" of faith for future generations.

The obvious appeal of this reconstruction is attested by its many adherents. It provides for development and conflict within Paulinism. It suggests that the Pastorals, with Acts and Ephesians, were part of the movement of "early Catholicism" that resisted Gnosticism while domesticating the more radical Paul of the authentic letters.

This reconstruction has serious deficiencies. Even if the writing of epistolary pseudepigrapha soon after Paul's death can be granted, the Pastorals were accepted as genuine by the ancient church, in contrast to clearly Pauline counterfeits (*3 Corinthians, Letter to Laodiceans, Letters of Paul and Seneca, Acts of Paul and Thecla*) that were almost as universally rejected. A mid-second century dating must dismiss the allusion in Polycarp's *Letter to the Philippians* (4.1) to 1 Tim. 6:7, 10, and reject the express statement of Tertullian (*Against Marcion* V. 21) that Marcion excluded the Pastorals from his canon—both of which would seem to necessitate an earlier origin of the material.

The common reconstruction falters most by failing to provide a convincing life setting for the production of three such similar yet quite different letters, and by paying too little attention to their self-presentation and literary form. It has been suggested, for example, that the letters were intended to rehabilitate a Paul fallen into disrepute because of his popularity among heretics. But Paul's authority is never at issue in the letters; it is always assumed. Nor is specific attention given to his "image." The suggestion also presupposes a consciousness of fine distinctions in doctrine such as exists only among scholars. For anyone seriously doubting or misplacing Paul's worth, furthermore, it is unlikely that the rather banal material in the Pastorals would prove an effective antidote. Even in other scenarios, such as an orthodox leader like Polycarp creating and then distributing the letters as a Pauline discovery, there are problems. Besides being inconsistent with Polycarp's situation such as we know it, this hypothesis makes us wonder why more use was not made of this creation by Polycarp himself. Moreover, would such a ploy be successful at a time when Paul was apparently a figure of controversy and rival communities were compiling their lists of acceptable and unacceptable writings on the basis of apostolic origin?

Another suggestion places the letters' production within a school setting in which the imitation of literary models took place. This is a sensible solution, since such schools were known to exist after the life of a founder. It would be a stronger suggestion if we could be as confident about the existence of such a school after Paul's death as we are of its existence during his lifetime. However sensible, the suggestion is not altogether satisfying. If Pauline models were being imitated, why were letters not produced that imitated Paul's correspondence to churches—as was most typical for Paul—rather than letters to individual delegates (only Philemon was addressed to an individual, and he was not a delegate)? Why were the style and form of the undisputed letters not followed more accurately? The fragment hypothesis is of little help here. It is hard to see why tiny autobiographical notes would be preserved in the first place, and then lifted into new compositions so clumsily. Further, if a pseudepigrapher had authentic fragments before him, why could he not imitate their style more convincingly? To complicate matters even more, the differences in style between the three letters themselves do not allow for simplistic theories of compositional imitation.

An enduring difficulty for the conventional reconstruction is the presence of variety in the Pastorals. Why would three such letters be produced, each of which was directed to a situation that was internally consistent yet very difficult to match with the situations of the other two? Here we would have a forger subtly able to create the verisimilitude of an established community in Ephesus and a new church in Crete, together with the appropriate sort of directions to each, and yet not able to imitate more convincingly the available Pauline samples.

No real progress will be made in the understanding of the Pastorals until they are restored to separate but equal status within the Pauline collection. It may well be, for example, that 2 Timothy can lay a far better claim to authenticity on every count than 1 Timothy. The first sustained questioning of their authenticity applied initially only to 1 Timothy, and then only on the point of diction. The declaration of inauthenticity for all three has been a more recent development, largely resulting from the association of 2 Timothy and Titus with 1 Timothy. But it is theoretically possible, for example, that 1 Timothy is pseudonymous, based on an authentic 2 Timothy. Such possibilities must be entertained, although any particular configuration is difficult to prove.

In the final analysis, it is difficult to make any assured claims about either the authenticity or the inauthenticity of the Pastorals as a whole or as individual letters. Yet, what we lose for our reconstruction of the "historical" Paul, we gain for the understanding of early Christianity: in the Pastorals we catch a glimpse of early Christian leadership, structure, and social world that might otherwise be unknown to us. Consequently, attention is appropriately directed to the literary self-presentation of each of the letters in turn and to their respective shaping of the Christian message within the Pauline tradition.

Paul's Delegates

The letters are written to Paul's most important delegates. We have repeatedly seen Timothy's prominence within the Pauline mission: co-sponsor of five letters (see 2 Cor. 1:1; Phil. 1:1; Col. 1:1; 1 Thess. 1:1; 2 Thess. 1:1), he was Paul's go-between with the Macedonian churches (see Acts 18:5; 19:22) of Thessalonica (1 Thess. 3:2) and Philippi (Phil. 2:19), as well as with the Corinthians (Rom. 16:21). According to 1 Tim. 1:3, he played the same role for the Ephesian church. In Acts 16:1, he is said to have a Greek father, which would make it likely that he had some Greek education as well. From what Paul says of him in the undisputed letters, his special role and his place in Paul's affections is obvious. When Paul wants the restive Corinthians to "imitate" him (1 Cor. 4:16), he adds (4:17):

> Therefore, I sent to you Timothy, my beloved and faithful child in the Lord, to remind you of my ways in Christ, as I teach them everywhere in the church.

We notice here the role of memory and imitation, and the portrayal of Timothy as the "reminder" of Paul's teaching and an example to a local community.

Paul clearly anticipated that Timothy would be received in the same manner Paul himself would be (1 Cor. 16:10-11):

> When Timothy comes, see that you put him at ease among you, for he is doing the work of the Lord, as I am. Let no one despise him.

When writing to the Philippians, Paul says of Timothy (2:19-23):

> I hope in the Lord Jesus to send Timothy to you soon, so that I may be cheered by news of you. I have no one like him, who will be genuinely anxious for your welfare. They all look after their own interests, not those of Jesus Christ. But Timothy's worth you know, how as a son with a father, he has served with me in the gospel. I hope therefore to send him just as soon as I see how it will go with me.

Finally, in 1 Thess. 3:2, Paul reports of Timothy:

> And we have sent Timothy, our brother and God's servant in the gospel of Christ, to establish you in your faith and to exhort you, that no one be moved by these afflictions.

There is a remarkable agreement between these random characterizations and the portrayal of Timothy in the Pastorals. He is a "beloved" (2 Tim. 1:2) or "genuine" child (1 Tim. 1:2). He is a "servant of God" (*doulos*; 2 Tim. 2:24; cf. same in Phil. 1:1, and *diakonos* in 1 Thess. 3:2). He is to "exhort" others (1 Tim. 6:2; 2 Tim. 4:2), and to "remind" churches of Paul's teaching (2 Tim. 2:14), providing them an example of it (1 Tim. 4:12) even as he himself has an example to follow in Paul (2 Tim. 1:13).

Two different but reasonable explanations can account for this evident agreement between the Pastorals and the genuine letters. First, the letters accurately report Paul's habitual perceptions of his delegate. Second, a pseudepigrapher had available to him the full range of such epithets when he drew up his imitation. The more important point, though, is that 1 and 2 Timothy present Timothy in a role that corresponds exactly to that explicitly given him in the undisputed letters: he is Paul's troubleshooter.

The undisputed letters tell us much less about Titus. He was of Greek origin (Gal. 2:3), and Paul makes much of his not having to be circumcised when he accompanied Paul to Jerusalem (Gal. 2:1-3). Although this is speculative, he may be the Titus (or Titius) Justus whom Acts 18:7 refers to as a "God-fearer" and whose house Paul uses after leaving the synagogue. He is, in any case, a notable associate of Paul's Corinthian ministry (2 Cor. 2:13; 7:6, 13, 14), especially Paul's collection efforts (2 Cor. 8:6, 16, 23; 12:18). He is not the representative of a local church but is Paul's "fellow-worker" (*koinōnos*; 2 Cor. 8:23). He is not, however, pictured as being on intimate terms with Paul.

The same sense is given by the Letter to Titus, in which he is called "genuine child" (Titus 1:4) but is not shown the sort of affection found in 1 and 2 Timothy. His duty in Crete may well also have included fund raising (see Titus 3:14). According to 2 Tim. 4:10, Titus also worked in Dalmatia, which would fit within the broad range of the Pauline mission (cf. Rom. 15:19).

In writing letters to delegates with such responsibilities, we would anticipate discussion of matters less appropriate for epistles written for community consumption. These could include: personal encouragement for the delegate's difficult task of dealing with lively Pauline communities; reminders of the ideal one should follow; hostile dismissals of rival teachers; *ad hoc* directions concerning local leadership positions and structural conflicts. Rather than lengthy doctrinal treatises, we would expect only formulaic allusions. As a means of encouragement, we might envision a shaping of the gospel that emphasized its godliness (*eusebeia*), a Christology in which the coming "appearance of the savior" figured dominantly, and ethical teaching that stressed virtue and the avoidance of vice. No doubt many of these same aspects would have had further appeal to the reader immersed in the educative culture of the Greco-Roman world. Moreover, such letters would likely combine attention to the delegate's personal disposition as well as to the attitudes appropriate to the office of teaching.

As so often in the Hellenistic world, there were precedents for letters like these. Second Timothy can be read as a personal parenetic epistle, and 1 Timothy and Titus can be understood as *mandata principis* letters. The following analysis will therefore proceed on the basis of genre rather than canonical order.

2 Timothy: A Personal Parenetic Letter

Paul writes to Timothy from prison (1:16; 2:9; 4:16). Although he still has workers around him, he is sensitive to the apostasy of others (1:15; 4:10, 16). He struggles to proclaim the gospel (4:17) and to direct the mission through delegates (4:10-12) and correspondence (4:13). He faces active opposition himself (4:14). Thus, despite feeling close to death (4:6-8), Paul writes to encourage and admonish Timothy in his own struggles. The letter is dominated by its unswerving attention to Timothy. Whatever is said about others is sooner or later turned back to Timothy: "but you . . ." The most frequent verb form in the letter is the second-person singular imperative. Nothing new is being communicated to Timothy, only reminders of what he already knows, together with the exhortation to hold fast to it.

Because we find here an aging, even dying, religious figure instructing his follower on the struggles to come and the need for perseverance, many who regard these letters as pseudonymous find the most appropriate literary category for 2 Timothy to be the farewell discourse, such as we find it in the *Testaments of the Twelve Patriarchs* or even Acts 20:17-35. A more likely parallel, and one closer in content and function, is the personal parenetic letter.

Rhetorical handbooks describe an *epistolē parainetikē* as a letter written to "exhort someone advising them to pursue something and to abstain from something." The sample letter given by Pseudo-Libanius reads:

> Always be an emulator, dear friend, of the virtuous. For it is better to be well spoken of when imitating good individuals, than to be reproached by all for following evil ones.

This short sample contains the elements of imitation and the antithetical expression of options: do this, avoid that. In actual parenetic discourses such as Pseudo-Isocrates' treatise *To Demonicus*, the form is followed exactly: the presentation of a model and appeal to memory (*Dem* 3–11) is followed by a series of moral maxims often expressed antithetically (12–49), and at the conclusion there is a re-presentation of models for imitation (50–51). So also in 2 Timothy we find the elements of memory, model, and maxims.

This classification helps explain the polemic against false teachers. We are given little specific information about them, despite the naming of Phygelus, Hermogenes (1:15), Hymenaeus, and Philetus (2:17). They claim that the resurrection is already past (2:18), but apart from that, they are characterized mainly by their methods, which involve harsh disputation (2:16, 23) and the intellectual seduction of uneducated women (3:6), as well as their morals, which are obviously poor. Much of this takes the form of stereotypical slander, like that used by Hellenistic philosophers when attacking each other. Yet Paul never attacks them directly. His concern is for his delegate, and he thus alternates characterizations of them with direct commands to Timothy. The false teachers thereby become the negative model Timothy is to avoid. The same use of polemic can be found in protreptic (i.e., exhortatory) discourse addressed to would-be philosophers: slander establishes a counter-type to the ideal teacher (cf. Dio *Oration* 77/78; Lucian *Demonax*; Epictetus *Discourses* III.22).

Second Timothy has the overall form of a personal parenetic letter, with the elements of polemic being utilized to develop more fully what Timothy is to avoid. The structure of 2 Timothy therefore is: the presentation of Paul as a model (1:3—2:13); maxims for Timothy as a teacher, presented in contrast to the false teachers (2:14—4:5); and the re-presentation of Paul as a model (4:6-18).

Paul, the Model for Teaching and Suffering (2 Timothy 1:3—2:13)

The motifs of memory and model open the letter. In the face of the opposition and success of rival teachers, Timothy is encouraged to "endure," particularly since his "father" Paul has little hope for release from prison. The thanksgiving typically anticipates Paul's main point: he "remembers" Timothy (1:3), "remembers" his tears (1:4), and "remembers" the sincere faith he had learned from his mother and grandmother (1:5). When Paul adds, ". . . a faith, which I am sure, dwells in you" (1:5), he reveals his true emphasis: he clearly wants to "remind" Timothy of the qualities and dispositions to which he was called. He was not given a spirit of timidity (or, cowardice: *deilia*) but one of "power and love and self-control" (1:7). Paul wants to "stir up" in him (1:6) this gift of power and confidence, so he will persevere in his ministry. The prevalent early Christian motif of "endurance" and "steadfastness" in the midst of trials takes on a practical edge here in 2 Timothy (cf. James 1:12).

Paul presents himself as a model for Timothy, who can find in him the "pattern of healthy teaching" (1:13). Timothy can preserve it, since it has been entrusted to him by "the Holy Spirit dwelling in us" (1:14). Paul is more than a source of proper teaching. He is the example of how to suffer for the gospel amidst adversity. Timothy is told, "Don't be ashamed" of testifying to the Lord; he is to "take a share of suffering for the gospel" (1:8). Paul too had been appointed a "preacher and apostle and teacher" of this "good news" (1:11), and "therefore I suffer as I do, but I am not ashamed" (1:12). Timothy should not therefore draw back because of suffering he may encounter for the "good news." He is able to keep going because of God's power (1:8), the indwelling Spirit (1:14), and the certainty of God's promise (1:12).

The mention of Onesiphorus in 1:15-18 is not beside the point. Because he provided help ("often refreshed me") and did so despite Paul's captivity, he provides Timothy with another example: "He was not ashamed of my chains" (1:16). As Paul can look forward to a reward from God for his suffering (1:12), so he can pray, "May the Lord grant to him to find mercy from the Lord on that day" (1:18). Timothy, in other words, is not alone in "sharing the suffering" for the good news, and should take encouragement in that fact.

The second aspect of Timothy's role is suggested in 2:2. He is to entrust the "sound teaching" to others who in turn will be able to teach. Timothy is not only a Christian who lives the gospel and suffers for it. His suffering occurs precisely because he is a teacher of the "good news." The focus therefore turns to his ministry of teaching, particularly regarding the attitudes he himself should have and should inculcate in others. Before turning to that role (2:14—4:5), however, Paul offers a series of models to which Timothy can look for encouragement. The advice, "Take your share of suffering as a good soldier of Jesus Christ" (2:3), suggests the first. The soldier, athlete, and farmer are all stock examples for exhortation in Hellenistic moral teaching (cf. 1 Cor. 9:7-27). Paul here emphasizes their attention to duty. The soldier does not get distracted by extraneous affairs; the athlete competes by the rules; and the farmer works hard. Reward only follows upon this devotion: the soldier pleases his recruiter; the athlete receives the crown; and the farmer enjoys the first fruits of the crop (2:3-6).

Paul saves his most important example till last: "Remember Jesus Christ, risen from the dead, descended from David, as preached in my gospel" (2:8). Once again, we see here the note of memory. Further, Paul specifies his gospel as ". . . the gospel for which I am suffering" (2:9). In fact, Paul endures suffering so that others might attain salvation (2:10). The implication is that Jesus likewise suffered and died, "so that life and immortality might be brought to light through the gospel" (1:10). Here, then, as in chapter 2 of Philippians, Jesus becomes the model par excellence for imitation. So Paul reminds Timothy of the "faithful word" (2 Tim. 2:11-13):

> If we have died with him we shall also live with him. If we endure, we shall reign with him. If we deny him, he will also deny us. If we are faithless, he remains faithful, for he cannot deny himself.

The first three lines of this apparently traditional saying have perfect internal symmetry: as we are toward God, so God will be toward us. Suffering now with Jesus will bring glory later with Jesus; endurance will bring rule; denial, denial. But the final line is a surprise, and in it we find a typical Pauline emphasis: God is faithful despite human infidelity.

As Paul offered the Philippians a series of examples of "life for others" that included Jesus and himself (Phil. 2:1—4:3), so here we find the same rhetorical technique. He provides Timothy with a series of concrete examples of suffering in the hope of reward: Onesiphorus, the soldier, athlete, and farmer; himself; and Jesus who suffered and died.

The Ideal Teacher (2 Timothy 2:14—4:5)

Paul fills out the model with maxims, set in a series of antitheses. The attitudes and actions of Timothy stand in contrast to those of the false teachers. They are given to disputatiousness (2:14) and godless chatter (2:16), which spreads like a gangrenous sickness (2:17). They have revolutionary impulses (2:22) and engage in senseless and useless quarrels (2:23). They are filled with all manner of vice (3:2-5). The opponents are charlatans (3:13) who prey on the uneducated and curious (3:6-7). They are like the magicians of Pharaoh's court who opposed Moses, "men of corrupt mind and counterfeit faith" (3:8). Timothy and those he instructs (2:14) are to avoid such practices and people (2:14, 16, 22, 23; 3:5).

In an intriguing rhetorical strategy, Paul uses a spatial imagery throughout this section. The opponents are always on the move: they "go from house to house" (3:6); they fall away and turn away (2:18); they "stand against" (3:8); and they "advance" (2:16; 3:13). In contrast, Timothy is to "remain" (3:14) and "stand fast" (3:14; 4:2). Paul is using the opponents as a foil to develop the endurance theme for the faithful believer: the steadfastness of Timothy is viewed as a response to the "unsteady" behavior of the unrighteous.

The end results will, according to Paul, justify his exhortation: although the opponents "make progress," Paul assures Timothy, "they will not advance" (3:9). Such comfort is all the more welcome since the opponents are obviously enjoying considerable success. Paul characterizes these as the "last days," when people will be "lovers of pleasure rather than lovers of God" (3:4). And it will only get worse. People will not even be willing to listen to sound teaching but will seek charlatans willing to shape their teaching to expectations (4:3). The fact that this behavior is indeed taking place in the present both confirms Paul's claim that the "last days" are upon them and encourages Timothy to remain firm in the faith: because the end is near, steadfastness and endurance in the face of this opposition are all the more urgent.

Against the tide of indifference and apostasy, Paul can only tell Timothy to remain steady, to endure suffering, and to fulfill his ministry (4:5). Timothy cannot cut truth to fit the season, but must remain constant (4:2):

> Preach the word; be urgent in season and out of season; convince, rebuke, exhort, be unfailing in patience and in teaching.

Timothy can once more look to Paul as a model of such endurance in the face of adversity. Paul reminds Timothy (3:10-11):

> You have observed my teaching, my conduct, my aim in life, my patience, my love, my steadfastness, my persecutions, my sufferings, what befell me at Antioch, at Iconium, and at Lystra, what persecutions I endured; yet from them all the Lord rescued me.

Paul too faced resistance to the truth, and as he held on, so should Timothy. The gospel ministry bears with it the necessity of suffering. For a sick world, health is a threat: "All who would desire to lead a godly life in Christ will be persecuted" (3:12). But as Paul was delivered—"From them all the Lord rescued me" (3:11)—so will Timothy be delivered.

In light of the apparent harshness and success of the opponents' attack, the advice given to Timothy is remarkable. The use of medical imagery was common in the contemporary moral literature, so it is not unusual for Paul to contrast "healthy" and "sick" teaching. Indeed, this is what gives the polemic against the moral behavior of the opponents its force, for the ancients had the correct perception that action does follow on perceptions, and bad ideas can lead to bad actions. Philosophers who used such language, however, disagreed about the proper medical approach to "sick thought." Some advocated harshness and scorn. They operated like surgeons. Others considered gentleness and care to be more useful for healing moral illness. That is the approach Paul advocates for Timothy. As Paul had characterized himself as being "as gentle as a nurse" (1 Thess. 2:7), so he wants Timothy to be gentle. Even when reproving, he is not to engage in harsh quarrels. Indeed, Paul sees such an attitude as opening the possibility for the adversaries' return to the truth (2:24-26):

> The Lord's servant must not be quarrelsome but kindly to everyone, an apt teacher, forbearing, correcting his opponents with gentleness. God may perhaps grant that they will repent and come to know the truth, and may escape the snare of the devil.

In this process there are resources available to the Christian teacher. Timothy can look to the education he has received in the faith from his maternal ancestors (1:5; 3:14). He has in Paul the source of sound teaching (1:13), the example of steadfastness in the ministry (3:10), and the model of suffering for the "good news" (3:11; 4:6). And, like Paul, he has the guidance of Torah, which he has known from his youth. It instructs him "for salvation through faith in Jesus Christ" (3:15). And because it is inspired by God, it is (3:16-17)

> profitable for teaching, for reproof, for correction, and for training in righteousness, that the man of God may be complete, equipped for every good work.

Paul, Model of Suffering in Hope (2 Timothy 4:6-18)

Paul concludes by again presenting himself as a model for Timothy. Even in prison, Paul continues to be opposed (4:14). Despite that, he does not turn from his ministry (4:17):

> The Lord stood by me and strengthened me to proclaim the word fully that all the Gentiles might hear it. So I was rescued from the lion's mouth.

The point for Timothy is clear. He should not be cowardly but imitate the perseverance of Paul and take "his share of suffering for the gospel." He can count on the Lord's supporting him, as well, and must rely on that support, since Paul himself is about to die. Paul closes with his own hope, that "Henceforth there is laid up for me the crown of righteousness which the Lord, the just judge, will award to me on that day," and extends that hope to Timothy as well, "and not only to me, but also to all who have loved his appearing" (4:8).

If this letter is written by Paul, it is evident that he believes his death is near. Moreover, the hardship of a lifetime has been brought to bear on his reflection of the ministry. Paul is concerned about securing a faithful transmission of his message and ministry to the next generation of leadership. Growing division in the church and hostility from without are reminders that such a transition will be difficult, achieved only at great personal cost to Paul and his delegates. Steadfastness, endurance, and faithfulness therefore take on an even more practical urgency. It is these values 2 Timothy seeks to inculcate. It is not that Timothy has been unfaithful. Rather, as Paul passes on the torch, he wants to "remind" Timothy of the importance of enduring despite suffering and opposition. The teacher earnestly desires that his disciples and delegates face suffering the same way he—in imitation of Jesus—did. In this way the gospel itself will endure.

1 Timothy: Life in God's Household

First Timothy comes closest to the stereotypical picture of the Pastorals. Elements of a personal parenetic letter are present in it: Paul is an example (now of God's mercy to sinners, 1:16), and Timothy is to be a model for the church (4:12). Timothy's attitudes are also contrasted with those of the false teachers (1:3-20; 4:1-16; 6:2b-16, 20-21). The letter, however, has less overall literary coherence than 2 Timothy. It gives only the merest hint of personal circumstance: Paul left Timothy in Ephesus on his way to Macedonia (1:3). He hopes to return soon (3:14) and in the meantime writes instructions to his delegate (3:15),

> so that you may know how one ought to behave in the household of God, which is the church of the living God, the pillar and bulwark of the truth.

These instructions give 1 Timothy its special character. They deal with prayer (2:1-5); the role of women in the liturgical assembly (2:8-15); the qualifications for bishops (3:1-7), deacons (3:8-13), and deaconesses (3:11); the care of widows (5:3-16); the payment of elders (5:17-19); the resolution of charges against elders (5:19-22); the attitudes of slaves (6:1-2); and the rich (6:17-19). The most disconcerting feature of 1 Timothy is the haphazard way these elements are put together. If one isolated the passages concerned with Timothy and the opponents, a letter much like 2 Timothy would be the result. If one kept only the prescriptions, the writing would provide the nucleus of later "church orders," albeit with a random and provisional air. And yet, a pattern not unlike that found in 2 Timothy emerges: the warnings against false teachers—occurring predominantly at the beginning, midpoint, and conclusion of the letter—provide a counter-example for the positive instructions on church order. Indeed, the framework for Paul's "rules" on proper ecclesial structure is provided by the false teachers, supplying strong notes of urgency and seriousness to the unfolding subject matter.

The model for this type of letter can be found in the Hellenistic royal correspondence known as the *mandata principis* letters, which are directives issued by rulers to their delegates who are governing territories. They were written to officials of a city or to specific individual representatives, carrying instructions for the delegate to execute. Although technically private correspondence, the directives most often were intended for larger audiences (the subject matter naturally dealt with aspects of civic life), and in this spirit the letters were sometimes inscribed on monuments for public reading. One interesting example—a letter to a newly appointed Egyptian official (PTeub. 703)—not only lists duties that are to be carried out, but also goes into details of expected conduct of the official, including being an exemplary model. This clearly corresponds to what we find in 1 Timothy. Overall, the *mandata principis* letters indicate the widespread practice of leaders establishing contact with their delegates and taking responsibility for activities occurring in other locales through their designated representatives. Paul's concern for the well-being of the community is thus expressed not to the community as a whole or to a local leader but to a delegate who is expected to attend to the problematic aspects of a local church's life.

A precise reconstruction of the situation in the Ephesian community is difficult. On the whole, the letter gives the impression of a relatively mature community, with its basic structures firmly in place. As so frequently, however, there is also the problem of deviance within the community. The names Hymenaeus and Alexander occur here again (1:20), now together (cf. 2 Tim. 2:17; 4:14). We are told little about them, except that "by rejecting conscience they have made shipwreck of their faith," so that Paul was forced to hand them over to Satan so that they might turn again to the truth (1:19-20; cf. 1 Cor. 5:5; 2 Tim. 2:25). They are, therefore, members of the church who appear to have been excommunicated. Otherwise, only "certain people" *(tines)* are mentioned (1:3, 6; 6:21). Timothy is to charge these not to teach other doctrines *(heterodidaskein;* 1:3).

The reference to other doctrines is not clear. Some people want to be considered "teachers of the law" (1:7) and are preoccupied with "myths and endless genealogies" (1:4). Some "liars whose consciences are seared with a hot iron" are against marriage for Christians and advocate dietary restrictions (4:2-3) and possibly other forms of asceticism (4:7-8). Some seek money for their teaching (6:5). Paul's final characterization is that they are involved with "godless chatter and contradictions which they have falsely called knowledge [*gnosis*]" (6:20). The traits can be combined and aligned with those of opponents in other Pauline writings. When the elements of Pauline slander (e.g., the accusation of cupidity) are removed, however, they resemble the sort of elitist esoteric groups we so often encounter in the religiosity of the Hellenistic world.

Several features distinguish 1 Timothy from 2 Timothy on the issue of the false teachers. (1) No mention is made in 1 Timothy of their aggressive missionary tactics or what effect these might be having. (2) In 1 Timothy they do not appear as teachers from the outside, but rather as ambitious and elitist members who were once part— or perhaps are still part—of the community itself. (3) In contrast to 2 Timothy, this letter does not stress rebuke or correction; rather, these negative characters supply the motive and context for Paul's message for Timothy and the community. (4) On the other hand, Paul responds to them with more than polemic: he clarifies the proper understanding of those things the opponents are distorting.

In response to their wishing to be teachers of the law (1:7), Paul specifies the nature and function of the law (1:8-10). In response to the forbidding of marriage and food, he stresses the essential goodness of creation and its capacity to be sanctified by prayer (4:3-5). He counters the claims for physical asceticism with those of "training in godliness" (4:7-8). He clarifies exactly what sort of "gain" one can expect from godliness, in response to those who sought monetary rewards for their teaching (6:5-10). It is very difficult, however, to draw a direct or explicit connection between what is said of, or in response to, the troublemakers, and the concrete directives concerning community life. Certainly, one can extrapolate from certain emphases to commotions caused by divergent teachings: from Paul's insistence that prayer should be free of disputation, his refusal to give women a teaching role (2:8-15), his concern for widows becoming gadabouts and gossips (5:13), his warning against the hasty appointment of elders (5:22), and his injunctions to slaves to obey believing owners (6:2). But the explicit connections are more difficult to establish.

Regarding its content, 1 Timothy contains allusions to familiar Pauline teaching, particularly in the emphasis on God's salvific will for all humanity (see 1:15-16; 2:3-6; 4:9-10; 6:13-16). There is a fascinating reference to Paul's conversion—seen as an example of God's mercy (1:12-16)—plus allusions to the trial and testimony of Jesus (2:6; 6:13). There is also this hymnic expression of the "mystery" in 3:16:

> He was manifested in the flesh, vindicated in the Spirit, seen by angels, preached among nations, believed on in the world, taken up in glory.

These elements are dominated, however, by the practical instructions and the context of moral exhortation, with its "sound teaching" (1:10; 6:3), "training in godliness" (1:4; 4:7), and "good conscience" (1:5, 19; 3:9).

The Household of God

First Timothy does not provide a full and satisfying picture of the community structure of the Ephesian church. The instructions deal with matters of immediate pertinence to the author and his delegate, rather than to the historian's curiosity.

The author calls the church the household of God (*oikos tou theou*; 3:15). In other letters, Paul uses the expression "the church in the household of . . ." (cf. Rom. 16:5; 1 Cor. 16:19; Col. 4:15), although he can also speak metaphorically of community members as "household servants" (Rom. 14:4) or "members of a household" (Gal. 6:10; Eph. 2:19). It is important to note here that the church as intentional community is not completely assimilated to the household structure. A distinction is made several times between "one's own household" and the community (1 Tim. 3:4-5, 12; 5:4). In fact, the most important function of the household in this letter is to provide an analogy for leadership: administrative abilities and leadership skills demonstrated in one structure carry implications for another. There is also a distinction—however unclear to present-day readers—drawn between the life and responsibilities of individual households and the life and responsibility of the church (see 5:4, 8, 16). The church imitates the household in many respects, but is not subsumed by it. Since early Christians met in houses—within the sphere of the household—such associations were inevitable.

Paul's directions to Timothy apply to several different spheres of the community's life. Some are directed to the life of individual households and the community members living within them. Such are the remarks about slaves belonging to Christian masters (6:1-2) and those about rich members of the community who are not to rely on their wealth but use it for helping others (6:17-19). Similar is the demand that individual children within households provide for widows (5:4, 8, 16) and the banal yet pertinent advice on the attitudes that Timothy should display toward diverse age and gender groups (5:1-2). There is little dramatic in this advice and nothing implausible. The author wants order, propriety, and graciousness in the domestic lives of believers.

Some—not much—attention is paid to the liturgical life of the community, but with a focus different from the instructions concerning the Lord's Supper and charismatic gifts in 1 Corinthians 11–14. Three very specific directives are given. First, prayers are to be said for all people, especially rulers (2:1-4). This is certainly unexceptional, as is the second instruction, which is that the male members, who pray with uplifted arms, should not have anger or quarreling among them (2:8).

The instructions about women are somewhat more problematic. The contrast between luxurious external adornment and the life of internal virtue (2:9-10) is commonplace in Jewish and Greco-Roman Hellenistic moral teaching. But the prohibition against women teaching in the assembly or having authority over men (2:11-12) is more difficult to contextualize. The command here lacks something of the tension found in 1 Cor. 11:2-16 and 14:34-36. There, the context was one of charismatic worship in which women were certainly prophesying and praying. Here, the instruction focuses narrowly on the cultural unacceptability of women teaching in public. They are to give instruction only in private for their children (2:15, taking "they" as referring to "her children"; cf. 2 Tim. 1:5; Titus 2:3). The justification for the prohibition is harsh, and the account of the sin of Eve (2:13-14) is sharper than in Paul's other reference to this part of the Genesis story (2 Cor. 11:2-3).

What we learn overall from these few remarks about worship is that it involves public prayer and teaching, and that both of these activities are male prerogatives. As much as one may seek a context for this in Diaspora Jewish synagogues, the participation of women appears more multifaceted there than what we see here in 1 Timothy, and more in line in with what we see in Paul's other letters. Of course, details are missing that might point to specific church problems (cf. 5:3-16) or perhaps even outside influences, such as the cult of Artemis, which was popular among women in Ephesus. Overall, however, Paul's message is consistent: order in the household and the church is essential for witness to the world. He clearly perceives the issue of female leadership as fitting into this in some way.

The most extended attention is given to the officers of the Ephesian church. The office of bishop (*episkopos*; 3:1-7) and deacon (*diakonos*; 3:8-10, 12-13) have been encountered before, albeit briefly (Phil. 1:1), as have deaconesses (3:11; cf. Rom. 16:1). The reference to women deacons is debated, but the repetition of "likewise" with the similarity of required behaviors in 3:11 (cf. 3:8) seems to demand that the women of 3:11 be viewed as parallel to, rather than the wives of, the deacons in 3:8. The existence of deaconesses in Ephesus indicates that although teaching was not an allowable activity for women, some ministerial roles were open to them. The office of elder (*presbyteros*; 5:17-22) is not found in other Pauline letters, although Acts associates elders with Pauline churches (14:23) and specifically with Ephesus in 20:17.

The instructions do not describe job responsibilities but personal qualifications. The bishop (or overseer) is obviously an administrator above all, and his position demands appropriate capabilities, although the bishop is also expected to be an "apt teacher" (3:2). Sound moral qualities and leadership ability are paramount (3:1-7). The work of deacons is also such that administrative abilities (proved by the management of a household) are desirable (3:12). Because specific cases are raised, we learn a little more about elders. Those who "rule well" are to be paid double, "especially those who labor in the word and teaching" (5:17). This suggests a board of elders (*presbyterion*, 4:14) who perform administrative functions, among whose number some may also teach or preach. The other directives concerning elders are a reminder of human frailty in every position of authority. Charges can be brought against them and must be carefully considered (5:19). Timothy may be forced to rebuke an elder publicly—seemingly the role of an outside delegate, not of someone in the same community (5:20). In the light of these possibilities, Paul gives the sound advice that appointment to such positions should not be made with haste (5:22). His concluding injunction is classically Pauline: "Keep these rules without favor; do nothing from partiality" (5:21).

The discussion of widows (5:3-16) is the most problematic for our understanding of the Ephesian community structure. The question clearly seems to be who should be supported by community funds, for a distinction is made on the basis of support available from private families (5:4, 8). The resources of the community as a whole are not to be burdened unnecessarily (5:16): the community's obligation is to help those who are "real widows" (5:16). But the discussion becomes more complicated at the point of who constitutes a "real" widow. Paul distinguishes between those whose husbands have died and those who are truly "left alone and have hoped in God" (5:5). Some women whose husbands have died are self-indulgent (5:6)—which means they have resources—or are not wholeheartedly committed to the community's life. If they got the chance, they would like to remarry. Some of them are idlers on the community dole, meddling and gossiping (5:13) instead of serving the community. Paul's solution would have widows of a marrying age remarry if possible. Only older widows and those without other resources ("left alone") should be enrolled (5:9, 11). But does the term "enroll" indicate a special order of widows? Paul complicates the question by appearing to provide a list of qualifications as he does for other offices (5:9-10).

The simplest and best explanation is that the Ephesian church followed the model of Diaspora Judaism in providing assistance on a regular and organized basis for the needy of the community (cf. Acts 6:1-7). One of the most important tasks of every Jewish community was the carrying out of this obligation. It was never easy. The obvious categories of those who required aid were the strangers, orphans, and widows. Orphans and strangers were easy to identify and relatively easy to provide for. The case of widows was always far more ambiguous and difficult. Paul wants Timothy in this case to be sure that only the truly needy are cared for by the community as a whole—and then only those with no other resources available to them (i.e., their Christian families should care for them first). They should be enrolled on a list that would certify their qualification for help. In return, they were to give themselves not to their own interests but to the service of the community as a whole.

The community structure at Ephesus according to 1 Timothy is not complicated. It resembles what little we know of the structure of Diaspora Jewish synagogues (see chap. 3, pp. 74–79). In them, a leader (*archisynagogos*) and a board of elders (*gerousia*) did administrative work and settled disputes. Their obligations included running the community charity efforts, both the raising of funds and their disbursement. They were helped in these functions by assistants (*chazzan/diakonos*) who performed more menial tasks in the liturgy and community charity functions. There is nothing in this that is not fully compatible with the church in Paul's lifetime. Moreover, there is nothing in this letter that approaches a hierarchical, much less a monarchical, order. No office is theologized or otherwise legitimated. The community structure is task-oriented and practical: it is established to meet the very real needs of the Ephesian Christian community.

The fact, however, that attention is given to these matters implies that there is more here than Paul simply detailing the obvious. Rather, as the instructions themselves make partially clear, there were problems with elders and with widows. But the need may also have come from the disruptions caused by those who, "with ideas in their heads," unsettled others. Certainly, a concern for order and for the good reputation of the community with outsiders runs through these instructions, a concern not alien to Paul elsewhere. The bishop should not be a recent convert who is easily led astray, thus falling into Satan's trap and giving outsiders a negative view of the church (3:7). The bad behavior of would-be widows can make outsiders revile the community (5:14). Slaves who refuse to serve their Christian masters will cause the gospel to be defamed (6:1). The overall goal is internal stability and external peace—here approached through the instructions given to a delegate. This is not much different from what is expressed in the most charismatic of Paul's letters (1 Cor. 14:37-40):

> If anyone thinks that he is a prophet or spiritual, he should acknowledge that what I am writing to you is a command of the Lord. If anyone does not recognize this, he is not recognized. So, my brethren, earnestly desire to prophesy, and do not forbid speaking in tongues. But all things should be done decently and in order.

In 2 Timothy, Paul was concerned with the preservation of his gospel through the person of Timothy—Paul's delegate. In 1 Timothy, the community as a whole is in view and Timothy's function is more critical here: he is the delegate who mediates instruction for the well-being of the church. As in Ephesians, the Christian household and community are witnesses to the world of "faith and truth" (2:7). But only a community that is orderly and harmonious—displaying the best of the values and virtues of the larger Greco-Roman culture—can truly be the "household of God." Indeed, only as an orderly "household" can the community stand as a witness among the Gentiles to the great mystery in Christ (3:16), with a leadership that will be "pillars and supports for the truth."

Titus: An Infant Church in the Outpost

In Titus, the segments that make up the puzzle of the Pastorals are pieced together in still another fashion. Unlike 1 Timothy, this letter gives a bit more autobiographical information. Paul is apparently in mid-career. His whereabouts are not indicated, but he expects to winter in Nicopolis (3:12) and anticipates that Titus will return to him from his temporary duty in Crete upon Paul's sending Artemas and Tychichus to relieve him (3:12). To fill out this picture, two reasons are given for Paul's having "left" Titus on Crete: Titus is to take care of unfinished business left by Paul, and he is to appoint elders in each city (1:5). Much of the letter is taken up with instructions on these matters.

There is nothing in this information that is itself implausible, except that we do not know of any Pauline mission in Crete; Acts only mentions Paul's being there as a prisoner on his way to Rome by ship (Acts 27:7-15). And if the Apollos of 3:13 is the same as the one in 1 Cor. 3:1-6, it is perhaps a little strange to see him as a helper of Titus (though cf. Acts 18:27; 1 Cor. 16:12). Tychichus, of course, we have met before (Acts 20:4; Col. 4:7; Eph. 6:21; 2 Tim. 4:12).

While the Letter to Titus bears a close correspondence to 1 Timothy by virtue of its being a *mandata principis*, stylistically it stands between 1 Timothy and 2 Timothy. It appears neither distinctively Pauline throughout (as is the case with 2 Timothy) nor only remotely Pauline (as is the case with 1 Timothy). Rather, it alternates short sections whose Pauline rhythms none would deny (see, e.g., 1:15; 2:11-14; 3:4-7) with longer stretches of a seemingly quite different style. In contrast to 2 Timothy, the parenetic elements are minimal. Titus is only told (2:7-8):

> Show yourself a model of good deeds and in your teaching show integrity, gravity, and sound speech that cannot be censured, so that an opponent may be put to shame, having nothing evil to say of us.

Moreover, much more than in 1 or 2 Timothy, there seems to be a direct relationship between the opponents and the instructions concerning "what is defective." In sum, Titus is best understood when considered on its own terms as a genuine piece of correspondence, addressing a specific and real situation.

The Situation of Titus

Everything in the letter supports the picture (suggested by 1:5) of a new, developing community. In 1 Timothy, the church at Ephesus already had bishops, elders, and deacons in place. Indeed, the provision could be made that the bishop not be a "recent convert" (1 Tim. 3:6), suggesting that the community has been in existence for some time. By contrast, in Titus it is stated that the elder or bishop (the transition in 1:5-7 is not altogether clear) ought to have children who are believers and that these should not be "open to the charge of being profligate or insubordinate" (1:6). Presumably there were Christian households in the community that could still have children who were unconverted, indicating the relatively new growth of Christianity in the region. A further clue to the context of this community is offered in the catalog of this bishop's qualities, especially those given in addition to the list in 1 Tim. 3:1-7: the bishop is not to be "arrogant or quick tempered or violent" (1:7; in the Greek these terms are quite strong).

We are led to wonder about the population among which Christianity is trying to strike roots. In the eyes of the author, the populace is unattractive: "Cretans are always liars, vicious brutes, lazy gluttons" (1:12). In fact, such a view of the Cretan population seems to have enjoyed almost proverbial status in antiquity. The sharpness with which the contrast between the Cretans and Christians is developed suggests the social formation rhetoric of a newly developing community, which must draw unmistakable borders of demarcation between the old life and the new. There may even be some hints in this language that the demarcation process is not meeting with full success, although the language of incivility ultimately functions as a foil to develop positive Christian traits.

The climate for evangelization is made stormier by opponents who are competing for the religious allegiance of the populace. In Titus, these opponents are outsiders, evidently Jewish rivals. They are "from the circumcision" (1:10), have "Jewish myths" (1:14), are stressing legal observance in some form (1:14), and claim to "know God" (1:16). The opponents are seemingly successful, and the degree of their success provides an important insight into the emphasis of Titus: "They are upsetting whole households by teaching for base gain what they have no right to teach" (1:11). A fragile Christian community, therefore, is being threatened not only by the problems accompanying recent converts in an apparently unsupportive environment but also by the ability of rival Jewish missionaries to persuade the newly converted that they have a more attractive vision for being God's people.

Here there is no possibility for dialogue. The survival of an infant church is at stake. Titus is therefore told by Paul, "They must be silenced" (1:11); and those being seduced by the Jewish opponents are to be "rebuked sharply" so that "they may be sound in the faith" (1:13). Titus himself is to avoid "stupid controversies, genealogical discussions, and quarrels over the law" (3:9). If anyone in the community remains factious, that person is to be warned repeatedly, then cut off (3:10). These are serious remedies for a tough situation. The bishop, likewise, is not simply to be an apt teacher (*didaktikos*) as in 1 Tim. 3:2. He has a more vigorous task (1:9):

> He must hold firm to the sure word as taught, so that he might be able to give instruction in sound doctrine, and also to confute those who contradict it.

The Teaching of Titus

It is important to observe that the *only* specific element of "church order" in Titus is the remarks about the bishop. Otherwise, the focus of practical instruction is on the household and civic responsibilities of Christians. In 2:1-10, Paul provides a list of attitudes that are appropriate, if somewhat bland, for older men (2:2) and women (2:3), younger women (2:4-5) and men (2:6), followed by an exhortation to slaves (2:9-10). In 3:1-2, general civic attitudes of submission to authority and basic rules of civility are recommended. All of these can be summed up as the doing of good works (*kala erga*; 2:14; 3:8, 14) that express the new Christian identity, in contrast to the wicked deeds of the opponents (1:16).

A closer look at the specific instructions raises some interesting questions. Why should older women need to be told not to be winebibbers (2:3)? Do their daughters really require teaching to "love their husbands and children" (2:4)? Are Christian slaves in need of instruction not to pilfer their masters' goods and not to be stubborn and untrustworthy (2:9-10)? Do Christians generally need to be told to seek "honest work" and that they should not be revolutionary (3:1-2)? The problem is this: behavior this ordinary should fall into the category of "what goes without saying," but here we find basic instructions being given in civility, the rudiments of civilized behavior. Since, as we have seen, "households" are being overturned by the success of the Jewish missionaries, these instructions are intended—in response—to strengthen the basic familial unit of the community by implicitly contrasting Christian behavior with that of the opponents: the opponents represent the opposite of the civility that ought to be found among members of the Christian household. Through this type of insider-outsider distinction, the gospel teaching is given a framework in which it might be able to grow securely, closing off the opportunity for further damage by the opponents. In Titus, therefore, the gospel itself takes on a civilizing function: it teaches people how to be members of society, a nuance often disguised by the English translation of the Greek.

In this light, we can better understand the two remarkable kerygmatic statements in Titus in which the Pauline language is most pronounced. These statements, we should note, frame and interpret the concrete directives. In 3:3-7, the author quotes a "faithful saying" that takes the form of a before-and-after statement, with the pivotal point being people's baptism as a response to the "good news." Before, they had shared in all the hostile attitudes of their neighbors, passing their days in malice and envy, "hated by people and hating one another" (3:3). But they had been given a new identity (3:4-7):

> But when the goodness and loving kindness of God our Savior appeared, he saved us, not because of deeds done by us in righteousness, but in virtue of his own mercy, by the washing of regeneration and renewal in the Holy Spirit, which he poured out upon us richly through Jesus Christ our Savior, so that we might be justified by his grace and become heirs in hope of eternal life.

Here we see that the qualities of God's gift—the goodness and kindness and mercy—should themselves shape Christian identity, both renewing and regenerating it. This statement is followed by the final command, "Insist on these things, that those who have believed in God might apply themselves to good deeds" (3:8). In short, specific forms of Christian behavior ought to follow upon the adoption of this new identity given by God.

The other statement (2:11-14) is found in the middle of the elementary civic instruction and is even more illuminating:

> *For* the grace of God has appeared for the salvation of all, *training* us to renounce irreligion and worldly passions, and to live sober, upright, and godly lives in this world, awaiting our blessed hope, the appearing of the glory of our great God and savior Jesus Christ, who gave himself for us to redeem us from all iniquity and to purify for himself a people of his own who are zealous for good deeds.

The most important word in this passage may well be the first—"For"—which connects the specific instructions to their basis: the grace of God itself. But the next most important word is surely "training" (*paideuousa*). For Paul, the grace of God itself has an educative function: it trains people toward the goal of becoming human social creatures. Here, as elsewhere in Paul, the Christian life involves a transformation from the old life to the new. Just as Christians had become "slaves to righteousness" (Rom. 6:18), so here they are to be "zealous for good works." In the context of Titus, this takes on an even more pragmatic meaning because the community seems still to be in the process of formation and stabilization. God's grace actually becomes a pedagogue for the new believers, training them in civic and social duties.

In a fascinating shift, Christianity here establishes its own distinctive "training," rivaling yet adapting the Greco-Roman pedagogical emphases. The point of all this is simple: the Christian household now represents the societal and cultural ideal. This serves to reinforce the boundaries that separate the insiders from those "vicious brutes" on the outside, which in turn solidifies and cements this community firmly in the tradition of the Pauline church.

In the end, we see why the general populace is portrayed the way it is in Titus. Throughout, Paul wants to contrast the life of the believer with the people of the world, and he does this by sharpening the distinctions between the two, subtly transposing their respective positions vis-à-vis cultural ideals. For Paul, the Christian solution is obvious: the gospel itself can provide a rooting in the world and the possibility of growth. The grace that comes to people in baptism can change their hearts from hostility to civility, and can begin to shape their behavior in ways compatible with their new identity. Life together in the social structures of "this world" demands of Christians that they leave behind irreligion, worldly passions, and hostility, adopting instead sober, godly, and upright patterns of behavior.

Scholars have often labeled this type of ethic as a "domesticated virtue," reflecting Christian cultural and social adaptation over time. Yet, in Titus, this ethic is much more that of eschatological witness, as 2:13 makes evident. Here we see the sharpness of Paul's thought elsewhere: the Christian lives on the cusp of the new age and the old (2:12-13). Indeed, the admonition for Christian faithfulness rests in these two fundamental and widely attested Pauline axioms: Jesus has redeemed his people (2:14) and he is coming in glory to establish them eternally (2:13).

Study Questions

1. What difference would it make in our understanding of Paul if he did not write these letters? In our understanding of the history of the church?

2. Considering all the New Testament references, what was Paul's relationship with Timothy?

3. What difference does it make that these letters are addressed to individuals rather than congregations?

4. How does attention to "letter types" help in the interpretation of these compositions?

5. What role do metaphors of the family and household play in these letters? What would account for this?

Bibliographical Note

Good summaries of the issues pertaining to authenticity are found in W. G. Kümmel, *Introduction to the New Testament*, trans. H. C. Kee (Nashville: Abingdon Press, 1975), 366–87; and E. E. Ellis, "The Authorship of the Pastorals: A Resume and Assessment of Recent Trends," in his *Paul and His Recent Interpreters* (Grand Rapids: Eerdmans, 1961), 49–57. For the discussion of specific points, see the classic study by P. N. Harrison, *The Problem of the Pastoral Epistles* (London: Oxford Univ. Press, 1921), as well as the more recent ones by R. F. Collins, *Letters That Paul Did Not Write: The Epistle to the Hebrews and the Pauline Pseudepigrapha* (Wilmington: Michael Glazier, 1988), 88–131; L. R. Donelson, *Pseudepigraphy and Ethical Argument in the Pastoral Epistles* (Tübingen: J.C.B. Mohr [Siebeck], 1986); K. Graystone and G. Herdan, "The Authorship of the Pastorals in the Light of Statistical Linguistics," *NTS* 6 (1959–60): 1–15; and J. D. Miller, *The Pastoral Letters as Composite Documents* (SNTSMS, 93; Cambridge: Cambridge Univ. Press, 1997). See also the vocabulary studies by D. Cook, "2 Timothy IV.6–8 and the Epistle to the Philippians," *JTS* 33 (1982): 168–71; and "The Pastoral

Fragments Reconsidered," *JTS* 35 (1984): 120–31. For well-balanced discussions, see C. F. D. Moule, "The Problem of the Pastoral Epistles: A Reappraisal," *BJRL* (1965): 430–52; and B. Metzger, "A Reconsideration of Certain Arguments Against the Pauline Authorship of the Pastoral Epistles," *Exp Tim* 70 (1958): 91ff. The most extensive recent attempt to place the Pastorals within the framework of Acts is J. A. T. Robinson, *Redating the New Testament* (Philadelphia: Westminster Press, 1970), 67–85. The Lukan connection is pursued in different ways by S. G. Wilson, *Luke and the Pastoral Epistles* (London: SPCK, 1979); and J. Quinn, "The Last Volume of Luke: The Relation of Luke-Acts to the Pastoral Epistles," in C. H. Talbert (ed.), *Perspectives on Luke-Acts* (Danville, Va.: Assn. of Baptist Professors of Religion, 1978), 62–75.

The standard view of the pastorals as pseudonymous, second- or third-generation productions is found (with variations) in R. Bultmann, *Theology of the New Testament*, 2 vols. (New York: Charles Scribner's Sons, 1955), 2:95–118; J. M. Ford, "A Note on Protomontanism in the Pastoral Epistles," *NTS* 17 (1976): 338–46; H. von Campenhausen, *Ecclesiastical Authority and Spiritual Power in the Church of the First Three Centuries*, trans. J. Baker (Stanford: Stanford Univ. Press, 1969); C. K. Barrett, "Pauline Controversies in the Post-Pauline Period," *NTS* 20 (1973–74): 229–45; E. Käsemann, "Paul and Early Catholicism," in his *New Testament Questions of Today* (Philadelphia: Fortress Press, 1969), 236–51; and M. C. de Boer, "Images of Paul in the Post-Apostolic Church," *CBQ* 42 (1980): 359–80. For the argument that the Pastorals responded to the threat posed by the egalitarian demands of second-century women, see J. Bassler, "The Widow's Tale: A Fresh Look at 1 Tim. 5:3-16," *JBL* 103 (1984): 23–41; and R. D. MacDonald, *The Legend and the Apostle: The Battle for Paul in Story and Canon* (Philadelphia: Westminster Press, 1983).

For the structure of the synagogue, see chapter 3. For the effort of organized charity in Judaism and the larger Greco-Roman world, see G. Hamel, *Poverty and Charity in Roman Palestine, First Three Centuries C.E.* (Berkeley: Univ. of California Press, 1990); G. E Moore, *Judaism in the First Three Centuries of the Christian Era*, 2 vols. (New York: Schocken Books, 1971 [1927]), 2:162–79; and B. A. Pearson, "Philanthropy in the Greco-Roman World and in Early Christianity," in his *The Emergence of the Christian Religion: Essays on Early Christianity* (Harrisburg, Pa.: Trinity Press Int'l, 1997), 186–213. On the relationship of early church and synagogue, see especially J. T. Burtchaell, *From Synagogue to Church: Public Services and Offices in the Earliest Christian Communities* (Cambridge: Cambridge Univ. Press, 1992). On elders in early Christianity and Judaism, see R. A. Campbell, *The Elders: Seniority within Earliest Christianity* (Edinburgh: T. & T. Clark, 1994).

For various aspects of offices in the early church as they relate to the argument of this chapter, see B. L. Blackburn, "The Identity of the 'Women' in 1 Tim. 3:11," in C. D. Osburn (ed.), *Essays on Women in Earliest Christianity: Volume 1* (Joplin, Mo.: College Press, 1995), 303–19; J. N. Collins, *Diakonia: Reinterpreting the Ancient Sources* (New York: Oxford Univ. Press, 1990); J. P Meier, "*Presbyteros* in the Pastoral Epistles," *CBQ*

35 (1973): 323–45; B. Reicke, "The Constitution of the Early Church in the Light of
Jewish Documents," in K. Stendhal (ed.), *The Scrolls and the New Testament* (New
York: Harper & Row, 1957), 143–56; J. Reumann, "Church Office in Paul, Especially in
Philippians," in B. H. McLean (ed.), *Origins and Method: Towards a New Understand-
ing of Judaism and Christianity* (JSNTSup, 86; Sheffield: Sheffield Academic Press,
1993), 82–91; J. H. Stiefel, "Women Deacons in 1 Timothy: A Linguistic and Literary
Look at 'Women Likewise . . .'," *NTS* 41 (1995): 442–57; and B. B. Thurston, *The Wid-
ows: A Women's Ministry in the Early Church* (Minneapolis: Fortress Press, 1989). On
the relevance of ancient associations and *collegia*, see J. S. Kloppenborg, "Edwin Hatch,
Churches and *Collegia*," in *Origins and Method*, 212–38; and B. H. McLean, "The
Agrippinilla Inscription: Religious Associations and Early Christian Formation," in
Origins and Method, 239–70.

For the example of the parenetic letter, see A. J. Malherbe, *Ancient Epistolary Theorists* (SBLSBS, 19; Atlanta: Scholars Press, 1988), 69, 75. Also see the relevant studies by
B. Fiore, *The Function of Personal Example in the Socratic and Pastoral Epistles* (AnB,
105; Rome: Biblical Institute Press, 1986); and M. M. Mitchell, "New Testament Envoys
in the Context of Greco-Roman Diplomatic and Epistolary Conventions: The Example of Timothy and Titus," *JBL* 111 (1992): 641–62.

The use of polemic in these letters is examined by R. J. Karris, "The Background
and Significance of the Polemic of the Pastoral Epistles," *JBL* 92 (1973): 549–64; F. H.
Colson, "Myths and Genealogies—A Note on the Polemic of the Pastoral Epistles," *JTS*
19 (1917–18): 265–71; and L. T. Johnson, "II Timothy and the Polemic Against False
Teachers: A Re-examination," *JRS* 6/7 (1978–79): 1–26, which provides the basic
framework for the analysis in this chapter.

On the community context reflected in the Pastorals, see R. M. Kidd, *Wealth and
Beneficence in the Pastoral Epistles: A "Bourgeois" Form of Early Christianity?* (SBLDS,
122; Atlanta: Scholars Press, 1990); M. Y. MacDonald, *The Pauline Churches: A Socio-
Historical Study of the Institutionalization in the Pauline and Deutero-Pauline Writings*
(SNTSMS, 60; Cambridge: Cambridge Univ. Press, 1988), 159–234; and D. C. Verner,
The Household of God: The Social World of the Pastoral Epistles (SBLDS, 71; Chico,
Calif.: Scholars Press, 1983). Also helpful is H. O. Maier, *The Social Setting of the Min-
istry as Reflected in the Writings of Hermas, Clement, and Ignatius* (Waterloo, Canada:
Wilfrid Laurier Univ. Press, 1991).

For various thematic aspects of the three letters, see J. W. Aageson, "2 Timothy and
Its Theology," *SBLSP* 36 (1997): 692–714; J. A. Allen, "The 'In Christ' Formula in the
Pastoral Epistles," *NTS* 10 (1963): 115–21; L. R. Donelson, "Studying Paul: 2 Timothy
as Remembrance," *SBLSP* 36 (1997): 715–31; E. E. Ellis, "Traditions in the Pastoral
Epistles," in C. A. Evans and W. F. Stinespring (eds.), *Early Jewish and Christian Exege-
sis* (Atlanta: Scholars Press, 1987), 237–53; G. D. Fee, "Toward a Theology of 2 Timo-
thy—from a Pauline Perspective," *SBLSP* 36 (1997): 732–49; M. J. Goodwin, "The
Pauline Background of the Living God as Interpretive Context for 1 Timothy 4.10,"

JSNT 61 (1996): 65–85; R. H. Gundry, "The Form, Meaning, and Background of the Hymn Quoted in I Tim 3:16," in W. Gasque and R. P. Martin (eds.), *Apostolic History and the Gospel* (Grand Rapids: Eerdmans, 1970), 203–22; A. T. Hanson, *Studies in the Pastoral Epistles* (London: SPCK, 1968); M. J. Harris, "Titus 2:13 and the Deity of Christ," in D. Hagner and M. J. Harris (eds.), *Pauline Studies* (Grand Rapids: Eerdmans, 1980), 262–77; D. Horrell, "Converging Ideologies: Berger and Luckmann and the Pastoral Epistles," *JSNT* 50 (1993): 85–103; G. W. Knight III, *The Faithful Sayings in the Pastoral Letters* (Grand Rapids: Baker Book House, 1979); A. Y. Lau, *Manifest in Flesh: The Epiphany Christology of the Pastoral Epistles* (WUNT, 2.86; J. C. B. Mohr [Siebeck], 1996); H. Marshall, "Salvation in the Pastoral Epistles," in H. Cancik et al. (eds.), *Geschichte-Tradition-Reflexion*, 3 vols. (Tübingen: J. C. B. Mohr, 1996), 3:449–69; N. J. McEleny, "The Vice-Lists of the Pastoral Epistles," *CBQ* 36 (1974): 203–19; A. J. Malherbe, "'In Season and Out of Season:' 2 Timothy 4:2," *JBL* 103 (1984): 235–43; idem, "Medical Imagery in the Pastorals," in W. E. March (ed.), *Texts and Testaments* (San Antonio: Trinity Univ. Press, 1980), 19–35; idem, "'In Season and Out of Season': 2 Timothy 4:2," *JBL* 103(1982): 23–41; I. H. Marshall, "Salvation, Grace and Works in the Later Writings in the Pauline Corpus," *NTS* 42 (1996): 339–58; M. Prior, *Paul the Letter-Writer and the Second Letter to Timothy* (JSNTSup, 23; Sheffield: Sheffield Academic Press, 1989); P. H. Towner, *The Goal of Our Instruction: The Structure of Theology and Ethics in the Pastoral Epistles* (JSNTSup, 34; Sheffield: Sheffield Academic Press, 1989); and F. Young, "The Pastoral Epistles and the Ethics of Reading," *JSNT* 45 (1992): 105–20. For a more general treatment, see M. Davies, *The Pastoral Epistles* (Sheffield: Sheffield Academic Press, 1996); and F. Young, *The Theology of the Pastoral Epistles* (Cambridge: Cambridge Univ. Press, 1994).

For critical commentary, see M. Dibelius and H. Conzelmann, *The Pastoral Epistles*, ed. H. Koester, trans. P. Buttolph and A. Yarbro (Hermeneia; Philadelphia: Fortress Press, 1972); G. W. Knight III, *The Pastoral Epistles* (NIGTC; Grand Rapids: Eerdmans, 1992); and J. D. Quinn, *The Letter to Titus* (AB; New York: Doubleday, 1990). For more general commentary, see L. T. Johnson, *Letter to Paul's Delegates: 1 Timothy, 2 Timothy, Titus* (Valley Forge, Pa.: Trinity Press Int'l, 1996); and J. N. D. Kelly, *A Commentary on the Pastoral Epistles* (HNTC, New York: Harper & Row, 1963).

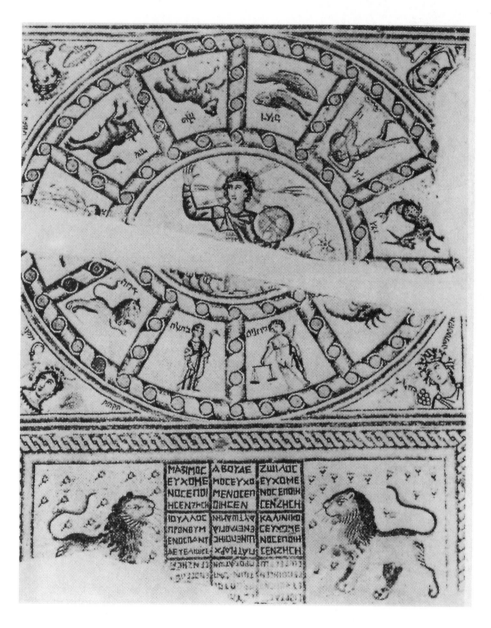

Mosaic zodiac and votive inscriptions in the floor of the synagogue at Hammath Tiberias (mid-fourth cent.)

PART FIVE

Other Canonical Witnesses

THE LIMITS OF the historical-critical model are perhaps best illustrated by its embarrassment at, and frequent neglect of, the writings we next consider: Hebrews, 1 Peter, 2 Peter, Jude, and James. Due both to the centrality of Paul for constructing the theological and chronological center of early Christianity and to the difficulty of placing these other writings within that framework, these epistles have often been neglected in modern scholarship. So strong is the developmental instinct (and so intrinsic to the model) that these writings are almost always regarded as later and often inferior productions, rather than simply representing different manifestations of the Christian movement and message.

Their variety in style and substance makes it difficult to fit them into a developmental framework. The category usually applied to them is "Early Catholicism," by which is meant a form of Christianity that has shifted in the direction of incipient institutionalization, moving away from the supposedly more charismatic and free-flowing ethos of the Pauline churches. This is a dubiously flexible rubric, stretching to fit almost anything that is thought to be non-Pauline: concern for church order and tradition, diminished eschatological expectation, and domesticated ethics. But these writings provide so little support for those characterizations that the category's inadequacy is clear.

Indeed, the variety of the letters makes any sort of classification difficult. The substantive range is so wide that simple formal categories offer the best possibility for grouping. These writings all present themselves, for example, as letters. This would be helpful were it not for the evidence that Hebrews and James only approximately accommodate themselves to the epistolary form. Sometimes these writings (together with the three Johannine letters, which I consider separately) are called general, or catholic, epistles, accounting for their seeming lack of specifically addressed congregations, which, in turn, gives them a certain universal character. Certainly James and

455

1 Peter could be read as being addressed to a readership wider than a single congregation. There is nothing about Hebrews, Jude, and 2 Peter, however, that is incompatible with their being writings aimed at specific individual churches. But since we do not know the identity of the readers, we can categorize these as general letters also. They could also be called letters to gentile churches, but while more or less plausible arguments can be made that 1 Peter and Hebrews (and even 2 Peter and Jude) are written to exclusively gentile churches rather than Jewish or mixed congregations, the assessment cannot be certain, and has as its main attraction its convenience.

The writings are also sometimes grouped together on the basis of their pseudonymous character. But although few would challenge pseudonymity in the case of 2 Peter, it is still possible to find supporters for the composition of 1 Peter by the apostle himself. More importantly, very little is gained by saying that James and Jude are pseudonymous. We know so little about their putative eponyms that no light is shed on the meaning of the texts by the mere assertion of the author's identity. Hebrews, of course, is viewed as pseudonymous only because of the tradition of Pauline attribution. The text does not identify the author. It is, properly speaking, an anonymous composition.

The lesson may simply be that our compulsion to categorize does a fundamental disservice to these writings. Their greatest contribution to our historical understanding of early Christianity may be the constant reminder that the movement cannot be reduced to Paul and his opponents, and that these short messages from the past represent many other voices whom the accidents of history have left silent.

The writings are of value, moreover, not simply for what they can tell us about the past but also for each one's distinctive witness to life before God in the light of the experience of Jesus. In Hebrews we find one of the richest and most complex interpretations of the Christian experience in the canon; in 1 Peter, an exhortation of rare grace; in 2 Peter and Jude, the voice of outrage and a defense of community identity in the face of deviance and defiance; in James, the unswerving and uncompromising translation of conviction into action. Each demands attention to its own voice. And together, their very capacity to slip the chains of simplistic categorization gives classifiers, too, some freedom.

20. The Letter to the Hebrews

LIKE ITS OWN description of Melchizedek (Heb. 7:3), Hebrews appears "without father or mother or genealogy," yet so impressively that its place in the canon seems due not to its author or circumstances but simply to its intrinsic merit. Although the Western church was slower in allowing it a position in the canon, the East gave it immediate and lasting popularity, so that its imagery helped shape liturgical prayer and its substance provided disputants of the third and fourth century with a rich resource for christological argument.

Contemporary scholars find Hebrews fascinating for the subtle combination it gives to diverse philosophical and religious symbols of the first century. For a writing of such beauty and power, however, Hebrews goes largely unread by ordinary Christians who are nourished by John and Paul. One reason might be that Hebrews is a sustained argument from beginning to end. Only a complete reading enables one to appreciate its full force. The few self-contained pericopes it can provide for liturgical lectionaries lose a great deal by being excerpted. A second reason is that in Hebrews a truth that can remain implicit and unacknowledged in other NT writings cannot be ignored: the symbolism of the ancient world is alien to our own, discouraging casual readings of the text.

Despite its complex symbolization, Hebrews provides a witness to the Christian experience that is clear and compelling. No pretense of an adequate reading will be found in this treatment; I want only to provide a framework that might help connect Hebrews with its ancient symbolic context, illuminating—at the very least—the way the letter ought to be read.

Preliminary Profile

The author's apology for "writing briefly" (Heb. 13:22) is a literary convention (cf. 1 Pet. 5:12). Hebrews is shorter than only Romans and 1 Corinthians among NT epistles. But then Hebrews is not really a letter. Besides the lack of formal epistolary elements, the circumstances of the writer are only briefly mentioned, almost as an afterthought (Heb. 13:23-25). The author appears as a subject only in 13:18, with an assurance that he (or she) has a pure conscience and hopes for a rapid return to the readers (13:19). There is news that Timothy, called "our brother," has recently been released from prison (13:23), and the author sends greetings from "those who come from Italy" (13:24). These notes establish a rather obvious connection to the Pauline mission, but take us no further, and certainly do not suggest any deliberate attempt at forgery as there is no reference at all to Paul.

As a theological treatise, Hebrews could comfortably stand next to Romans as a reflection on the mystery of God's work in Christ. But Hebrews also has an intense, immediate, and consistent pastoral orientation. It most resembles a *homily*. The author says he has written a word of exhortation (*logos tēs paraklēseōs*; 13:22). The style agrees with that description: the author uses the first-person plural ("we") throughout, only shifting to direct address for emphasis. References to speaking occur throughout: "... of which we are speaking" (2:5), "... about this we have much to say, which is hard to explain, since you have become dull of hearing" (5:11), "... though we speak thus" (6:9).

The rhetorical organization of the homily is masterful. Exposition and exhortation alternate throughout, building on each other with such force that the cumulative impact is persuasive and the conclusions undeniable. The exposition of 1:1-14, for example, leads directly to exhortation (2:1-4); the argument of 2:5-18 is turned directly into an application by 3:1; and the discussion of 3:2-6 is driven home by the "therefore" of 3:7-13. Then, more rapidly, the exposition of 3:14-19 is applied in 4:1; that of 4:2-10 in the exhortation of 4:11-16; and so on through the sermon. In the process, the writer puts forth themes that are only later developed, creating a wavelike, cumulative force. Thus, Jesus' fellowship with humans (2:14-18) is made thematic in 5:1-10; his faith (3:1-6) is made explicit in 12:1-3; his role as priest (4:14; 5:1-10) is developed more fully in 7:1—9:28.

By designating Hebrews as a homily, I am not suggesting that it was necessarily delivered orally: I am suggesting only that it retains, as does Paul's "diatribe," the air of speech rather than writing. Whether homily or letter, it was intended to be read aloud to an audience. The title "To Hebrews [*pros hebraious*]" was appended early but probably represents an early Christian attempt to designate an originally anonymous and addressless text as one written to the Jews. It certainly does not mean (as has been suggested) "against the Hebrews." Without any external controls, it is not surprising to find many candidates for the audience: the Colossians, the Corinthians, converted priests in Jerusalem, converts from Qumran, converts from Alexandrian Judaism, or Diaspora Jews in Jerusalem on pilgrimage. The suggestions all depend on the same internal evidence.

The audience certainly consisted of Christians (see 6:1-3) who knew the Scriptures rather well. One cannot always argue from a writer's use of texts to a reader's appreciation of them, but in Hebrews the argument relies so heavily on citations and the ability to recognize their import, that if the audience was deficient in this respect, the writer was a poor communicator. The thematic elements are also of interest here. For instance, the author puts the angels in their proper place (1:5-14; 2:2), much as Paul had to do in Galatia (Gal. 3:19; 4:9) and Colossae (Col. 1:16; 2:18). Hebrews also puts Moses in his place (3:2-6), as Paul did in Gal. 3:19 and 2 Cor. 3:7-18. Most of all, the Levitical (Aaronic) priesthood is put in its place (chaps. 5–10), reflecting a concern unparalleled in the NT, although rival claims to the priesthood are found in contemporaneous Jewish writings. The author makes disparaging remarks about diverse teachings and about legislation dealing with food and drink (9:10; 13:9). These remind us of similar remarks in Col. 2:20-22, 1 Cor. 8:1-13, and Rom. 14:1-23. The comments here are made in passing, however, so that their significance for reconstructing the situation of the readership is unclear.

Of more importance for the overall presentation of the document are clues concerning the social context of the audience. The community has already experienced some suffering for its commitment to the Messiah (10:32-35; 12:3-13) and can look forward to more (13:13-14). They have not yet suffered unto death (12:4), but they knew and had visited some who had been imprisoned (10:34). Further, they had either themselves experienced or knew of those who had faced "public abuse and affliction" (10:33). Of most interest to us is the remark that the readers "joyfully accepted the plundering of [their] property, since [they] knew that [they themselves] had a better possession and an abiding one" (10:34). Like the sectarians at Qumran, some of them had experienced despoliation of their property.

This small clue is important. It enables us to appreciate some specific instructions to the hearers: they are to show hospitality (13:2), keep free from love of money (13:5), be content (13:5), and share what possessions they have (13:16). Even more, it provides a context for much of the homily's imagery, which relies on many property metaphors. Already in 10:34, we notice the contrast between the property that was taken and their "better and more lasting possession." Throughout the writing, property language symbolizes relationships and realities (see, e.g., 2:14; 3:1; 6:13-18; 7:4-10; 9:16-22)—most impressively and climactically in 11:1—12:17.

Corresponding to the community's physical losses is a spiritual condition of discouragement, even despair. The most obvious concern of the author is that the community's members are developing "drooping hands and weak knees" (12:12). Their discouragement places them in the tempting situation (2:18) of turning away from their commitment (12:16-17), as a way, perhaps, to relieve some of the oppressive measures brought upon them. The author thus writes against the "dullness of hearing" (5:11) that leads to disobedience, and the failure both of nerve and of faith (2:3; 3:12-4:1; 4:11, 14; 5:11-14; 6:4-8; 10:24-29). The Christian message, instead, is one of steadfastness and faithfulness in the face of opposition.

The text gives us a considerable amount of evidence about the readers. But we meet here again the methodological problem epistolary writing always involves: can we pull these elements together to form a consistent identity of the community behind the text? It is difficult to know whether the thematic elements all point to one specific situation. For instance, it might be possible to identify the hearers as, say, priestly converts from Qumran, whose loss of property and prestige as a result of their conversion shakes their confidence, tempting them to return to their former priestly order. The literary artistry of the writer gives us pause, however, for an accomplished rhetorician need not rely on the actual conditions of his hearers for the generation of themes to motivate them. Some may derive simply from the imagination, others from the literary momentum created by the primary themes. We must in the end be content with the certain knowledge that the hearers were Christians who knew enough of the Scriptures to appreciate such a learned and literary tour de force and who were, in the estimation of the homilist, in need of such encouragement as might be given by this "word of exhortation" (13:22).

A search for the author of Hebrews is no less frustrating than the search for his audience. Attribution to Paul is reflected in canonical lists and manuscripts, such as second- or third-century papyrus manuscript designated as P[46] where it is among Paul's letters. But Pauline attribution was vigorously questioned by such early writers as Tertullian, who thought the connection with Timothy made Barnabas a likely candidate, and Origen, who suggested Luke might have translated Paul's thought, but then confessed that "only God knows" (Eusebius *Ecclesiastical History* III.38.2). Certainly Hebrews contains a number of touches that we would otherwise have considered Pauline, such as "access" to God given by Christ (4:16; 10:19-22; cf. Rom. 5:1; Eph. 2:18), God's promise to Abraham (6:13-18; cf. Gal. 3:16-18), Abraham's response of faith (11:8-12; cf. Rom. 4:1-25), and the faith of Jesus understood as obedience (5:1-10; 12:1-3; cf. Rom. 5:12-21). In some other respects, Hebrews resembles the Gospel of John: it begins with a preexistent word (1:2-5; cf. John 1:1-18) and does not regard "flesh" (2:14; 5:7; 10:20) as an attitude hostile to God (as in Paul) but as a symbol of human mortality and frailty (cf. John 1:13-14; 3:6; 8:15). Yet, Hebrews puts all these elements together in an entirely distinctive fashion, and therefore the characterizations "Pauline" and "Johannine" are equally misleading.

The quest for authorship has led many to search for someone who was learned in the Scripture, who knew the technical modes of argumentation associated with both the rabbis and Philo, whose perceptions were influenced by the symbolic world of Alexandrian Judaism, and who had argumentative clarity, rhetorical skill, fervor in exhortation, and moral severity. Martin Luther hit upon a rather obvious candidate: Apollos. We met him as an associate of Paul (Acts 19:1; 1 Cor. 1:12; 3:4-22; 4:6; 16:12; Titus 3:13). In Acts 18:24-28 there is a portrait of him that sounds like a job description for the writer of Hebrews:

> Now a Jew named Apollos, a native of Alexandria, came to Ephesus. He was an eloquent man, well versed in the Scriptures. He had been instructed in the way of the Lord; and being fervent in spirit, he spoke and taught accurately the things concerning Jesus, though he knew only the baptism of John. He began to speak boldly in the synagogue; but when Priscilla and Aquila heard him,

they took him and expounded to him the way of God more accurately. . . . He powerfully confuted the Jews in public, showing by the Scriptures that the Christ was Jesus.

If Apollos were the author, several of the connections of Hebrews with 1 Corinthians would be clarified, for he was associated with Corinth: the question of foods (9:10; 13:9; cf. 1 Cor. 8:1-13); the comparison of the congregation to the people in the desert (3:7–4:13; cf. 1 Cor. 10:1-13); and the contrast between infants' food and that of adults (5:11-14; cf. 1 Cor. 3:1-3). Paul's concern at once to associate Apollos with himself (1 Cor. 3:5-9; 4:6), yet to distance himself from a ministry based on rhetorical skill (1 Cor. 2:1-5), would also take on a sharper edge. The suggestion that Apollos might have written a letter like Hebrews to the Corinthian congregation before Paul wrote 1 Corinthians raises just enough interesting possibilities to keep it from being dismissed. Yet, the authorship of Hebrews by Apollo must remain only conjecture. Indeed, the same evidence that supports the authorship by Apollos has been used to argue that Paul's staunch co-worker Priscilla, who had herself instructed Apollos, was the author. Whoever the author might have been, the writing testifies to yet another remarkable intellect in the Christian movement's first generation.

Hebrews was composed early enough to be quoted extensively by *1 Clement*, written to the Corinthian church around 95 C.E. The dating is sometimes thought to depend on the question of whether such temple imagery as used by Hebrews would be plausible before the destruction of the Jerusalem temple in 70. But this is a false issue on two counts. First, the appropriation of temple imagery by dissident groups was both possible and popular long before the temple's destruction, as both Qumran and Paul attest. Second, Hebrews does not focus on the physical temple and its cult in Jerusalem but centers on Torah's description of the idealized rule for worship to be carried out in the "tent in the wilderness" (cf. Exod. 25:10-40). The argument is thus carried out not by comparison to a stone edifice but by literary allusion. The sermon could therefore have been written any time between 35 and 95 C.E.

Hebrews as a Christian Witness

Because the interpretation of Jesus' work that is offered by Hebrews is so distinctive, it may be helpful to begin with those aspects of the writing that connect it to the wider Christian movement. The author twice refers to matters he presupposes but does not treat. In Heb. 2:3-4 we find something similar to a kerygmatic statement that sounds much like the story line of Luke-Acts: a great salvation first declared by the Lord and attested (cf. Luke 1:2) by signs, wonders, powerful deeds (cf. Acts 2:43; 5:12; 2 Cor. 12:12), and gifts of the Spirit (Acts 2:1-4; 1 Cor. 12:11; Eph. 4:2-7). In 6:1, the author mentions the "elementary doctrine of Christ," which he presupposes as he moves on to more mature teaching. Here is an important clue to the nature of the writing: it is preceded by the same contrast between "milk for babes" and "solid food for the mature" (5:11-14) that Paul employs in 1 Cor. 3:1-3. But whereas Paul thought the Corinthians incapable of mature teaching since they were full of rivalry and strife (1 Cor. 3:3), this author chides his hearers for their "dullness" in order to push them toward a deeper understanding, one fit for "teachers" (5:12). Hebrews thus does not advance an interpretation that conflicts with shared Christian traditions but promotes one that builds on those traditions for hearers who are able to move to greater levels of engagement and insight.

The author lists some elements of the common tradition: repentance from dead works and faith toward God (cf. 1 Thess. 1:9); instruction about "baptisms" or "ablutions;" the laying on of hands; the resurrection of the dead; and the future judgment. Surprising in this list of rudimentary Christian tradition is the lack of christological formulae, but of course, that is the author's primary theme in the letter. Another conviction shared with the rest of the Christian movement, but not requiring statement, is that Torah is authoritative and inspired by the Holy Spirit: "The Holy Spirit says . . ." (3:7) and "The Holy Spirit also bears witness to us, saying . . ." (10:15). This is found most emphatically in the prologue: "In many and diverse ways, God spoke of old to our fathers by the prophets . . ." (1:1).

That statement of the prologue concludes with the real focus of Hebrews: "In these last days, God has spoken to us by a Son" (1:2). Here the author clarifies that the sermon about to unfold will develop the christological basis for God's new word to the faithful. The focus on Christology is clear from the start, and develops with an extraordinary fullness and complexity: it contains a clear statement of the Son's preexistence (1:2; 10:5), of his incarnation (2:14-18; 10:5-7), and of his sacrificial, atoning death (1:3; 2:9; 6:6; 7:27). The resurrection of Jesus is found explicitly in 1:3 but also provides the dominating premise of the sermon, so much at the heart of the exposition that it requires no direct statement. Hebrews is, indeed, largely a midrashic working out of the implications of Psalm 110, the classic resurrection psalm of the early Christian movement. Finally, Hebrews has a definite statement that Christ will return again for judgment (9:28; 10:25). The range and grandeur of the Christology of Hebrews is suggested by its stark, yet strangely allusive, summary: 'Jesus Christ is the same, yesterday, today, and forever" (13:8).

No less substantially connected to the discussion of Christology is the teaching of Hebrews on Christian existence. In the first place comes faith, which finds in this sermon its fullest exposition next to that in Romans. As with Paul, faith is a response to God that involves trust and obedience. But Hebrews puts the most emphasis on the "enduring" quality of faith, its "fidelity" (see, above all, Heb. 11-12). Fidelity is rooted in the reliability of God's promises, enabling Christians to have hope, all the more secure since it is "anchored" in the resurrection and exaltation of Jesus (see 6:18-20). Christian love is also touched on (13:1), being explicated in terms of hospitality (13:2), care for prisoners (13:3), respect for marriage fidelity (13:4), and the sharing of possessions (13:16). Little is said about the internal life of communities, apart from their holding regular assemblies (10:25) and saying prayers of praise as sacrificial offerings to God (13:15). The audience is also exhorted to obey and submit to its leaders (13:17). They are told as well (13:7):

> Remember your leaders, those who spoke to you the word of God; consider the outcome of their life, and imitate their faith.

The "imitation of faith," in Hebrews, inevitably involves suffering. This writing emphasizes the essential connection between the life of faith and the experience of suffering, raising it to a level of a theme (see, e.g., 5:1-10; 12:3-13).

The Argument of Hebrews

Hebrews contains the longest sustained argument in the NT. A simple form of midrashic logic gives structure to the sermon as a whole. Grasping it means understanding much of the writer's mode of argumentation. We have met the basic argument before, most fully in Rom. 5:12-21. It was used widely in the rabbinic tradition where it probably was borrowed from Greek rhetoric. It is the argument *a minore ad maius*—"from the lesser to the greater"—or, in its Jewish form, *qal we chomer*—"the light and the heavy." Reduced to its bare bones, the argument looks like this: If such and such is the case with *x*, which is a small matter, then it is even more the case with *y*, which is a greater matter.

The argument obviously involves analogy. As in all analogy, two things are required: an element of similarity or continuity and an element of dissimilarity or discontinuity. In a typical midrashic application of the argument, for instance, we find God's way with Israel compared to an earthly king's manner with his people (cf. *Sifre on Numbers* 86). The element of continuity is the relationship of rule and submission; that of discontinuity, the greater magnitude of God's rule over all creatures compared with a king's over a city. The logic runs thus: if an earthly king acts in this way, how much more will the king of the universe do the same?

The element of continuity in Hebrews is provided by the word of God spoken to the people: God spoke in the past and continues to speak in the present (1:1-2; 2:1-4; 3:5-7; 4:12-13; 7:28). The author speaks of the Christian confession as a word (6:1; 13:7), and understands the discourse of Hebrews as such a word as well (4:13; 5:11; 13:22). God's consistency in speaking—through prophets or Son—is what provides the ground of comparison: God's word does not change, even though the mode of revelation may. The latter naturally leads us to the point of discontinuity.

The element of discontinuity is the agent that brings the word. The contrast is sharply drawn between the mediation of God's word by prophets, angels, Moses, and Torah (with its cult) on the one hand, and Christ, on the other. The critical step in the argument is therefore to establish the "heavy" as opposed to the "light," the "greater" over against the "lesser." The linchpin of Hebrews is the supremacy of the word spoken through the Son of God. So, the author shows in sequence—from Torah itself—that although angels are God's ministering spirits, Jesus is God's Son (1:1-14); that although Moses was a servant within God's house (i.e., the people), Jesus is Son and builder of the house (3:5-6); that the cultic acts of the Aaronic priests had to be repeated through time because of their inefficacy, but because by his resurrection Jesus is eternal Son and thus his offering endures forever (chaps. 5–10). It is the greater magnitude of the revelation of God's word in Christ that provides the basis of discontinuity.

The word spoken through the Son holds a greater promise and a more certain fulfillment than that spoken of old (12:22-24). The term *bebaios*—"fair," "certain," "reliable," "sure"—recurs frequently in characterizing this word (2:2; 3:6; 6:19; 9:17; 13.9). Because the present word is more sure and powerful, it demands a greater obedience than the word of old, and disobedience bears a greater punishment (see 2:2; 4:1-2; 6:6-8; 12:17). It is easy to see how the logic of the argument moves toward that of exhortation, as the contrast is now between the *people in the desert* and the *people of God today*. The desert generation failed to hear and obey, so it did not enter the land of Canaan, which was the lesser "rest." The people of God in the writer's own day also have a promised "rest": the life of God into which the resurrected Jesus has entered once for all, which is the greater "rest." This promise also demands a response of obedience, and failure will be more grievous than in the former case. Thus, the urgency of the exhortation in 4:11-13:

> Let us therefore strive to enter that rest, that no one fall by the same sort of disobedience. For the word of God is living and active, sharper than any two-edged sword, piercing to the division of soul and spirit, of joints and marrow, and discerning the thoughts and intentions of the heart.

The Symbolism of Hebrews

The symbolism of Hebrews is complex, deriving from a variety of traditions. The search for a perfect correspondence between one tradition and this writing is futile, for Hebrews reshapes the available symbols around the figure of a crucified and exalted Messiah, giving a distinctive configuration to its content. A discussion of the symbolic framework is valuable only insofar as it helps us understand the new contours. It has recently been argued, for example, that Hebrews most resembles the thought world of the Qumran sectarians. Both there and here, we find a New Covenant community, separation from cult with appropriation of its symbols, the expectation of a priestly as well as kingly messiah, even an interest in the figure of Melchizedek. The elements of disagreement, however, are also noteworthy: Hebrews rejects the laws of purity and diet about which the sectarians were obsessive, has no mythic explanation for the world's division into good and evil, and indeed lacks such dualism entirely. More important, the Qumran connection does not really help us to grasp the author's basic conviction concerning what constitutes "the greater."

The long-standing opinion that Hebrews reflects a kind of Platonic worldview is sufficiently accurate to include its author as first among the Christian Platonists of Alexandria. I use the term "worldview," because by the first century, Plato's classic metaphysical theories, as expressed, for example, in the *Republic* 509D–521B, had been filtered through many schools and permutations, becoming in the process as much a common consciousness as a theoretical doctrine.

In broad terms, this is a view of reality that draws a sharp distinction, indeed, a dividing line, between the *phenomenal* world, which is the realm of materiality, characterized by movement, change, and corruption—and, therefore, only partial knowledge—and the *noumenal* world, characterized by changelessness and incorruptibility because it is spiritual in nature. This is the world of pure "forms" or "ideas." The distinction is metaphysical (one realm of being is denser and more "real" than the other), epistemological (the world of change allows only approximate perceptions—i.e., "opinions"—whereas ideas can be truly "known") and axiological (the noumenal world is "better" than the phenomenal).

That which we do not see, therefore, is more real and more worthwhile than that which can be seen. As the perceived world is only a "shadow" or "reflection" of the noumenal world, the physical manifestation of a thing is infinitely inferior to its ideal essence and purity: the idea of "cat" is finer and more real than any furry moving creature that catches mice. The two realms are related by a certain formal causality. Noumenal being is primordial; the phenomenal world is derivative. If the ideal world is the stamp, the phenomenal bears its seal. The spiritual realm is one of types; the material world has antitypes, which correspond only roughly to their ideal models.

The Platonism of Hebrews resembles that of Philo and the Book of Wisdom, a version well on its way to what is called middle Platonism. Found also in Hermetic and Gnostic literature, it is a hybrid of Platonic metaphysics and Semitic cosmology. In Jewish tradition this most often involved interaction with the Genesis creation accounts. There, the heavens (*ha shemaim*) is the realm where God dwells, and the earth (*ha aretz*) the place of human activity. A great distance lies between them: "As far as the heavens are above the earth, so great is his steadfast love for those who fear him" (Ps. 103:11); "God is in heaven, you are on earth; therefore let your words be few" (Qoh. 5:2); "Thus says the Lord, heaven is my throne and the earth is my footstool" (Isa. 66:1). In this understanding, the temple can be regarded as a place of access between the two realms: "The Lord is in his holy temple, the Lord's throne is in heaven" (Ps. 11:4).

Not a great step is required to identify the heavens with the world of forms, and the earth with the material realm. Philo, for example, observes the double account of human creation in Gen. 1:26-27 and 2:7. He notices that the first account was "according to the divine image" and the second "from the dust of the earth." He most naturally views the first creation as the ideal "form" of humanity and the second as its material realization. In Exod. 25:40, likewise, Philo reads that Moses is told to construct a place of worship in the desert according to the pattern of what God showed him on the mountain. In Philo's Greek version (LXX), it read: ". . . according to the type [*typos*]" that Moses was shown (cf. Acts 7:44). It follows, then, that earthly worship is only an imperfect representation of that divine ideal or model (cf. chap. 3, pp. 84–86).

The static, ahistorical character of Platonism has often been noted. In Philo's version, the "oracles of God" in Scripture are like the oracles at Delphi, timeless messages whose original context and meaning are not as critical as their enduring message for Philo's own present. God's word is spiritual and timeless but is clothed in human speech, which is temporal and changing. Human interpretation must take account, therefore, of diverse levels of meaning. The same words can at once bear a material (i.e., literal) meaning, a psychic (i.e., moral) sense, and a spiritual (i.e., allegorical) significance. So Philo reads the exodus story at once as the literal freeing of Israel from Egypt, as a passage from vice to virtue, and as the ascent of the soul to spiritual freedom and ecstasy.

Hebrews shares not only the language of this outlook, but also some of its fundamental perceptions. The Son, for example, is said to "reflect the glory of God and bear the very stamp of his nature" (1:3), which recalls Wis. 7:26. The worship of priests in the tent is called a shadow and copy of true worship (8:5), and the authority cited is the same LXX text from Exod. 25:40 as Philo used. The law is a shadow (*skia*) rather than the real image (*autēn tēn eikona*) of "the good things to come" (10:1). Torah provides "examples" that anticipate "the real" (4:11; 9:23). Jesus, for example, enters the real tent (*skēnēs alēthinēs*) in his resurrection (8:2) and is said to go into a sanctuary "not made by hand, a copy of the true one, but into heaven itself" (9:24). In contrast to the repeated offerings of earthly priests through time, his priestly act is one that is "once for all" because it takes place in the realm of "true being," heaven.

Platonism is, however, entirely reworked by Hebrews. First, Hebrews shows a very acute awareness of history: God spoke of old, and speaks now in different ways. The past also serves as a type or example for the present, which is greater and "more real" (see 4:11). Second, the distinction between heaven and earth is not only cosmological, it is also ontological. "Heaven" describes God's eternal existence and all that participate in it, whereas "earth" denotes merely passing human existence. Third, Hebrews exalts rather than denigrates the physical. Only because Jesus was and had a body could he be a priest. His body, furthermore, is not cast off at death but exalted. Thus, the sharpness of the dualism is undercut: corporeal existence, although inferior, is clearly incorporated into God's plan. Fourth, Hebrews emphasizes change: Christ came once and will come again; he was, for a little while, lower than the angels, but now is exalted and enthroned. Platonism is here stretched and reshaped around belief in a historical human savior whose death and resurrection enriched both his body and, consequently, the earthly realm as a whole. Christ sacralizes the inferior material sphere so that life is worth living in the present because of him, thus circumventing any form of resignation from the process and pressures of earthly existence. Hebrews shows us what Philo might have written had he been a Christian. It contributes to the transformation of Hellenism that, with the Christian Platonists Origen, Clement, Athanasius, and Cyril, fundamentally affected the development of western philosophy.

The Use of Scripture in Hebrews

Hebrews quotes widely from Torah (mostly the LXX version), using the Law, the Prophets, and the Writings. The author introduces the texts with a variety of formulae (see, e.g., 2:5; 3:7; 4:4; 7:17). He particularly exploits texts (e.g., Pss. 110:4 and 95:11) that have God swearing oaths, for when God swears, a promise is doubly sure. Hebrews sometimes alters a text to make a point. For instance, the LXX version of Ps. 40:6-8, "Sacrifices and offerings thou hast not desired, but ears you have prepared for me," becomes ". . . a body you have prepared for me" (10:5), which nicely fits the argument of 10:10: "We have been sanctified through the body of Jesus Christ once for all."

The longest citation is from Jer. 31:31-34 (in Heb. 8:8-12), which is used because it refers to a new covenant unlike the one made in the wilderness. The author's comment is revealing: "In speaking of a new covenant, he treats the first as obsolete."

Hebrews also uses a variety of interpretive techniques. It follows the rule of aligning two texts in which the same word occurs so that they mutually interpret each other (see, e.g., the use of Pss. 110:1 and 8:4-6 in Heb. 1:13 and 2:6). The writer sometimes makes elliptical citations, expecting the readers to catch the further implications based on a knowledge of the larger context of the citation (see, e.g., 2:12-13). The following three examples illustrate the range of the author's technique and the way scriptural interpretation carries the argument.

A Midrash on Ps. 95:7-11 (Heb. 3:7—4:13)

In this section, the author establishes his most dramatic image of existence before God, that of pilgrimage. It stretches from the patriarchs to the present, and only in Jesus is the goal of that pilgrimage (access to God) finally accomplished. The key words from the psalm are "*today* if you hear my voice" and "as I *swore* in my wrath, they will never enter my *rest*." Here we have God speaking and swearing through

David, long after the event of the exodus. The "today" of the psalm must, therefore, be an eternal call of God. Therefore, the word of Scripture addresses the present hearers directly. They are not to harden their hearts as the people did in the desert, for which reason God did not let them enter the "rest" of Canaan (3:19). But if God can still speak of a "today," his promise too must remain: "Therefore the promise of his rest remains" (4:1).

But what sort of "rest" could the Scripture mean? Here, the text of Gen. 2:2 provides the clue: ". . . and God rested on the seventh day from all his works." It is, then, the "Sabbath rest" of God himself (cf. Exod. 20:11) that the Scripture still extends, one the people of old did not achieve. They had entered the land, certainly, but they did not attain the rest that is God's life, the one intended for them upon entrance into the land of "milk and honey" (4:8). The first "Jesus" (the Greek form of the Hebrew "Joshua") could not bring them so far; otherwise the "today if you hear his voice" would not still challenge them. Since the offer remains open, the promise must still be open as well: "So then, there remains a Sabbath rest for the people of God. For whoever enters God's rest also ceases from all their labors as God did from his" (4:9-10). Here we see most clearly the "lesser to greater" use of Torah.

An Encomium on the Ancestors in the Faith (Heb. 11:1-40)

As in Romans 9–11, the history of the people is reread from the perspective of faith, here not the faith that justifies but the one that endures. This, of course, is not a major shift from Paul. The difference between Hebrews and Paul is not in the conception of faith itself, since for Paul, also, faith is primarily a matter of obedience. Rather, the major shift is in emphasis, as faithful obedience takes on an even more urgent dimension for the writer of Hebrews. As in the midrash of Rom. 4:1-25, Abraham appears here as the supreme example of faith among the patriarchs and matriarchs; the aspect of his faith that is stressed is its endurance even through testing. But also, Abraham exemplifies the one who lives as though seeing things others do not; he wandered homeless, yet was convinced that he was headed for a "city that has foundations, whose builder and maker is God" (11:10). In this, he showed by example how faith is "the assurance of things hoped for, the conviction of things not seen" (11:1), and, as the pattern Abraham set indicates, faith or trust in God leads to obedience and faithful living.

The term "conviction," sometimes translated "substance" (from the Greek *hypostasis*), has legal connotations: it is a down payment or a pledge of property. For those whose property had been plundered and who were told that they had a "better possession and an abiding one," the example of the ancestors was most pertinent. They all acted in view of what had not yet appeared (11:3, 7, 8, 13, 26-27). The repeated formula "by faith . . . by faith" has a powerful, almost hypnotic effect, culminating at last in the powerful exhortation of 12:1:

Therefore since we are surrounded by such a cloud of witnesses, *let us also* lay aside every weight and sin that clings so closely, and run with perseverance the race that is set before us.

It is both a stirring call to join in the pilgrimage to the heavenly homeland (11:4) and an exhortation to the pilgrims lest they might fall by the way (12:12-13). Here we see, then, the paradigmatic use of Torah by the writer of Hebrews.

An Allegory on Torah (Heb. 7:1-17)

Melchizedek appears only once in the narratives of Torah, when he meets Abraham after the slaughter of the kings (Gen. 14:18-22). He reappears in Ps. 110:4. The author of Hebrews is the only NT writer to read past the first verse of this resurrection psalm—"The Lord said to my Lord, sit at my right hand"—to find "The Lord has sworn and will not go back, you are a priest forever according to the order of Melchizedek" (Ps. 110:4). The author finds in this text evidence that the resurrected Jesus is not only a kingly messiah—"the Lord sends forth from Zion your mighty scepter" (Ps. 110:2)—but a priestly one as well. In the light of this, he re-reads the story of Abraham and Melchizedek in Genesis.

Etymology is a favorite resource for allegorical interpretation. The name Melchizedek can be construed *melek-zedekah*, that is, "king of righteousness." And, since he is the king of Salem, he is also king of peace (*shalom* = play on Salem; Heb. 7:2). And this surely anticipates the messianic age, when "righteousness and peace shall kiss" (Ps. 85:10). Of all the important figures in Genesis, moreover, this king alone has no genealogy. But, according to the rabbinic logic of Hebrews, if something is not in Torah, neither is it in the world (*non in tora non in mundo*). Thus, the author can legitimately conclude that Melchizedek had no ancestry (7:3, 6). And since Torah does not relate his death, neither did he die, "but resembling the Son of God, he continues as a priest forever" (7:3). When Jesus also gains "indestructible life" through the resurrection, he attains that eternal priesthood of Melchizedek (7:15-17). Such an interpretation, of course, could come only from one who first knew of such a Son of God and who was reading Torah with the view that the text speaks directly of Christ.

Abraham, moreover, gave tithes to Melchizedek, thereby recognizing him as "priest of God most High" (7:2, 4). But since Abraham, as patriarch, bore the whole line of Levitical priests of the Israelite people, his gesture was, in effect, the recognition by Torah itself that the priesthood that descended from Melchizedek was superior (7:6-10). Rabbinic tradition contains an interesting parallel. A talmudic passage (Babylonian Talmud, *Nedarim* 32b) says God wanted to give the priesthood to Melchizedek, but because in his blessing he had named Abraham before God, the priesthood was taken from him and given to Abraham instead. In the citation of Ps. 110:4, the same words that the writer of Hebrews understands as "according to the order of Melchizedek," the rabbis understood as "because of the words of Melchizedek."

It is tempting to see in the rabbinic interpretation a response to just the sort of use of Melchizedek we find in Hebrews (cf. *Genesis Rabbah* 43.6-8). Christian interpretation saw the psalm as prophetically pointing to Jesus' priesthood as qualitatively different than that of Levi. Although the precise relationship between Jesus and Melchizedek is not made clear in Hebrews, Melchizedek clearly represents Jesus and provides a marvelous way for the writer to interpret Ps. 110 in light of the belief in Jesus' resurrection from the dead. Here midrashic argument, in concert with allegorical interpretation, has been used to underscore a christological proof from Torah.

The Christology of Hebrews

Hebrews is unusually full in its use of titles for Jesus. Many of them are traditional. The author has a predilection for the name "Jesus," corresponding to an interest in the human side of the Messiah (2:9; 3:1; 4:14; 6:20; 7:22; 10:19; 12:24; 13:12, 20), as well as for the title "Christ," reflecting interest in the messianic role (3:6, 14; 5:5; 6:1; 9:11, 14, 24, 28). He uses the combination "Jesus Christ" only three times (10:10; 13:8, 21). He speaks often of the "Son" (1:2, 5, 8; 3:6; 5:5, 8; 7:28), as well as "Son of God" (4:14; 6:6; 7:3; 10:29), "Lord" (1:10; 2:3; 7:14; 13:20), and "Son of man" (2:6; cf. Ps. 8:4). We also find here one of the very few attributions in the NT of the title "God" (*theos*) to Jesus, implicitly in 3:4 and explicitly in 1:8 (by a citation of Ps. 45:6-7).

Other titles in Hebrews are either unique or rare. Jesus is called an "heir" (1:2), "firstborn" (1:6), "great shepherd of the sheep" (13:20), "pioneer" (2:10; 12:2), and "perfecter" (12:2). He is "sanctifier" (2:11), "apostle" (3:1), and "builder of the house" (3:3). He is "cause of salvation" (5:9), "forerunner" (6:20), "guarantor" (7:22), "minister" (8:2), and "mediator" (8:6; 9:15; 12:24). When viewed in concert with one another, these special titles illustrate two aspects of the Christology of Hebrews: Jesus is one who brings salvation from God to humanity (apostle, cause, sanctifier, shepherd, minister, builder, guarantor), and he is also the human being who first reaches what is the plan of God for all humans (heir, firstborn, pioneer, perfecter, forerunner). As one who bridges humanity and divinity, he is, preeminently, mediator.

These aspects come together in the title that is unique to Hebrews among the NT writings: Jesus is "priest"/"high priest" (2:27; 3:1; 4:14; 5:5, 10; 6:20; 7:26; 8:1; 9:11; 10:21). Alongside the traditional priestly imagery drawn from the cult (e.g., sacrifice, mediator), Hebrews also develops the royal aspects of the title, and this, in fact, becomes a predominant emphasis in the letter. The combination occurs in Ps. 110:1-4, one of the classic texts for NT messianic exegesis. This psalm provides the image of royal enthronement that runs throughout Hebrews (1:3, 8, 13; 2:5, 7, 9; 4:16; 7:1, 2; 8:1; 10:12; 12:2, 28). The significance of this connection is clarified when one recalls that the Qumran sectarians, among other apocalyptic communities, expected a priestly as well as a royal messiah. The writer of Hebrews, however, combines the two roles often separated elsewhere. Thus, it is not descent from David that makes Jesus king, though in Hebrews Jesus does comes from the tribe of Judah (7:14). Rather, since his resurrection is a royal enthronement (1:13), his exaltation also becomes the completion of the priestly work that began with his death (9:11-12):

> But when Christ appeared as a high priest of the good things that have come, then through the greater and more perfect tent (not made with hands, that is, not of this creation), he entered once for all into the holy place, taking not the blood of goats and calves but his own blood, thus securing eternal redemption.

Priesthood and kingship are both attained by resurrection, which indelibly links the two functions (10:12-13):

> But when Christ had offered for all time a single sacrifice for sins, he sat down at the right hand of God, there to wait till his enemies be made a stool for his feet (cf. Ps. 110:1).

Death (with its priestly overtones) and resurrection (with its royal emphases) together form the movement of Jesus to the Holy Place that is God's presence (9:24):

> Christ has entered, not into a sanctuary made with hands, a copy of the true one, but into heaven itself, now to appear before the presence of God in our behalf.

Because Jesus continues to live as the resurrected one, his mediation of salvation is once and for all an acceptable offering to God. Because this passage of a human being from death "through the veil of the flesh" into God's life is the organizing conviction of the author, the imagery of the tent and its furniture in Hebrews 8–9 is complex. It does not help to compare notes with the original in Torah, for the Christian confession stretches those symbols into almost unrecognizable forms. Precisely the confused state of the symbolism reminds us that the starting point of Hebrews, as for all the NT writings, is the paradoxical experience of a crucified and raised Messiah. Drawing upon the Platonic thought outlined above—the distinction between the ideal and the real—the life into which Jesus moved after the resurrection is the ideal of which human life in this world is but a copy. It is the fullness and completeness of Jesus' new life that transforms the old symbols of the tabernacle used by Israel in the wilderness into an inferior representation of Jesus' new location in the Holy Sanctuary of God.

Because Jesus is priest, the Christology of Hebrews must be both "high" and "low." To offer a truly efficacious sacrifice, Jesus must be the eternal Word, the true Son of

God, living "by the power of indestructible life" (7:16). But to be an effective mediator, he must be fully human as well. Thus we find the emphasis on the body of Jesus in 10:5-10, and this striking passage in 2:14-18:

> Therefore since the children share in flesh and blood, he himself partook of the same nature, that through death he might destroy him who has the power of death, that is, the devil, and deliver all those who through fear of death were subject to life-long bondage. For surely it is not with angels that he is concerned but the children of Abraham. Therefore he had to be like his people in every respect that he might become a merciful and faithful high priest in the service of God, to make expiation for the people. For because he himself has suffered and been tempted, he is able to help those who are tempted.

From the side of divinity, he was a "merciful" priest, a mediator; from the side of humanity, he was "faithful," an exemplar.

The last line of the previous citation leads us to the most profound aspect of the Christology of Hebrews. The God-man Jesus was not a fleshly puppet controlled by a divine *logos*: he was fully human, a person who, because of his obedient response to God, was "made perfect" (5:7-10):

> In the days of his flesh, Jesus offered up prayers and supplications, with loud cries and tears, to him who was able to save him from death, and was heard for his godly fear. Although he was a son, he learned obedience through what he suffered, and being made perfect, he became source of eternal salvation to all who obey him, being designated by God a high priest after the order of Melchizedek.

While it is not certain that this passage shows awareness of the Synoptic Gospels' Passion accounts, it is clear that for Hebrews Jesus' obedience demands suffering. Indeed, the obedience itself is a form of suffering, as Jesus learns ever more fully what it means to be a son. The author here plays on a commonplace of Hellenistic education: "Learning is suffering [*mathein, pathein*]."

As a human, therefore, Jesus progressively became an obedient son, moving by faith toward the God who called him. His perfection (maturity) as son was not granted outright, but was developed in him by obedient faith. Thus, since he stepped through the veil of the flesh into the Holy Place, he has opened a way for all humans to follow. The significance for those whose human lot Jesus shared totally, apart from sin, is that every human is thus capable of being perfected. The "capacity for God," which has been placed in humans by their creation according to God's image, has been realized in a single and specific human being—"the pioneer and perfecter of our faith" (12:2)—who has shown the way:

Consider Jesus, the apostle and high priest of our confession—he was faithful to the one who appointed him (3:1-2) . . . [and] being made perfect, he became the source of eternal salvation (5:9).

The Christology of Hebrews therefore also becomes the basis for its exhortation. At first, the insistence that God disciplines those he loves in 12:5-11 appears trite, a throwback to the moral insensitivity of Job's friends. Only when we remember one of the nuances of the Greek word "discipline" (*paideia*) do we grasp the depth of the exhortation: "Endure for the sake of an education (*eis paideian hypomenete*)" (12:7). Discipline is here not punishment but "education." The human experience of suffering shapes Christians in the pattern of him who "learned to be son" through his suffering. It is the process of learning to become children of God, as Jesus himself did. He is the pioneer who blazed the way and he is also the "finisher" who gives those who follow the power to complete the journey. If they remain faithful as he did, then they will attain a full share in the inheritance that as heir (1:4) he has obtained for them (Heb. 12:1-2):

Therefore since we are surrounded by such a cloud of witnesses, let us also lay aside every weight and sin which clings so closely, and let us run with perseverance the race that is set before us, looking to Jesus, the pioneer and perfecter of our faith, who for the joy that was set before him, endured the cross, despising the shame, and is seated at the right hand of the throne of God.

We see here, then, the exhortatory goal of the christological argument of Hebrews from the beginning. The letter is thus much more than mere praise or encomium for what Jesus has achieved. It is an argument for faithful human obedience to God: Jesus did it, and has therefore created the possibility for all other humans to follow. The argument intends to inspire the believer's "confidence to enter the sanctuary by the blood of Jesus" (10:19) "with a true heart in full assurance of faith (10:22)." Faithful living is the essential element of Christian existence, ensuring salvation for those who persevere to the end (10:36-39).

Study Questions

1. What genre of literature best describes Hebrews? What are the characteristics of that genre? How does that affect our reading of Hebrews?

2. In what ways does Hebrews resemble Platonism? What accounts for this?

3. What is the dominant image for Jesus in Hebrews? What is its function?

4. How does Hebrews appeal to the great "heroes" of the faith?

Bibliographical Note

For a variety of topics related to the General Epistles, see R. P. Martin and P. H. Davids, *Dictionary of the Later New Testament and Its Developments* (Downers Grove: Inter-Varsity Press, 1997).

For some discussion of issues raised in this chapter regarding authorship and destination, see C. P. Anderson, "Hebrews among the Letters of Paul," *SR* 5 (1975–76): 258–66; F. F. Bruce, "'To the Hebrews': A Document of Roman Christianity?" *ANRW* II.25.4 (1987): 3496–521; R. F. Collins, *Letters That Paul Did Not Write: The Epistle to the Hebrews and the Pauline Pseudepigrapha* (Wilmington: Michael Glazier, 1988), 19–56; R. Hoppin, *Priscilla, Author of the Epistle to the Hebrews and Other Essays* (New York: Exposition Press, 1969); B. P. Hunt, "The Epistle to the Hebrews: An Anti-Judaic Treatise?" *SE* 2 (1964): 408–10; L. D. Hurst, "Apollos, Hebrews, and Corinth: Bishop Montefiore's Theory Examined," *SJT* 38 (1985): 505–13; T. W. Manson, "The Problem of the Epistle to the Hebrews," *BJRL* 32 (1949–50): 1–17; W. Manson, *The Epistle to the Hebrews: A Historical and Theological Reconsideration* (London: Hodder & Stoughton, 1951); and J. C. McCullough, "Recent Developments in Research on the Epistle to the Hebrews," *IBS* 2 (1980): 141–65, 3 (1981): 28–45.

For genre, structure, and argument, see B. Lindars, "The Rhetorical Structure of Hebrews," *NTS* 35 (1989): 382–406; T. H. Olbricht, "Hebrews as Amplification," in S. E. Porter and T. H. Olbricht (eds.), *Rhetoric and the New Testament* (JSNTSup, 90; Sheffield: Sheffield Academic Press, 1993), 375–87; J. Swetnam, "On the Literary Genre of the 'Epistle' to the Hebrews," *NovT* 11 (1969): 261–69; idem, "Form and Content in Hebrews 1–6," *Bib* 53 (1972): 368–85; idem, "Form and Content in Hebrews 7–13," *Bib* 55 (1974): 333–48; and A. Vanhoye, *Structure and Message of the Epistle to the Hebrews* (Rome: Biblical Institute Press, 1989).

On the general background, see the full survey by L. D. Hurst, *The Epistle to the Hebrews: Its Background of Thought* (SNTSMS, 65; Cambridge: Cambridge Univ. Press, 1990). The Hellenistic aspects of Hebrews are emphasized by L. K. K. Dey, *The Intermediary World and Patterns of Perfection in Philo and Hebrews* (SBLDS, 25; Missoula, Mont.: Scholars Press, 1975); R. S. Eccles, "The Purpose of the Hellenistic Patterns in the Epistle to the Hebrews," in J. Neusner (ed.), *Religions in Antiquity* (Leiden: E. J. Brill, 1968), 207–26; J. W. Thompson, *The Beginnings of Christian Philosophy: The Epistle to the Hebrews* (CBQMS, 13; Washington, D.C.: Catholic Biblical Assn., 1982); R. Williamson, *Philo and the Epistle to the Hebrews* (Leiden: E. J. Brill, 1970); and idem, "Platonism and Hebrews," *SJT* 16 (1963): 415–24. The symbolic world of Gnosticism and the *anthropos* myth are vigorously exploited by E. Käsemann, *The Wandering People of God: An Investigation of the Letter to the Hebrews*, trans. R. A. Harrisville and I. L. Sandberg (Minneapolis: Augsburg Pub. House, 1984). The connection to the symbols of Qumran is pursued by F. C. Fensham, "Hebrews and Qumran," *Neot* 5 (1971): 9–21; and M. DeJonge and A. S. van der Woude, "11Q Melchizedek and the New Testament," *NTS* 12 (1965–66): 301–26.

The use of Scripture in Hebrews is analyzed by P. M. Eisenbaum, *The Jewish Heroes of Christian History: Hebrews 11 in Literary Context* (SBLDS, 156; Atlanta: Scholars Press, 1997); idem, "Heroes and History in Hebrews 11," in C. A. Evans and J. A. Sanders (eds.), *Early Christian Interpretation of the Scriptures of Israel: Investigations and Proposals* (JSNTSup, 148; Sheffield: Sheffield Academic Press, 1997), 380–96; J. Fitzmyer, 'Now This Melchizedek . . .' Heb 7:1," in his *Essays on the Semitic Background of the New Testament* (Missoula, Mont.: Scholars Press, 1974), 221–43; C. A. Gieschen, "The Different Functions of a Similar Melchizedek Tradition in *2 Enoch* and the Epistle to the Hebrews," in *Early Christian Interpretation of the Scriptures of Israel*, 364–79; A. T. Hanson, "Christ in the Old Testament According to Hebrews," *SE* 2 (1964): 393–407; idem, "Hebrews," in D. A. Carson and H. G. M. Williamson (eds.), *It Is Written: Scripture Citing Scripture* (Cambridge: Cambridge Univ. Press, 1988), 292–302; F. L. Horton, *The Melchizedek Tradition: A Critical Evaluation of the Sources to the Fifth Century AD and in the Epistle to the Hebrews* (SNTSMS, 30; Cambridge: Cambridge Univ. Press, 1976); F. Howard, "Hebrews and the Old Testament Quotations," *NovT* 10 (1968): 208–16; G. Hughes, *Hebrews and Hermeneutics: The Epistle to the Hebrews as a New Testament Example of Biblical Interpretation* (SNTSMS, 36; Cambridge: Cambridge Univ. Press, 1979); J. C. McCullough, "The Old Testament Quotations in Hebrews," *NTS* 26 (1979–80): 363–79; S. G. Sowers, *The Hermeneutics of Philo and Hebrews: A Comparison of the Interpretation of the Old Testament in Philo Judaeus and the Epistle to the Hebrews* (Richmond: John Knox Press, 1965); and J. Swetnam, *Jesus and Isaac: A Study of the Epistle to the Hebrews in Light of the Aqedah* (AnB, 94; Rome: Biblical Institute Press, 1981).

For various thematic aspects of the letter, see H. Anderson, "The Jewish Antecedents of the Christology of Hebrews," in J. H. Charlesworth (ed.), *The Messiah: Developments in Earliest Judaism and Christianity* (Minneapolis: Fortress Press, 1992), 512–35; M. R. D'Angelo, *Moses in the Letter to the Hebrews* (SBLDS, 42; Chico, Calif.: Scholars Press, 1979); C. K. Barrett, "The Eschatology of the Epistle to the Hebrews," in D. Daube and W. D. Davies (eds.), *The Background of the New Testament and Its Eschatology* (Cambridge: Cambridge Univ. Press, 1964), 363–93; W. E. Brooks, "The Perpetuity of Christ's Sacrifice in the Epistle to the Hebrews," *JBL* 89 (1970): 205–14; F. F. Bruce, "The Kerygma of Hebrews," *Int* 23 (1969): 3–19; C. N. Croy, *Endurance in Suffering: Hebrews 12:1–3 in Its Rhetorical, Religious, and Philosophical Context* (SNTSMS; Cambridge: Cambridge Univ. Press, 1998); J. Dunnill, *Covenant and Sacrifice in the Letter to the Hebrews* (SNTSMS, 75; Cambridge: Cambridge Univ. Press, 1992); M. R. Cosby, *The Rhetorical Composition and Function of Hebrews 11 in Light of Example Lists in Antiquity* (Macon: Mercer Univ. Press, 1988); F. Filson, *"Yesterday": A Study of Hebrews in the Light of Ch. 13* (London: SCM Press, 1967); D. Hamm, "Faith in the Epistle to the Hebrews: The Jesus Factor," *CBQ* 52 (1990): 270–91; L. D. Hurst, "The Christology of Hebrews 1 and 2," in L. D. Hurst and N. T. Wright (eds.), *The Glory of Christ in the New Testament* (New York: Clarendon Press, 1987), 151–64; M. E.

Isaacs, *Sacred Space: An Approach to the Theology of the Epistle to the Hebrews* (JSNTSup, 73; Sheffield: Sheffield Academic Press, 1992); W. G. Johnson, "The Pilgrimage Motif in the Book of Hebrews," *JBL* 97(1978): 239–51; C. R. Koester, *The Dwelling of God: Tabernacle in the Old Testament, Intertestamental Jewish Literature, and the New Testament* (CBQMS, 22; Washington, D. C.: Catholic Biblical Assn., 1989), 152–83; S. Lehne, *The New Covenant in Hebrews* (JSNTSup, 44; Sheffield: Sheffield Academic Press, 1990); B. Lindars, "Hebrews and the Second Temple," in W. Horbury (ed.), *Templum Amicitiae* (JSNTSup, 48; Sheffield: Sheffield Academic Press, 1991), 410–33; G. W. MacRae, "Heavenly Temple and Eschatology in the Letter to the Hebrews," *Semeia* 12 (1978): 179–99; D. Peterson, *Hebrews and Perfection: An Examination of the Concept of Perfection in the "Epistle to the Hebrews"* (SNTSMS, 47; Cambridge: Cambridge Univ. Press, 1982); J. Schaefer, "The Relationship between Priestly and Servant Messianism in the Epistle to the Hebrews," *CBQ* 30 (1968): 359–89; K. Schenck, "Keeping His Appointment: Creation and Enthronement in Hebrews," *JSNT* 66 (1997): 91–117; J. M. Scholer, *Proleptic Priests: Priesthood in the Epistle to the Hebrews* (JSNTSup, 49: Sheffield: Sheffield Academic Press, 1991); D. A. deSilva, *Despising Shame: Honor Discourse and Community Maintenance in the Epistle to the Hebrews* (SBLDS, 152; Atlanta: Scholars Press, 1995); and D. Worley, "God's Faithfulness to Promise: The Hortatory Use of Commissive Language in Hebrews" (Diss., Yale Univ., 1981; Worley's analysis of the possession language in Hebrews particularly influenced my reading of Hebrews).

For critical commentary and full bibliography, see H. W. Attridge, *The Epistle to the Hebrews*, ed. H. Koester (Hermeneia; Philadelphia: Fortress Press, 1989); G. W. Buchanan, *To the Hebrews* (AB; Garden City, N.Y.: Doubleday, 1972); P. Ellingworth, *Commentary on Hebrews* (NIGTC; Grand Rapids: Eerdmans, 1993); and W. L. Lane, *Hebrews*, 2 vols. (WB; Waco: Word Books, 1991). For a more general and readable treatment, see V. C. Pfitzner, *Hebrews* (Nashville: Abingdon Press, 1997).

21. 1 Peter

FIRST PETER'S PLACE in the canon undoubtedly owes something to its attribution to the apostle who walked with Jesus and who was one of the pillars of the early Christian community. But since other writings bearing the same apostle's name did not enter the canon (*The Gospel of Peter*, *Apocalypse of Peter*), a greater reason for this writing's authority is its intrinsic merit. Martin Luther included it among the NT writings that "show thee Christ" (German Bible, 1522).

Understanding 1 Peter presents the opposite problem from understanding Hebrews. With Hebrews, the problem is coming to grips with the reshaping of so complex a symbolic world that its shared traditions are not immediately visible. With 1 Peter, the problem is that its distinctive voice might be missed, at first reading, because it shares so much common tradition. Having another letter in the canon also attributed to Peter (2 Peter) does not help, for its appearance is so drastically different as to raise more questions than it answers. The real character of 1 Peter yields only to repeated and careful reading; in the space here available I will examine certain critical questions that emerge from the description of the text itself.

Literary Form and Relationships

First Peter has the appearance of being a real letter. Because of its heavy use of baptismal imagery, some have thought that it originated as a paschal liturgy or even a baptismal ritual. It has also been considered a homily (on Psalm 34) preached on the occasion of baptism. Whatever its antecedents may be, 1 Peter bears the marks of representing a genuine piece of epistolary correspondence. The greeting (1:1-2) is classic. The addressees are "exiles of the Dispersion [Diaspora]" and the "elect." They live in the provinces of Pontus, Galatia, Cappadocia, Asia, and Bithynia. This is, then, a general letter, addressed to a wide group of early Christian communities and, consequently, lacking reference to local circumstances of specific churches. The odd geographical sequence of provinces may indicate the route of delivery. The author is identified simply as "Peter, an apostle of Jesus Christ" (1:1). He later calls himself a "fellow elder and witness of [or, to] the sufferings of Christ" (5:1).

A blessing formula—"Blessed be God" (1:3-9)—follows the greeting (cf. 2 Cor. 1:3-7; Eph. 1:3-14). First Peter's style makes the exact determination of transitions difficult, but the blessing is followed by a statement (1:10-12), leading to the body of the letter (1:13). The author's careful use of connectives throughout the letter makes for a fairly seamless fabric. The repetition of "I exhort"—the first time to all the readers (2:11), the second time to the leaders (5:1)—is probably of greater structural significance than the frequently observed transition in 4:11-12. The final remarks in 5:12-14 are brief, but tell us something of the author's circumstances. He sends greetings from the "fellow-elect sister" in "Babylon" (5:13), which probably means the church at Rome (cf. Rev. 17:1, 5). He has with him Mark, whom he calls "my son" (5:13), and he is writing "through Silvanus" (5:12). He characterizes his epistle as one that "exhorts and bears witness that this is the true grace of God" (5:12).

However straightforwardly the letter presents itself, its origin and authorship are not entirely clear. An ancient tradition associates a Mark with Peter in Rome (see Eusebius *Ecclesiastical History* II.14-15). Mark is, of course, one of the most common names in the Roman Empire. Still, the only Mark we know in the NT is the cousin of Barnabas and occasional companion of Paul (cf. Acts 15:37; Col. 4:10; Phlm. 24; 2 Tim. 4:11). We also know something of a Silvanus (or Silas). He began as a delegate of the Jerusalem church (Acts 15:22-24) and after Paul and Barnabas split (over Mark!), he became Paul's co-worker in ministry (Acts 15:40), spending part of the time with Timothy (Acts 17:14-15; 18:5). With them, he helped evangelize Corinth (2 Cor. 1:19). He also co-sponsored the two Thessalonian letters (1 Thess. 1:1; 2 Thess. 1:1). Thus, Silvanus is clearly part of the *Pauline* mission.

The connection to Pauline Christianity appears to extend beyond the simple use of names. It has been said that if the letter did not claim to be from Peter, no one would doubt it came from Paul. This somewhat exaggerated assertion is supported by the dense midrash found in 1 Pet. 2:4-10, which uses the same Scripture texts as Rom. 9:25-33. The language, such as "die to sin and live to righteousness" (2:24; cf. Rom. 6:2, 11), "put to death in the flesh, but alive in the spirit" (3:18; cf. Rom. 6:10; Eph. 2:18), and "Jesus Christ, who has gone into heaven, and is at the right hand of God, with angels, authorities, and powers subject to him" (3:22; cf. Phil. 2:10-11; Col. 2:15; Eph. 1:20-21), certainly seems to echo Paul. So does the description of gifts in 4:10-11 (cf. Rom. 12:3-8). Despite these sometimes striking resemblances, however, the writer of 1 Peter gives such language his own distinctive turn.

Besides, there are even more substantive contacts with the Letter of James. Among many small points, there is the remarkable parallelism in the discussion of "faith tested by trials" in 1 Pet. 1:6-8 and James 1:2-4 (cf. also Rom. 5:1-5). Even more impressive is 1 Pet. 5:5-9, in which there is a point-by-point correspondence to James 4:6-10, down to the citation of Prov. 3:34.

Some scholars think that such literary similarities and parallels demand the hypothesis of literary dependency. In this view either James (the usual suggestion) or Peter is dependent on Paul with the other one then dependent on it. In such theories the concept of authorship tends to be very mechanical. First Peter is also thereby pushed well beyond the point of possible Petrine authorship, particularly if Ephesians is the Pauline letter thought to be copied, as it is generally considered to be written later than Paul. A more likely hypothesis, one increasingly adopted by scholars, is that the writer of 1 Peter used liturgical, apologetic, and parenetic traditions in his composition, just as Paul and the writer of James utilized shared traditions when composing their letters. Thus, the concatenation of texts from Torah on the rejection of Israel (2:4-10) could be drawn by both Paul and Peter—and used somewhat differently by each—from an early Christian apologetic source. So also with the use of liturgical and parenetic materials. First Peter need not be dependent on any Pauline writing, so the composition's date cannot be based on the traditions it uses.

The questions we have been considering obviously touch on the issue of the letter's authenticity. Could the Peter who was a follower of Jesus have written such a letter, or must it be pseudonymous? The Greek style is sometimes thought to preclude Petrine authorship. It is spare but expressive, with a rich use of participles, generally more subtle and less vivid than the Greek of the "typical" Pauline letter. Was such finesse within the range of the Peter we know from the Gospels? He appears there as something of a rustic, whose accent betrays his origins (Matt. 26:73). Luke goes out of his way to call him and John uneducated, common men (*agrammatoi kai idiōtai*; Acts 4:13). The issue of style is not decisive, however, for the following reasons: (1) Acts is making a literary point by contrasting, in good Hellenistic style, the bold barbarians and the sophisticated authorities. The "Hebrew" learning of the "rulers, elders, and scribes" (Acts 4:5) is countered by the "ignorant" but possibly Greek-speaking Galileans. (2) All the evidence suggests that earliest Christianity grew up in a Greek-speaking environment and that from early on the language had a direct impact on the traditions and expressions of the incipient movement. Moreover, many Galilean Jews—such as Peter and John—appear to have come into regular contact with Greek-speaking Gentiles of the Decapolis and the surrounding regions through business and other transactions. (3) The letter could have been dictated to a secretary fluent in Greek. The phrase "through Silvanus" (5:12), although possibly meaning that he was the postman, could also indicate that he was the amanuensis. In the final analysis, one cannot dismiss Petrine authorship on the basis of the Greek alone, so there is nothing intrinsically improbable in Peter the apostle "writing" 1 Peter.

The Situation of the Readers

The issues of authorship and dating hinge most of all on a decision concerning the situation addressed in 1 Peter. A proper assessment of that context is also necessary to appreciate the author's response. Peter speaks to his readers as if they came from a pagan background: "As obedient children, do not be conformed to the passions of your former ignorance" (1:14); "You know that you were ransomed from the futile ways inherited from your fathers" (1:18); and "Let none of you suffer as a murderer, or a thief, or a wrongdoer, or a mischief-maker" (4:15). These remarks would ill befit those who had been observers of Torah. Peter also applies Hos. 1:9 to them: "Once you were no people, but now you are God's people" (2:10). Alerting his readers to the change required of them, Peter says, ". . . no longer live by human desires . . . The time is past for doing what the Gentiles like to do . . . They are surprised that you do not now join them in the same wild profligacy" (4:2-4; note the "no longer" in 4:2). Clearly the cumulative effect of these statements suggests that the community consisted of gentile converts from paganism.

If his readers are largely of gentile origin, however, we have hit upon another problem for the attribution of Petrine authorship. In Paul's version of the Jerusalem Council, Paul was to preach to Gentiles, and *Peter to the circumcised* (Gal. 2:8). Why then would he be writing to gentile Christians? There are some indications that Peter's ministry was extensive (cf. Gal. 2:11-12; 1 Cor. 1:12; 9:5), and the tradition of his sojourn in Rome is well attested. A circular letter to gentile churches from Peter in Rome may be surprising, but it is not impossible. We cannot allow the fragmentary nature of the information on early Christianity to dictate the patterns of the early Christian churches. Paul is most predominantly connected with the gentile mission in the NT, but there were other missionaries among the early Christians. Pauline co-workers were not the only missionaries to the Gentiles. Moreover, there is no indication that Peter actually founded the churches addressed in 1 Peter and nothing precludes a Jerusalem leader from addressing concerns for gentile churches abroad (cf. Acts 15).

The believers to whom Peter writes are clearly undergoing some form of suffering. "Various trials" are testing their faith (1:6). They are being "spoken against" as evildoers (2:12); they may "endure pain while suffering unjustly" (2:19); they may be abused and reviled and suffer (3:16). Despite this, they are not to return "evil for evil or reviling for reviling, but on the contrary, bless . . ." (3:9; cf. Rom. 12:14, 17), for if they suffer for righteousness' sake, they will be blessed (3:14; cf. Matt. 5:10). They should not be surprised at the "fiery ordeal" they are experiencing (4:12). They "share Christ's sufferings" (4:13), being "reproached for the name of Christ" (4:14) and suffering "as a Christian" (4:16).

The fact of their suffering is clear, but the nature of it is disputed. Some scholars take the expressions "for the name of Christ" (*en onomati Christou*; 4:14) and "as a Christian" (*hōs Christianos*; 4:16) as indicating an organized state persecution such as that carried out under Trajan (ca. 112) by Pliny the Younger in Bithynia, the region mentioned in 1:1. In fact, Pliny's letter to Trajan asks whether Christians should be punished for bearing "the name itself" (*Letters* X.96) or only if they are guilty of other crimes as well. In such an imperial or otherwise state-sponsored persecution, Christians were forced to choose between Christ and death. Since the first such persecution was the local one in Rome under Nero, and we know of none in the East until Domitian (93–96), and since tradition suggests that Peter was killed in Rome under Nero (64–68), the implications of this construal for both dating and authorship are obvious. The letter would date at the earliest from the end of the first century, and Peter the apostle could not have written it.

Taken as a whole, however, the letter does not support the hypothesis of a state persecution. Apart from the "fiery ordeal" (*pyrōsis*) in 4:12, which may well pick up the image of fire from 1:7 (*dia pyros*; cf. 1 Cor. 3:10-15), the author's depiction of the believers' suffering points to a context of social ostracism. Except for the term "suffering" (*paschō*; 2:19-20; 3:14, 17; 4:15, 19; 5:10), the terms used suggest verbal rather than physical attacks: "speaking against" (or, "slandering" [*katalaleō*] 2:12; 3:16), "insulting" (*epēreazō*; 3:16), "reproaching" (*oneidizō*; 4:14), and "reviling" (*loidoreō*; 2:23; 3:9). They are certainly experiencing hostility, and the possibility of random local mob action cannot be excluded. Such was the lot of Jews everywhere in the Diaspora, and of Christians from the beginning (see Acts 18:12-17; 19:23-40; 1 Thess. 2:14). Yet, overall, what seems to be at the heart of the circumstances is the internal stress experienced by intentional communities within a pluralistic context: a sense of conflict with the larger cultural and social ethos, combined with the actual confrontation from one's neighbors that naturally results from difference.

This perception is supported further by the nature of Peter's response. There is in this letter no trace of a martyr piety— seeking death in imitation of Jesus—or apocalypticism—eagerly anticipating the end of the suffering through God's cataclysmic intervention—though both are frequently stimulated by persecution. Christians are told, rather, to avoid conflict by maintaining exemplary behavior (2:12). The presupposition is that such a tactic will be effective. Peter therefore assumes the reasonableness and essential good will of the outsiders. Members of the communities should be prepared to offer a reasoned account (*apologia*) of their convictions, with gentleness and reverence, "to anyone asking of you an account" (3:15). This does not suggest a formal hearing before a judge, but a response to the individuals who are reviling them. There is the hope that the Christians' good behavior "will put those to shame" (3:16). Peter's attitude toward civil authority is utterly incompatible with a situation of state persecution. Civil government is, to say the least, viewed positively. We read in 2:13-14, 17:

> Be subject for the Lord's sake to every human institution, whether it be the emperor as supreme, or to governors as sent by him to punish those who do wrong and praise those who do right . . . Honor the emperor.

This is clearly not a description of the anti-Christ, but reflects instead the attitude of a group seeking to make a home for its new identity within a larger cultural context, rejecting but also accepting key elements of the dominant culture along the way.

Suffering is no less real, however, just because it does not lead to death. Since scorn and contempt are slow-working acids that corrode individual and communal identity, social alienation should not be viewed as a trivial form of suffering. Persecution may bring death, but the martyr has the advantage of dying with meaning. Societal scorn, however, threatens meaning and identity. In the face of outside hostility or contempt, intentional communities often respond by portraying the outsiders as evil. It is remarkable, therefore, that 1 Peter advocates such an open attitude toward the larger society, which, according to the writer, only needs to be shown that the Christian way is harmless.

The Form of Christian Identity

Peter does not attack the outsiders. Instead, he calls his readers to a renewed sense of their own identity. I will touch on three aspects of the teaching: the basis of their hope in the power of God; the implications of their baptismal initiation; and the conformity of their identity to the pattern set by Jesus. Then I will look at the communal context of the readers themselves.

Faith and Hope in God

The opening prayer is a powerful reminder of community identity. The first unit (1:3-5) is tightly structured. The statement "God has given us a rebirth" immediately implies that Christians live on a plane different both from their neighbors and from their former selves. Peter goes on to state three specific implications. First, they have a "living hope." They do not share the futile fantasies of idol worshipers; rather, Christian hope rests in a "living God," demonstrated "through the resurrection of Jesus Christ from the dead" (1:3). Second, they have by this birth come into an "inheritance," which is "imperishable, undefiled, and unfading, kept in heaven for you" (1:4). In contrast to the instability of this world, they live in reference to a future that is already realized in the life and power of God. Third, their new life has a definite goal: the "salvation ready to be revealed in the last time" (1:5). Therefore, between their "already" (rebirth) and their "not yet" (salvation), they live in hope.

Peter immediately offers two further elements of encouragement. All of the prophecies of Scripture point to his readers' own time: Christians stand, therefore, within a history that continues and is legitimated by the sacred writings of Israel. Second, these writings certify that the Christians' "trials," (1:6) like those of the Messiah (1:11), will have the effect of leading—through the "refinement" of their faith—to the "salvation of their souls" (1:9). Just as Christ's sufferings led to his "subsequent glory" (1:11), so will the suffering of the readers lead to the salvation of their souls. Here is the characteristic outlook of 1 Peter: a serene confidence that what has been given is secure and what is hoped for is certain. This is because their entire existence is shaped by the overwhelming power of God revealed in the death and resurrection of Jesus: "Through him you have confidence in God, who raised him from the dead and gave him glory, so that your faith and hope are in God" (1:21-22).

Baptism

Baptism lies at the heart of the message of 1 Peter. Baptism provides the point of transition from the old life into the new one of confidence and assurance in God, which in turn leads to living a life in imitation of Christ. First Peter's basic argument is clear, although it is complicated by some obscurity in detail.

The basic thrust of 1 Peter's argument is that what happened in Jesus extends to all Christians: "He himself bore our sins in his body on the tree, that we might die to sin and live to righteousness. By his wounds you have been healed" (2:24; cf. Isa. 53:4-5). The theme of the suffering servant runs throughout 1 Peter, and relates directly to the suffering the Christians experience. Indeed, the immediate setting for 1 Peter's treatment of Baptism occurs in the context of 3:13-18, which speaks of suffering despite one's doing good. Thus, first and foremost, the act of Baptism is used as a foil to develop the basics of the Christian life: one will suffer just as Christ suffered.

But the writer's encouragement moves in more complex directions. Just as Jesus was vindicated by the resurrection, leading to his glorification at the right hand of God and the subjection of all authorities and powers (3:22), so Christians also await the time of their vindication and glorification (1:7; 4:7; 3:13). In this way, one can see the subtle but real connection between 3:18-22 and 4:1-6. It is the power of Jesus over the cosmic forces and history that gives the believer assurance and confidence that the process begun by baptism can and will be carried out by God.

Though the cosmic and historical implications of the power of Jesus' resurrection are critical to the author's overall argument, the texts where he expresses them—3:18-22 and 4:1-6—have numerous difficulties. In 3:18-22, the author says (I am summarizing) that when Christ was made alive in the spirit, he went and preached to the spirits in prison, people who in the past had not obeyed God, all the way back to the days of Noah. With 4:1-6, the major difficulty is in verse 6: "This is why the gospel was preached even to the dead, that though judged in the flesh as humans, they might live in the spirit like God."

Both these texts are notoriously obscure. The first, 3:18-22, is often viewed as being dependent on the mythology of Gen. 6:1-4 (the "sons of God"), as it was developed in apocalyptic literature (cf., e.g., *1 Enoch* 10.5-15; 15.10-12; 18.15—19.1; 22.4). If dependent on that mythology, Jesus is here seen announcing judgment and God's victory to those demonic forces imprisoned by God. But the reference in 4:6 to the proclamation of the gospel to the dead—those "judged by the flesh"—seems, despite the reticence of many scholars, to refer to the events alluded to in 3:18-22. This at least makes sense of the literary connections. If such is the case, it is difficult to see how the "spirits" could be demonic figures. More likely, then, the "spirits" are the mass of unredeemed people who waited in captivity for God's definitive salvation; those who had rejected God's plan before the ultimate manifestation of his power in Jesus.

The author is evidently relying on a complex intersection of motifs and traditions, and it is unclear precisely what aspect of Jesus' resurrection experience is in view. His primary point, however, is that God, through Jesus, controls both history and the cosmic forces. To this end, the mythic account of 3:19-20 is fitted between two kerygmatic fragments (3:18, 21-22) that frame the assertion of the power for salvation with a confession of God's power manifest in Jesus' resurrection:

> Christ died to sins once for all, the righteous for the unrighteous, that he might bring us to God, being put to death in the flesh but made alive in the spirit . . . (cf. 4:6).

And:

> . . . through the resurrection of Jesus Christ who has gone into heaven, and is at the right hand of God, with angels, authorities, and powers, subject to him.

By the reference to the preaching to the spirits the writer means to demonstrate the ultimate nature of both these statements: the powerful nature of the salvation accomplished through Jesus' death, and the irreversible impact on history and the cosmos wrought by God through the resurrection of Jesus from the dead.

Since the larger context for these statements is the call to follow Jesus' example (3:13-18), one is not surprised to find a reference to Baptism nestled in the middle. As the writer attests, eight persons in Noah's time were "saved through water" (3:20). This seems somewhat odd, since in Genesis, it was the water that destroyed and the ark that saved (Gen. 7:17). The image, however, is governed by its immediate application, in which water serves as an instrument: "Baptism, which corresponds to this, now saves you . . . through the resurrection of Jesus Christ" (3:21). The power of God, released in the resurrection of Jesus and extending to all creation, reaches also to these new believers through the ritual of Baptism. We see, then, how the various elements come together to serve the larger argument of 1 Peter: just as Noah was separated from the wicked people of his day through "water," so Baptism now separates the believers from the world around them. What began with Jesus' death and resurrection now continues through Baptism, and what will be consummated at Jesus' return can and will be achieved by the power of God, the one who both literally and figuratively brings life out of death.

Throughout 1 Peter we see an emphasis on the immediacy of the readers' experience of a transition from the past to the present (1:12) and a stress on the now of their new identity (see 1:21; 2:10, 25; 3:21). Baptism is one moment in this transition that Peter calls rebirth (1:23). Its most extended treatment is in 1:22—2:3:

Having purified your souls by your obedience to the truth for a sincere love of the fellow Christians, love one another earnestly from the heart. You have been born anew, not of perishable seed but imperishable, through the living and abiding word of God. For all flesh is grass, and all its glory like the flower of the grass. The grass withers and the flower fades, but the word of the Lord abides forever. This is the good news which was preached to you. So put away all malice and guile and insincerity and envy and all slander. Like newborn babes, long for the pure spiritual milk, that by it you may grow up to salvation, for you have tasted that the Lord is good.

Here, obedience to the gospel proclamation and the ritual of Baptism are brought together as the pivotal experience of "rebirth" into a new identity. Peter's readers have been "purified" (1:22) and "reborn" (1:23). They have, and should continue to, "put off" their old qualities as one puts off clothing. Since they are only babes and have yet to grow into maturity, the pure spiritual milk (*logikon adolon gala*) is appropriate food (cf. 1 Cor. 3:1-3; Heb. 5:11-14). The allusion to Ps. 34:8 in 2:3 contains a deliberate pun. The Greek reads, "Taste and see that [or, because] the Lord is sweet [*chrētsos*]." The Christian messianist sees here in Scripture the plain statement: "The Lord is *Christ*."

The syntax of this verse is such that two construals are possible. Either the "guileless milk of the word" is to be the basis of their growth (i.e., "by it"), or Jesus himself is to be that basis—they have tasted, now they can grow up "in him." Both are likely implied, as Jesus is implicitly identified with the "milk." In any case, the transformation before them is one that will shape them according to the pattern of Jesus as found already in the Scripture.

Thus, 1 Peter's main concern here is the function of Baptism: the transition from the old life to the new. In a manner similar to Rom. 6, the significance of Baptism is that it denotes the beginning of a new life for those who have been immersed. It is easy to see why many scholars have considered 1 Peter a baptismal homily, since it could easily contain elements actually preached to those being baptized. Yet, as in the case of Rom. 6, the baptismal language is utilized to get at the larger issue of what it means to live the Christian life. Thus the baptismal language here functions to refocus believers back on the nature of their call: to imitate Jesus in all things.

Imitation of the Suffering Jesus

The Christology of 1 Peter is closely tied to the experience of the believers in two ways. First, in its affirmation of a personal love for Christ: "Without having seen him you love him; though you do not see him, you believe in him with unutterable and exalted joy" (1:8). Even love for God is not frequently mentioned in the NT (cf. Matt.

22:37; Mark 12:30; Luke 10:27; Rom. 8:28; 1 Cor. 2:9; 8:3; 2 Tim. 4:8; James 1:12; 2:5). Only in the Fourth Gospel (14:23-24; 21:15-16) do we find the equivalent personal response to the Messiah.

Second, Jesus is consistently portrayed as one who suffers (1:11, 19; 3:18; 4:1). Therefore, when Christians suffer for their faith, they share in his suffering (4:13). Jesus also left them an example (*hypogramma*) of his suffering, so that they might "follow in his footsteps" (2:21). Indeed, to this role they have been "called" (2:21). They are not called, however, to replicate his death; as indicated earlier, there is no martyr piety in 1 Peter. Rather, they are to imitate the *manner of his endurance* before his death. Since they may have to suffer even though they have done nothing wrong (2:19), they can therefore look to Jesus, who suffered even though he had "committed no sin; no guile was found on his lips" (2:22). And this was the manner of his suffering (2:23):

> When he was reviled, he did not revile in return; when he suffered, he did not threaten; but he trusted to him who judges justly.

Therefore, when *they* are reviled, they should not revile in return but bless (3:9) and place their trust in God (1:21).

In this description of Jesus, we see once more the pervasive influence of the passage about the suffering servant (Isa. 53:4-9) on the early Christian ethos. And although this passage is formally directed to those who are household servants (*oiketai*; 2:18), it is clear that the attitudes of patient endurance, submission, and fidelity contained in the image of the servant are intended to be ideals for the whole community (as 3:8-17 indicates; cf. esp. 3:13-17 with 2:18-23; 4:1, 12-13). Baptism has brought these believers into a new life, one that models itself on Jesus.

The Church as God's House

First Peter has no elaborate church order. Ministries of speech and service are exercised according to the "gift of God" (4:9-11). Elders are instructed by their "fellow elder" (5:1), to "tend their flock" willingly. They are not to be domineering but to be "examples to the flock" (5:3). The flock image is extended by 5:4: "When the chief shepherd is manifested you will receive the unfading crown of glory" (cf. 2:25: "You were straying like sheep but have now returned to the shepherd and guardian [bishop] of your souls").

In the biblical tradition, the flock is an image for the people of Israel (2 Sam. 5:2; Ezek. 34:12; Isa. 40:11; Jer. 31:10). One of the most distinctive aspects of this letter is its identification of *gentile* believers with Israel. The addressees are called "exiles of the Diaspora" and "elect" (1:1); they are to conduct their lives in fear "throughout the time of exile" (1:17); they are "aliens and exiles" (2:11). The scattered gentile Christians are thus viewed as the spiritual equivalent of the Jewish Diaspora, which is defined in contrast to the homeland, Palestine.

These gentile believers, of course, are not exiled from their geographical location or even, as suggested earlier, alienated in their social status. Rather, the stance they adopt toward the world alienates them in society. Wherever they live, they are not "at home," for they are fundamentally defined by their relationship to God. Their inheritance is "kept in heaven for them" (1:4; cf. Heb. 13:14; Phil. 3:20). Christians live within the world but are not completely defined by it. Therefore, they should refuse to grow comfortable within its structures, for they are called by one who transcends the world's measure. In this sense, the gentile Christians inherit the attributes of Diaspora Judaism.

First Peter sees no tension between believing and unbelieving Jews; the sort of historical tension that characterizes Romans 9–11 is not found in this letter. For the first time in the NT, we can speak accurately of the consciousness of a "new Israel." This is shown dramatically in 2:9-10, where Peter applies the most treasured epithets of Israel directly to gentile Christians. *They* are now the "chosen race" (cf. Isa. 43:20; Deut. 7:6; 10:15), the "royal priesthood" (cf. Exod. 19:6), and "God's own people" (cf. Exod. 19:5; Isa. 43:21). The Gentiles, being called out of darkness (cf. Isa. 9:2), have now received mercy, becoming God's people as a result (cf. Hos. 2:23). This should not be construed as evidence for a later form of Christianity that was distanced both chronologically and theologically from its Jewish beginnings. Rather, it reveals what was inherent in early Christianity from the start: God was forming a new people through Christ and all those who believe—both Jew and Gentile—are God's "chosen." The emphasis on Gentiles in 1 Peter is simply a function of its situation—the letter is addressed to *gentile* communities.

The Christian community also appropriates to itself the image of the temple. It is a "house of the Spirit" where "spiritual offerings" are made to God (2:4-5). No less complex than Eph. 2:19-22, the church is here portrayed as a living place of worship built up on the "cornerstone' of Jesus. Rejected by humans, he has been made a "living stone" by God (2:4, 7-8). Although these believers are aliens and exiles with regard to the world, they have a home in God's creation: they are the house built by the Spirit of the living Lord, and God dwells in this new community just as in the temple of old.

The image of a spiritual house wherein prayers are offered to God "through Jesus Christ" (2:5) corresponds to that of the household of God (*oikos tou theou*), which consists of those who believe the "gospel of God" (4:17). Peter provides a list of duties for this household (2:13—3:7). He begins with submission to the emperor, who was regarded as the *paterfamilias* or head of the extended household of the empire (cf. Rom. 13:1), and to other civil authorities. We see at once the motivation that runs through these directives. Like the Jews of the Diaspora, Christians must show by their good behavior and domestic order that they are neither dangerous nor a threat to the social fabric.

Peter turns next to the attitudes of slaves (2:18-25), but he has no corresponding exhortation for masters. This could be an indication of the social status of many of the believers, but it could also be due to the author's desire that everyone in the community—by following in the footsteps of Christ—should cultivate the attitudes of domestic servants (*oiketai*) within the "household of God." Characteristically, women are to prefer internal to external adornment and to obey their own husbands. Husbands, in turn, are to regard their wives as "fellow sharers in the gift of life" (3:5-7). Although clearly dependent upon the larger Greco-Roman value system, these directives are given a distinctive Christian function and motivation that places them in line with the similar commands given elsewhere in the NT: the pattern of Christ dictates the pattern of church, household, and family relations.

The household duties, though, are basically outward looking, a way for the Christian Diaspora to disarm its critics. The truer norm for its internal life is the concept of holiness, which also corresponds to the notion of a spiritual temple. Christians are measured not by the standards of others but by the one who called them and gave them their new identity: "As he who called you is holy, be holy yourselves in all your conduct, since it is written, 'You shall be holy, for I am holy' [Lev. 11:45]" (1 Pet. 1:15-16). That the church should be characterized by holiness was axiomatic in the Christian movement (cf. 1 Thess. 4:3; 1 Cor. 6:9-11; 2 Tim. 1:9). Thus, Christians could not adapt themselves completely to the world. Since they were always "called by God" and always "purified by the word of truth," they would always be different. Even in the "house of God," therefore, they were not totally at home, but remained "in exile," waiting for the one who was to appear (1:7), bringing about the salvation of their souls (1:9). They could maintain the tension in confidence and hope (1:21) with the assurance (5:10) that:

> after you have suffered a little while, the God of all grace, who has called you to his eternal glory in Christ, will himself restore, establish, and strengthen you.

Study Questions

1. How does the discussion of authorship and dating of 1 Peter help illuminate the character of the letter?

2. How is suffering portrayed in 1 Peter? Does 1 Peter discuss suffering in general, or only with regard to specific circumstances?

3. What role does the discussion of baptism play in 1 Peter? Are the metaphors connected to baptism different from those used elsewhere in the New Testament?

4. How are "temple" and "household" used as metaphors in 1 Peter? For whom would these metaphors resonate?

Bibliographical Note

A survey of the data on Peter can be found in R. E. Brown et al., *Peter in the New Testament: A Collaborative Assessment by Protestant and Roman Catholic Scholars* (Minneapolis: Augsburg Pub. House, 1973); and P. Perkins, *Peter: Apostle for the Whole Church* (Columbia: Univ. of South Carolina Press, 1994). Also see J. K. Elliott, "Peter, Silvanus and Mark in 1 Peter and Acts: Sociological-Exegetical Perspectives on a Petrine Group in Rome," in W. Haubach and M. Bachmann (eds.), *Wort in der Zeit* (Leiden: E. J. Brill, 1980), 250–67; and M. L. Soards, "1 Peter, 2 Peter, and Jude as Evidence for a Petrine School," *ANRW* II.25.5 (1988): 3828–49. On the purpose and nature of the letter, see J. H. Elliott, *A Home for the Homeless: A Sociological Exegesis of 1 Peter* (Philadelphia: Fortress Press, 1981); and C. F. D. Moule, "The Nature and Purpose of 1 Peter," *NTS* 3 (1956–57): 1–11. For a good cross-section of essays on the epistle, see C. H. Talbert (ed.), *Perspectives on First Peter* (Macon, Ga.: Mercer Univ. Press, 1986).

The possible liturgical background to the letter is explored by F. L. Cross, *I Peter: A Paschal Liturgy* (London: A. R. Mowbray & Co., 1954); A. R. C. Leaney, "I Peter and the Passover: An Interpretation," *NTS* 10 (1963–64): 238–51; and T. C. G. Thornton, "1 Peter, A Paschal Liturgy?" *JTS* 12 (1961): 14–26.

The dependency of 1 Peter on Ephesians is explored by J. Coutts, "Ephesians 1:3-14 and I Peter 1:3-12," *NTS* 3 (1956–57): 115–27; and C. L. Mitton, "The Relationship Between I Peter and Ephesians," *JTS* 1 (1950): 67–73. An approach closer to mine—shared NT parenesis—is found in P. Carrington, *The Primitive Christian Catechism* (Cambridge: Cambridge Univ. Press, 1940); and A. C. Sundberg, "On Testimonies," *NovT* 3 (1959): 268–81. For the relation of 1 Peter to the gospel tradition, see E. Best, "I Peter and the Gospel Tradition," *NTS* 16 (1970): 95–113; and R. H. Gundry, "'Verba Christi' in I Peter: Their Implications Concerning the Authorship of I Peter and the Authenticity of the Gospel Tradition," *NTS* 13 (1966–67): 336–50.

Some significant thematic aspects of the letter are treated in P. J. Achtemeier, "Newborn Babes and Living Stones: Literal and Figurative in 1 Peter," in M. P. Horgan and P. J. Kobelski (eds.), *To Touch the Text* (New York: Crossroad, 1989), 207–36; F. H. Agnew, "I Peter 1:2: An Alternative Translation," *CBQ* 45 (1983): 68–73; J. K. Applegate, "The Co-Elect Woman of 1 Peter," *NTS* 38 (1992): 587–604; D. L. Balch, *Let Wives Be Submissive: The Domestic Code in I Peter* (SBLMS, 26; Chico, Calif.: Scholars Press, 1981); E. Best, "I Peter II 4–10: A Reconsideration," *NovT* 11 (1969): 270–93; O. S. Brooks, "1 Peter 3:21: A Clue to the Literary Structure of the Epistle," *NovT* 16 (1974): 290–305; W. J. Dalton, *Christ's Proclamation to the Spirits: A Study of 1 Peter 3:18—4:6,*

2nd ed. (AnB, 23; Rome: Biblical Inst. Press, 1989); J. H. Elliott, "Backward and Forward in His Steps" in F. Segovia (ed.), *Discipleship in the New Testament* (Philadelphia: Fortress Press, 1985), 184–209; idem, *The Elect and the Holy* (NovTSup, 12; Leiden: E. J. Brill, 1966); B. Gärtner, *The Temple and the Community in Qumran and the New Testament* (SNTSMS, 1; Cambridge; Cambridge Univ. Press, 1965), 72–88; D. Hill, "On Suffering and Baptism in 1 Peter," *NovT* 18 (1976): 181–89; J. Knox, "Pliny and I Peter: A Note on I Pet 4:4-16 and 3:15," *JBL* 72 (1973): 187–89; T. W. Martin, *Metaphor and Composition in 1 Peter* (SBLDS, 131; Atlanta: Scholars Press, 1992); T. P. Osborne, "Guide Lines for Christian Suffering: A Source-Critical and Theological Study of 1 Peter 2, 21-25," *Bib* 64 (1983): 381–403; B. Reicke, *The Disobedient Spirits and Christian Baptism* (Copenhagen: Munksgaard, 1946); W. L. Schutter, *Hermeneutic and Composition in I Peter* (WUNT, 2.30; Tübingen: J. C. B. Mohr [Siebeck], 1989); E. G. Selwyn, "Eschatology in I Peter," in D. Daube and W. D. Davies (eds.), *The Background of the New Testament and Its Eschatology* (Cambridge: Cambridge Univ. Press, 1954), 394–401; L. Thurén, *Argument and Theology in 1 Peter: The Origins of Christian Paraenesis* (JSNTSup, 114; Sheffield: Sheffield Academic Press, 1995); and W. C. Van Unnik, "The Teaching of Good Works in I Peter," *NTS* 1 (1954): 92–110.

For critical commentary, see P. J. Achtemeier, *1 Peter: A Commentary on First Peter*, ed. E. J. Epp (Hermeneia; Minneapolis: Fortress Press, 1996); F. W. Beare, *The First Epistle of Peter*, 3rd ed. (Oxford: Basil Blackwell, 1970); P. H. Davids, *The First Epistle of Peter* (NICNT; Grand Rapids: Eerdmans, 1990); L. Goppelt, *A Commentary on I Peter*, ed. F. Hahn, trans. J. E. Alsup (Grand Rapids: Eerdmans, 1993 [1978]); J. R. Michaels, *1 Peter* (WBC; Waco: Word Books, 1988); and E. G. Selwyn, *The First Epistle of Saint Peter* (London: Macmillan & Co., 1958). For a more general treatment, see J. N. D. Kelly, *A Commentary on the Epistles of Peter and Jude* (HNTC; New York: Harper & Row, 1969).

22. 2 Peter and Jude

THE SECOND LETTER of Peter and the letter of Jude are marginalized in the NT canon, disliked when not disowned. Even those who find merit in them do not rank them among the important NT writings. They are seldom read and less often studied. Since there is almost surely a literary connection between them, they are also invariably joined together, so that even each one's distinctive witness to the Christian faith is obscured.

They are most vigorously detested by those who see in them the exemplification of "early Catholicism." They contain nothing about church order, but most of the other themes that are typically associated with a second-generation "decline" in Christianity are found in them: faith not as existential response but as the shared belief of the community (2 Pet. 1:1, 5; Jude 3, 20); tradition as the transmission of a body of truth (2 Pet. 2:21; Jude 3); salvation as a present possession more than a future hope (2 Pet. 3:15; Jude 3); God and Christ regarded almost exclusively as Savior (2 Pet. 1:1, 11; 2:20; 3:2, 18; Jude 25); deviation from community norms being viewed as a serious offense (2 Pet. 2:17-22; Jude 12-16); and eschatology reduced to a defense of the second coming (2 Pet. 3:4-13). This portrait is, of course, a stereotype, as these same features are found in the earliest Christian writings. Moreover, the qualities of Jude and 2 Peter are not so easily reduced to formulaic assertions, but reveal much more vibrant and multifaceted dimensions.

In truth, the letters are not easy to read. They are not, first of all, pleasant reading, since they consist in large part of polemic and threat against unsavory characters. Neither are they easy to understand. In broad terms they are simple enough: both defend the common heritage against distortion and corruption. But their allusions presuppose traditions no longer fully available to us. Reading them requires a greater decoding ability than is needed for other parts of the NT. This problem is only exacerbated by their relative isolation within the NT collection: while they are clearly related to each other, their connections to other traditions are more difficult to determine.

The Documents Together

The two letters are joined by the sharing of a substantial amount of material. Jude is much shorter, consisting almost entirely of polemic. Most of Jude's material is also found in 2 Peter 2, altered and fitted within quite a different kind of letter. Was Jude written first and later incorporated into 2 Peter? Or was there dependence in the other direction, with Jude being an abbreviated version of 2 Peter 2? Despite the obvious points of contact between them, however, even the shared material is not used in an identical way, and there is the third possibility that they independently employed a common source.

Most scholars think that there is a direct literary dependence, with the direction going from Jude to 2 Peter 2. Once that is said, however, little is learned about either writing. I argue here that each has its own voice, and that Jude in particular is done a disservice by being reduced to the level of a source for 2 Peter.

Pseudonymity is generally asserted or assumed for both letters. The implications are clearly much weightier in the case of 2 Peter, since another letter attributed to Peter is also in the canon. A few scholars still support the attribution to "Simeon Peter, a servant and apostle of Jesus Christ" (2 Pet. 1:1) for both Petrine epistles. They point to 2 Pet. 3:1, which explicitly states that this is the second letter written "by way of reminder" to the readers. They observe that the autobiographical elements in 2 Peter (esp. in 1:1, 13-18) are so explicit that if it is not authentic, the letter must be considered either a deliberate forgery or a transparent and presumably harmless fiction. They note also the few thematic connections between the two letters, such as the role of prophecy in Scripture (2 Pet. 1:19-21; 1 Pet. 1:10-12) and the rescue of Noah from the flood (2 Pet. 2:5; 1 Pet. 3:20-21). Finally, they argue that the dissimilarity in the style of the letters could be due to the use of an amanuensis in 1 Peter (see 5:12).

The two Petrine letters have, however, so many and such great differences that a majority of scholars conclude that they come from different authors. Even if not a necessary conclusion, this certainly seems plausible. Barring an amanuensis, the styles are significantly different. The Greek of 1 Peter is clear and direct; that of 2 Peter is convoluted and deliberately arcane in its vocabulary. More difficult to account for are the several indications that 2 Peter derives from a second generation Christian. The author speaks of "all the letters" of "our beloved brother Paul," and whereas the second phrase might be used by Peter, the first would be very unlikely, presuming as it does a Pauline epistolary collection of some sort. These letters, furthermore, are given the status of "the other Scriptures," and a history of interpretation and misinterpretation of them is presupposed (3:15-16). The reference to the predictions made by Jesus and "your apostles" is also somewhat strange if this is itself written by an apostle (3:2), and can only be explained with some difficulty. Further, part of the problem this letter addresses is caused by a lapse of time since those predictions were made that is lengthy enough to create doubts about their fulfillment. The phrase "since the fathers fell asleep" (3:4) need not refer to the first Christian generation, but it certainly indicates a lapse of time. Finally, the two letters have a different outlook. In the face of revilement from the outside, 1 Peter offered comfort but also the exhortation to be open to outsiders. Second Peter fights deviance within the community caused by teachers seeking their prey among "unsteady souls" (2:14). In response, 2 Peter is as bellicose as 1 Peter is irenic.

The letter closest in tone and outlook to 2 Peter is, of course, Jude. This has led to the hypothesis that the "first letter" referred to in 2 Peter 3:1 was really Jude. In fact, Jude 3 can be read as though a longer exhortation on "our common salvation" was interrupted by the pressing need to deal with troublemakers. In this theory, Jude was sent off as a stopgap response to a crisis, then had its material incorporated as chapter 2 of the longer treatment that had been planned from the start. The hypothesis is clever and complicated. It requires a confusion in attribution very early in the manuscript tradition. It also demands that 2 Peter and Jude both address fundamentally the same problem; and that may be to demand too much. Moreover, one would want to know why two different pseudonyms were used rather than a common one. The theory does remind us that we know so little about these writers and their relationships that we cannot be overly confident about who wrote what and when it was written.

The claim that Jude is pseudonymous is even less illuminating. The author is a "brother of James" and a "servant of Jesus Christ" (v. 1). His readers apparently knew which James this was, but we do not. Was it James "the brother of the Lord" (Gal. 1:19; 2:9), James the son of Alpheus (Matt. 10:3; Mark 3:18), or James the Son of Zebedee (Matt. 4:21; Mark 1:19)? Was this Jude, then, himself the "brother of the Lord" (Matt. 13:55; Mark 6:3) or the apostle "Jude the son of James" (Luke 6:16; Acts 1:13; John 14:22)? There is, of course, no way of knowing. There is also no way to date the letter accurately. There is nothing about Jude that would prohibit its being a letter written by a follower of Jesus in Palestine during the first generation of the Christian movement. It was probably written before 2 Peter, whose date is equally uncertain. Certainly 2 Peter is one of the last of the NT writings to be composed, but it could well have been written before the end of the first century.

Both letters are usually included among the General Epistles, signifying that they were written for a broader readership than that of a specific community. This designation may not be accurate for either. Unlike James and 1 Peter, these letters simply do not identify their audience. But it is possible that each of them was written for a specific community addressing particular problems.

Jude

Despite the amount of space it devotes to polemic, Jude is not a direct attack on opponents. It is, rather, a letter of exhortation (*parakalōn*) written for insiders—those who are "called" (v. 1) and "beloved" (vv. 1, 3, 17, 20)—to encourage their struggle for the faith, "once for all delivered to the saints" (v. 3). Several components of a parenetic letter can be spotted (cf. discussion on 2 Timothy, pp. 433–34). The author "reminds" his readers of what they already know (v. 5) but also calls them to "remember" (v. 17) both the apostolic words that predicted the troubles they now face and the examples (*deigma*) that Scripture provides of how wicked people are always punished by God (v. 7). These examples all point to the present situation (vv. 8, 10, 12, 16, 19). After characterizing the opponents, however, Jude twice turns to the readers, "but you, beloved" (vv. 17, 20), exhorting them not to have the attitudes of the opponents.

Jude does not lack literary grace. The repetition, ". . . these are the ones . . . [*houtoi eisin*]" (vv. 8, 10, 12, 16, 19), is rhetorically effective. An effective play on the word "keeping" (using both *tēreō* and *phylassō*) runs through the letter. The addressees are those God has "kept for Jesus Christ" (v. 1). The wicked angels did not "keep" their place and were punished by being "kept" in chains (v. 6). In similar fashion, the "nether gloom of darkness" is being "kept" for contemporary rebels (v. 13). The readers are to "keep" themselves in the love of God (v. 21). And, finally, God is the one who can "keep" them from falling (v. 24).

The identity of those disturbing the community is particularly hard to determine because of the stereotypical polemic. All opponents, we have by now learned, are pleasure seekers (vv. 7–8) and braggarts (v. 16), arrogant (v. 10), rapacious (vv. 11, 16), driven by desires (v. 16), and given to nastiness (v. 4). There is no indication in this letter of false teachers or of a specific doctrine supporting such immoral behavior. The closest thing to a doctrinal comment is that some ungodly people have surreptitiously entered the community (cf. Gal. 2:4), "perverting grace into licentiousness" and "denying our only Master and Lord, Jesus Christ" (v. 4). The contemporary reader, conditioned by Paul's letters, may be tempted to understand "perverting grace" as involving a theological position, but it could also be simply a matter of behavior: the ungodly twist the gift by their licentiousness. The "denial" of the "Master and Lord" does not represent a christological position but, as in Titus 1:16, stands for a practical rejection. Just as ancient sinners, these ungodly ones reject authority (*kyriotēta*; v. 8; notice the possible play on *kyrios* ["Lord"], cf. v. 4). They deny the implications of an allegiance to God and Christ by their faithlessness, arrogance, and rebellion.

The specific injury they commit against the church is connected with their behavior at love feasts, but in a way that is left unclear, except that they apparently have too good a time (v. 12). The phrase "shepherding themselves" (v. 12) means either that they were church leaders or that they refused any guidance from authority. Otherwise, they are malcontent (v. 16) and, not surprisingly, divisive (v. 19). So inconsistent is their behavior with the life guided by the Spirit that Jude calls them "worldly people [*psychikoi*], not having the Spirit" (v. 19).

Jude's outrage is obvious. He wants to protect the church's "most holy faith" (v. 20). His readers can be comforted by the fact that the rebellious are already experiencing the consequences of their immoral behavior (v. 10) and they will surely also be punished like those God repaid in the past, who came out of Egypt but were destroyed for their faithlessness (v. 5; cf. 1 Cor. 10:1-13; Heb. 3:7—4:13). The angels (undoubtedly those of Gen. 6:1-4 and *1 Enoch*) were punished for not holding their proper place (v. 6). The cities of Sodom and Gomorrah combined lust with the breaking of natural boundaries (v. 7).

Jude's reference to the dispute between Michael and the devil over the body of Moses does not appear in Torah, but seems to come from an apocryphal work entitled the *Assumption of Moses*. The point of the reference is to underscore the "reviling speech" practiced by the opponents. Moreover, since they "walk in the way of Cain," we surmise that they are envious (cf. Gen. 4:5 LXX; 1 John 3:12). Because they are like Balaam in their desire for gain (Num. 22:7; 31:16), we know that they are avaricious. Since they also "perish in Korah's rebellion" (Num. 16:3-50), we know that they are arrogant and defiant of authority. Thus, through a variety of negative associations, the writer of Jude paints a vivid picture of the depravity of the enemies of the faith. Furthermore, the fate of Cain, Balaam, and Korah is well known from Torah, and points to the fact that the opponents in Jude will also be judged by God.

The symbols used by Jude derive from an apocalyptic context. In addition to the use of the *Assumption of Moses*, we find a direct citation from *1 Enoch* 1.9 (in vv. 14-15). The author obviously regarded him "who lived in the seventh generation after Adam" (cf. *1 Enoch* 60.8) as an inspired prophet (cf. Gen. 5:24; Heb. 11:5) and his writing as Scripture. He reminds his readers as well of Christian apocalyptic sayings, "the things said beforehand by the apostles of our Lord Jesus Christ": "In the last time there will be scoffers, following their own ungodly passions" (v. 17). The closest we come again to such a statement in the NT writings is 2 Pet. 3:3 and 2 Tim. 3:2-5.

The troublemakers are rootless—"wandering stars" (vv. 12–13). In contrast, Jude wants his readers to root themselves in the "common salvation" (v. 3). They are to be "built up" in the most holy faith. They are, in contrast to those who do not have the Spirit, to "pray in the Holy Spirit." They are to "keep" the love of God and wait for the mercy of the Lord Jesus (vv. 20–21). They are, in short, to stand fast, just as God will enable them to do (v. 24). While they maintain the integrity of their Christian identity, avoiding even the hint of corruption ("the garment spotted by the flesh"), they are also to reach out to those whom they might help (vv. 22–23):

> Convince some, who doubt; save some, by snatching them out of the fire; on some have mercy with fear.

Jude, then, is not simply about the vilification of outsiders, but the solidification of the faith of those believers inside the church. By making clear the fate of those who oppose God and by portraying in vivid terms the degrading character of those who stand outside the community, the writer both creates the motivation for obedience and, through contrast with the opponents, establishes the basic substance of faithfulness for the believer.

2 Peter

The distinctive voice of 2 Peter can be detected immediately in the use made of the material in chapter 2 that is shared with Jude. In contrast to Jude, the moral condemnation here definitely serves as a polemic against false teachers who propagate destructive doctrines (2:1). Peter also has a wordplay that illustrates the author's preoccupation throughout this section: the adversaries teach "destructive heresies," but they themselves are heading toward "destruction." Jude left the judgment of God largely implicit in his polemic, but it is this element that 2 Peter makes explicit and emphatic. The redactional interest is clear in 2:3: the opponents exploit others with false words, but the Scripture will show ("from of old") that their "destruction has not been asleep."

In the recitation of examples, 2 Peter stresses not the angels' rebellion but the fact that God did not spare them (2:4). A figure lacking in Jude is introduced in 2:5: the story of Noah shows that God saves the righteous even while the ungodly are being destroyed. The narrative of Lot demonstrates the same: Jude sees only the evil cities, but Peter gives us Lot "vexed in his righteous soul" and saved (2:7-8). Since both figures appear as examples of eschatological judgment also in Luke 17:26-32, we may have here an early Christian tradition. Yet, 2 Peter puts this tradition to a specific purpose, demonstrating that the divine judgment is both real and discriminating: the wicked are punished and the righteous saved (2:9).

After 2:10, much of the polemic matches Jude closely, but the distinctive Petrine touch is found in the donkey's voice (cf. Num. 22:21-35) by which Balaam was "rebuked for his own transgression" (2:16) and in the description of the opponents as teachers. They are trying to seduce the newly converted by promising them freedom (2:18). This freedom consists of an offer of a life free from the threat of God's presence and power. They deny divine retribution, suggesting that people can live as they please, with God powerless to respond. Licentiousness now is joined to theory as practical atheism ("the fool says in his heart there is no God," Ps. 14:1) is linked to an intellectual posture claiming God's impotence to judge the world.

Peter closes in on the opponents' self-deception. Their vaunted freedom is really a slavery to corruption (2:19). Christians who follow the false teachers end up worse off than when they were pagans (2:20). Before they converted, after all, they were ignorant. But once they have come to the knowledge of "our Lord and Savior," their apostasy is knowing and willful, and a denial of their own experience (2:21). Their leap to this alleged freedom is in reality a turning back: a habituated compulsion like that which drives dogs to eat their vomit (2:22). This intentional slander illustrates their true animal desires and nature.

Second Peter's use of this polemical material reveals both its situation and its method. A theoretical doctrine is now supporting the disruption of the newly converted, as false teachers proselytize among the naive. The writer of 2 Peter must not only slander them but must also show that their intellectual pretensions are empty. This is accomplished by showing from scriptural examples how God's judgment was effective in the past, and that it was a judgment that responded to the actions of human beings: the good were rewarded and the evil punished. The clear implication is that the readers are accountable to the living God, one for whom human actions are real and important. The point will be made even more explicit in the chapters that frame this middle section.

The Defense of God's Judgment (2 Peter 3)

Peter now answers the intellectual challenge of the opponents. Not merely the delay of the Parousia (3:3-4) is at issue, for the opponents question whether God judges at all. Both experience and reason, they claim, show that everything continues as it has from the beginning (3:4), implying a world that lies outside the power of God. The writer of 2 Peter claims that these opponents have forgotten the point of the scriptural examples (3:5): God judges and punishes the wicked. The argument of 2 Peter in 3:5-7 depends on the validity of the scriptural witness as well, but with a deeper theological connection. First, the world we inhabit is not independent or accidental; it is created by God's word—by God's freedom and power (3:5). Second, the very stuff of its making (i.e., water) can be used by God for destruction, as the Genesis story of the flood shows (3:6). Third, the same word of God remains with power to judge those who scorn it: the judgment last time was by water; next time it will be by fire (3:7; cf. 3:10, 12). God's power to judge is defended on the basis of Scripture, experience, and reason. The rationalists are wrong; God is the source of all reality and continues to shape the world freely according to the divine will. Humans are thus not on their own.

The writer of 2 Peter turns next to the deficiency in the theological imagination of the opponents. They think of God and humans in univocal terms. God, however, cannot be "tardy," for temporal categories do not apply to divinity (3:8). If we as temporal creatures cannot avoid thinking in temporal terms, we must at least qualify our conclusions by a reminder of the qualitative distance between God and humans: God's measure is not ours (3:8). Even if the time seems long to us, the judgment is no less sure. Indeed, as the tradition knows, "the day of the Lord will come like a thief" (3:10; cf. Matt. 24:43; Luke 12:39; 1 Thess. 5:2; Rev. 3:3), and when it does, there will certainly be judgment. Then, those whose only hope is placed in this world will find that hope dissolved—with the world—in fire (3:10, 12).

The writer's argument makes sense less as a comfort to those dismayed at the delay of Jesus' second coming—there is only a hint of that—than as a fundamental defense against those who, for a life of "freedom," deny God's rule. Second Peter is fundamentally a Christian theodicy. On the basis of Scripture and logic, it demonstrates that the "scorning of Lordship" (2:1) leads to a corrupt life, which also calls down on itself the very judgment it denies.

The debate here resembles that in Hellenistic philosophy between the upholders of divine providence (such as the Stoics) and its deniers (such as the Epicureans). Among Jewish sects, the Epicurean position was associated with the Sadducees, while the

Pharisees represented the defense of God's providence. The intellectual component in this discussion derives from those Hellenistic and Jewish roots rather than from a christological heresy or theosophical position like Gnosticism. Behind the question of providence, of course, is the complex issue of creation and of the relation between God and the world.

Second Peter's point, however, is not primarily an abstract one but one about "what sort of persons ought you to be" (3:11). Those who view the world as contingent and dependent on God live in accordance with that reality: in "holiness and godliness" (3:11). So the writer wants them to remain "stable" in the face of the skeptics (3:17), growing in the knowledge of "our Lord and Savior Jesus Christ" (3:18). The apparent delay of God's wrath is interpreted in traditional Jewish categories, as a sign that the living God is also loving, having forbearance. God wants humans to repent (3:9), delaying judgment in order to allow time for the human choice between life and death. It is in this connection that we find 2 Peter's fascinating reference to "all Paul's letters," containing thoughts that are sometimes difficult to understand (3:15). The theme of God's forbearance scarcely dominates the letters of Paul that we know, but the writer's essential point here is found in the letter known to the Roman church, Romans 2:3-6. As Peter puts it, the lack of punishment of the wicked within our experience is not a sign of divine impotence but mercy: "Count the forbearance of the Lord as salvation" (3:15).

Literary Form

Second Peter has been characterized as a farewell discourse in epistolary form. Thus, we find the aged apostle shortly before his death (1:14). He prepares his followers for what will happen "after his departure" (1:15). The emergence of false teachers (2:1) will alert them to the fact that these are the "last days," when such opponents were prophesied to arise (3:2-3). In the face of opposition, the faithful are to hold to the teaching that comes from him and are not to be seduced by dangerous novelty (1:12, 20-21). The appropriate understanding of the tradition is therefore critical, including the proper interpretation of Scripture. Scripture is the source of truth—and the basis of 2 Peter's argument—but it must be interpreted in accordance with the Spirit who inspired it, and that Spirit is active in the church's tradition (1:19-21). Since Paul's writings also are regarded as Scripture, the same care must be taken not to misinterpret them (3:16). Thus, measures are put in place to ensure that opponents do not distort the true foundations of the Christian faith. Here we have the development—*in nuce*—of the later Christian appeal to church tradition in its polemic with heretics, who are characterized as distorting that original truth.

Within the testamentary form, the credentials of the writer to speak authoritatively for the tradition are important. Second Peter's use of the transfiguration story (1:16-18) known to us from the Synoptic Gospels (Matt. 17:1-8; Mark 9:2-8; Luke

9:28-36), has precisely this certifying function. Whether the writer is a fictional Peter or not, a connection to an eyewitness account of the revelation of Jesus as God's beloved son is asserted. What is important is the claim to an experience of God's revelation and its being rooted in the gospel story. This is what becomes the authoritative basis for the writer's interpretation of Scripture. In contrast to the "cleverly concocted myths" (1:16) that are the sign of "false prophets" (2:1), this writer claims a share in the very story of God's personal involvement with the world, which in turn underscores the argument of chapters 2 and 3: "We have the prophetic word made more secure" (2:1).

Second Peter can be read as a farewell discourse. But in terms of its form and function, it is more accurately a parenetic letter, because of its deliberate use of memory, models, and maxims. In the author's statement of purpose (1:12-15), we see that the goal is to *remind* the readers of the truth they already know and to *motivate* them by way of that reminder: In 3:1-2, again, the writer stirs them to remembrance in order that they might *recall* the prophetic witness. On the other hand, the false teachers *forget* their past experience of forgiveness (1:9). Indeed, the opponents forget that judgment is inevitable: they *forget* the punishment of the flood (3:5).

The writer of 2 Peter wants the readers not to *forget* but to *remember* (3:8). To this end, his list of scriptural stories that illustrate God's judgment functions paradigmatically; it provides negative and positive *models*, a point that is made explicit in 2:6: "[God] made them an example [*hypodeigma*] to those who were to be ungodly." As for maxims, these are succinctly stated in the exhortation with which the author begins (1:5-7):

> Supplement your faith with virtue, and virtue with self-control, and self control with steadfastness, and steadfastness with godliness, and godliness with Christian affection, and Christian affection with love.

Thus, 2 Peter seeks not only to warn opponents of their impending fate but, even more so, to keep the believers from abandoning their faithful obedience to God. Through both positive content and negative counter-example, the letter of 2 Peter accomplishes both these ends.

Study Questions

1. What do 2 Peter and Jude share in terms of theme, perspective, and style? What do you conclude from these connections?

2. What are the most important connections between Jude and literature outside the New Testament? Are these connections in theology, vocabulary, style, theme?

3. Against whom is the polemic in these two letters directed? What sort of change are they looking for?

4. What distinguishes 2 Peter from Jude?

Bibliographical Note

On the state of research, see the older treatment by J. Rowston, "The Most Neglected Book in the New Testament," *NTS* 21 (1974–75): 554–63 (for Jude), as well as the more recent studies by R. J. Bauckham, "2 Peter: An Account of Research," *ANRW* II.25.5 (1988): 3713–52; and idem, "The Letter of Jude: An Account of Research," *ANRW* II.25.5 (1988): 3791–3826. Also see M. L. Soards, "1 Peter, 2 Peter, and Jude as Evidence for a Petrine School," *ANRW* II.25.5 (1988): 3828–49.

For an attempt to place Jude at a specific time and place in second-century Egypt, see J. J. Gunther, "The Alexandrian Epistle of Jude," *NTS* 30 (1984): 549–62. For the placement of Jude in the mission of the relatives of Jesus, see the intriguing study by R. J. Bauckham, *Jude and the Relatives of Jesus in the Early Church* (Edinburgh: T. & T. Clark, 1990). For Jude as an anti-heretical polemic, see F. Wisse, "The Epistle of Jude in the History of Heresiology," in M. Krause (ed.), *Essays in the Nag Hammadi Texts* (Leiden: E. J. Brill, 1972): 133–43.

On specific points, see J. D. Charles, "Literary Artifice in the Epistle of Jude," *ZNW* 82 (1991): 106–24; idem, *Literary Strategy in the Epistle of Jude* (Scranton: Univ. of Scranton Press, 1993); E. E. Ellis, "Prophecy and Hermeneutic in Jude," in his *Prophecy and Hermeneutic in Early Christianity* (Grand Rapids: Eerdmans, 1978), 221–36; I. H. Eybers, "Aspects of the Background of the Letter of Jude," *Neot* 9 (1975): 113–23; J. Fossum, "Kyrios Jesus as the Angel of the Lord in Jude 5–7," *NTS* 33 (1987): 226–43; S. J. Joubert, "Language, Ideology and the Social Context of the Letter of Jude," *Neot* 24 (1990): 335–49; idem, "Persuasion in the Letter of Jude," *JSNT* 58 (1995): 75–87; L. Thurén, "Hey Jude! Asking for the Original Situation and Message of a Catholic Epistle," *NTS* 43 (1997): 451–65; and A. F. J. Klijn, "Jude 5 to 7," in W. C. Weinrich (ed.), *The New Testament Age* (Macon: Mercer Univ. Press, 1984), 237–44.

Jude's use of *1 Enoch* is examined by M. Black, "The Maranatha Invocation and Jude 14, 15 (I Enoch I:9)," in B. Lindars and S. S. Smalley (eds.), *Christ and Spirit in the New Testament* (Cambridge: Cambridge Univ. Press, 1973), 189–96; C. D. Osburn, "The Christological Use of 1 Enoch 1:9 in Jude 14, 15," *NTS* 23 (1976–77): 334–41; and idem, "I Enoch 80:2–8 (67:5–7) and Jude 12–13," *CBQ* 47 (1985): 296–303. Jude's use of the Assumption/Testament of Moses is thoroughly analyzed in R. J. Bauckham's commentary, *Jude, 2 Peter* (see below), 65–76. Also see J. D. Charles, "Jude's Use of Pseudepigraphical Source-Material as Part of a Literary Strategy," *NTS* 37 (1991): 130–45; and idem, " 'Those' and 'These': The Use of the Old Testament in the Epistle of Jude," *JSNT* 38 (1990): 109–24.

For studies taking into account both Jude and 2 Peter, see M. Desjardins, "The Portrayal of the Dissidents in 2 Peter and Jude: Does It Tell Us More About the 'Godly' than the 'Ungodly'?" *JSNT* 30 (1987): 89–102; J. Knight, *2 Peter and Jude* (Sheffield: Sheffield Academic Press, 1995); and D. F. Watson, *Invention, Arrangement, and Style: Rhetorical Criticism of Jude and 2 Peter* (SBLDS, 104; Atlanta: Scholars Press, 1988). On the issue of polemic in both letters, see A. du Toit, "Vilification as a Pragmatic Device in Early Christian Epistolography," *Bib* 75 (1994): 403–12.

The connections of 2 Peter to 1 Peter are considered by G. H. Boobyer, "The Indebtedness of 2 Peter to Peter," in A. J. B. Higgins (ed.), *New Testament Essays* (Manchester: Manchester Univ. Press, 1959), 34–53; and W. J. Dalton, "The Interpretation of 1 Pet. 3:19 and 4:6: Light from 2 Peter," *Bib* 60 (1979): 547–55. On the connection of 2 Peter to Jude, see J. Kahmann, "The Second Letter of Peter and the Letter of Jude: Their Mutual Relationship," trans. P. Judge, in J.-M. Sevrin (ed.), *The New Testament in Early Christianity* (BETL, 86; Leuven: Leuven Univ. Press, 1989), 105–21; and J. A. T. Robinson in his *Redating the New Testament* (Philadelphia: Westminster Press, 1976), 140–99.

For a general treatment of the setting of 2 Peter, see T. Fornberg, *An Early Church in a Pluralistic Society: A Study of 2 Peter* (ConBNT, 9; Lund: CWK Gleerup, 1977). One of the more important studies on 2 Peter is J. H. Neyrey, "The Form and Background of the Polemic in 2 Peter," *JBL* 99 (1980): 407–31, to which my treatment of 2 Peter is indebted. For individual points, see H. C. C. Cavallin, "The False Teachers of 2 Peter as Pseudo-Prophets," *NovT* 21 (1979): 263–70; J. D. Charles, *Virtue Amidst Vice: The Function of the Catalog of Virtues in 2 Peter 1.5-7* (JSNTSup, 150; Sheffield: Sheffield Academic Press, 1997); F. W Danker, "2 Peter 1: A Solemn Decree," *CBQ* 40 (1978): 64–82; D. Farkasfalvy, "The Ecclesial Setting of Pseudepigraphy in Second Peter and Its Role in the Formation of the Canon," *SC* 5 (1985): 3–29; A. B. Kolenkow, "The Genre Testament and Forecasts of the Future in the Hellenistic Jewish Milieu," *JSJ* 6 (1975): 57–71; J. H. Neyrey, "The Apologetic Use of the Transfiguration in 2 Pet. 1:16-21," *CBQ* 42 (1980): 504–19; C. P. Thiede, "A Pagan Reader of 2 Peter: Cosmic Conflagration in 2 Peter 3 and the *Octavius* of Minucius Felix," *JSNT* 26 (1986): 79–96; and G. Vermes, "The Story of Balaam in the Scripture: Origin of Haggadah," in his *Scripture and Tradition in Judaism* (SPB, 4; Leiden: E. J. Brill, 1961), 127–77. For 2 Peter as the quintessential example of "early Catholicism," see E. Käsemann, "An Apologia for Primitive Christian Eschatology," in his *Essays on New Testament Themes* (Philadelphia: Fortress Press, 1982 [1964]), 169–95; and C. H. Talbert, "II Peter and the Delay of the Parousia," *VC* 20 (1966): 137–45.

For recent scholarly commentary with full bibliography, see R. J. Bauckham, *Jude, 2 Peter* (WBC; Waco: Word Books, 1983); and J. H. Neyrey, *2 Peter, Jude* (AB; New York: Doubleday, 1993). Also helpful for its critical notes is the older commentary by J. B. Mayor, *The Epistles of Jude and II Peter* (Grand Rapids: Baker Book House, 1979 [1907]). For more general treatment, see J. N. D. Kelly, *The Epistles of Peter and Jude* (HNTC; New York: Harper & Row, 1969).

23. The Letter of James

THE LETTER OF James still suffers from the marginal status assigned it by one wing of the Protestant Reformation. Martin Luther did not include it among the "chief proper books"; compared to them, he thought it a "right strawy epistle." Since it contained "many a good saying," however, it could be read with profit (*German Bible*, 1522). Luther disliked James because he thought it contradicted Paul's teaching on faith-righteousness (in 2:14-26) and because it did not have any "gospel character," that is, did not "show thee Christ."

Luther's view was not that of the early church, which regarded James as a powerful moral exhortation. Its late formal canonization in some areas was due not to concern about its content but to doubts about its apostolic origins. Luther's opinion was not shared by other reformers—John Calvin, for instance, wrote an appreciative commentary on James. Influential critics of the nineteenth century, however, forcefully adopted Luther's position, interpreting this letter as part of the historical dialectic between Pauline and Judaizing movements in early Christianity (cf. Gal. 2:12; Acts 15:1). Although such an interpretation is rarely advanced today, James continues to be studied almost entirely in terms of its relationship to Paul. This is doubly unfortunate. It unfairly makes Paul the sole criterion for canonical acceptance, and it disastrously reduces the significance of James to a few misunderstood verses. Those who have managed to read James on its own terms discover in it a writing of rare vigor and life, which interprets the "faith of our Lord Jesus Christ of glory" (2:1) in a distinctive and compelling manner.

Literary Form and Relations

We know little about the circumstances of the composition. The author is James, "a servant of God and of Jesus Christ" (1:1), sufficiently well known to be recognizable even by such a modest designation (cf. Jude 1). Of course, we no longer can recognize the author so simply, be he the "brother of the Lord" (Mark 6:3; Gal. 1:19; 2:9; 1 Cor. 15:7; Acts 12:17; 15:13; 21:18) or another James of the first generation (Matt. 10:3; Mark 15:40; Luke 6:15-16; Acts 1:13). One must also entertain the possibility that this is a pseudonymous writing, one which intended to make reference to a noteworthy individual—probably, then, the brother of Jesus, one of the pillars of the early church. We simply cannot know which is the case.

The details in the letter are of little help. The Greek is generally good Koine; there are some Semitisms, and a degree of literary artistry as well. The letter uses some rather rare vocabulary as well as the rhetorical techniques of assonance and alliteration. A few small details suggest a Palestinian (1:1; 5:17-18) or at least Jewish-Christian provenance (2:1-7). But like the varying depictions of the audience as (possibly) both poor and wealthy (1:9-10; 2:5-7), oppressing and oppressed (5:1-6), persecuted (1:2-4, 12-15; 5:7-11) and belligerent (4:1-2), such evidence is difficult to weigh, for the author is less likely to be reflecting local circumstances or crises than employing literary allusions or *topoi* (see, e.g., 3:13—4:10).

An argument for the pseudonymity of the letter usually depends on the Hellenistic character of the writing—meaning its good Greek and its knowledge of Greek literary and philosophical turns—which presumably would place it late and outside Palestine. A second basis for supposing pseudonymity is James' presumed knowledge of Paul's teaching, reflected in the discussion of faith and works in 2:14-26. The first point does not have merit. A first-generation Christian in Palestine could write good Greek and know something of the commonplaces of Greek rhetoric and philosophy. The Pauline connection, furthermore, is less certain than is sometimes supposed. True, the combination "faith and works" is otherwise known to us only in Paul. But then we do not know all of the earliest Christian writings nor all the traditions of first-century Judaism (see e.g., the often overlooked reference in 1 Macc. 2:51-52). And it is at least possible that this writing could have stimulated Paul's combination rather than the reverse.

But these observations still miss the mark, for they allow the presumption to stand that James and Paul were addressing the same topic. They were not. In Paul, the contrast between faith and works was one between the faith in and of Jesus, as a soteriological principle, and the observance of the commandments of Torah, with its promise of life. The contrast in James is one that was common among Hellenistic moral philosophers: between speech and action (cf. Epictetus II.1.31; II.9.21; III.22.9; Dio *Oration* 35.2). James decries a merely verbal profession of faith that fails to be lived out in appropriate behavior. The Paul who called for "faith working through love" (Gal. 5:6) would certainly agree, and indeed he makes the explicit declaration that humans are judged by God on the basis of their "works" (Rom. 2:6-8). In James, it is faith itself that works, not faith that is abandoned in favor of human achievement.

The Pauline connection, therefore, does not help us place James. This writing could be the earliest of all the Christian compositions, penned by the brother of Jesus, or it could be one of the latest of the canonical witnesses, written pseudonymously by a teacher (see 3:1) concerned about the misuse or misunderstanding of Pauline slogans. Whichever is the case, it is certainly not a monument to a Judaizing movement. The letter represents a form of Christian self-understanding neither Pauline nor anti-

Pauline but uniquely its own. Its spiritual heirs are the Christian writings usually called "apostolic," namely, *1 Clement* and the *Shepherd of Hermas*.

The epistolary character of James is restricted to its greeting, addressed to the "twelve tribes of the Dispersion" (1:1). As in 1 Pet. 1:1-2, the designation seems to refer less to the readers' ethnic background or geographical location than to their connection to the traditions of Torah. The greeting also suggests that James is not responding to the problems of a specific community but addressing issues pertinent to a general Christian readership. James thus appears not to be a real piece of correspondence but a composition fitted to the epistolary genre, although this point is sometimes debated.

Though James, like Hebrews, does not appear to be a sustained homily, much of it has a definite homiletic character. It is liberal in its use of the direct address: "brethren," and "beloved brethren" (1:2, 16, 19; 2:1, 5, 14; 3:1, 10; 4:11; 5:7, 9, 10, 12, 19). It also contains several essays or discourses that are relatively free-standing, such as those on faith (2:14-26), the use of the tongue (3:1-12), and envy (3:13—4:10). In them, we find stylistic features associated with the diatribe, such as the use of rhetorical questions (2:14, 21; 3:13; 4:1, 5), the presence of an imagined interlocutor (2:18-19; 4:13; 5:1), and apostrophe (4:4). These give James much of its color and life. They also remind us that, as with Paul's use of the diatribe form, we are dealing primarily with a *teaching* instrument.

Apart from the essays, James consists mainly of short sayings and commands, which sometimes alternate with longer exhortations. Finding the argument in James is not always easy, for this writing is closer to the form of Jesus' "discourses" in the Gospel of Matthew or to the type of units one finds in the Book of Proverbs. Similar to Jesus' words in the Synoptic Gospels, many of the letter's aphorisms—shorter, seemingly independent units—are connected by catchword association, particularly in chapter 1. The first exhortation, "Count it all joy [*charan*]" (1:2), picks up the "Greeting [*chairein*]" of 1:1. Then, the "steadfastness [*hypomonē*]" of 1:3 is linked to the "steadfastness [*hypomonē*]" of 1:4; the "lacking [*leipomai*]" in 1:4 to the "lacking [*leipomai*]" in 1:5; the "asking [*aiteō*]" in 1:5 to the "asking [*aiteō*]" in 1:6a; and the "doubting [*diakrinomai*]" in 1:6a to the "doubting [*diakrinomai*]" in 1:6b.

Such a mechanical arrangement at first appears not only artificial but also deficient in providing a context for interpreting specific sayings. But even a purely formal ordering of disparate sayings brings them into a greater whole and provides a new constellation of meaning. The teaching in James cannot be reduced to a single proposition or argument, and, as in all wisdom literature, its reference is not to logic but to the observable realities of life: statements are to be tested not against their internal consistency but against their correspondence to reality. The writer thus creates a larger framework for a variety of the premises of Christian theology and ethics.

The "structureless structure," furthermore, holds mainly for the first chapter. Isolated sayings do occur later (see 4:11-12; 5:12), but short discourses dominate the rest of the composition. When the sayings of chapter 1 are examined more closely, in fact, they appear as an index to topics treated more expansively in the essays. The theme of enduring trials (1:2-4, 12-15) is developed in 5:7-11; the contrast of rich and poor (1:9-11) is treated more fully in 4:13—5:6; the proper use of the tongue (1:19-21) is greatly expanded in 3:1-12; the emphasis on doing the word (1:22-26) is enlarged in 2:14-26; the nature of true wisdom (1:5-8, 16-18) is argued in 3:13—4:10; and the prayer of faith (1:6-7) is amplified in 5:13-18. Thus, as recent studies of James have increasingly demonstrated, there is an overall coherence to the letter's argumentation.

In the broadest sense, then, James is a form of moral exhortation or parenesis. The dominant mood is the imperative. The readers are reminded of what they already know and urged to act on that knowledge (see 1:3; 3:1; 4:4; 5:20). The "mirror of forgetting" in 1:23-24 at least suggests the motif of memory, so familiar in parenesis. Moreover, the author presents models for his readers to emulate: Abraham (2:21-23), Rahab (2:25), Job (5:11), and Elijah (5:17). These elements are not so tightly structured and connected as in 2 Timothy, and it thus is more precise to designate James as parenesis within an epistolary framework rather than as a parenetic letter per se.

The writer of James is one of the premier teachers in the NT canon, and therefore this letter is most fairly compared to other parenetic material—not Romans 3–5 but Romans 12–13; not Ephesians 1–3 but Ephesians 4–6; not Galatians 1–4 but Galatians 5–6. James does not develop theories but reminds the readers of accepted truths; it does not expound theology but exhorts to virtue. And as is often seen in such moral teaching, the materials used by James are not necessarily specific to the Christian movement but employ the rich materials made available by the wisdom tradition of Judaism and Hellenism alike. Parallels to the sayings in James are found not only in Torah but in the Jewish writings of Philo, the *Testaments of the Twelve Patriarchs*, and the *Sentences of Pseudo-Phocylides*, as well as in Greco-Roman moralists like Seneca, Dio Chrysostom, and Epictetus.

But James is not so traditional that it fails to be distinctively Christian, although some scholars have suggested this option. Luther, we remember, saw no "gospel character" in it. Some scholars have suggested that James originated as a Jewish writing that was taken over with only minor editing for use by Christians. The name Jesus occurs only twice (1:1; 2:1), each time with sufficient awkwardness to make the suggestion of an interpolation at least possible. James certainly has nothing about the death and resurrection of Jesus, except by a stretch in the interpretation of 5:11. But neither for that matter does Romans 12–13. A distinction is important here. The search for what is distinctively Christian—that is, idiosyncratically Christian—should neither be identified totally with a search for Christology nor become the basis for a theological judgment on the value of a particular text. Too often, a subtle form of theological anti-Judaism enters into these discussions, as though only what differed from Judaism was valuable in earliest Christianity. But that direction leads toward Marcionism.

In fact, however, James has many specifically Christian features, beginning with the ambiguity of his use of "Lord." The "Lord Jesus Christ" (1:1) and "Lord of glory" (2:1) certainly presume the resurrection and exaltation traditions of early Christianity (cf. Phil. 2:9-11). In other cases, James's use of "Lord" wavers tantalizingly between reference to God and reference to Christ, probably deliberately bringing both into play (see esp. 5:7-8 and 5:14-15). Other turns of language may not be exclusive to the Christian movement but are certainly comfortable within it (see, e.g., 1:16, 21; 2:7; 5:6). The most striking connection to Paul does not come in the discussion of faith and works (2:14-26), but in those places where both Paul and James presuppose the attitudes of traditional Jewish piety (cf. James 1:2-4/Rom. 5:1-5; James 2:5/Rom. 8:28 and 1 Cor. 2:9; James 2:10/Gal. 5:3). Even more impressive are the multiple points of contact with 1 Peter—James 1:1/1 Pet. 1:1; James 1:2/1 Pet. 1:6; James 1:3/1 Pet. 1:7; James 1:10-11/1 Pet. 1:24; James 4:6-10/1 Pet. 5:5-9; James 5:20/1 Pet. 4:8—illustrating a mutual indebtedness to common Christian tradition.

James's most fascinating appropriation of Christian traditions is found in the awareness and use of what we know as the gospel tradition, particularly the sayings of Jesus, although in James these are unattributed. The command to pray without doubting (1:5-6) is very similar to that given by Jesus (Matt. 7:7-8; Mark 11:23). The threat that "the judge stands at the door" (5:9) echoes Jesus' words in Matt. 24:33. The prohibition of oaths (5:12) is remarkably close to that spoken by Jesus (Matt. 5:34-37). The threat against rich oppressors (5:1-2) resembles the woe against the rich in Luke 6:24. Above all, James contains in 2:8 the command to love one's neighbor as oneself from Leviticus 19:18, which is enunciated by Jesus as well (Matt. 22:39; Mark 12:31; Luke 10:27). Many other turns of speech remind the discerning reader of the teachings of Jesus, especially those found in Matthew's Sermon on the Mount (cf. James 1:22/Matt. 7:26; James 2:13/Matt. 5:7; James 2:14/Matt. 7:21; James 3:18/Matt. 5:9; James 5:17/Luke 4:25).

In James, the experience of Jesus and the symbolic world shared with Judaism stand in much less dialectical tension than in Paul. The term "Judaizing," however, is totally inappropriate. That term has significance only where Christ and Torah are opposed as soteriological principles, such as we find in Paul's discussion. James knows nothing of that opposition. The writer can consequently speak naturally of the law of freedom (1:25; 2:12), by which is not meant the ritual demands of Torah in and of themselves, but a new understanding of *all* of Torah provided by the teachings of Jesus.

James makes available to Christians, first, the *wisdom tradition* of Torah not only because wisdom is thematically important (1:5; 3:13-18), but because its exhortations resemble most the practical ethical instructions found in Proverbs, Ecclesiastes, and Sirach. James also transmits to Christians the *prophetic tradition* of Torah. The writing contains many allusions to Hosea, Isaiah, and Zechariah (see 1:9-11; 2:23; 3:18; 4:4, 8, 14; 5:2, 4); the voice of Isaiah and Amos can be heard in the call to conversion in 3:13—4:10, as well as in the condemnation of oppressors in 5:1-6. James also reinterprets Torah as law in a way unique among the NT writings, mediating the *halachic tradition* to Christians. The way this is accomplished will be more obvious as we turn to the teaching of James.

The Practical Faith of Christians

James teaches an ethics of faith and love. The term "faith" does not carry the heavy theological weight here that it does in Paul. But neither does it mean merely an intellectual assent to divine revelation. James caricatures such a faith as empty and dead: "You believe that God is one; you do well. Even demons believe and shudder" (2:19). James's own rich understanding of faith is found in the four OT figures who stand as models at the climax of three thematic developments, beginning respectively in 2:1, 5:7, and 5:13. Abraham and Rahab exemplify the *works of faith* (2:23-25). Job is the model for the *endurance of faith* (5:11). Elijah provides the example for the *prayer of faith* (5:17-18).

As a moralist, the writer of James has concern for the way people carry out in action what they profess in speech. The contrast drawn is not between faith and law but between the empty profession of religion and its living expression. The target is the double-minded person (*dipsychos*; 1:7-8; 4:8) who claims allegiance to God but lives by the world's standard. James regards such a person as self-deluded (1:26-27):

> If anyone thinks oneself religious but does not govern the tongue, that one is deceiving oneself and one's religion is empty. Pure religion pleasing to God and the Father is this: to visit orphans and widows in their affliction, and to keep oneself unstained from the world.

And like all moralists, James questions the "usefulness" or "profit" of convictions if they are not put into practice (2:15-16):

> If a brother or sister is ill clad and in lack of daily food, and one of you says to them, "Go in peace, be warmed and filled," without giving them the things needed for the body, what does it *profit*?

It is in this framework that 2:14 must be understood: "What does it *profit* . . . if a person says he or she has faith, but has not works? Can their faith save them?" For James, a faith that is not articulated in action is "empty" (2:20), as "dead" as a body lacking its spirit (2:17, 26)—no faith at all. Since faith is manifested in a person's way of acting (2:18), James declares boldly of Abraham that he was justified by his works (2:21). It is imperative, however, to read as well the next verse, for the participial phrase that follows shows exactly what sort of work James had in mind. Not observance of

Torah but the radical obedience of *faith* itself is intended. Scripture makes plain that Abraham's call to sacrifice his son Isaac was a testing of his *faith* (Gen. 22:1-19). The sacrifice of Isaac was faith in action (cf. Heb. 11:17-19). James says therefore that faith was active with Abraham's works (or, literally in the Greek: "faith co-worked the works") and it was *faith* that was "perfected" by this "testing" (see 1:2-4). Faith is the subject of both parts of 2:22.

James also offers both Abraham and Rahab (cf. Heb. 11:31) as examples of how faith expresses itself in "works of mercy." The background to this allusion is the "hospitality" shown by both Abraham (Gen. 18:1-15) and Rahab (Josh. 2:1-21) when they gave shelter, food, and protection to those in need. They demonstrated how the verse that opens this section is fulfilled: "Judgment is without mercy to the one who does not show mercy; but mercy conquers over judgment" (2:13). As we see in 2:16-17, it is the lack of mercy that rejects needy fellow believers with only an empty and ineffectual word. Such is the counterexample of "dead" and "useless" faith: speech without action. In James, faith is spelled out by endurance, prayer, and acts of mercy. What, then, is the meaning of law?

The Law of Liberty

James sees the law of liberty (or, freedom [*eleuthēria*]) as the measure of Christian identity (1:25), the norm for life, and the basis for judgment: "So speak and act as ones who will be judged by the law of freedom" (2:12). This law includes the Decalogue—the "ten words" revealed through Moses (2:11; cf. Rom. 13:8-10)—kept in its entirety (2:10). But the specific law that structures the kingdom of God (2:5) is the royal law (or, "law of the kingdom" [*nomos basilikos*]; 2:8): the law of love for one's neighbor. Paul refers to this as the fulfillment of the whole law (Rom. 13:10; Gal. 5:14) and Jesus announced it as next to "love of God" (Matt. 19:19; 22:39; Mark 12:31; Luke 10:27).

Leviticus 19:18, "You shall love your neighbor as yourself," is pivotal within James. The writer seems deliberately to have based some of the text on a careful reading of that commandment of Torah in its original context. When it is said, "If you really keep the royal law *according to the Scripture*, you do well" (2:8), the writer means for it to be taken literally: the text of Leviticus gives guidance to the full meaning of love for one's neighbor. Leviticus 19:15 forbids judging with partiality; James says discrimination in judging is incompatible with faith (2:1-12). Leviticus 19:16 forbids slander and evil talk in the land; James 4:11-12 does not allow evil speech against a fellow believer. Oppression and the withholding of wages from laborers are forbidden by Leviticus 19:13 as they are also by James 5:4. Vengeance and grudge-holding are discouraged by Leviticus 19:18a; James 5:9 warns against holding grudges against one another. Leviticus 19:12 forbids the taking of oaths, just as James 5:12 does. In Leviticus 19:17, one is told to reason with neighbors rather than hate them; James 5:20 commands turning back an erring Christian from his or her way. We notice as well that each of these negative commands in James is accompanied by an explicit mention of law or judgment (2:9-13; 4:11; 5:9, 12).

The reading of Leviticus, however, is qualified by an understanding of life given by Jesus the Messiah. Thus partiality is prohibited because of its incompatibility with the faith of "our Lord Jesus Christ" 2:1). The prohibition of slander and judging therefore recalls the command of Jesus in Matt. 7:1. The command not to hold a grudge stands under the imminent coming of Jesus as judge (5:8). The prohibition of oaths is found also in Jesus' mouth (Matt. 5:34-37). The ideal of fraternal correction also reflects a saying of Jesus (Matt. 18:15; Luke 17:3). Thus, we find in James a messianic halachic midrash: the implications of the law of love are found enunciated in the text of Torah and ratified by the teaching of Jesus.

Life in Community and World

The perfection James seeks from the readers (1:4) is one not of solipsistic virtue but of faith and mercy directed toward the neighbor. The neighbor is first of all the brother and sister (see 2:15) who meet together in the "assembly" (2:2). This community is aware of bearing a special name (2:7) and promise (2:5). It is called not to destroy but to build up its common identity (4:11; 5:9). The members pray for others as well as themselves (5:16). They confess sins to each other and engage in mutual correction (5:15-16, 19-20). The elders of the church are to gather at the bed of the sick person for prayer and anointing (5:14-15).

Because it uses more universal traditions, however, James also reaches beyond the enclave of the assembly to the larger world. More than other NT writings, James provides the basis for a social ethic. Religion is to be proved, for example, by the care taken for those perennially dispossessed in a patriarchal society: widows and orphans (1:27). The sick too are to receive care (5:13-16). James does not allow for the compatibility of discrimination on the basis of social status with the identity of this community (2:1-7). War and murder are traced to their roots in envy and the insatiable desire for more pleasure, possessions, and power (3:18—4:3). Those doing business in the world are called to recognize the arrogance implicit in untrammeled entrepreneurship (4:13-17). Those who for profit practice oppression, fraud, and murder are condemned (5:1-6). These principles are available, James suggests, not by contemplation of the "natural face" but of the "perfect law of liberty" (1:23-25).

Friendship with the World and God

The ethic in James is, moreover, in the strictest sense a theological ethic. All human activity is referred to the God who is creator, sustainer, savior, and judge. "Every good and perfect gift" comes from God (1:17). As humans were created in God's image (3:9), so have Christians been "chosen" as heirs of the kingdom (2:5) and "brought forth by the word of truth, that we should be a kind of first fruits of [God's] creatures" (1:18). Christians have been shaped by the "truth." Therefore, they must put away all wickedness (1:21) and above all any form of deceitful or destructive speech (1:13, 19, 26; 2:16; 4:11, 16; 5:12). James considers the control of speech the hardest of all human skills (3:1-12), making it all the more necessary that believers "receive the implanted word which is able to save [their] souls" (1:21).

Humans are not independent moral agents, for they are defined by their relationship to God. James thus does not think in terms of virtue and vice, but in terms of "sin leading to death" (1:15; 5:20) that is sponsored by the devil (4:7), and of the "crown of life" that God has promised to those who are faithful (1:12). While James has no Christology to speak of, it is among the richest of NT writings in its theology, which is found above all in the form of warrants for right action (see 1:5, 12, 13, 16, 20, 27; 2:5, 11, 13, 19, 23; 3:9; 4:4, 6, 8, 10, 15; 5:4, 9, 10, 11, 15).

The living God alone saves and destroys (4:12), gives grace to the humble while opposing the proud (4:6), answers the prayer of individuals (1:5) and of the community (5:15), and turns testing into the maturity of faith (1:2). James knows that "if we approach God, God will approach us" (4:8), for God is a "Lord rich in mercy and compassion" (5:11). God is also the ultimate judge whose recompense is measured by the way humans treat one another: "Judgment is without mercy to one who has shown no mercy; yet mercy triumphs over judgment" (2:13).

Judgment is most clearly spelled out in James's attack on oppressors. James shares with the Lukan beatitudes and woes (Luke 6:20-26) the perspective of the kingdom: the poor are blessed and the rich are filled with woe (1:9-11; 2:6). In the present scheme of things, however, the rich dominate. They oppress the poor and drag them into court (2:6). They defraud their laborers by withholding their wages, even murdering them (5:1-6). James does not call for a revolt but for patience and endurance like that of Job (5:7-11). The reason for this stress is that a reversal is certain: the oppressors will taste the misery they now inflict on the poor when the Lord returns (5:8), for God is the final Judge of all (4:12).

James understands that human behavior flows from a fundamental commitment of the heart. A person can choose to respond to the gift of the word (1:21), the wisdom from above (3:15), and the Spirit God made to dwell in humans (4:5), living according to the measure of the kingdom and the perfect law of freedom. Or one can choose to live by the measure of the "world," which is opposed to that of God. It is characterized by self-aggrandizement, untrammeled desire, pleasure seeking, and above all, envy (1:14, 21; 3:14, 16; 4:1-3). In the call to conversion (3:13—4:10), James puts this choice in the evocative language of friendship. Those who are double-minded, who want to be friends with everyone and live by both measures at once, cannot: they must choose (4:4):

> Faithless creatures! Do you not know that friendship with the world means enmity with God? Therefore whoever wishes to be a friend of the world makes oneself an enemy of God.

If the "friend of the world" lives by the measure of selfishness and envy, the "wisdom that comes from below" (3:14-16), how does the "friend of God" live? He or she imitates Abraham and lives by the perspective of faith: "Abraham believed God and it was reckoned to him as righteousness; and he was called friend of God" (2:23). This person lives not in arrogance (4:6, 16) but in humility (4:7, 10), knowing that one's life comes not from his or her own efforts but from God's gift. Such a one has the simplicity that comes from purity of heart (4:8), and seeks not selfish benefit but the fulfillment of the perfect law of freedom (2:8): love for the neighbor in faithful obedience to God.

Study Questions

1. What accounts for the marginalization of James in the history of interpretation? If you had been asked, would you include it in the New Testament? Why or why not?

2. What are the most important connections between James and the teachings of Jesus?

3. What books in the Old Testament is James most like? Why?

4. What does James mean by "friendship with the world" (4:4)?

Bibliographical Note

For studies pertaining to James, the brother of Jesus (the person most frequently associated with the Epistle of James), see R. J. Bauckham, *James* (New York: Routledge, 1999); J. Painter, *Just James: The Brother of Jesus in History and Tradition* (Columbia: Univ. of South Carolina Press, 1997); and R. B. Ward, "James of Jerusalem," *ANRW* II.26.1 (1992): 792–810. For the letter in recent research, see P. H. Davids, "The Epistle of James in Modern Discussion," *ANRW* II.25.5 (1988): 3621–45.

For recent studies dealing with the general framework of James, including specific issues of interpretation, see J. B. Adamson, *James: The Man and His Message* (Grand Rapids: Eerdmans, 1989); T. B. Cargal, *Restoring the Diaspora: Discursive Structure and Purpose in the Epistle of James* (SBLDS, 144; Atlanta: Scholars Press, 1993); and T. C. Penner, *The Epistle of James and Eschatology: Re-reading an Ancient Christian Letter* (JSNTSup, 121; Sheffield: Sheffield Academic Press, 1996). For a discussion of context and related issues, see L. T. Johnson, "The Social World of James: Literary Analysis and Historical Reconstruction," in L. M. White and O. L. Yarbrough (eds.), *The Social World of the First Christians* (Minneapolis: Fortress Press, 1995): 178–97.

The Pauline connection is variously pursued by V. Limberis, "The Provenance of the Caliphate Church: James 2.17-26 and Galatians 3 Reconsidered," in C. A. Evans and J. A. Sanders (eds.), *Early Christian Interpretation of the Scriptures of Israel: Investigations and Proposals* (JSNTSup, 148; Sheffield: Sheffield Academic Press, 1997), 397–420; J. G. Lodge, "James and Paul at Cross-Purposes? James 2:22," *Bib* 62 (1981): 195–213; and D. O. Via, "'The Right Strawy Epistle' Reconsidered: A Study in Biblical Ethics and Hermeneutics," *JR* 49 (1969): 253–67. Aspects of genre are treated by L. G. Perdue, "Paraenesis and the Epistle of James," *ZNW* 72 (1981): 241–56; and F. O. Francis, "The Form and Function of the Opening and Closing Paragraphs of James and I John," *ZNW* 61 (1970): 110–26.

For the relation of James to various aspects of the symbolic world, see W. R. Baker, *Personal Speech-Ethics in the Epistle of James* (WUNT, 2.68; Tübingen: J. C. B. Mohr [Siebeck], 1995); M. A. Jackson-McCabe, "A Letter to the Twelve Tribes in the Diaspora: Wisdom and 'Apocalyptic' Eschatology in the Letter of James," *SBLSP* 35 (1996): 504–17; L. T. Johnson, "James 3:13—4:10 and the *Topos PERI PHTHONOU*," *NovT* 25 (1983): 327–47; idem, "The Mirror of Remembrance (James 1:22-25)," *CBQ* 50 (1988): 632–45; idem, "Taciturnity and True Religion: James 1:26–27," in D. L. Balch et al. (eds.), *Greeks, Romans, and Christians* (Minneapolis: Fortress Press, 1990): 329–39; idem, "The Use of Leviticus 19 in the Letter of James," *JBL* 101(1982): 391–401; J. Marcus, "The Evil Inclination in the Epistle of James," *CBQ* 44 (1982): 606–21; P. Minear, "'Yes and No': The Demand for Honesty in the Early Church," *NovT* 13 (1971): 1–13; S. E. Porter, "Is *dipsychos* (James 1,8; 4,8) a 'Christian Word'?" *Bib* 71 (1990): 469–98; O. J. F. Seitz, "The Relationship of the Shepherd of Hermas to the Letter of James," *JBL* 63 (1944): 131–40; and M. H. Shepherd, "The Epistle of James and the Gospel of Matthew," *JBL* 75 (1956): 40–51.

For studies of particular themes and passages, see L. Alonso Schökel, "James 5,2 [sic; = 5:6] and 4,6," *Bib* 54 (1973): 73–76; W. R. Baker, "'Above All Else': Contexts of the Call for Verbal Integrity in James 5.12," *JSNT* 54 (1994): 57–71; J. H. Elliott, "The Epistle of James in Rhetorical and Social Scientific Perspective: Holiness-Wholeness and Patterns of Replication," *BTB* 23 (1993): 71–81; L. E. Elliott-Binns, "James 1:18: Creation or Redemption?" *NTS* 3 (1957): 148–61; P. H. Davids, "James and Jesus," in D. Wenham (ed.), *Jesus Tradition Outside the Gospels* (Sheffield: JSOT Press, 1985),

63–84; P. J. Hartin, *James and the Q Sayings of Jesus* (JSNTSup, 47; Sheffield: Sheffield Academic Press, 1991); L. T. Johnson, "Friendship with the World/Friendship with God: A Study of Discipleship in James," in F. Segovia (ed.), *Discipleship in the New Testament* (Philadelphia: Fortress Press, 1985), 166–83; J. A. Kirk, "The Meaning of Wisdom in James: Examination of a Hypothesis," *NTS* 16 (1969): 24–38; S. Laws, "'Does Scripture Speak in Vain?': A Reconsideration of James 4:5," *NTS* 20 (1974): 210–15; S. R. Llewelyn, "The Prescript of James," *NovT* 39 (1997): 385–93; L. Thurén, "Risky Rhetoric in James?" *NovT* 37 (1995): 262–84; D. J. Verseput, "Reworking the Puzzle of Faith and Deeds in James 2.14-26," *NTS* 43 (1997): 97–115; R. B. Ward, "Partiality in the Assembly," *HTR* 62 (1969): 87–97; idem, "The Works of Abraham: James 2:14-26," *HTR* 61(1968): 283–90; D. F. Watson, "James 2 in Light of Greco-Roman Schemes of Argumentation," *NTS* 39 (1993): 94–121; and idem, "The Rhetoric of James 3.1-12 and a Classical Pattern of Argumentation," *NovT* 35 (1993): 48–64.

The classic commentary on James is M. Dibelius, *James: A Commentary on the Epistle of James*, rev. H. Greeven, trans. M. A. Williams (Hermeneia; Philadelphia: Fortress Press, 1976 [1964]). The older commentary by J. B. Mayor, *The Epistle of St. James*, 3rd ed. (London: Macmillan & Co., 1913), also contains much useful information. For more recent critical commentary, see P. H. Davids, *Commentary on James* (NIGTC; Grand Rapids: Eerdmans, 1982); L. T. Johnson, *The Letter of James* (AB; New York: Doubleday, 1995); and R. P. Martin, *James* (WBC; Waco: Word Books, 1988). More straightforward guides through the text are S. Laws, *A Commentary on the Epistle of James* (HNTC; San Francisco: Harper & Row, 1980), and R. W. Wall, *Community of the Wise: The Letter of James* (Valley Forge, Pa.: Trinity Press Int'l, 1997).

In this miniature from a twelfth-century Latin manuscript of Josephus's Antiquities *(Paris, BN, Lat. 5047), Christ is portrayed as the Creator-Logos and Cosmocrator. The central medallion is Sapientia–Ecclesia ("Woman Wisdom–Church"); the surrounding medallions depict the six days of creation.*

PART SIX

The Johannine Traditions

CERTAIN PERSISTENT FEATURES are present in all the NT writings. They show the impact of the religious experience and continuing societal struggles of Christian groups. They are written for churches, and they use traditions developed by communities. At the same time, none is simply a community production. The traditions are selected and shaped by creative minds. Neither Gospels nor letters conform to the grid of a collective mentality. All bear the impress of poets, preachers, and prophets.

In all the NT writings, furthermore, the figure of Jesus Messiah stands in tension with the symbols employed by the community to interpret his significance for their lives. Jesus is the catalyst for reflection and its organizing principle. The symbols drawn from Torah and from the wider cultural milieu are not incidental: they are the medium of community self-understanding and communication. But knowledge of the symbolic world in all its dimensions does not lead directly to the understanding of any NT writing. In them, every symbol is reshaped by the experience of the crucified and raised Messiah and the conviction that he is the living Lord.

The writings of the Johannine tradition reflect these same tensions between community, symbolic world, and the interpretation of Jesus. So fascinating in fact are the puzzles presented by these documents that the focus of our discussion must be resolutely set from the beginning. The Johannine documents can be read for the reconstruction of the believing community that was their setting—an interesting subject but not our own. They can be studied to determine which symbols from which part of Hellenistic culture most affected these believers—a more plausible project but still not ours. They can, finally, be read as witnesses to the life of God in Jesus. This is the real subject of the writings and is our subject as well. Our way into that task will be cleared, however, by a few remarks about the other two projects I have mentioned, both of which concern the complex relationship of these writings to a possible history of a Johannine Christianity.

The Johannine traditions are found in a narrative in the gospel genre, three letters, and an apocalyptic document. The way that these writings—the Gospel of John or the Fourth Gospel (FG); 1, 2, and 3 John; and the Apocalypse or Book of Revelation—relate to each other, to the rest of the NT witnesses, and to the community for which they were written have been variously described.

Most scholars consider the FG and the three letters to have the same provenance if not authorship. Many also conclude on the basis of genre, style, and theology that Revelation must belong elsewhere. Yet Revelation provides the only firm connection between these writings: the tradition's eponym (John) and communities in a specific location (Asia Minor). Without Revelation, the Johannine community floats entirely free of any historical constraints. The Book of Revelation, furthermore, despite the transmutations effected by the apocalyptic form, shares far more points of fundamental outlook and symbolism with the Johannine writings than with any other part of the canon.

Nevertheless, much of the contemporary discussion of Johannine Christianity tends to leave Revelation to one side, concentrating almost entirely on the FG and the three letters. The implications of this omission for any reconstruction of a Johannine history are obvious. Apart from the random patristic references to John and the Ephesian church, all evidence for Johannine Christianity comes from these writings. The excision or inclusion of a single document, as well as assumptions about the order of the writings' composition, dramatically affects any history based exclusively on them. Circularity in such circumstances, of course, cannot be avoided. Hence the intrinsic fragility of such reconstructions, which a short example can illustrate.

It is plausible to regard some version of the FG as the oldest Johannine writing, bearing within itself intimations of tensions that later, as the letters would indicate, divided the community. But nothing prevents us from reversing this order of composition, in which case the FG would appear quite differently: it was written in light of the problems reflected in the epistles. The progression would become even more uncertain if Revelation were included. Indeed, it is questionable whether the writings ought to be viewed as necessarily representing sequential stages in a particular community's existence: reconstructing history based purely on a few literary sources is a hazardous enterprise.

What we mean by "Johannine community" is also uncertain. Is something more meant than simply the Johannine readership? If so, what form of social organization is implied? Some have taken the FG as suggesting in its communal preoccupations and language the setting of an intentional group like a school. Others have observed that the letters appear to presuppose a cluster of loosely organized local house-churches. Still others have remarked that all these writings share fundamentally sectarian attitudes: they define themselves as much by what they oppose as by what they affirm. Are these various characterizations compatible? Do they fit with the impression given by

Revelation of many communities in diverse cities, some of which are in competition with other groups?

Not only is the social organization of the Johannine community or communities unclear, the ethnic background of the believers is as well. Once more, the writings tell us various things: there was at some point conflict and separation from some form of Judaism (John 9); there was a Samaritan connection (4:4-42); Greek-speaking Gentiles or Diaspora Jews were brought into the fold (7:35; 12:20), so that even common Hebrew terms required translation (1:38, 41, 42; 9:7); and some of the believers referred to outsiders as "pagans" (3 John 7). What this information amounts to, however, is less than clear.

If the documents do not provide a history or sociology of Johannine Christianity, they do reveal something of the great tensions that existed for those Christians who read these extraordinary texts. More than any other part of the NT, the Johannine writings bear the signs of the stress and conflict that so deeply influenced the interpretation of the "good news" in Jesus.

In no other NT writings do we find the ideal of peace, unity, and love so clearly expressed, and yet so evidently at odds with the community's own experiences. All of these writings make a sharp distinction between insider and outsider. In the Gospel, the historical conflict between the Jews and Jesus represents the continuing conflict between the world and Jesus' "friends." In the letters, the issue of who is an insider and who is not tragically spells out the division *within* the community, as different parties claim exclusive rights to the truth. And in Revelation, the battlefront is double: there is hostility and persecution from the world outside, as well as division and corruption from within.

Their origin aside, then, the symbolism of all these Johannine writings is bold and clear: there is good and evil, darkness and light, truth and falsehood, death and life, them and us—and one must choose sides in these historic and cosmic conflicts. In each of these writings, furthermore, it is the figure of Jesus that stands at the center of the conflict. In the Gospel, allegiance to him demands separation from the synagogue but also invites identity as his friend. In Revelation, true witness to Jesus against falsehood and idolatry continues his witness to the truth, leading, perhaps, to a death like his. In the letters, the community divides precisely over the proper understanding of Jesus. The dialectic, therefore, between experience and interpretation, present in all the NT writings, is manifestly and indelibly impressed into the very fabric of the Johannine symbolic world.

24. The Gospel of John

THE CENTERPIECE OF the Johannine writings is the Fourth Gospel (FG), a witness to Jesus so simple and powerful that its influence on Christian consciousness is unsurpassed. Like the Synoptic Gospels, the FG tells the story of Jesus' life, death, and resurrection. Matthew, Mark, and Luke gave distinctive shape to the same basic storyline by editing and altering their shared traditions. John more fundamentally transmutes the story as a whole, giving the term "Gospel" still another dimension.

The FG has always been attributed to a John, whom Irenaeus says was the disciple of the Lord who wrote at Ephesus (*Against Heresies* III.1.1). The narrative itself invites speculation concerning an anonymous disciple (John 1:35-42; 18:15-18) identified only as one "whom Jesus loved" (13:23; 19:26; 20:2-9). He is identified as the authoritative witness behind the writing (19:35; 21:20-24). Since nothing is ever said in this Gospel about a John, and the Synoptic sons of Zebedee are mentioned only incidentally (21:2), it is not unreasonable to identify the beloved disciple with John the son of Zebedee (cf. Matt. 10:2; Mark 3:17; Luke 6:14; Acts 1:13), who was a "pillar" of the first Jerusalem church (Acts 3:1; 4:13; 8:14; Gal. 2:9). The beloved disciple is important because he roots this version of Jesus' story in an eyewitness account. The readers of the FG regarded him as their "founder" (19:26), and his death was sufficiently unexpected that it created the need for interpretation (21:20-23).

The claim to such firsthand traditions was once regarded as entirely fictitious, but the FG shows as good a knowledge of first-century Palestinian terrain, customs, and ideology, as do the Synoptics (see, e.g., 3:23; 4:5, 9, 20, 25; 5:16-18; 6:1, 59; 9:11; 11:54; 12:20; 18:13). Archaeology in fact has verified some specific facts that earlier critical scholars had dismissed as spurious (see 5:2; 19:13).

The FG does not, however, appear simply as the account of an eyewitness. Rather, it reveals several stages of composition. The most obvious is the addition to the story in John 21, after the solemn conclusion of 20:30-31. The scribal uncertainty about the placement of the passage about the adulterous woman (7:53—8:11) also testifies to a certain fluctuation in the text. Not surprisingly, the nature and number of redactional stages have been vigorously debated by scholars. One of the simplest theories is that an originally radical version was thoroughly reworked by a later "ecclesiastical redactor," who modified the spiritualizing tendencies of the original along more orthodox lines. As a consequence, the "real" FG can be recovered only by excerpting and rearranging our present canonical text.

Other hypotheses are considerably more complex if no less fragmenting, positing as many as five stages of composition. Many contemporary scholars are convinced that in one stage of the process an original "signs source" (the ending of which was 20:30-31) was joined to a "sayings source." The putative discovery of seams and sources is sometimes also connected to "stages in the community's life." The text is thereby treated as an archaeological site whose layers reveal buried social history. The reconstructions are, however, sufficiently numerous and unconvincing to diminish confidence in the method itself.

The FG we now read does not have the look of a composition by committee or of a haphazard outcome of heavy-handed editing. Only to minds obsessively concerned with a certain level of consistency are seams always indicators of sources. To other readers, they appear as literary signals, and in their view the FG does not require reconstruction. It stands today as it has for two thousand years, as a coherent, profound, and challenging witness, itself sufficient evidence that the Johannine community had within it at least one great theologian and writer.

The FG has always been considered the latest of the Gospels. Some nineteenth-century critics argued it was a late second-century production. Their dating was based on the assumption that its symbols came from Hellenistic philosophy, which, it was believed, would necessitate its composition outside Palestine, and that its high Christology demanded a long period of development. The archaeological discovery of Greek manuscripts of John's Gospel in Egypt dating from the late (P[75], P[66]) or even early second century (P[52]) makes a late second-century date impossible. One closer to the turn of the first century is more likely. Neither redactional nor doctrinal elements require a long period of development. John's Christology is certainly different from that of Paul or Hebrews, but it is no "higher" than any other NT writing. The compositional complexity of John is no greater than that of Matthew or even Mark. And in the light of better historical knowledge it is no longer necessary to postulate a long sojourn in the Hellenistic world to account for John's symbols.

The symbols we encounter in the FG are certainly different from those in the Synoptic Gospels. In this case, the term "symbolic world" is accurate, for moving from the Synoptics to John is truly like entering another universe. Jesus does not speak in neat aphorisms or in parables of the kingdom. He does not meet Pharisees and Sadducees in short bursts of controversy. Instead we find longer discourses, heavy with abstract substantives like "light," "truth," and "life," being combined in complex patterns with verbs like "believing," "seeing," and "knowing." Jesus speaks more in allegories than parables, and his speech points to himself rather than to a kingdom—all metaphors meet in him. His self-referential speech describes an ethical and possibly even a metaphysical dualism: humans are faced with a choice between what is from above and what is from below, what is light and what is dark, what is true and what is false, what leads to death and what leads to life (see 3:5-21; 5:30-47; 12:44-50). This dualistic universe is intersected by the "man from heaven" (3:31), who enters the world to reveal himself and the one who sent him (14:9-11) before returning to his previous place (16:28). The path of descent and ascent defined by the revealer provides the way for his chosen ones to follow (14:6-7).

It is small wonder scholars have tried to find in one tradition or another the key to unlocking the Johannine symbolic system. Older studies saw a Platonic dualism and traces of Stoicism's *logos* theology. The history of religions school found the symbols in John closest to those of gnostic writings, whether Hermetic or Mandean. Recent scholarship has reaffirmed native Jewish elements, not only in obvious resemblances to Philo Judaeus but to Pharisaic preoccupations as well. Further, the perceptions of the Samaritans, particularly their "prophet like Moses" messianism, can be traced in the FG. Virtually all of John's dualistic elements can be found even more sharply present in the sectarian writings from Qumran. Thus, the interconnections are at once diverse and multiple, and, at the same time, baffling.

Although such investigations have not isolated a single dominant influence on the symbols of the FG, they have made three aspects clear. First, all elements of John's symbolic structure are present and important in the Judaism of first-century Palestine. Second, no less than in other NT writings, the symbols of Torah play a critical role. Third, the symbols are given their coherence by the figure of Jesus.

The reason for the writing of the FG is as complex as its symbolic world. Suggestions on its purpose have not been lacking, but they have tended to exaggerate one thematic element to the neglect of others. Some have thought the Gospel to have primarily an apologetic function, asserting the superiority of Jesus over John (1:6-8, 15, 19-28; 3:22-30; 5:35; 10:41) or demonstrating Jesus' messianic credentials to Jewish unbelievers (5:39-47; 7:21-52; 10:31-38; 12:37-50). Others have emphasized John's persuasive functions, suggesting that it was written to persuade Diaspora Jews not yet cut off from the synagogue, or even Gentiles, to convert to the Christian messianic movement (see 1:9, 38, 41, 42; 4:21-26; 7:35; 9:22; 10:16; 11:52; 12:20-22, 32, 42). Still others have emphasized its polemical aspects, arguing that it was written to undermine perceived heresies in Christology (such as docetism) or in certain forms of Gnosticism. It is doubtful that a composition as rich as this can be reduced to a single function. Indeed, even the Gospel's own stated intention (20:30-31) has a certain ambiguity:

> Now Jesus did many other signs in the presence of his disciples, which are not written in this book; but these are written that you may believe that Jesus is the Christ, and that believing you may have life in his name.

That signs should lead to belief and belief to life is clear enough. The ambiguity comes in the precise construction given to the phrase "that you may believe." We are not certain whether the tense of the verb should be present or aorist. If it is aorist, then the phrase would read, "that you might believe," and the purpose would be conversion.

But if it is present tense, then the phrase would read, "that you might go on believing," and the purpose would be reinforcement and encouragement. The present tense is the reading better supported by the manuscript evidence, and the whole tenor of the Gospel suggests less a document for proselytism than one of pastoral concern for the converted. One of the most perceptive observations on the literary structuring of John suggests that the very movement of the story corresponds to the perceptions of a community that defined itself through opposition to unbelievers, and that the complex coding of the narrative prohibits understanding by those who do not share the symbolic system and convictions of the community.

John and the Synoptic Tradition

The special character of John's Gospel can be seen immediately when it is systematically compared to the Synoptic Gospels. So many and great are the points of divergence that one might at first wonder whether they really tell the same story.

Both chronology and geography have a decidedly different character. Matthew and Luke provide an account of Jesus' human origin through Joseph and Mary; John's prologue (1:1-18) gives an account of Jesus' divine origin as the "Word" (*logos*). In all the Synoptics, Jesus' ministry begins in Galilee, and then moves dramatically toward Jerusalem for his one fatal visit to that city. In the FG, Jesus moves back and forth between Galilee and Judea during the course of his ministry. He appears first in Judea, then goes to Galilee (1:28, 43). He makes a brief trip to Jerusalem for a Passover (2:13). While there, he purifies the temple (2:13-22), an event the Synoptics make the climax of his ministry rather than the hallmark of its initiation. Jesus then goes from Jerusalem to Judea (3:22) and from Judea back to Galilee through Samaria (4:3, 45). He returns to Jerusalem for another feast (5:1). For his second Passover (6:4), however, he is back in Galilee (6:1). He goes to Jerusalem again for the Feast of Booths (7:1-10), and is still there for the feast of the rededication of the temple (10:22). He goes from Jerusalem to Judea (10:40), where he sojourns until returning for his final Passover (12:12). This review indicates three ways in which the Johannine presentation of Jesus' ministry differs from the Synoptic version. First, his ministry centers in Judea, not in Galilee. Second, his ministry lasts three years, not one. Third, his ministry is inextricably connected to the observance of the great pilgrimage feasts of Judaism.

Even the time of Jesus' death is different. In contrast to the Synoptics, Jesus is crucified on the day of preparation for the Passover (19:31); and thus the last supper is not a Passover meal in the FG. In contrast to the Synoptics, Jesus is already anointed before his burial (19:39-42) and Mary Magdalene comes to the tomb alone and discovers Jesus missing (20:1) before she tells Peter and John (20:2-10). The pattern and order of the resurrection-appearance stories also differ. Jesus appears once to Mary alone (20:11-18) and twice to his disciples in Jerusalem (20:19-29). His sole Galilean appearance is at the seaside rather than on a mountaintop (21:1-14). It is impossible, in short, to reconcile fully the account of Jesus' life and death in the FG with that in the Synoptics.

A more significant difference in the FG is the character of Jesus' deeds and words. These will demand closer attention. For now, I simply note that the exorcisms, so important in the Synoptics, are missing altogether. Jesus does perform three healing miracles and one resuscitation, but not nearly the number of miracles attributed to him in the Synoptics. Further, his actions are called signs (*sēmeia*) and have an obvious symbolic importance. Regarding his words, in the mouth of Jesus we find none of the Synoptic parables, although Jesus does use some "figures" (10:6; 16:25). Rather, Jesus carries out lengthy discourses, and even the confrontations with his opponents become occasions for disputatious monologues in which not Jesus' deeds so much as the claims implicit in them are at issue (see esp. 5:10-47; 6:41-65; 9:35—10:39).

Despite the differences, the FG also contains definite points of contact with the Synoptic tradition. Specific miracles in John show a greater or lesser resemblance to miracles in the Synoptics: the healing of the official's son (4:46-53; cf. Matt. 8:5-10 and Luke 7:1-10); the healing of the paralytic (5:2-9; cf. Mark 2:1-12; pars.); the multiplication of the loaves (6:1-13; cf. Mark 6:34-44; pars.); and the walking on the water (6:16-21; cf. Mark 6:45-51; Matt. 14:22-27). Other events are found both in John and the Synoptics: John's baptism (1:25; 3:23; cf. Mark 1:4; pars.) and arrest (3:24; cf. Mark 1:14; pars.); Peter's confession (6:68-69; cf. Mark 8:29; pars.); the purification of the temple (2:14-16; cf. Mark 11:15-18; pars.); the anointing at Bethany (12:1-8; cf. Mark 14:3-9; Matt. 26:6-13; and possibly Luke 7:36-50); the entry into Jerusalem (12:12-15; cf. Mark 11:9-10; pars.); and, above all, the Passion narrative (18:1—19:42), which, despite its distinctive elements such as the amplified role of Pilate (18:29—19:22), is recognizably the same as in the Synoptics, having a particularly large number of contacts with Luke's version.

Other thematic elements that the Synoptic Gospels present as single events can be discerned in the FG in a more diffused manner. Thus, the Synoptic temptation account (Mark 1:12-13; pars.) finds its equivalent in John 6:14-15 and 7:3-4, and the agony in the garden (Mark 14:32-42; pars.) in 12:27-29 and 18:11. It is even possible to detect the reworking of Synoptic sayings material in places such as John 1:42; 12:24-26; 13:12-20; and 21:22. Despite these few examples, however, most of what is in John is not in the Synoptics, and vice versa.

The question of the relationship of the FG to the Synoptics has a long history of discussion. Some patristic writers considered John as the *supplement* to the synoptic tradition (see, e.g., Eusebius, *Ecclesiastical History* III.24.7-13, and Augustine, *On the Harmony of the Evangelists* IV.7, V.8). If the assertion is understood only in terms of the FG containing material not found in the Synoptics, it is an inaccurate description of the relationship. But in a deeper sense, the FG does perform just such a supplemental function to the rest of the gospel tradition: it does this through explicit *theological reflection in the form of a story*. Several distinctive features of the FG will make this clear.

First, John is an ecclesiastical Gospel. Now, the word "church" never occurs in it, and there is nothing in the Gospel about church organization. Yet no other Gospel so consciously states its relationship to the community of its readers and its narrator's own point of view. This self-consciousness is shown by the narrator's reason for writing (20:30-31), by the way the future presence of Jesus among his followers is promised before his death (14:25-31; 15:1-11), and, above all, by the way there is repeated acknowledgment of the greater insight that came about through the resurrection (2:17-22; 12:16; 14:25; 20:9). Because of these clues to the reader, John is free to collapse the distance between the story of Jesus and the story of the church. While there is the distinct awareness of the difference between Jesus' time and the time of the church (14:15-31; 16:7-15, 19-28, 31-33), the reality of the *now* permeates the narration of the *then* in much more explicit and conscious ways than was possible in the Synoptics. The signs worked by Jesus are recognizable as the church's own signs. The conflicts faced by Jesus are those faced by the community (9:22; 12:42): "If the world hates you, it hated me first" (15:18).

Second, John is a sacramental Gospel. While it contains no institution account except that of the foot washing (13:1-14), the Gospel is pervaded by a consciousness of liturgical traditions, both of the Jews—shown by its fascination with Jewish feasts—and of the Christian community. The FG shows how the sacraments of the church are rooted in the signs of Jesus and, at a deeper level, in the sign that Jesus himself is. The sacramental character of the FG has been disputed. But whether original or due to a later redactor, the present text bears language unmistakably suggestive of Baptism (3:5; 7:37-39; 19:34) and the Eucharist (6:35-58).

Third, John's eschatology is predominantly realized. As with the sacramental character of the Gospel, this feature is really another aspect of the ecclesiastical focus of the FG. While there are important statements that maintain the future expectation of resurrection and judgment (5:28-29; 11:24), the major emphasis of the Gospel is that the end time is a present reality. For the community of believers, "the time is coming and *now is*" (4:23; 5:25). This point, however, requires qualification. Unlike Gnosticism, the FG does not suggest that the believers themselves are living the heavenly life in their present. The point, rather, is that the offer of life and the critical judgment of the world have definitively taken place in the coming of Jesus. He is "the resurrection and the life" (11:25), and God's judgment on humans is based on their response to him (5:25-27). And, at least in the sense that those who believe in him can be called "children of God" (1:12), they too share in eternal life in the present (3:18-21): "This is eternal life, that they know thee the only true God and Jesus Christ whom thou hast sent" (17:3). This is not such a strange phenomenon if we remember that the Qumran community also held a realized eschatology in complete concert with futuristic expectations. From the standpoint of the cult, church, and community, the emphasis is on the realized nature of the present experience of God. From the standpoint of the enemies of the community and the motivation for moral action, the stress is placed on the coming judgment of God.

Fourth, John's presentation of Jesus is more symbolic than literal. The previous three points find their summation in this one, which requires an even more careful qualification. A fuller presentation of John's Christology will follow. For the moment we should note that his portrayal of Jesus is sometimes called a "naive docetism." That is, Jesus is *said* to be human but he does not really appear so. Some have suggested that the FG so emphasizes Jesus as revealer that his humanity is diminished if not lost. In contrast, for instance, to Mark's Jesus, who obviously suffers, this Jesus is a superhuman figure.

This contrast, however, is often overdrawn. The Jesus of Mark's Gospel is scarcely just another human. When compared to the symbolic framework operating in Mark's Gospel, he appears just as alien as the Jesus of the FG. Traditional Christian piety, in fact, sees in John what scholars sometimes miss: while Jesus is "God's Word," he is also emphatically "made flesh" (1:14). John's is in many ways the most human portrayal of Jesus. Jesus experiences fatigue (4:6) and anguish (12:27; 13:21). His whole being is shaken at the death of Lazarus, and he weeps (11:33-35). Jesus changes his mind (7:1-10). Jesus converses with real people in real places: with Nicodemus (3:1-13), the Samaritan woman (4:7-26), the cripple (5:2-9), the blind man (9:35-38), Mary and Martha (11:17-37), and his disciples (1:38-51; 4:31-38; 6:66-71; 9:1-5; 11:1-16; 13:31—14:31). His controversies with opponents are not quickly finished with a polished one-liner, but are passionately drawn out (6:41-65; 7:14-36; 8:12-58; 10:22-39). This Jesus performs a miracle simply for human pleasure (2:1-11), shows irritation (2:4; 6:26; 7:6-8; 8:25) and suspicion (2:24-25), and asks for a positive human response (6:66-71). Only this Jesus is portrayed as having friends (11:1—12:9; 15:13-15). He has a disciple he prefers to others (13:23; 19:26; 20:2; 21:20); and he asks Simon three times, "Do you love me more than these?" (21:15-17).

How then do we account for the other side of John's Christology, which shows Jesus as more than human, speaking "as no man has ever spoken" (7:46)? This side is a function above all of the theological nature of John's narrative and its literary expression. What is left implicit in the Synoptic Gospels is made explicit in the FG. The whole drama of God's relationship with humanity is played out in the FG, with Jesus as the central character. This is the most consistently christocentric of the Gospels, and for that reason, Jesus functions far more symbolically in John.

He is the one who—through his person—"exegetes" the Father to the world (1:18). God is always turned toward the world implicitly by his unseen power and presence; the FG makes this explicit, in a specific time and place, in the figure of Jesus. Therefore, the human response to Jesus represents as well the human response to God. The FG fully establishes that Jesus represents God, and it spells out the consequences of this for human decision: commitment to Jesus is a choice for life, light, and truth—for God.

Hostility toward Jesus is a choice against light for darkness, against truth for falsehood, against life for death—against God for self. Because of this function, Jesus always points beyond himself to the one he represents. The FG is certainly theology: it makes explicit what is implicit in the story of Jesus. But it is a narrative theology: John retells the story in such a way that the narrative itself bears all the deeper resonances of reflection on the figure of Jesus.

Style and Structure in John

The FG is stylistically simple yet symbolically dense. Its generally clear and correct "schoolchild" Greek is so apparently artless that the subtlety of the Gospel's literary technique can easily be missed. The following points are meant to illustrate something of the Gospel's art.

Irony is a favorite and multifaceted literary technique in the FG. The readers always know more than the characters in the narrative and can appreciate their words and actions at quite another level. Characters are given lines that state the truth far beyond their own intentions, as when Caiaphas declares that Jesus should die for the whole people (11:50), or when the people respond to Pilate's "enthronement" of Jesus (19:12-14) by shouting, "We have no king but Caesar" (19:15). Apparently prosaic expressions turn out to have deeper significance. When the disciples first meet Jesus, they ask him, "Where do you stay [or "remain"; *menō*]?" and Jesus tells them, "Come and see" (1:38-39). Only later do we discover the implications of "remaining with Jesus" (15:4-11). So also the expression "lifted up" (*hypsoō*) evokes both the crucifixion of Jesus as well as his glorious exaltation (3:14; 8:28; 12:32-34). Even single words like "sign," "hour," "glory," and "truth" carry several levels of meaning within the narrative, as when Pilate asks the one standing before him (whom the reader has known from the beginning to be "full of grace and truth," 1:14, and who has just told Pilate that he has come to "witness to the truth"), "What is truth?" (18:37-38).

Many of the dialogues of the FG are also structured ironically. A statement or deed of Jesus perfectly plain to the readers is misunderstood by the character functioning as Jesus' dialogue partner. The more Jesus explains, the deeper grows the misunderstanding. The reader, of course, enjoys the whole process. The community's "inside" knowledge makes the words of Jesus transparent. Only outsiders do not understand. Thus, Jesus is approached by Nicodemus, a Jewish teacher superficially attracted to this "man from God" (3:2). Jesus tells Nicodemus that a person cannot enter God's kingdom unless born *anōthen*. The adverb can—depending on the context—mean either "again" or "from above," or both. Nicodemus naturally takes it in its crudest form: "How can a person enter a second time (*deuteron*) his mother's womb and be born?" (3:4). By this misunderstanding Nicodemus shows that he is not "from above" but from below (3:6-8). The community, however, knows the true meaning (3:11). The dialogue with Nicodemus imperceptibly becomes a monologue, first by Jesus (3:10-15), then by the narrator (3:16-21), explicating this more adequate knowledge of the community.

Likewise, Jesus tells the Samaritan woman that if she knew his identity she would ask him for living water (4:10). Missing the point, she goes on about the depth of the well and his lack of a bucket (4:11-12). She cannot grasp that he means quite another kind of water (4:13-14), but the readers do. Again, when Jesus tells his opponents that where he is going they cannot come (7:33; 8:21), they think he is going to the Diaspora (7:35) or planning suicide (8:22). But the reader knows Jesus is going to the Father, and that if people don't believe in him they cannot follow (14:28). The dialogues invite the reader into the process by which the community defines itself against a hostile environment. Jesus spoke "from above" and was misunderstood by all except those "who received him, who believed in his name" (1:12). So does the community that now faces hostility from the outside find in the encoded speech of this Gospel reinforcement for its convictions.

Almost everything in the FG has a symbolic value, including names (1:42, 47; 9:7) and numbers (2:1, 6; 6:13, 70; 21:11). Individual persons represent others: Nicodemus stands for all teachers of the Jews, Martha for all believers, Thomas for all doubters. This representative function accounts for the stock character of the Johannine drama, just as Jesus' representative function gives his figure a certain artificiality. The symbolic role of individuals is most apparent in the case of the "Jews." John does not altogether collapse the distinctions between first-century Jewish sects; the term "Pharisee" occurs only seven fewer times than in Luke. But the Gospel's tendency is to group all Jews together. The distancing term "Jew" (*Ioudaios*) is used some seventy times, compared to five in Luke. The impression given, therefore, is that all Jews—without distinction—were opposed to Jesus. As a result, despite its clear statement that salvation is *from the Jews*" (4:22) and that Jesus is portrayed as arguing *as a Jew* (8:12-58), the FG is often regarded as anti-Jewish. But the Jews of this narrative have as *symbolic* a function as Jesus does: just as Jesus shows how God is toward the world, the Jews represent the tendency of *all humans* to reject the truth of God. John does not intend to evaporate either Jesus or the Jews from history altogether; but their narrative portrayal results from the Gospel's attempt to make of history something more than merely a chronicle of the past.

The symbiotic relationship of the Johannine symbols to Judaism is exemplified by the Gospel's use of the Jewish feasts. We have seen that the narrative places Jesus in the context of the great feasts of Passover (2:13; 6:4; 12:12), Booths (7:1-10), and Hanukkah (10:22). The Gospel also appropriates the symbols traditionally associated with these feasts and applies them to Jesus, so that he personifies all the holy times and places of Judaism (see 1:51): he is the slain lamb (1:29, 36; 19:36) and living bread (6:32-51) of the Passover; the living water (7:37-39) and light (8:12; 9:4-5) of Booths; he is the tent where God's glory dwells (1:14), and his body the new temple (2:21).

Structurally the FG has four major parts. The *prologue* (1:1-18) announces major themes of the story. The *Book of Signs* (1:19—12:50)—the original ending of which is sometimes considered 20:30-31—dramatizes the proposition of the prologue: "The light shines in the darkness and the darkness cannot accept [or, overcome] it" (1:5). The *Book of Glory* (13:1—20:31) shows how "those who believe in him become children of God" (1:12). It has two subdivisions: the revelation of Jesus' glory to his disciples through his teaching (13:1—17:26) and the manifestation of Jesus' glory through his death and resurrection (18:1—20:31). An *appendix* (21:1-25) shows the readers how Peter was restored after his betrayal and how the death of the beloved disciple is to be interpreted.

From another standpoint, the structure of the Gospel is manifestly christocentric. That is, it circles about the figure of Jesus. Linear plot development is less important here than in the other Gospels. There is neither suspense nor surprise but only irony. Patristic writers compared John to the figure of an eagle. Like birds of prey who circle their target, this evangelist describes outer and inner circles around the figure of Jesus. In this discussion, therefore, the reader should look for the measurement of a series of radii that point to an identical center, observing how John can say the same thing in numerous and varied ways.

The Book of Signs: The Deeds of the Messiah

The Prologue (1:1-18)

Characters in Torah are introduced by genealogies (*toledoth*). Matthew and Luke both begin their gospels by tracing Jesus' origins back to biblical ancestors: Abraham in Matthew and Adam in Luke. In contrast, John begins with a prologue that makes the story of Jesus begin in the very bosom of God (1:1). Jesus represents in the world the absolute beginning or origin (*archē*)—God. The prologue consists in a series of rhythmic strophes, some of them chiastic in form. The poetry is twice interrupted by prose interjections dealing with John the Baptist (1:6-8, 15). The prologue's cyclic pattern (the Word comes from God, dwells with humanity, returns to God) defines the dominant spatial movement of the whole Gospel: descent and ascent. The literary antecedents of the prologue are less likely gnostic hymns than the biblical traditions associated with Wisdom (Prov. 8:22-31; Sir. 24:3-34; Wis. 7:22-8:1), which are used elsewhere in the NT to express the conviction that meeting Jesus meant encountering God (Col. 1:15-20; Heb. 1:1-3).

The prologue anticipates many of the Gospel's themes. We find (1:3-4) that the Word (*logos*) bears both light (*phōs*; cf. 3:19-21; 8:12; 9:5; 11:9-10; 12:35, 36, 46) and life (*zōē*; cf. 3:15-16, 36; 4:14, 36; 5:24, 26, 29, 39, 40; 6:27; 8:12; 10:10, 28; 11:25; 12:25, 50; 14:6; 17:2-3; 20:31). Light and life are primal metaphors for the very essence of God. We see as well that the light is locked in conflict (1:5) with a darkness that can neither "accept" nor "overcome" the light (the verb *katalambanō* can mean either one; cf. 3:19; 6:17; 8:12; 12:35, 46). In the "testimony" of John (1:7) is anticipated as well the mission of Jesus in the world (cf. 2:25; 3:11; 4:44; 5:31; 18:37). Jesus' testimony, however, is that of a light "coming into the world" (1:9; cf. 1:15, 30; 3:8, 19, 31; 4:25; 5:43; 8:14; 14:3), and he thus personifies the truth (*alētheia;* 1:14; cf. 3:21; 4:23-24; 5:33; 8:32; 14:6, 17; 15:26; 16:7, 13; 17:17, 19; 18:37). Against every form of counterfeit claim based on human pretension, he offers "genuine" life based on the gift of God (cf. 3:33; 4:18; 5:31-32; 6:55; 7:18; 8:13-14, 17, 26; 10:41; 19:35; 21:24).

In the prologue as well we find already the contrast between those in the world who refused to know him as he was (1:10; cf. 1:50; 2:24-25; 5:42; 6:15, 70; 8:28, 32, 55; 10:14, 38; 14:7; 16:3; 17:3) and those who beheld and accepted him as he was (1:14; cf. 2:23; 4:19; 6:2, 40, 62; 7:3; 12:45; 14:17, 19; 16:10; 17:24): the only begotten Son of God (1:14; 18; cf. 3:16-18). A second contrast in the prologue is between what was found only partially in Torah (*nomos;* 1:17; cf. 1:45; 7:19, 23, 49; 8:17; 10:34; 12:34; 15:25; 18:31; 19:7)—including that found in the figure of Moses (1:17; cf. 1:45; 3:14; 5:45-46; 6:32; 7:19, 22-23; 8:5; 9:28-29)—and what was realized in its fullness (*plērōma;* 1:16) in Jesus. This is the "grace and truth" (*chesed we emeth;* 1:14, 16, 17—found over 100 times in the Gospel) that are both the gift and the attributes of the Father, whom Jesus reveals and represents in his flesh. It is this flesh that, like the tabernacle of Torah, is the tenting place of God's glory in the world (1:14; cf. 6:51-63).

An element of the prologue not found in the FG narrative is the designation of Jesus as the "Word" (*logos*). The prologue in this case gives explicit expression to the constant assumption behind the deeds and words of Jesus: he acts and speaks as the incarnate expression of God's speech. As word gives body to thought, so does Jesus give visible expression in the world to the invisible power and presence of God.

The prologue's final words perfectly summarize the literary and theological function of Jesus in the narrative of the FG: "No one has ever seen God; the only begotten Son, who is in the bosom of the Father; he has made him known" (1:18). The Greek phrase "has made him known" (*exegēsato*) contains the sense both of revealing and interpreting (as in "exegesis"). In its literal meaning of "leading out," it may also be an allusion to the exodus, subtly bringing the figure of Moses into play. While Moses could reveal law, he could not illuminate the very grace and truth of God, which Jesus—as the tent of God's presence (1:14)—can. While Moses could lead the people to the land, only Jesus can lead the people to the bosom of the Father, for only he came from that place. Everything in the FG presupposes this highly explicit framework. In contrast to the Gospel of Mark, then, there is no "secret" in John's narrative except for outsiders: at the outset of the story we know who Jesus is, why he was sent, and the nature of those who will follow him back to the Father.

Jesus and John the Baptist

The touch of the evangelist is masterly in the portrayal of John the Baptist. We can guess from this account that the Baptist was an independent and important prophet with a great following, one that for a time rivaled Jesus' own (1:19; 3:22-30; 4:1). The FG had to acknowledge that he was "a man sent from God" (1:6), while simultaneously showing him subordinate with respect to Jesus.

The prose interpolations in the prologue brilliantly accomplish both ends. John the Baptist is a witness to the light but is not the light (1:6-8); and his entire testimony is that a greater one than himself will come after him (1:15). The relativization is all the more convincing since it is placed in the Baptist's own mouth. He himself then walks out of the numinous haze of the prologue into the lucid foreground of the Jordan River in 1:19, making a narrative bridge between the eternal Word and the earthly Jesus. The problem of having Jesus baptized by John is avoided in the FG: there is no baptism scene, only John bearing testimony to the descent of the Spirit, attesting, "This is the Son of God" (1:31-34).

John the Baptist twice denies that he is the Christ, each time concluding with a statement reminiscent of the synoptic tradition (1:19-23, 24-27). A third time he reminds the crowds that he never claimed to be the Messiah (3:28). John plays perfectly the role of witness. He points away from himself toward Jesus, "the Lamb of God" (1:29, 36). He frees his disciples to follow another (1:37), and with noble poignancy defines himself as "the bridegroom's friend" who is thrilled to hear the groom's voice (3:29) but knows as well that his role is to decrease, while that of Jesus is to increase (3:30). There is nothing accidental in this portrayal. Jesus later refers to the Baptist: "He was a burning and shining lamp, and you were willing for a while to rejoice in his light. But the testimony I have is greater than that of John . . ." (5:35-36). None of the other evangelists managed to articulate so clearly and forcefully the Christian understanding of John's relationship to Jesus.

Naming Jesus (1:29-51)

As in the Synoptics, Jesus' ministry begins with the gathering of his followers, two of whom—in a distinctive Johannine touch—are prior disciples of the Baptist (1:35-40). The process in the FG is considerably more complex than in the Synoptics. First, it is greatly concentrated, with the action carried by a series of questions and answers. The technique is used again in the dialogue between Jesus and these same figures at the last supper (13:36—14:24). Second, the calling of disciples involves a process of assigning names to Jesus. We already heard the crowds seek a name for John the Baptist (1:19-23). Those who now encounter Jesus give him the whole range of titles found in the Synoptics, even those that were "secret." John the Baptist begins the process by calling Jesus the "Lamb of God who takes away the sins of the world" (1:29, 36). This is the first epithet given to Jesus in the narrative, and its imagery is repeated at his death (19:31-37). John also calls Jesus the "Son of God" (1:34).

John's two disciples, who play a significant role in this Gospel (6:5-8; 12:21-22; 14:8-9), are the first to call Jesus "Rabbi" (1:38). Andrew follows by calling him the "Messiah" (1:41), and Philip comes next with a longer designation: "the one spoken of by Moses and all the prophets, Jesus, son of Joseph, from Nazareth" (1:45; cf. 6:42). Finally, Nathaniel calls Jesus "Rabbi, Son of God, King of Israel" (1:49). In the biblical tradition, the act of naming is an exercise of power: it demonstrates the authority of one person over another. In the Johannine progression, however, as the disciples attempt to name Jesus, they come under *his* power: they become his disciples. Indeed, in an ironic twist, rather than merely "naming" Jesus, it turns out they have been "identifying" his person and significance, establishing, in the process, his inherent authority over the world. When Jesus goes on to reverse the process of naming (1:42, 47), he confirms what the narrative has already implied.

It is typical for John's narrative that the identifications of Jesus made by others are not inaccurate, just inadequate. Only Jesus can most fully name himself. He responds to Nathaniel with a self-designation: "You will see the heaven opened and the angels of God ascending and descending upon the Son of man" (1:51). Here the enigmatic synoptic title is again found in the mouth of Jesus, framed by a deliberate allusion to the dream of Jacob in Gen. 28:12-17. Jacob saw the angels ascending and descending and concluded, "This is the house of God, this is the gate of heaven" (Gen. 28:17). In a single deft allusion, John has Jesus identify himself as the Holy Place where humans encounter God, the one who has descended from God and will ascend again, becoming the "gate" through whom others can go to the Father (see 10:7).

The New Creation

The FG, in another allusion to Genesis, makes a further point about Jesus in the narrative sequence that reaches from the prologue through the wedding at Cana. The first words of the prologue, "In the beginning," deliberately recall the opening of Genesis. The Word is present and active in creation on "the first day." The succeeding incidents are marked by an apparently casual dating: "the next day" (1:29), "the next day" (1:35), "the next day" (1:43). This brings us through four days. The wedding feast at Cana is "on the third day" (2:1). At that feast, as we know, Jesus transforms a natural substance (water) into a new creation (wine). What is at work here is not the simple processes of life (*bios*), but true Life (*zōē*)—the power of God.

The symbolism of John is rarely one-layered. The phrase "on the third day" could not but remind Christian readers of the resurrection "on the third day," enabling them to recognize at work in Jesus the power of the resurrection life: "I am the resurrection and the life" (11:25). They could not easily avoid noticing that the water was transformed into wine, a symbol at once for the blood of the lamb and their new Pasch—

the Christian eucharist—in memory of Jesus. In Jesus, then, the power of a new creation is at work, which does not deny but transforms the world he himself, as Word, helped shape. And lest any reader miss the significance of the miracle, the evangelist concludes at 2:11:

> This, the first of his signs, Jesus did at Cana in Galilee, and manifested his glory; and his disciples believed in him.

In the deeds and words of Jesus, the reader of the Gospel (like the disciples at Cana) will recognize the "Word made flesh" who makes present the "glory," that is, the effective power of God (1:14). All Jesus' deeds are symbolic: they are signs that point beyond themselves—and even beyond him—to God, present in the world and re-creating the cosmos through Jesus.

The Signs of the Messiah

Jesus' signs were to reveal the presence of God in him, leading to faith (2:11; 20:30-31). The FG has Jesus perform seven such signs, corresponding to the seven days of the new creation: the wedding at Cana (2:1-11), the healing of the official's son (the "second sign"; 4:46-53), the healing of the paralytic (5:2-9), the multiplication of the loaves (6:1-13; cf. "When the people saw the sign . . . ," 6:14), the walking on water (6:16-21), the healing of the man born blind (9:1-12), and the raising of Lazarus from the dead (11:17-44).

To borrow from Aristotelian categories used in later sacramental theology, all the signs have both matter and form. Their matter is water (Cana, the pool, the walking), bread (the multiplication), light (the blind man), and life (the official's son, Lazarus). Their form is given by Jesus' words that explicate the meaning of the actions. He is the "living water" (4:10), the "bread of life" (6:35), the "light of the world" (8:12), and the "resurrection and the life" (11:25). The signs point to Jesus and he, in turn, points to the presence of God in the world.

But despite the confident assurance of 20:30-31 that the signs lead to belief, they are in fact an ambiguous dimension of the Johannine narrative. For believers, the signs can confirm belief (2:11; 20:30). At other times the words of Jesus lead to commitment: "You have the words of eternal life" (6:68; cf. 11:27, and see the contrast in 4:48). Yet, for those who do not believe, the gestures of Jesus are neither convincing nor self-validating. After he prophetically cleaned the temple, his opponents asked, "What sign have you?" (2:18). After he multiplied the loaves, the crowd cried, "What sign do you do that we may see and believe you?" (6:30). For Nicodemus (3:2) and the crowds who flocked to Bethany after the raising of Lazarus (12:18), the signs were spectacular evidences of a holy man or magician. For the crowd in the desert, the multiplication of food was important not as a sign but as a means of gratification:

"You seek me not because you saw signs but because you ate your fill of the loaves" (6:26).

The signs by themselves may fascinate and even lead to superficial assent (see 2:23), but not to the full commitment of faith. This is made plain at the close of Jesus' public ministry (12:37-43): all of Jesus' signs did not lead to belief in him (12:37). Like Mark explaining the lack of perception regarding Jesus' parables, John makes use of two citations from Isaiah to interpret this rejection. Isaiah 53:1 identifies Jesus as the suffering servant who has not been believed (12:38; cf. Rom. 10:16) and Isaiah 6:10 expresses the motif of blindness and hardening that is so extensively employed by the Synoptics (cf. Mark 4:12; Matt. 13:14-15; Luke 8:10; Acts 28:26-27). They saw but did not really see, heard but did not really hear.

We have, here, an open secret that still cannot be grasped except by faith. Isaiah 6:1-13 recounts the prophet's vision of the glory of God in the temple and his prophetic call. John seems to allude to this when he tells the reader, "Isaiah said this because he saw *his* glory and spoke of *him* [i.e., Jesus]" (12:41; cf. 8:56-58). This witness thus attests that the presence and power of God are one, and, as they were at work in the past, so are they now in Jesus, with the "fullness of grace and truth" (1:14). But, if Isaiah could "see" this in the past, why could God's power and presence not be grasped in the present?

To answer this troubling question John plays on two meanings of the Greek noun *doxa*: "reputation"/"opinion" over against "presence"/"glory." Faced with the choice in Jesus, "they loved more the glory [i.e., opinion] that comes from humans than the glory [i.e., presence] that comes from God" (12:43). The explanation only deepens the mystery, but it does enable the evangelist to close Jesus' open ministry with a final prophetic call (12:44-50) before turning to the private instruction of the disciples (13:1—17:26) which precedes his death (18:1—19:42). The mystery in John seems to be this: the more clearly the claim of God is made, the more violent is the world's rejection of it.

The Book of Signs: The Claims of Jesus

The FG shows a constant attempt to identify Jesus. And with the exception of the charges that he had a demon and that he was a Samaritan (7:20; 8:48), virtually everything said of him has some element of truth. There are, however, circles within circles. For instance, what is revealed through the various disputes within the Book of Signs is discovered to be a parabolic form of what is revealed to believers in the Book of Glory. Even within the context of the public ministry there are inner and outer circles of identification. I will touch here on what is said about Jesus by outsiders, then by believers, and finally by Jesus himself. These levels circulate inward, increasingly becoming more adequate for designating who Jesus is.

Identification by Outsiders

While the titles of "Messiah" ("Christ"), "Prophet," and "King" are all applied to Jesus by outsiders, only the Christian reader understands the way in which Jesus both fulfills and exceeds the expectations associated with such designations. John the Baptist aroused messianic expectations because of his preaching and baptizing (1:25)—although he did no signs (10:40) and had to reject the titles of "Messiah" (1:20, 25; 3:28), "Elijah" (1:21), and "prophet" (1:21). The populace then shifts its speculation to Jesus, wondering whether he might be the Messiah (4:29) or whether the leaders might secretly know him to be (7:26). In the process, the FG tells us a considerable amount about popular messianic expectation. The crowd knows that the Messiah is to come from Bethlehem (7:42), although it is also said that the Messiah's origin will be unknown (7:27). The Messiah is to reveal all things (4:25), perform great signs (7:31), and remain forever (12:34). In the eyes of Jesus' opponents, of course, Jesus meets none of these requirements. But the narrator and the reader know how Jesus does reveal all things, does perform great signs, does have his ultimate origin hidden from them, and does "remain forever." Here we see how the Christian messianic understanding subtly transforms and mutates the symbols of Judaism in light of the confession and expression of faith.

The titles "Prophet" and "King" appear to be associated particularly with the expectation of a messiah who would be a "prophet like Moses." While Jesus is termed "*a* prophet" because he could read hearts (4:19) and perform signs (6:14; 9:17), it is only when he multiplies loaves in the wilderness—like Moses had done in Torah—that the people cry out that he is "*the* Prophet," and seek to make him king (6:15). Yet, in the Passion narrative—where the theme of Jesus' kingship is most dominant (see 18:33-39; 19:12-22)—the content of kingship and the prophetic task are drastically reinterpreted. Thus, "prophet" and "king" in the FG are significantly altered versions of popular Second Temple Jewish messianic expectations. John has reshaped these expectations in light of the larger symbolic framework of Jesus' death, resurrection, and ascension. This is a critical element that the FG shares with the Synoptics, and indicates the larger perspective of shared early Christian belief: Jesus was the "Expected One," but he was not the individual people expected him to be.

Identification by Believers

Jesus is called "Messiah" by those coming to belief in him (1:41; 11:27). The appropriateness of this title is certified by its use by Jesus himself (17:3) and by the narrator (1:17), who is writing so that his readers may continue to believe that Jesus is "the Christ, the Son of God" (20:31). The title "Son," as we shall see, is Jesus' own, so it provides the "inner" understanding of the traditional role of the Messiah. John the Baptist refers to Jesus as "Son of God" (1:34), and Nathaniel expands on this title: "Son of

God, king of Israel" (1:49). Martha surely represents all believers when she confesses, "I believe that you are the Christ, the Son of God, he who is coming into the world" (11:27), a designation fully in agreement with the prologue (1:9, 14, 17).

Jesus is called "Savior of the world" by the Samaritans who believed in him (4:42), and he could also be called "Lord" (9:38), though this title is used indiscriminately in the sense of "master." Peter calls Jesus "the Holy One of God" (6:69). The FG also uses the title God (*theos*) of Jesus, albeit sparingly. We find it first in the prologue, "the Word was God" (1:1), and possibly, "the only God who is in the bosom of the Father" (dependent on a variant reading of 1:18). Thomas therefore is not out of sympathy with the view of the narrator when he confesses after the resurrection, "My Lord and my God" (20:28).

Self-Identification by Jesus

The most distinctive identifications of Jesus are found in his own mouth. This style of self-referential speech most sets apart the Jesus of the FG from the Jesus of the Synoptics. Like the understanding of Jesus' deeds as signs, such self-designations reflect the continuing reflection of believers on Jesus' identity. I will consider here, in turn, his use of the title "Son of man," the phrase "I am," and the language related to sonship.

SON OF MAN

This title is found frequently in the Synoptics. It is thus not surprising to encounter it in the speech of Jesus in the FG. In the Synoptics, the title has a threefold reference: to Jesus' present ministry, to his suffering, and to his eventual role as judge when he would "come on the clouds." In the FG it occurs once as a simple self-designation that calls for a response of belief: "Do you believe in the Son of man?" (9:35). But as reflected in its first occurrence (1:51), the title's predominant use in the FG is within a pattern of descent and ascent. Jesus is the one who will be "lifted up" in his crucifixion (3:14; 8:28), which will also be his exaltation (13:31). When he is lifted up, the Son of man will draw all people to himself (12:32-34) so that they may have eternal life (3:15).

But this Son of man is also one who has already "descended"—and here we see an example of the Johannine "realized eschatology." The traditional expectation was for the "descent" to take place in the future. In the FG, however, Jesus has already descended from heaven. He is the "man from heaven" who is uniquely capable of revealing the things "from above" (3:12, 31; cf. 8:23). So when the Son of man is lifted up, he returns to where he was before (6:62).

Unlike the Synoptics, where the Spirit descends on Jesus but he only ascends after his death and resurrection, the FG makes Jesus' prior existence and being critical to the salvific scheme of the Gospel. Indeed, his exaltation at death hinges upon his prior existence in the "bosom of God." Moreover, since for John "no one has seen the Father except him who is from God" (6:46), the Son-of-man language establishes a pattern of descent and ascent that validates and indeed combines Jesus' role as revealer and judge: "No one has ascended into heaven but he who descended from heaven, the Son of man" (3:13; cf. 5:27). Here we see explicitly what is only implicit in the Synoptics: Jesus reveals who he is and people either accept or reject this revelation, upon which basis they are then judged. Thus, for the FG, "Son of man"—in one title—captures both the elements of revelation and judgment (cf. 8:14-16).

"I AM"

Distinctive to the FG are statements made by Jesus using "I am" (*egō eimi*) in several different forms. The first is in the form "I am X," by which Jesus identifies himself with something already known to the hearers. There are seven of these statements, corresponding to the seven signs and days of the new creation. In each of them, there is at least an implied contrast between the accepted and sometimes counterfeit versions of "X" and the "genuine" realization of it in Jesus. In all of them as well, *beneath the metaphor* is a claim to be the source of that life (*zōē*) which comes from God.

After multiplying the loaves, Jesus declares, "I am the bread of life" (6:35, 48). This is a play on the manna Moses gave to the people in the desert. According to Exod. 16:4, the bread "came from heaven", but, according to Jesus, while it gave sustenance to the body, it was not truly "bread from heaven" in terms of offering eternal life (6:32). Only Jesus is the genuine bread (6:55), because he descends from God and offers the life that comes from God, "for the bread of God is that which comes from heaven and gives *life* to the world" (6:33).

At the Feast of Booths, Jesus claims, "I am the light of the world" (8:12; 9:5). Before his coming, people lived in darkness (3:19-21; 11:10). He now brings the revelation of God, which in turn reveals the world for what it is (1:9; 12:46). The person who sees this light also sees the one who sent it—God (12:45). But the light brings with it judgment (3:19). Before its coming, there was neither light nor darkness, only reality; but when the light shines, then for the first time there is a choice—people can tell the light from the darkness. The choice made between light and darkness also brings judgment on those making it. Those who claim to see without this light are proved blind (9:39-41). But those who see by this light (9:35-38) also live by the life it brings: "In him was life and the life was the light of men" (1:4).

Three of the "I am" statements emphasize the relationship between Jesus and his followers. In contrast to thieves and robbers who destroy the sheep (10:8), Jesus declares, "I am the door of the sheep" (10:7). Those who enter by him will be saved (10:9) and given life: "The thief comes only to steal and kill and destroy. I come that they may have life and have it abundantly" (10:10). In a second, closely related contrast, Jesus says, "I am the good shepherd" (10:11). He is not like the hireling who has no care for the sheep. He demonstrates his care for the sheep by laying down his life for them (10:17). The third statement particularly stresses Jesus as the source of life for his followers: "I am the true vine" (15:1). Those who are cut off from him will wither and die (15:6), but those who stay joined will live and bear fruit (15:2).

All these statements are clearly metaphorical. In contrast, the final two in the form of "I am X" are more straightforward claims to *be* what in fact the metaphors suggest: the source of life. In response to the crisis of Lazarus's death and Martha's belief in a future resurrection (11:24), Jesus says, "I am the resurrection and the life" (11:25). Those who believe in him will never "die"—in the eternal sense—but will live with God's life (11:26). Finally, Jesus tells his disciples at the last supper, "I am the way and the truth and the life; no one comes to the Father but by me" (14:6). This last statement makes clear what all the rest have suggested: in contrast to every form of human self-aggrandizement and pursuit of life, Jesus brings the genuine life that can come only from God. He is revealer and life-giver.

A second kind of "I am" statement is more mysterious. In some cases, it appears to be a rather straightforward response of identification, "I am he." So Jesus tells the Samaritan woman who says the Messiah will reveal everything, "*Egō eimi* speaking to you" (4:26), which simply means: "I, the one speaking to you, am he [i.e., the Messiah]." Likewise, when the disciples are frightened at seeing Jesus walking on the water, he says to them, "*Egō eimi*, do not be afraid" (6:20), which probably means, "It is I." But the dramatic impact of the phrase is suggested in the arrest scene. Jesus asks twice, "Whom do you seek?" When he is told, "Jesus," he responds, "*Egō eimi*" (18:5, 6). This would appear to mean simply, "I am he [i.e., Jesus]" except that, when they hear this, the men fall to the ground (18:6). Undoubtedly the narrator is attempting to tell the reader something, and this becomes apparent when this later incident is read in light of the disputation in John 8:12-58.

In that passage, the expression "*Egō eimi*" occurs three times and is particularly ambiguous. Jesus tells the Jews, "You will die in your sins unless you believe that *Egō eimi*." They, understandably, ask, "Who are you?" (8:24-25). A second time he says to them, "When you have lifted up the Son of man then you will know that *Egō eimi*" (8:28). Does this mean they will know that he is the Son of man or simply that he *is* in some unspecified sense?

The reason this question is pertinent is seen in the final use of the expression. Jesus tells his opponents that Abraham has seen him; they mock him. He replies, "Truly, truly, I say to you, before Abraham was, *Egō eimi*" (8:58). That his opponents recognize the deeper implications of the statement is indicated by their attempt to stone him for blasphemy (8:59). Later, they will say that they wanted to stone him because, "being a human being, he makes himself God" (10:33). This, of course, is exactly what the absolute use of *Egō eimi* would suggest. His opponents, and the Gospel's percipient readers, would recognize in all this talk of *Egō eimi* the self-identification of the Lord God to Moses in the burning bush, "I am who I am" (Exod. 3:14; cf. Isa. 41:4; 43:10). Thus, both implicitly and explicitly throughout the narrative, Jesus identifies himself as "I am"—the self-designation of YHWH in Torah. In this play on the ambiguity of

Egō eimi, we find perhaps one of the strongest statements anywhere in the NT of the early Christian belief that Jesus was God manifested in the flesh.

SON OF THE FATHER

We have seen that the title "Son of God" supplies the appropriate content for messianic belief. And in Jesus' language about himself as Son, we find the deepest and most intimate level of his self-revelation in the Book of Glory. Jesus was sent into the world as an only begotten son (1:18; 3:16-17). Like human sons who observe their fathers at work, Jesus confesses that he can do nothing of himself, but only what he observes his Father doing: he works as his Father works (5:19). This means that he carries out the same functions as the Father in the world. As the Father is the source of life, so does the Son have this life (5:21) that he gives to others (5:26; 6:40, 57). The Son is a judge as the Father is a judge (5:22) and should receive honor just like the Father (5:23). It is as the Father's son that he bears witness (5:30): he hears the words spoken by the Father and communicates them to the world. He is, therefore, an obedient Son (8:26, 28). The Father, in return, loves the Son (3:35; 5:20) and gives him glory (8:54; 12:28).

The blindness of the Son's opponents can be summarized in this way: "They did not know he spoke the Father to them" (8:27). Similarly, the gift to the disciples is summarized thus: "He who has seen me has seen the Father" (14:9). In the language of a filial relationship that is expressed by obedience and love, Jesus himself provides the inner meaning of the title "only Son of God" (1:14, 18).

A Christological Controversy (chaps. 7–8)

The distinctive way in which the Christology of the FG unfolds in the Book of Signs can perhaps best be illustrated by looking at a single section in greater detail.

Chapters 7 and 8 form a single long controversy between Jesus and his opponents. It is interrupted, however, by the pericope of the adulterous woman (7:53—8:11). Although the pericope appears in this location in all printed editions of the Gospel, it is very doubtful that it is in its right place or that it even comes from the same writer. The vocabulary bears much more of a synoptic than Johannine stamp, and the character of the confrontation is closer to the pericope style of the Synoptics. It also sits uneasily between the two parts of the christological argument. Finally, the passage has an unusual textual history. Many of the manuscripts that have it in this part of the FG are late and belong to a common textual tradition. Many other manuscripts also have it here, but they include critical signs indicating doubts as to its proper placement. Yet other manuscripts put the passage after 7:36 or 21:25, while some even place it in the Gospel of Luke (after either 21:38 or 24:53). The best and most ancient manuscripts, however, omit the passage altogether. The weight of the textual evidence suggests, then, that this story, which has deservedly enjoyed great popularity, is, like the longer ending of Mark, part of the canonical collection but so mechanically

placed in its present location that a literary consideration of the Gospel can legitimately work around it.

After some initial indecision (7:1-9), Jesus decides to return to Jerusalem for the
Feast of Booths (7:2, 10). While in the city, he engages in a running disputation with
the Jews, who are full of speculation concerning his identity (7:11-13). John typically
uses symbols associated with this feast in reference to Jesus. The Mishnah (*Sukkah* 5.2-
4 and 4.9) indicates that a ceremonial libation of water and a procession carrying
torches of light were traditional elements of this celebration. The FG therefore has
Jesus cry out (7:37-38) on "the last day of the feast, the great day":

> If anyone thirst, let him come to me and drink, who believes in me. As the
> Scripture has said, "Out of his heart shall flow rivers of living water."

And shortly thereafter, Jesus also announces, "I am the *light* of the world" (8:12).

The controversy in chapters 7 and 8 is in reality part of the longer running battle
between Jesus and the opposition, in which the same points are touched on repeatedly.
There is a marked resemblance, for example, between 7:27-28 and 8:14c-d; 7:24 and
8:15; 7:28 and 8:19; 7:30 and 8:20; 7:33-36 and 8:21-22. These chapters also pick up
elements of the earlier disputation caused by Jesus' healing of a paralytic (cf. 8:16 and
5:30; 8:14 and 5:31; 8:18 and 5:37). Throughout this series of controversies, themes
first suggested in 3:19-21 re-emerge, as the points of the present battle build toward
the further confrontations coming in 10:31-38 and 12:27-50.

In the present section of the dispute there is an ever-greater identification of the
issues that are leading to the growing alienation between Jesus and his interlocutors.
Jesus and the Jews talk past each other, as though they really were on different planes
(7:23). The pattern of the passage is dialogical, but in fact the questions and answers
resemble more a judicial cross-examination. Only the reader knows that the ones
doing the examining are in fact the ones being examined. Many of Jesus' answers
could not have been intelligible to his opponents but are so to the reader. Characteristic of the deep lack of understanding is Jesus' repeated statement, "Where I am going
you cannot come" (7:34; 8:21). Jesus himself indicates that this is because "I go to the
one who sent me" and the reader rightly understands this to be God. But the Jews
think, first, that he is going to the Diaspora (7:35) and then that he is going to commit
suicide (8:22). Each conclusion is mistaken. Yet so dense is the Johannine irony that
each conclusion is true at another level. The Gospel *will* go to the Greeks, or the Greeks
will come to it (12:20) and Jesus *will* "lay down his life himself" for the sake of others
(10:17-18). Another example of this layered discourse and narrative is provided at the
very beginning of the controversy: Jesus asks his interlocutors, "Why do you seek to kill
me?" (7:19), and they vigorously reject the charge; yet, by the end of the dispute, they
are indeed trying to kill him (8:59).

The fundamental problem of the adversaries, the evangelist suggests, is their unwillingness to accept the claims to which Jesus' deeds themselves attest. They avoid the simple equation that for Jesus—and the narrator—is the only correct one: when they ask, "Where is your father?" Jesus answers, "You know neither me nor my father; if you knew me you would know my father also" (8:19). The circularity and frustration of the controversy are suggested by their exasperated question, "Who are you?" and Jesus' response, which in Greek can mean either "Even what I told you from the beginning" or "Why do I talk to you at all?" (8:25). Both answers fit this exchange, the function of which is to demonstrate how the darkness cannot grasp or overcome the light.

Throughout the dispute, of course, Jesus is speaking less to his opponents than to the Christian readers of the FG. And they learn a great deal about the nature of Jesus' claim to be God's Son, as well as the nature of Jesus' opponents—the ones later to become the opponents of the Christian readers themselves. They see that the Jews claim Abraham as their father (8:33) and charge Jesus with having a demon (8:48). But Jesus says that his Jewish opponents have not lived up to their descent from Abraham. The principle, as we have seen, is that children act like their parents (5:19). Since they seek to kill Jesus, they show that their real father is the devil, "who was a murderer from the beginning" (8:44)—Abraham never acted thus (8:40). As for their claim to be free children (8:33), it is an illusion since they are slaves of sin (8:34). Only the truth can make them free (8:31-32); that is to say, only the free Son can liberate them (8:36). If God were their Father, they would love Jesus (8:42).

Jesus is the free Son because he is the obedient Son: "I declare to the world what I have heard from [God]" (8:26). He speaks from his Father's authority, not his own (8:28). And since Jesus always does what is pleasing to the Father, he is not left alone (8:29): his Father is with him (8:16). Indeed, since the Father is always "with" Jesus, he is a second witness to Jesus' words. This fulfills the requirement of Jewish law that the witness of two people is required (8:17-18; cf. Deut. 19:15). Here we meet the Johannine theme that the law revealed by Moses finds its "fullness" in the "grace and truth" revealed in Jesus (1:16-17). If Torah is not read in the light of that fulfillment, it is misread. In the controversy of chapter 5, Jesus told the Jews, "You search the scriptures, because you think in them you have eternal life; and it is they that witness to me" (5:39). His opponents not only cannot hear the Word incarnate; they even fail to understand the import of their own authoritative texts: "It is Moses who accuses you, on whom you set your hope. If you believed Moses, you would believe me, for he wrote of me" (5:45b-46; cf. Deut. 18:18). This is similar to the midrashic treatment of Ps. 82:6, which shows that Jesus is scripturally justified in calling himself "Son of God": if those to whom Torah was revealed were called God's sons, how much more the one whom God sanctified and sent into the world (10:34-36). If the people were really faithful to Torah, they would also have faith in Jesus: "He who is of God hears the words of God; the reason you do not hear them is that you are not of God" (8:47).

In this controversy, the revelation made through Jesus is seen as continuous with that made through Moses. Openness to one would mean understanding the other: Jesus speaks God's truth. If some have chosen falsehood in lieu of this, they have forsworn their own heritage, choosing slavery, sin, and death over life: "if anyone keeps my word he will never see death" (8:51). The functions of Torah are totally subsumed by Jesus: he reveals God's will, he judges, he offers the spirit, he gives light, he liberates, he gives life. What Torah was as text, Jesus is as living Son: God's Word.

The Book of Glory: Jesus Teaches His Disciples

The great and dramatic shift in the FG is from the open ministry to an inner revelation, from those in the world—"though he had done so many signs before them, yet did not believe in him" (12:37)—to "his own"—"having loved his own in the world he loved them to the end" (13:1). The FG has no direct teaching on discipleship except in the Book of Glory, first by Jesus' words and then by his example in death and resurrection.

Jesus' teaching is set at a supper "before the feast of Passover" (13:1-2). The meal is not emphasized, and there is no "institution" of the Eucharist—John's "eucharistic discourse" in 6:48-58 serves that function. The only ritual action is the foot washing (13:4-12), which is given as an example for imitation (13:15). This opening scene has elements that resemble those in the Synoptics, although thoroughly reworked (13:16/Matt. 10:24, Luke 6:40; 13:17/Matt. 7:24, Luke 11:28; 13:20/Matt. 10:40, Luke 10:16; 13:21-26/Matt. 26:21-25, Mark 14:17-21, Luke 22:21-23). In a mirror image of the pattern established by the Book of Signs, Jesus' symbolic actions give rise to a dialogue, made up largely of questions and answers. When first called, the disciples "named" Jesus; now they question him in turn (Simon Peter, 13:36; Thomas, 14:5; Philip, 14:8; Judas, 14:22). The dialogue then shifts to a monologue interrupted only by a final common question (16:17-18) and exclamation (16:29-30), culminating in the solemn prayer of 17:1-26.

Jesus' last-supper discourse (13:1—17:26) interprets his ministry as well as the future of the disciples. We find in it therefore the confluence of themes that appeared earlier in the narrative. We have repeatedly been told that Jesus' "hour" has not yet arrived, without being told the precise nature of that "hour" (2:4; 7:30; 8:20). In the climactic scene of the open ministry, this theme was intensified: "The hour has come for the Son of man to be glorified" (12:23) and "Save me from this hour" (12:27). Now we are told, "Jesus knew his hour had come to depart" (13:1) and Jesus himself says, "Father, the hour has come; glorify thy Son that the Son may glorify you" (17:1). At the crucifixion, in turn, the narrator tells us that "from that hour" the beloved disciple took care of Jesus' mother (19:27).

The hour of Jesus is therefore at once his death and his glorification. When we remember the precise way John uses "glory," we see that Jesus' death is the moment when God's presence is, paradoxically, most powerful. The notion of Jesus' glory (1:14; 2:11; 11:4, 40; 12:41) and of his "being glorified" (7:39; 8:54; 11:4; 12:16, 23, 28), which was associated with his signs, is now intensified by association with the great sign that is his death and resurrection: "Now is the Son of man glorified and in him God is glorified; if God is glorified in him, God will also glorify him in himself and glorify him at once" (13:31-32; cf. 14:13; 15:8; 16:14; 17:1, 4, 10, 22, 24). It is the hour as well of Jesus' "going away," to use the expression that so confused his opponents (7:33; 8:21). Now the reader is told plainly that Jesus is going away to the Father from whom he came (13:1, 3, 33, 36; 14:3, 12, 19, 28, 30; 16:5-7, 16, 28; 17:11, 13).

The Johannine theme of conflict and judgment that arises in the last-supper discourse evinces three aspects in the Book of Glory, illustrating how the event of the last supper is paradigmatic for the FG. First, the conflict between light and darkness is clearly identified as one between God and Satan. We have seen in the earlier controversies that Jesus was called a demoniac (8:48) and that he charged the Jews with having the devil as a father (8:44). Now we see that it was the "devil" who put it in Judas' heart to betray Jesus (13:2), possessing Judas—as it were—to do such things (13:27). When Jesus is arrested, it is understood as the coming of "the ruler of this age" (14:30); when the comforter comes, it is understood to be the judgment of the "ruler of this age" (16:10).

Second, there is conflict and judgment within the group of disciples. Peter is tested in the foot washing (13:6-10), but Jesus does not refer to him when he says, "You are not all clean" (13:11). This refers to Judas, who breaks fellowship by his betrayal. The portrayal of this event in the FG is chilling indeed. Already in 6:70 Jesus says, "Did I not choose you the Twelve, and one of you is a devil," whom the evangelist identifies as Judas (cf. 13:2, 27). The actual scene of betrayal is powerfully depicted. Jesus has withdrawn from the world of darkness with his disciples, retreating to the upper room. As in the Synoptics, the disciples ask who will betray him. But only in John does Jesus tell the beloved disciple that it is the one to whom he gives the dipped bread. Given the dense symbolism of bread in this Gospel, the body language here is most dramatic. Jesus takes the bread and gives it to Judas. As he takes the morsel, Satan enters into him (13:27). The narrator then states: "So, after receiving the morsel, he immediately went out; and it was night" (13:30). From the perspective of the FG, this unquestionably represents a complete and utter rejection by Judas of who Jesus is and why he came: the choice for darkness against light; the choice for death against the bread of eternal life.

The third kind of conflict and judgment is the one the disciples will face after the departure of Jesus. The alienation between the world and them, between the insiders and the outsiders, will continue. As the world hated him so it will hate them (15:18-27; 16:2-4, 8, 20, 33; 17:13-19). But the remedy for this situation unfolds in the other major speech in the Book of Glory—the farewell discourse

This discourse makes clear to the readers what was hidden from unbelievers, namely, Jesus' ultimate origin and destination: "I came from the Father and have come into the world; again, I am leaving the world and going to the Father" (16:28; cf. 13:1, 3; 14:2, 12, 28; 16:16; 17:5, 8,13). Jesus is also the way by which others can go to the Father (14:4-7). The relationship between Jesus and the Father is expressed in terms of the greatest intimacy: he and the Father are one (14:8-11; 16:15; 17:21). But Jesus is not the Father. He remains united to God through obedience and love (14:10, 31; 15:9, 15; 17:4, 12, 13). This pattern is also one for the disciples to imitate. To this end, Jesus leaves only one commandment for his followers: they are to love one another (13:34; 15:12, 17). By so doing, they will "abide" in the love of Jesus (15:9-10, 14). Such a spiritual abiding reveals the deeper implications of the hints dropped in the earlier narrative about abiding or remaining (*menō*; cf. 1:38-39; 5:38; 6:27, 56; 8:31, 35; 12:34; 14:10, 17, 25). The allegory of the vine and the branches establishes a relationship of mutual life and love between Jesus, his disciples, and the Father. They are to remain in Jesus (15:4), just as Jesus remains in the Father (15:10). They do this by obeying the commandment of mutual love.

The earlier narrative suggested that Jesus would be the source of a loving spirit for those who believed in him (4:13-14; 7:37-39). Jesus now makes clear that his departure will lead to a new mode of God's presence (and of his own presence) among his friends: through the Holy Spirit, who is called "Paraclete" or "Comforter" (*paraklētos*). This is the Spirit of truth (14:17) that will lead them into all truth (16:13). Specifically, the Spirit will "bring to remembrance all that I have said to you" (14:26). So the Spirit continues the witness of Jesus (15:26) in and through the disciples. This witness will "convict" the world in exactly the way Jesus does, concerning sin, righteousness, and judgment (16:7-11). But since the disciples continue to represent Jesus in the world, they can expect a fate like his. They too will be hated by the world (15:18—16:4) and experience great sorrow (16:20). And since they have the love of God within them (15:10), even this sorrow will be changed into joy (15:11; 16:22). The final prayer of Jesus states that the disciples too have been given eternal life (17:3) and glory (17:22), being sanctified (17:19), all because the love of God is in them as it was in Jesus (17:26).

In the FG, as we have seen, both ecclesiology and soteriology are rooted in Jesus. This is a community of "friends" bound together by their love for each other, which comes from the love Jesus first showed them, the very love of God. It is present among them in the Holy Spirit, sent from both Father and Son, to draw them into unity. No better expression can be found for the life of the Spirit than, "that they may be one even as we are one" (17:22). We are forewarned, then, that this is a community for which disputes over true and false spirits, or any form of disunity at all, would create the most severe sort of identity crisis (cf. below, on 1, 2, 3 John). Unity is understood to be the grounding—and indeed the very essence—of the community in the Spirit.

The Book of Glory: The Son

Passion and Death

John's Passion narrative includes a considerable amount of material also found in the Synoptics, such as the arrest in the garden (18:1-11), including Peter's slicing off the ear of the high priest's servant (18:10); Peter's betrayal (18:15-27); the trial before Pilate (18:29—19:16), including the offer of Barabbas (18:39-40); the place of crucifixion (19:17); the title on the cross (19:19); the execution of two others (19:18); and the dividing of the garments (19:23-24). Even the shared elements, however, are given a specific Johannine shading. Thus Judas appears as the leader of the mob (18:2), and when Jesus identifies himself, "I am he," the crowd falls back (18:4-6). Jesus' response to Peter's violence amounts to a version of the synoptic Gethsemane account: "Put your sword into its sheath; shall I not drink the cup which the Father has given me?" (18:11; cf. 12:27-29). As in the Synoptics, Peter's betrayal is juxtaposed to Jesus' witnessing. In John, however, the contrast is sharper because the two accounts are interwoven (18:15-27), and an astute reader will not miss the point of Peter's reaching out to a fire for warmth while the light of the world is captured by the powers of darkness (18:18).

The distinctive thematic element in the FG's Passion concerns the kingship of Jesus. John has no trial before the Sanhedrin, only private hearings before the priests Annas and Caiaphas (18:19-23, 24, 28), with Jesus quickly shunted to Pilate afterward. His trial before the Roman procurator becomes an extended dialogue on the reality and nature of his kingship. Pilate functions in the role the Jews played in the earlier controversies: in response to Pilate's dull questions (18:33, 35, 37, 38; 19:10), Jesus makes clear that his kingship is not of this world (18:33) and that earthly political power is an illusion (19:11). Jesus' kingship consists in his witnessing to the truth (18:36-37). But when Pilate asks the critical question of the FG, "Where are you from?" Jesus says nothing at all (19:9).

The climax of the trial comes in 19:12-16, when the narrator pulls Pilate's gestures into the ironic framework of the entire narrative up to this point, signaling the event's importance by telling us the time and place (19:14). Pilate had already dressed Jesus in royal robe and mock crown (19:5); now he deliberately places Jesus (the text demands this transitive translation of *kathizō* instead of "Pilate sat down") on his own judgment seat—the symbol of Pilate's authority that now also becomes the symbol of Jesus' (19:13). Pilate cries out, "Here is your king"—referring to Jesus on the seat— to which the chief priests respond: "We have no king but Caesar" (19:15). Through this ironic narrative, the reader is told that the people have in fact chosen to be ruled by human powers, rejecting the kingship of God.

The deliberateness of the irony in the kingship imagery is made clear by the exchange between Pilate and the Jews on the appropriateness of the title "King of the Jews" written on the sign (19:21), and by Pilate's response, "What I have written, I have written" (19:22). In other words, while Pilate's actions are aligned with the statement "Jesus believed himself to be the king of the Jews," his ironic confession—in writing and in speech—attests the truth: "Jesus *is* king of the Jews." What is thus denied by one character at one level in the narrative, is confirmed by that same character at another level.

The figure of Pilate is important for our understanding of the FG, for it shows that the Johannine treatment of the Jews is not really a form of anti-Jewish sentiment: Pilate also represents the world that refuses the truth about God and itself. Faced with one who came only to bear witness to the truth and who said, "Everyone who is of the truth hears my voice" (18:37), Pilate can only answer, "What is truth?" (18:38). In this way, the trial narrative—and particularly the confrontation of Jesus and Pilate—paradigmatically confirms both who Jesus is and his rejection by the world.

Turning to the crucifixion scene, we see that it looks very different than in the Synoptics. Jesus is not abandoned by his disciples; rather he has released them (18:8). At the cross, he is still surrounded by Mary his mother, Mary the wife of Cleopas, Mary Magdalene, and the beloved disciple (19:25-26). As Jesus had loved his friends to the end (13:1), so do they love him till his end. This is the second appearance of Jesus' mother in the FG. The first was when Jesus showed his glory in a sign of resurrection life at the wedding in Cana (2:1-11). The second is for his glorification in death. For the Johannine community, as for the Lukan community, the figure of Mary has an important symbolic value: she represents the intimacy that exists between Jesus and his followers.

Consistent with the whole Johannine presentation, Jesus is fully conscious on the cross. He knows that now "all has been brought to completion" (19:28), declaring "It is finished" (see 13:1; 17:4). As Jesus had said he would "hand over his life" (10:18), the evangelist now shows that to be the case: he bows his head and "hands over" his spirit (19:30). No less than in the Synoptics, but with different texts, this scene is interpreted by the symbols of Torah. Thus, Jesus' words "I thirst" (19:28) are said to fulfill Ps. 69:21. And the image of Jesus as the lamb whose bones are not broken (19:36; cf. 1:36) recalls Exod. 12:46.

The strangest element of the Johannine crucifixion scene is also the most revealing of the author's intentions. The narrator begins by stressing the presence of the eyewitness—a way of alerting the reader that something significant is taking place (19:35). The writer then goes on to relate that the soldiers came and broke the legs of the others, but not the legs of Jesus: Jesus is the Paschal Lamb, which does not have the bones broken (Exod. 12:46). Jesus is then pierced in the side, and water and blood flow from it (19:34). This happens, we see, immediately after Jesus says, "It is finished," and "hands over" his spirit (19:30). We only grasp the meaning and importance of this sequence when we consult the full context of Zech. 12:10 to which the narrator points in 19:37: "They shall look on him whom they have pierced." The larger passage in Zechariah (12:10; 13:1) reads:

> And I will *pour out* on the house of David and the inhabitants of Jerusalem a
> *spirit* of compassion and supplication, so that, when they *look on one whom*
> *they have pierced*, they shall mourn for him as one weeps for an only child, and
> weep over him as one weeps for a firstborn. . . . *On that day*, there shall be a
> *fountain opened* for the house of David and the inhabitants of Jerusalem to
> cleanse them of sin and uncleanness.

The eyewitness sees just such a fountain in the side of Jesus. The water and blood have a dual—yet unified—symbolism: the blood signals atonement and the cleansing of sin, while the water signals the outpouring of the Spirit. In the case of the water, the reader remembers the "water bubbling up to eternal life" (4:14), and that "out of his heart shall flow rivers of living water," which, we were told, was "the Spirit which those who believed in him were to receive" (7:38-39). Now, he is glorified, atonement has been achieved, and the Spirit is given. The irony of the FG does not cease even here: it is from the side of the one who cries, "I thirst," that the living waters flow.

The Resurrection

The powerful grip of the resurrection traditions on Christian communities is indicated by their inclusion in the FG, which could so easily have done without them. Once more in these accounts we can find traces of shared gospel traditions, thoroughly reworked according to Johannine perspectives. The empty-tomb account (cf. Mark 16:1-8; pars.) focuses on Mary Magdalene (20:1-2) and the footrace between Peter and the beloved disciple (20:3-9), but above all it focuses on the fact that the beloved disciple was the first to "believe." The account of the mistaken-identity (cf. Luke 24:13-35) also involves Mary Magdalene, who thinks Jesus is the gardener (20:11-18). John includes a double appearance to the gathered disciples (cf. Luke 24:36-49), the second to accommodate the doubting Thomas (20:19-29). Finally, in a story reminiscent of Peter's call to discipleship in Luke 5:3-7, Jesus appears to all the disciples in Galilee (21:1-14), restoring Peter (21:15-19) and clarifying the fate of the beloved disciple (21:20-24).

The stories have, overall, the same functions as in the Synoptic Gospels: the empty tomb certifies that Jesus is not among the dead, even though he has already been extravagantly anointed and buried (19:39-42). The failure of people to recognize Jesus shows that he now lives in a new way and he will be recognized by those who know his voice when he calls them by name (20:16; cf. 10:3). The transformation of Jesus also has implications for his disciples and their world. He enters rooms locked by fear, because the power of his life drives away fear and brings peace (20:19). He shows his wounds so that his friends may know that the one who lives is also the one who was slain, and that he bears forever on his body the marks of wounded humanity (20:20). Further, he is mysteriously present to the disciples as they work and eat together (21:1-14).

But as always in this Gospel, the words of Jesus himself provide the transition from the gospel narrative to the story being lived out by the community addressed by the FG. The members of the community live with the assurance that he ascended to the Father as he told them he would (20:17). They know that they possess the Spirit that comes directly from him so that they can be to the world what he was (20:21-23). They are those who now are not seeing yet are believing and being blessed (20:29). They are those who are to show their love for Jesus by their care for the "sheep," the Messiah's community. They live by the last words from the risen one, which tell them what all the Gospels say, "*you* follow me" (21:22).

Study Questions

1. What effect did the discovery of early fragments of the Gospel of John on papyri (P^{52}, P^{66}, P^{75}) have on the dating of the Gospel?

2. What are some of the key metaphors of the Gospel of John?

3. Identify some of the specific ways in which the Gospel of John is different from the Synoptic Gospels.

4. How does the Gospel of John use irony? Give some examples.

5. What metaphors are used in the "I am" sayings? What is distinctive about these sayings?

6. What is distinctive about the ending of John? What might that tell us about its composition?

Bibliographical Note

For a variety of topics related to the Johannine literature, see R. P. Martin and P. H. Davids, *Dictionary of the Later New Testament and Its Developments* (Downers Grove: InterVarsity Press, 1997). A helpful review of recent Johannine scholarship as a whole is R. Kysar, *The Fourth Evangelist and His Gospel* (Minneapolis: Augsburg Pub. House, 1975); idem, "The Fourth Gospel: A Report on Recent Research," *ANRW* II.25.3 (1980): 2389–440; and D. M. Smith, "The Contribution of J. Louis Martyn to the Understanding of the Gospel of John," in R. T. Fortna and B. R. Gaventa (eds.), *The Conversation Continues: Studies in Paul & John* (Nashville: Abingdon Press, 1990), 275–97. For useful collections of essays, see J. Ashton (ed.), *The Interpretation of John*, rev. ed. (Edinburgh: T. & T. Clark, 1997); idem, *Studying John: Approaches to the Fourth Gospel* (New York: Clarendon Press, 1994); C. K. Barrett, *Essays on John* (Philadelphia: Westminster Press, 1982); R. A. Culpepper and C. C. Black (eds.), *Exploring the Gospel of John* (Louisville: Westminster/John Knox Press, 1996); M. de Jonge, *Jesus: Stranger from Heaven and Son of God*, trans. and ed. J. E. Steely (SBLSBS, 11; Missoula, Mont.: Scholars Press, 1977); J. L. Martyn, *The Gospel of John in Christian History* (New York: Paulist Press, 1978); S. Porter and C. A. Evans (eds.), *The Johannine Writings* (BS, 32; Sheffield: Sheffield Academic Press, 1995); and D. M. Smith, *Johannine Christianity: Essays on Its Setting, Sources, and Theology* (Columbia: Univ. of South Carolina Press, 1984). For treatments of the FG as a whole, see J. Ashton, *Understanding the Fourth Gospel* (New York: Clarendon Press, 1991); J. Painter, *The Quest for the Messiah: The History, Literature and Theology of the Johannine Community*, 2nd ed. (Nashville: Abingdon Press, 1993); and S. S. Smalley, *John: Evangelist and Interpreter* (London: Paternoster Press, 1978).

For various aspects of the Johannine community and literature, see O. Cullmann, *The Johannine Circle*, trans. J. Bowden (Philadelphia: The Westminster Press, 1976 [1975]); R. A. Culpepper, *The Johannine School* (SBLDS, 26; Missoula, Mont.: Scholars Press, 1975); M. Hengel, *The Johannine Question*, trans. J. Bowden (London: SCM Press; Philadelphia: Trinity Press Int'l, 1989); E. Schüssler Fiorenza, "The Quest for the Johannine School: The Apocalypse and the Fourth Gospel," in her *The Book of Revelation: Justice and Judgment* (2d ed.; Minneapolis: Fortress Press, 1998), 85–113; D. M. Smith, "Johannine Christianity: Some Reflections on Its Character and Delineation," *NTS* 21 (1975): 222–48; F. Vouga, "The Johannine School: A Gnostic Tradition in Primitive Christianity?" *Bib* 69 (1988): 371–85; and D. E. H. Whiteley, "Was John Written by a Sadducee?" *ANRW* II.25.3 (1980): 2481–2505. On the Beloved Disciple, see R. J. Bauckham, "The Beloved Disciple as Ideal Author," *JSNT* 49 (1993): 21–44; J. H. Charlesworth, *The Beloved Disciple: Whose Witness Validates the Gospel of John?* (Valley Forge, Pa.: Trinity Press Int'l, 1995); R. A. Culpepper, *John the Son of Zebedee: The Life and Legend* (Columbia: Univ. of South Carolina Press, 1994), 56–88; and M. de Jonge, "The Beloved Disciple and the Date of the Gospel of John," in E. Best and R. McL. Wilson (eds.), *Text and Interpretation* (Cambridge: Cambridge Univ. Press, 1979), 99–114.

Studies that seek the history of the community in the FG include J. Bassler, "The Galileans: A Neglected Factor in Johannine Community Research," *CBQ* 43 (1981): 243–57; R. E. Brown, *The Community of the Beloved Disciple* (New York: Paulist Press, 1979); J. L. Martyn, *History and Theology in the Fourth Gospel*, rev. ed. (Nashville: Abingdon Press, 1979); J. Painter, "The Farewell Discourses and the History of Johannine Christianity," *NTS* 27 (1980–81): 525–43; J. D. Purvis, "The Fourth Gospel and the Samaritans," *NovT* 17 (1975): 161–98; U. Schnelle, *Antidocetic Christology in the Gospel of John: An Investigation of the Place of the Fourth Gospel in the Johannine School*, trans. L. M. Maloney (Minneapolis: Fortress Press, 1992 [1987]); U. C. von Wahlde,

"Community in Conflict: The History and Social Context of the Johannine Community," *Int* 49 (1995): 379–89; R. A. Whitacre, *Johannine Polemic: The Role of Tradition and Theology* (SBLDS, 67; Chico, Calif.: Scholars Press, 1982); and D. B. Woll, *Johannine Community in Conflict: Authority, Rank, and Succession in the First Farewell Discourse* (SBLDS, 60; Chico, CA: Scholars Press, 1981).

The perennial problem of the relationship between John and the Synoptic Gospels is examined by P. Borgen (with response from F. Neirynck), "John and the Synoptics," in D. L. Dungan (ed.), *The Interrelations of the Gospels* (BETL, 95; Macon, Ga.: Mercer Univ. Press, 1990), 408–58; T. L. Brodie, *The Quest for the Origins of John's Gospel: A Source-Oriented Approach* (New York: Oxford Univ. Press, 1993); A. Denaux (ed.), *John and the Synoptics* (BETL, 101; Leuven: Leuven Univ. Press, 1992); C. H. Dodd, *Historical Tradition in the Fourth Gospel* (Cambridge: Cambridge Univ. Press, 1965); J. A. T. Robinson, *The Priority of John*, ed. J. F. Coakley (London: SCM Press, 1985); and D. M. Smith, *John among the Gospels: The Relationship in Twentieth-Century Research* (Minneapolis: Fortress Press, 1992).

On the use and reconstruction of multiple sources in the FG, see D. A. Carson, "Current Source Criticism of the Fourth Gospel: Some Methodological Questions," *JBL* 97 (1978): 411–29; R. T. Fortna, *The Fourth Gospel and Its Predecessor: From Narrative Source to Present Gospel* (Philadelphia: Fortress Press, 1988); B. Lindars, *Behind the Fourth Gospel* (London: SPCK, 1971); D. M. Smith, *The Composition and Order of the Fourth Gospel* (New Haven: Yale Univ. Press, 1965); H. M. Teeple, *The Literary Origin of the Gospel of John* (Evanston, Ill.: Religion and Ethics Inst., 1974); and U. C. von Wahlde, *The Earliest Version of John's Gospel: Recovering the Gospel of Signs* (Wilmington: Michael Glazier, 1989).

On the use of the Old Testament in the FG, see M.-E. Boismard, *Moses or Jesus: An Essay in Johannine Christology*, trans. B. T. Viviano (Minneapolis: Fortress Press; Leuven: Peters Press, 1993); C. A. Evans, "Obduracy and the Lord's Servant: Some Observations on the Use of the Old Testament in the Fourth Gospel," in C. A. Evans and W. F. Stinespring (eds.), *Early Jewish and Christian Exegesis* (Atlanta: Scholars Press, 1987), 221–36; A. Guilding, *The Fourth Gospel and Jewish Worship: A Study of the Relation of St. John to the Ancient Jewish Lectionary System* (London: Clarendon Press, 1960); A. T. Hanson, *The Prophetic Gospel: A Study of John and the Old Testament* (Edinburgh: T. & T. Clark, 1991); M. Hengel, "The Old Testament in the Fourth Gospel," in C. A. Evans and W. R. Stegner (eds.), *The Gospels and the Scriptures of Israel* (JSNTSup, 104; Sheffield: Sheffield Academic Press, 1994), 380–95; and B. G. Schuchard, *Scripture within Scripture: The Interrelationship of Form and Function in the Explicit Old Testament Citations in the Gospel of John* (SBLDS, 133; Atlanta: Scholars Press, 1992).

Various other aspects of the FG's symbolic world are investigated by C. K. Barrett, *The Gospel of John and Judaism*, trans. D. M. Smith (Philadelphia: Fortress Press, 1975 [1970]); P. Borgen, *Bread from Heaven: An Exegetical Study of the Concept of Mana in the Gospel of John and the Writings of Philo* (NovTSup, 10; Leiden: E. J. Brill, 1965); J. H. Charlesworth (ed.), *John and the Dead Sea Scrolls* (New York: Crossroad, 1990); C. H. Dodd, *The Interpretation of the Fourth Gospel* (Cambridge: Cambridge Univ. Press, 1968); C. A. Evans, *Word and Glory: On the Exegetical and Theological Background of John's Prologue* (JSNTSup, 89; Sheffield: Sheffield Academic Press, 1993); J. M. Ford, *Redeemer—Friend and Mother: Salvation in Antiquity and in the Gospel of John* (Minneapolis: Fortress Press, 1997); J. J. Kanagaraj, *"Mysticism" in the Gospel of John: An Inquiry into Its Background* (JSNTSup, 158; Sheffield: Sheffield Academic Press, 1998); W. A. Meeks, "'Am I a Jew?' Johannine Christianity and Judaism," in J. Neusner (ed.), *Christianity, Judaism, and Other Greco-Roman Cults: I. New Testament* (SJLA, 12; Leiden: E. J. Brill, 1975), 163–86; idem, "The Man from Heaven in Johannine Sectarianism," *JBL* 91(1972): 44–72; and idem, *The Prophet-King: Moses Traditions and the Johannine Christology* (NovTSup, 14; Leiden: E. J. Brill, 1967).

Helpful exegetical and thematic studies include P. N. Anderson, *The Christology of the Fourth Gospel: Its Unity and Disunity in the Light of John 6* (Valley Forge, Pa.: Trinity Press Int'l, 1996); D. M. Ball, *"I Am" in John's Gospel: Literary Function, Background and Theological Implications* (JSNTSup, 124; Sheffield: Sheffield Academic Press, 1996); J. Beutler and R. T. Fortna (eds.), *The Shepherd Discourse of John 10 and Its Context* (SNTSMS, 67; Cambridge: Cambridge Univ. Press, 1991); G. M. Burge, *The Anointed Community: The Holy Spirit in the Johannine Tradition* (Grand Rapids: Eerdmans, 1987); D. Burkett, *The Son of Man in the Gospel of John* (JSNTSup, 56; Sheffield: Sheffield Academic Press, 1991); C. M. Carmichael, *The Story of Creation: Its Origin and Its Interpretation in Philo and the Fourth Gospel* (Ithaca: Cornell Univ. Press); R. J. Cassidy, *John's Gospel in New Perspective: Christology and the Realities of Roman Power* (Maryknoll: Orbis Books, 1992); M. Davies, *Rhetoric and Reference in the Fourth Gospel* (JSNTSup, 69; Sheffield: Sheffield Academic Press, 1992); E. Franck, *Revelation Taught: The Paraclete in the Gospel of John* (ConBNT, 14; Lund: CWK Gleerup, 1985); E. Harris, *Prologue and Gospel: The Theology of the Fourth Evangelist* (JSNTSup, 107; Sheffield: Sheffield Academic Press, 1994); J. J. Kanagaraj, *'Mysticism' in the Gospel of John: An Inquiry into Its Background* (JSNTSup, 158; Sheffield: Sheffield Academic Press, 1998). E. Käsemann, *The Testament of Jesus: A Study of the Gospel of John in the Light of Chapter 17*, trans. G. Krodel (Philadelphia: Fortress Press, 1968); C. R. Koester, *Symbolism in the Fourth Gospel: Meaning, Mystery, Community* (Minneapolis: Fortress Press, 1995); A. J. Köstenberger, *The Missions of Jesus and the Disciples according to the Fourth Gospel* (Grand Rapids: Eerdmans, 1998); R. Kysar, "Anti-Semitism and the Gospel of John," in C. A. Evans and D. A. Hagner (eds.), *Anti-Semitism and Early Christianity: Issues of Polemic and Faith* (Minneapolis: Fortress Press, 1993), 113–27; R. G. Maccini, *Her Testimony Is True: Women as Witnesses according to John* (JSNTSup, 125; Sheffield: Sheffield Academic Press, 1996); E. L. Miller, "The Johannine Origins of the Johannine *Logos*," *JBL* 112 (1993): 445–57; P. Minear, "The Original Functions of John 21," *JBL* 102 (1983): 85–98; F. J. Moloney, *The Johannine Son of Man*, 2nd ed.

(Rome: LAS, 1978); G. C. Nicholson, *Death as Departure: The Johannine Descent-Ascent Schema* (SBLDS, 63; Chico, Calif.: Scholars Press, 1983); J. H. Neyrey, *An Ideology of Revolt: John's Christology in Social-Science Perspective* (Philadelphia: Fortress Press, 1988); K. Quast, *Peter and the Beloved Disciple: Figures for a Community in Crisis* (JSNTSup, 32; Sheffield: Sheffield Academic Press, 1989); D. Rensberger, "The Politics of John: The Trial of Jesus in the Fourth Gospel," *JBL* 103 (1984): 395–411; F. F. Segovia, *The Farewell of the Word: The Johannine Call to Abide* (Minneapolis: Fortress Press, 1991); and F. Thielman, "The Style of the Fourth Gospel and Ancient Literary Critical Concepts of Religious Discourse," in D. F. Watson (ed.), *Persuasive Artistry* (JSNTSup, 50; Sheffield: Sheffield Academic Press, 1991), 169–83.

For literary studies of the FG, see R. A. Culpepper, *Anatomy of the Fourth Gospel: A Study in Literary Design* (Philadelphia: Fortress Press, 1983); J. P. Heil, *Blood and Water: The Death and Resurrection of Jesus in John 18–21* (CBQMS, 27; Washington: Catholic Biblical Assoc., 1995); G. O'Day, *Revelation in the Fourth Gospel: Narrative Mode and Theological Claim* (Philadelphia: Fortress Press, 1986); L. P. Jones, *The Symbol of Water in the Gospel of John* (JSNTSup, 145; Sheffield: Sheffield Academic Press, 1997); D. A. Lee, *The Symbolic Narratives of the Fourth Gospel: The Interplay of Form and Meaning* (JSNTSup, 95; Sheffield: Sheffield Academic Press, 1994); F. J. Moloney, *Belief in the Word: Reading John 1–4* (Minneapolis: Fortress Press, 1993); idem, *Signs and Shadows: Reading John 5–12* (Minneapolis: Fortress Press, 1996); A. Reinhartz, *The Word in the World: The Cosmological Tale in the Fourth Gospel* (SBLMS, 45; Atlanta: Scholars Press, 1992); M. W. G. Stibbe, *John as Storyteller: Narrative Criticism and the Fourth Gospel* (SNTSMS, 73; Cambridge: Cambridge Univ. Press, 1992); and D. Tovey, *Narrative Art and Act in the Fourth Gospel* (JSNTSup, 151; Sheffield: Sheffield Academic Press, 1997).

The classic commentary on the FG, however flawed by its redactional hypotheses, is R. Bultmann, *The Gospel of John: A Commentary*, trans. G. Beasley-Murray et al. (Philadelphia: Westminster Press, 1971 [1966]). For further critical commentary, see C. K. Barrett, *The Gospel According to John*, 2nd ed. (Philadelphia: The Westminster Press, 1978); G. R. Beasley-Murray, *John* (WBC; Waco: Word Books, 1987); R. E. Brown, *The Gospel According to John*, 2 vols. (AB; Garden City, N.Y.: Doubleday & Co., 1966–70); E. Haenchen, *John*, 2 vols., trans. and ed. R. W. Funk (with U. Busse) (Hermeneia; Philadelphia: Fortress Press, 1984 [1980]); and R. Schnackenburg, *The Gospel According to John*, 3 vols., trans. K. Smythe et al. (New York: Crossroad, 1968–82 [1965–75]). For more general commentary, see T. L. Brodie, *The Gospel According to John: A Literary and Theological Commentary* (New York: Oxford Univ. Press, 1993); and C. H. Talbert, *Reading John: A Literary and Theological Commentary on the Fourth Gospel and the Johannine Epistles* (New York: Crossroad, 1992).

25. 1, 2, and 3 John

THE THREE LETTERS attributed to John emerge from a context of conflict and at first appear to provide a window onto the history of Johannine Christianity. Close examination of the letters, however, leads to the conclusion that they provide a basis less for a precise historical reconstruction of a community's story than for an appreciation of the distinctive Johannine understanding of Christian existence.

Since our knowledge of a "Johannine" church is at best vague, it is impossible to assign these three very short writings to precise moments in that church's putative history. A complete lack of external controls prohibits reconstructing any history in the full sense. The best one can hope for is to find traces of an internal development within the group. And even this depends entirely on reading between the lines of the writings themselves. This approach, however, has several problems. First, the same community might not be in view in all three letters; the letters could, for instance, have been written at intervals and addressed to different communities, making it difficult to decipher stages in the conflict. Second, although it is likely that these documents had a common authorship, one cannot be entirely certain; indeed, a common style and symbolic structure would be expected from both sides of a divided community. Third, one cannot be totally confident that the letters were written in the particular sequence in which they are now found, making reconstruction of stages of conflict very difficult. Indeed, it is quite possible that they were all sent at once. In this case, one could not trace any development in the community, since the letters would describe only a single point in its history.

Even the attempt to describe the situation to which these letters were addressed, therefore, must to some extent consist of a recital of the difficulties confronting any such description.

The Setting: Conflict and Division

Each of the letters indicates in its own way that there is conflict among the readers. In 3 John, the dispute appears at first reading to be purely political, taking the form of a conflict between rival leaders. In 2 John, that conflict is connected to the issue of proper teaching. And in 1 John, doctrinal and moral disagreements dominate. The conflict appears to be one generated from within rather than from without. In contrast to the Gospel of John, the issue is not hostility or persecution from the world but internal disputes and rivalries.

The surface issue concerns the proper understanding of Jesus, but the dimensions or even the precise nature of the conflict are not easy to recover. First and Second John clearly indicate that convictions concerning Jesus have become—if not the cause of the divisions—at the very least the banners of the respective parties. In the most explicit fashion, the content of belief, rather than simply the assent of faith, becomes here a criterion for membership. The terms "orthodoxy," "heterodoxy," and "heresy" are appropriate ones in these letters. Thus, we find the use of the verb "to confess" (*homologeō*, *exhomologeō*; 1 John 2:23; 4:2, 3, 15; 2 John 7) and "to deny" (*arneomai*; 1 John 2:22-23). In a shift from the Fourth Gospel, the opponents are thus not unbelievers but fellow Christians; they are not purely outsiders but ones who had at first belonged to the author's own group: those "who went out from us" (1 John 2:19). Now, they are given traditional titles of disdain: they are "false prophets" (1 John 4:1) and "antichrists" (1 John 2:18, 22; 4:3). In the description of 2 John 7, they are above all "deceivers who have gone out into the world."

These designations do not, however, establish what doctrinal points separate the various Johannine groups. For instance, one could question how literally the author understands the term "antichrist": does the individual completely deny Christ or simply hold to a different view of Jesus as Christ? A number of creedal statements in 1 and 2 John are pertinent here. In 1 John we find the phrases "he who denies that Jesus is the Christ" and "he who denies the Father and the Son"; together, these statements designate a liar and an antichrist (2:22). In contrast, the readers are to "believe in the name of the Son Jesus Christ" (3:23). A similar opposition appears later between "every spirit which confesses that Jesus Christ has come in the flesh" and "every spirit that does not confess Jesus" (4:2-3). In the same chapter, the orthodox group testifies "that the Father has sent the Son as Savior of the world," and this is placed next to "whoever confesses that Jesus is Son of God" (4:14-15). A series of confessional phrases follows in chapter 5: "whoever believes that Jesus is the Christ" (5:1); "whoever believes that Jesus is the Son of God" (5:5); "whoever believes in the Son of God" (5:10); "believe in the name of the Son of God" (5:13); and "we know that the Son of God has come" (5:20). Finally, 2 John 7 has, "who will not acknowledge the coming of Jesus Christ in the flesh."

These phrases make fairly obvious what this orthodox group confesses. But it is not at all clear what the content of the "heterodox" belief is. It is not certain that everything the author's group affirms is being denied by their opponents. Nor does it appear that the denials add up to a coherent confession. According to the writer, the antichrist denies that "Jesus is the Christ," denying the Father and the Son (1 John 2:22). But it is difficult to determine whether the denials of Jesus (1 John 4:3) and "that Jesus Christ has come in the flesh" (2 John 7) represent expansions, refinements, or equivalents to the rejection of Jesus as the Christ. We cannot confirm whether the opponents challenge the confession that Jesus is the Messiah, that he is the Son of God, or that he is truly human. Perhaps they denied that Jesus "came" as God's son, believing instead that he was "adopted" as God's son in the resurrection. Moreover, we cannot be certain that the author actually knew the precise position of those who had separated themselves from the community. Indeed, given the ancient practice of vilifying opponents—depicting them as having all forms of doctrinal and moral failures—we must also question how much of the portrayal may be owed to the author. Nevertheless, the writer does seem convinced that the opponents are deficient in their understanding and appreciation of *Jesus*. The figure who was, according to the Fourth Gospel, the abiding center of their life and unity, is here the focal point of dissension and division.

Any attempt to reconstruct a coherent position for the "opponents" must deal with two methodological difficulties. First, we cannot assume from every positive statement or exhortation that the opposition held a direct counterview. The author's insistence on love, and particularly on the practical expression of love, may reflect a lack of care among the opposition party; on the other hand, it need not. Second, we cannot assume that the theological framing of the division was either more or less important than the social dimensions of that conflict. These were at least twofold: the mutual withholding of hospitality, and rival claims to leadership (see 2 John and 3 John). We do not have sufficient information to decide whether the political and social conflicts preceded, accompanied, or followed the theological disagreement. Moreover, we must always keep in mind that, in early Christianity, to deny hospitality to a fellow Christian was also to deny Christ. Thus, there may be a confluence of conceptions here, so that the theological conflict expresses at a higher level the reality of the social dissension.

Whatever the precise nature of the disputes, any sort of division would be a severe crisis for a church that lived within the symbolic framework we have seen in the Fourth Gospel. The farewell discourse of Jesus (John 15:1—17:26) portrays a community of friends. They share in one Spirit; being joined to Jesus as Jesus is to the Father, in a fellowship of unity and love. For a community with such a self-understanding, any dissension and deviance would be difficult to understand or assimilate. But a clash over the right understanding of Jesus, and a division leading to mutual excommunication, would challenge this community's very identity and existence.

A Three-Letter Packet from the Elder

The three letters were probably sent at the same time to the same destination, for it would be difficult to account for the preservation of letters as unassuming as 2 and 3 John were they not the companions of a more significant writing. The function of each writing will be considered in more detail as we examine them in turn. For the moment, we should note that 3 John was most likely a letter of recommendation from the elder to Gaius, certifying that the carrier of the other two letters, Demetrius, was to be received with open arms. Second John was to be read to the entire assembly as an introduction and cover letter for 1 John, which is not really a letter at all but an exhortation, closer in nature to a homily. The Johannine letters thus make most sense when viewed as parts of the same epistolary package. As for the identity of the elder who wrote the letters or the location of the recipients, there have been many theories but few widely acknowledged solutions.

3 John: Letter of Commendation from the Elders

Third John is a genuine personal letter and provides us with the only specific names in the dispute generating the Johannine correspondence: Gaius, Demetrius, and Diotrephes. The good Greco-Roman names indicate the presence of a gentile component in the Johannine communities. The short farewell indicates that these churches call themselves "friends" (v. 15), following the teaching of Jesus (John 15:12-15). The elder who writes aligns himself with the "true witness" of the Fourth Gospel: "You know that our testimony is true" (v. 12; cf. John 19:35; 21:24). The author calls Gaius "beloved" (vv. 1, 2, 5, 11), but this individual is otherwise unknown to us. He appears to be the head of a household, since the elder praises him for his hospitality to traveling Christians (vv. 5-6).

The elder is pleased that Gaius is doing well and, above all, that his emissaries have testified to the fact that Gaius "walks in the truth" (v. 3). There appears to be considerable communication between these local churches. Those who provide hospitality for the messengers and missionaries become, in turn, "fellow workers for the truth" (v. 8).

The hospitality of Gaius and his household is all the more important for the elder as neither his letters nor his emissaries are being accepted by another church leader, Diotrephes. Diotrephes here appears as a rival to the elder, one who seeks primacy of place among the Johannine churches (v. 9). His bid for power is exemplified by his refusal to accept those sent by the elder. What is more, he expels from the assembly those who do accept them (v. 10).

At the very least, then, 3 John shows us a power struggle between two church leaders—the elder is pitted against a figure characterized as ambitious and malicious, perhaps a leader of those "who went out from us" (1 John 2:19; 2 John 7). It is difficult to know, however, if a deeper doctrinal division is hinted at in 3 John: the emphasis on "walking in the truth" (vv. 2-3) could indicate theological problems (i.e., the author is implicitly urging the readers not to depart from specific Christian truths). Yet, in light of the dominance of the theme of hospitality in the letter (vv. 5-8, 10, 11-12), it is quite possible that this emphasis simply attempts to inculcate a spirit of openness toward the emissaries.

Gaius, in contrast, is a local leader still in communion with the elder and willing to receive his delegates and teaching. Without such hospitality, the elder's branch of the church would face extinction, for those who traveled "for the name" would or could take no support from "pagans" (v. 7). This small aside reminds us of the sectarian tendencies inherent in all forms of Johannine Christianity. Now, however, those "outside" may even include dissident Christians. Those who provided refreshment and new outfitting ("sending them on," v. 6) for these messengers became their "fellow workers" and "friends"; the sharing of their possessions symbolized as well the sharing in their spiritual ideals.

The pertinence of all the talk about hospitality is revealed by the specific purpose of this short note: it seems to accompany the other two letters—"I have written something to the church" (v. 9). The epistolary aorist ("written") seems not to refer to a previous communication but to the exhortation that the elder now wants read in the assembly—1 John. Thus, 3 John serves as a letter of recommendation for the messenger who carries these letters—Demetrius, who is well attested by everyone and "by the truth itself" (v. 12). Gaius can therefore safely accept him and his messages. The "many things" the elder does not want to commit to paper (v. 13) but is postponing for a face-to-face meeting (v. 14) concern practical matters, such as dealing with the Diotrephes situation. In the meantime, with a classic parenetic flourish, the elder reminds Gaius not to follow the example of Diotrephes in refusing hospitality to the elder's emissaries: "Do not imitate the evil but the good" (v. 11). Nothing could sound more Greek. But the motivation given for such behavior places us once again within the distinctively Johannine symbolic world: the one who does good is "from God," whereas the one who does evil "has not seen God" (v. 11).

2 John: Cover Letter to the Church

The second of the short letters carried by Demetrius is a note from the elder to Gaius's community—the introduction to the longer letter of 1 John. The "elect lady with her children" (v. 1) is a honorific title for the community, as the closing also suggests: "the children of your elect sister greet you" (v. 13). The letter supposes a collective audience (vv. 2, 3, 6, 8, 10, 12). The greeting is more extended than in 3 John but with the same emphasis on "truth": "all who have come to know the truth" love this community, on the basis of "the truth dwelling within us" (vv. 1-2). The elder prays that his reader receive grace, mercy, and peace "in truth and love" (v. 3), and he rejoices to see them "walking in the truth" (v. 4). The closing suggests again that the elder defers personal matters for a later face-to-face conference, when he hopes "their joy might be made full" (v. 12; cf. 3 John 10, 13-14).

The issue of false teaching emerges explicitly in this letter. The elder warns his readers of the "many deceivers who have gone out into the world" (v. 7). We are reminded by this of the deep ambivalence of the Johannine writings toward that entity called the "world." In the Fourth Gospel, the world is at once the arena for the revelation of Jesus and the object of God's love and salvation (John 1:9; 3:16-17; 4:42; 6:14, 33, 51; 8:12; 9:5; 10:36; 11:27; 12:46-47; 17:21-24) and, because of its rejection of God in Jesus, it is a place characterized by the absence of God and hostility toward believers (John 1:10; 7:4-7; 8:23; 11:9; 12:25, 31; 14:17-31; 15:18-19; 16:8, 11, 33; 17:6, 9, 11, 14, 16, 18, 25). The same tension is carried over with equal intensity in 1 John: "the world" was the recipient of God's love and salvation through Jesus (1 John 2:2; 4:9, 14, 17) but exists now as a place dominated by a power other than God's (5:19), reflecting this in its perverted values and hatred for the "children of God" (1 John 2:15-17; 3:1, 13; 4:1-5; 5:4-5).

Those who have left the elder's community and "gone out into the world" therefore partake of its values. They are collectively "the deceiver and the antichrist" (2 John 7). Whether by their explicit teaching or their actions, their deception amounts to this: "They deny Christ's coming in the flesh" (v. 7). The elder portrays them as those who do not hold fast to the community traditions: "Whoever goes forward [*proagei*] and does not remain in the teaching of Christ does not have God" (v. 9). The ambiguity of the expression "teaching of Christ" may be deliberate. It includes teaching "about Christ," that is, a proper understanding of Christ, for that is required to "have both the Father and the Son" (v. 9). But it may also include the teaching "from Christ," meaning the commandment that Jesus himself taught them "from the beginning," to love one another (v. 5).

Concern for false teaching is here combined with practical directives on hospitality. What the elder complained of in the practice of Diotrephes (3 John 10) he now recommends to this church: believers are not to receive into their houses anyone not espousing the proper teaching. They are not even to greet such people (v. 10). With Diotrephes, of course, the failure to accept the emissaries was a rejection of the elder's authority. Here in 2 John we see the survival techniques of intentional communities faced with deviance: shunning and excommunication. The stakes are outlined succinctly: "Whoever greets them makes fellowship [*koinōnei*] with their evil deeds" (v. 11).

This compact observation contains a complex of interconnected concepts. First, as we have seen often in the NT writings, hospitality means more than the sharing of space and food—it implies a spiritual communion. Second, as we saw in the Pastorals and 2 Peter, evil behavior is thought to follow directly from wrong thinking. Thus, in this view, listening to wrong teaching about Jesus leads to evil deeds against Jesus. The refusal of hospitality in this case is therefore not an act of hostility toward individual persons but a defensive measure against error and evil by a community fighting to maintain its own identity.

The elder alerts his readers to the message of 1 John, which they will also hear in the assembly: they are to hold to the commandment they learned from the beginning, not wandering off but staying in place (vv. 5–6). This single all-inclusive commandment—that they love one another—came to them from Jesus (John 15:12, 17) and is, the elder insists, still the necessary and sufficient way for this community to define itself.

1 John: Exhortation to Faithfulness

We would not expect a writing so beautiful or compelling as 1 John to emerge from the difficult circumstances suggested by 2 and 3 John. This is the "something written for the church" that Demetrius carried to the household of Gaius. Although clearly a written composition (see 2:1, 7, 8, 12, 13, 14, 21, 26; 5:13), it has no epistolary character at all, retaining instead a distinctive homiletic style of exhortation. The elder "announces" or "proclaims" (1:2, 3, 5) to his audience a message (1:5) that really has no new content (2:7) but is a simple reminder and exhortation to live by that commandment which was "from the beginning": love one another (1:1; 2:7, 13, 14, 24; 3:11).

The style of 1 John is much like that of the Fourth Gospel. Its Greek is, if anything, even simpler, while its vocabulary is more abstract. The combination makes it a difficult composition to read sequentially, as the same points appear to be made repeatedly with only slight variations. The style can be deceptive, for it sometimes contains the form of argument while lacking its logic. Thus from 1:6 to 2:5 we read eight conditional sentences. Each of them has an internal coherence. But when read in sequence, not only the connection between them but also their individual points are easily forgotten.

The most striking stylistic element in 1 John is the apparent self-contradiction regarding the believer and sin that is found throughout the letter: one sentence affirms something that another appears to deny. For instance, the writer claims that anyone who says they are without sin is a liar and makes a liar of God (1:8-10). Yet, the writer also maintains further on that anyone who sins is a "child of the Devil" and does not abide in Jesus (3:4-10). Not surprisingly, various source theories have been invoked to account for this phenomenon. They are not necessary, however. The function of the phraseology is an important key to deciphering the elder's meaning: what is granted by way of proposition ("everyone sins") in one place is taken away by way of exhortation ("do not sin") in another. The vacillation between affirmation and exhortation in 1 John derives not from a multiplicity of sources and editors but from the internal tension created by the author's task: encouraging faithfulness to God in a context where many of the community have left to "walk in the darkness."

This composition shares the same symbolic world as the Fourth Gospel. We find in it many of the Gospel's major themes: the distinctions between light and darkness (1:5;

2:8-9, 10), truth and falsehood (1:6; 2:4, 21, 27; 3:19; 4:6, 20; 5:7), the community and "the world" (2:15; 3:1, 13; 4:3, 4, 5; 5:19), and life and death (1:2; 3:14-15; 5:11, 13). Moreover, in 1 John we find the same conviction of being in touch with the "beginning." It occurs here in several senses: chronological, ontological, and existential. Chronologically, they have received truth from the traditions passed on to them "from the beginning" (1:1; 2:24; 3:11); ontologically, they "know"/"abide in" Jesus who is himself "from the beginning" (2:13-14; cf. John 1:1); existentially, they are in direct communion with the Holy Spirit (2:20, 27; 3:24; 4:2, 6, 13; 5:7). The believers are those who are "born of God" (3:1, 2, 10; 4:4, 7; 5:1, 4, 18, 19). They "bear testimony" (4:14; 5:7, 10) to what they "see and hear" (1:3; 2:24; 3:2, 6), even as they "abide" (2:6, 10, 17, 24-25; 3:6, 24; 4:12, 13, 15) both in the commandment (2:3; 3:22; 5:2) and in the love (3:11, 14, 18; 4:7, 11-12, 21) revealed to them in the Son of God (4:7-10).

What distinguishes the shaping of these symbols in 1 John, however, is that none of them can be affirmed as straightforwardly as in the Fourth Gospel. This is a community divided: some have "gone out from us" (2:19). And although the elder insists that if they "had really been of us" they would not have left, the identity of this community that defines itself in terms of its share in the Spirit—its unity and its love—is severely shaken. At least two groups now lay claim to being the community of the beloved disciple, and their claims appear to be mutually exclusive. Thus the task before the elder is to assert the traditional claims for his readers, but at the same time to take into account the new circumstance of division and dispute.

The remarkable thing about 1 John is that it does not consist of a bitter polemic against those who departed or a sustained refutation of their claims. The focus of this writing is not on the outsiders but on those who remain. However, they are not simply congratulated for holding on to the truth. Rather, they are challenged to a renewed affirmation of their identity, which cannot be simply a matter of correct doctrine. It is a practical exhortation throughout: it begins with: "I am writing to you so that you may not sin" (2:1); and ends with: "Little children, keep yourselves from idols" (5:21).

In 1 John we find the rare phenomenon of a perfectionistic and sectarian community dealing with failure and division not by blaming those who left but by renewing community identity through a recollection of the fundamentals of community belief. The faithful remnant is encouraged to cultivate a new alertness to its own failures. And these failures, it becomes clear, are those of complacency: an unheeding and comfortable confidence in the sufficiency simply of being an insider. But it is not enough, any longer, to claim the Spirit; now everyone must "test every spirit to see whether they are of God" (4:1). It is not enough to claim distinction from "the world"; the departure of some has shown that "the world" is not simply out there but also inside the community itself. Thus, the response to division is the cultivation of stronger borders of community identity in order to solidify group cohesion.

The community of the elder is therefore required to examine its symbols to discover elements of a shared tradition that will engender this cohesion. So, for example, it is imperative for the community to acknowledge its own sinfulness (1:8, 10), in the confidence that Jesus will be their expiation and advocate with the Father (1:7, 9; 2:2; 4:10). No longer can they be content with the simple affirmation that the one born of God does not sin (3:9; 5:18). That conviction is true in the sense that those "walking in the light" are to strive for complete obedience to God. Yet, it must now be understood in a new way: the denial of sin is not only self-deception (1:8) but may itself be the "sin unto death" (5:16-17), for it places confidence in one's own perfection, not in the mercy of God. This community, however, confesses its sin and prays for its members who sin (5:14). Its confidence is thus not in its own perfection but in the gift of life that came from the side of the crucified (5:6-8; cf. John 19:34). This emphasis both reestablishes reliance on God and refocuses the community's attention inward toward each other, leveling, in the process, any ambitious pretensions among individuals (cf. 3 John 9).

Furthering the goal of establishing community cohesion, the elder moves to a second major premise: the truth cannot remain simply the abstract confession of Jesus as Son of God come in the flesh, as important as that is (2:22-23; 3:23; 4:2-3, 14; 5:1, 10-11, 20); it must be translated into appropriate behavior. This means a real and effectual love, which stands in contrast to the hatred so characteristic of the world (2:15; 3:1, 13; 4:3, 4, 5; 5:13, 19) and those false brethren who have joined it (2:9-10; 3:14-15; 4:20). The sad fraternal relationship between this community and those who have departed is suggested by the example of Cain. He murdered his brother simply because "his own deeds were evil and his brother's righteous" (3:12-13; cf. Gen. 4:8-16).

In contrast, the members of this community must "perfect" their love, removing the defensiveness that comes from fear and opening their hearts to each other in care (2:5; 4:12, 17-18). They cannot any longer remain isolated as though the identity of the community would be maintained no matter what they did. They must reestablish the bonds of love between them, so that the community can stand firm in the midst of adversity and crisis. They are to pray for each other and correct each other (5:14-17). They are to care for each other in as practical and direct a fashion as God's love in Christ operates (1 John 3:16-18):

> By this we know love, that he laid down his life for us; and we ought to lay down our lives for our fellow believers. If anyone has the world's goods and sees one's fellow believer in need, yet closes one's heart against that one, how does God's love abide . . . ? Little children, let us love not in word or speech but in deed and in truth.

By cultivating love in the community, the identity and borders of this group of believers are strengthened, and any malicious behavior (cf. 3 John 10) is cut off at its root.

Thus the community must now face up to the task of renewing its integrity in action and understanding. This accounts for the apparent inconsistency in the composition, between assertion and exhortation. There is a sense in which this community can continue to assert that it has the message of life (1:1-4) and has experienced victory over the evil one (2:12-14). Its members can state with truth that their sins have been forgiven (2:12), that they have knowledge of truth (2:20-21) and are God's children (3:2). They can even declare that no one born of God sins (3:9-10; 5:18) and that their own hearts do not condemn them (3:21). They are sure that they do abide in God (3:24) and have overcome the antichrist (4:4). They have the Spirit (4:13) and love is perfected among them (4:17). Their faith overcomes the world (5:4). They bear a testimony within themselves (5:10) and have confidence (5:14) that they are in the God who is true (5:20).

But even while they assert these convictions, which form the very structure of their symbolic world, they must affirm as well the imperatives that arise from the failure of the community to live by those same convictions. If they say they have no sin, they deceive themselves (1:8) and make God a liar since he sent Jesus as expiation for their sins (1:10). If they hate their fellow believers they are still in the dark (2:9). They must hate the world and refuse to live by its standards (2:15). They are to abide in God (2:27). They must cleanse themselves (3:3) and are commanded to love one another (3:11) not just in word but in deed (3:18). The elder is here exhorting the community to establish common bonds in Christ, eradicating any form of spiritual hierarchy and pretension: all are the same before God, in Christ, and in the community.

In short, then, the elder indicates to this remnant community that its symbols of self-understanding are true and correspond to reality. But the reason for the community's failure—division—is that it did not appreciate that the gift carried with it an imperative. They need to realize once more that it was not *their* perfection that made them "children of God," but that this was a gift of God. They need to look once again at the source of their identity, to learn the pattern for their lives together (1 John 4:7-12):

> Beloved, let us love one another; for love is of God, and whoever loves is born of God and knows God. Whoever does not love does not know God, for God is love. In this the love of God was made manifest among us, that God sent his only Son into the world, so that we might live through him. In this is love, not that we loved God, but that God loved us and sent the Son to be the expiation for our sins. Beloved, if God so loved us, we also ought to love one another. No one has ever seen God; if we love one another, God abides in us and God's love is perfected in us.

Here we see the two-pronged approach of the elder. First, he establishes humility as the basis for community existence. Second, he defines the life of the group as the imitation of the unity and love found in God. The solution to the problem of division and discord is thus found through the identity, cohesion, and concord that come from faithfully imitating the love of God. Only in this way is further division prevented, existing breaches repaired, estranged former members brought home, and opened wounds healed.

Study Questions

1. What sort of conflict appears in each of the three letters?

2. What accusations are made against those who left the community?

3. What do the Johannine epistles share in common with the Gospel of John in terms of vocabulary, theme, and perspective?

4. Identify the "family" metaphors in these letters. What does this tell you about the author's understanding of church? What relationships do these terms describe?

Bibliographical Note

Much of the literature cited for the Gospel of John is also relevant here. For an overview of scholarship on the epistles, see the introduction by F. F. Bruce, "Johannine Studies Since Westcott's Day," in B. F. Westcott's *The Epistles of St. John* (Grand Rapids: Eerdmans, 1966), lix–lxxvi. For the reconstruction of the historical setting of the letters, see R. E. Brown, *The Community of the Beloved Disciple* (New York: Paulist Press, 1979), 93–144; idem, "'Other Sheep Not of This Fold': The Johannine Perspective on Christian Diversity in the Late First Century," *JBL* 97 (1978): 5–22; idem, "The Relationship to the Fourth Gospel Shared by the Author of 1 John and by His Opponents," in E. Best and R. McL. Wilson (eds.), *Text and Interpretation* (Cambridge: Cambridge Univ. Press, 1979), 57–68; J. Painter, "The 'Opponents' in 1 John," *NTS* 32 (1986): 48–71; and P. Perkins, "*Koinōnia* in I Jn 1:3-7: The Social Context of Division in the Johannine Letters," *CBQ* 45 (1983): 631–41.

For general issues related to the epistles as a whole, see C. C. Black, "The Johannine Epistles and the Question of Early Catholicism," *NovT* 28 (1986): 131–58; R. E. Brown, "The Qumran Scrolls and the Johannine Gospel and Epistles," in his *New Testament Essays* (New York: Paulist Press, 1965), 102–31; R. B. Edwards, *The Johannine Epistles* (Sheffield: Sheffield Academic Press, 1996); J. J. Gunther, "The Alexandrian Gospel and the Letters of John," *CBQ* 41 (1979): 581–603; W. F. Howard, "The Common Authorship of the Johannine Gospel and Epistles," *JTS* 48 (1947): 12–25; J. M. Lieu, *The Theology of the Johannine Epistles* (Cambridge: Cambridge Univ. Press, 1991); idem, "What Was from the Beginning: Scripture and Tradition in the Johannine Epistles," *NTS* 39

(1993): 458–77; J. A. T. Robinson, "The Destination and Purpose of the Johannine Epistles," *NTS* 7 (1960): 56–65; and J. C. Thomas, "The Order of the Composition of the Johannine Epistles," *NovT* 37 (1995): 68–75.

On 1 John, see J. Bogart, *Orthodox and Heretical Perfectionism in the Johannine Community as Evident in the First Epistle of John* (SBLDS, 33; Missoula, Mont.: Scholars Press, 1977); J. C. Coetzee, "The Holy Spirit in I John," *Neot* 13 (1979): 43–67; A. Feuillet, "The Structure of 1 John: Comparison with the Fourth Gospel," *BTB* 3 (1973): 194–216; F. O. Francis, "The Form and Function of the Opening and Closing Paragraphs of James and 1 John," *ZNW* 61 (1970): 110–26; M. de Jonge, "The Use of the Word *Christos* in the Johannine Epistles," in C. K. Barrett (ed.), *Studies in John* (NovTSup, 24; Leiden: E. J. Brill, 1970), 66–74; J. M. Lieu, "Authority to Become Children of God: A Study of I John," *NovT* 23 (1981): 210–28; E. Malatesta, *Interiority and Covenant: A Study of einai en and menein en in the First Letter of Saint John* (AnB, 69; Rome: Biblical Inst. Press, 1978); P. S. Minear, "The Idea of Incarnation in I John," *Int* 24 (1970): 291–302; B. Noack, "On 1 Jn 2:12-14," *NTS* 19 (1972): 236–41; J. C. O'Neill, *The Puzzle of 1 John: A New Examination of Origins* (London: SPCK, 1966); O. Piper, "I John and the Didache of the Primitive Church," *JBL* 66 (1947): 437–51; F. F. Segovia, *Love Relationships in the Johannine Tradition: Agapē/Agapan in I John and the Fourth Gospel* (SBLDS, 58; Chico, Calif.: Scholars Press, 1982); J. S. Sibinga, "A Study in 1 John," in *Studies in John*, 194–208; P. J. Thompson, "Psalm 119: A Possible Clue to the Structure of the First Epistle of John," *SE* 2/TU 87 (1964): 487–92; J. Townsend, "The Sin Unto Death: 1 Jn 5:16ff," *Restoration Quarterly* 6 (1962): 147–50; U. C. von Wahlde, *The Johannine Commandments: 1 John and the Struggle for the Johannine Tradition* (New York: Paulist Press, 1990); D. F. Watson, "Amplification Techniques in 1 John: The Interaction of Rhetorical Style and Invention," *JSNT* 51 (1993): 99–123; and B. Witherington III, "The Waters of Birth: John 3.5 and 1 John 5.6-8," *NTS* 35 (1989): 155–60.

On 2 and 3 John, see R. W. Funk, "The Apostolic Presence: John the Elder," in his *Parables and Presence* (Philadelphia: Fortress Press, 1982), 103–10; J. Lieu, *The Second and Third Epistles of John: History and Background*, ed. J. Riches (Edinburgh: T. & T. Clark, 1986); A. J. Malherbe, "Hospitality and Inhospitality in the Church" in his *Social Aspects of Early Christianity*, 2nd ed. (Philadelphia: Fortress Press, 1983 [1977]), 92–112; U. C. von Wahlde, "The Theological Foundation of the Presbyter's Argument in 2 Jn (vv 4–6)," *ZNW* 76 (1985): 209–24; D. F. Watson, "A Rhetorical Analysis of 2 John According to Greco-Roman Convention," *NTS* 35 (1989): 104–30; and idem, "A Rhetorical Analysis of 3 John: A Study in Epistolary Rhetoric," *CBQ* 51 (1989): 479–501. On the formal elements of the letter of recommendation, see C. H. Kim, *Form and Function of the Familiar Greek Letter of Recommendation* (SBLDS, 4; Missoula, Mont.: Scholars Press, 1972).

For critical commentary, see R. E. Brown, *The Epistles of John* (AB; Garden City, N.Y.: Doubleday, 1982); R. Bultmann, *A Commentary on the Johannine Epistles*, trans.

R. P. O'Hara et al. (Hermeneia; Philadelphia: Fortress Press, 1973 [1967]); R. Schnack-enburg, *The Johannine Epistles: Introduction and Commentary*, trans. R. and I. Fuller (New York: Crossroad, 1992 [1975]); S. S. Smalley, *1, 2, 3, John* (WBC; Waco: Word Books, 1984); and G. Strecker, *The Johannine Letters*, ed. H. W. Attridge, trans. L. M. Maloney (Hermeneia; Minneapolis: Fortress Press, 1996 [1989]). For more general treatment, see D. Rensberger, *1 John, 2 John, 3 John* (Nashville: Abingdon, 1997); and G. S. Sloyan, *Walking in the Truth: Perseverers and Deserters—The First, Second, and Third Letters of John* (Valley Forge, Pa.: Trinity Press Int'l, 1995).

26. The Book of Revelation

FEW WRITINGS IN all of literature have been so obsessively read with such generally disastrous results as the Book of Revelation (= the Apocalypse). Its history of interpretation is largely a story of tragic misinterpretation, resulting from a fundamental misapprehension of the work's literary form and purpose. Insofar as its arcane symbols have fed the treasury of prayer and poetry, its influence has been benign. More often, these same symbols have nurtured delusionary systems, both private and public, to the destruction of their fashioners and to the discredit of the writing.

Misunderstandings appear to be invited by the text itself, for it claims to offer a "revelation from Jesus Christ" which makes known to the readers "what is going to happen shortly" (1:1). No wonder it has often been taken as a divinely certified blueprint for the future. Already in the second century, Papias found in passages like Rev. 20:4-6 a promise of a literal earthly thousand-year (millennial) reign of the saints preceding the end of time:

> They came to life and reigned with Christ a thousand years. The rest of the dead did not come to life until the thousand years were ended. This is the first resurrection. Over such the second death has no power, but they shall be priests of God and of Christ, and they shall reign with him a thousand years (20:4-6; cf. Eusebius *Ecclesiastical History* III.39.12).

Papias was among the first of many "millenarians"—including Irenaeus, the Montanists, Joachim of Fiore, and some radical reformers of the sixteenth century—who found in Revelation a guide to the restored heaven and earth (21:1-2). People in every age could also find in these pages—with the text's own whispered injunctions to read between the lines (13:18; 17:9)—the identity of *their* "beast" (13:18). Rulers and usurpers from Nero to Saddam Hussein have unwittingly borne the epithet "666." Moreover, Revelation (in passages such as 21:1-8), when read in conjunction with the idealized picture of the primitive church in Acts 4:32-37, seemed to offer a basis for utopian, egalitarian projects that sought by human effort to bring about the vision of a heavenly Jerusalem. The ideal is born again in every age, including our own, when many Christians use Revelation as the essential guidebook to determine the time of an inevitable Armageddon (16:16). In short, the Book of Revelation is one of those rare compositions that speaks both to the deepest longings of the human heart for health and well-being and to the obscure corners of the human heart that tend toward illness.

This history of interpretation has several constant emphases. Most important among these, the book is considered a literal prophecy of future events. Two aspects of this definition are significant: first, "prophecy" is taken in its narrowest sense to mean "prediction": the text's frame of reference is not the author's own historical period but the one contemporary to the reader. The reading of contemporary events is therefore an essential part of reading this text: how does the pattern of world affairs as known to the reader connect with the signs of the approaching end time as outlined in Revelation? Second, the symbolism of the writing is treated as though it were a prophetic cryptogram: the reader is concerned not with intertextual connections or allusions to the religious heritage of the writer but only with the ways in which textual symbols can be aligned—point by point—with aspects of the reader's present situation. This process of interpretation has shown itself to be incapable of being disconfirmed by experience. If the reading of contemporary events turns out to be erroneous—if in fact the end does not come—it is never the nature of the text or of the interpretive process that is blamed; the calculations were merely off. Rather than telling people something about *how* Christian existence might be lived in the face of evil and apparent hopelessness, the text becomes something akin to a train schedule.

The problem here is that exegesis is swallowed up in hermeneutics. The conviction that God's Word speaks directly to every age has not been accompanied by the appreciation that it does so as mediated through its initial historical expression. The contemporary significance of any NT writing does not derive from the fact that it was written expressly for our age but from the conviction that a truth spoken to the first age of Christians can and does remain a truth for every age of believers. Failure to appreciate the historical fashioning and function of Revelation has bred great mischief. The remembrance of things past in this case means freedom from a prison of literalism and openness to the fresh message that the text can offer out of its historical context.

Above all for the Book of Revelation, therefore, the perspective provided by historical-critical analysis enables us to grasp the literary conventions within which the book's meaning is formed and expressed. From it, we learn to read the Book of Revelation as a writing in the apocalyptic genre, and discover how the frame of that genre is itself reshaped by the experience of a crucified and raised Messiah.

Revelation and Apocalyptic

Since there is a fairly extensive discussion of apocalyptic in an earlier section of this book (chap. 2), I will here review only some salient points of that outlook and literature. It arose as a form of literary prophecy within Judaism in response to an erosion of values from within and an attack on those values from without. It found classic expression in the Book of Daniel (chaps. 7–12) written during the Maccabean period, and it proliferated in a large number of pseudonymous writings both Jewish and Christian. To those wavering in their convictions it counseled fidelity; to those holding firm in obedience to God it encouraged endurance; to those who were losing their life through martyrdom it promised reward; and to those persecuting the faithful it pronounced judgment. Apocalyptic offered the oppressed and persecuted comfort by providing an interpretation of history. Writing in the name of a prophet or sage of the past, a contemporary writer assumed the mantle of prophecy and with it the authority of antiquity in the analysis of the writer's contemporary situation. Thus, present circumstances were retrojected into a prophecy that appeared to the reader to come from the past.

Apocalyptic is essentially a revelational literature. In the spirit, a prophet ascends to heaven, or has portentous dreams, or is transported to nether regions, so that the prophet can see both the present transcendental reality and its future historical realization, then communicate these to others by means of recording the revelations. Such visions of the future and the predictions they breed always have a fictive quality. We have seen as well that apocalyptic uses a standard range of symbols, with a heavy emphasis on numerology, cosmic catastrophes, and fabulous beasts.

The Book of Revelation obviously shares many of the same characteristics. It is, first, a self-consciously *written* composition: "Blessed is whoever reads . . . hears . . . what is *written* [1:3] . . . [and] keeps the words of prophecy of this *book* . . . [22:7]" (cf. 2:1, 8, 12, 18; 3:1, 7, 14; 22:9). The writing is also *visionary* in nature. A "revelation" is, in the apocalyptic tradition, generally something to be beheld. We see this already at the beginning of the writing: John is told, "Write what you see in a book" (1:10). The visions recorded in the book, however, are not the raw experience of mystical states but their literary distillation. The text can be called an "apocalypse [or, revelation] of Jesus Christ" (*apocalypsis Iēsou Christou*; 1:1), with the phrase "of Jesus Christ" understood both in the sense that the revelation comes from him, and is about him. John is told, "Come up hither and I will show you what must take place after this" (4:1), and as he passes through the open door of heaven, he "sees" and "hears" both what now is happening "there" and what will happen on earth. The most characteristically apocalyptic expression in this writing is "I saw" (1:2, 12, 17; 4:1; 5:1-2, 6, 11; 6:1-12; 7:1-2, 9; 8:2, 13; 9:1, 17; 10:1, 5; 13:1-2, 11; 14:1, 6, 14; 15:1, 2, 5; 16:13; 17:3-18; 18:1; 19:11, 17, 19; 20:1, 4, 11-12; 21:1, 2, 22).

Revelation shares with other apocalyptic writings a standard set of symbols. Numbers are important, for they combine an aura of precision with mystery. The number seven is most prominent: lampstands and stars standing for angels and churches (1:20), spirits of God (1:4; 3:1; 4:5), seals (5:1), horns and eyes of the lamb (5:6), trumpets (8:2), thunders (10:3), heads of the dragon (12:3) and of the beast (13:1), bowls (15:7), plagues (15:1), kings (17:9), and thousands killed (11:13). The number four occurs with the living creatures (4:6-8), horsemen (6:1-8), and the angels at the corners of the earth (7:1). In the biblical tradition, multiples of the number twelve gain an obvious significance by association with the tribes/patriarchs of Israel. So we find that the heavenly Jerusalem has twelve gates and foundation stones, corresponding to twelve apostles and angels (21:12-14); that the tree of life gives twelve fruits (22:2); that the woman clothed with the sun has a crown with twelve stars (12:1); that there are in heaven twenty-four elders and twenty-four thrones (4:4); and that the number of the elect is one hundred forty-four thousand, which equals twelve thousand from each of Israel's twelve tribes (7:4; 14:1-5). The point of all these numbers, of course, is that there is no point to them: they are not precise calculations by the writer. Rather, numbers lend a sacred character to certain realities and the replicated patterns of numbers indicate the existence of a God-ordered cosmos unfolding through a God-ordained plan, a critical element of the apocalyptic framework.

Revelation also has a well-stocked apocalyptic menagerie. On one side there is the "four living creatures" (4:6-8), the "Lamb who was slain yet lives" (5:6), the four horses (6:1-8), the eagle (8:13; 12:14), locusts like cavalry (9:3-11), and the white horse (19:11-16). On the opposite side there is the red dragon (12:3; also known as the ancient serpent, cf. 12:9), a "beast out of the sea" (13:1-2; this beast combines the qualities of leopard, bear, and lion), another "beast out of the earth" (13:11), and the scarlet beast (17:3, 7-12).

There is also no lack of cosmic phenomena. There are heavens that open (4:1), earthquakes, eclipses, dissolutions (6:12-17), angelic guards who hold the four corners of the earth like a carpet and prevent the winds (7:1), thunder, earthquake, lightning (8:5), a series of plagues (8:7-12), and a woman clothed with the sun and with a crown of stars (12:1). The feel of this imagery is perhaps best illustrated by Rev. 10:1-3:

> Then I saw another mighty angel coming down from heaven, wrapped in a cloud, with a rainbow over his head, and his face was like the sun, and his legs like pillars of fire. He had a little scroll open in his hand. And he set his right foot on the sea, and his left foot on the land, and called out with a loud voice, like a lion roaring; when he called out the seven thunders sounded.

These fantastic images can, possibly, be teased into some coherent picture, but the exercise would be quite beside the point. No particular number, beast, or star is significant in and of itself; it is the cumulative effect that creates the sense of mystery and transcendence essential for the dramatic impact of the revelation.

Revelation is like other apocalyptic works in this respect as well: despite its elaborate symbolism, it presents a rather straightforward interpretation of history. Appearances to the contrary, God is in charge of the world. Even though God's people suffer tribulations and evil appears to be triumphant (12:7—13:8), God will intervene decisively on behalf of the oppressed (14:14—20:15), bringing history to its goal: the communion of God with humans (21:1—22:5). Moreover, this climax to history is to come "quickly" (1:1; 2:16; 3:11; 11:14; 22:6, 7, 12, 20).

The function of this emphasis is exhortatory: since the outcome is certain and soon, those suffering are given the strength to hold on till the end. The text tells the reader at critical moments, "Here is a call to the endurance and faith of the saints" (13:10; again in 14:12). The final vision of the heavenly Jerusalem descending to earth is accompanied by this assurance: "Whoever conquers shall have this heritage" (21:7). Those who remain steadfast are "victorious" (see 2:7, 11, 17, 26; 3:5, 12, 21), and by their suffering they share in a victory over evil and death (15:2) that was first won by the Lamb who was slain yet now still lives (5:6; 17:14). Thus, as in classical apocalyptic, the motivation of the writer is to secure obedience and faithfulness from a people in the midst of crisis.

In three important ways, however, Revelation also breaks the mold of the "ordinary" apocalypse and secures its unique place among such writings. First, it is a work of great artistry. One need only read snippets of *1 Enoch* to appreciate this point. There is nothing accidental or haphazard in the composition of Revelation: however obscure it appears to the reader, one of the fascinating qualities of the book is the sense of an active and subtle intelligence at work. Even its almost barbarous Greek seems to be deliberate, an evocation of the "sacred" and "biblical" world. Although Revelation contains no direct citation from the OT, it is an elaborate reworking of scriptural texts so seamless and creative that the reworking genuinely results in its own "language"; a work steeped in the diction, terminology, rhythm, motifs, and ethos of the classic OT prophets. Revelation makes particularly heavy use of the classical prophetic texts, such as Amos and Isaiah, and even more of Revelation's predecessors in apocalyptic— Zechariah, Daniel, and most of all, Ezekiel. From Ezekiel we recognize the heavenly throne chariot, the living creatures, the sea of glass, the sealing of the thousands, the eating of the scroll, the living waters through Jerusalem, and the measuring of the temple. All of this Revelation brings alive in a new and powerful synthesis.

Second, Revelation has elements that resemble the writings stemming from Jewish Merkabah (chariot) mysticism. Such Hekhalot literature (named for the "halls" in the heavenly places visited by the seer) itself derived from the esoteric interpretation of Ezekiel, so the connections are not altogether surprising: the ascent to the "throne chariot" and the description of the "heavenly halls." Thus, the ascent of the seer to the heavenly places (4:1) in Revelation is standard. But the furnishings of the heavenly court are particularly interesting: the throne with someone seated on it (4:2), the rainbow of gems (4:3), the living creatures (4:6), the sea of glass (4:6), the torches of fire (4:5), the attendant and praising angels (4:6-9), the fiery glassy sea (15:2), the lake of fire (19:20), and the courts of the heavenly city paved with gems (21:15-21). Above all, Revelation resembles the Hekhalot writings with its sacred hymns sung by the angels (4:11), elders (11:16), and saints (15:2-4). Interspersed throughout the visions, they give those visions a quality of liturgy and prayer (see 4:9-11; 5:9-12; 7:10-12; 11:15b,

17-18; 16:5b-7; 19:1-4). The hymns also function, in the style of Greek drama, to give an authorized commentary on the proceedings.

Third, Revelation transcends the apocalyptic genre because of the Christian experience of Jesus. Like all the writings of the NT, its expectations concerning the future are shaped by its acute awareness of God's present power demonstrated by the resurrection of Jesus and the gift of the Spirit. So we find not an anonymous or pseudonymous writing but one written by a contemporary individual well-known to the readers, who tells them of his experience of the risen Lord at a specific time and place (1:9-10). Moreover, John does not engage only in the fictional predictive prophecy of apocalyptic. In the letters to the seven churches of Asia Minor, he addresses what is happening among them now, pronouncing blessings and curses in true prophetic style (2:1—3:22). Thus, classical prophecy is here combined with, rather than merely subsumed by, the apocalyptic mode of communication. The Christ of the church is present to the believers in their present, so the judgment in the community now is as important for the writer as the judgment to come.

Most of all, the conviction that Jesus has risen from the dead as Lord transforms the symbols of apocalyptic. We read not only a revelation *about* Jesus but one that comes *from* him (1:1). His is the voice that speaks through the prophet in the letters. The Son of man is not simply one who will come as judge (14:14) but one who lives now (1:13): "I am the living one; I died and I am alive forevermore" (1:18). Jesus stands before the throne of God as the Lamb who was slain but is now alive (5:6; 7:10). He sits on the white horse bearing the title "Faithful and True" (19:11); his garments are, like the servant's, dipped in blood (Isa. 63:3), and he is called the "Word of God" (19:13). He is "King of kings and Lord of lords" (19:16). He is the bridegroom of the new Jerusalem (21:9) as well as her "temple" (21:22) and "lamp" (21:23).

For Revelation, therefore, the triumph of God over evil and death is not only a future expectation; it has already been realized *in heaven*. Jesus' resurrection is the pledge of God's cosmic victory over evil. The hope of the saints does not rely simply on the promise of God made in the distant past. It is based on the present power of God—manifest in the resurrection of Jesus—and on the proleptic realization of those hopes by the saints who have now joined him in heaven: already the church shares in the resurrection victory through those who have gone ahead. As the visions reveal to the readers, then, the essential victory has already been won. The outcome is not in doubt; the visions of the future simply spell out the inevitable consequences of the triumph already accomplished by Jesus. In the Book of Revelation, as elsewhere in the NT, the characteristic Christian experience of the "already" and the "not yet" transforms the symbols of apocalyptic itself.

Revelation and the Johannine Literature

For a writing preoccupied with the heavenly places, Revelation is firmly rooted in the world of human experience. The seven churches of Asia to which John writes (1:4) are located in well-known cities: Ephesus, Smyrna, Pergamum, Thyatira, Sardis, Philadelphia, and Laodicea. The letters contain small touches that may reflect knowledge of local conditions and traditions. The churches in Philadelphia and Smyrna also received letters from Ignatius of Antioch early in the second century, and Ephesus was the destination of letters written by both Paul and Ignatius. Laodicea is also mentioned in Paul's epistle sent to the Colossian community (Col. 4:13-16).

In the seven "spirit letters" that follow his opening vision (1:9-19), John—the writer and seer—addresses the conditions of these churches. He names allies (like Antipas, the faithful witness; 2:13) and opponents (like Jezebel, the prophetess; 2:20-23). Some opponents are designated as "false apostles" (2:2) and another group is called the "Nicolaitans" (2:6, 15). The latter advocated a liberal policy regarding eating idol meat (2:6, 14, 20), a practice reprehensible to the writer (cf. 1 Cor. 8:1-13). John also refers to "false Jews" (3:9), the "synagogue of Satan" (2:9), "Satan's throne" (2:13), and "the deep things of Satan" (2:24). The allusive nature of these identifications suggests that those so designated were already well known to the readers. The opposition is more elaborately disguised in the visions, but the harlot—"Babylon the great, the mother of whores"—who brings destruction on the saints (17:4-6), clearly is intended to represent the Roman Empire (cf. 17:9-14).

The major question that arises is whether these concrete references suffice to place Revelation within the Johannine world familiar to us from the epistles and the Gospel. The debate in early Christianity over whether the "elder" of the Johannine epistles was to be identified with the "beloved disciple" who wrote the Fourth Gospel carried over into the discussion of the authorship of Revelation. There was never a unanimous consensus on this issue in the early church; the "elder" and the "beloved disciple" where often viewed as separate people. Thus, Papias thought that the writer of Revelation was the "elder" (see Eusebius *Ecclesiastical History* III.39.5-14). But Polycrates, the late second-century bishop of Ephesus, traced the ancient tradition of the Asian churches associated with Revelation back to Philip and John, the beloved disciple (Eusebius *Ecclesiastical History* V.24.2-5).

In either case, some scholars have great difficulty imagining this writing's outlook as existing side by side with that of the letters and the Gospel. They can find a place for it only by placing it very early or very late in a chronological development. Others think of Revelation as another product of the circle or school of Johannine Christianity. They attribute its differences less to the passage of time than to the transformations required by the apocalyptic genre—as opposed to the epistolary or narrative genre. Because of the lack of evidence, however, such connections are open to debate. As for the dating of the work, the clear data it presents of active and organized persecution makes a date toward the end of the first century the most likely.

Once it is granted that the apocalyptic genre drastically reshapes the view of the world, the deep harmony in outlook and symbolization between Revelation and the other Johannine writings is all the more impressive. Only a few points can be touched on here, beginning with the designations for Jesus. In the Fourth Gospel, the title "Lamb of God" was applied to him (1:29, 36). In Revelation, the title becomes the central image for the crucified and raised Messiah. He is the Lamb who was slain but now lives (5:6-8, 12-13; 6:1, 16; 7:9, 10, 14, 17; 12:11; 13:8, 11; 14:1, 4, 10; 15:3; 17:14; 19:7-9; 21:9, 14, 22, 23, 27; 22:1-3). He is also "Son of man" (1:13; 14:14; cf. John 1:51) and "Son of God" (2:18; cf. John 11:27; 20:31; 1 John 3:8). He is the "Word of God" (*logos tou theou*; 1:2, 9; 6:9; and, above all, 19:13; cf. John 1:1-14), and "king"/"King of kings" (1:5; 15:3; 19:16; cf. John 18:29—19:22). As in the other Johannine writings, Jesus is the "faithful witness" (1:5; 3:14; 19:11; cf. John 5:32; 8:14; 1 John 5:9), the one who "loved us and freed us from our sins by his blood" (1:5; cf. 1 John 1:7; 5:6-8; John 19:34), and "the one who comes" (1:4, 8; 2:5; 3:11; cf. John 1:9; 11:27; 1 John 4:2; 5:6; 2 John 7).

Even more striking are some designations associated solely, in the NT, with the Johannine writings. Jesus, for example, identifies himself by "I am" sayings (1:8, 17; 2:23; 21:6; 22:13, 16; cf. John 6:35; 8:12). He is also called "the beginning [*archē*] of God's creation" (3:14) as well as the "beginning and the end" (21:6; 22:13; cf. John 1:1-2; 1 John 1:1). Picking up on Jesus' characteristic speech in the Fourth Gospel, Revelation calls him simply the "Amen" (3:14; cf. John 1:51; 5:19). Jesus also refers to "my Father" (2:28; 3:5, 21; cf. John 5:17, 43; 14:2) and "my God" (3:2, 12; cf. John 20:17). In another distinctively Johannine phrase, Jesus says that just as he has received authority from the Father, he also gives it (2:26-28; cf. John 1:12; 17:2). And the Johannine metaphors of water, light, and life are—each in its own way—attached to Jesus in Revelation: Jesus is the one who will give the thirsty a drink from the fountain of the water of life (7:17; 21:6; 22:1, 17; cf. John 4:14; 7:37-39); from him comes life (2:10; 3:5; 11:11; 22:2, 14, 19; cf. John 1:4; 3:15); and he is the light of the new Jerusalem (21:24; 22:5; cf. John 8:12; 1 John 2:8). Thus, the language used to describe Jesus has real resonance and congruity with the images and expressions from the Fourth Gospel.

The conflicts and loyalties of this community are also symbolized in a manner similar to that in the other Johannine writings. The community's members stand in opposition to those they call "false Jews" (2:9; 3:9), members of the "synagogue of Satan" (2:9; 3:9). We remember how the Fourth Gospel placed Jesus in conflict with the Jews (see esp. John 8:12-58), and believers in conflict with the synagogue (John 9:22). As in the Johannine letters (1 John 3:7; 4:6; 2 John 7), the opponents here are "deceivers" (Rev. 2:20; 12:9; 13:14; 18:23; 19:20; 20:3, 8, 10) who speak with an ungodly spirit (Rev. 13:15; 16:13-14; 18:2; cf. 1 John 4:1-3, where the antichrist is characterized thus). Ultimately, the community's conflict is with Satan, as was the case with Jesus in the Fourth Gospel (Rev. 2:9, 13, 24; 3:9; 12:9, 12; 20:2, 7, 10; cf. John 6:70; 8:44; 13:2, 27). And like the beloved disciple and the believers of the letters, the community in the Book of Revelation is one of "witnesses" (1:2; 2:13; 6:9; 11:3, 10; 19:10; cf. John 19:35; 21:24; 1 John

1:2; 4:14; 5:9-12; 3 John 3, 12) who have, by their faith and love, become "conquerors" over evil and falsehood (Rev. 2:7, 11, 17, 26; 3:5, 12, 21; 21:7; cf. 1 John 2:13-14; 4:4; 5:4-5) just as Jesus has already conquered (Rev. 5:5; 17:14; cf. John 16:33).

The similarities of ostensible setting, context, self-designation, and description of Jesus are indeed striking. If not written by the same person or within the same school, it appears that the seer of Revelation was at least thoroughly familiar with either the Fourth Gospel and epistles or with the symbolic world reflected in those same writings.

Of course, at some point the Johannine symbolic world coalesces with the symbolic world of early Christianity more generally. We cannot say, for instance, that the Johannine symbolic world must be identified solely with the communities associated with the Johannine texts, nor that those same communities necessarily are the point of origin of the Johannine symbolic world itself. In the final analysis, early Christianity was a much more dynamic movement than this, with ideas and motifs constantly intersecting and intermingling. This dynamism is perhaps reflected nowhere else better than in Revelation, where the symbolic world so grounded in one segment of the NT corpus can be utilized in such similar ways in such an obviously different framework. If nothing else, this demonstrates that even a seemingly "renegade" NT writing like Revelation is ultimately grounded in the very heart and soul of early Christian tradition.

A Prophetic Community

Each of the NT writings gives us some sense of the writer's understanding of the church in its social structure and its relationship to Israel and the world. This understanding is conveyed in various ways, including images and titles for community leaders. We have already seen the church designated as temple (1 Cor. 3:16; Eph. 2:21), house of God (Heb. 3:2; 10:21; 1 Pet. 2:5; 4:17), and the saints (1 Cor. 1:2; Eph. 1:1; Heb. 13:24; 1 Pet. 1:15; Jude 3). Among the titles for leaders, we have met apostles, prophets (1 Cor. 12:28-30; Eph. 4:11-12; Rom. 12:6), teachers (Acts 13:1; 1 Cor. 12:28; Eph. 4:11; James 3:1), bishops (Acts 20:28; Phil. 1:1; 1 Tim. 3:2; Titus 1:7), elders (Acts 11:30; 15:2; 20:17; 1 Tim. 5:1-19; Titus 1:5; James 5:14; 1 Pet. 5:1), and deacons (Rom. 16:1; Phil. 1:1; 1 Tim. 3:8, 12).

When we look at the Johannine writings apart from Revelation, we are struck by the relative paucity of such designations. The term "apostle" occurs only once, in a nontechnical sense (John 13:16). The only "prophet" is Jesus (John 4:19; 6:14; 9:17), just as the only "teacher" is Jesus (John 1:38; 3:2; 11:28; 13:13-14; 20:16). There are no "bishops" or "deacons," and the only "elder" is the author of 2 and 3 John.

A similar reticence can be observed in Revelation. The term "apostle" is used three times. Twice it refers to contemporaries of the writer: it is used with reference to people "who call themselves apostles but are not" (2:2; cf. Didache 11.3-12) and those who will rejoice at the fall of Babylon—the "saints, apostles, and prophets" (18:20). The third occurrence is in 21:14, where the walls of the new Jerusalem have twelve foundations, "and on them the twelve names of the twelve apostles of the Lamb." These few passages remind us that the symbolism of the Twelve is by no means confined to Luke-Acts, and that the apostles were regarded as playing a foundational role (cf. Eph. 2:20). Except for pretenders, however, the role of the apostle appears to be one relegated to the past.

The term "elder" is used by Revelation in a very restricted way. The seer is not identified by that title, nor is any other human figure on earth. The term "elder" is reserved for the twenty-four elders in heaven (4:4, 10; 5:5, 6,8,11,14; 7:11,13; 11:16; 14:3; 19:4). As for the designations "teacher," "bishop," and "deacon," they do not occur at all.

In contrast, Revelation prefers the language of *prophecy* when speaking of the community. The title "prophet" is used eight times (10:7; 11:10, 18; 16:6; 18:20, 24; 22:6,9), the verb "to prophesy" twice (10:11; 11:3), and the noun "prophecy" seven times (1:3; 11:6; 19:10; 22:7, 10, 18, 19). More important than the number of uses is the pattern. First, the language is used not only of specific leaders or holders of office but of the community as a whole. Second, the language intersects repeatedly with other favorite terms. Some of these connections deserve attention.

The author frequently uses the term "servant" (*doulos*) for believers (1:1; 2:20; 7:3; 13:16; 15:3; 19:2, 5, 18; 22:3, 6), and several times it is found in combination with the noun "prophet" (10:7; 11:18; 22:9 [cf. 19:10 where it is occurs with verb "to prophecy"]). The language of "witness" or "testimony"—in various forms—is used of the community, carrying with it prophetic resonances throughout. The verb "to bear witness" or "to testify" (*martureō*) is used four times (1:2; 22:16, 18, 20), most interestingly in the combination with "prophecy": "I *testify* to everyone who hears these words of *prophecy*" (22:18). The noun "witness" (*martus*)—as in "one who witnesses/attests/testifies"—is used of Jesus (1:5; 3:14), Antipas (2:13), the mysterious "two witnesses" (11:3), and the martyrs who died and "witnessed in their blood" (17:6). The noun "testimony" or "witness" (*marturia*)—as in the substance of "witnessing"—is used some eight times, and when it appears as *marturia Iēsou* it means both witness "*to* Jesus" and "*by* Jesus" (literally, "witness of Jesus" understood both objectively and subjectively; see 1:2, 9; 6:9; 11:7; 12:11, 17; 19:10; 20:4). The most fascinating occurrence again has the explicit connection to prophecy: "The witness [*marturia*] of Jesus is the spirit of prophecy [*prophēteias*]" (19:10).

The term "saints" or "holy ones" (*hagioi*) is another frequent designation. In the singular it refers to God (4:8; 6:10) or Jesus (3:7) as the Holy One. In the plural it refers to believers on earth and the elect in heaven who have triumphed over death (see 5:8; 8:3, 4; 13:7, 10; 14:12; 17:6; 18:20; 19:8; 20:6, 9; 22:21). As with the term "servant," the author brings this term into combination with the language of prophecy: enemies "have shed the blood of saints and prophets" (16:6; cf. 11:18; 18:24).

These combinations suggest that the author of Revelation regards the church as a *prophetic community*. It is a community of saints and of servants, whose prophetic office is carried out by their bearing witness to Jesus; like the prophets of the OT, they testify to God's truth and judgment in an overtly hostile environment. We notice as well that these terms are applied alike to those struggling on earth, to those triumphant in heaven, and to Jesus; there is a continuity in the prophetic vocation in Revelation—a fellowship of prophetic witness. The prophetic image is further enhanced by the way language about the Spirit (*pneuma*) is used. As we have already seen, this simple equation can be drawn: "The witness of Jesus ["to Jesus"] is the *spirit of prophecy*" (19:10). And God can be called "the Lord . . . of the *spirits* of the prophets" (22:6). Further, it is both the Spirit and the Bride (the community) who call out to the Bridegroom (Christ), "Come" (22:17). Thus, the "Spirit of God" is intimately connected to the understanding of the believers as prophetic witnesses: the spirit is upon them and they are prophesying/testifying in the last days (cf. Joel 2:28-32; Acts 2:17-21).

The description of the representative figures of the church also employs the language of prophecy. First, there is the seer himself—he has written a "book of prophecy" (1:3; 22:18-19). When he addresses the seven churches, it is the "Spirit" who speaks through him (2:7, 11, 17, 29; 3:6, 13, 22; cf. 14:13), indicating that the prophetic revelation is from God (22:16). This is further confirmed by the fact that in his visions, he is carried away "in the Spirit" (1:10; 4:2; 17:3). After eating the scroll in imitation of the great OT prophet Ezekiel (10:9-10; cf. Ezek. 2:8-3:3), he is told, "You must again prophesy about many peoples and nations and tongues and kings" (10:11). Indeed, the seer and his community are explicitly singled out as "prophets" by the angel, their fellow "servant" (22:9). Thus, the seer is first and foremost a prophet, one who imitates, but also surpasses, the classic Israelite prophets of the OT.

The other representative figures of the community are the "two witnesses" (11:3-13). They appear during an interlude following the command of the angel to John that he should "prophesy again" (10:11). They are not named but are sufficiently known to the readers to be recognizable by the titles "olive trees" and "lampstands" (11:4). The terms "witnessing" and "prophesying" are used interchangeably of them. We read, "I will grant my two witnesses power to prophesy" (11:3), and find that "the days of their prophesying" (11:6) are the same as the period of "their witnessing" (11:7). Their works, furthermore, recall those of the prophets Elijah and Moses (11:6), and their end is like that of the witness/prophet Jesus. They are killed as he was "in the city where their Lord was crucified" (11:8). The one responsible for their death is the "beast that ascends from the bottomless pit and makes war on them" (11:7). This beast anticipates the "beast from the Sea" in 13:1, who also "makes war on the saints to conquer them" (13:7). Like Jesus also, the two witnesses/prophets rose from the dead, going "up to heaven in a cloud" (11:12). Commentators debate whether they are real, specific individuals within the community or representative of the community as a whole. In any case, one can thus trace the succession: first Jesus, then the community that follows Jesus, and, finally, its representatives—are all prophets who bear witness to the revelation of God's righteous judgment in the world.

The prophetic imagery affects the picture of the community's opponents as well. In the letter to Thyatira, the rival leader "Jezebel"—not her real name but an allusion to the idol-worshiper and great opponent of the prophet Elijah (cf. 1 Kings 16:31)—is termed a "prophetess" (2:20), whose encouragement to her followers to eat idol meat amounts to teaching "the deep things of Satan" (2:20, 24). In the visions, the demonic opponents of the saints possess caricatured prophetic features. Just as Jesus is a "faithful witness" who is seen as a slain lamb, so the second beast—the one from the earth, the second representative of the dragon Satan (12:13—13:2)—is pictured as having "two horns like a lamb" but a voice "like a dragon" (13:11-18). This beast is later referred to as a "false prophet" (16:13-14):

> I saw issuing from the mouth of the dragon and from the mouth of the beast and from the mouth of the false prophet, three foul spirits like frogs, for they are demonic spirits, performing signs.

We also read, "The beast was captured, and with it the false prophet who in its presence had worked the signs by which it deceived those who had received the mark of the beast" (19:20). And the final victory is achieved when "the devil who had deceived them was thrown into the lake of fire and sulphur where the beast and the false prophet were" (20:10). Thus, both the human and grander demonic opponents of the earthly community and its heavenly counterpart are portrayed as mirrors of the Christian prophetic witness. As the Christian prophets speak "in and through the Spirit," these false prophets speak through foul demonic spirits. Much like the ancient "contest" between Moses and the magicians of Egypt (Exod. 7:8-25), the present is also a "contest" between the prophets of God bearing witness to the truth and the prophets of the Devil testifying to falsehood and deception.

The Witness of Jesus Is the Spirit of Prophecy

Christians continue and imitate the witness first presented by Jesus. He was the faithful and true witness (1:5; 3:14) who came into the world to "bear witness to the truth" (John 18:37). Because of his testimony, he was killed by a hostile world, and his witness was therefore sealed with his blood (1:5; 5:9; 7:14; 19:13). As in the other Johannine writings, Revelation views the Spirit's function as continuing the witness of Jesus in the world through the lives of Christians (cf. John 16:7-11). Insofar as Jesus continues to "speak" through the Spirit, his prophetic role continues even in this book, which is a "revelation from Jesus Christ" (1:1) and a "witness by Jesus" (19:10). But as Christians continue to keep God's commandments, living in obedience to God by Jesus' faith, they also "witness to Jesus" (19:10) in the world.

Witness in Tribulation and Temptation: The Letters (2:1—3:22)

In the Book of Daniel the esoteric message of the visions (chaps. 7–12) is preceded by a series of folk tales that contain the same basic message in exoteric form (chaps. 1–6). So are the great visions of the Book of Revelation preceded by seven letters to the churches of Asia Minor, which prepare for the visions by addressing similar issues through straightforward exhortation.

In the letters, the voice of prophecy is open and direct. The prophet speaks in the name of Jesus and with his Spirit. Jesus is revealed in the opening vision as "standing in the midst of the lampstands" (1:13), which, we are told, "are the seven churches" (1:20). Here is the resurrected Lord present to the church through the Spirit. Such prophetic speech as we find here may reflect the liturgical practice of the primitive community (cf. 1 Cor. 12-14). We find in the prophetic utterances sayings that also appear in other NT writings (cf. Rev. 3:3 and 1 Thess. 5:2, Matt. 24:43; Rev. 3:20 and Matt. 24:33, James 5:9; see chap. 6, above).

The letters—or, more formally, decrees or edicts—follow a strict four-stage pattern:

(1) Each begins with the command to the seer that he should write to a specific church—"to the angel of the church at Ephesus, write" (2:1; cf. 2:8, 12, 18; 3:1, 7, 14). The addressee is actually the "angel" of the church, the heavenly counterpart to the individual communities (1:20). Moreover, each opening statement contains a reference to Jesus as the one who speaks.

(2) Jesus is then identified by a series of epithets: He is the one "who holds the seven stars in his right hand, who walks among the seven golden lampstands (2:1); "the first, the last, who died and came to life" (2:8; cf. 1:17; 22:13); the one "who has the sharp, two-edged sword" (2:12; cf. 1:16); the "Son of God" (2:18); the one who has the "seven spirits of God and the seven stars" (3:1; cf. 1:4; 5:6; 22:6); the "Holy One, the True One, who has the key of David" (3:7; cf. 5:5; 22:16); and the "Amen, the faithful and true witness, the Beginning of God's creation" (3:14). This assemblage of names and titles is strongly reminiscent of the process of "naming Jesus" in the opening sequence of the Fourth Gospel (John 1:29-51). The epithets, which are explicitly based on the opening vision (1:9-20), provide literary signals that connect the letters to the later visions of the book as well.

(3) There follows the statement "I know," which leads to the description of the churches' respective situations (2:2, 9, 13, 19; 3:1, 8, 15), containing commendation or judgment. For some of the communities, there is praise: they have patiently endured (2:2, 3, 19; 3:10); come through tribulation and poverty (2:9); held fast to the name (2:13); and have kept love, faith, and service (2:19). Other communities receive mostly

blame: they have abandoned love (2:4); fallen into idolatry and immorality (2:14-15, 20-22); and developed a tepid Christian practice (3:15).

(4) Every one of the communities receives an exhortation (2:5, 7, 10-11, 16-17, 25, 29; 3:3-4, 11, 18-19) and a promise (2:7, 11, 17, 26-28; 3:5, 12, 20-21), placed in the context of the repetition of the phrase: "let everyone who has an ear listen to what the Spirit is saying to the churches" (2:7, 11, 17, 29; 3:6, 13, 22).

Despite the rich symbolism, the message of the letters is straightforward: patiently endure and hold fast to the convictions and practice of the Christian life, being faithful to God in the face of the present trials. Despite their tribulation and poverty, the communities are to continue their witness. Moreover, they are to resist the temptation to idolatry and immorality. Just as in the stories of Daniel, there is nothing complicated in this exhortation. Jesus, as the resurrected Lord, is present with them in their experience; he knows what they suffer, and will reward them if they endure and punish them if they fall away. By maintaining their fidelity to Jesus, they continue to bear prophetic testimony in the world.

Witness in Persecution and Death: The Visions

Once the seer passes through the open door of heaven (4:1), he and the readers are swept into a world quite unlike any other. The visions of Revelation are dazzling in their imagery, even if not altogether coherent. I will not add here to the endless store of studies devoted to the structure, sequence, and symbolism of these visions. Beneath the complex sequences of seals, trumpets, bowls, and beasts, four fundamental convictions are expressed.

The first conviction is that "in heaven" the victory over evil and death has already been won by God and the Messiah. The idolatrous powers strutting the earth are illusory; there is but one power controlling history. Second, the apparent dominance of evil in human affairs is itself part of God's triumphant plan, and those who come through suffering and persecution faithfully receive the reward of eternal life with God. God is in control of the world, and evil is not running rampant; rather, everything is taking place according to God's design. Third, the history of humans has a goal even on earth: the time of the suffering of the saints will come to an end, the visible and effective rule of God among humans will be established, and the wicked will be judged. Fourth, those who share the witness of Christ on earth in the face of death will share as well in heaven his victory over death.

In the visions, we see that the witness of believers *to* Jesus can lead to the shedding of their blood (6:10; 7:14; 12:11; 16:6; 17:6; 18:24). More than the avoidance of idolatry and immorality may be demanded of the Christian; the giving of one's life itself may be necessary. And if it is, there is the knowledge that those who so die share in the witness of the one "who was slain but now lives" (5:6) and who ransomed humans by his blood (5:9). Indeed, the garments of the saints are "washed in the blood of the Lamb" and made pure (7:14), indicating that those who imitate the death of Jesus are saved by his atoning death for them. Now we understand the logic of being a witness (*martus*), as it culminates in "martyrdom." There is also a reversal: just as the blood of Jesus and the saints is spilled now, so the blood of the wicked will soon be on the garments of Christ when he comes to judge with a vengeance (19:13; cf. Isa. 63:1-6).

That the Christians addressed by the visions faced real death cannot be doubted. The seer observes in heaven "under the altar the souls of those who had been slain for the word of God, and for the witness they had borne" (6:9); and in the battle against the dragon, "they have conquered him by the blood of the Lamb and by the word of their testimony, for they loved not their own lives even unto death" (12:11). The beast from the earth—the false prophet—makes war on the saints, trying to conquer them (13:7); he marks everyone with his seal, making them slaves (13:16). The Christians, again, bear witness in these battles by laying down their lives in imitation of Jesus.

The persecution suffered by the saints is one sponsored by the great harlot Babylon (14:8; 17:1-18). Just as the Babylon of old waged war on God's people Israel, so too the new Babylon—the Roman Empire—is devoted to the destruction of God's people in Christ. Even though 18:2—19:8 is a hymn celebrating her great fall, for those whose lives are still within her grasp she remains a powerful and demonic presence: "In her was found the blood of the prophets and saints and of all who have been slain on the earth" (18:24).

Here there can be no positive evaluation of the governing powers such as we saw in Rom. 13:1-7 or 1 Pet. 2:13-17. The reason is simple: the state has usurped powers never intended for it, becoming a "beast" that demands ultimate allegiance; making idolatrous claims that cannot be acknowledged by Christians. It is in this context that one must understand the significance of Jesus being called "Lord of lords": Christians cannot accept the power of any institution as supreme because Christ reigns over all. At the same time, Revelation does not advocate a violent or armed rebellion against the iniquitous power of the state. It essentially promotes a passive resistance. While Christians do not organize a revolt against Rome, they also do not obey its idolatrous commands. They must keep the commandments of God and the faith of Jesus, even if it results in their death. The message underlying all the visions comes down, therefore, to precisely the same exhortation as in the Johannine letters: "Here is a call for the endurance of the saints, those who keep the commandments of God and the faith of Jesus" (14:12; cf. 13:10).

This prophetic church can bear such witness because of its conviction, rooted in the experience of the resurrection of Jesus, that this earthly life is not all there is, that there remains a heavenly reward for a life now given in prophetic witness to the truth of God's claim over the world. Indeed, such Christians are convinced that their very suffering and death help speed the realization of God's victory (12:10-11):

Now the salvation and the power and the kingdom of our God and the authority of the Messiah have come, for the accuser of our comrades has been thrown down, who accuses them day and night before our God. And they have conquered him by the blood of the Lamb and by the word of their testimony, for they loved not their lives even unto death.

The final and glorious vision in Revelation is, of course, that of the heavenly Jerusalem, coming down from above, together with the ringing affirmation from the throne (21:3):

Behold, the dwelling of God is with humans. [God] will dwell with them, and they shall be [God's] people, and God will be with them.

Here is the final reconciliation of earth and heaven—of God's life and creation—by which Revelation draws full circle back to Genesis 1–2. The end of time is a new creation of heaven and earth; a returning but also a transformation of God's original work. It cannot be accomplished by human effort, but can only come from the source of all reality, who declares, "Behold, I make all things new" (21:5). Only with this final restoration will evil truly be banished from the earth (21:8, 27). And despite the threat of eternal punishment for those who reject this gift, there is still the hope for a universal extension of this life. By the light of the Lamb even the nations shall walk (21:24), and "the leaves of the tree are for the healing of the nations" (22:2):

There shall no more be anything accursed, but the throne of God and of the Lamb shall be in it and the servants shall worship [God]. They shall see [God's] face and [God's] name shall be on their foreheads. And night shall be no more; they need no light of lamp or sun, for the Lord God will be their light, and they shall reign for ever and ever (22:3-5).

In Jewish tradition, no one was allowed to see God's face nor speak the holy name. Here, however, the very "face" and "name" of God are manifested to the faithful prophets who have endured until the end. God's glory—revealed only partially and proleptically before—has finally come to dwell fully among humans as they reign with God in the new temple. This reign of the saints is described as an eternal act of worship: they have been called to be a "kingdom of priests" (1:6; 5:10; 20:6), whose final and best *witness* is to join the heavenly creatures in praising God. In Revelation, prayer is both a prophetic act and the most powerful political posture.

Study Questions

1. What do the terms "millenarian" and "apocalyptic" mean? In what senses is Revelation an apocalypse? How is it different?

2. What does Revelation share in common with the Gospel of John in terms of vocabulary, theme, and perspective?

3. How would you state the central message of the letters to the seven churches in your own words? How was this message particularly important in the first century? In what sense is it an enduring message?

4. What role does persecution play in Revelation? What do we know about the persecutions of the early church in the first century?

Bibliographical Note

A sense of the interpretation of Revelation in Christian history can be gained from R. K. Emmerson and B. McGinn (eds.), *The Apocalypse in the Middle Ages* (Ithaca: Cornell Univ. Press, 1992); C. A. Patrides and J. Wittreich (eds.), *The Apocalypse in English Renaissance Thought and Literature* (Ithaca: Cornell Univ. Press, 1984); and A. W. Wainwright, *Mysterious Apocalypse: A History of the Interpretation of the Book of Revelation* (Nashville: Abingdon Press, 1993). A useful overview of the writing is provided by M. E. Boring, "The Theology of Revelation: 'The Lord Our God the Almighty Reigns,'" *Int* 40 (1986): 257–69; M. Rissi, "The Kerygma of the Revelation of John," *Int* 22 (1968): 3–17; and E. Schüssler Fiorenza, "Composition and Structure of Revelation," in her *The Book of Revelation: Justice and Judgment* (2d ed.; Minneapolis: Fortress Press, 1998), 159–80. Also see J. Court, *Myth and History in the Book of Revelation* (Atlanta: John Knox Press, 1979), and A. Yarbro Collins, *Crisis & Catharsis: The Power of the Apocalypse* (Philadelphia: Westminster Press, 1984).

For the symbolism and outlook of apocalyptic generally, see first the bibliography for chapter 2. The background of Merkabah mysticism is provided by I. Gruenwald, *Apocalyptic and Merkavah Mysticism* (AGJU, 14; Leiden: E. J. Brill, 1980). The relationship of the Book of Revelation to apocalyptic is examined in various ways by D. E. Aune, "The Apocalypse of John and the Problem of Genre," *Semeia* 36 (1986): 65–96; J. J. Collins, "Pseudonymity, Historical Reviews, and the Genre of the Revelation of John," *CBQ* 39 (1977): 329–43; J. Kallas, "The Apocalypse—An Apocalyptic Book?" *JBL* 86 (1967): 69–80; C. Rowland, *The Open Heaven: A Study of Apocalyptic in Judaism and Early Christianity* (London: SPCK, 1982), 403–41; D. S. Russell, *Method and Message of Jewish Apocalyptic* (Philadelphia: Westminster Press, 1964), 205–34; and P.

Vielhauer and G. Strecker, "Introduction," in E. Hennecke and W. Schneemelcher (eds.), *New Testament Apocrypha*, 2 vols., rev. ed., trans. R. McL. Wilson (Louisville: Westminster/John Knox Press; Cambridge: James Clark & Co., 1991–92), 2:542–602. On the ethos, environment, and literature of early Christian apocalypticism more generally, see E. Schüssler Fiorenza, "The Phenomenon of Early Christian Apocalyptic: Some Reflections on Method," in D. Hellholm (ed.), *Apocalypticism in the Mediterranean World and the Near East*, 2nd ed. (Tübingen: J. C. B. Mohr [Siebeck], 1989), 295–316; L. L. Thompson, "Social Location of Early Christian Apocalyptic," *ANRW* II.26.3 (1996): 2615–56; and A. Yarbro Collins, "Early Christian Apocalyptic Literature," *ANRW* II.25.6 (1988): 4665–711.

On the connection of prophecy/prophets to Revelation, see D. E. Aune, "The Prophetic Circle of The John of Patmos and the Exegesis of Revelation 22.16," *JSNT* 37 (1989): 103–16; M. D. Goulder, "The Apocalypse as an Annual Cycle of Prophecies," *NTS* 27 (1980–81): 342–67; D. Hill, "Prophecy and Prophets in the Revelation of St. John," *NTS* 18 (1971–72): 401–18; F. D. Mazzaferri, *The Genre of the Book of Revelation from a Source-Critical Perspective* (BZNW, 54; New York: W. de Gruyter, 1989); and E. Schüssler Fiorenza, "*Apocalypsis* and *Propheteia*: Revelation in the Context of Early Christian Prophecy," in *The Book of Revelation*, 133–56. On the theme of "witness," see B. Dehandschutter, "The Meaning of Witness in the Apocalypse," in J. Lambrecht (ed.), *L'Apocalyptique johannique et l'Apocalyptique dans le Nouveau Testament* (BETL, 53; Leuven: Leuven Univ. Press, 1980), 283–88; A. A. Trites, "*Martus* and Martyrdom in the Apocalypse," *NovT* 15 (1973): 72–80; and idem, *The New Testament Concept of Witness* (SNTSMS, 31; Cambridge: Cambridge Univ. Press, 1977).

For a discussion of Revelation's historical and cultural interconnections, see C. K. Barrett, "Things Sacrificed to Idols," *NTS* 11 (1964–65): 138–53; A. A. Bell, "The Date of John's Apocalypse: The Evidence of Some Roman Historians Reconsidered," *NTS* 25 (1978–79): 93–102; P. Borgen, "Polemic in the Book of Revelation," in C. A. Evans and D. A. Hagner (eds.), *Anti-Semitism and Early Christianity: Issues of Polemic and Faith* (Minneapolis: Fortress Press, 1993), 199–210; C. J. Hemer, *The Letters to the Seven Churches of Asia in Their Local Setting* (JSNTSup, 11; Sheffield: Sheffield Academic Press, 1989); J. T. Kirby, "The Rhetorical Situations of Revelation 1–3," *NTS* 34 (1988): 197–207; H. Koester (ed.), *Pergamon—Citadel of the Gods* (Harrisburg, Penn.: Trinity Press Int'l, 1998); J. N. Kraybill, *Imperial Cult and Commerce in John's Apocalypse* (JSNTSup, 132; Sheffield: Sheffield Academic Press, 1996); L. L. Thompson, *The Book of Revelation: Apocalypse and Empire* (New York: Oxford Univ. Press, 1990); idem, "Cult and Eschatology in the Apocalypse of John," *JR* 49 (1969): 330–50; idem, "A Sociological Analysis of Tribulation in the Apocalypse of John," *Semeia* 36 (1986): 147–74; B. Newman, "The Fallacy of the Domitian Hypothesis," *NTS* 10 (1963–64): 133–39; J. N. Sanders, "St. John on Patmos," *NTS* 9 (1962–63): 75–85; S. J. Scherrer, "Signs and Wonders in the Imperial Cult: A New Look at a Roman Religious Institution in the Light of Rev. 13:13-15," *JBL* 103 (1984): 559–610; E. Schüssler Fiorenza,

"The Quest for the Johannine School: The Book of Revelation and the Fourth Gospel," in *The Book of Revelation*, 85–113; idem, "Visionary Rhetoric and Social-Political Situation," in *The Book of Revelation*, 181–203; A. Yarbro Collins, "Myth and History in the Book of Revelation: The Problem of Its Date," in B. Halpern and J. D. Levenson (eds.), *Traditions in Transformation: Points in Biblical Faith* (Winona Lake, Ind.: Eisenbrauns, 1981), 377–403; and idem, "Persecution and Vengeance in the Book of Revelation," in D. Hellholm (ed.), *Apocalypticism in the Mediterranean World*, 729–49. For general treatment of the political context, see P. Keresztes, "The Imperial Roman Government and the Christian Church: I. From Nero to the Severi," *ANRW* II.23.1 (1979): 247–315.

For overall treatment of the symbolism of Revelation, see R. J. Bauckham, *The Climax of Prophecy: Studies on the Book of Revelation* (Edinburgh: T. & T. Clark, 1993); and B. J. Malina, *On the Genre and Message of Revelation: Star Visions and Sky Journeys* (Peabody, Mass.: Hendrickson Pubs., 1995); as well as, more generally, A. Farrer, *A Re-Birth of Images: The Making of St. John's Apocalypse* (London: Dacre Press, 1949); and P. Minear, *I Saw a New Earth: An Introduction to the Visions of the Apocalypse* (Washington, D.C.: Corpus Pub., 1968). On the imagery and literary context of specific visions, symbols, and motifs, see D. E. Aune, "The Apocalypse of John and Graeco-Roman Revelatory Magic," *NTS* 33 (1987): 481–501; R. J. Bauckham, "The List of Tribes in Revelation 7 Again," *JSNT* 42 (1991): 99–115; M. Black, "The 'Two Witnesses' of Rev. 11:3f. in Jewish and Christian Apocalyptic Tradition," in E. Bammel et al. (eds.), *Donum Gentilicium* (Oxford: Clarendon Press, 1978), 226–38; A. Feuillet, *Johannine Studies* (New York: Alba House, 1965), 183–292; J. M. Ford, "The Heavenly Jerusalem and Orthodox Judaism," in E. Bammel et al. (eds.), *Donum Gentilicium*, 215–26; L. W. Hurtado, "Revelation 4–5 in the Light of Jewish Apocalyptic Analogies," *JSNT* 25 (1985): 105–24; L. J. Lietaert Peerbolte, *The Antecedents of Antichrist: A Traditio-Historical Study of the Earliest Christian View on Eschatological Opponents* (Leiden: E. J. Brill, 1996); J. W. Mealy, *After the Thousand Years: Resurrection and Judgment in Revelation 20* (JSNTSup, 70; Sheffield: Sheffield Academic Press, 1992); P. Minear, "The Wounded Beast," *JBL* 72 (1953): 93–101; M. Rissi, *The Future of the World: An Exegetical Study of Rev 19:11-22:15* (London: SCM Press, 1966); H. Ulfgard, *Feast and Future: Revelation 7:9-17 and the Feast of Tabernacles* (ConBNT, 22; Stockholm: Almqvist & Wiksell, 1989); A. Yarbro Collins, *The Combat Myth in the Book of Revelation* (HDR, 9; Missoula, Mont.: Scholars Press, 1976); idem, "The History of Religions Approach to Apocalypticism and 'The Angel of the Waters' (Rev 16:4-7)," *CBQ* 39 (1977): 367–81; idem, "Numerical Symbolism in Jewish and Early Christian Apocalyptic Literature," *ANRW* II.21.2 (1984): 1221–87; and idem, "Revelation 18: Taunt Song or Dirge?" in *L'Apocalyptique johannique*, 185–204.

Other thematic aspects are treated by D. E. Aune, "The Form and Function of the Proclamation to the Seven Churches (Revelation 2–3)," *NTS* 36 (1990): 182–204; G. K. Beale, "The Hearing Formula and the Visions of John in Revelation," in M. Bockmuehl and M. B. Thompson (eds.), *A Vision for the Church: Studies in Early Christian Ecclesiology* (Edinburgh: T. & T. Clark, 1997), 167–80; idem, *John's Use of the Old Testament in Revelation* (JSNTSup, 166; Sheffield: Sheffield Academic Press, 1998); P. Borgen, "Emperor Worship and Persecution in Philo's *In Flaccum and De Legatione Gaium* and the Revelation of John," in H. Cancik et al. (eds.), *Geschichte-Tradition-Reflexion,* 3 vols. (Tübingen: J. C. B. Mohr, 1996), 3:493-509; P. R. Carrell, *Jesus and the Angels: Angelology and Christology in the Apocalypse of John* (SNTSMS, 95; Cambridge Univ. Press, 1997); J. Fekkes, *Isaiah and Prophetic Traditions in the Book of Revelation: Visionary Antecedents and their Development* (JSNTSup, 93; Sheffield: Sheffield Academic Press, 1994); R. L. Jeske, "Spirit and Community in the Johannine Apocalypse," *NTS* 31 (1985): 452–66; M. de Jonge, "The Use of the Expression *ho christos* in the Apocalypse of John," in *L'Apocalyptique johannique,* 267–81; T. Pippin, *Death and Desire: The Rhetoric of Gender in the Apocalypse of John* (Louisville: Westminster/John Knox Press, 1992); L. T. Stuckenbruck, *Angel Veneration and Christology: A Study in Early Judaism and in the Christology of the Apocalypse of John* (WUNT, 2.70; Tübingen: J. C. B. Mohr [Siebeck], 1995); J. P. M. Sweet, "Maintaining the Testimony of Jesus: The Suffering of Christians in the Revelation of John," in W. Horbury and B. McNeil (eds.), *Suffering and Martyrdom in the New Testament* (Cambridge: Cambridge Univ. Press, 1981), 101–17; A. Yarbro Collins, "The Political Perspective of the Revelation to John," *JBL* 96 (1977): 241–56; and idem, "The 'Son of Man' Tradition and the Book of Revelation," in J. H. Charlesworth (ed.), *The Messiah: Developments in Earliest Judaism and Christianity* (Minneapolis: Fortress Press, 1992), 536–68.

The classic commentary on Revelation is R. H. Charles, *Revelation,* 2 vols. (ICC; Edinburgh: T. & T. Clark, 1920). For more recent critical commentary, see D. E. Aune, *Revelation,* 3 vols. (WBC; Dallas: Word Books, 1997–98); G. K. Beale, *The Book of Revelation* (NIGTC; Grand Rapids: Eerdmans, 1998); and J. M. Ford, *Revelation* (AB; New York: Doubleday, 1975). More general treatment can be found in G. B. Caird, *A Commentary on the Revelation of St. John the Divine* (HNTC; New York: Harper & Row, 1966); and J. Roloff, *Revelation,* trans. J. E. Alsup (Minneapolis: Fortress Press, 1993).

Caves near Qumran where many of the Dead Sea scrolls were discovered. (Photo by Marshall D. Johnson. Used by permission.)

Epilogue
The New Testament
as the Church's Book

I HAVE REFERRED throughout this book to the New Testament as though it were a self-evident reality. As a historical reality of the Christian religion, it is. But as a religious and theological issue within contemporary Christianity, it is much disputed. We have examined the individual writings that make up this collection, including the process of their creation and their respective reshaping of the symbolic world of Torah. It is therefore appropriate to consider the collected NT writings as just that—a collection. Our subject is the NT canon and its implications for the community that accepts the NT writings as authoritative for faith and practice.

Framing the Discussion

The subject draws us immediately into a well-trodden battleground of divided Christianity: the relationship between Scripture and tradition—between the Bible and the church. The clearest and in some ways the most tragic result of the Reformation debates on the subject was that terms making sense only in relationship were distorted by their separation. Martin Luther's cry of *sola scriptura* ("Scripture alone") in response to perceived ecclesiastical abuses was countered by the Catholics with the slogan *scriptura et traditio* ("Scripture and tradition")." This debate, from its inception, led to distortion on both sides.

In Protestantism, an emphasis on Scripture as the sole and self-validating norm for Christian life led not only to a diminished appreciation of the community as the bearer of the book but also, paradoxically, to the breaking up of the book itself. Already in Luther we find the application of content criticism (*sachkritik*) to the NT writings from the standpoint of the "pure gospel" found in Paul; an approach that would later grow into the notion of a "canon within the canon": the conviction that within the historically transmitted canon there must be located a pristine and essential core. The result of this process was an effectively narrowed collection. On the Catholic side the distortion was no less grievous. The term "tradition," which had been intended to stress the *context* for the reading of Scripture, was taken to be an independent source of authority—another norm for Christian life. Increasingly, tradition became identified with the magisterium of the church and its elaborate legal system, so that in effect, the canon of Scripture was swallowed by canon law.

The distortions and diminutions resulted from the separation and isolation of realities that had meaning only in their conjunction. Far from being opposing principles or independent norms, Scripture and tradition represent two moments of the same dialectical process by which the church in every age rediscovers and reaffirms its identity as one that is continuous with the church in previous generations. It is a process that was there from the beginning. The very birth of the church is its first exemplification. The coming into being of the canon itself is its most visible and enduring symbol.

The Process of Canonization

For the historical process of canonization to be understood properly, it is necessary to distinguish five separate but interconnected stages. Only the last stage is really visible to us now, and it is therefore often taken to be the most important; but this is not the case. This last stage is ratification, when in response to challenges of various kinds, the church began to draw up definitive lists, offering reasons why these books were its own to the exclusion of others. Naturally enough, the reasons given have a certain artificiality, since they represent rationalizations of a process far more organic and spontaneous in nature.

Long before ratification and the crises that provided the catalyst, there was a gradual growth of a collection: the increasing accumulation of Christian texts that were customarily used in the various Christian communities. This collection would later provide the substantial basis for the official decisions of the church. Those first stages of the process are now mostly hidden from our view, but from the few glimpses that the remaining evidence offers, we are able to make a reasonable reconstruction of the process. It is most important to maintain the reality of this process, for otherwise what was largely a natural and organic development over a period of many years would appear to be a late, arbitrary, and artificial imposition by the ecclesiastical establishment. Although strictly speaking it is only proper to speak of the "canon of the New Testament" at the stage of its ratification—for that was when such language came into play—it would be overly cautious to deny the existence of substantially the same collection of writings long before that time, as evidenced in the customary usage of the churches. Indeed, we are only able to appreciate the nature of the Christian canon when we retrace, as best we can, those earlier stages in the process of canonical formation.

Composition

It is obvious that the church came into being before the NT. The writings themselves arose as crystallizations of community traditions. Form and redaction analysis of the letters and Gospels alike show how earlier oral and written traditions were given new settings within those writings that sought to address the changing circumstances of specific Christian communities. The varying community contexts of preaching, worship, and teaching are reflected in the sayings and stories of the Gospels. The letters bear fragments of, and make allusions to, liturgical formulae, hymns, ritual practices, and prophecies. Above all, as we have repeatedly observed, the NT writings give new symbolic shape to the Scripture the first Christians shared with Judaism, the writings of Torah. In the most proper sense, the NT always remains a commentary on the Torah. What Christians eventually came to call the Old Testament remains an essential component of the Christian Bible, although always interpreted in light of God's New Word—Jesus.

Use

The first Christian writings were not composed for private devotion or edification. They were public writings, intended for reading in the assembly. Increasingly, they were read in the liturgy alongside selected readings from the Law and the Prophets. Not surprisingly, such liturgical use hastened the perception of the NT writings themselves as Scripture and the Word of God—they came to share in the convictions held concerning Torah. Because of such public and liturgical use, these writings also came to be employed in the preaching and teaching activities of the church. Thus, as writings, they increasingly helped shape the continuing tradition of the community, being quoted as authorities alongside passages from Torah.

From the very beginning, as well, writings were exchanged between churches for the purpose of being read aloud in the assembly. The practice is reflected in Acts 15 where the apostolic letter is sent to gentile believers in Antioch, Syria, and Cilicia (Acts 15:23). Second Corinthians is sent to "all the saints who are in the whole of Achaia" (2 Cor. 1:1). Galatians is written for all the churches of that province (Gal. 1:2). The Colossians and Laodiceans are to exchange the letters Paul wrote to each (Col. 4:16). Ephesians and 1 Peter are circular letters, intended for numerous churches throughout a particular region. These last two examples are especially interesting, as they indicate that already in the first Christian generation, news and admonition from an apostle or teacher to one community in particular became a source of encouragement for other communities as well.

Collection

As writings were exchanged, local churches began to build collections that were more extensive than those written specifically to them. This is the critical step toward the formation of a canon. By collecting and copying texts originally composed for others, and by reading these in its own assembly, a community asserts the relevance for itself of that which was written for others: the particular bears the possibility of becoming general.

The evidence suggests that Paul's letters were the first Christian writings gathered into a collection. We have previously noted the hypotheses that connect the composition of Acts or Ephesians to this process. Whatever the validity of such theories, it is clear that within thirty years of his death, Paul's letters were being used by churches other than the ones for whom they were originally written, and indeed were regarded as having a special authority. Only a few traces of this process can still be detected in the Christian writings of the late first- and early second century.

Clement of Rome wrote a letter of exhortation to the Corinthian congregation (ca. 95 C.E.). In it, he explicitly refers to Paul's First Letter to the Corinthians (*1 Clem.* 47.2–4). In addition, he makes extensive and unmistakable use of the Letter to the Hebrews (*1 Clem.* 17.1–6; 36.1–6; cf. Eusebius *Ecclesiastical History* III.38.1). This means simply that both documents had by that time not only reached the Roman church but also attained significant authority there. Some twenty years later (ca. 115 C.E.), Ignatius, the bishop of Antioch in Syria, wrote to the Ephesian church as he made his way to Rome and his eventual martyrdom. He tells its members that Paul "in all his letters mentions your union with Christ Jesus" (Ign. *Eph.* 12.2). We do not know how many of Paul's letters were known by Ignatius. Certainly he knew 1 Corinthians (cf. Ign. *Eph.* 16.1; 18.1; *Magn.* 10.2; *Trall.* 2.3), and quite probably Romans (cf. Ign. *Eph.* 8.2; 18.2) and Ephesians (cf. *Smyrn.* 1.2; *Pol.* 5.1; 6.2).

Shortly thereafter, Polycarp, the bishop of Smyrna, wrote to the Philippians, sending them his collection of the letters of Ignatius (*Letter to the Philippians* 13.2). He not only recalls Paul's personal presence in that community, but refers to letters Paul wrote to them (3.2). The style of Polycarp's letter makes the definite identification of specific Pauline texts difficult, but it is obvious that he knows and uses a large number of Pauline letters, including—in my judgment—the Pastorals (4:1). We have also seen that the author of 2 Peter speaks of "all" Paul's letters, regarding them as being "like other Scriptures" (2 Pet. 3:16). These references suggest that collections of some or many of Paul's letters were extant by the end of the first decade of the second century in such major centers of Christianity as Rome, Corinth, Antioch, Smyrna, Ephesus, and Philippi, and that for such churches Paul's letters were already well on the way toward—if not already having arrived at—the status of "Scripture."

Progress toward a Gospel collection is more difficult to trace. If the two-source solution to the Synoptic problem is correct, then we know that by the year 85 at the latest, Matthew, or a Matthean scribal group, possessed the Gospel of Mark. Luke, likewise, makes reference to earlier attempts at writing gospel narratives, and he certainly used Mark (Luke 1:1). In his *Letter to the Corinthians*, Clement of Rome tells them to "recall the words of our Lord Jesus" (*1 Clem.* 13.2; 46.8–9) and follows with what appear to be mixed citations or reminiscences of Gospel passages, most resembling sections of Matthew. Ignatius of Antioch shows probable use of the Fourth Gospel (cf. Ign. *Eph.* 5.2; *Magn.* 7.1; *Rom.* 7.2-3; *Phld.* 7.1; 9:1) and Matthew (cf. Ign. *Eph.* 14.2; *Smyrn.* 1:2; 6:1). Polycarp's *Letter to the Philippians* also shows some use of Matthew (7.2; 12.3), numerous Pauline letters (3:3; 4:2; 5:1-3; 11:4; 12:1), 1 Peter (2:1; 5:3; 8:1), as well as 1 John (7:1). The *Didache* (ca. 90–100 c.e.) contains many allusions to Gospel sayings and has what appears to be an extended citation from Matthew 6:9-11 in its version of the Lord's Prayer (Did. 8:2).

This pattern of use continues into the middle of the second century. In his *First Apology* (ca. 155 c.e.), Justin Martyr describes the Christian worship service as including both reading and preaching from the apostles and prophets (67). He refers to the "memoirs" of the apostles in the plural, and cites them (66). Likewise, in his *Dialogue with Trypho*—an extended disputation with a Jew involving debates over messianic texts in Torah—Justin again makes both frequent allusion to the "memoirs of the apostles" (101, 105, 106, 107) and explicit citations of the Gospels (12, 18, 32, 49, 76, 78, 112, 125, 133).

In addition to the testimony of Justin that the NT writings formed the content of preaching, we have direct evidence that such was the case from the homily entitled *2 Clement* (ca. 150), which quotes Mark 2:17 as Scripture: ". . . and another Scripture says, 'I did not come to call the righteous but sinners'" (*2 Clem.* 2:4; cf. 3:2; 6:1-2; 11:5-7). In the apologetic literature of the middle and late second century we find some explicit citations of the NT, as in Theophilus of Antioch's *To Autolycus* (III.14), Athenagoras' *Supplication for the Christians* (12, 32, 33), and the *Epistle to Diognetus* (12.5).

Three points should be made to summarize this outline of evidence. First, the citations of NT writings are not numerous, and they are obviously not made from a "New Testament" as such. Second, the citations, on the other hand, are frequent enough to be noticed, and more important, are cited as authoritative, even at times as the equivalent of Torah. Finally, it is even more striking that we do not find other Christian writings cited in preference to, or alongside of, these that later are to be called the NT. In other words, as few as these citations are, they support the primacy of place and authority from the start of those writings that would later form the NT corpus.

Exchange and collection were critical factors in the process of many churches forming a larger unity—the one church. This development, if not begun, was at least foreshadowed by both Paul's collection for the Jerusalem church among his gentile congregations and the circular letters he wrote. By reading the same texts, communities would inevitably be shaped according to a shared identity, growing increasingly aware of the catholicity of their faith. Three statements were made by the communities that assembled such collections. First, by viewing the writings of "apostles and prophets" as foundational documents and placing them alongside Torah for reading in the liturgy, they asserted at once the continuity of their identity with that expressed in those writings, as well as the authority of these writings—as God's Word—to shape the worshiping community. Second, they affirmed their communion with other local churches throughout the inhabited world (*oikoumenē*) who were reading the same writings. Third, they stated that these writings had a universal pertinence: what Paul said to the Corinthians in past generations applies as well to the Smyrneans in this generation, and therefore to every generation of the church in every place thereafter.

Selection

The Christian movement produced many more texts than the ones that found their way into the canon. Some of them were written later than those now in the NT canon. This is the case with most if not all of the "gnostic gospels." But others, such as the *Didache* or *1 Clement,* were probably written earlier than some that were canonized (e.g., 2 Peter). The second century in particular produced many gospels, apocalypses, and acts of various apostles. Communities therefore had to choose which of these they wanted read in the worship, and which, in turn, would serve as the basis of proclamation and teaching.

From the beginning, not all churches agreed on every choice. Some churches had local favorites they regarded as Scripture, while rejecting another choice favored elsewhere. For example, we have sparse evidence for the Western church regarding James as Scripture until the late fourth century (although there was no active rejection of it either). In the East, in contrast, James was regarded as Scripture already by the time of Origen (184–254 c.e.). On the other hand, the *Shepherd of Hermas* enjoyed strong local popularity for a period in the West, and the *Apocalypse of Peter* found the same favor in the East. Because of the enthusiastic excesses of the prophetic movement called Montanism in the late second century, the Book of Revelation was regarded with deep suspicion by some writers and churches, as was also the Fourth Gospel—there was much debate over each before their full inclusion in the canon was realized.

For the most part, however, our earliest evidence shows that there was a rather remarkable degree of unanimity from the start concerning the great majority of the writings. Even so eclectic a thinker as Clement of Alexandria, who was capable of drawing inspiration from anywhere and everywhere, made some distinctions on the basis of the church's tradition: "We do not find this saying in the *four gospels that have been handed down to us,* but in that according to the Egyptians" (*Stromata* III.13). By the turn of the third century, writers as diverse as Irenaeus, Tertullian, and Origen have a canon substantially the same as that accepted today.

One of the earliest canonical lists available to us is a fragmentary Latin text called the *Muratorian Fragment*. There are two major positions on its relevance: it represents either the canonical list of the Western church in the late second century or of the Eastern (or possibly Western) church in the fourth century. The precise date or provenance of the document is of less importance to us here than its witness to the process and principles of canonization.

The document is both fascinating and confusing. In it, we find listed most of the writings of the present canon: the four Gospels and Acts; the letters of Paul, including the Pastorals; two letters of John (1 and 2); the letter of Jude; and the Apocalypse of John—twenty-two of the twenty-seven writings. More interesting are the variations. There is no mention of a third letter of John, Hebrews, James, or—and this seems strange for a Western provenance—any letters of Peter. None of these documents is necessarily rejected; they are simply not listed. On the other hand, the *Muratorian Fragment* includes the Jewish apocryphal Wisdom of Solomon, as well as the Christian *Apocalypse of Peter*, although it acknowledges that not everyone agrees that the latter should be "read in church." A middle ground is held by the *Shepherd of Hermas*. It can be read by the faithful—its popularity attested in fact by the discussion of it in this list—but it should not be read publicly in the church or included among the "apostles and prophets." From this we see how the key factor for canonization is not whether documents can be read or used by individuals but whether they are to be read publicly in worship. Finally, the *Muratorian Fragment* vehemently excludes the fictitious letters that claim to come from Paul but are in reality forgeries by Marcion: these "cannot be accepted in the catholic church." Equally vigorous is the rejection of the writings by gnostic teachers such as Valentinus and Basilides.

The process of selection inevitably involved the rejection of some writings. This aspect of canonization was accelerated by the challenge of Marcionism in the middle of the second century. Marcion broke from the great church, establishing a dissident form of Christianity complete with a "canon" that was made up solely of Paul's letters—excluding the Pastorals (see Tertullian *Against Marcion* V.21)—and an expurgated version of Luke's Gospel, which Marcion claimed Paul meant when referring to "my gospel."

The same obsessive dualism that led Marcion to identify the visible world as the work of an evil demiurge from which the good news of Jesus freed humans led him to regard Torah as the work of that demiurge and all other NT writings—except Paul's—as the "corruptions" of a Judaizing spirit. Some scholars have thought that Marcion's abbreviated canon made up of a gospel (*to euangelion*) and apostle (*to apostolikon*) provided both the impetus and structural principle for the creation of an "orthodox" canon. This is probably to overstate the case. Yet, Marcion's truncated version of the church's inchoate canon certainly forced orthodox leaders to look more closely at their communities' lists and their reasons for holding them.

Another second-century challenge to the canon was posed by the composition of the *Diatessaron* by Tatian (ca. 170). This cleverly woven version of the gospel story used all four Gospels, seeking to replace their messy multiplicity with a single harmonized rendition. The *Diatessaron* was enormously popular in Syria. Indeed, it was—in practice—the canonical version there for several centuries, being read in worship and serving as the basis for preaching, and was not displaced until the fifth century. The *Diatessaron* did not enjoy the same favor elsewhere, however; the rest of the churches did not accept this harmony as a replacement for the four Gospels. They thereby demonstrated that they did not regard the Gospels as merely historical sources but as separate and valuable witnesses precisely in their literary diversity.

Perhaps an even greater threat came from the expansion of Christian literature from the side of Gnosticism. Writings claiming to be from apostles contained secret revelations that would shape Christianity in the direction of an individualistic, mystical, and anti-institutional spirituality. The issue of "what to read" in various communities was very much connected to different ideas of "who we are."

Ratification

The repeated threats posed by expansion and contraction of the NT canon were neither mild nor temporary in nature. The *Diatessaron* flourished in Syria; Marcionism was the dominant form of Christianity in many parts of the empire; and Gnosticism had many forms and adherents. If orthodoxy was to survive, or, to put it another way, if Christian identity was to avoid being fragmented in diverse directions, limits needed to be set. Thus, the discussion over the matter of definition became increasingly precise.

Early in the fourth century Eusebius, Bishop of Caesarea, states that "the writings of the New Testament" consist of the four Gospels (the "Holy tetrad"), the Acts of the Apostles, the letters of Paul, 1 John, 1 Peter, and—with some hesitancy on his part—the Book of Revelation. If we include Hebrews as one of Paul's letters (an association often made in the ancient church), Eusebius' canon has twenty-two writings. These he calls the recognized books (*homologoumenoi*), about which he asserts there is unanimity. He then adds five writings that he calls disputed (*antilegomenoi*): James, Jude, 2 Peter, and 2 and 3 John. Combined, we have the present canon of twenty-seven writings. Eusebius goes on to list works he calls "non-genuine," by which he means works that may have enjoyed canonical status at some times and places but that should not be regarded as such—writings such as the *Shepherd of Hermas* and the *Apocalypse of Peter*. Finally, he rejects altogether the gospels and acts that go by names of apostles but that have been "put forward by heretics." These are not only spurious but in his view "wicked and impious."

Eusebius thus shows us a firm but still somewhat flexible canon. He is not certain about Revelation. He is clear, however, about the majority of writings that belong and those that do not. It is also instructive to note the critical spirit Eusebius brings to the discussion: the reasons for rejecting the gospels and acts of the "heretics" are that they have not previously appeared as Scripture in the writings of orthodox Christians, their phraseology is not consonant with that associated with the apostolic age, and their contents and perspective differ greatly from orthodoxy. Three criteria—use in the church, apostolic derivation, and theological consistency—are here operative (see Eusebius *Ecclesiastical History* III.25.1–7). Here we see quite clearly the defensive posture of the established church, as it seeks to define itself over against perceived hostile outside influences.

The defensive stance adopted in the ratification process is best illustrated by the *Paschal Letter* of Athanasius (39th), bishop of Alexandria, written in 367 C.E. He lists the twenty-seven writings of the present NT canon, calling them the "springs of salvation" (10). He also approves of other writings for use in instruction, such as Wisdom of Solomon, Esther, Judith, and the *Shepherd of Hermas*. But he is even more vehement than Eusebius in rejecting other writings: "There is nowhere mention of the secret writings, but they are a device of heretics, who write them when they will, furnishing them with dates, and adding them, that bringing them forth as ancient, they might thus have an excuse for deceiving the undefiled" (12).

Finally, we can note the list put out by the North African Council of Carthage (397 C.E.), which corresponds precisely to the canon of the present church (article 39):

> . . . apart from the canonical Scriptures nothing is read in church under the name of the divine Scriptures. The canonical writings are . . . [there follows a list of the OT writings] . . . and of the New Testament, four books of the Gospels; of the Acts of the Apostles, one book; of Paul's letters, thirteen; of the same [i.e., Paul] to the Hebrews, one; of the apostle Peter, two; of John, three; of James, one; of Jude, one; of the Apocalypse of John, one book. Let the church across the sea be consulted for the confirmation of this canon.

We observe that for this North African church, communication with Rome on this matter was important. We also notice the canonical principle: these are the writings that "are to be read in the church as divine Scripture."

Thus by the end of the fourth century not only had the organic process of canonization been accomplished for some time, but ratification was complete. Apart from the remaining dissidents of a gnostic persuasion, this was the canon of all Christians for the next millennium. In response to Luther's reopening of the issue of canonicity by his demotion of Hebrews, James, Jude, and Revelation from "the proper books," and to Ulrich Zwingli's rejection of Revelation, the Council of Trent in 1546 reaffirmed a canon of twenty-seven writings, as did also the Articles of the Church of England (1562/1571) and the Westminster Confession (1647).

Principles of Canonization

From this process two things immediately become apparent about the nature of the canon. First, the rejection of Marcionism by the church shows that the canon is *in principle pluralistic.* Whatever the dissonances between OT and NT, between Paul and James, the canon is not the isolation of a single "correct" theology that becomes the measure of everything else. With this rejection of Marcionism and its truncated canon there can be read an implied rejection of any sort of "canon within the canon"—for Marcion simply proposed a bolder version of that concept.

Second, the ultimate rejection of Tatian's *Diatessaron* also tells us that the canon is made up of a plurality of witnesses rather than a single unified version. Equally important, the maintenance of four Gospels affirmed that the canon is, above all, a *collection* of writings. For the life of the church, neither the life of Jesus nor the history of the church is normative. Rather, the Gospels precisely in their particularity relate the "good news" of Jesus Christ. This is a "four-form gospel" (Irenaeus *Against Heresies* III.11.8): it is "good news according to" these four witnesses. Matthew does not supplant Mark because it is fuller; John is not rendered invalid because of its disagreements with the Synoptics. They are not competing histories but convergent witnesses, interpreting—each in their own way—the Word of God in Jesus.

So much seems to be clear. What is less obvious are the criteria used for the canonization of some writings and the rejection of others. Certainly custom played a role and should not be neglected as a factor. The opinion of learned people in the churches also counted, as we are told by Eusebius (*Ecclesiastical History* III.25.6; cf. Augustine *Against Faustus* XXII.79). These Christians were able to make reasoned judgments on such matters as previous citation as Scripture, apostolic style, and theological coherence.

On the other hand, inspiration—a criterion for canonization we might expect to play a great role—is not a factor. The *Shepherd of Hermas* and many other writings either claimed inspiration or had it claimed for them, yet were neither universally nor ultimately accepted as canonical. In contrast, no NT writing claims inspiration for itself. The statement in 2 Tim. 3:16 that all Scripture is inspired by God (*theopneustos*) refers to Torah. Second Peter 3:16 refers to Paul's letters as though they were Scripture but does not say they were "inspired." In Revelation, "inspiration" is certainly implied but not explicitly claimed. No doubt there was an increasingly widespread conviction that the NT writings were divinely inspired, but that notion did not appear to factor in as a criterion for canonization.

The criterion of apostolic origin or association, on the other hand, does find explicit expression. The influence of Paul was undoubtedly important in this regard, but equally so was the fight against gnostic teachers who claimed a secret succession (*diadochē*) for the transmission of their esoteric books. The orthodox claim of apostolic origin stated that the NT writings did not emerge out of nowhere or only recently: they could be traced along the public and universally recognized lines of ecclesial tradition. This argument carries the implicit judgment that the earlier the writing, the more original and theologically pure it is. Yet, the earliest church was also very conscious of having descended from "eyewitnesses" to the work of God in Christ, and connecting tradition back to these "eyewitnesses" made obvious sense. Thus, Papias, for example, was concerned to connect all the authoritative writings to an apostle: Mark's Gospel comes from Peter's companion and translator; Luke's from a companion of Paul; Matthew and John from apostles; and the letters of Paul, John, James, Jude, and Peter from apostles as well.

Two important claims were made against the Gnostics by this principle of apostolic origin. The first was the claim of historical priority: these were the writings that first gave expression to the Christian identity. The second is the claim of historical continuity: the church of today reads and understands—as though written to itself—the writings of Jesus' first followers. It requires no esoteric code for understanding their plain meaning; the context was given with the text, in the church's public life. The criterion of apostolic origin was important, but it was also somewhat artificial and it was certainly not decisive (see Augustine *On the Harmony of the Evangelists* I.I.2) as many of the writings that were attributed to apostles were not accepted, such as the *Gospel of Thomas, Gospel of Peter*, and the *Apocalypse of Peter*. The Gospels of Luke and Mark, on the other hand, were accepted for reasons clearly transcending their apostolic pedigree.

Canonization evidently involved the communal recognition of a writing's authority, but once more this was scarcely an absolute norm. There were authoritative writings in the early church that were not canonized or that enjoyed only local acceptance—for example, the *Didache* and the "church orders" that followed it (such as the *Didascalia Apostolorum* and the *Apostolic Constitutions*). So are the letters of Ignatius of Antioch, which were regarded as important enough to be collected and distributed by Polycarp. An important distinction should be made here between a local or temporary authority and a general and permanent one. The writings finally accepted into the canon were understood to have transcended simply local or temporary authority, having the capacity to address the church in every place and time.

If we search for the intrinsic qualities in the writings that were perceived as giving them authority, we are told little by the ancient sources and must rely on guesswork. Certainly, some judgment on the content of the writings was involved. It is apparent in the writings of many patristic authors that there is a *regula fidei*—"rule of faith"— that provides the proper framework for Christian understanding. The *regula* (simply the Latin version of "canon") is not spelled out definitively but appears as a transition point between the NT kerygma and the fully developed creeds of the councils. We find explicit reference to such a *regula* in writers as diverse as Clement of Alexandria (*Stromata* 1), Irenaeus (*Against Heresies* I.8.1; 1.22.1) and Tertullian (*On the Prescription of Heretics* XIII; XXXVI.1–5; *Against Praxeas* II.1–2; *Against Marcion* I.21). Even so adventuresome a theologian as Origen pays explicit and sincere tribute to the *regula* as the essential framework for his investigations (*On First Principles* I. pref. 3–4).

The significance of this *regula* is that it provides a framework as well for the reading of orthodox writings. Although some circularity is inevitably involved—the *regula* itself is understood to be derived from the same orthodox writings it uses to establish as orthodox—the deduction of a basic principle is possible. It is clear, for example, that the orthodox teaching in both its kerygmatic and its creedal forms places great emphasis on the incarnation of the Word and the crucifixion and death of Jesus. It is no accident that gospels with a docetic (i.e., Jesus was not truly human) Christology—whatever their apostolic attribution—are not found in the canon, nor are gospels that treat the death of Jesus as either unimportant or only an embarrassing episode on the way to Jesus' apotheosis. Of course, to term this doctrinal norm "orthodoxy" is somewhat of a misnomer, since this category only takes on meaning in retrospect. Yet, it does indicate that there was a perceived congruity between the theology of the earliest Christian writings we possess—essentially the entire NT canon—and the later articulation of the church.

Such a doctrinal norm is not inconsistent with the outlook of the NT writings themselves, for we have observed throughout this book how each, in its own fashion, fought against deviance in teaching as much as in behavior. As important as the *regula fidei* was, however, it did not stand alone. Irenaeus, in his battles with the heretics, combined it with both the argument from traditional citation of the NT writings as Scripture and the principle of apostolic succession (*Against Heresies*, III). And even this combination would be convincing only to those who already shared those convictions. The *regula* also focused mainly on doctrinal elements. It provided a negative measure, not a positive one. Perfectly orthodox writings such as the *Shepherd of Hermas* and the *Didache* still did not find their way into the canon, and one needs to account for this by a more positive criterion, since those texts were not viewed as heretical and were used and read frequently in many Christian communities.

The Sense of the Church

There was in all likelihood not a single criterion for canonization. The best historical account of the process may be to attribute it to what is in fact a theological category, the sense of the church (*sensus ecclesiae*). This is an expression that denotes both a process and a perception. The process is the way in which the church as a whole makes its decisions. The perception reflects the church's way of seeing itself. This "sense of itself" is what ultimately, I would suggest, determined canonicity and the final shape of the NT.

For those inside the community, the process is one guided by the Holy Spirit that inspired the writings. But for all that, it is not a mystical process. It is, rather, the greater communal awareness of many individual communities, sharpened and tested by interchange, disputation, and debate. It is not made all at once but over the course of time. It is not a decision made by a special authority or office; rather, it involves the discernment of all in the church.

The perception involved in the *sensus ecclesiae* is that these writings have a deep congruence with the church's own sense of its identity: not only what the church is now but also what it is called to be. It is the sense that these writings, taken in concert, accurately and authentically represent what the church is and ought to be, though none of the writings alone states that perception fully. More important still, these writings are seen to have the ability to reshape that identity and regenerate that life for succeeding generations of the church.

The *sensus ecclesiae* perceives that these writings possess catholicity of authority. They not only address the past or even the present but have the power to address future situations as well, creating, for those who read them, capacities for Christian existence that are authentic and continuous with the experience of the first Christians. This potency, we note, is one aimed not primarily at individuals but at communities. This collection of writings can bring the church into being, shaping it according to the pattern of its first best realizations.

It is not by accident, I suggest, that the canon of the NT does not include writings that dissolve the difference between Christ and Christians into mystical unity, that cut the bonds of this people with their Jewish ancestors, that systematically distinguish between the elite and the herd, or that make the denial of creation the mark of authentic holiness. Such tendencies work precisely to destroy community. The present writings of the NT have as their almost exclusive focus the shaping of communities into a common identity. That is why they were chosen in preference to others that had no such interest.

Such a *sensus ecclesiae* is difficult to defend on strictly historical grounds. It has been asserted in the past, and more urgently in the present, that the process of canonization was one that was inherently corrupt. According to this view, entirely worthy writings of diverse forms of Christian life were ruthlessly suppressed by orthodox leaders out of unworthy motives. Because of this, the whole issue of canonization ought to be reopened, with all the writings produced by earliest Christianity given equal weight as this generation decides what its "Bible" ought to be.

According to this argument, the most important stage of the canonization process was that of the ratification by the bishops. These bishops, however, were both politically motivated and conditioned by the cultural attitudes of their day. In every decision, they chose that which was conservative over that which was radical; chose institution rather than charism; fought for hierarchy rather than egalitarianism; preferred doctrine to mysticism; and suppressed women in favor of men. The canon we now have, therefore, is not the canon of the whole church, but only of a victorious segment of that church. In this view, all Christians have been shaped by a sectarian canon that, while different, is no less tendentious than Marcion's.

This is not the place to engage that position in detail. Only a few points need to be made here by way of response. First, a realistic appreciation of history and historical processes is important. All human decision making involves politics and power. The church has never been the new Jerusalem; its grasp on the truth is always fragile, often faithless, and sometimes even grotesque. These things cannot be disputed. That said, however, we must not romanticize the opposition any more than we romanticize the orthodox: there were dirty tricks enough to go around for all parties in those ancient disputes. Despite that, one cannot discount that higher motivations than the simple drive for power were often at work.

Second, although the process of canonization is historical in nature, the canon itself is a theological datum. It results from the decision of the church in every age to reaffirm and ratify those earlier decisions. This the church does by reading these and only these writings in its public worship and by using these texts alone in its debate over the nature of the kingdom. The decision for or against the canon never has been, nor should it have been, based on the purity of the process by which the writings were selected and ratified.

Third, the critical contemporary question with regard to the canon is not the motivation or means of the first ratifiers. The question is, rather, whether those other factors betrayed the *sensus ecclesiae* in a fundamental way. Did those bishops, in other words, still make the right decision, even if for the wrong reasons (if indeed their reasons and motivations were questionable)? This is the appropriate subject for the debate, discernment, and decision of the church in this age and the next, for it concerns not the past process but the present prophetic voice of these writings. In this connection, when the credentials of other ancient or modern candidates for canonization are presented, or when canonical writings are considered for rejection, critical questions need to be asked: What sort of Christian identity will these writings generate in the succeeding generations? Do these writings enable the church to maintain not only its connection to the identifiable past but also its capacity to embrace humans in every circumstance of place and time?

Canon and the Church

Canonicity, in sum, is a statement of relevance. By it the church affirms that the particular and historically conditioned meaning of these writings is not their only meaning. They are not utterly defined by their first circumstances but possess enduring worth and normative force. They can bring the church of every place and time into being and shape it according to the "mind of Christ" (see 1 Cor. 2:16).

The term "relevance," however, needs qualification. Relevance is not the same in every time and place. For this reason, the whole *collection* of writings must be kept alive if the church in every time and place is to live. In times of reform, it may be the voice of Paul that is most pertinent; in times of moral lassitude, that of James or Matthew. In periods of persecution, the Book of Revelation is read in ways quite different than in periods of calm. In times of alienation, 1 Peter reveals new and rich significance to its readers. In the face of moral corruption, even the often neglected Jude suddenly seems pertinent. Before rationalistic skepticism, 2 Peter becomes surprisingly contemporary. Nor is this only a matter of different times. The church is universal and exists in very different circumstances simultaneously. Here, the church may enjoy prosperity and position; there, it is persecuted and poor. In this place, it may require the voice of prophecy; there, the comfort of promise. The canon must be able to address every time and place where the church exists.

Nor is the relevance of these writings to be found in them individually; rather, it is found in them precisely as parts of a collection related dialectically to all the other parts of that collection. The church holds in a creative tension the very human Jesus of Luke's Gospel and the transcendent Jesus of the Fourth Gospel. It walks delicately between the gift of freedom from Paul and the law of freedom from James. It is precisely the way these writings work *together* to shape Christian identity that makes the canon such an important and intricate organism—one which reveals the principle of a "canon within the canon" as a fundamentally arrogant proposition. Such a proposition claims to know for every age and time which documents possess relevance, and is willing to close the possibility that other canonical witnesses might testify to new ages and realizations of the church.

Some Canonical Theses

I want to close this book with ten theses on the canon as the book of the church, and a concluding proposal. By now the reader surely knows that all these statements make sense only within the context of a commitment to the reality we call "the church." My main point is that the entity called "the New Testament" only makes full sense within that larger commitment and framework.

1. The canon is simply the church's working bibliography. Whatever else is read or studied by individual Christians, these are the writings to which the church as such turns for debating and defining its identity. These are the public documents of the church, the framework for its discussions. They are public in the sense that they are read aloud in worship. They are also public because they offer themselves to the whole community, providing the basis for debate and discernment as new issues and experiences are confronted.

2. The canon is more than the residue of a historical process. It requires a commitment of faith by the church in every age and place. The acceptance of these specific writings by a community, not in council but in liturgical use, is the most fundamental issue for identity that the community will confront. The selection excludes any contemporary writings that may attempt to win the complete allegiance garnered by the NT canon, and it asserts the church's continuity with the historical manifestations of the church in the past. By this selection, the church assumes as well the

responsibility for transmitting the same measure—in its entirety—to the church in the ages to come.

3. The canon and the church are correlative concepts. The canon establishes discrete writings from the past as Scripture. Without the church there is no canon; without canon there is no Scripture in the proper sense. As the church stands under the norm of Scripture in every age—finding life and meaning in the reading of it—so do these writings find their realization as Scripture by being so read by a community, age after age, as the measure of its life and meaning.

4. It is the nature of a canon to be closed. An unlimited canon is no longer a "rule," just as a twelve-inch ruler cannot gain inches and still be a one-foot ruler. Because it is closed, the canon is able to perform its function of mediating a specific identity through the successive ages of the church. Because the church today reads the very same writings as were read by Polycarp, Augustine, Thomas Aquinas, Luther, and Bonhoeffer, it remains identifiably the same community. Only such a steady measure can provide such continuity. If a lost letter of Paul's should be discovered, there would undoubtedly be great excitement. But there should be no expansion of the canon, for that letter, from the time of its composition until the present, has not shaped the identity of the universal church.

5. It is because the canon is closed and exclusive that it can be truly catholic, having universal and enduring pertinence. This is only an apparent paradox. A measure that can be altered by addition or subtraction at any time and place cannot have the capacity to address every time and place. It is because the canon is closed that it can give rise to an open process of interpretation.

6. What distinguishes the theologian from the historian of ideas and the student of literature is the effective acceptance of the canon. For history and literature as such, the concept of canon is meaningless, except as a convenient categorization or the recognition that a certain group of writings achieved classical status for a certain period of history. But such recognition does not affirm the distinctive interrelationship between texts and a living community over an extended period of time, which is essential to the notion of canon.

7. The ecclesial decision to regard these writings as Scripture bears with it the recognition that they have a peculiar and powerful claim on the lives of individuals and the community as a whole. The community asserts that it does not control these writings but that these texts, in a very real sense, control the community, by providing the definitive framework for its self-understanding. Within this community, the critical questions that readers pose to the texts are far less significant than the critical questions the texts pose to readers.

8. Implicit in the recognition of the canonical writings as Scripture is the acknowledgment that they not only speak in the voice of their human authors but also speak for another. These texts speak prophetically to every age, and essential to the concept of prophecy is the speaking of God's Word. These texts play a role in the process of

God's revelation. Within their time-conditioned words and symbols, which come from many persons in the past, there speaks as well the single Word of God, which endures through all ages. This conviction can be expressed by the statement that the texts are "divinely inspired," for to speak of the Word of God is to speak as well, by implication, of the work of God's Spirit. "Divine inspiration" is one of the ways of expressing the unique authority of the writings in the canonical collection. Explanations and interpretations of inspiration, however, vary widely. They range from psychological theories that virtually equate it with literary inspiration, through metaphysical distinctions between primary and secondary causality, to the attribution of the whole creative process of composition within the social context of earliest Christianity, to the real but subtle working of the Holy Spirit as part of the constitutive force behind the founding of the church. However it is conceived, the fact that "God speaks" is foundational. Ultimately, of course, unlike Torah that is itself God's word, the NT canon reflects first and foremost that God's final Word is in Jesus as the Christ, a Word that, it is understood, the NT writers interpret through the prism of Torah and in the light of human experience.

9. Since the canon consists of a disparate collection of writings, with both the OT and NT forming the Christian Bible, it resists reduction to any single unifying principle imposed from the outside. If it excludes by its nature any "canon within the canon," it certainly also resists any conceptual mold that either relativizes or removes the texts themselves in all their concrete particularity. This resistance applies as well to any "New Testament theology." In all its forms, NT theology is simply another attempt to reduce the many to the one by the discovery of some abstract and unifying principle, whether it is called "salvation history," "justification by faith," "liberation theology," "kerygma," "regula fidei," "narrativity," or "existential decision." All such principles—no matter how appropriate at one level—demand the selection of some texts as more central and governing than others. All fit the writings themselves to frames of greater or lesser abstraction, often imputing wholly external criteria in the process. The canon resists such attempts precisely because it is made up of multiple and irreducible writings. They cannot, without distortion, be shaped into a static and synthetic symbolic system.

On the other hand, because of this diversity, the canon opens the possibilities for doing theology in the church, which is quite another sort of enterprise. In this enterprise, the articulation of the experience of God in the lives of contemporary persons and events is brought into a faithful and critical dialogue with all the writings of the OT and NT, not in an attempt to fix their meaning but to engage in a living conversation that ranges freely, opening up new, sometimes surprising, avenues for life.

10. Since the canon has meaning first of all as the public documents of a community that are intended for reading in the assembly, the church requires a hermeneutic appropriate to the nature of the canon. Such a hermeneutic would not be concerned primarily with the reading of texts by individuals for their pleasure or transformation.

There have been no end of interpretive models for this sort of reading, from allegory to existential interpretation to reader-response theories. There is nothing wrong with such methods in and of themselves, for freedom and fantasy open the minds and hearts of individuals in every age. But the key word here is "individual," since such models of interpretation scarcely reach to the neighbor. Moreover, while there is nothing ostensibly wrong or even misguided about someone expanding the canon for their own personal spirituality, the whole debate about expansion misses the fundamental function of the canon, which is *to mediate the identity of the church as church*. Commitment to the church demands a commitment to its canon, for in that collected group of texts known as the New Testament the church recognizes that God speaks to the community of believers, and in its reading the community of believers today recognizes that it stands in continuity with the communities of believers in every age.

What is needed, then, is a properly *ecclesial hermeneutic*, one that places the writings in their proper canonical context and that involves the entire faith community—past and present—in the interpretive process. For such a hermeneutic to work, there must be the active discernment of the work of God in the lives of contemporary believers, raised to the level of a narrative of faith; at the same time, there must be the active discernment of the canonical texts in the light of these experiences and narratives. And this process must occur in a public context that enables discussion, debate, disagreement, and decision. In this creative, if tension-filled, context, the canonical witnesses can again shape the identity of the Christian community in every age.

A Modest Proposal

I began this book with the search for a model. I close it with a modest suggestion.

The formation of an ecclesial hermeneutic can follow the example of the process by which the writings themselves came into existence, allowing the dialectic of experience and interpretation to take place again.

The experience of God continues, however darkly. But now, not only the texts of Torah but those of the NT canon form the symbolic world that will be reshaped and renewed by such experience, coming to new clarity in the life of the church. In describing a model for grasping the nature of these writings and their appearance, I suggested early on that midrash was a useful tool. Here, I renew that suggestion with regard to a hermeneutical model.

The Christian church can again learn something from Judaism by regarding the NT canon as analogous to the Talmud. The Talmud was a crystallization of a long history of interpretation of Torah mediated by new experiences; it became authoritative for the Jewish tradition not as the replacement of Torah but as the inescapable prism through which Torah would be read and understood. The NT writings can be regarded as crystallizations of reflection on Torah in light of the experience of Jesus as resurrected Lord. The NT writings remain authoritative and normative for the Christian tradition not as the replacement of Torah but through their offering interpretations of God's new Word in Jesus—the indispensable prism through whom Torah is to be read and understood.

There is this difference: in the Talmud there are not separate writings, but voices, whereas in the NT there are diverse literary forms that speak with multiple voices.

But there is this even more important similarity: In the study of Talmud one never listens to only one voice or authority. One never follows the views of Rabbi Judah through every tractate. Nor is there ever any single abstractable answer that need not be reinterpreted in the light of new circumstances. Indeed, the whole point of midrash is to hear the various voices in all their conflicts and disagreements, for it is precisely in those elements of plurality and even disharmony that the texts open to new meanings, so that they are allowed to speak to the disharmonies and disjunctions of contemporary life.

In exactly this fashion, I suggest, Christians should learn to read the canon of the NT, not in search of an essential core or purified "canon within the canon"—not, in other words, within the frame of a single abstract principle—but in a living conversation with all the writings in all their diversity and divergence. Only in this way can they continue to speak.

Study Questions

1. What are the earliest indicators that Paul's letters circulated as a collection among the early churches?

2. What is the *Muratorian Fragment* and why is it important in reconstructing the use of NT books?

3. What role did Marcion play in moving the church toward creating a canon of the NT?

4. How is what Tatian did in the *Diatessaron* similar and dissimilar from how Matthew and Luke used Mark?

5. What is meant by the phrase "the sense of the church" (*sensus ecclesiae*)?

6. How is a "midrashic model" of Christian hermeneutics continuous with the process of the NT's composition?

Bibliographical Note

For the historical process of NT canonization, see the primary sources in D. J. Theron, *Evidence of Tradition* (Grand Rapids: Baker Book House, 1958); and the discussions by H. von Campenhausen, *The Formation of the Christian Bible* (Philadelphia: Fortress Press, 1972), 103–268; W. R. Farmer and D. M. Farkasfalvy, *The Formation of the New Testament Canon: An Ecumenical Approach* (New York: Paulist Press, 1983); H. Y. Gamble, *The New Testament Canon: Its Making and Meaning* (GBS; Philadelphia: Fortress Press, 1985); L. M. MacDonald, *The Formation of the Christian Biblical Canon*, rev. ed. (Peabody, Mass.: Hendrickson Pubs., 1995), 137–249; B. M. Metzger, *The Canon of the New Testament: Its Origin, Development, and Significance* (Oxford: Clarendon Press, 1987); C. F. D. Moule, *The Birth of the New Testament*, 3rd ed. (New York: Harper & Row, 1982), 235–69; W. Schneemelcher, "The History of the New Testament Canon," in E. Hennecke and W. Schneemelcher (eds.), *New Testament Apocrypha*, 2 vols., rev. ed., trans. R. McL. Wilson (Philadelphia: Westminster/John Knox Press, 1991–92), 1:10–50; and B. F. Westcott, *A General Survey of the History and Canon of the New Testament*, 6th ed. (Grand Rapids: Baker Book House, 1980 [1889]). The OT canonical process has not been emphasized here, but on it, besides von Campenhausen and MacDonald above, see R. Beckwith, *The Old Testament Canon of the New Testament Church* (Grand Rapids: Eerdmans, 1985); and A. C. Sundberg, *The Old Testament of the Early Church* (HTS, 20; Cambridge, Mass.: Harvard Univ. Press, 1964). On more general issues of relevance, see J. T. Barrera, *The Jewish Bible and the Christian Bible: An Introduction to the History of the Bible*, trans. W. G. E. Watson (Grand Rapids: Eerdmans; Leiden: E. J. Brill, 1998), and P. M. Blowers (ed. and trans.), *The Bible in Greek Christian Antiquity* (Notre Dame: Univ. of Notre Dame Press, 1997).

   For a treatment of the criteria used in the canonizing process, see R. M. Grant, *Heresy and Criticism: The Search for Authenticity in Early Christian Literature* (Louisville: Westminster/John Knox Press, 1993). A consideration of specific historical problems connected with canonization is found in O. Cullmann, "The Plurality of the Gospels as a Theological Problem in Antiquity," in his *The Early Church*, ed. A. J. B. Higgins (Philadelphia: Westminster Press, 1956), 39–58; N. A. Dahl, "The Particularity of the Pauline Epistles as a Problem in the Ancient Church," in *Neotestamentica et Patristica* (NovTSup, 6; Leiden: E. J. Brill, 1962), 261–71; E. Käsemann, "The Canon of the New Testament and the Unity of the Church," in his *Essays on New Testament Themes*, trans. W. J. Montague (Philadelphia: Fortress Press, 1964), 95–107; and A. C. Sundberg, "Towards a Revised History of the New Testament Canon," *SE* 4 (1968): 452–61. On tradition and the *regula fidei*, see R. P. C. Hanson, *Origen's Doctrine of Tradition* (London: SPCK, 1954); and idem, *Tradition in the Early Church* (Philadelphia: Westminster Press, 1962). On the *Muratorian Fragment*, see G. M. Hahneman, *The Muratorian Fragment and the Development of the Canon* (Oxford: Clarendon Press, 1992); K. Stendahl, "The Apocalypse of John and the Epistles of Paul in the Muratorian Fragment," in W. Klassen and G. F. Snyder (eds.), *Current Issues in New Testament Study* (New York: Harper & Row, 1962), 239–45; and A. C. Sundberg, "Canon Muratori: A Fourth Century List," *HTR* 66 (1973): 1–41.

On the use and reception of the NT texts by early Christian writers, see B. Dehandschutter. "Polycarp's Epistle to the Philippians: An Early Example of 'Reception'," in J. -M. Sevrin, *The New Testament in Early Christianity* (BETL, 86; Leuven: Leuven Univ. Press, 1989), 275–91; R. M. Grant, "Scripture and Tradition in Ignatius of Antioch," in his *After the New Testament: Studies in Early Christian Literature and Theology* (Philadelphia: Fortress Press, 1967), 37–54; D. A. Hagner, *The Use of the Old and New Testaments in Clement of Rome* (NovTSup, 34; Leiden: E. J. Brill, 1973), 135–350; C. N. Jefford, *The Sayings of Jesus in the Teachings of the Twelve Apostles* (Leiden: E. J. Brill, 1989); H. Koester, *Ancient Christian Gospels: Their History and Development* (Philadelphia: Trinity Press Int'l, 1990), 349–402 (on *2 Clement* and Justin Martyr); A. Lindemann, "Paul in the Writings of the Apostolic Fathers," in W. S. Babcock (ed.), *Paul and the Legacies of Paul* (Dallas: Southern Methodist Univ. Press, 1990), 25–54; É. Massaux, *The Influence of the Gospel of Saint Matthew on Christian Literature before Saint Irenaeus*, 3 vols., trans. N. J. Belval and S. Hecht, ed. A. J. Bellinzoni (Macon: Mercer Univ. Press, 1990–93); F. Neirynck, "The Apocryphal Gospels and the Gospel of Mark," in *The New Testament in Early Christianity*, 123–75; and C. M. Tuckett, "Synoptic Tradition in the Didache," in *The New Testament in Early Christianity*, 197–230.

Various writers and texts of the early church have been mentioned throughout this chapter. On the "heretics" and their relationship with the church, see G. Lüdemann, *Heretics: The Other Side of Early Christianity*, trans. J. Bowden (Louisville: Westminster/John Knox, 1996 [1995]); on Marcion (including his impact on canonization), see E. C. Blackman, *Marcion and His Influence* (London: SPCK, 1948); and A. von Harnack, *Marcion: The Gospel of the Alien God*, trans. J. E. Steely and L. D. Bierma (Durham: Labyrinth Press, 1990 [1924]); on Tatian, see W. L. Peterson, "Tatian's Diatessaron," in H. Koester, *Ancient Christian Gospels*, 403–30; and idem, *Tatian's Diatessaron: Its Creation, Dissemination, Significance, and History in Scholarship* (Leiden: E. J. Brill, 1994); on the numerous early Christian writers noted in this chapter, see the introductions in J. Quasten, *Patrology*, 3 vols. (Westminster, Md.: Christian Classics, 1983 [1950]); and on the various apocryphal texts mentioned, see the introductions in E. Hennecke and W. Schneemelcher (eds.), *New Testament Apocrypha*, 2 vols., rev. ed., trans. R. McL. Wilson (Louisville: Westminster/John Knox Press; Cambridge: James Clark & Co., 1991–92).

A sense of the contemporary debate over the reopening of the canon can be gained from D. L. Dungan, "The New Testament Canon in Recent Study," *Int* 29 (1975): 339–51; and A. C. Sundberg, "The Bible Canon and the Christian Doctrine of Inspiration," *Int* 29 (1975): 352–71. The stimulus for this discussion has come from a variety of quarters: the development of a feminist critique of Christian origins that questions some of the basic lines of early Christian development, on which see

E. Schüssler Fiorenza, *In Memory of Her: A Feminist Reconstruction of Christian Origins* (New York: Crossroad, 1983); the discovery of the gnostic documents that are often interpreted as sponsoring a more egalitarian vision of community, on which see E. Pagels, *The Gnostic Gospels* (New York: Random House, 1979); and various studies that challenge the orthodox vision and content of earliest Christianity, on which see J. M. Robinson and H. Koester, *Trajectories through Early Christianity* (Philadelphia: Fortress Press, 1971); and R. Cameron, "Alternate Beginnings—Different Ends: Eusebius, Thomas, and the Construction of Christian Origins," in L. Bormann et al. (eds.), *Religious Propaganda & Missionary Competition in the New Testament World* (Leiden: E. J. Brill, 1994), 501–25. For an example of the view of canon that results, see E. Schüssler Fiorenza, *Searching the Scriptures; Vol. 1: A Feminist Introduction* and *Vol. 2: A Feminist Commentary* (New York: Crossroad, 1994–95).

Recent critical scholarship has taken up the challenge of several scholars to trace the interpretive consequences of a serious acceptance of the canon. The fullest attempt to push this beyond the programmatic stage has been the work of B. Childs, *The New Testament as Canon: An Introduction* (Philadelphia: Fortress Press, 1985), esp. 3–33; and idem, *Biblical Theology of the Old and New Testaments: Theological Reflection on the Christian Bible* (Minneapolis: Fortress Press, 1993). Also see W. J. Abraham, *Canon and Criterion in Christian Theology* (London: Oxford Univ. Press, 1998); J. Barton, *Holy Writings, Sacred Text: The Canon in Early Christianity* (Louisville: Westminster/John Knox Press, 1997); F. Kermode, "The Argument About Canons," in F. McConnell (ed.), *The Bible and the Narrative Tradition* (New York: Oxford Univ. Press, 1987), 78–96; P. R. Noble, *The Canonical Approach: A Critical Reconstruction of the Hermeneutics of Brevard S. Childs* (Leiden: E. J. Brill, 1995); A. C. Outler, "The 'Logic' of Canon-Making and the Tasks of Canon-Criticism," in W. E. March (ed.), *Texts and Testaments* (San Antonio: Trinity Univ. Press, 1980), 263–76; J. A. Sanders, *Canon and Community: A Guide to Canonical Criticism* (GBS; Philadelphia: Fortress Press, 1984); and C. J. Scalise, *Hermeneutics as Theological Prolegomena: A Canonical Approach* (Macon, Ga.: Mercer University Press, 1994). On the issue of inspiration, see W. J. Abraham, *The Divine Inspiration of Holy Scripture* (New York: Oxford Univ. Press, 1981); P. J. Achtemeier, *The Inspiration of Scripture: Problems and Proposals* (Philadelphia: Westminster Press, 1980); L. Alonso Schökel, *The Inspired Word: Scripture in the Light of Language and Literature*, trans. Francis Martin (New York: Herder & Herder, 1965); K. Rahner, *Inspiration in the Bible* (New York: Herder & Herder, 1961); J. L. McKenzie, "The Social Character of Inspiration," *CBQ* 24 (1962): 115–24; C. H. Pinnock, *The Scripture Principle* (San Francisco: Harper & Row, 1984); and K. R. Trembath, *Evangelical Theories of Biblical Inspiration: A Review and Proposal* (New York: Oxford Univ. Press, 1987).

Representative statements on the history and nature of biblical theology are found in J. Barr, "Trends and Prospects in Biblical Theology," *JTS* 25 (1974): 265–82; B. Childs, *Biblical Theology in Crisis* (Philadelphia: Westminster Press, 1973); G. Ebeling, "The Meaning of 'Biblical Theology'," in his *Word and Faith*, trans. J. W. Leitch

(Philadelphia: Fortress Press, 1960), 79–97; S. J. Kraftchick et al. (eds.), *Biblical Theology: Problems & Perspectives* (Nashville: Abingdon Press, 1995); H. G. Reventlow, *Problems of Biblical Theology in the Twentieth Century*, trans. J. Bowden (Philadelphia: Fortress Press, 1986 [1983]); K. Stendahl, "Biblical Theology: A Program," in his *Meanings: The Bible as a Document and as Guide* (Philadelphia: Fortress Press, 1984), 11–44; and F. Watson, *Text and Truth: Redefining Biblical Theology* (Grand Rapids: Eerdmans, 1997).

Specifically on NT theology, see A. K. M. Adam, *Making Sense of New Testament Theology: "Modern" Problems and Perspectives* (Macon: Mercer Univ. Press, 1995); H. Boers, *What Is New Testament Theology?* (GBS; Philadelphia: Fortress Press, 1979); N. A. Dahl, "The Neglected Factor in New Testament Theology," in his *Jesus the Christ: The Historical Origins of Christological Doctrine*, ed. D. H. Juel (Minneapolis: Fortress Press, 1991), 153–63; idem, "Rudolf Bultmann's *Theology of the New Testament*," in *Jesus the Christ*, 187–216; G. Hasel, *New Testament Theology: Basic Issues in Current Debate* (Grand Rapids: Eerdmans, 1978); R. Morgan (ed. and trans.), *The Nature of New Testament Theology: The Contribution of William Wrede and Adolf Schlatter* (London: SCM Press, 1973); idem, "New Testament Theology," in *Biblical Theology*, 104–30; and H. Räisänen, *Beyond New Testament Theology: A Story and a Programme* (Philadelphia: Trinity Press Int'l, 1990). More theoretical statements on the failure, future, or possibility of NT theology are found in E. Käsemann, "The Problem of a New Testament Theology," *NTS* 19 (1972–73): 235–45; G. Ladd, "The Search for Perspective," *Int* 25 (1971): 41–62; C. Peter, "The Role of the Bible in Roman Catholic Theology," *Int* 25 (1971): 78–94; and L. Keck, "Problems of a New Testament Theology," *NovT* 7 (1964): 217–41.

Various approaches to doing NT theology are exemplified by H. Braun, "The Problem of a New Testament Theology," *JTC* 1 (1965): 169–83; R. Bultmann, *Theology of the New Testament*, 2 vols. (New York: Charles Scribner's Sons, 1951, 1955); G. B. Caird, *New Testament Theology*, ed. L. D. Hurst (Oxford: Clarendon Press, 1994); O. Cullmann, *Salvation in History* (New York: Harper & Row, 1967); J. D. G. Dunn, *Unity and Diversity in the New Testament: An Inquiry into the Character of Earliest Christianity*, 2nd ed. (Philadelphia: Trinity Press Int'l, 1990); L. Goppelt, *Theology of the New Testament*, 2 vols., ed. J. Roloff, trans. J. Alsup (Grand Rapids: Wm. B. Eerdmans, 1981–82 [1975–76]); A. Schlatter, *The History of the Christ: The Foundation of New Testament Theology*, trans. A. J. Köstenberger (Grand Rapids: Baker Books, 1997); and H. Schlier, "The Meaning and Function of a Theology of the New Testament," in his *The Relevance of the New Testament* (New York: Herder & Herder, 1968), 1–25.

A helpful survey of hermeneutics through the history of Christianity is provided by R. M. Grant (with D. Tracy), *A Short History of the Interpretation of the Bible*, 2nd ed. (Philadelphia: Fortress Press, 1984); and J. B. Rogers and D. K. McKim, *The Authority and Interpretation of the Bible: An Historical Approach* (San Francisco: Harper & Row, 1979). A more extensive survey is found in *The Cambridge History of the Bible*, 3 vols.

(Cambridge: At the Univ. Press, 1963–70). Specialized studies of respective periods are R. M. Grant, *The Letter and the Spirit* (London: SPCK, 1957); M. Simonetti, *Biblical Interpretation in the Early Church*, trans. J. A. Hughes (Edinburgh: T. & T. Clark, 1994); F. M. Young, *Biblical Exegesis and the Formation of Christian Culture* (Cambridge: Cambridge Univ. Press, 1997); J. Danielou, *From Shadows to Reality: Studies in the Biblical Typology of the Fathers*, trans. W. Hibberd (London: Burns & Oates, 1960); R. P. C. Hanson, *Allegory and Event: A Study of the Sources and Significance of Origen's Interpretation of Scripture* (London: SCM Press, 1959); R. E. McNally, *The Bible in the Early Middle Ages* (Atlanta: Scholars Press, 1986 [1959]); B. Smalley, *The Study of the Bible in the Middle Ages*, 3rd ed. (Oxford: Blackwell, 1984); J. S. Preus, *From Shadow to Promise: Old Testament Interpretation from Augustine to the Young Luther* (Cambridge, Mass.: Harvard Univ. Press, 1969); R. A. Muller and J. L. Thompson (eds.), *Biblical Interpretation in the Era of the Reformation* (Grand Rapids: Wm. B. Eerdmans, 1996); H. G. Reventlow, *The Authority of the Bible and the Rise of the Modern World*, trans. J. Bowden (Philadelphia: Fortress Press, 1984 [1980]); K. Scholder, *The Birth of Modern Critical Theology: Origins and Problems of Biblical Criticism in the Seventeenth Century*, trans. J. Bowden (Philadelphia: Trinity Press Int'l, 1990 [1966]); J. C. O'Neill, *The Bible's Authority: A Portrait Gallery of Thinkers from Lessing to Bultmann* (Edinburgh: T. & T. Clark, 1991); H. Frei, *The Eclipse of Biblical Narrative: A Study of Eighteenth and Nineteenth Century Hermeneutics* (New Haven: Yale Univ. Press, 1974); R. A. Harrisville and W. Sundberg, *The Bible in Modern Culture: Theology and Historical-Critical Method from Spinoza to Käsemann* (Grand Rapids: Eerdmans, 1995); A. C. Thiselton, *The Two Horizons: New Testament Hermeneutics and Philosophical Description with Special Reference to Heidegger, Bultmann, Gadamer, and Wittgenstein* (Grand Rapids: Eerdmans, 1980); and D. Kelsey, *The Uses of Scripture in Recent Theology* (Philadelphia: Fortress Press, 1975).

Further conversation pertinent to the constructive proposal made in this chapter can be found in R. E. Brown, *The Critical Meaning of the Bible* (New York: Paulist Press, 1981); S. E. Fowl, *Reading in Communion: Scripture and Ethics in Christian Life* (Grand Rapids: Eerdmans, 1991); idem (ed.), *The Theological Interpretation of Scripture: Classic and Contemporary Readings* (Cambridge, Mass.: Blackwell Pubs., 1997); H. Frei, "The 'Literal Reading' of Biblical Narrative in the Christian Tradition: Does It Stretch or Will It Break?" in *The Bible and the Narrative Tradition*, 36–77; J. Goldingay, *Models for Interpretation of Scripture* (Grand Rapids: Eerdmans, 1995); idem, *Models for Scripture* (Grand Rapids: Eerdmans, 1994); G. Green (ed.), *Scriptural Authority and Narrative Interpretation* (Philadelphia: Fortress Press, 1987); S. Hauerwas, *Unleashing the Scripture: Freeing the Bible from Captivity to America* (Nashville: Abingdon Press, 1993); R. B. Hays, *The Moral Vision of the New Testament: Community, Cross, New Creation* (San Francisco: HarperCollins, 1996); L. T. Johnson, "Fragments of an Untidy Conversation: Theology and the Literary Diversity of the New Testament," in *Biblical Theology*, 276–89; idem, *Scripture and Discernment: Decision-Making in the Church*

(Nashville: Abingdon Press, 1996); D. Kelsey, "The Bible and Christian Theology," *JAAR* 48 (1980): 385–402; G. A. Lindbeck, *The Nature of Doctrine: Religion and Theology in a Postliberal Age* (Philadelphia: Westminster Press, 1984); G. Loughlin, *Telling God's Story: Bible, Church, and Narrative Theology* (Cambridge: Cambridge University Press, 1996); S. M. Schneiders, *The Revelatory Text: Interpreting the New Testament as Sacred Scripture* (San Francisco: HarperCollins, 1991); and F. Watson, *Text, Church and World: Biblical Interpretation in Theological Perspective* (Grand Rapids: Eerdmans, 1994).

Appendix 1
New Approaches to the New Testament

THE MAIN TEXT of this book approaches the writings of the New Testament from the framework of an experience/interpretation model that respects the anthropological, historical, literary, and religious dimensions of the text. Since the time of its first publication in 1986 there has been a proliferation of new approaches and methods within the field of New Testament studies. In writing the present edition, I decided to touch on some of them in this appendix rather than trying to incorporate them into the main body of the text. One reason is that the approach taken in the book has its own integrity; another is that methods and approaches wax and wane—even within the time between the first edition of the book and this one! We live in an age much fascinated by "methodology," and the currents move rapidly. Structuralism has already come and gone, chiastic analyses no longer proliferate, and the perspectival pummeling of parables seems for the moment at least to have slowed. It is no longer absolutely necessary to include Levy-Straus, Greimas, Ricoeur, Habermas, Foucault, Derrida, or Girard in the first paragraph of a dissertation. The following rapid survey touches only on those developments that appear to have some staying power.

Each of the new approaches develops more fully one of the dimensions of the text mentioned above. The historical dimension has been expanded in several ways. The first is through an unparalleled explosion of new knowledge about the Mediterranean world, especially the discovery, editing, translating, and publishing of archaeological and literary evidence. More information about the world of the New Testament is available to more scholars than at any previous time. The historical approach has also definitively been released from the constraints of the canon, recognizing that if historical reconstruction of the past is the point, then all available sources should be used without respect to their canonical status. The study of early Christian history has also learned to pay attention to local realities and development. One manifestation of this focus—the value of which still remains to be determined—is the effort to reconstruct the histories of communities by detecting layers of redaction within literary compositions. A more salutary result is the recognition that in addition to ideas, the social processes of communities are also an important element in history.

The anthropological dimension of the text has received much attention as well. The most straightforward development has been the enhancement of the historical-critical method by an appreciation of social realities. Historical study is beginning to concern itself not only with singular events in the past but also enduring social patterns, not only with the words and actions of great people but also the social interactions and customs of ordinary people. Virtually every activity or practice of the first Christians makes sense within a cultural context that is becoming increasingly better known. Research into the social world has revealed the significance of patronage and benefaction within a stratified social system, the meaning and importance of honor and shame within that system, the lives of slaves, the roles of women, the patterns of property, and the functions of sexuality. There has also been the application of social-scientific theory to the writings of the New Testament. The basic premise here is that theory applies cross-culturally, so that patterns of behavior observed in one cultural setting can be used to fill in deficient data in another setting. Johannine literature has thus been approached from the perspective of theories concerning sectarianism or millenarianism. The Parables of Jesus have been read against the backdrop of peasant culture existing within an imperial economic system. Anthropological observations concerning everything from table manners to burial practices have been brought to bear on the New Testament. Such studies often yield stunning insight into specific details of texts. Sometimes, however, the theoretical model exercises excessive control over fragmentary data.

Appreciation for the literary dimension of New Testament compositions has also taken several forms. Uniting them is the conviction that the final form of a writing is not only the appropriate object of analysis but also the most important guide to its meaning. The disciplines of form-criticism and redaction-criticism each prepared the way by paying attention to the form of materials and the ways in which editing shapes and creates meaning. In the Gospels, forms of narrative criticism have dominated recent study. Borrowing freely from literary critics, scholars have freely invoked the categories of implied author and implied or ideal readers, reliable and unreliable narrators, plot analysis and characterization. The importance of genre has also been stressed, and the narrative character of the Gospels has been illuminated by comparison to other ancient narratives such as novels, biographies, and histories.

A major breakthrough in the study of New Testament epistolary literature (and to some extent the Gospels as well) has been the recovery of an appreciation for ancient rhetoric not simply as a matter of style or ornamentation, but above all as a form of argumentation and persuasion. Analysis of the types of rhetoric and their patterns of demonstration has enabled a much more precise appreciation of the literary structure and argument not only in Paul's letters but also in the Letter of James and the Epistle to the Hebrews. If "literary criticism" tends to take its categories from contemporary readers of fiction, "rhetorical criticism" seeks to employ the categories of the ancient orators and speech writers. Both kinds of analysis have their value. The development of socio-rhetorical criticism attempts to combine the insights of rhetorical and social-world analysis, recognizing that ancient rhetoric always functioned within a given cultural context and sought to shape that context. For instance, research into the values of honor and shame within the culture combines with the analysis of epideictic discourse to good effect.

While narrative and rhetorical criticism resemble traditional exegesis in their concern to discover and honor the meaning of the text "as it was intended" (that is, the meaning immanent in the text so far as it can be discerned), other developments have given more explicit attention to the active and even creative role of the reader. "Reader-response" criticism is another element borrowed from contemporary literary studies. In some New Testament work, it simply takes the form of trying to imagine how the "implied reader" of the text might have constructed meaning from a narrative or argument within the framework of options available in the ancient world. A more dramatic departure from the constraints of the text is the form of reader-response that pays closest attention to the reader as reader: the meanings (some textual and some not) that accrue in and through the act of reading irrespective of—or, perhaps, in spite of—the ancient cultural context. Even further down the road of subjectivity in reading are forms of post-modernist interpretation in which the process of reading involves subverting and deconstructing the intentionality of the text. In such analysis the balance of authority between text and reader is tipped decisively in favor of the reader; the text is mainly "pretext" for the process of creative and playful reflection on contemporary issues. Thus, the resemblance between some post-modernist interpretation and ancient allegory is not accidental, but attests to the enduring human need to close the gap that exists between our world and the world of the text.

Finally, the period between the first and second editions of this book has seen the birth and rapid development of what has come to be called Ideological Criticism. To some extent, it has its roots in the classical historical critical model, which already in the Tübingen School exercised a "hermeneutics of suspicion" with regard to the writings of the New Testament through the identification of their theological tendencies within early Christian conflicts. To some extent, it shares the perceptions of social-scientific approaches by its focus upon social status and the economic substructure of social symbols, both within the text and within contemporary reading communities. Ideological criticism also has affinities with reader-response and post-modernist literary criticisms in the way it privileges the perspective of the contemporary reader's critical stance over against the ancient text, and the manner in which it challenges the values embedded in that text. What is distinctive to ideological criticism is not its self-conscious adoption of a contemporary ideology and praxis as the consistent perspective from which both to read and to evaluate the New Testament, for that is what the church has always done. Rather, it is the self-conscious adoption of an ideology and praxis defined in terms of social class or group that identifies itself as oppressed or marginalized with respect to race, gender, sexual orientation, or any form of social, economic, and political status. Ideology criticism seeks to uncover the ideological agendas both of ancient texts (how they suppress or marginalize certain groups) and of contemporary readers and interpreters. Thus, in the case of feminist criticism, it is not only the social realities of antiquity having to do with the marginalization of women that come into question, and not only the rhetoric in the New Testament that confirms or even exacerbates such marginalization, but also the ideological tendencies within contemporary communities that dictate such readings of these ancient texts.

All of these developments reflect the progressive sociological shift of the discipline of New Testament studies from ecclesial and theological institutions to the setting of the university. Conversations with colleagues in the humanities and social sciences have affected the development of new approaches. The long-term effect of a study of sacred texts within a secular academy detached from the convictions of communities for whom these texts have existential significance remains to be seen.

Bibliographical Note

For a comprehensive survey and introduction to new interpretive methods and their development, see A. C. Thiselton, *New Horizons in Hermeneutics: The Theory and Practice of Transforming Biblical Reading* (Grand Rapids: Zondervan, 1992); and The Bible and Culture Collective, *The Postmodern Bible* (New Haven: Yale Univ. Press, 1995); as well as J. B. Green (ed.), *Hearing the New Testament: Strategies for Interpretation* (Grand Rapids: Eerdmans, 1995). The journal *Semeia: An Experimental Journal for Biblical Criticism* (Atlanta: Scholars Press, 1974–) has produced numerous issues related to new methodologies. One should also consult the journal *Currents in Research: Biblical Studies* (Sheffield: Sheffield Academic Press, 1993–) for up-to-date treatment and assessment of new methods and approaches.

On social-scientific and anthropological approaches, see J. H. Elliott, *What Is Social-Scientific Criticism?* (GBS; Minneapolis: Fortress Press, 1993); J. D. Kingsbury (ed.), *Gospel Interpretation: Narrative-Critical and Social-Scientific Approaches* (Harrisburg, Penn.: Trinity Press Int'l, 1998); R. Rohrbaugh (ed.), *The Social Sciences and New Testament Interpretation* (Peabody, Mass.: Hendrickson Pubs., 1996); B. J. Malina, *Christian Origins and Cultural Anthropology: Practical Models for Biblical Interpretation* (Atlanta: John Knox Press, 1986); and idem, *The New Testament World: Insights from Cultural Anthropology*, rev. ed. (Louisville: Westminster/John Knox Press, 1993). On rhetorical criticism, see G. A. Kennedy, *New Testament Interpretation through Rhetorical Criticism* (Chapel Hill: Univ. of North Carolina Press, 1984); B. L. Mack, *Rhetoric and the New Testament* (GBS; Minneapolis: Fortress Press, 1990); S. E. Porter and T. H. Olbricht, *Rhetoric and the New Testament* (JSNTSup, 90; Sheffield: Sheffield Academic Press, 1993); and D. F. Watson and A. J. Hauser, *Rhetorical Criticism of the Bible: A Comprehensive Bibliography with Notes on History and Method* (Leiden: E. J. Brill, 1994). On socio-rhetorical criticism, see V. K. Robbins, *Exploring the Texture of Texts: A Guide to Socio-Rhetorical Interpretation* (Valley Forge, Pa.: Trinity Press Int'l, 1996); and idem, *The Tapestry of Early Christian Discourse: Rhetoric, Society and Ideology* (New York: Routledge, 1996).

For a variety of literary-critical methods, see W. A. Beardslee, *Literary Criticism of the New Testament* (GBS; Philadelphia: Fortress Press, 1969); W. Egger, *How to Read the New Testament: An Introduction to Linguistic and Historical-Critical Methodology*, ed. H. Boers (Peabody, Mass.: Hendrickson Pubs., 1996); N. Frye, *The Great Code: The Bible and Literature* (New York: Harcourt Brace Jovanovich Pubs., 1982); idem, *Words with Power: Being a Second Study of "The Bible and Literature"* (New York: Penguin Books, 1990); E. V. McKnight, *Meaning in Texts: The Historical Shaping of a Narrative Hermeneutics* (Philadelphia: Fortress Press, 1978; E. V. McKnight and E. S. Malbon (eds.), *The New Literary Criticism and the New Testament* (Valley Forge, Pa.: Trinity Press Int'l, 1994); S. D. Moore, *Literary Criticism and the Gospels: The Theoretical Challenge* (New Haven: Yale Univ. Press, 1989); D. Patte, *The Religious Dimensions of Biblical Texts: Greimas's Structural Semiotics and Biblical Exegesis* (Atlanta: Scholars Press, 1990); idem, *Structural Exegesis for New Testament Critics* (Minneapolis: Fortress Press, 1990); idem, *What Is Structural Exegesis?* (GBS; Philadelphia: Fortress Press, 1976); N. R. Petersen, *Literary Criticism for New Testament Critics* (GBS; Philadelphia: Fortress Press, 1978); S. E. Porter (ed.), *Handbook to Exegesis of the New Testament* (NTTS, 25; Leiden: E. J. Brill, 1997); M. A. Powell, *What Is Narrative Criticism?* (Minneapolis: Fortress Press, 1990); and R. A. Spencer (ed.), *Orientation by Disorientation: Studies in Literary Criticism and Biblical Literary Criticism* (Pittsburgh: Pickwick Press, 1980).

For various ideological and reader-critical approaches, see A. K. M. Adam, *What Is Postmodern Biblical Criticism?* (GBS; Minneapolis: Fortress Press, 1995); T. K. Beal and D. M. Gunn (eds.), *Reading Bibles, Writing Bodies: Identity and the Book* (New York: Routledge, 1996); B. K. Blount, *Cultural Interpretation: Reorienting New Testament Criticism* (Minneapolis: Fortress Press, 1995); A. Brenner, *The Intercourse of Knowledge: On Gendering Desire and 'Sexuality' in the Hebrew Bible* (Leiden: E. J. Brill, 1997); M. G. Brett (ed.), *Ethnicity and the Bible* (Leiden: E. J. Brill, 1996); C. H. Felder (ed.), *Stony the Road We Trod: African American Biblical Interpretation* (Minneapolis: Fortress Press, 1991); N. K. Gottwald (ed.), *The Bible and Liberation: Political and Social Hermeneutics* (New York: Orbis Books, 1983); David Jobling (ed.), *The Bible and the Politics of Exegesis* (Cleveland: Pilgrim Press, 1991); D. L. Jeffrey, *People of the Book: Christian Identity and Literary Culture* (Grand Rapids: Wm. B. Eerdmans, 1996); S. D. Moore, *God's Gym: Divine Male Bodies of the Bible* (New York: Routledge, 1996); idem, *Mark & Luke in Poststructuralist Perspective: Jesus Begins to Write* (New Haven: Yale Univ. Press, 1992); idem, *Poststructuralism and the New Testament: Derrida and Foucault at the Foot of the Cross* (Minneapolis: Fortress Press, 1994); D. Patte, *Ethics of Biblical Interpretation: A Reevaluation* (Louisville: Westminster/John Knox Press, 1995); D. Rutledge, *Reading Marginally: Feminism, Deconstruction and the Bible* (Leiden: E. J. Brill, 1996); E. Schüssler Fiorenza, *Bread Not Stone: The Challenge of Feminist Biblical Interpretation*, rev. ed. (Boston: Beacon Press, 1995); idem, *But She Said: Feminist Practices of Biblical Interpretation* (Boston: Beacon Press, 1992); idem (with S. Matthews), *Searching the Scrip-*

tures; Vol. 1: A Feminist Introduction (New York: Crossroad, 1993); D. Seeley, *Deconstructing the New Testament* (Leiden: E. J. Brill, 1994); F. F. Segovia and M. A. Tolbert (eds.), *Reading from This Place: Social Location and Biblical Interpretation*, 2 vols. (Minneapolis: Fortress Press, 1995); J. L. Staley, *Reading with a Passion: Rhetoric, Autobiography, and the American West in the Gospel of John* (New York: Continuum, 1995); and H. C. Washington, et al. (eds), *Marking Boundaries: Essays on/in Feminist Theological Hermeneutics* (Sheffield: Sheffield Academic Press, 1998).

Appendix 2
The Historical Jesus

SOME READERS of this book's first edition were startled at the lack of attention I paid to the ministry of Jesus. So standard a feature of New Testament introductions is a sketch of Jesus' career preceding an account of Christianity's initial expansion that its absence here seemed to demand some explanation. There are basically two reasons why I continue to omit such a sketch in this second edition. The first is that this is not a history of the Christian movement, but rather an introduction and interpretation of the *writings* of the New Testament. How Jesus appears and is interpreted by each of the canonical writings is the focus. The second reason is that all the representations of Jesus in the canonical writings—Gospels as well as Epistles—are from the perspective of that powerful experience of him we call the resurrection. So profoundly does this faith perspective affect all statements about Jesus in the New Testament that the construction of a satisfying historical account faces severe difficulties.

The difficulties go beyond the faith perspective of the Gospel writers. The Gospels at best cover only three years of Jesus' activity, and include accounts that escape any historical verification, such as healings, exorcisms, transfigurations, and resurrections. When they describe events that are potentially verifiable, the Gospels diverge substantially on points that are fundamental to a historical rendering: the sequence and location of events, the manner and content of Jesus' speech, and the identity, character, and motivations of his followers and opponents.

I am by no means skeptical concerning the possibility of demonstrating with the highest degree of probability not only Jesus' existence, but also a fair number of important historical statements concerning his human life. Jesus' existence and his identity as a first-century Palestinian Jew are overwhelmingly verified both by the literature generated in his name and by the converging lines of evidence provided by the Christian writings as well as the few fragmentary testimonies extant from Greco-Roman and Jewish sources (see chap. 4 for the most important of these). These converging lines touch on Jesus' work among the Jewish people involving both teaching and wonderworking, resistance to him among Jewish leaders, his death by crucifixion under the Roman Prefect Pontius Pilate, and the continuation of a movement in his name after his death.

The broad patterns of Jesus' work can also be confirmed through the convergence of evidence from New Testament epistolary and narrative writings. That Jesus spoke in parables, healed the sick, interpreted Torah, spoke of God as his father, announced God's kingdom, and associated with religiously and socially marginal people is virtually certain. It is also possible to state with a high degree of probability that some

627

specific incidents reported in the Gospel narratives are historical: that Jesus was baptized by John in the Jordan, for example, chose followers, created a disturbance in the temple, and underwent some form of legal process before his death.

When historians try to push past the limits imposed by the sources, however, both the subject of inquiry and the methods of proper historiography become distorted. This is the case in particular when the search for a historical Jesus is not really so much about history as it is about theology. Since the Enlightenment, Christians uncomfortable with the witness and interpretation of the Gospels have sought a "historical Jesus" to serve as the measure of genuine Christianity. The main thing that such questers sought was a Jesus from whom any element of the supernatural or miraculous was removed. Only such a Jesus, they thought, could address a world measured by the severe standards of rationality. In order to find that Jesus, it was necessary to peel away the faith of the church; and since that faith permeated all the Gospels, it eventually meant peeling away parts of the Gospels as well.

The classic quest of the historical Jesus described by Albert Schweitzer in his 1906 study advanced by stages: first, to eliminate the miraculous in order to secure that which is truly historical; next, to eliminate the Gospel of John since it disagreed so fully with the witness of the Synoptics; next, to determine which of the Synoptics was earliest in order to secure—it was thought—a source that was neutral and reliable. And when the Gospel of Mark was finally located as the first of the Gospels, it was necessary to decide whether it really was a reliable source or itself a rendering of the church's faith. If Mark was reliable, then the apocalyptic Jesus it presented was not at all useful to modern scholars. If Mark was a creation of the church's faith, then the search must be declared over and a failure.

The new quest for the historical Jesus, over the last thirty years, has much in common with the first. It is still driven by usually unstated theological premises. Rather than search for a single source, however, the new search proceeds first by deconstructing all the Gospels (canonical as well as non-canonical) as literary compositions, then excavating from all Gospels (both canonical and non-canonical) pieces of the tradition that are considered to be the authentic voice or deed of Jesus. The criteria used to determine which pieces are authentic and which ones are not are themselves of dubious scientific value. But more significant, a selection of pieces out of the Gospels is still dependent on the earlier selection made by the believing church and the evangelists; the process does not yield any new or independent information about Jesus.

A more severe difficulty is that a pile of pieces does not by itself yield a satisfying picture of Jesus. It is necessary to fit these pieces into an alternative framework than the one provided by the Gospels. At this point, the subjective character of the entire enterprise becomes evident: the framework chosen often reveals as much about the investigator as it does about Jesus. When scholars, all using the same methods and studying the same materials, derive such a variety of "historical" Jesuses—a revolutionary zealot, a cynic radical, an agrarian reformer, a gay magician, a charismatic cult reformer, a peasant, a guru of oceanic bliss—then one may well wonder whether anything more than a sophisticated and elaborate form of projection has taken place. And when such images of Jesus are proposed as a more reasonable and culturally acceptable measure for Christianity than the Jesus portrayed in the canonical Gospels, then it becomes clear that a theological and cultural agenda is the driving force rather than a desire to do better history. There are other, more superior and effective ways of establishing the relevance and meaningfulness of the Gospel tradition for the modern world.

There is nothing in the least blameworthy about trying to find out as much as one can about the historical figure of Jesus, so long as one respects the difficulties facing that endeavor. There is certainly everything to praise about learning as much history as possible in order to better comprehend the Jesus portrayed in the Gospels. Such efforts require clarification and perhaps even resistance, however, when the "historical" becomes the only measure of truth, or when a "historical" reconstruction of Jesus is proposed as the measure of the church's identity rather than the Jesus of the Gospels, who is both the Christ of the church and the resurrected Lord of faith.

Bibliographical Note

For a thorough and compelling summary of life-of-Jesus research through the centuries, see C. Allen, *The Human Christ: The Search for the Historical Jesus* (New York: The Free Press, 1998). On specific periods, see H. Anderson, *Jesus and Christian Origins: A Commentary on Modern Viewpoints* (New York: Oxford Univ. Press, 1964); M. J. Borg, *Jesus in Contemporary Scholarship* (Valley Forge, Penn.: Trinity Press Int'l, 1994); C. Brown, *Jesus in European Protestant Thought 1778–1860* (Grand Rapids: Baker Books, 1985); R. M. Grant, *The Earliest Lives of Jesus* (London: SPCK, 1961); J. H. Hayes, *Son of God to Superstar: Twentieth Century Interpretations of Jesus* (Nashville: Abingdon Press, 1976); D. L. Pals, *The Victorian "Lives" of Jesus* (San Antonio: Trinity Univ. Press, 1982); A. Schweitzer, *The Quest of the Historical Jesus*, trans. W. Montgomery (Baltimore: Johns Hopkins Univ. Press, 1998 [1961]); and B. Witherington III, *The Jesus Quest: The Third Search for the Jew of Nazareth* (Downers Grove: InterVarsity, 1995). For a general introduction to recent research, see R. Shorto, *Gospel Truth: The New Image of Jesus Emerging from Science and History, and Why It Matters* (New York: Riverhead Books, 1997). On the anti-Jewish undercurrent of much earlier life of Jesus research, see S. Heschel, *Abraham Geiger and the Jewish Jesus* (Chicago: Univ. of Chicago Press, 1998).

For a sample of recent studies on the historical Jesus, see D. C. Allison, *Jesus of Nazareth: Millenarian Prophet* (Minneapolis: Fortress Press, 1998); H. Boers, *Who Was Jesus? The Historical Jesus and the Synoptic Gospels* (San Francisco: Harper & Row, 1989); M. J. Borg, *Jesus a New Vision: Spirit, Culture, and the Life of Discipleship* (San

Francisco: Harper & Row, 1987); J. D. Crossan, *The Historical Jesus: The Life of a Mediterranean Jewish Peasant* (San Francisco: HarperCollins, 1991); F. G. Downing, *Jesus and the Threat of Freedom* (London: SCM Press, 1987); R. W. Funk, *Honest to Jesus: Jesus for a New Millennium* (San Francisco: HarperCollins, 1996); J. Gnilka, *Jesus of Nazareth: Message and History*, trans. S. S. Schatzmann (Peabody, Mass.: Hendrickson Pubs., 1997); M. de Jonge, *Jesus, The Servant-Messiah* (New Haven: Yale Univ. Press, 1991); J. P. Meier, *A Marginal Jew: Rethinking the Historical Jesus*, 2 vols. (New York: Doubleday, 1991, 1994); B. F. Meyer, *The Aims of Jesus* (London: SCM Press, 1979); S. J. Patterson, *The God of Jesus: The Historical Jesus and the Search for Meaning* (Harrisburg, Pa.: Trinity Press Int'l, 1998); J. M. Robinson, *A New Quest of the Historical Jesus and Other Essays* (Philadelphia: Fortress Press, 1983); E. P. Sanders, *Jesus and Judaism* (Philadelphia: Fortress Press, 1985); E. Schillebeeckx, *Jesus: An Experiment in Christology*, trans. H. Hoskins (New York: Crossroad, 1979 [1974]); M. Smith, *Jesus the Magician* (San Francisco: Harper & Row, 1978); G. Vermes, *Jesus the Jew: A Historian's Reading of the Gospels* (Philadelphia: Fortress Press, 1973); N. T. Wright, *Jesus and the Victory of God* (Minneapolis: Fortress Press, 1996); and B. H. Young, *Jesus the Jewish Theologian* (Peabody, Mass.: Hendrickson Pubs., 1995).

For comprehensive analysis of issues related to the historical Jesus, see B. Chilton and C. A. Evans (eds.), *Studying the Historical Jesus: Evaluations of the State of Research* (NTTS, 19; Leiden: E. J. Brill, 1994); and G. Theissen and A. Merz, *The Historical Jesus: A Comprehensive Guide*, trans. J. Bowden (Minneapolis: Fortress Press, 1998). Also see C. A. Evans, *Life of Jesus Research: An Annotated Bibliography* (NTTS, 24; Leiden: E. J. Brill, 1996). On various aspects related to life-of-Jesus research, see the following: on the passion, see the bibliography in chapter 6. On the resurrection, see the bibliography in chapter 5. On the sayings of Jesus, besides the bibliographies in chapters 7 and 8, see J. D. Crossan, *In Fragments: The Aphorisms of Jesus* (San Francisco: Harper & Row, 1983); idem, *In Parables: The Challenge of the Historical Jesus* (San Francisco: Harper & Row, 1973); C. H. Dodd, *The Parables of the Kingdom*, rev. ed. (New York: Charles Scribner's Sons, 1961); C. W. Hedrick, *Parables as Poetic Fictions: The Creative Voice of Jesus* (Peabody, Mass.: Hendrickson Pubs., 1994); J. Jeremias, *Rediscovering the Parables of Jesus* (New York: Charles Scribner's Sons, 1966); E. Linnemann, *Parables of Jesus: Introduction and Exposition* (London: SPCK, 1966); and B. H. Young, *Jesus and His Jewish Parables: Rediscovering the Roots of Jesus' Teaching* (New York: Paulist Press, 1989).

On other aspects of the teaching of Jesus, see M. J. Borg, *Conflict, Holiness, and Politics in the Teachings of Jesus* (Harrisburg, Pa.: Trinity Press Int'l, 1998 [1984]); B. Chilton, *Pure Kingdom: Jesus' Vision of God* (Grand Rapids: Eerdmans, 1996); J. Jeremias, *New Testament Theology: The Proclamation of Jesus*, trans. J. Bowden (New York: Charles Scribner's Sons, 1971); E. P. Meadors, *Jesus: The Messianic Herald of Salvation* (Peabody, Mass.: Hendrickson Pubs., 1997 [1995]); and M. Reiser, *Jesus and Judgment: The Eschatological Proclamation in Its Jewish Context*, trans. L. M. Maloney (Minneapolis: Fortress Press, 1997 [1990]).

On various other aspects of Jesus' life, see E. Bammel and C. F. D. Moule (eds.), *Jesus and the Politics of His Day* (Cambridge: Cambridge Univ. Press, 1984); E. Bammel (ed.), *The Trial of Jesus* (London: SCM Press, 1970); B. Chilton, *A Galilean Rabbi and His Bible: Jesus' Use of the Interpreted Scripture of His Time* (Wilmington: Michael Glazier, 1984); idem, *The Temple of Jesus: His Sacrificial Program Within a Cultural History of Sacrifice* (University Park, Pa.: Pennsylvania State Univ. Press, 1992); S. L. Davies, *Jesus the Healer: Possession, Trance, and the Origins of Christianity* (New York: Continuum, 1995); P. R. Eddy, "Jesus as Diogenes? Reflections on the Cynic Jesus Thesis," *JBL* 115 (1996): 449–69; M. Hengel, *The Charismatic Leader and His Followers*, trans. J. Greig (New York: Crossroad, 1981 [1968]); P. W. Hollenbach, "The Conversion of Jesus: From Jesus the Baptizer to Jesus the Healer," *ANRW* II.25.1 (1982): 196–219; D. Seeley, "Jesus and the Cynics Revisited," *JBL* 116 (1997): 704–12; G. H. Twelftree, *Jesus the Exorcist: A Contribution to the Study of the Historical Jesus* (Peabody, Mass.: Hendrickson Pubs., 1993); and S. Westerholm, *Jesus and Scribal Authority* (ConBNT, 10; Lund: CWK Gleerup, 1978).

On the cultural and historical context of Jesus' life, see J. H. Charlesworth, *Jesus within Judaism: New Light from Exciting Archaeological Discoveries* (New York: Doubleday, 1988); J. H. Charlesworth (ed.), *Jesus and the Dead Sea Scrolls* (New York: Doubleday, 1992); J. H. Charlesworth and L. L. Johns (eds.), *Hillel and Jesus: Comparisons of Two Major Religious Leaders* (Minneapolis: Fortress Press, 1997); J. D. M. Derrett, "Law and Society in Jesus' World," *ANRW* II.25.1 (1982): 477–564; S. Freyne, *Galilee, Jesus and the Gospels: Literary Approaches and Historical Investigations* (Philadelphia: Fortress Press, 1988); K. C. Hanson and D. E. Oakman, *Palestine in the Time of Jesus: Social Structures and Social Conflicts* (Minneapolis: Fortress Press, 1998); A. E. Harvey, *Jesus and the Constraints of History* (London: Duckworth, 1982); G. Vermes, *The Religion of Jesus the Jew* (Minneapolis: Fortress Press, 1993); and M. Wilcox, "Jesus in Light of His Jewish Environment," *ANRW* II.25.1 (1982): 131–95.

For my own approach, see L. T. Johnson, *The Real Jesus: The Misguided Quest for the Historical Jesus and the Truth of the Traditional Gospels* (San Francisco: HarperCollins, 1996), and *Living Jesus: Learning the Heart of the Gospel* (San Francisco: HarperCollins, 1998). For a similar treatment, see M. Bockmuehl, *This Jesus: Martyr, Lord, Messiah* (Edinburgh: T. & T. Clark, 1994). Also see W. M. Thompson, *The Struggle for Theology's Soul: Contesting Scripture in Christology* (New York: Crossroad, 1996). For a sustained critique of my earlier book, see R. J. Miller, "The Jesus of Orthodoxy and the Jesuses of the Gospels: A Critique of Luke Timothy Johnson's *The Real Jesus*," *JSNT* 68 (1997): 101–20. For a variety of approaches to the development of Christology in the early church, see W. Bousset, *Kyrios Christos: A History of the Belief in Christ from the Beginnings of Christianity to Irenaeus*, trans. J. E. Steely (Nashville: Abingdon Press, 1970 [1964]); M. Casey, *From Jewish Prophet to Gentile God: The Origins and Development of New Testament Christology* (Louisville: Westminster/John Knox Press, 1991); J. D. G. Dunn, *Christology in the Making: A New Testament Inquiry into the Origins of the Doctrine of the Incarnation*, 2nd ed. (Grand Rapids: Eerdmans, 1989); P. Fredrickson, *From Jesus to Christ: The Origins of the New Testament Images of Jesus* (New Haven: Yale Univ. Press, 1988); R. H. Fuller, *The Foundations of New Testament Christology* (New York: Charles Scribner's Sons, 1965); F. Hahn, *The Titles of Jesus in Christology: Their History in Early Christianity*, trans. H. Knight and G. Ogg (New York: World Pub. Co., 1969 [1963]); M. J. Harris, *Jesus as God: The New Testament Use of* Theos *in Reference to Jesus* (Grand Rapids: Baker Books, 1992); M. Hengel, *The Son of God: The Origin of Christology and the History of Jewish-Hellenistic Religion*, trans. J. Bowden (Philadelphia: Fortress Press, 1976); idem, *Studies in Early Christology* (Edinburgh: T. & T. Clark, 1995); A. J. Hultgren, *Christ and His Benefits: Christology and Redemption in the New Testament* (Philadelphia: Fortress Press, 1987); L. W. Hurtado, *One God, One Lord: Early Christian Devotion and Ancient Jewish Monotheism* (Philadelphia: Fortress Press, 1988); R. Jewett (ed.), *Christology and Exegesis: New Approaches*; *Semeia* 30 (1984); M. de Jonge, *Christology in Context: The Earliest Christian Response to Jesus* (Philadelphia: Westminster Press, 1988); S. Kim, *The Son of Man as the Son of God* (Grand Rapids: Wm. B. Eerdmans, 1985 [1983]); R. N. Longenecker, *The Christology of Early Jewish Christianity* (London: SCM Press, 1970); I. H. Marshall, *The Origins of New Testament Christology*, updated ed. (Downer's Grove: InterVarsity Press, 1990); A. J. Malherbe and W. A. Meeks, *The Future of Christology* (Minneapolis: Fortress Press, 1993); C. F. D. Moule, *The Origin of Christology* (Cambridge: Cambridge Univ. Press, 1977); P. Pokorny, *The Genesis of Christology: Foundations for a Theology of the New Testament*; E. Schillebeeckx, *Christ: The Experience of Jesus as Lord*, trans. J. Bowden (New York: Crossroad, 1980 [1977]); E. Schüssler Fiorenza, *Jesus—Miriam's Child, Sophia's Prophet: Critical Issues in Feminist Christology* (New York: Continuum, 1994); I. G. Wallis, *The Faith of Jesus Christ in Early Christian Traditions* (SNTSMS, 84; Cambridge: Cambridge Univ. Press, 1995); and B. Witherington III, *The Christology of Jesus* (Minneapolis: Fortress Press, 1990).

Index

Index of Scriptural Passages

Index of Ancient Authors

Index of Modern Authors

Index of Subjects